# Writing with POWER

Contributing Author
**Joyce Senn**

Senior Consultants
**Constance Weaver**
**Peter Smagorinsky**

## Language

## Composition

## 21st Century Skills

Perfection Learning®

## Editorial

| | |
|---|---|
| **Editorial Director** | Carol Francis |
| **Executive Editor** | Jim Strickler |
| **Editorial Team** | Gay Russell-Dempsey, Terry Ofner, Kate Winzenburg, Sue Thies, Andrea Stark, Paula Reece, Sheri Cooper |

## Design

| | |
|---|---|
| **Art Director** | Randy Messer |
| **Design Team** | Tobi Cunningham, Deborah Bell, Emily Greazel, Mike Aspengren, Jane Wonderlin, Dea Marks, Lori Zircher, Jill Kimpston |
| **Illustration/Diagrams** | Mike Aspengren, Sue Cornelison |
| **Image Research** | Anjanette Houghtaling |

**Joyce Senn** taught both middle and high school before putting her experience and love of language to work in her distinguished career as educational consultant and author. Specializing in grammar, Senn was a pioneer in textbook publishing in her use of themed activities, helping to provide a context for once-isolated grammar, usage, and mechanics practice. Senn's other publications include the acclaimed children's reference book *Quotations for Kids* (Millbrook Press, 1999) and *Information Literacy: Educating Children for the 21st Century* (with Patricia Breivik, National Education Association, 2nd Ed., 1998).

Special thanks to Joan McElroy, Ph.D., for contributions to the research strand of *Writing with Power*, and to David Kulieke, English instructor and consultant, for his review of the grammar, usage, and mechanics chapters.

Copyright © 2012
by Perfection Learning® Corporation
1000 North Second Avenue
P.O. Box 500
Logan, Iowa 51546-0500
Tel: 1-800-831-4190 • Fax: 1-800-543-2745
perfectionlearning.com

1 2 3 4 5 6 7 WC 16 15 14 13 12 11 10

ISBN 13: 978-1-61563-636-5
ISBN 10: 1-61563-636-6

# Senior Consultants

**Peter Smagorinsky** wrote the activities that form the project-centered "structured process approach" to teaching writing at the heart of the composition units of *Writing with Power*. A high school English teacher for fourteen years, Smagorinsky has also taught in the English Education programs at the University of Oklahoma (1990-1998) and University of Georgia (1998-present). In addition to numerous articles, he has published books through Heinemann (*Teaching English by Design*, 2007, and *The Dynamics of Writing Instruction: A Structured Process Approach for the Composition Teacher in the Middle and High School,* with Larry Johannessen, Elizabeth Kahn, and Thomas McCann, 2010); through Teacher's College Press (*Research on Composition: Multiple Perspectives on Two Decades of Change*, ed., 2006); through Cambridge University Press (*Vygotskian Perspectives on Literacy Research: Constructing Meaning through Collaborative Inquiry*, with Carol D. Lee, 2000); and through the National Council of Teachers of English (NCTE) Press (*Standards in Practice, Grades 9–12*, 1996). For NCTE, he also chaired the Research Forum, co-edited *Research in the Teaching of English*, co-chaired the Assembly for Research, chaired the Standing Committee on Research, chaired the Research Foundation, and served as President of the National Conference on Research in Language and Literacy.

**Constance Weaver** developed the "power" concept and features for *Writing with Power,* identifying strategies for using grammatical options to add power to writing and thinking as well as developing the "Power Rules," beginning with ten "must know" conventions for success in school and the workplace and expanding into features more relevant for advanced writers. Weaver has shaped English education for more than thirty years, illuminating the relationship between grammar and writing and providing practical, effective teaching guidance, from her earliest works on the subject, the best-selling *Grammar for Teachers* (NCTE, 1979) and the widely acclaimed *Teaching Grammar in Context* (Boynton/Cook, 1996), to her most recent *Grammar Plan Book* (Heinemann, 2007) and *Grammar to Enrich and Enhance Writing* (with Jonathan Bush, Heinemann, 2008). She has also long been a leader in literacy and reading. Her book *Reading Process and Practice* (Heinemann, 1988) is authoritative in its field. In 1996, Weaver was honored by the Michigan Council of Teachers of English with the Charles C. Fries award for outstanding leadership in English education. Weaver is the Heckert Professor of Reading and Writing at Miami University, Oxford, Ohio, and Professor Emerita of English at Western Michigan University, Kalamazoo.

# National Advisory Panel

*Writing with Power* was developed under the guidance of outstanding educators—teachers, curriculum specialists, and supervisors—whose experience helped ensure that the program design was implemented in a practical, engaging way for every classroom.

## Middle School

**DeVeria A. Berry**
Curriculum Specialist
Frank T. Simpson-Waverly School
Hartford Public School
Hartford, Connecticut

**Marylou Curley-Flores**
Curriculum Specialist
Reading/Language Arts
Curriculum and Instruction
San Antonio Independent School District
San Antonio, Texas

**Karen Guajardo**
Curriculum Specialist
Reading/English Language Arts
Curriculum and Instruction
San Antonio Independent School District
San Antonio, Texas

**Tina DelGiodice**
English Teacher/Staff Developer (retired)
Jersey City Public Schools
Jersey City, New Jersey

**Julie Hines-Lyman**
Curriculum Coach
Agassiz Elementary School
Chicago Public Schools
Chicago, Illinois

**Marcia W. Punsalan**
Language Arts Department Chair
Clay High School
Oregon City Schools
Oregon, Ohio

**Melanie Pogue Semore**
Director of Upper School
Harding Academy
Memphis, Tennessee

## High School

**Nathan H. Busse**
English Language Arts Teacher
Fox Tech High School
San Antonio Independent School DIstrict
San Antonio, Texas

**Joyce Griggs**
Instructional Specialist
Peoria Unified School District
Peoria, Arizona

**Jill Haltom**
English Language Arts/Reading Director
Coppell Independent School District
Coppell, Texas

**Lynn Hugerich**
Retired English Supervisor
Secaucus Public School District
Secaucus, New Jersey

**Linda M. Moore, M.Ed.**
English Instructor
Coppell High School
Coppell Independent School District
Coppell, Texas

**Debora Stonich**
Secondary English Curriculum Specialist
Humanities Teacher
Lovejoy Independent School District
Lovejoy High School
Allen, Texas

## Student Contributors

*Writing with Power* proudly and gratefully presents the work of the following students, whose writing samples—from effective opening sentences to in-depth literary analyses—show so clearly the power of writing.

**From Lucyle Collins Middle School**
**Fort Worth, Texas**
Marbella Maldonado
Victor Ramirez

**From Evanston Township High School**
**Evanston, Illinois**
Morgan Nicholls

**From Canton South High School**
**Canton, Ohio**
Griffin Burns
Cody Collins
Marti Doerschuk
Reanna Eckroad
Erica Gallon
Lindsay Kerr
Elise Miller
Katie Smith
Natalie Volpe

# CONTENTS IN BRIEF

# COMPOSITION

# COMPOSITION

# COMPOSITION

# COMPOSITION

UNIT
3

# Research and
## Report Writing    356

# COMPOSITION

# COMPOSITION

## Part II Communication and Collaboration

# COMPOSITION

# GRAMMAR

# GRAMMAR

# GRAMMAR

## 19 Subject and Verb Agreement

# GRAMMAR

# GRAMMAR

# GRAMMAR

# Writing with POWER

Language

Composition

21st Century Skills

Perfection Learning®

# Unit 1

# Style and Structure of Writing

Who are your favorite writers? You can be certain that few of them, if any, acquired their skills in isolation. More likely they were in the company of other writers, at least figuratively, as they developed and organized their ideas. It is also likely that in their first attempts to write they studied and practiced the style, rhythm, tone, and precision of other writers' work. This unit will help you develop your writing skills in much the same way, by connecting you with other writers. At the same time it will help you recognize and develop the unique voice—the verbal fingerprint—that is your own.

*I've always seen myself in sentences. I begin to recognize myself, word by word, as I work through a sentence.*

— Don DeLillo

# A Community of Writers

**This book** is called *Writing with Power.* Its goal is to help you develop powerful writing and necessary and useful communication skills that you can carry with you beyond high school for successful participation in the 21st century. This chapter will lay the foundation for the writing instruction and activities presented in future chapters. It will review the writing process and also present strategies for participating effectively within a community of writers.

# Writing with Power

Every day, people read texts. You can usually tell when a text has been written with power. Texts written with power usually:

- demonstrate the **six traits** of good writing
- use **language in varied, interesting ways** to show relationships and provide details
- follow the **conventions** appropriate for the purpose, occasion, audience, and genre

This program will help you write with power and enable you to accomplish your goals through your writing.

##  The Six Traits

### IDEAS

Strong writing includes a clear idea, message, or **theme.** To this foundation, writers add vivid details that help bring their ideas to life. Powerful writing helps you focus your thinking so that readers can easily follow what you are trying to say.

### ORGANIZATION

Well-organized writing typically has a clear beginning, middle, and ending, presenting details in a logical order. To accomplish this effect, writers often use the transitional words and phrases listed in the chart below.

| WRITING PURPOSE | ORGANIZATIONAL PATTERNS | COMMON TRANSITIONS |
| --- | --- | --- |
| **Expository (to explain or inform)** | Order of importance<br>Cause/effect<br>Comparison/contrast | *First, next, most important*<br>*As a result, for that reason, because*<br>*Similarly, in contrast, on the other hand* |
| **Narrative (to tell a real or imaginary story)** | Chronological (time) order | *First, yesterday, the next day, last year, next, until* |
| **Descriptive** | Spatial (location) order | *At the top, near the middle, to the right, on the other side, next to, behind* |
| **Persuasive** | Order of importance | *The most important, equally important, in addition, also, in fact* |

# VOICE

**Voice** is the quality in writing that lets readers know a real, unique individual is behind the words. Your voice is your personal signature: People who read your writing can tell right away what kind of person with whom they are engaging. Your writing voice should fit the expectations for the situation. You would undoubtedly, for instance, use one voice for writing a college application essay and a different one for consoling a sad friend.

| WRITING PURPOSE | WHAT THE WRITER'S VOICE SHOULD CONVEY |
|---|---|
| Expository and persuasive writing | Genuine interest in the subject, often including personal insights about why the subject is important to the writer and what the reader might expect to gain from it; respect for differing viewpoints; confidence without swagger |
| Descriptive and narrative writing | A genuine, not phony, personality; often some personal statements that show a willingness to trust readers with sensitive ideas |

# WORD CHOICE

Your writing is more likely to affect your readers if you use specific and lively language appropriate to the situation. Strategies for producing captivating texts include using active-voice verbs, employing precise nouns and modifiers, and adding colorful and figurative language. (You will learn more about word choice in Chapter 2.)

# SENTENCE FLUENCY

Your sentences should flow together. You can achieve this effect when you employ transitional words or phrases, repeated words, and pronouns that refer back to an earlier word. These devices give your sentences a sense of flow. Few writers produce fluid texts the first time around; most return to their early drafts and revise so that readers can follow their thinking easily. (You will learn more about sentence fluency in Chapter 2.)

# CONVENTIONS

Clear writing is free of problems with grammar, spelling, capitalization, punctuation, and word choice. It includes sentences that follow rules for grammar and usage and paragraph breaks that occur where you change topics. Writing that follows these rules makes a positive impression on readers. If you use conventions that are inappropriate for the occasion, such as writing a business memo in the style of a personal journal entry, you may confuse or turn off your readers. (You will learn more about some of the most important conventions on pages 8–10.)

**Learning Tip**

Choose a passage from your favorite writer and explain how it demonstrates the six traits of good writing.

## ② The Power of Language ⚡

The number of unique sentences that you could conceivably produce is theoretically infinite. Simple pictures can communicate an idea such as "DeWayne whipped up a meal," but language can add detail, meaning, subtlety, and feeling to that idea in seemingly endless ways: "DeWayne hated to cook, but he was hungry, and no one was around to help him prepare lunch, so he made a quick peanut butter and jelly sandwich and grabbed an apple."

Fluent writers generate power through their careful and deliberate use of language. To help you develop this ability, each composition chapter in this program contains a warm-up activity called "The Power of Language." These activities help you to create interesting and varied sentence patterns. Each language strategy has two names. The first identifies the language concept. The second name, after the colon, reflects its purpose or function. The "Power of Language" strategies in this book are:

- Appositives: Who or What? page 61

- Parallelism: The Power of 3s, pages 120 and 301

- Absolutes: Zooming In, page 142

- Adverbial Clauses: Scene Setters, page 169

- Adjectives and Adjectival Phrases: Modifiers Come Lately, page 193

- Participial Phrases: Getting into the Action, page 241

- Dashes: Dash It All, page 340

- Wordiness: Less Is More, page 367

- Fluency: Let It Flow, page 430

Using these strategies will help you transform your writing from "DeWayne whipped up a meal" to an endless variety of detailed, interesting, and original expressions, giving your language significant *power*.

### Learning Tip

With a partner, take the simple sentence "DeWayne whipped up a meal" and use your language power to expand it with details and subtlety of meaning. Share your revised sentence with the class.

# ❸ The Power Rules

The ways in which you use language can help you to determine your own destiny. The words you use, the structure of your sentences, the rules you follow all signify your membership in a social group. With friends and family, you speak in a casual vernacular. Different families follow different speech patterns; while one family might say, "Where the ketchup at?" another might say, "Where is the catsup?" The language you use tends to sound like the speech of the people you spend time with or hope to spend time with. This kind of speech is the language of power in these social situations. You use it comfortably, and it feels natural and right to you.

However, the language of power in familiar surroundings is not necessarily the language of power in other situations. In many situations, "Standard English," such as the language used in many workplaces, is the norm. Its conventions may depart from the speech you use with friends and family. However, if you hope to succeed in school, college, or a profession, you benefit from learning the language of power that dominates those settings. The speech conventions that follow are therefore not absolutely right or wrong. Rather, good communicators learn how to "code switch," adjusting their speech so that the conventions that they follow meet the expectations for each particular situation.

English professors have found that certain grammatical and syntactic errors, such as errors in pronoun usage, create more negative impressions than others. Since these errors can influence how people perceive you, you should learn how to edit your writing so that it meets the standards expected in workplaces and educational settings. The list below identifies 10 of the most important conventions to master.

## EDITING FOR MAINSTREAM CONVENTIONS: THE POWER RULES

**1. Use only one negative form for a single negative idea.** (See pages 866–867.)

| Before Editing | After Editing |
|---|---|
| Max looked through his binoculars but *didn't* see *nothing*. | Max looked through his binoculars but *didn't* see *anything*. |
| There *wasn't scarcely* any time to call. | There *was* scarcely any time to call. |

**2. Use mainstream past tense forms of regular and irregular verbs.** (See pages 750–776.) You might try to recite and memorize the parts of the most common irregular verbs.

| Before Editing | After Editing |
|---|---|
| Amelia *eat* at my house last night. | Amelia *ate* at my house last night. |
| Alicia *walk* Wags around the block. | Alicia *walked* Wags around the block. |
| We *have did* nothing all day. | We *have done* nothing all day. |
| I *thinked* about it all night. | I *thought* about it all night. |

3. **Use verbs that agree with the subject.** (See pages 826–853.)

| Before Editing | After Editing |
|---|---|
| I *shovels* the driveway after each snow. | I *shovel* the driveway after each snow. |
| My cats and my dog *eats* from the same bowl. | My cats and my dog *eat* from the same bowl. |
| Either the guitars or the tuba *are* out of tune. | Either the guitars or the tuba *is* out of tune. |
| Neither Marsha nor the Bryan brothers *is singing* in tune. | Neither Marsha nor the Bryan brothers *are singing* in tune. |

4. **Use subject forms of pronouns in subject position. Use object forms of pronouns in object position.** (See pages 790–801.)

| Before Editing | After Editing |
|---|---|
| *Her* and Chase have been deputized. | *She* and Chase have been deputized. |
| *Him* and his posse look ridiculous. | *He* and his posse look ridiculous. |
| *Her* and *me* are soul sisters. | *She* and *I* are soul sisters. |

5. **Use standard ways to make nouns possessive.** (See pages 964–966.)

| Before Editing | After Editing |
|---|---|
| The *cups* handle is broken. | The *cup's* handle is broken. |
| All the *cup's* handles are broken. | All the *cups'* handles are broken. |
| The *earths* texture is quite loamy. | The *earth's* texture is quite loamy. |
| I just love that *bottles* color. | I just love that *bottle's* color. |
| *Conans* favorite dessert is lima bean pie. | *Conan's* favorite dessert is lima bean pie. |

6. **Use a consistent verb tense except when a change is clearly necessary.** (See pages 762–776.)

| Before Editing | After Editing |
|---|---|
| I *dive* off the board when I *went swimming* last night. | I *dove* off the board when I *went swimming* last night. |
| Dinah *was walking* home when she *hears* the siren. | Dinah *was walking* home when she *heard* the siren. |

7. **Use sentence fragments only the way professional writers do, after the sentence they refer to and usually to emphasize a point. Fix all sentence fragments that occur before the sentence they refer to and ones that occur in the middle of a sentence.** (See pages 661–663.)

| Before Editing | After Editing |
|---|---|
| *Today.* Zippy is hiding in his cage. | *Today,* Zippy is hiding in his cage. |
| Studying for a test. *When I'm at a football game is distracting.* So I'd better study at home. | Studying for a test *when I'm at a football game is distracting, so* I'd better study at home. |
| We cancelled our subscription. *The reason being that we didn't like the magazine.* | We cancelled our subscription *because we didn't like the magazine.* |

8. **Use the best conjunction and/or punctuation for the meaning when connecting two sentences. Revise run-on sentences.** (See pages 736–738.)

| Before Editing | After Editing |
|---|---|
| Grant rubbed the lantern, a genie came out. | *When* Grant rubbed the lantern, a genie came out. |
| The rain started pouring, I put on my poncho. | *After* the rain started pouring, I put on my poncho. |
| I called, Heidi answered. | I called, *and* Heidi answered. |

9. **Use the contraction *'ve* (not *of*) when the correct word is *have*, or use the full word *have*. Use *supposed* instead of *suppose* and *used* instead of *use* when appropriate.** (See pages 889, 896, and 899.)

| Before Editing | After Editing |
|---|---|
| Hammond should *of* ordered rice and beans. | Hammond *should've* ordered rice and beans. |
| We might *of* studied too hard for this test. | We might *have* studied too hard for this test. |
| Haywood would *of* come over if we'd invited him. | Haywood would *have* come over if we'd invited him. |
| I am *suppose* to be home by nine o'clock. | I am *supposed* to be home by nine o'clock. |
| I *use* to like my pancakes with syrup, but now I prefer them with chocolate chips. | I *used* to like my pancakes with syrup, but now I prefer them with chocolate chips. |

10. **For sound-alikes and certain words that sound almost alike, choose the word with your intended meaning.** (See pages 874–903.)

| Before Editing | After Editing |
|---|---|
| Rhoda wanted *too* drive my new car. (*too* means "also" or "in addition") | Rhoda wanted *to* drive my new car. (*to* is part of the infinitive *to drive*) |
| *You're* new phone looks fancy. (*you're* is a contraction of *you are*) | *Your* new phone looks fancy. (*your* is the possessive form of *you*) |
| *They're* phones were not charged. (*they're* is a contraction of *they are*) | *Their* phones were not charged. (*their* is the possessive form of *they*) |
| *Their* goes my weekend. (*their* is the possessive form of *they*) | *There* goes my weekend. (*there* means "in that place") |
| *Its* possible that Stella will win the prize. (*its* is the possessive form of *it*) | *It's* possible that Stella will win the prize. (*it's* is a contraction of *it is*) |

Writers often use the following proofreading symbols to indicate where they need to make changes when they edit. These symbols help writers to know where their writing should be revised to follow the Power Rules.

# PROOFREADING SYMBOLS

| | | |
|---|---|---|
| ∧ | insert | We went on a ^fantastic journey. |
| ∧ | insert comma | Meg enjoys hiking, skiing ∧ and skating. |
| ⊙ | insert period | Gary took the bus to Atlanta⊙ |
| ℣ | delete | Refer ~~back~~ to your notes. |
| ¶ | new paragraph | ¶ Finally Balboa saw the Pacific. |
| no ¶ | no paragraph | no ¶ The dachshund trotted away. |
| . . . | let it stand | I appreciated her ~~sincere~~ honesty. |
| # | add space | She will be#back in a moment. |
| ⌒ | close up | The airplane waited on the run‿way. |
| t℣ | transpose | They only have two dollars left. |
| ≡ | capital letter | We later moved to the south. |
| / | lowercase letter | His favorite subject was /Science. |
| ⓈⓅ | spell out | I ate 2 oranges. |
| ℣ ℣ | insert quotes | "I hope you can join us," said my brother. |
| ∧ | insert hyphen | I attended a school‑related event. |
| ∨ | insert apostrophe | The ravenous dog ate the cat's food. |
| ◯→ | move copy | I usually on Fridays go to the movies. |

## Learning Tip

Write the following sentence on a piece of paper, just as it's written here:

Emily tookthe bus to new york to see her brothers freind.

Add proofreading symbols to show corrections. Compare your work with a partner's. Did you find the same errors and mark them the same way?

CHAPTER 1

# ④ Writing in the 21st Century

Most teenagers are experts on using electronic communication. Like your peers, you probably send over a hundred text messages a day. You may spend over an hour a day on the Internet, not only reading but responding on interactive Web sites. You probably write countless e-mail, text, and instant messages. You may maintain a social networking site and write notes to friends on theirs. You share photos, videos, and music files, and people often respond to them. You "talk" with friends in chat rooms. You use the Internet to find information you need and have learned to discriminate between good information and bad on Web sites. For each of these types of 21st century writing, you follow unique and evolving conventions.

You also write in school, although in this setting you are often writing in response to other people's questions instead of your own. You write essays on tests, analyze stories and poems for English, take notes and write research papers in social studies, and write lab reports for science classes. In addition to your e-texts, you write other things outside school: shopping lists, notes, poems and stories, and other pieces that are part of the structure of your life.

## THE RIGHT KIND OF WRITING?

There is no single way to write that is "right" for every occasion. The right way to write is the way that's appropriate for the situation, your reasons for writing, and the expectations of your readers. In other words, writing should be "in tune" with what is appropriate for the situation.

## GLOBAL INTERACTIONS

Technology helps you to connect with people across the globe. The Internet enables you to buy what you want from anywhere in the world. You might play real-time computer games with people from around the earth, and you can probably understand and repair your technological tools much more easily than can the grown-ups in your life.

Those who make it in this electronically-connected world benefit from the ability to **work creatively and cooperatively with others.** For success in the 21st century, you need to be able to **think critically, reason logically,** and **solve all manner of problems** effectively. You will need to know how to **communicate,** and to **master the technologies** through which you engage in virtual exchanges with others. Writing according to the conventions of a social group and setting can help you develop all of those skills and prepare you to live a satisfying and fulfilling life.

> **Learning Tip**
>
> For one day, keep a log of how many times you write, and under what circumstances. Include text messaging. Compare your log to those of your classmates and look for patterns.

# Collaborating Through the Writing Process

The writer is often depicted as someone on an island, detached from others and writing in solitude. Some parts of the writing process are indeed accomplished alone, but most people write with other people in mind and with others who help at different points of the process. People talk over their ideas with others before, while, and after they write in order to get ideas and feedback. They often have an editor, teacher, or supervisor who reads and critiques their writing. For the writing in this program, you and your classmates will create and participate in a **community of writers** and work in **collaboration** throughout the writing process, often in groups of three to four students.

##  Prewriting: Getting Started

### STRATEGIES FOR FINDING A SUBJECT

Writing ideas lurk everywhere—in a memory, a friendship, a conversation, an ocean wave. Following are strategies that will help you tap this vast store of writing subjects.

***Taking an Inventory of Personal Interests*** You write more effectively when you write about a subject you personally find interesting. Complete statements like the following to explore your personal interests.

- The most interesting projects I have completed are . . .
- In the next five years of my life, I would like to . . .
- I disagree with my friends about . . .
- I would like to know more about . . .

***Freewriting*** Freewriting is one way to uncover ideas that lie buried in your mind. **Freewriting** means writing down anything and everything without pausing to reflect. You can begin writing about anything, or you can do focused freewriting, using a word, a topic, or a question to start your mind moving. Write words, phrases, or sentences— whatever encourages your thoughts.

***Keeping a Journal*** A **journal** is a notebook in which you make daily entries about your experiences, observations, and reflections. Date each entry in order to chronicle certain stages of your life. You will find this record of your personal feelings, opinions, and observations to be a rich source for writing ideas.

***Reading, Interviewing, and Discussing*** You can also develop ideas for writing subjects using the following strategies. In each case, keep a record in your journal of the ideas that surfaced.

### Strategies for Thinking of Subjects

- Do some background reading on topics that interest you. If you are interested in space exploration, for example, find some recent articles to read in the library or on the Internet.
- Interview someone who knows more about a subject than you do.
- Discuss subjects of mutual interest with classmates, friends, and/or family to find interesting and fresh angles on a subject.

*Keeping a Learning Log* A Learning Log is a section of your journal where you can write down ideas or information about math, science, history, health, or any other subject that interests you. You can use it to capture what you know about a subject and what you still need or want to learn about it. You can also use it to record your progress as a writer.

## CHOOSING AND LIMITING A SUBJECT

Writing gives you the opportunity to know yourself better and to present your ideas and interests to others. Make the most of this opportunity by writing about subjects you find personally stimulating. The following guidelines will help you choose such subjects.

### Guidelines for Choosing a Subject

- Choose a subject that genuinely interests you.
- Choose a subject that will interest your readers.
- Choose a subject you can cover thoroughly through your own knowledge or a reasonable amount of research.

Once you have chosen a subject, you may have to limit it, or narrow it so that it is more manageable. To limit a broad subject, use the following strategies.

### Guidelines for Limiting a Subject

- Limit your subject to one person or one example that represents the subject.
- Limit your subject to a specific time or place.
- Limit your subject to a specific event.
- Limit your subject to a specific condition, purpose, process, or procedure.

A student writer named Leroy came up with the broad subject, *performing before audiences.* He narrowed that subject in the following way.

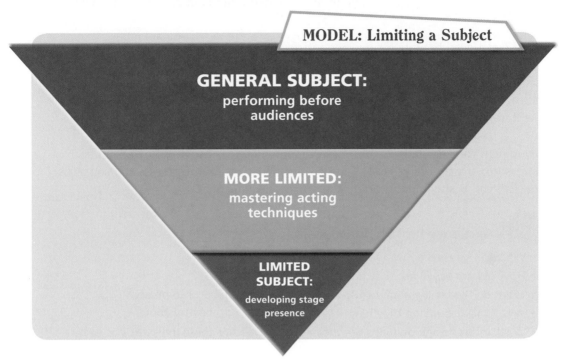

**MODEL: Limiting a Subject**

**GENERAL SUBJECT:**
performing before
audiences

**MORE LIMITED:**
mastering acting
techniques

**LIMITED
SUBJECT:**
developing stage
presence

## CONSIDERING PURPOSE, OCCASION, AUDIENCE, AND GENRE

**Purpose** is your reason for writing or speaking. Whatever your purpose is for a particular piece of writing, define it clearly before you begin writing. The following chart lists the most common purposes and forms (genres).

| WRITING PURPOSES | POSSIBLE FORMS (GENRES) |
| --- | --- |
| **Expository**<br>to **explain** or **inform;** to focus on your subject matter and audience | **Factual writing**<br>scientific essay, research paper, business letter, summary, descriptive essay, historical narrative, news story |
| **Creative (literary)**<br>to **create;** to focus on making imaginative use of language and ideas | **Entertaining writing**<br>short story, novel, play, poem, dialogue |
| **Persuasive**<br>to **persuade;** to focus on changing your readers' minds or getting them to act in a certain way | **Convincing writing**<br>letter to the editor, persuasive essay, movie or book review, critical essay (literary analysis), advertisement |
| **Self-expressive**<br>to **express** and **reflect** on your thoughts and feelings | **Personal writing**<br>journal entry, personal narrative, reflective essay, personal letter |

**Occasion** is why you write—the factor that prompts you to decide on your process for communicating. Occasion usually can be stated well using one of the following sentences.

- I feel a need to write for my own satisfaction.
- I have been asked to write this by [name a person].
- I want to write an entry for [name a publication].
- I want to enter a writing contest.

As you plan your writing, you also need to remember the **audience** you will be addressing, or who will be reading your work. What are their interests and concerns? How can you best communicate to this particular audience?

**HERE'S HOW**

## Audience Profile Questions

- Who will be reading my work?
- How old are they? Are they adults? teenagers? children?
- What do I want the audience to know about my subject?
- What background do they have in the subject?
- What interests and opinions are they apt to have? Are there any words or terms I should define for them?

The **genre,** or form of writing, you choose will also shape your subject. (See the chart on the previous page for a listing of common forms or genres of writing.) Each genre has several characteristics that make it different from the others, and readers expect these characteristics to be present when they read. If you are reading a biography, for example, you expect that there will be well-researched information provided about

**Learning Tip**

In your Learning Log, write a few sentences explaining the importance to a writer of purpose, occasion, audience, and genre.

someone's life, probably in a fairly formal style. If you begin reading and you find instead that the entire biography consists of one long rap song, you wouldn't know what to make of it, even if it did tell the story of someone's life. Similarly, if a prospective employer asks you to submit a résumé and instead you send a series of dramatic vignettes about your background and experience, the employer's expectations would be thrown off.

An acronym may help you remember the essentials of prewriting. Think of **SOAP** (subject, occasion, audience, and purpose) as a strategy to help you keep these aspects in mind when you plan to write.

# Collaboration in Action

## Prewriting

Derek, Leroy, and Maria are in a writing group together. It's their first writing activity of the year. They are supposed to come up with a topic and choose the purpose and audience for their writing. Here's how their discussion might go.

**Derek:** So Leroy, you're going to write on stage presence, eh?

**Leroy:** Yeah, I think I have my topic pretty well limited. I need to think about purpose and audience now I guess.

**Maria:** So what are some possible purposes?

**Leroy:** I could just inform people. I suppose I could entertain if I tried to make it funny.

**Derek:** Who would you be writing for?

**Leroy:** I could write for new theater students, I guess. Or I could write for a general audience. Rather than give advice, I could just give information.

**Derek:** Which sounds like more fun?

**Leroy:** The advice, for sure.

**Maria:** That's the way you should write it then.

**Derek:** Or maybe what it's like to get ready to act. I think most people don't get how much work you do.

**Leroy:** Thanks for the ideas.

Talking and listening help Leroy clarify his purpose and audience. After the group finishes talking about his topic, they have a similar conversation about the subjects Maria and Derek will write about.

## Collaboration Practice

Meet with a small group for 10 minutes. Use what you have learned to try to come up with a good writing topic for each member.

# ❷ Prewriting: From Ideas to a Plan

## DEVELOPING A SUBJECT

Once you have chosen a subject, limited it, and determined your purpose, occasion, audience, and genre, you can flesh out your ideas with supporting details. **Supporting details** are the facts, examples, incidents, reasons, or other specific points that back up your main idea. The following strategies will help you gather supporting details.

*Brainstorming* **Brainstorming** is an effective way to discover details for an essay, once you have chosen and limited your subject. To brainstorm, work with a partner or a group of classmates and freely list all ideas related to your subject as they occur to you. Just let them flow from one to another until you have unearthed a large store of ideas.

### Collaborating: Guidelines for Group Brainstorming

- Set a time limit, such as 15 minutes.
- Write the subject on a piece of paper and ask someone to be the recorder. If your group meets frequently, take turns recording ideas.
- Start brainstorming for details—facts, examples, incidents, reasons, connections, and associations. Since you can eliminate irrelevant ideas later, contribute and record any and all ideas.
- Build on the ideas of other group members. Add to those ideas or modify them to make them better.
- Avoid criticizing the ideas of other group members.

*You can learn more about group discussions on pages 584–586.*

When you have finished brainstorming, you should get a copy of all the ideas from the group recorder. Then, from the group list, select the details that are best for your own essay.

*Clustering* **Clustering** is a visual form of brainstorming that involves listing and connecting ideas. Begin with a single word or phrase. Arrange associated ideas around that nucleus, linking the ideas back to the original word or phrase. In the end you have a diagram that provides you not only with details but also with the paths that connect them. As a result, you can see groups, or clusters, of related details. The following is part of a cluster developed by the student planning an essay on stage presence.

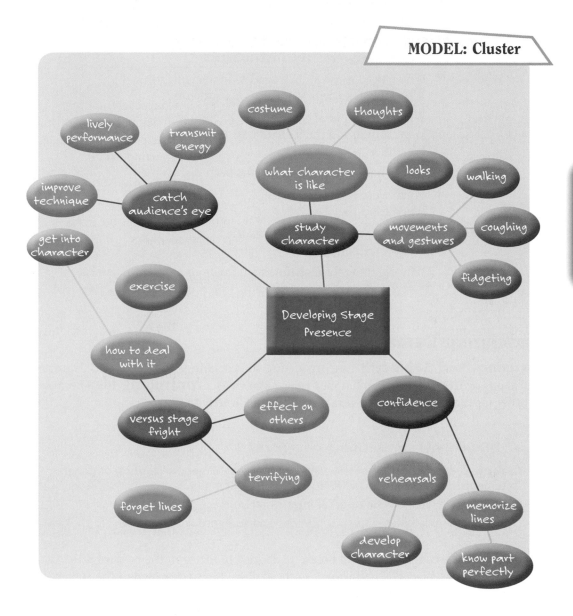

**Inquiring** To explore a writing topic, you can also use the technique of inquiring. Ask questions that begin with *who, what, where, when, why,* and *how.* The model on the next page shows some questions one writer used as a guide in finding details about early musical instruments. Notice that the writer developed more than one question using *who, what, when,* and *how.*

| **MODEL: Inquiring to Develop Supporting Details** | |
|---|---|

### Early Musical Instruments

| | |
|---|---|
| **Who?** | Who played musical instruments in ancient times? |
| | Who invented the first musical instruments? |
| **What?** | What are the oldest instruments known? |
| | What sounds did the instruments make? |
| | What did they look like? |
| **Where?** | Where have ancient instruments been discovered? |
| **When?** | When were they discovered? |
| | When were they created? |
| **How?** | How were the instruments made? |
| | How were they played? |
| **Why?** | Why did different instruments develop in different places? |

## ORGANIZING DETAILS

***Focusing Your Subject*** Before organizing your details, you first need to determine your focus or **main idea.** A main idea is also known as a **controlling idea** because all other ideas and details in the text need to relate directly to it.

### Guidelines for Deciding on a Focus

- Look over your supporting details. Think of meaningful generalizations, or general statements, that you can draw from some or all of the details.
- Choose a main idea that holds great interest for you.
- Choose a main idea that suits your purpose and audience and works well in the genre.

After Leroy reviewed his prewriting notes, he decided to focus on the best ways to develop stage presence. As a performer in school plays, he is interested in the subject and can say something meaningful about it. His purpose is to write an essay that informs his classmates. His main idea suits this purpose, and since all students have participated in performances in some way, his audience is likely to find the subject appealing.

## CLASSIFYING AND ORDERING DETAILS

The supporting details you collect for an essay are likely to fall into certain categories. If you are explaining weather forecasting, for example, some of the details may deal with kinds of weather, some with forecasting methods, and some with forecasting successes and failures. If you are comparing and contrasting the U.S. Congress and the British Parliament, your details will fall into the categories of similarities and differences.

When you classify, be sure to use categories that fit your purpose and main idea. If some details do not fit into any category, set them aside. You may be able to use them in your introduction or conclusion. Leroy classified his details into two groups: *during rehearsals* and *before performance*.

Next, order your details so that they progress logically from one to the other. A clear method of organization helps your reader follow and understand the details you present.

### WAYS TO ORGANIZE DETAILS

| Types of Order | Definition | Examples |
| --- | --- | --- |
| Chronological | the order in which events occur | story, explanation, history, biography, drama |
| Spatial | location or physical arrangement | description (top to bottom, near to far, left to right, etc.) |
| Order of Importance | degree of importance, size, or interest | persuasive writing, description, evaluations, explanations |
| Logical | logical progression, one detail growing out of another | classifications, definitions, comparison and contrast |

The order you choose will depend on your writing purpose and supporting details. For example, Leroy, whose purpose was to inform, chose a combination of chronological order and order of importance, going from most to least important. Following is his list.

## MODEL: Ordering Details

**During rehearsals**
—develop confidence
—know your part perfectly
—practice movements, gestures as well as script
—study your character
—practice staying in character
—practice reacting to what's happening onstage

**Before performance**
—rechannel nervous energy
—exercise; stretch, shake
—do not practice lines
—get into character

### Learning Tip

With a partner, use brainstorming, clustering, or inquiring to develop ideas for a topic of your choice. Decide how you will organize your ideas. Share your work with the rest of the class.

## 3 Drafting

When you write a first draft, you draw together your ideas on paper, pulling your prewriting notes into complete sentences and forming an introduction, a body, and a conclusion. You write more than one draft to assure a worthwhile essay. In your additional drafts, you will be able to look for more ideas, rethink your ideas, or even find a more workable subject. However, even though your first draft is just a preliminary version, it should be in a form that a reader can understand. The following strategies will help you prepare a draft.

### Strategies for Drafting

- Write an introduction that will capture the reader's interest and express your main idea clearly. You may want to return to your introduction at a later stage to evaluate its effectiveness in reaching your audience and addressing your purpose.
- After the introduction, use your organized prewriting notes as a guide, but depart from those notes when a good idea occurs to you.
- Write fairly quickly. Do not worry about spelling or phrasing. You will have the opportunity to go back and fix such problems when you revise.
- Stop frequently and read what you have written. This practice will help you move logically from one thought to the next.
- Do not be afraid to return to the prewriting stage if you find that you need more ideas or need to clarify your thinking. You can always stop and freewrite, brainstorm, or cluster to collect ideas.
- Write a conclusion that drives home your main idea.

The following model shows the first draft of Leroy's essay on stage presence. Notice that even as he drafts he is doing some revising, as the cross-outs indicate. Also notice these three features:

- The first paragraph serves as an introduction and asks a question to catch the reader's attention; the last paragraph serves as the conclusion and wraps up Leroy's ideas.
- The draft follows the planned order of details and ideas (see pages 20–21).
- Leroy made several mistakes in spelling, grammar, and punctuation. These mistakes will be corrected at a later stage in the writing process.

### MODEL: First Draft

~~There are certain perfo Do you~~ Have you ever felt yourself watching a minor character in a play instead of the star? Some actors always ~~hold~~ catch and hold the audience's eye, ~~even if they have~~ no matter how small a part they play. These performers have stage presence. This is a certain something that is transmitted and sent to the audience. Stage presence is not magic. You too can have it. Just work on your technique during rehearsals. Also learn to ~~control~~ channel your emotions at performance time.

~~Be conf~~ Stage presence is based on confidence. Your first and most important step then is to learn your part. Know it as if it was really part of you. Try different deliveries, moves, and gestures until you find just the right ones. Then rehearse them until they come naturally. Another important thing is to ~~work on your movements~~ develop your character ~~you are playing~~ as you rehearse. Think about what the person is like. Practice staying in character every moment. Listen and react to everything that happens onstage. Do that even when you have no lines. Finally, consentrate onthe way you move. Avoid halfway movements. If you grin grin from ear to ear. if you do turn your head, really turn it. Transform yourself into the character so that you behave like the character. When performance time arrives you ~~will~~ can expect to be nervous. Expereinced actors do not try to calm themselves. They draw on their nervous energy instead. That way they can increase their energy level. By the way, avoid the temtation to practice you're lines, especially trouble some ones. Misteaks only will end up making you nervouser. The best way to rechanel your nervus energy is to get into character. Chat with others as your character would walk around as your character would. Another importent strategy is Exercise. Even just a healthy stretch and shake of your limbs, head and body will help.

~~What is Achieving stage presence~~ Stagepresence depends on wor concsciousnes–of your character, of your emotions, and of your audience above all. According to Ms Keller Drama Teacher "There are no small parts, only small actors. When you use the techniques above, you can always be a big actor.

## Writing Tip

When using a word processor, remember to save your work regularly. Click on the Save icon whenever you pause in your writing or select Save from the pull-down file menu. You can also program your computer to save automatically.

## DRAFTING A TITLE

The final step in writing the first draft is to think of a suitable title. A good title will express the main idea of the essay and at the same time catch the reader's attention. Many times words or phrases found within the essay can be used as titles.

# 4 Revising

If you can answer *no* to any question in the first column, try the fixes in the second.

| REVISING STRATEGIES | QUICK FIXES |
| --- | --- |
| **Check for Clarity and Creativity**<br>• Are your ideas interesting, fresh, and original, rather than familiar and overused?<br>• Does the text satisfy its purpose? Have you taken some risks? | • Insert a personal experience or example.<br>• Think of an unlikely comparison between your subject and something else.<br>• Talk with others to get ideas. |
| **Elaborate by Adding Details**<br>• Does your writing seem fully developed?<br>• Are your ideas fully supported?<br>• Have you used details that would help bring a scene or idea to life for a reader? | • Use one of the prewriting strategies on pages 13–14 and 17–20 to come up with lively elaborations.<br>• Tell who or what with appositives (page 61), zoom in on details with absolutes (page 142), set the scene with adverbial clauses (page 169), add adjectives and adjectival phrases (page 193), get into the action with participial phrases (page 241), and dash it all by adding extra information separated by dashes (page 340).<br>• Show, don't tell.<br>• Take a mental snapshot and write what you see. |
| **Rearrange Out-of-Order Items**<br>• Check the organization of your words, sentences, and ideas. Does one idea lead logically into another? Have you combined ideas clearly and efficiently? | • Use your word processor to rearrange and reorganize your sentences or paragraphs so the reader can easily follow your thoughts.<br>• Use transitions to show the relationships between ideas. |
| **Delete Unnecessary Words or Details**<br>• Do all the details relate to your controlling idea? | • Delete, or remove, unrelated details and delete any extra or unneeded words and repetitive sentences. |
| **Substitute Words and Sentences**<br>• Are all parts of your draft clear?<br>• Are your words lively and precise? | • Ask a "test reader" for suggestions.<br>• For a dull, general word, find a richer and more vivid synonym. |

# Using a Six-Trait Rubric

A rubric like the one below can help you determine what you need to do to improve your draft. You can also use it to evaluate the work of your writing group partners. For each trait, "4" is the highest score.

| | | | | |
|---|---|---|---|---|
| **Ideas** | **4** The main idea is clear. Plenty of details such as facts, examples, and anecdotes provide support. | **3** The main idea is clear. There is enough support for the main idea to back it up adequately. | **2** The main idea could be clearer. There are some supporting details, but more details would be helpful. | **1** The main idea statement is missing or unclear. Few examples and facts are provided in support. |
| **Organization** | **4** The organization is clear with abundant transitions. | **3** A few ideas seem out of place or transitions are missing. | **2** Many ideas seem out of place and transitions are missing. | **1** The organization is unclear and hard to follow. |
| **Voice** | **4** The voice sounds natural, engaging, and unique. | **3** The voice sounds natural and engaging. | **2** The voice sounds mostly natural but is weak. | **1** The voice sounds mostly unnatural and is weak. |
| **Word Choice** | **4** Words are specific, powerful, and appropriate to the task. | **3** Words are specific and language is appropriate. | **2** Some words are too general and/or misleading. | **1** Most words are overly general and imprecise. |
| **Sentence Fluency** | **4** Varied sentences flow smoothly. | **3** Most sentences are varied and flow smoothly. | **2** Some sentences are varied but some are choppy. | **1** Sentences are not varied and are choppy. |
| **Conventions** | **4** Punctuation, usage, and spelling are correct. The Power Rules are all followed. | **3** Punctuation, usage, and spelling are mainly correct and Power Rules are all followed. | **2** Some punctuation, usage, and spelling are incorrect but all Power Rules are followed. | **1** There are many errors and at least one failure to follow a Power Rule. |

**Learning Tip**

Try using this rubric to evaluate Leroy's first draft. Assign each trait a score based on this rubric.

## USING A CHECKLIST

A checklist like the one below is another tool for improving a draft.

### Evaluation Checklist for Revising

✓ Do you clearly state your main idea? (pages 20–23 and 87–89)

✓ Does your text have a strong introduction, body, and conclusion? (pages 22, 106, and 108–122)

✓ Do you support your main idea with enough details? (pages 18–21, 24, and 90–91)

✓ Do your details show instead of merely telling what you want to say? (pages 18–21 and 90–91)

✓ Do you present your ideas in a logical order? (pages 5 and 20–21)

✓ Do all of your sentences relate to the main idea? (pages 21–22 and 90–91)

✓ Are your ideas clearly explained? (page 24)

✓ Are your words specific? (pages 6 and 47–48)

✓ Have you removed any words or ideas that were repeated unnecessarily? (pages 24 and 68)

✓ Are your sentences varied and smoothly connected? (pages 59–66)

✓ Is the purpose of your text clear? (pages 5–6 and 15)

✓ Is your writing suited to your audience? (pages 15–16)

✓ Is your writing suited to the occasion? (page 16)

✓ Does your writing include the defining characteristics of the genre you have chosen? (pages 15–16)

✓ Is your title effective? (page 23)

Using some of these tools, Leroy began a first-pass revision.

**MODEL: Revision**

## Stage Presence

Have you ever felt yourself watching a minor character in a play instead of the star? Some actors always catch and hold the audience's eye, no matter how small a part they play. These performers have stage presence. ~~This is~~ *poise and energy* a certain ~~something~~ that is transmitted ~~and sent~~ to the audience. Stage presence is not magic. ~~You can have it too. Just~~ ~~work~~ *By working* on your technique during rehearsals, ~~Also learn~~ *and* to channel your *ing* emotions at performance time, *you too can project that special quality when you step onstage.*

# CONFERENCING

You have been **conferencing,** meeting with others to share ideas or identify and solve problems, throughout the writing process. Conferencing is especially helpful during revising when weaknesses in the writing can be addressed. However, offering something that might sound like criticism isn't an easy thing to do. At the same time, you don't help your writing group members if you are not honest with them. The trick is to be positive and specific and to offer praise as well as any suggestions for improvement.

## Guidelines for Conferencing

### Guidelines for the Writer

- List some questions for your peer. What aspects of your work most concern you?
- Try to be grateful for your critic's candor rather than being upset or defensive. Keep in mind that the criticism you are getting is well intended.

### Guidelines for the Critic

- Read your partner's work carefully. What does the writer promise to do in this text? Does he or she succeed?
- Point out strengths as well as weaknesses. Start your comments by saying something positive like, "Your opening really captured my interest."
- Be specific. Refer to a specific word, sentence, or section when you comment.
- Be sensitive to your partner's feelings. Phrase your criticisms as questions. You might say, "Do you think your details might be stronger if ... ?"

# Collaboration in Action

## Revising

Leroy's writing group has already discussed Derek's and Maria's drafts. They made notes on their papers about where they could make improvements based on their peers' feedback. Now it is Leroy's turn to have his paper discussed.

**Leroy:** Alright, I've written about how to get ready to act. But I'm a better actor than writer, so I might need some help.

**Derek:** I thought it was really good. I learned a lot from it.

**Leroy:** Thanks. Was there anything that wasn't clear?

**Maria:** Your middle section is really cramped, I think. You packed so much into it. Maybe you need more than one body paragraph.

**Leroy:** I was wondering that, too.

**Derek:** I think that middle section also jumped around a little.

**Maria:** Stronger transitions in the middle section would also help avoid the feeling of jumping around.

**Leroy:** Thanks. I'll go back and read it over and maybe rearrange a few things. Do you think the piece is right for my audience, new theater students?

**Derek:** I think so. You didn't talk down to them, but you also were really informative.

**Leroy:** Alright, I'll see what I can do.

## Collaboration Practice

Choose a paper you are working on or have completed previously and make a copy for each member of your group. Conference with one another to improve your drafts.

*Collaborating*

# USING FEEDBACK FROM YOUR TEACHER

Your teacher is a member of the community of writers and an excellent collaborator. He or she is probably with you for each stage of the writing process. The chart shows different ways your teacher can provide feedback and how you can use that feedback to improve your writing.

| TEACHER FEEDBACK | HOW TO USE FEEDBACK |
|---|---|
| **During prewriting your teacher might:**<br>• meet briefly with you to discuss and approve your topic<br><br>• suggest ways you might gather information and other supporting materials<br><br>• comment on your organization | **You can use this feedback to improve your work by:**<br>• rethinking if necessary to come up with a sharply focused topic<br><br>• following the suggestions with an open mind<br><br>• experimenting with different organizational patterns |
| **During drafting your teacher might:**<br>• move from desk to desk to offer suggestions on your process of drafting (for example, continually going back and rereading what you've written)<br><br>• offer suggestions or concerns about a direction your draft seems to be taking | **You can use this feedback to improve your work by:**<br>• trying out the suggestions, even if they are uncomfortable at first<br><br>• saving your work and then coming back to it with a fresh eye to try to see the concerns your teacher raised<br><br>• asking questions if you don't understand the concerns your teacher has |
| **During revising your teacher might:**<br>• meet with you to go over some issues face to face<br><br>• make written comments on your work about ideas, organization, and flow | **You can use this feedback to improve your work by:**<br>• making a good effort to change the things you discussed<br><br>• using the comments as positive guides rather than negative criticisms |
| **During editing your teacher might:**<br>• identify errors<br><br>• offer mini-lessons on challenging points | **You can use this feedback to improve your work by:**<br>• making corrections and adding items to your personalized checklist |
| **During publishing your teacher might:**<br>• give you presentation ideas<br><br>• help you reach your audience | **You can use this feedback to improve your work by:**<br>• gaining confidence in sharing your work with readers and being willing to take risks |

# ⑤ Editing and Publishing

## EDITING FOR WORDINESS: EDITING STAR

Reputable large home appliances are certified by the Environmental Protection Agency to assure customers of their "energy star" efficiency. A refrigerator that is marked with an energy star is guaranteed to get the same results as one that uses more energy. The less power required to complete a job, the more energy-efficient the product is.

Word power is like energy power in that efficiency is a desirable quality. The fewer words needed to get the job done, the more efficient the writing is. In the following two examples, note how much stronger the efficient version is.

> **Word Guzzler**     The military colonel petted and stroked his animal friend and pet, his feline cat.
>
> **Fuel Efficient**     The colonel petted the cat.

Throughout the composition chapters in this book, you will see the language arts version of the energy star logo: the editing star. It will accompany a brief activity that can remind you to cut out wordiness.

## USING A GENERAL EDITING CHECKLIST

Good writers often use an editing checklist to help them avoid forgetting things. The best way to use such a list is to go over your work several times, each time looking for a different kind of problem. For instance, you might look for spelling errors in one reading and comma errors in the next. The following checklist will help you.

### Editing Checklist

✓ Are your sentences free of errors in grammar and usage?
✓ Did you spell each word correctly?
✓ Did you use capital letters where needed?
✓ Did you punctuate each sentence correctly?
✓ Did you indent paragraphs as needed and leave proper margins on each side of the paper?

## Using a Manual of Style

Writers often consult style guides or handbooks to review rules for grammar, spelling, mechanics, and usage. As you edit, you may wish to consult one of the following:

- *A Manual for Writers of Research Papers, Theses, and Dissertations.* Kate Turabian. 7th ed. Chicago: University of Chicago Press, 2007.
- *The Chicago Manual of Style: The Essential Guide for Writers, Editors, and Publishers.* 15th ed. Chicago: University of Chicago Press, 2003.
- *MLA Handbook for Writers of Research Papers.* 7th ed. New York: Modern Language Association of America, 2009.

## Creating a Personalized Editing Checklist

A **Personalized Editing Checklist** is a section of your journal in which you keep a list of errors that recur in your writing. These may include words you frequently misspell; usage mistakes, such as forgetting to use the possessive case before a gerund; and mechanical errors, such as overusing commas. When you edit an essay, you should read your work against this checklist as well as the standard list in your text.

## Proofreading

**Proofreading** means "reading and marking corrections." You may become so familiar with your essay while revising that you skip over mistakes. Proofreading during the editing stage will help give you the distance to pick up mistakes that you missed earlier. The following techniques will help.

 **Proofreading Techniques**

- Focus on one line at a time.
- Exchange your work with a partner and check each other's papers for errors.
- Read your essay backward, word by word. By changing the way you read your work, you will find that you will spot many errors.
- Read your essay aloud, very slowly.
- Use a college dictionary for spelling and a handbook for grammar, usage, and mechanics to double-check anything you are unsure of.
- Use the proofreading symbols on page 11.

The following model shows how Leroy edited a section of his essay on developing stage presence.

¶When performance time arrives you can expect to be nervous. Experienced actors, rather then trying to calm themselves draw on their nervous energy to increase their energy level. The best way to rechanel your nervus energy is to get into character. Chat with others as your character would, walk around as your character would. Another important strategy is Exercise. Even just a healthy stretch and shake of your limbs, head and body will help.

# PUBLISHING

Following are just a few ways you could share your writing.

## Publishing Options

### In School

- Read your work aloud to a small group in your class.
- Display your final draft on a classroom bulletin board.
- Read your work aloud to your class or present it in the form of a radio program or videotape.
- Create a class library and media center to which you submit your work. The library and media center should be a collection of folders or files devoted to different types of student writing and media presentations.
- Create a class anthology to which every student contributes one piece. Use electronic technology to design a small publication. Share your anthology with other classes.
- Submit your work to your school literary magazine, newspaper, or yearbook.

### Outside School

- Submit your written work to a newspaper or magazine.
- Share your work with a professional interested in the subject.
- Present your work to an appropriate community group.
- Send a video based on your written work to a local cable television station.
- Post your work on your online blog.
- Enter your work in a local, state, or national writing contest.

*Using Standard Manuscript Form* The appearance of your essay may be almost as important as its content. A marked-up paper with inconsistent margins is difficult to read. A neat, legible paper, however, makes a positive impression on your reader. When using a word-processing program to prepare your final draft, it is important to know how to lay out the page and how to choose a typeface and type size.

Use the following guidelines for standard manuscript form to help you prepare your final draft. The model on pages 34–35 shows how the writer used these guidelines to prepare his final draft on performing. Some manuals of style have specific requirements for preparing manuscripts. Be sure to check the guidelines your own school uses before preparing your final manuscript.

## Standard Manuscript Form

- Use standard-sized 8½-by-11-inch white paper. Use one side of the paper only.
- If handwriting, use black or blue ink. If using a word-processing program or typing, use a black ink cartridge or black typewriter ribbon and double-space the lines.
- Leave a 1.25-inch margin at the left and right. The left margin must be even. The right margin should be as even as possible.
- Put your name, the course title, the name of your teacher, and the date in the upper right-hand corner of the first page. Where applicable, follow your teacher's specific guidelines for headings and margins.
- Center the title of your essay two lines below the date. Do not underline or put quotation marks around your title.
- If using a word-processing program or typing, skip four lines between the title and the first paragraph. If writing by hand, skip two lines.
- If using a word-processing program or typing, indent the first line of each paragraph five spaces. If handwriting, indent the first line of each paragraph 1 inch.
- Leave a 1-inch margin at the bottom of all pages.
- Starting on page two, number each page in the upper right-hand corner. Begin the first line 1 inch from the top. Word-processing programs give you the option of inserting page numbers.

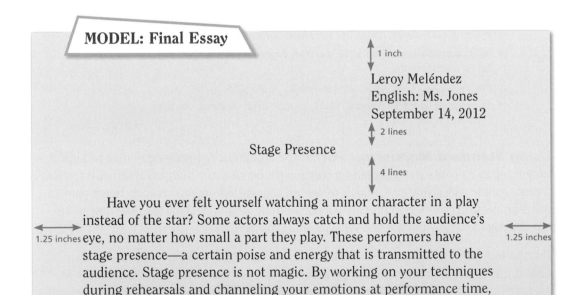

**MODEL: Final Essay**

1 inch

Leroy Meléndez
English: Ms. Jones
September 14, 2012

2 lines

Stage Presence

4 lines

1.25 inches    Have you ever felt yourself watching a minor character in a play instead of the star? Some actors always catch and hold the audience's eye, no matter how small a part they play. These performers have stage presence—a certain poise and energy that is transmitted to the audience. Stage presence is not magic. By working on your techniques during rehearsals and channeling your emotions at performance time, you too can project that special quality when you step onstage.    1.25 inches

Stage presence is based on confidence. Your first and most important step, then, is to learn your part. Know it as if it were really part of you. Practice different deliveries, moves, and gestures until you find just the right ones. Then rehearse them until they come naturally.

Another important tactic is to develop your character as you rehearse. Think about what the person is like—how he or she talks, feels, thinks, moves, and sleeps. Learn to transform yourself into the character so that you automatically walk as the character walks, cough as the character coughs, even fidget as the character fidgets. Practice staying in character every moment, listening and reacting appropriately to everything that happens on stage—even when you have nothing to say. Finally, concentrate on the way you move. Avoid halfway movement. If you grin, grin from ear to ear. If you turn your head, really turn it.

When performance time arrives, you can expect to be nervous. Experienced actors, rather than trying to calm themselves, draw on their nervousness to increase their energy level. The best way to rechannel your nervous energy is to get into character. Chat with others as your character would. Walk around as your character would. Another important strategy is exercise. Even just a healthy stretch and shake of your limbs, head, and body will help. Finally, avoid the temptation to practice your lines, especially troublesome lines. Mistakes will only end up making you more nervous.

Stage presence depends on consciousness—of your character, of your emotions, and of your audience above all. According to Ms. Keller, drama teacher, "There are no small parts, only small actors." Using the techniques sketched above, you can always be a big actor.

1 inch

## KEEPING A WRITER'S PORTFOLIO

A good way to track your progress as a writer is to keep a **portfolio**—a collection of your work that represents various types of writing and your progress in them. When you add a piece to your portfolio, be sure to date it so you will later have an accurate chronological record of your work.

You may be asked to write evaluations of your progress as a writer throughout the year. You should include these evaluations in your portfolio along with your writings. This will help you examine both your successes as a writer and the areas of your work that could be stronger still. At the term's end, you may be asked to write a "cover letter" for your portfolio in which you summarize its contents, explain why you included each piece, and evaluate your overall progress, strengths, and weaknesses.

The following guidelines will help you make the most of your portfolio.

### Guidelines for Including Work in Your Portfolio

- Date each piece of writing so you can see where it fits in your progress.
- Write a brief note to yourself about why you have chosen to include each piece—what you believe it shows about you as a writer.
- Include unfinished works if they demonstrate something meaningful about you as a writer.

Throughout the writing activities, you will be asked to take "Time Out to Reflect." Reflecting on your experience as a writer will give you an opportunity to develop your process even further. Use these reflections to think about what you have learned, what you want to learn, and how you can continue to grow as a writer. You may wish to add these written reflections to your portfolio.

You have now traveled through the five stages of the writing process. Take a moment to write down your understanding of the writing process. How closely does this process match your previous experiences as a writer? What might account for any differences between the writing process as described in this chapter and the writing process as you have previously experienced it? How would you define a "community of writers"?

# Timed Writing: On Your Own

There are times in school, such as during testing, when you will not be able to benefit from collaboration. The more you collaborate when you can, however, the less alone you will feel in those situations. You will no doubt be able to remember things your writing partners have said during your group meetings and then use them in your solo writing as well. For example, you might catch yourself writing a word or phrase that your group members thought was overused and too general. Or you might remember that time after time, your group members reminded you to use transitions to connect ideas. Use these memories to help you do your very best on timed writing tasks.

The following chart shows the stages of a timed writing experience. In each, imagine what your writing partners would be saying to help you.

## Working Through Timed Writing Tasks

- Begin by understanding the task. Read the prompt carefully. Identify the key words in the directions: they will tell you what kind of writing to produce. Ask yourself what your audience—the examiners—will be looking for, and try to provide it.
- Think about the time you have for the test and make a budget. Leave the most time for drafting, but build in time for planning and revising as well.
- Plan your writing by jotting down ideas, making lists, or using any other format that helps you (such as a cluster diagram). When you have good ideas to work with, arrange them in a logical order.
- Think through how to begin your writing. Begin drafting when you know what your main idea will be and you have ideas for introducing it.
- Use your notes to draft the body of your work.
- Remember what you have learned about strong conclusions and write a good ending to your work.
- Read over your work. If something seems confusing or out of place, fix it.
- Check your work for errors in grammar, usage, mechanics, and spelling. Try to remember the mistakes you have made in the past so that you can avoid them.

Like everything else, writing under time pressure gets easier with practice. Each composition chapter in this book ends with a timed writing activity that you can use to practice. There is also more information on timed writing and essay tests on page 493.

# Developing Style and Voice

**Y**our **writing style** is the distinctive way you express yourself through the words you choose and the way you shape your sentences.

As a writer, you use unique styles to express thoughts about different subjects. You choose words and shape sentences to make your writing powerful and concise. The words and sentences mix to create a great variety of styles that depend on your individual choice, the purpose of your writing, and your intended audience. You also develop a voice that comes through in your writing. (See page 6.) You choose the appropriate voice for your purpose and audience.

> **Voice** is the quality in writing that makes it sound as if there is a real and unique person behind the words, a verbal fingerprint.

As you develop your writing style, focus on one basic goal: to write as clearly as you can with your audience in mind. As you try to reach this goal, you will discover and develop your writing style and voice. The end result will be written words that say what you want them to say in a style that your audience will want to read.

## Writing Project    Parody

*Just for the Fun of It* Use vivid words, varied sentences, and humor to write a parody by completing the following project.

*Think Through Writing* A **parody** is a type of writing in which a particular style is imitated and exaggerated for a humorous effect. On television, *Saturday Night Live* often uses parody to make fun of individuals and groups of people by exaggerating and poking fun at the things that can make them look silly. Parody also often appears when a film "spoofs" a genre, such as horror movies, spy movies, commercials, and other types that are turned into comedies by imitation and exaggeration. Think of a parody with which you are familiar, and write about it. Do you find it funny? Why? What do the authors do to turn a serious person, genre, or other subject into a silly one? Write for ten minutes, without worrying about grammar or other aspects of form.

**Talk About It** In your writing group, discuss the parodies you have written about. What is being mocked? What makes the parodies funny? What strategies seem to work well?

**Read About It** In the following selection, author Russell Baker retells the story of Little Red Riding Hood. Instead of telling it as a children's story, he uses the voice and style of contemporary and cliché-happy professionals. Read the story, noting how Russell makes people who use such a style sound ridiculous.

> **MODEL: Parody**

# Little Red Riding Hood Revisited

*Russell Baker*

Once upon a point in time, a small person named Little Red Riding Hood initiated plans for the preparation, delivery and transportation of foodstuffs to her grandmother, a senior citizen residing at a place of residence in a forest of indeterminate dimension.

> In just one sentence, Baker manages to use one cliché, two euphemisms, one instance of redundancy, and two instances of wordiness. He also uses general and abstract words. Can you find all of these?

In the process of implementing this program, her incursion[1] into the forest was in midtransportation process when it attained interface[2] with an alleged perpetrator. This individual, a wolf, made inquiry as to the whereabouts of Little Red Riding Hood's goal as well as inferring that he was desirous of ascertaining the contents of Little Red Riding Hood's foodstuffs basket, and all that.

"It would be inappropriate to lie to me," the wolf said, displaying his huge jaw capability. Sensing that he was a mass of repressed hostility intertwined with acute alienation, she indicated.

> By taking the use of bloated language to an extreme, Baker parodies people who use such language: politicians, business workers, lawyers, sociologists, and psychologists.

"I see you indicating," the wolf said, "but what I don't see is whatever it is you're indicating at, you dig?"

Little Red Riding Hood indicated more fully, making one thing perfectly clear—to wit, that it was to her grandmother's residence and with a consignment[3]

---

1 **incursion:** An entering in or into.
2 **interface:** Meeting.
3 **consignment:** Delivery.

of foodstuffs that her mission consisted of taking her to and with.

At this point in time the wolf moderated his rhetoric[4] and proceeded to grandmother's residence. The elderly person was then subjected to the disadvantages of total consumption and transferred to residence in the perpetrator's stomach.

"That will raise the old woman's consciousness," the wolf said to himself. He was not a bad wolf, but only a victim of an oppressive society, a society that not only denied wolves' rights, but actually boasted of its capacity for keeping the wolf from the door. An interior malaise[5] made itself manifest[6] inside the wolf.

"Is that the national malaise I sense within my digestive tract?" wondered the wolf. "Or is it the old person seeking to retaliate for her consumption by telling wolf jokes to my duodenum[7]?" It was time to make a judgment. The time was now, the hour had struck, the body lupine[8] cried out for decision. The wolf was up to the challenge. He took two stomach powders right away and got into bed.

The wolf had adopted the abdominal-distress recovery posture when Little Red Riding Hood achieved his presence.

"Grandmother," she said, "your ocular[9] implements are of an extraordinary order of magnitude."

"The purpose of this enlarged viewing capability," said the wolf, "is to enable your image to register a more precise impression upon my sight systems."

"In reference to your ears," said Little Red Riding Hood, "it is noted with the deepest respect that far from being underprivileged, their elongation and enlargement appear to qualify you for unparalleled distinction."

"I hear you loud and clear, kid," said the wolf, "but what about these new choppers?"

> In an extreme case of "diplomatic" or neutral language, Baker reduces "was eaten" to "was subjected to the disadvantages of total consumption and transferred to residence in the perpetrator's stomach."

> While thoughtful people might agree with the concept of an oppressive society furthering crime, Baker uses such a ludicrous example—wolves' rights—that the concept itself gets held up to the light for closer examination.

> Throughout, the wolf talks in idioms and slang.

---

4 **rhetoric:** Verbal communication.
5 **malaise:** A vague sense of mental or moral ill-being.
6 **manifest:** Easily understood or recognized by the mind.
7 **duodenum:** Part of the small intestine.
8 **lupine:** Wolfish.
9 **ocular:** Of or relating to the eye.

"If it is not inappropriate," said Little Red Riding Hood, "it might be observed that with your new miracle masticating[10] products you may even be able to chew taffy again."

This observation was followed by the adoption of an aggressive posture on the part of the wolf and the assertion that it was also possible for him, due to the high efficiency ratio of his jaw, to consume little persons, plus, as he stated, his firm determination to do so at once without delay and with all due process and propriety, notwithstanding the fact that the ingestion of one entire grandmother had already provided twice his daily recommended cholesterol intake.

This entire paragraph is one long, rambling sentence that describes simple events in ridiculously abstract ways and uses jargon.

There ensued flight by Little Red Riding Hood accompanied by pursuit in respect to the wolf and a subsequent intervention on the part of a third party, heretofore unnoted in the record.

Due to the firmness of the intervention, the wolf's stomach underwent ax-assisted aperture[11] with the result that Red Riding Hood's grandmother was enabled to be removed with only minor discomfort.

---

10 **masticating:** Chewing.
11 **aperture:** Opening.

The wolf's indigestion was immediately alleviated with such effectiveness that he signed a contract with the intervening third party to perform with grandmother in a television commercial demonstrating the swiftness of this dramatic relief for stomach discontent.

"I'm going to be on television," cried grandmother.

And they all joined her happily in crying, "What a phenomena!"

> Baker pokes fun at people who use big words but don't realize *phenomena* is plural.

**Respond in Writing** Respond to Baker's parody of Little Red Riding Hood. Did you find it funny? Why or why not? What does he do that makes this piece of writing a parody? In what other styles could he have written the story for humorous effect?

**Develop Your Own Ideas** Work with your classmates to develop your ideas for your writing.

**Small Groups:** In small groups, construct a list of devices of an effective parody. (Exaggeration, for instance, is one type of device.) Reread the sidebar comments on pages 39–42 for ideas. Use a graphic organizer like the following to identify the devices of parody; an example of each device from film, television, the Internet, writing, or other source; and why you find the device humorous or not.

| What Makes Something Funny? | | |
|---|---|---|
| Device | Example | Effect |
|  |  |  |
|  |  |  |
|  |  |  |

**Whole Class:** Make a master chart of all of the devices of parody that the writing groups have identified, and discuss the examples provided as humorous or not. As a result of this discussion, you should have a list of many parodic devices and an understanding of why you find them effective in different examples.

**Write About It** You will next write a parody. Your parody might take any of the following directions.

| Possible Topics | Possible Audiences | Possible Forms |
| --- | --- | --- |
| • parody of a genre, such as truck commercials, a type of music, or advice columns<br><br>• parody of a well-known person, such as a politician or author<br><br>• parody of a specific television program, film, novel, or other work of art<br><br>• parody of a tradition, ritual, or other cultural practice | • other teenagers<br><br>• the type of person being parodied<br><br>• people who enjoy the subject you are parodying<br><br>• people who dislike the subject you are parodying<br><br>• visitors to a public video-sharing Web site | • video<br><br>• article for a newspaper that parodies the news<br><br>• fake article in your school newspaper<br><br>• track on a CD |

# Understanding the Varieties of English

Although English has many different dialects (for example, British, Australian, and the U.S. dialects of the South, the Southwest, and New England), none is so different that one group cannot understand another.

## 1 American Dialects

Humorist and essayist Roy Blount, Jr., wrote of the differences between the northern dialect and the southern dialect, "The language needs a second-person plural, and *ya'll* is manifestly more precise, more mannerly and friendlier than *you people* or *y'uns*." As Blount points out, dialects differ from one another in vocabulary, pronunciation, and even grammar.

### ● Practice Your Skills

#### *Identifying Dialects*

With your peers decide what type of dialect you speak. Provide examples of your vocabulary, pronunciation, and grammar that characterize your dialect. What culture has influenced your dialect? Compare and contrast your examples with the dialects of other parts of the country (a southern dialect compared to a southwestern dialect, for example). Make a chart, index, or dictionary of words to introduce your regional dialect to people from other parts of the country.

---

### PROJECT PREP  *Prewriting*  *Choosing a Topic*

1. In your writing group, identify a subject for your parody. What would be fun to make fun of? Feel free to draw on any of the topics that you originally wrote about or that other classmates suggested. It is fine if more than one person selects the same topic.

2. Think about the characters in your parody. How could you use dialect to make them seem real? Write five examples of sentences in a dialect that your characters might speak.

## ② Formal and Informal American English

The variety of English you use depends on your purpose and audience. As a writer, you can learn to adjust what you write to the circumstances.

### STANDARD AMERICAN ENGLISH

When writing an informative essay, it is best to use Standard English. **Standard English** is the formal English taught in school and used in newspapers, scholarly works, and many books.

**Writing Tip**

Use **Standard English** when writing for school and for a large general audience.

● **Practice Your Skills**

*Comparing Dialects with Standard English*

After you have developed a list of examples of your regional dialect, compare and contrast them with Standard English. Make a T-chart, with the dialect words and phrases in one column and the Standard English version in the other.

### COLLOQUIALISMS, IDIOMS, SLANG, AND JARGON

When you speak to your friends, you probably use various types of informal language. These are described in the chart below.

| Informal Language | Definition | Example |
|---|---|---|
| Colloquialism | informal expressions used in conversation but usually not in writing | Cecil was dog-tired after running twenty laps around the track. |
| Idiom | a phrase or expression that has a meaning different from the literal translation of the words | Mark was driving by the hardware store when a car cut him off. |
| Slang | colorful or exaggerated expressions and phrases that are used by a particular group | Hope missed the fiesta last night because she went to the flicks with Leonard. |
| Jargon | a specialized vocabulary most often used in a technical, scientific, or professional field | Whatever cyber-punk hacked the mainframe has ultra-killer apps. |

## ● Practice Your Skills

### Using Appropriate Standard English

Substitute words or phrases in Standard English for the underlined colloquialisms, idioms, jargon, and slang expressions in the following sentences.

1. When Jason explained that I should purge my disk cache, reboot, and rebuild my desktop, I nodded, but I really had no idea what he was talking about.

2. Arturo sleeps like a log.

3. When Rose gets caught up in a book, she's oblivious to the noise around her.

4. The week before finals, Juan hit the books every night.

5. The reporter had a gut feeling about the person's innocence.

6. Between midnight and one in the morning, the cops pulled over twelve cars.

7. After studying all weekend, the test was a piece of cake.

8. He got up on the wrong side of the bed and spent the entire morning in a crabby mood.

9. The pitcher threw a splitter and a hook, but his best pitch was his change.

10. The woman's computer was a hand-me-up from her nephew.

---

## PROJECT PREP  *Prewriting*  *Analyzing Language*

In your writing group, identify the language used by a key character in your parody. Does he or she use specialized vocabulary, as Baker's narrator does? Does your character change his or her pronunciation to appeal to a specific audience? For example, some politicians drop the "g" sound from words ending in *-ing* as a way to sound folksy. Does your character use certain sentence structures or other traits that people will recognize as typical of the speaker?

# Choosing Vivid Words

Words with rich, precise meanings give life to your thoughts and your writing. Look for vivid words in this scene, which describes a famous moment in horror-story history.

> **MODEL: Vivid Words**
>
> It was on a dreary night of November that I beheld the accomplishment of my toils. With an anxiety that almost amounted to agony, I collected the instruments of life around me, that I might infuse a spark of being into the lifeless thing that lay at my feet. It was already one in the morning. The rain pattered dismally against the panes, and my candle was nearly burnt out. Then, by the glimmer of the half-extinguished light, I saw the dull yellow eye of the creature open. It breathed hard, and convulsive motion agitated its limbs.
>
> — Mary Shelley, *Frankenstein*

Just as Dr. Frankenstein sparks life into his creature, Shelley sparks life into her writing with carefully chosen words. Indeed, her own words may have helped her to visualize the scene as she wrote—just as they have helped readers ever since.

## ❶ Specific Words

Use specific words to convey clear messages and create clear images. In each example below, a general word is replaced by one of the specific words Mary Shelley uses in the preceding passage. The specific word may be a more precise synonym or a word with a different, richer sense.

> **Writing Tip**
>
> Choose **specific words** over general words.

| | |
|---|---|
| **General Verb** | The rain **fell** against the window. |
| **Specific Verb** | The rain **pattered** against the window. |
| **General Adjective** | The **big** blast shook the house. |
| **Specific Adjective** | The **convulsive** blast shook the house. |

● **Practice Your Skills**

*Choosing Specific Words*

Write two specific words for each of the following underlined general words.

**1.** Nothing ever stopped Lou and Henry from <u>talking</u>.

**2.** The <u>book</u> kept Andrew reading late into the night.

**3.** As the rocket blasted off, the earth <u>moved</u>.

**4.** It was an <u>awful</u> defeat, but the season had just begun.

**5.** Whenever Anna <u>came</u> into a room, everyone knew it.

**6.** The new state champions marched <u>happily</u> around the field.

**7.** That summer was a <u>great</u> time for the entire Diaz family.

**8.** Prince never behaved like an ordinary <u>dog</u>.

**9.** Surprisingly all three beginners skated <u>well</u>.

**10.** The <u>nice</u> breeze carried the scent of lilacs.

**PROJECT PREP** *Analyzing* **Specific Language**

Consider the specific language choices your key character might make. For example, you may want to take turns in your group completing the activity above as if you were your character. What specific words would your character choose to replace the general ones? Take notes of the specific words you come up with so you can use them in your parody.

# The Language of **Power**  *Possessive Nouns*

**Power Rule:** Use standard ways to make nouns possessive. (See pages 964–966.)

**See It in Action**  When making your language as specific as possible, you may want to use possessive nouns. To make a noun show ownership or possession, you must change its form by adding an apostrophe. To form the possessive of a singular noun, simply add *-'s,* as in the following examples.

| | |
|---|---|
| **Singular Possessive** | At this point in time the wolf moderated his rhetoric and proceeded to grandmother's residence. |
| **Singular noun ending in** *-s* | Little Red Riding Hood poured milk to the glass's rim. |

To form the possessive of a plural noun, you need to do one of two things: Add only an apostrophe to a plural noun that ends in *-s*, or add *-'s* to a plural noun that does not end in *-s*.

| | |
|---|---|
| **Plural Possessive** | Thinking she heard wolves' howls, the grandmother hushed the children's crying. |

**Remember It**  Record this rule and examples in the Power Rule section of your Personalized Editing Checklist.

**Use It**  Read through your project to make sure you have formed possessives correctly. Before making a noun possessive, determine if it is singular or plural.

# ② Denotation and Connotation

When you look up a word in the dictionary, you will find its denotative meaning. Some words, however, have an additional meaning based on how the word is emotionally perceived by the reader or listener. This is called the connotative meaning. For example, *photo* and *snapshot* have a similar denotative meaning. *Snapshot*, however, connotes (or suggests) something more casual than *photo*.

● **Practice Your Skills**

*Identifying Denotation and Connotation*

The following pairs of words all have similar denotative meanings. Describe their connotative differences.

**1.** mirror, looking-glass    **3.** old, ancient

**2.** lanky, svelte    **4.** noodles, pasta

Create five pairs of your own, using the dictionary as needed. Your pairs should all have similar denotative meanings but different connotative meanings. When you have completed your five pairs, share them with the class.

---

## PROJECT PREP    *Analyzing*    *Mood*

In your writing group, identify the mood you want your parody to convey and think about words with connotations that will help you create that mood. The author Edgar Allen Poe, for instance, used language that suggested something dark or sinister, as in the following passage that opens the short story "The Tell-Tale Heart":

> "TRUE!—nervous—very, very dreadfully nervous I had been and am; but why *will* you say that I am mad? The disease had sharpened my senses—not destroyed—not dulled them. Above all was the sense of hearing acute. I heard all things in the heaven and in the earth. I heard many things in hell. How, then, am I mad? Hearken! and observe how healthily—how calmly I can tell you the whole story."

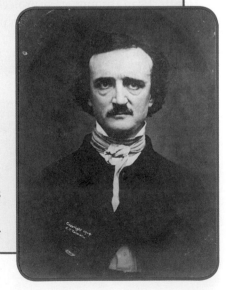

Talk through some ideas with your group members until you have at least five words your key character can use to establish the mood you desire.

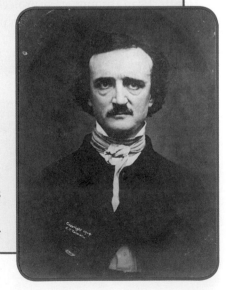

# 3 Figurative Language

A good writer knows how to use language figuratively as well as literally—to stretch the literal meaning of words so that they appeal to the imaginations of readers. **Literal language** uses words for their exact, direct meaning. **Figurative language** is usually composed of **figures of speech,** also known as **tropes**—expressions that use words in inventive ways. Compared to literal language, figurative language creates stronger images.

| Literal Language | The moon appeared in the cloudy sky. |
| Figurative Language | The moon was a ghostly galleon tossed upon cloudy seas. |
| | —Alfred Noyes, "The Highwayman" |

Here the poet appeals to the reader's imagination with his choice of imagery. Rather than simply stating that the night sky was cloudy, the poet compares the moon to a galleon, or ship, being tossed upon a sea of clouds.

## SIMILES AND METAPHORS

The two most common tropes are similes and metaphors, which fire the imagination by making unusual comparisons. **Similes** use *like* or *as* to make a comparison. **Metaphors,** on the other hand, imply a comparison without using *like* or *as,* or they simply state that one thing is another. Such figures of speech can enrich your writing and help your reader view ideas or things in new ways.

> **Writing Tip**
>
> Use **figurative language** to appeal to your reader's imagination.

| Simile | Here he stopped again, and glanced suspiciously to right and left, **like a rabbit that is going to bolt into its hole.** |
| | —E. M. Forster |
| Metaphor | The days ahead **unroll in the mind, a scroll** of blessed events in the garden and the barn. |
| | —E. B. White |

Forster uses *like* to compare a suspicious man to a rabbit. White implies a comparison between the days ahead and a scroll.

When you use figurative language, beware of the mixed metaphor. In a **mixed metaphor,** two different comparisons are illogically combined.

| | |
|---|---|
| **Mixed Metaphor** | His car was a spoiled child, drowning him in the waves of its demands. |
| **Improved** | His car was a spoiled child, eternally whining for his attention. |

A spoiled child cannot drown someone in its waves, but a spoiled child can certainly whine for attention.

## PERSONIFICATION

When you attribute human qualities to objects or ideas, you are using personification. Here are examples.

| | |
|---|---|
| **Personification** | The book **beckoned** to me from the shelf. |
| | The trees **danced** to the rhythm of the wind. |
| | Darkness **crept** silently into the house. |
| | The mountain **dared** me to try its slopes. |

Of course, books cannot beckon, trees cannot dance, darkness cannot creep, and mountains cannot dare. Yet the meaning of each sentence is clear, since the actions described are understandable human actions. Through personification, objects and ideas take on fresh, new identities.

## ONOMATOPOEIA

Some figures of speech rely on the sounds of words to create vivid impressions. **Onomatopoeia,** for example, is a figure of speech in which the word's sound matches its meaning. Some examples of onomatopoeia are *crash, slither, ooze, thump, hiss, quiver, boom, whistle, jangle, purr, swoop,* and *sizzle*.

Onomatopoeia is a figure of speech that is more widely used in poetry than in prose. Used sparingly, however, it can enrich prose writing by calling on the reader's sense of hearing to bring a passage to life.

## ● Practice Your Skills

### Experimenting with Onomatopoeia

Write one sentence about each subject. Use onomatopoeia to add sound effects appropriate to the subject.

**1.** doorbell          **2.** surf          **3.** busy office

## ● Practice Your Skills

### Identifying Figures of Speech

The following sentences are from a novel by Stephen Crane. Identify the underlined figure of speech in each case by writing *personification, simile, metaphor,* or *onomatopoeia.*

**1.** The <u>voices of the cannon</u> were clamoring in interminable chorus.

**2.** The red sun was pasted in the sky <u>like a wafer.</u>

**3.** There was <u>a little flower of confidence</u> growing within him.

**4.** The guns <u>belched</u> and <u>howled.</u>

**5.** The <u>regiment was a machine</u> run down.

## ● Practice Your Skills

### Using Figurative Language

Write a paragraph about something that moves, such as the ocean, clouds, or a car. Include literal language, a simile or a metaphor, and personification.

**PROJECT PREP**    *Analyzing*    *Figurative Language*

In your writing group, consider the role figurative language might play in your parody. For example, if the key character employs simile, metaphor, onomatopoeia, or personification, identify why and to what effect. Note any use of figurative language that you can parody.

# Think Critically

## Comparing

When you compare, you think of similarities or differences between people, places, things, or even ideas. One effective way to compare is to create a simile or metaphor. For example, if you compared the human brain to a computer, you would find several similarities. Both a brain and a computer process large amounts of information quickly. They both have extensive memories, and they both can classify related pieces of information into groups.

Effective similes and metaphors use creative comparisons that allow people to see things in new and different ways. Following is an example.

Angered by events, the crowd of people flew down the street **like a swarm of bees.**

Making a chart like the following one will help you write your own powerful comparisons. Begin by identifying the qualities of your subject that you wish to convey.

| COMPARISON CHART | | |
| --- | --- | --- |
| **Identify:** What are the subject's (crowd's) qualities? | **Ask:** What other subjects share those qualities? | **Choose:** Which conveys the connotation or feeling I am after, and why? |
| –angry, threatening | –swarm of bees | The swarm of bees comes closer because it gives the feeling of anger and of many individuals forming a dangerous group. |
| –moving fast | –avalanche of snow | |

## Thinking Practice

Make a comparison chart for one of the following phrases. Then write a resulting simile.

1. The truck was like . . .
2. A friendship is like . . .
3. The bridge spanned the bay like . . .

# 4 Language to Avoid

## CLICHÉS

A **cliché** is an overused comparison that has lost its power to evoke a strong mental image. If you find clichés in your writing, replace them with new similes. The following are some examples.

Clichés

Andrea was **happy as a lark** with her examination score.

Dad used to be **stubborn as a mule** about my allowance.

On the subject of classroom hours, her word was as **good as gold.**

## TIRED WORDS, EUPHEMISMS, AND LOADED LANGUAGE

When expressing and explaining your thoughts and ideas, it is important to realize that certain common expressions have become so overused that they are no longer precise or vivid. Similarly, there are other expressions that are misleading. Using these words and expressions without being aware of it can weaken your writing.

Note: There are times when writers purposely use euphemisms and loaded language. In political flyers, commercials, editorials, and other forms of persuasive text, euphemisms and loaded language are used to create a desired effect.

| Type of Expression | Definition | Example |
|---|---|---|
| Tired Words | language that has been exhausted of strength or precision through overuse | I went surfing in Mexico last month and it was really fun. |
| Euphemism | the substitution of a mild, indirect term for one considered blunt or offensive | When the old steam radiator began leaking water all over the floor, Neal called the facility engineer. |
| Loaded Language | words that are weighted with meaning or emotional importance | Many people will tell you that they have a natural-born right to watch television. |

### Writing Tip

Avoid **clichés, tired language, euphemisms,** and **loaded language.** Your writing will be more precise, vivid, and accurate.

## ● Practice Your Skills

### *Identifying Language*

Read the following sentences. Identify clichés, tired words, euphemisms, and loaded language.

1. It's a shame that Amy's car broke down, but that's the way the cookie crumbles.

2. After unpacking, we piled our empty boxes next to the curb for the sanitation engineer to haul away.

3. The destruction of the world's coral reefs was described by one environmentalist as "an insult to Mother Nature."

4. After the cashier rang up my purchase and wished me a nice day, I left the store.

5. When Senator McGalliard accused the president of being a hawk, the media blasted him for being a liberal.

---

**PROJECT PREP**  *Fresh Language*

1. With your writing group, identify any tired words or worn-out clichés you associate with a key character in your parody and discuss specific ways in which you could parody those.

2. Review all the notes you took from discussions you have had with your writing group on language choices and their role in your parody. Then write a first draft of your parody, making the most out of opportunities to parody your subject's word choices.

# Using a Word Choice Rubric

Evaluate your word choice with the following rubric.

| 4 Words are specific and powerful, rich in sensory images. | 3 Words are specific and some appeal to the senses. | 2 Some words are overly general and/or tired. | 1 Most words are overly general and tired. |
|---|---|---|---|
| • I used Standard English if required. I used Nonstandard English, with colloquialisms, if appropriate.<br><br>• I used words with connotations that match my intended meaning precisely.<br><br>• I used fresh, not tired words.<br><br>• I used words that appeal to all senses. | • I made reasonable choices between Standard and Nonstandard English.<br><br>• The connotations of the words I used generally convey my meaning.<br><br>• I used clear but unoriginal words.<br><br>• I appealed to the senses but could have done more. | • I made some confusing choices between using Standard and Nonstandard English.<br><br>• A few of the connotations of my words might mislead readers.<br><br>• I used a few tired expressions.<br><br>• I appealed to only one or two senses. | • I was not aware of differences between Standard and Nonstandard English and made confusing choices.<br><br>• The connotations of my words often do not match my intended meaning.<br><br>• Few of my words are specific or vivid.<br><br>• I didn't appeal to many senses. |

## PROJECT PREP  *Evaluating*  *Word Choice*

The above rubric is useful when evaluating your straightforward writing, but it needs some adjustment to be a good measure of your language use in a parody, where exaggeration often distorts good style. For example, if a key character in your parody is known for using dull language, then you would want to avoid rich, colorful language completely.

With a partner, then, revise the word choice rubric so that it is suitable for use with a parody. Share your rubric with the rest of the class and as a whole class develop a master rubric from these ideas that everyone can use.

# In the Media

## Television and Language

Since television became widespread in American culture in the 1950s, popular shows and advertisements have been shaping language. Talented writers create vivid, colorful words or phrases that become part of everyday speech, at least for a few months. Among the earliest expressions to enter the language were "Come on down!" from a game show called *The Price is Right,* "How sweet it is!" from a comedy called *The Jackie Gleason Show*, and "Just the facts, ma'am," from a crime show called *Dragnet*.

One of the most popular television shows in recent years, *The Simpsons*, has contributed several expressions to general speech. Among these are "D'oh!" and "Don't have a cow."

## Media Activity

With a group of your peers, brainstorm in order to come up with at least five expressions from television shows. Consider TV comedies, dramas, game shows, talk shows, and even news shows. Your expressions should be comments that you have heard outside of TV. Share your examples with the class. After all the expressions have been shared, discuss the influence of television on your own speech.

---

### QUESTIONS FOR ANALYZING TELEVISION VOCABULARY

- What expressions do you use that come from television?
- How do you feel letting other people create language for you?
- What expressions have you ever coined?
- What goals do you have for your own vocabulary?

# Creating Sentence Variety

Clothing with an appealing style flatters the human form. Similarly an appealing writing style shows ideas to their best advantage. One important feature of writing style is sentence construction. An interesting pattern of sentences appeals to the reader's ear and gives a graceful shape to ideas.

Short, choppy sentences suffer from two serious weaknesses. First, their rhythm soon becomes tiresome to the reader. Second, they obscure the relationships among ideas.

Compare the following two examples. The first presents a series of short, choppy sentences, while the second combines the short sentences into one. Notice how the relationships among the ideas become clearer when the sentences are combined.

**Short Sentences**   Alfonso beat John in the mile race. John was Alfonso's best friend. John was also Alfonso's chief rival in track. Alfonso felt proud of his victory. He also felt sorry about John's defeat.

**Combined**   After Alfonso beat John in the mile race, Alfonso felt proud of his victory but sorry about the defeat of his best friend and chief rival in track.

The techniques of sentence combining will help you link related ideas and vary the lengths of your sentences.

> **Writing Tip**
>
> Vary the length and structure of your sentences.

# ① Combining Sentences with Phrases

Two sentences can be combined by turning one sentence into a phrase that modifies the main idea expressed in the other sentence.

CHAPTER 2

A.     Police departments today use computers. **Computers store important information about suspects.**

Police departments today use computers **to store important information about suspects.** (infinitive phrase)

B.     In 1967, the first computer system used to fight crime was developed. **The FBI developed it.**

In 1967, the first computer system used to fight crime was developed **by the FBI.** (prepositional phrase)

C.     The National Crime Information Center provides information by computer. **It aids police nationally.**

The National Crime Information Center provides information by computer, **aiding police nationally.** (participial phrase)

D.     Catch can call up a picture of a suspect on a computer screen. **It is a highly advanced system.**

Catch, **a highly advanced system,** can call up a picture of a suspect on a computer screen. (appositive phrase)

## ● Practice Your Skills

### Combining Sentences with Phrases

Combine each of the following sets of sentences, using one or more of the preceding techniques. Add commas where needed.

1. Birds navigate the long distances of their migration routes. They use innate compasses and clocks.
2. The arctic tern holds the distance record. It flies a round-trip distance of 23,000 miles. It goes from the Arctic to the Antarctic every year.
3. Many birds use the sun. It helps them navigate.
4. Tens of millions of shearwaters land on islands off Australia. The time they will arrive is one November day.

> **PROJECT PREP** *Revising* **Combining Sentences**
>
> In your writing group, review each person's draft and identify possible sentences to combine to improve the flow.

# The Power of Language ⚡

## Appositives: Who or What?

As you have seen, you can use appositive phrases to combine ideas into one sentence. An **appositive** is a element that identifies or adds identifying information to a preceding noun. Appositives can be single words, phrases, or clauses. Baker writes:

> This individual, a wolf, made inquiry as to the whereabouts of Little Red Riding Hood's goal. . . .

The words "a wolf" add details that identify "the individual."

Often, as in the following example, the noun or pronoun being clarified is repeated in the appositive, and more information is added.

> He was not a bad wolf, but only a victim of an oppressive society, a society that not only denied wolves' rights, but actually boasted of its capacity for keeping the wolf from the door.

Some appositives are essential to a sentence and others are not. In the first example, "a wolf" is not essential. That is, it could be left out and the sentence would still be meaningful. Since it is not essential, a comma precedes and follows it. In other sentences the appositive is essential, and therefore no commas are used. (See pages 691 and 953.) If you read the following sentence without the appositive, it would not make sense.

**Essential**    Aspiring actress Little Red Riding Hood authored a book.

## Try It Yourself

Write six sentences with appositives that might fit in your parody. In three of the sentences, the appositive should be essential to the sentence. In the other three, it should not. If possible, use these sentences in your draft. During revision, see if using appositives will make your writing more interesting.

### Punctuation Tip

Use commas before and after an appositive that is not essential. Do not use commas if the appositive is nonessential. To determine whether an appositive is essential, try reading the sentence without it.

# ❷ Combining Sentences by Coordinating

Ideas of equal importance can be joined with a coordinating conjunction (*and, but, or, for, nor, yet,* and *so*). Following are some examples of sentences that were combined by coordination.

**A.**    In many science fiction novels, robots grow too powerful. They try to take over the world.

In many science fiction novels, robots **grow** too powerful **and try** to take over the world. (compound verb)

**B.**    Robots in most early works were dangerous. In *Star Wars,* C3PO and R2D2 are friendly.

Robots in most early works were dangerous, **but** in *Star Wars,* C3PO and R2D2 are friendly. (compound sentence)

**C.**    One famous movie robot is Gort in *The Day the Earth Stood Still.* Another is Robbie the Robot in *Forbidden Planet.*

Two famous movie robots are **Gort** in *The Day the Earth Stood Still* and **Robbie the Robot** in *Forbidden Planet.* (compound predicate nominative)

## ● Practice Your Skills

### Combining Sentences by Coordinating

Combine each of the following pairs of sentences, using the conjunction shown in parentheses.

**1.** Animals' tails are used for communication. They are also used for locomotion. (and)

**2.** The position in which an animal holds its tail may indicate aggression. The position may also be an indicator of the animal's social rank. (or)

**3.** Running cheetahs bend their tails in the direction they want to turn. Running wolves bend their tails in the direction they want to turn. (and)

**4.** For many animals, tails are rudders. For many animals, tails are balances. (both/and)

---

**PROJECT PREP** *Revising* **Combining Sentences**

In your writing group, review each person's draft and identify possible sentences to combine to improve the flow.

---

# ③ Combining Sentences by Subordinating

Ideas of unequal importance can be combined by **subordination**—by turning the less important idea into a subordinate clause. Following are some words that introduce subordinate clauses.

| RELATIVE PRONOUNS | | SUBORDINATING CONJUNCTIONS | |
|---|---|---|---|
| who | that | after | because |
| whom | which | until | whenever |
| whose | whoever | unless | although |

**A.** Capitol pages have a chance to see government in action. They are aides to lawmakers.

Capitol pages, **who are aides to lawmakers,** have a chance to see government in action. (adjective clause)

**B.** The Supreme Court uses only three students as pages. The chances of becoming a Supreme Court page are slim.

**Because the Supreme Court uses only three students as pages,** the chances of becoming a Supreme Court page are slim. (adverb clause)

**C.** A person may want to become a Capitol page. That person should write to his or her senator and representative for information.

**Whoever wants to become a Capitol page** should write to his or her senator and representative for information. (noun clause)

CHAPTER 2

## ● Practice Your Skills

### Combining Sentences by Subordinating

Combine each of the following sentences, using the joining word given in parentheses. Add commas where needed.

1. Senate pages may be between fourteen and seventeen years old. Pages in the House must be high school juniors or seniors. (while)
2. The *Capitol Page School Handbook* tells pages about their jobs. It is issued by the House of Representatives. (which)
3. The tasks of Capitol pages are varied. They include running errands and handling phone calls. (which)
4. Parliamentary rules must be followed strictly. Pages sound bells to call House members to a vote. (because)
5. Capitol pages serve out the terms to which they are appointed. They must still attend school. (while)
6. The school is part of the Washington, D.C., public school system. The schedule is adjusted for the pages. (although)
7. Regular classes begin in the morning. Capitol pages have already finished their special early classes. (when)
8. Pages attend school. They rush to Capitol Hill for a day's work. (after)
9. Someone may come from outside Washington, D.C., to be a page. He or she must arrange for room and board. (whoever)
10. Pages are well paid. Living expenses are high. (although)

---

## PROJECT PREP  Revising  *Combining by Subordinating*

In your writing group, review each person's draft, looking for places where sentences can be combined. Count the number of words in each sentence, and note especially short ones. Highlight the shortest sentences, and identify possible sentences to combine by subordinating.

# 4 Varying Sentence Structure and Beginnings

By combining sentences, you can create sentences with different lengths and structures. Using a mix of the four basic sentence types will improve your writing.

| | |
|---|---|
| **Simple** | Rita read the letter. (one independent clause) |
| **Compound** | Rita read the letter, and Sam waited. (two or more independent clauses) |
| **Complex** | While Rita read the letter, Sam waited. (one independent clause and one or more subordinate clauses) |
| **Compound-Complex** | While Rita read the letter, Sam waited, but she never uttered a word. (one or more independent clauses and one or more subordinate clauses) |

Beginning every sentence with a subject can become monotonous. Use the following sentence starters for a change of pace.

| | |
|---|---|
| **Adverb** | **Probably** the largest meteor to fall within recorded history landed in Siberia in 1947. |
| **Adjective** | **Brittle** as glass, the meteor broke into thousands of pieces on its way to Earth. |
| **Prepositional Phrase** | **In its original form,** it probably weighed 200 tons. |
| **Infinitive Phrase** | **To trace the source of the meteor,** scientists studied the debris at the site. |
| **Participial Phrase** | **Landing with great destructive force,** the meteor felled all trees within 40 miles. |
| **Adverbial Clause** | **If the meteor had fallen two hours later,** it would have hit Leningrad. |

## ● Practice Your Skills

### Varying Sentence Beginnings

Write a paragraph that contains at least one example of each of the four different sentence types. Try to vary your sentence beginnings.

**PROJECT PREP** *Revising* *Combining Sentences*

In your writing group, review each person's draft. Highlight the first three words in each sentence. Do any sentence patterns seem repetitive? Suggest ways to vary the sentence structure or sentence beginnings.

# Using a Fluency Rubric

Evaluate your fluency with the following rubric.

| 4 Sentences are varied in length and structure. Every sentence matters. | 3 Sentences are mostly varied in length and structure. A few words and sentences seem unnecessary. | 2 Many sentences are the same in length and structure. A number of words and sentences seem unnecessary. | 1 Most sentences are the same in length and structure. A number of words and sentences seem unnecessary. |
|---|---|---|---|
| • I combined short, choppy sentences into varied, longer ones.<br><br>• I used coordinating and subordinating conjunctions to improve the flow and show the relationship of ideas.<br><br>• I started my sentences in a variety of ways, not always with the subject first.<br><br>• I avoided rambling sentences. | • I combined some short, choppy sentences into varied, longer ones, but in a few places there is still some choppiness.<br><br>• I sometimes used coordinating and subordinating conjunctions to improve the flow and show the relationship of ideas.<br><br>• I started most of my sentences in a variety of ways, not always with the subject first.<br><br>• I avoided rambling sentences. | • A few parts of my work flow, but there is still choppiness.<br><br>• I used a few conjunctions to improve the flow and show relationships, but I see now that I could have used more.<br><br>• Many of my sentences start the same way, with the subject.<br><br>• A few of my sentences ramble or contain unnecessary information. | • I didn't quite achieve a flow. My writing seems to start and stop.<br><br>• I didn't often combine ideas into one sentence to improve the flow and show relationships.<br><br>• Most of my sentences start the same way, with the subject.<br><br>• Several of my sentences ramble or contain unnecessary information. |

## PROJECT PREP  *Revising*  *Fluency*

In your writing group, evaluate each writer's composition for fluency, using the rubric above. Based on the feedback from your group, revise some of your sentences to create greater variety unless you have purposely limited variety in service of your parody. For example, maybe you decided to reverse Baker's approach and tell a very sophisticated and complex story as a children's story with a simplified, repetitive style.

# Writing Concise Sentences

Just as a hiker carries only the essentials in order to move easily, a writer should use only the words needed to communicate clearly. Lighten your reader's load by avoiding needless words. Keep your sentences **concise** by eliminating needless words and phrases.

## ① Rambling Sentences

Sentences that ramble on and on are usually the result of excessive coordination. To break up rambling sentences, separate ideas into concise sentences of their own.

> **Writing Tip**
>
> Keep your sentences **concise** by eliminating needless words and phrases.

| | |
|---|---|
| **Rambling** | Some lions live in groups, which are called prides, and the lions who live this way can be said to be more fortunate than solitary lions, because the members of a pride of lions share all of the important tasks—for example, tasks such as hunting and protecting their turf—while solitary lions must feed themselves and must protect themselves on their own. |
| **Improved** | Lions who live in groups, called prides, are more fortunate than solitary lions. Members of a pride share important tasks such as hunting and protecting their turf, while solitary lions must feed and protect themselves. |

## ● Practice Your Skills

### Revising Rambling Sentences

Revise the following rambling sentence into shorter sentences.

> The Beatles were an immensely popular singing group in the years during the 1960s and 1970s, and they expressed in their words and in their music the feelings of the young people of those times, but even though they were controversial and their records and their appearances were banned in some places, still their popularity held steady for many years.

---

**PROJECT PREP** *Revising* *Sentence Structure*

In your writing group, analyze the sentence structure of the subject of your parody. Identify any sentence structures that might make your subject distinct, and note how you might exaggerate them for comic effect in your parody.

# ② Unnecessary Words

## REDUNDANCY

**Redundancy** means unnecessary repetition of words or phrases. Find the redundancy in the first sentence of each pair below. Then notice how it is eliminated without any loss of meaning in the second sentence.

| | |
|---|---|
| Redundant | Our **memorable** trip to London was **unforgettable.** |
| Concise | Our trip to London was unforgettable. |
| Redundant | **Animals** who are members of the **mammal family** are warm-blooded. |
| Concise | Mammals are warm-blooded. |

## EMPTY EXPRESSIONS

Fillers—words that contribute no meaning to a sentence—are called **empty expressions.** Reduce empty expressions to a single meaningful word or eliminate them entirely, as shown below.

| | |
|---|---|
| Empty | **The thing of it is that** I cannot turn in my paper **due to the fact that** I forgot it. |
| Concise | I cannot turn in my paper because I forgot it. |
| Empty | **It seems** there were 20 people at the party. |
| Concise | Twenty people attended the party. |

| COMMON EMPTY EXPRESSIONS | |
|---|---|
| on account of | so as you can see |
| what I want/believe/think is | the reason that |
| it seems as if | the thing of it is that |
| due to the fact that | there is/are/was/were |
| in my opinion | I believe/feel/think that |

# WORDINESS

The expression "less is more" makes good sense for writing. You can often sharpen your writing by using as few words as possible to make your point.

***Wordy Phrases and Clauses*** Constructions that use more words than necessary are referred to as **wordy.** Because wordiness detracts from your writing style, try to reduce each wordy construction to a shorter phrase or a single word.

**Phrase to Word**

| | |
|---|---|
| Wordy | Winds on Greenland's ice cap howl in **a fierce way.** (prepositional phrase) |
| Concise | Winds on Greenland's ice cap howl **fiercely.** (adverb) |
| Wordy | Dry snow, **having the quality of sand,** covers the ice. (participial phrase) |
| Concise | Dry, **sandlike** snow covers the ice. (adjective) |

**Clause to Phrase**

| | |
|---|---|
| Wordy | Because of the winds, scientists **who work in Greenland** do not venture far from their stations. (adjectival clause) |
| Concise | Because of the winds, scientists **working in Greenland** do not venture far from their stations. (participial phrase) —or— Because of the winds, scientists **in Greenland** do not venture far from their stations. (prepositional phrase) |
| Wordy | The ice cap, **which is a perilous wilderness,** appears serene from the air. (adjective clause) |
| Concise | The ice cap, **a perilous wilderness,** appears serene from the air. (appositive phrase) |

**Clause to Word**

| | |
|---|---|
| Wordy | A glare **that is blinding** rises from the ice cap on a sunny day. (adjectival clause) |
| Concise | A **blinding** glare rises from the ice cap on a sunny day. (adjective) |

## INFLATED LANGUAGE

Some writers tend to use inflated language—words with many syllables that sound impressive but do not communicate as effectively or concisely as simple, direct words. Avoid using long or pretentious words merely to impress your reader.

| | |
|---|---|
| **Inflated** | In the process of implementing this program, her incursion into the forest was in midtransportation process when it attained interface with an alleged perpetrator. |
| | —Russell Baker |
| **Concise** | On her way into the forest, she met a wolf. |

● **Practice Your Skills**

*Eliminating Redundancy, Empty Expressions, and Wordiness*

Revise the following sentences to eliminate redundancies, empty expressions, and wordy phrases and clauses. Some sentences may need more than one revision.

1. Many of the popular sports that many people enjoy in Japan are contests of strength and power.
2. There is *sumo* wrestling, for example, which pits two huge, giant men against each other.
3. The first wrestler to touch the floor before the other with anything but his feet loses the match.
4. Preceding the match the contestants enact a traditional ritual that they perform before the wrestling begins.
5. After clapping their hands, they extend their arms out with open hands to show the fact that they carry no weapons.
6. Kampsville, which is a center for archaeological research and training, is located in west central Illinois.
7. Every year young students who are interested in archaeology go to Kampsville in order to dig up the past.
8. The remains of 2,000 communities of prehistoric times are being uncovered.
9. Students are taught to dig in a very careful way.
10. Bones that come from animals can be very revealing.

**PROJECT PREP** *Revising* **Wordiness**

In your writing group, identify any wordiness there may be in each writer's composition. If it does not serve a purpose, make suggestions for eliminating it.

# In the Media

## Advertising Campaign

You receive a catalog in the mail from an outdoor clothing company. Flipping through the pages you see a rugged-looking jacket on a model with wind-blown hair. You stop and read the "copy," the written blurb that goes with it:

*You thought about turning back, but something in the wind kept you moving. And then, in the hush of nightfall, you heard the whimpers. A quick flash of white fur, and a mother wolf grabbed her pup by the scruff and trotted off into the darkness. The coat kept you warm through that starry night, and so did the memory of that rare glimpse into wolf motherhood.*

The copy writers have used evocative language to create an appealing scene that you now associate with that jacket. Chances are you'll never wear it on a starry night in the wilderness with a mother wolf and pup as companions, but the imaginative association may make you want the coat even more than ever. The message behind the ad is: *This coat will put you in harmony with nature, you rugged individual, and in it you will experience both unsurpassed coziness and a glimpse into nature's secrets.* In reality, a jacket can keep you warm, but all the rest of the implied benefits of that jacket are things the jacket itself simply cannot deliver.

The success of any ad campaign depends on the ability of the advertising team to combine creative, exciting language with compelling visuals to deliver a carefully chosen message to a targeted audience.

## Media Activity

In order to explore these challenges, imagine you work for an advertising agency that has won contracts to advertise the following products.

- a new line of cross-training shoes
- an unusual new Internet search engine
- a public interest group exposing dangers in the water supply
- a state-of-the-art planetarium funded by the state and local government

Divide into four teams, each of which will develop an advertising campaign for one of these products. Use the following questions to help you design your strategy.

## QUESTIONS FOR DEVELOPING AN ADVERTISING STRATEGY

- How will you create interest in the product?
- Who will be your audience?
- What characteristic of the product will you highlight?
- Will the tone of your campaign be amusing, dramatic, intelligent, emotional? Why?
- Which two media will be most effective?
- What slogan will you use?
- What kinds of text, visuals, and music will you use?
- What will be the roles of the team members?
- What equipment will you need? How will you get it?

Summarize your answers in a one-page strategy statement. Then prepare a detailed proposal to present to the client. In the proposal, lay out your strategy as clearly as possible, including sketches and approaches for each of the two media you identified.

Create one ad for each of the media. (If you are creating a video ad, refer to *Electronic Publishing,* pages 589–603, for help in creating the video.) Make a schedule showing what each team member will do by what target dates. You may want to refer back to your strategy statement frequently. Also develop a questionnaire eliciting constructive criticism to distribute to your class after they have had a chance to see your work. After showing your ads and receiving the completed questionnaires, write a summary of what you learned about your ad from the questionnaires.

*editing* ☆

Make the following wordy passage more "fuel efficient" by cutting out needless words and phrases.

> If you really desire to make many more friends, to engage in all kinds of more fun, and to make lots more more money, buy Carol's Amazing Lotion at any store that sells it.

# Correcting Faulty Sentences

Most writers, when writing their first drafts, concentrate on just the content and organization. Only later do they go back to polish their sentences and correct any errors. In this section, you will find ways to revise your sentences to eliminate some common sentence faults.

## 1 Faulty Coordination

You can prevent problems in faulty coordination in three ways. First, avoid using the wrong coordinator, which will blur the meaning of your sentence. Notice in the following example how the writer sharpens the meaning by supplying the appropriate coordinator.

| Faulty Coordination | I want to learn more about photography, **and** I am going to take lessons. |
|---|---|
| Correct | I want to learn more about photography, **so** I am going to take lessons. |

The following lists some common coordinators according to their use.

| SOME COMMON COORDINATORS | | | |
|---|---|---|---|
| **To Show Similarity** | **To Show Contrast** | **To Show Alternative** | **To Show Result** |
| and | but | either/or | so |
| both/and | still | neither/nor | therefore |
| furthermore | nevertheless | or, nor | as a result |

Second, coordinate only those ideas that are related to each other. If the ideas are not related, express them in separate sentences.

| Faulty Coordination | Planes fly over our house every hour, and flying is really a safe way to travel. |
|---|---|
| Correct | Planes fly over our house every hour. Flying is really a safe way to travel. |

Finally, coordinate only those ideas that are equally important. If the ideas are not equal, subordinate one of them by putting it in a phrase or a subordinate clause.

| Faulty Coordination | Inez forgot our phone number, and she did not call us. |
| Correct | **Forgetting our phone number,** Inez did not call us. (phrase) |
| Correct | **Since Inez forgot our phone number,** she did not call us. (subordinate clause) |

## PROJECT PREP *Revising* *Faulty Sentences*

In your writing group, analyze each writer's composition for incorrect sentence structure, especially faulty coordination. If you are writing a parody, think about whether incorrect use of language could become the source of parody. For example, satiric singer Tom Lehrer parodies folk singers in "The Folk Song Army," including the following verse:

> The tune doesn't have to be clever
> And it don't matter if you put a couple extra syllables into a line
> It sounds more ethnic if it ain't good English
> And it don't even gotta rhyme — excuse me — rhyne

If the subject of your parody employs Nonstandard or faulty English, note the ways he or she uses them and think about how you could exaggerate this use of English in your parody.

## ② Faulty Subordination

Subordination is used to show the relationship between ideas of unequal importance. Subordination can lead to two types of problems: (1) using the wrong subordinator and (2) subordinating the wrong idea.

To avoid the first problem use a word that shows exactly how the ideas are related.

| | |
|---|---|
| **Faulty Subordination** | Yuki trained for months **even though** he would be ready for the Olympic trials. |
| **Correct** | Yuki trained for months **so that** he would be ready for the Olympic trials. |

To avoid the second problem, use a subordinator and turn the less important idea into a subordinate clause. Then express the more important idea as an independent clause.

| | |
|---|---|
| **Faulty Subordination** | Although they took a walk in the park, it was snowing. |
| **Correct** | Although it was snowing, they took a walk in the park. |

This chart shows common subordinators, listed according to their use.

| SOME COMMON SUBORDINATORS | | | |
|---|---|---|---|
| **To Show Time** | **To Show Cause** | **To Show Purpose** | **To Show Condition** |
| after | because | that | if |
| before | since | so that | even though |
| whenever | as | in order that | unless |

The following guidelines will help you correct faulty coordination and faulty subordination as you revise your writing.

 **Correcting Faulty Coordination and Subordination**

- Use the connecting word that best expresses how the ideas are related.
- Express unrelated ideas in separate sentences.
- If related ideas are equally important, use a coordinating word to combine them.
- If related ideas are not equally important, turn the less important idea into a phrase or a subordinate clause.

● **Practice Your Skills**

*Correcting Faulty Coordination and Subordination*

Use the guidelines in the box above to revise each of the following sentences.

**1.** Tales of western cowhands depict adventurous heroes, and actually their lives were exhausting and dangerous.

**2.** On the range water was scarce and raiders were common; furthermore, cowhands on the open range endured many hardships.

**3.** The cowhands' most precious possessions were their horses; also horses were their only means of transportation.

**4.** A cowhand might give the last drop of water in his canteen to his horse since he himself was thirsty.

**5.** A western saddle was designed for support; because a cowhand could even nap in the saddle without falling.

**PROJECT PREP** *Revising* **Faulty Sentences**

In your writing group, review each author's work for faulty coordination and faulty subordination in your sentences. If you find any that do not serve some purpose, make suggestions for correcting the faulty sentences.

# ③ Faulty Parallelism

A parallel structure is one in which two or more ideas linked with coordinate or correlative conjunctions are expressed in the same grammatical form. Ideas being contrasted should also be parallel. **Parallelism** helps readers understand related ideas. **Faulty parallelism,** on the other hand, adds a jarring effect to a sentence.

| | |
|---|---|
| Faulty | The committee members were **enthusiastic, energetic,** and **of great diplomacy.** (two adjectives and one prepositional phrase) |
| Parallel | The committee members were **enthusiastic, energetic,** and **diplomatic.** (three adjectives) |
| Faulty | Neither soft **words** nor **offering treats** could coax the kitten down from the tree. (noun, gerund) |
| Parallel | Neither soft **words** nor **treats** could coax the kitten down from the tree. (both nouns) |
| Faulty | **Doing** your best is more important than **to win.** (gerund, infinitive) |
| Parallel | **Doing** your best is more important than **winning.** (both gerunds) |
| Parallel | **To do** your best is more important than **to win.** (both infinitives) |

## ● Practice Your Skills

### Correcting Faulty Parallelism

Revise the faulty parallelism in the following sentences.

**1.** Vernetta's goals are to study law and saving money.

**2.** Some toys are neither of any educational value nor safe.

**3.** After the audition, Tom felt both disappointed and relief.

**4.** Roberto proved himself trustworthy and a hardworking person.

**5.** The sense of smell is more powerful in evoking memories than how things sound.

---

**PROJECT PREP** *Revising* *Effective Style*

In your writing group, read one another's compositions as a whole. Note where the style is especially effective and where it could be improved. Use your peers' feedback to guide your revision as you polish your draft.

# 4 Active Voice

Writers always have a choice between the active and passive voice. The **active voice** stresses the doer of an action. The **passive voice** stresses the receiver of an action. In fact, the doer is sometimes left out of a sentence written in the passive voice. (See pages 777–779.)

**Active**       The plumber just fixed the kitchen sink.

**Passive**      The kitchen sink was just fixed by the plumber.

**Passive**      The kitchen sink was just fixed.

The passive voice not only requires more words, but it can also rob a sentence of its feeling of action. In general, choose the active voice over the passive except when the doer of the action is either obvious or unimportant.

**Passive**      The old library has been completely remodeled. (The focus is appropriately on the library, not on who did the remodeling.)

**Active**       José and Tina prepared the chicken and beef tacos. (If the context focuses on the cooks, active voice is stronger than passive.)

**Passive**      The chicken and beef tacos were prepared by José and Tina. (If the context focuses on the food, then passive voice might be appropriate to keep the emphasis on the dishes rather than the cooks.)

In a sentence such as "Barack Obama was elected President in 2008," where you wish to place emphasis on the receiver of the action, the passive voice is proper and useful.

Baker uses passive voice to serve his comic purposes in his retelling of Little Red Riding Hood.

> The elderly person was then subjected to the disadvantages of total consumption and transferred to residence in the perpetrator's stomach.

**Writing Tip**

Revise your sentences to eliminate faulty coordination, faulty subordination, faulty parallelism, and the overuse of the passive voice.

The sentence removes all real action from this dramatic event, a stark contrast to the more familiar "The wolf ate the grandmother," in which the subject is very clearly the doer of the action and very clearly acting upon the object, the grandmother.

## Practice Your Skills

### *Changing Passive Voice to Active Voice*

Rewrite each of the following sentences in the active voice.

**1.** A yard full of holes was dug by the persistent husky.

**2.** A decision was made by the company president to present employees with year-end bonuses.

**3.** A foul ball was called by the first-base umpire.

**4.** The plan for a new shopping mall was vetoed by the mayor.

**5.** Cinco de Mayo is celebrated by thousands of people.

**PROJECT PREP** *Publishing* **Sharing with an Audience**

Publish your work in the format you selected from page 43 or in another appropriate medium. Invite feedback from your audience.

# Writing Lab

## Project Corner

### Speak and Listen
### Take Notes

Discuss the various parodies produced by class members. What do they achieve? Is their goal simply humorous? Do they have an effect that makes a broader criticism of something in society? Discuss the role of parody in society and how it can help to improve people's conduct.

As people express their ideas, **take notes** about their comments. Then, discuss the notes that members of the class took. Did everyone consider the same information to be worth noting? Discuss any differences in what people wrote down.

### Collaborate and Create Try a New Form

In your writing group, select one parody and **produce it through a new form.** For example, if the parody is written, reproduce it through a different medium, such as a storyboard, an animation, or a performance.

### Post it Share with the World

**Send your parody** to a place where people outside your class can use it. You might upload a video to a file-sharing Web site, submit a parody to a satirical Web site, or contact a local newspaper to see if they might publish it.

### Reflect on your Writing Process
### Learn from Experience

For the parody you have written, **reflect on the process** you went through to generate it. Consider what was helpful, what was a waste of time, and how you might modify your process to produce a paper of this sort on a new occasion.

# In Academic Areas
## Poster for a Math Bee

1. As head math instructor at Brown High School, you want to promote an upcoming statewide math bee—a contest you feel Brown has a good chance of winning. *Design a poster* for the hallways of Brown, and write a short paragraph describing the math bee to students. Use vivid words and descriptions that will make the contest sound appealing. Keep your tone lively, convincing your student audience that the contest will be beneficial and fun to attend.

# For Oral Communication Speech to Campers

2. You are the head counselor at Camp Sunburn. You must prepare a speech to the campers—who range in age from 10 to 12—about ways to avoid the mosquitoes that are plaguing the area. *Prepare the speech* about how to avoid mosquitoes for the camp children. Make your speech lively and enjoyable by using vivid words and figurative language. Vary your sentence structures and sentence beginnings, and avoid rambling or faulty sentences.

# Timed Writing 🕐 Jargon-Free Story

3. Rewrite the first two paragraphs of Russell Baker's satirical passage about Little Red Riding Hood on page 39. Change the jargon-filled sentences into simple, direct language. Use an informal and playful tone as if you were telling the story to a group of your close friends.

*Before You Write* Consider the following questions: What is the subject? What is the occasion? Who is the audience? What is the purpose?

Prewrite to focus on using specific words to create clear images and to avoid using jargon. Use figurative language such as similes and metaphors to appeal to your reader's imagination. However, be sure to avoid clichés and mixed metaphors. You have 15 minutes to complete your work.

*After You Write* Evaluate your work using the six-trait evaluation forms on pages 25 and 66.

**CHAPTER 3**

# Structuring Your Writing

**T**he **structure** of a text is its organization, or the order of its parts.

Structures for texts take a variety of forms, as the following examples show.

- **A letter from a college** begins with a greeting, continues with the news that you have been accepted to attend, and ends with the closing "Sincerely."

- **A social networking Web site** displays your profile photo and name at the top, prominently features updates from your friends in the center, and shows links to games and groups for you to explore off to the side.

- **A newspaper article** begins with a high school soccer team winning the first round of the sectional tournament, moves on to describe the highlights of the game, then quotes key players and the coach about the challenges faced in the next round.

- **A history chapter** begins with background on the time period, describes key people and events, and summarizes the chapter information in a concluding paragraph.

## Writing Project *Analytical*

*History Close Up* Write an essay about an event in history in which one group of people was put down in some way by another.

*Think Through Writing* On the following page, you will read about what can happen to a group of people who are held back by misconceptions and prejudice. You are probably aware of instances in which people have been excluded based on appearance, beliefs, or social class. How did these people respond? What does history record about people like them? Write freely to answer these questions.

*Talk About It* In your writing group, discuss your ideas about historical events centered on race, ethnicity, religion, gender, or social bias.

*Read About It* In 1928, Virginia Woolf lectured the women students of Cambridge University, England, focusing on the position of women in society. Her talks were later published as one work entitled *A Room of One's Own*.

In the following excerpt from *A Room of One's Own,* Virginia Woolf focuses on the role of women in Elizabethan society. Her search for information about the Elizabethan woman, however, produced very little. In developing her essay, Woolf imagined that Shakespeare had a sister who was as gifted as he. Would this sister have had any of the opportunities afforded Shakespeare? Read the excerpt for Woolf's answer.

**MODEL: Essay**

# Shakespeare's Sister

*Virginia Woolf*

Here am I asking why women did not write poetry in the Elizabethan age, and I am not sure how they were educated; whether they were taught to write; whether they had sitting-rooms to themselves; how many women had children before they were twenty-one; what, in short, they did from eight in the morning 'till eight at night. They had no money evidently; according to Professor Trevelyan they were married whether they liked it or not before they were out of the nursery, at fifteen or sixteen very likely. It would have been extremely odd, even upon this showing, had one of them suddenly written the plays of Shakespeare, I concluded, and I thought of that old gentleman, who is dead now, but was a bishop, I think, who declared that it was impossible for any woman, past, present, or to come, to have the genius of Shakespeare. He wrote to the papers about it. He also told a lady who applied to him for information that cats do not as a matter of fact go to heaven, though they have, he added, souls of a sort. How much thinking those old gentlemen used to save one! How the borders of ignorance shrank back at their approach! Cats do not go to heaven. Women cannot write the plays of Shakespeare.

Be that as it may, I could not help thinking, as I looked at the works of Shakespeare on the shelf, that the bishop was right at least in this; it would have been impossible, completely and entirely, for any woman to have written the plays of Shakespeare in the age of Shakespeare. Let me imagine, since facts are so hard to come by, what would have happened had Shakespeare had a wonderfully gifted sister, called Judith, let us say. Shakespeare himself went, very probably—his mother was an heiress—to the grammar school, where he may have learnt Latin—Ovid,

> This introucotry paragraph begins in an informal, contemplative way and draws readers into a thoughtful frame of mind. It ends on a note of humor, keeping readers interested.

> The phrase "Be that as it may" lets the reader know that now information Woolf believes is more important will be given. Here Woolf introduces the thesis, or main idea, of her essay.

Virgil and Horace—and the elements of grammar and logic. He was, it is well known, a wild boy who poached rabbits, perhaps shot a deer, and had, rather sooner than he should have done, to marry a woman in the neighborhood, who bore him a child rather quicker than was right. That escapade sent him to seek his fortune in London. He had, it seemed, a taste for the theatre; he began by holding horses at the stage door. Very soon he got work in the theatre, became a successful actor, and lived at the hub of the universe, meeting everybody, knowing everybody, practicing his art on the boards, exercising his wits in the streets, and even getting access to the palace of the queen.

Meanwhile his extraordinarily gifted sister, let us suppose, remained at home. She was as adventurous, as imaginative, as agog to see the world as he was. But she was not sent to school. She had no chance of learning grammar and logic, let alone of reading Horace and Virgil. She picked up a book now and then, one of her brother's perhaps, and read a few pages. But then her parents came in and told her to mend the stockings or mind the stew and not moon about with books and papers. They would have spoken sharply but kindly, for they were substantial people who knew the conditions of life for a woman and loved their daughter—indeed, more likely than not she was the apple of her father's eye. Perhaps she scribbled some pages up in an apple loft on the sly, but was careful to hide them or set fire to them. Soon, however, before she was out of her teens, she was to be betrothed to the son of a neighboring wool-stapler. She cried out that marriage was hateful to her, and for that she was severely beaten by her father. Then he ceased to scold her. He begged her instead not to hurt him, not to shame him in this matter of her marriage. He would give her a chain of beads or a fine petticoat, he said; and there were tears in his eyes. How could she disobey him? How could she break his heart?

The force of her own gift alone drove her to it. She made up a small parcel of her belongings, let herself down by a rope one summer's night and took the road to London. She was not seventeen. The birds that sang in the hedge were not more musical than she was. She had the quickest fancy, a gift like her brother's, for the tune of words. Like him, she had a taste for the theatre. She stood at the stage door; she wanted to act, she said. Men

> This paragraph presents Woolf's main theories by describing the life of Shakespeare's gifted "sister."

> Just as a paragraph has supporting sentences that give details about the main idea, a composition has supporting paragraphs. Here Woolf gives more details to show why it would have been impossible for any woman to have written the plays of Shakespeare in his time.

laughed in her face. The manager—a fat, loose-lipped man—guffawed. He bellowed something about poodles dancing and women acting—no woman, he said, could possibly be an actress. He hinted—you can imagine what. She could get no training in her craft. Could she even seek her dinner in a tavern or roam the streets at midnight?

Yet her genius was for fiction and lusted to feed abundantly upon the lives of men and women and the study of their ways. At last—for she was very young, oddly like Shakespeare the poet in her face, with the same grey eyes and rounded brows—at last Nick Greene the actor-manager took pity on her; she found herself with child by that gentleman and so—who shall measure the heat and violence of the poet's heart when caught and tangled in a woman's body?—killed herself one winter's night and lies buried at some crossroads where the omnibuses[1] now stop outside the Elephant and Castle.[2]

That, more or less, is how the story would run, I think, if a woman in Shakespeare's day had had Shakespeare's genius. But for my part, I agree with the deceased bishop, if such he was—it is unthinkable that any woman in Shakespeare's day should have had Shakespeare's genius. For genius like Shakespeare's is not born among laboring, uneducated, servile people. It was not born in England among the Saxons and the Britons. It is not born today among the working classes. How, then, could it have been born among women whose work began, according to Professor Trevelyan, almost before they were out of the nursery, who were forced to it by their parents and held to it by all the power of law and custom? Yet genius of a sort must have existed among women as it must have existed among the working classes. Now and again an Emily Brontë or a Robert Burns blazes out and proves its presence. But certainly it never got itself on to paper.

When, however, one reads of a witch being ducked, of a woman possessed by devils, of a wise woman selling herbs, or even of a very remarkable man who had a mother, then I think we are on the track of a lost novelist, a suppressed poet, of some mute and inglorious Jane Austen, some Emily Brontë who dashed her brains out

In these two paragraphs, Woolf creates in the sister a flesh-and-blood person who represents many women of her era. Woolf's poetic appraisal adds poignancy to the description of the young woman's death.

That Woolf should agree with the bishop piques the reader's interest. We are alerted that she will share another insight on the subject.

By contrasting anonymous artists of the past with references to beloved authors of her (and our) time, Woolf leads the reader to imagine the women artists lost to us forever.

---

1 **omnibuses:** Buses.
2 **Elephant and Castle:** The name of a British inn.

on the moor or mopped and mowed about the highways crazed with the torture that her gift had put her to. Indeed, I would venture to guess that Anon, who wrote so many poems without signing them, was often a woman. It was a woman Edward Fitzgerald, I think, suggested who made the ballads and the folksongs, crooning them to her children, beguiling her spinning with them, or the length of the winter's night.

**Respond in Writing** Respond to Virginia Woolf's essay. Are her opinions well supported? Does her imagined life of Shakespeare's "sister" seem to you to reflect actual historical events? What have you learned about how bias and prejudice can affect a group of people? What strikes a familiar chord in your own life?

**Develop Your Own Ideas** Work with your classmates to develop your ideas about bias and prejudice throughout history.

**Small Groups:** In your writing group, make a chart like the one below to share your examples and analysis of historical bias and prejudice. Use the writing you have done, the excerpt from Virginia Woolf's lecture, and any other knowledge or sources available to help you develop your ideas.

| Bias or Prejudice | Its Effect on the Recipients | What We Can Learn from This |
|---|---|---|
|  |  |  |

**Whole Class:** Make a master chart of all of the examples and analysis generated by the small groups, and use these ideas for further discussion.

**Write About It** You will write an essay about a time in history when one group was ill-treated by another because of prejudice or bias. You may choose from any of the following possibilities.

| Possible Topics | Possible Audiences | Possible Forms |
|---|---|---|
| • a bias against a particular social group<br><br>• a prejudice about a certain religious (or nonreligious) group<br><br>• a bias against a certain socio-economic group<br><br>• a misconception about a particular racial group | • other teenagers<br><br>• parents<br><br>• school administrators<br><br>• the student council<br><br>• people who hold the prejudice you are writing about | • a history magazine or Web site<br><br>• a blog<br><br>• a letter<br><br>• a report to the class<br><br>• a memo |

Woolf's essay is a good example of one of the most valuable uses of writing: to explore an idea and create understanding. Each paragraph in her essay has a role to play in developing her idea. As a writer, you are expected to provide a message with substance. Paragraphs contribute to the logical structure of your writing.

A **paragraph** is a group of related sentences that present and develop one main idea.

## ❶ Paragraph Structure

Each paragraph is an entity all its own, with its own specific facts and ideas. Notice how the following well-written paragraph is easy to read and understand.

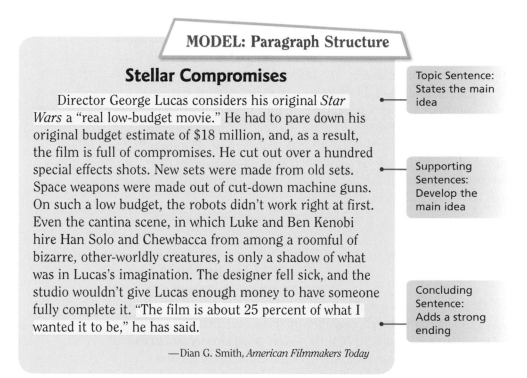

**MODEL: Paragraph Structure**

### Stellar Compromises

Director George Lucas considers his original *Star Wars* a "real low-budget movie." He had to pare down his original budget estimate of $18 million, and, as a result, the film is full of compromises. He cut out over a hundred special effects shots. New sets were made from old sets. Space weapons were made out of cut-down machine guns. On such a low budget, the robots didn't work right at first. Even the cantina scene, in which Luke and Ben Kenobi hire Han Solo and Chewbacca from among a roomful of bizarre, other-worldly creatures, is only a shadow of what was in Lucas's imagination. The designer fell sick, and the studio wouldn't give Lucas enough money to have someone fully complete it. "The film is about 25 percent of what I wanted it to be," he has said.

—Dian G. Smith, *American Filmmakers Today*

Topic Sentence: States the main idea

Supporting Sentences: Develop the main idea

Concluding Sentence: Adds a strong ending

CHAPTER 3

The structure of this paragraph is easy to follow. In this case, the **topic sentence** is the first one you read. In some paragraphs, it may come in the middle or at the end. The main idea may be implied rather than stated directly or the main idea may be expressed in two sentences. Most paragraphs that stand alone, however, have a clearly stated topic sentence, a body of **supporting sentences,** and a **concluding sentence**.

## TOPIC SENTENCE

A **topic sentence** states the main idea of the paragraph.

The topic sentence is more general than the other sentences in the paragraph. It gives an overall summary of what the paragraph will be about while being specific enough to focus on the main point of the paragraph.

### FEATURES OF A TOPIC SENTENCE

- A topic sentence states the main idea.
- A topic sentence focuses the limited subject to one main point that can be adequately covered in the paragraph.
- A topic sentence is more general than the sentences that develop it.

The following examples demonstrate a topic sentence and an implied main idea.

### MODEL: Topic Sentence in the Middle

Japan is a collection of large islands, strung along the eastern shore of the mainland of Asia. The islands are very rugged and very mountainous. High over all the other peaks rises the one supreme peak—the perfect cone of snowclad Fuji. Like most of the high mountains of Japan, Fuji is a volcano, sleeping, but far from dead. Compared to the Alps and the Himalayas, Fuji is not especially high. It seems high, however, because it rises in one superb sweeping curve right from the shore to the sky, a curve that can be seen for a hundred miles on every side.

—Richard Halliburton, *Complete Book of Marvels*

Topic Sentence

### MODEL: Implied Main Idea

When the newborn seal pup slips from the warmth of his mother's body onto the ice, crystals form on his wet little body and his skin temperature falls to 70°F. He shivers so vigorously that in about 45 minutes he has produced enough heat to bring his skin temperature to 93.4°F. Only a light coat of baby fur, the lanugo, protects him from the zero temperatures of the Antarctic spring. His metabolism, however, is exceedingly high during his early life, and he can take in great quantities of milk. Seal mothers' milk is richer than heavy cream; it is half butterfat. On this creamy diet the pup gains about 250 pounds in six weeks and has a good coating of fat.

—Lucy Kavaler, *Life Battles Cold*

Implied Main Idea: Seal pups have natural mechanisms to help them survive frigid temperatures.

## Practice Your Skills

### Identifying the Main Idea

Find and write the topic sentence of each paragraph. If the main idea is implied, write a sentence expressing that idea.

### 1. Forest Rangers

Park rangers' work includes planning and carrying out conservation efforts to protect plant and animal life in the parks from fire, disease, and heavy visitor traffic. Rangers plan and conduct programs of public safety, including law enforcement and rescue work. They set up and direct interpretive programs such as slide shows, guided tours, displays, and occasionally even dramatic presentations. These programs are designed to help visitors become aware of the natural and historic significance of the areas they visit.

—Walter Oleksy, *Careers in the Animal Kingdom*

### 2. Starry Neighbors

Easter Island is the loneliest inhabited place in the world. The nearest solid land the islanders can see is above in the firmament, the moon and the planets. They have to travel farther than any other people to see that there really is land closer. Therefore, living nearest the stars, they know more names of stars than of towns and countries in our own world.

—Thor Heyerdahl, *Aku-Aku*

## PROJECT PREP   *Prewriting*   *Paragraph Structure*

Write a paragraph, perhaps choosing from one of the topics listed on page 86. In your writing group, discuss each person's first rough draft. Since you were writing primarily to explore your own thoughts on the subject, the writing will probably not be very structured. Identify the topic sentence or implied main idea of each paragraph. Then discuss what each writer would need to do to provide structure to his or her writing.

# ② Paragraph Development

Not every paragraph with a topic sentence, supporting sentences, and a concluding sentence is an effective paragraph. What the sentences say is as important as how they are put together. The following chart shows some types of supporting details you can use.

| TYPES OF SUPPORTING DETAILS | | |
| --- | --- | --- |
| examples | incidents | facts/statistics |
| reasons | directions | steps in a process |
| sensory details | events | comparisons/contrasts |
| causes and effects | analogies | classifications |

When you choose your supporting details, keep in mind the purpose of the paragraph and the kinds of questions a reader may have about the subject.

## ADEQUATE DEVELOPMENT

Readers quickly lose interest when writing is insufficiently developed. No matter which method of development you use, your supporting details must be numerous and specific enough to make the main idea clear, convincing, and interesting. The evidence must be relevant and substantial. These characteristics ensure **adequate development.**

### MODEL: Adequate Paragraph Development

Around the turn of the last century child-labor practices led to a grueling life for many American children. In 1900 at least 1.7 million children under the age of sixteen worked for wages. Children working at night were kept awake by having cold water splashed in their faces. Some girls under sixteen worked sixteen hours a day in canning factories, capping forty cans per minute. Ten-year-old boys crouched over dusty coal chutes for ten hours a day to pick slate out of the coal sliding past. In city tenements many children seven years and younger made artificial flowers at night to be sold the next day at street stands. Some states began passing laws protecting child laborers after 1905. Not until 1938 was a federal law passed that prevented employers in most industries from hiring children under the age of sixteen.

—Clarence L. Ver Steeg, *American Spirit*

The paragraph begins with information gathered in 1900.

Five years pass before laws are passed.

The words "Not until" emphasize the passing of many years. A time span of 38 years is covered chronologically in this paragraph.

### Improving Development

Using the facts in the following table, revise the paragraph below so that the main idea is adequately developed. Retain the first sentence and the last sentence. (The last sentence is the topic sentence.)

**Writing Tip**

Use sufficient **specific details** to develop your main idea adequately.

## Cities Take Over

Between the years 1860 and 1910 the nation's population increased enormously. The new population moved to both rural and urban areas, but more people moved to cities. The number of cities increased dramatically. Since the early 1900s, the United States has been a nation of cities.

| Facts | 1860 | 1910 | % of Growth |
|---|---|---|---|
| overall population | 31 million | 92 million | 200 |
| rural population | 25 million | 50 million | 100 |
| urban population | 6 million | 42 million | 600 |
| number of cities | 400 | 2200 | 450 |
| number of immigrants from Europe (1865–1910): 19 million | | | |

### editing ☆

You don't need extra wording to successfully develop your ideas. Revise the following sentence to make it more concise.

> The wonderfully protective child labor laws that were passed in many forward-thinking states in 1905 were horrendously slow in becoming the law of our land.

CHAPTER 3

You can use a rubric like the one below to evaluate how well you have developed ideas in your writing.

## Idea Rubric

| 4 Ideas are presented and developed in depth. | 3 Most ideas are presented and developed with insight. | 2 Many ideas are not well developed. | 1 Most ideas are not well developed. |
|---|---|---|---|
| • I developed each idea thoroughly with specific details. | • I developed most ideas thoroughly with specific details. | • I tried to develop ideas but was more general than specific. | • I tried to develop ideas but was mostly overly general. |
| • My presentation of ideas was original. | • My presentation of some ideas was thoughtful. | • I listed rather than developed ideas. | • My ideas were not developed. |
| • I made meaningful connections among ideas. | • I made some connections among ideas. | • I made few connections among ideas. | • I did not make connections among ideas. |
| • I took some risks to make my writing come alive. | • I played it safe and did not put much of myself into the composition. | • I left a few things out, but I think my meaning comes across. | • I left some important things out, so my meaning wasn't really clear. |

## PROJECT PREP  *Prewriting*  *Developing Ideas*

In your writing group, discuss each person's main idea and ways to develop it adequately. You might want to expand the chart you used earlier to include supporting details.

| Bias or Prejudice Analysis Chart | | |
|---|---|---|
| **Bias or Prejudice** | **Its Effect on the Recipients** | **What We Can Learn from This** |
| | | |
| Details | Details | Details |
| • <br> • <br> • | • <br> • <br> • | • <br> • <br> • |

Using the feedback from your group, draft your paragraph and then evaluate it using the rubric above.

# 3 Unity

In a paragraph that has **unity,** all the sentences support and develop the main idea. If a paragraph is unified, the reader is not distracted by details that stray from the main point. In the following paragraph, the crossed-out sentences stray from the main idea.

**MODEL: Paragraph Unity**

Sammy Lee, a second-generation Korean American, has devoted his life to athletic excellence and physical fitness. In 1948 he won the Olympic medal for high diving. When he repeated his feat at the Olympics four years later, he became the first male diver to win two consecutive times. ~~Another Korean American, Richard You, was an Olympic weight lifting coach.~~ Lee also won the James E. Sullivan award for outstanding sports achievement in 1958. He now practices medicine and has served on the President's Council on Physical Fitness. ~~Richard You is also a doctor at present.~~

## Practice Your Skills

### Checking for Unity

Write the two sentences that stray from the subject in the paragraph below.

**Writing Tip**

Achieve **unity** by making sure all the supporting sentences relate to the topic sentence.

Although the alchemists of long ago are often regarded as superstitious magicians, they did help pave the way for some important discoveries. In their vain search for an elixir of life and a way to turn metals into gold, they discovered chemicals that are now common in such products as dye, varnish, medicine, glass, and steel. Alchemists also developed waterproofing, smelling salts, and some painkillers. Some alchemists, nonetheless, were undoubtedly frauds. One early alchemist developed a theory of gas, and others led the way to an understanding of blood circulation and enzymes and hormones. One famous alchemist, Merlin, may have existed only in legend. Although their work was limited by a lack of scientific knowledge, many alchemists were serious scientists whose discoveries opened new doors.

**PROJECT PREP** *Evaluating* **Unity**

In your writing group, evaluate one another's drafts looking for any sentences that destroy the paragraph's unity. Make changes in your draft based on the evaluation of your peers.

# ④ Coherence

In a **coherent** paragraph, ideas follow logically and smoothly.

The following chart shows the five most common ways to organize paragraphs and longer pieces of writing.

**Writing Tip**

Achieve **coherence** in a paragraph by ordering the ideas logically and using transition words.

## WAYS TO ORGANIZE IDEAS

| | |
|---|---|
| **Chronological Order** | Arrange details in the order in which they occurred (time order). |
| **Spatial Order** | Arrange details according to their location—near to far, top to bottom, for example. |
| **Order of Importance** | Arrange details from most to least or from least to most important. |
| **Developmental Order** | Arrange details in a logical progression in which one idea grows out of another. |
| **Comparison/Contrast** | Arrange details to show how two items are similar or different. Describe one item and then the other or compare and contrast by feature. |

A writer can use various devices, such as in the chart below, to help the reader understand how the ideas in a paragraph are related.

### HERE'S HOW  Strategies for Connecting Ideas

- Repeat key words occasionally to link ideas.
- Use synonyms to connect back to key words.
- Use pronouns to relate back to key nouns.
- Use transitions—words and phrases that show how ideas are related to one another.

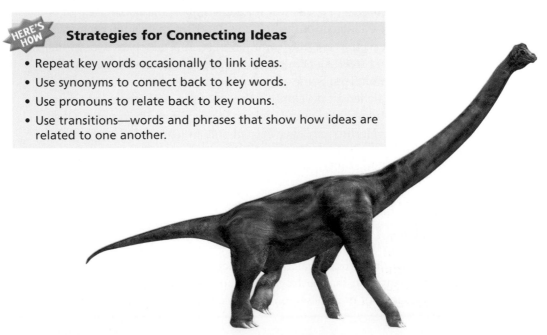

The following chart lists common transitions for particular types of organization. Most transitions can often be used with more than one kind of organization.

| KIND OF ORGANIZATION | COMMON TRANSITIONS |
|---|---|
| Chronological Order | first, second, then, by evening, in the beginning, soon, immediately, finally, years ago, tomorrow |
| Spatial Order | above, below, right, next to, beyond, inside, behind |
| Order of Importance | first, second, more, most important, the largest, above all, furthermore, also, another |
| Developmental Order | furthermore, besides, however, despite, another, as a result, therefore |
| Comparison/Contrast | similarly, like, just, as, but, on the other hand, in contrast to, however |

● **Practice Your Skills**

*Identifying Paragraph Organization*

Write *chronological, spatial, order of importance, developmental,* or *comparison/ contrast* to describe the organization of each of the following paragraphs.

**1. Zookeepers Then and Now**

The job of animal keeper in a zoo once required no advanced education. The primary responsibilities of the keeper were to feed the animals and keep their cages clean, and working with wild animals was not considered a desirable activity. Recently, however, more zoos have begun hiring college graduates as keepers. In contrast to earlier times, the job of animal keeper now includes more challenging roles, such as presenting educational programs to the public and studying the animals' habitats. Furthermore, unlike years ago, zoos are deluged with applications from college graduates eager to work with animals.

**2. Tail Snaring**

"Catch and release" has become a popular slogan for those who fish for sport rather than for food. As a result, devices that land fish without harming them are popular. The tail snare, which lassoes fish by their tails, is one such device. Besides being useful to people who fish, tail snares help conservationists tag fish. Furthermore, the device does not damage game fish. In short, tail snares are helpful to all.

**3. The Distant Past**

Throughout most of the Mesozoic era, sometimes called the Age of Reptiles, primitive mammals scurried about, lost in the shadows of the mighty dinosaurs who lumbered through the gloomy swamps and giant softwood forests. In the beginning of the Cretaceous, the period which marks the last chapter in the reign of the giant reptiles, the earth cooled. Inland seas receded, marshes dried up, and the monster dinosaurs clambered out onto the trembling uplands and began to live on open ground. Great hardwood forests soon covered the land. Life for the small, ancestral mammals was perilous, and while the terrible dinosaurs ruled, the little animals scurried about in the deep green shade of the forests or took refuge in the branches of bushes and trees, often venturing forth only at night. They waited, unaware of the kingdom they were soon to inherit, and used their wits and mammalian advantages to survive.

—Judith Grosch, *You and Your Brain*

#### 4. A Man of Many Talents

Benjamin Franklin accomplished many things in his eighty-four years. He was a recognized inventor. Franklin gave to the world the stove, bifocals, and the lightning rod. He invented a draft for fireplaces and a combination chair and stepladder for the kitchen. He was also a city planner. Franklin reorganized the British Post Office, established a city police system in Philadelphia, and a fire-control organization. Furthermore, Franklin was a military strategist. He organized a successful defense of his colony when it was threatened by attack by the French. He led a force of men into the wilderness near Bethlehem and supervised the building of three important forts in that area. Finally Franklin was an active statesman. He was a member of the committee which drew up the Declaration of Independence, a delegate to the Constitutional Convention, and an ambassador to England and France for over twenty-five years.

—P. Joseph Canavan

#### 5. Whose Desk Is It?

There was no name on the office door, but I recognized the desk immediately. Its surface was hidden beneath tall, precarious mounds of paper. Just visible behind a pile of folders stood a framed photo of my parents and me, smiling out over the rubble. On the wall above hung a painting I had done in second grade. "For Dad!" it proclaimed in shaky but bold green letters. Undoubtedly this was my father's desk.

### ● Practice Your Skills

#### *Recognizing Transitions*

Find and write the transitional words and phrases used in each of the paragraphs in the previous practice activity.

Use the following rubric to evaluate the order of your ideas and your use of transitions.

## Organization Rubric

| 4 Ideas progress smoothly and the organization clarifies meaning. | 3 Most ideas progress smoothly and the organization is clear. | 2 Some ideas progress smoothly but the organization is not consistent. | 1 Few ideas progress smoothly and there is no clear organization. |
| --- | --- | --- | --- |
| • My topic sentence states the main idea creatively and captures attention.<br><br>• I used the best organization pattern to present the supporting details.<br><br>• My concluding sentence provides a strong ending to the paragraph.<br><br>• My sentences flow smoothly. I used transitions throughout. | • I stated the main idea in the topic sentence and captured attention.<br><br>• I used an appropriate organization to present the supporting details.<br><br>• My concluding sentence helps make the paragraph feel complete.<br><br>• Most of my sentences flow smoothly. I used some transitions. | • I stated the main idea in the topic sentence but did not capture attention.<br><br>• I used an appropriate organization but had some things out of order.<br><br>• My conclusion provides an ending but it does not feel strong.<br><br>• I repeated some ideas unnecessarily. I could have used more transitions. | • I did not state my main idea clearly.<br><br>• I did not really use an organizational pattern.<br><br>• My concluding sentence does not provide an ending for the paragraph.<br><br>• I repeated some things and also had some things out of order or not related to the topic. I did not use transitions. |

## PROJECT PREP  *Prewriting*  *Achieving Coherence*

In your writing group, discuss the best way for each writer's ideas to be organized. Switch papers and write a few sentences of your partner's paragraph in its new organization. Be sure to include transitions. Look over the work your partner does on your paper and consider how effectively the writing achieves coherence.

# Paragraph Writing Workshops

## ① Narrative Paragraphs

When your purpose is to relate a series of events, you will write a narrative. **Rhetorical strategies,** such as introducing the subject in an interesting way, building suspense, and other techniques that hold the reader's attention, apply as much at the paragraph level as at the essay level. Practice these strategies as you create narrative paragraphs.

**Narrative writing** tells a real or an imaginary story with a clear beginning, middle, and ending.

### Structuring a Narrative Paragraph

- In the **topic sentence**, capture attention and make a general statement.
- In the **supporting sentences,** tell the story, event by event, often building suspense.
- In the **concluding sentence,** summarize the story or make a point about its meaning.

---

**MODEL: Narrative Paragraph**

## A Curious Clown

The polar bear has an insatiable curiosity, and sometimes he can be quite a clown. In 1969, a coast-guard vessel in the Canadian Artic received a visit from an adult male polar bear traveling atop a drifting ice floe. The animal was obviously bent on a shopping expedition, and the crew obliged by throwing it a carton full of black molasses which the bear soon spread all over itself and the ice. This was followed by some jam, salt pork, two salami sausages, an apple which it spat out in disgust, and a jar of peanut butter which disappeared in about two seconds flat. Eventually the food supply ran out, but the 363 kg (800 lb.) bear stuck its head through one of the port-holes in search of further nourishment. When nothing turned up, it decided to climb aboard, much to the alarm of the crew, who decided to open up the hoses on it. This was a big mistake, however, because the bear absolutely loved the drenching and raised its paws in the air to get the jet of water under its armpits. In the end the coastguards were forced to fire a distress rocket rather close to the interloper before it reluctantly moved away.

—Gerald L. Wood, *Animal Facts and Feats*

**Topic Sentence:** Makes a general statement

**Supporting Sentences:** Illustrate the bear's curiosity and clownishness

**Concluding Sentence:** Wraps up the story

You can use a graphic organizer like the one below to help you organize a narrative paragraph.

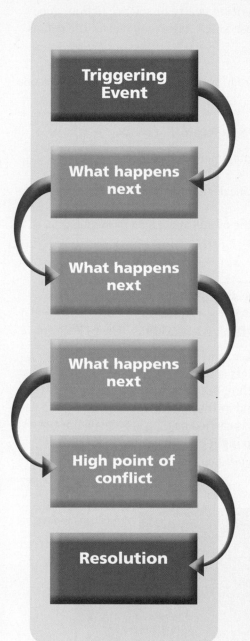

**Triggering Event**

**What happens next**

**What happens next**

**What happens next**

**High point of conflict**

**Resolution**

## QuickGuide for Writing Narrative Paragraphs

→ Brainstorm, write freely, or tell your story out loud to think of all the events in the story you want to tell. When you have them all, arrange them in chronological order.

→ Include the event that started the story in motion, the conflict and how it was approached, and the resolution.

→ Use transitions such as *first, the next day,* and *at last* to keep the order clear.

→ Include a clear introduction and conclusion.

### ● Create Real-World Texts

1. As a senior you are experiencing many "last times." Write a narrative telling the story of a "last time" in your life.

2. Write a narrative from your family's history that has become family lore. Make an audio recording of your story and play it for family members.

3. Write a humorous story about an embarrassing moment.

4. Write a paragraph for history class about a courageous leader who stood up against bias and prejudice.

# ② Descriptive Paragraphs

When you want your reader to picture a person, an object, or a place clearly, you need to write a good description. Whether writing poetry or science fiction, good descriptive writing helps your reader see, hear, smell, taste, and feel all the details you are describing.

**Descriptive writing** paints a vivid picture in words of a person, object, or scene.

 **HERE'S HOW**

### Structuring a Descriptive Paragraph

- In the **topic sentence,** make a general statement about the subject and suggest an overall impression.
- In the **supporting sentences,** supply specific details that help readers use their five senses to bring the picture to life.
- In the **concluding sentence,** summarize the overall impression of the subject.

---

## MODEL: Descriptive Paragraph

### Harbored for the Night

In the breeze-cooled cabin of the *Jodi-Lee*, daylight seems ages ago. Outside, the dark, cool waters splash in whispers against the hull in an ageless rhythm. Creaking ropes and mellow clangs of other boats blend in the harbor hush. The musty smell of wet wood is carried by the breeze. All around the harbor, the damp night air cools away the sunburns of the day. In the *Jodi-Lee*, the moon is a comforting night-light.

**Topic Sentence:** Is implied by the lush descriptions (a houseboat at night is a delight for the senses)

**Supporting Sentences:** Provide evocative sensory details

**Concluding Sentence:** Reinforces the sensory images and refers back to first sentence

You can use a graphic organizer like the one below to help you organize a descriptive paragraph.

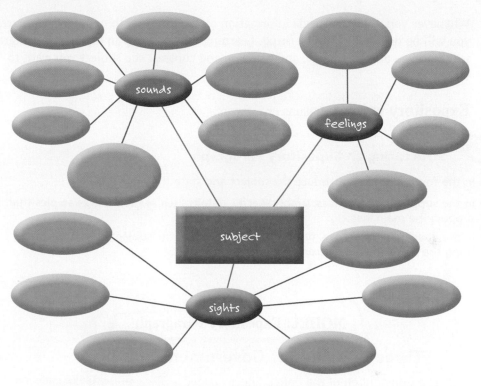

## QuickGuide for Writing Descriptive Paragraphs

→ Brainstorm or use a cluster diagram to compile vivid sensory details that bring your subject to life.

→ Choose details that convey a strong impression, and organize them in spatial order or another logical order.

→ Use transitions such as *beyond, outside,* and *all around* that suit the order you have chosen.

→ Include a clear introduction and conclusion.

## ● Create Real-World Texts

1. Write a paragraph describing an item you own that you want to sell.

2. Write a paragraph describing an ordinary setting that takes on extraordinary qualities when conditions change, such as a deserted movie theater or a street decked out for a festival.

3. Describe a person in the scene you created above.

4. Describe the place high school graduation is held an hour after graduation is over.

# ❸ Expository Paragraphs

Whenever you want to provide information or explain something to your readers, you will be using expository writing. Learning how to write an expository paragraph will help you analyze, define, and compare and contrast the subject you want to write about.

**Expository writing** explains or informs.

### HERE'S HOW  Structuring an Expository Paragraph

- In the **topic sentence,** introduce the subject and state the main idea.
- In the **supporting sentences,** supply specific details such as facts and examples that support the main idea.
- In the **concluding sentence,** draw a conclusion about the subject or in other ways bring the paragraph to a strong ending.

---

**MODEL: Expository Paragraph**

## Three Branches of Government

The Constitution of the United States created a national government with three distinct branches. They are the legislative branch (Congress), the executive branch (the president/Cabinet), and the judicial branch (the federal court system). No one branch has absolute power; each one has its own duties and limitations. For example, the President is the one to appoint Supreme Court justices, but those appointees must be approved by Congress. When Congress, on the other hand, makes a law, the President has the right to veto it, and the Supreme Court may determine whether it is constitutional or not. This separation of powers prevents any one branch or person from becoming too powerful.

Topice sentence: States the main theme

Supporting Sentences: Offer detailed information about the main idea

Concluding Sentence: Refers back to topic sentence and adds related information

You can use a graphic organizer like the one below to help you organize an expository paragraph.

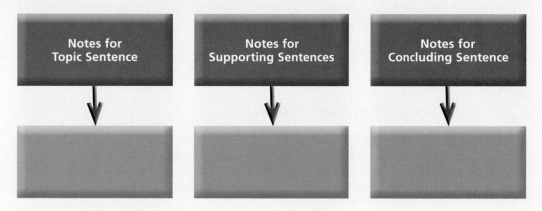

| Notes for Topic Sentence | Notes for Supporting Sentences | Notes for Concluding Sentence |

## QuickGuide for Writing Expository Paragraphs

→ Use brainstorming or clustering to think of subjects. Then use one of the methods of developing expository paragraphs listed above to explain your subject.

→ Use relevant and substantial evidence and well-chosen details to support your main idea. (See pages 90–91.)

→ Organize the parts of your expository paragraph in a logical order. (See pages 94–95.)

→ Use transitions such as *for example, on the other hand,* and *however* to keep the order clear.

→ Include a clear introduction and conclusion.

## ● Create Real-World Texts

1. Write an expository paragraph for your British Literature class explaining the key features of Victorian society.

2. Write an expository paragraph on physical fitness and health that relates to teenagers for a student newsletter.

3. Write how an accidental or chance incident affected your life in some important way.

4. Write a paragraph that explains the value or importance of high school traditions.

# ④ Persuasive Paragraphs

When you write persuasive paragraphs, you are trying to convince others that they should share your opinion or take a certain course of action. Learning how to write a persuasive paragraph will help you develop the skills for any kind of persuasive writing.

**Persuasive writing** asserts an opinion and uses facts, examples, and reasons to convince readers.

### Structuring a Persuasive Paragraph

- In the **topic sentence,** assert an opinion.
- In the **supporting sentences,** back up the opinion with facts, examples, reasons, and if necessary citations from experts. Acknowledge opposing views, and address them directly with reasoned arguments. Appeal to the reader's reason, but also engage the reader by appealing to emotion as well.
- In the **concluding sentence,** restate the opinion and make a final appeal.

In the following model, notice how supporting sentences enhance the topic sentence.

## MODEL: Persuasive Paragraph

## The Fall of Rome

Historians have long been fascinated by the fall of the Roman Empire and the causes of that fall. Although at one time most historians blamed Rome's collapse on the invasion of barbarians, a more careful study shows that Rome contained the seeds of its own destruction. For one thing, the economy of Rome was in serious disorder. The historian Max Weber argues that the decline of slavery and cities, coupled with the development of self-sufficient manors, left the city-based governments in poverty. At the same time, wealthy Romans indulged in lavish luxuries, widening the gap between the social classes. Another historian, Mikail Rostovtzeff, adds an intellectual crisis to the causes of Rome's collapse. He claims that the influx of conquered nationalities "barbarized" Rome, sapping it of its intellectual vigor. Perhaps most important, Rome's political structure was in disarray. Uncertainty over who held the ruling power, the people or the Senate nobles, led to revolutions and massacres. Although no single one of these forces would have been sufficient to topple the great empire, the combination of internal weaknesses ultimately left it unable to defend itself against the barbarian invaders.

Topic Sentence: States the main idea

Supporting Sentences: Develop the main idea

Concluding Sentence: Reiterates the main idea of the paragraph

You can use a graphic organizer like the one below to help you organize a persuasive paragraph.

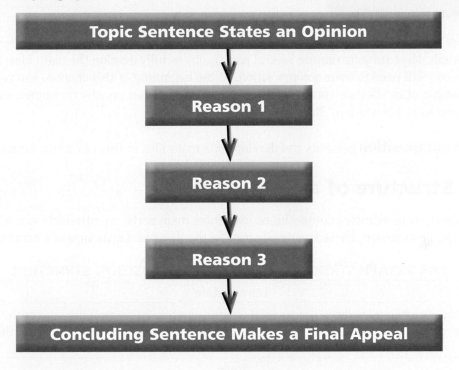

**Topic Sentence States an Opinion**

**Reason 1**

**Reason 2**

**Reason 3**

**Concluding Sentence Makes a Final Appeal**

## QuickGuide for Writing Persuasive Paragraphs

→ Explore your ideas by freewriting, and then choose one opinion that you feel strongly about that you think you can defend.

→ Gather the information you need to defend your opinion and convince others. Conduct interviews and include quotations from knowledgable sources.

→ Include a clear thesis or position based on logical reasons with various forms of support, such as hard evidence, reason, common sense, and cultural assumptions.

→ Arrange your arguments from least to most important.

→ Include a clear introduction and conclusion.

## ● Create Real-World Texts

1. Athletes are often recruited by colleges. Write a persuasive paragraph defending the recruitment of athletes or arguing why athletes should be held to the same standards as other students.

2. Write a paragraph in a letter to a post-secondary school you want to attend persuading the admissions officer to consider your application seriously.

# Compositions

Most of the writing you will do in and out of school will require more than a single paragraph. Most subjects require several paragraphs to fully develop the main idea. In short, you will need to write a composition. At the beginning of this chapter, you read an example of an effective composition—Virginia Woolf's essay on why no women wrote great works of literature in Shakespeare's time.

A **composition** presents and develops one main idea in three or more paragraphs.

## 1 Structure of a Composition

Carefully constructed compositions have three main parts: an introduction, a body, and a conclusion. These three parts parallel the three-part structure of a paragraph.

| PARAGRAPH STRUCTURE | COMPOSITION STRUCTURE |
|---|---|
| **Introduction** | |
| topic sentence introduces the subject/ expresses the main idea | introductory paragraph introduces the subject/expresses the main idea in a thesis statement |
| **Body** | |
| supporting sentences | supporting paragraphs |
| **Conclusion** | |
| concluding sentence | concluding paragraph |

As you read the composition about early humans using toothpicks that begins below, notice how the three main parts and the thesis statement work together to present a unified subject.

MODEL: Composition

### But Did They Floss?

As anthropologists imagine it, early humans sat by the fire after a hard day at the hunt, chewing on roasted mammoth and picking their teeth with sticks cut to sharp points. At other times, they just picked their teeth idly, while contemplating what a daub of paint might do for drab cave walls. The simple toothpick, recent discoveries reveal, may have been one of the first "tools" of human design.

Introduction

Thesis Statement

Evidence of Stone-Age toothpicks is indirect but compelling, anthropologists say. Fossil teeth, the most durable relics of early life, seem to tell the tale. Analysis of grooves on ancient teeth has led to a consensus that these are the marks of heavy toothpick use by early humans. The journal *Nature* has reported that the earliest known example of the grooved-teeth phenomenon was found in 1.8–million-year-old fossils. The grooves were especially common in the teeth of Neanderthals and other archaic *Homo sapiens* of Europe and Asia between 130,000 and 35,000 years ago. Researchers considered whether the grooves could have been the result of tooth decay, dietary grit or stripping and processing fibers in making domestic goods. "None of these, however, really fits the evidence," *Nature* reported. The similarity of the prehistoric grooves to toothpick-caused abrasions in historical and modern populations of American Indians and Australian Aborigines argued for the toothpick interpretation of the data.

**Body: Supporting paragraph**

In a recent article in *Current Anthropology,* Christy G. Turner II, professor of anthropology at Arizona State University, concluded, "As far as can be empirically documented, the oldest human habit is picking one's teeth."

**Conclusion**

—John Noble Wilford, *The New York Times*

CHAPTER 3

● **Practice Your Skills**

*Analyzing a Composition*

Write answers to these questions about what you have just read.

**1.** What is the main idea of the composition?

**2.** What audience might this be addressing? Is it effective?

**3.** How does the body paragraph support the main idea?

**4.** Evaluate the conclusion. Is it effective? Why or why not?

**PROJECT PREP** Expanding *From Paragraph to Composition*

In your writing group, discuss each writer's draft with a focus on how to expand it. Use the chart on page 106 to guide your thinking. For example, can the topic sentence be adapted to serve as a thesis statement? Can each supporting detail become the topic of a supporting paragraph? Make a plan for a rewrite.

# ② Introduction of a Composition

Just as you want to make a good impression when you make a presentation, you must make a strong first impression in your writing. Your introduction is that first impression. It should accomplish the goals below.

## Writing an Introduction

- Introduce the subject.
- Capture the reader's attention and prepare the reader for what is to follow.
- Establish the tone—your attitude toward both the subject and the audience.
- Present the controlling idea in a thesis statement.
- State or imply your purpose for writing.

"Always grab the reader by the throat in the first paragraph, sink your thumbs into his windpipe in the second, and hold him against the wall until the tag line," advises writer Paul O'Neil. Here are some less aggressive, but equally effective, ways to begin your composition so that your reader will be motivated to keep reading.

## Capturing the Reader's Attention

- Start with a story or anecdote.
- Tell how you became interested in your subject.
- Offer vivid and/or startling background information.
- Ask a hard-to-answer question.
- Describe in vivid detail something that relates to your main idea.
- Begin with a humorous or satirical statement.
- Start with a captivating quotation.
- Take a stand on an issue that is important to you.

## VOICE AND TONE

Despite the apparent silent nature of the written word, everything you read has a voice and tone.

> **Voice** involves the writer's word choices as well as the sound and rhythm of those choices.
>
> **Tone** is the writer's attitude toward his or her subject and audience.

In using your voice and setting the tone of a composition, consider your positive or negative feelings about the subject. For example, your tone may be serious or comical, admiring or critical, sympathetic or mocking, joyful or sad. Your voice will reveal your unique way of thinking. The following paragraphs are strong in both voice and tone.

The other day when a commercial came on, I automatically pressed "Muting" on the TV remote control and realized what a great modern development muting is. Essentially I've remained a 1950s guy, but I do recognize a good invention when I see it. "Seek and Scan" on my car radio you can have. I have never mastered seek and scan. I just don't know what they're for. I thought it was perfect when you had your on/off knob and a tuner to find the station. Period. That's it. Fine. Now you can seek or scan and lock in stations. What?

—Charles Grodin, "Modern Times"

## MODEL: Reflective Voice and Tone

The best teachers have showed me that things have to be done bit by bit. Nothing that means anything happens quickly—we only think it does. The motion of drawing back a bow and sending an arrow straight into a target takes only a split second, but it is a skill many years in the making. So it is with a life, anyone's life. I may list things that might be described as my accomplishments in these few pages, but they are only shadows of the larger truth, fragments separated from the whole cycle of becoming. And if I can tell an old-time story now about a man who is walking about, *waudjoset ndatlokugan,* a forest lodge man, *alesakamigwi udlagwedewugan,* it is because I spent many years walking about myself, listening to voices that came not just from the people but from animals and trees and stones.

—Joseph Bruchac, "Notes of a Translator's Son"

## Practice Your Skills

### Identifying Voice and Tone

Read each introduction below. Then write an adjective—such as *lighthearted, reflective,* or *bitter*—to describe the voice and tone of each one.

**1.** A proper holiday, coming from the medieval "holy day," is supposed to be a time of reflection on great men, great deeds, great people. Things like that. Somehow in America this didn't quite catch on. Take Labor Day. On Labor Day you take the day off, then go to the Labor Day sales and spend your devalued money with a clerk who is working. And organized labor doesn't understand why it suffers declining membership? Pshaw. Who wants to join an organization that makes you work on the day it designates as a day off? Plus, no matter how hidden the agenda, who wants a day off if they make you march in a parade and listen to some politicians talk on and on about nothing?

—Nikki Giovanni, "On Holidays and How to Make Them Work"

**2.** Vietnam is a black-and-white photograph of my grandparents sitting in bamboo chairs in their front courtyard. They are sitting tall and proud, surrounded by chickens and roosters. Their feet are separated from the dirt by thin sandals. My grandfather's broad forehead is shining. So too are my grandmother's famed sad eyes. The animals are obliviously pecking at the ground. This looks like a wedding portrait, though it is actually a photograph my grandparents had taken late in life, for their children, especially for my mother. When I think of this portrait of my grandparents in the last years of their life, I always envision a beginning. To what or where, I don't know, but always a beginning.

—Le Thi Diem Thuy, "The Gangster We Are All Looking For"

**3.** Before you even get the cone, you have to do a lot of planning about it. We'll assume that you lost the argument in the car and that the family has decided to break the automobile journey and stop at an ice-cream stand for cones. Get things straight with them right from the start. Tell them that there will be an imaginary circle six feet away from the car, and that no one—man, woman, or especially child—will be allowed to cross the line and reenter the car until his ice-cream cone has been entirely consumed and he has cleaned himself up. Emphasize: Automobiles and ice-cream cones don't mix. Explain: Melted ice cream, children, is a fluid that is eternally sticky. One drop of it on a car-door handle spreads to the seat covers, to trousers, and thence to hands, and then to the steering wheel, the gear shift, the rear-view mirror, all the knobs of the dashboard—spreads everywhere and lasts forever, spreads from a nice old car like this, which might have to be abandoned because of stickiness, right into a nasty new car, in secret ways that even scientists don't understand.

—L. Rust Hills, "How to Eat an Ice-Cream Cone"

## THESIS STATEMENT

In addition to introducing the subject and setting the tone, the introduction also contains the thesis statement.

> The **thesis statement** states the main idea and makes the purpose of the composition clear.

The model thesis statements on the following page both limit the subject and convey the purpose of the composition.

The performance of the stock market in the past year may have an impact on several industries in the coming year. (explains a subject)

To be better prepared for work in the international economy, students should learn more than one language. (states an opinion)

The time I spent camping in the mountains taught me about my own abilities and strengths. (expresses a feeling about an experience)

The thesis statement is the **controlling idea** of a composition. It must be broad enough to include the main points in your composition yet limited enough to cover your subject well. It creates a strong impression when used in your introduction. Your working thesis statement will probably be revised as you flesh out your composition.

● **Practice Your Skills**

*Identifying Thesis Statements*

Write the thesis statement in this introductory passage. If the thesis statement is not expressed, compose a sentence that expresses it. Then write a sentence telling what you would expect from the rest of the composition.

The voice I assume for children's bad behavior is like a winter coat, dark and heavy. I put it on the other night when my eldest child appeared in the kitchen doorway, an hour after he had gone to bed. "What are you doing here?" I began to say, when he interrupted: "I finished it!"

The [domineering] tone went out the window and we settled down for an old-fashioned dish about the fine points of *The Phantom Tollbooth*. It is the wonderful tale of a bored and discontented boy named Milo and the journey he makes one day in his toy car with the Humbug and the Spelling Bee and a slew of other fantastical characters who change his life. I read it first when I was ten. I still have the book report I wrote, which began "This is the best book ever." That was long before I read *The Sound and the Fury* or *Little Dorrit,* the Lord Peter Wimsey mysteries or Elmore Leonard. I was still pretty close to the mark.

All of us have similar hopes for our children: good health, happiness, interesting and fulfilling work, financial stability. But like a model home that's different depending on who picks out the cabinets and the shutters, the fine points often vary. Some people go nuts when their children learn to walk, to throw a baseball, to pick out the "Moonlight Sonata" on the piano. The day I realized my eldest child could read was one of the happiest days of my life.

—Anna Quindlen, "Enough Bookshelves"

## ● Practice Your Skills

### Writing a Thesis Statement

Write a thesis statement for the following subject and lists of details.

**Subject:** Training Dolphins

**Details:**
- Positive reinforcement is a key ingredient.
- Each successfully performed act is rewarded with a whistle or fish.
- Applause is also a reward.
- Breaking down a trick into its parts is another key ingredient.
- The dolphin learns each small part before putting it all together.
- The dolphin learns each new part by trial and error.
- Any movement toward the desired effect is rewarded.

**PROJECT PREP** *Drafting* *Introduction*

Following the plan you developed with your writing group, draft an introduction to your expanded paper. Refer to the charts on pages 106 and 108 to make sure your introduction accomplishes its purposes.

# ❸ Body of a Composition

When you are satisfied that your introduction will grab your reader's attention, your next task is to develop your preliminary working thesis statement, idea by idea, in the body of your composition.

## SUPPORTING PARAGRAPHS

In one way or another, all of the supporting paragraphs in the body of a composition relate to the main idea. Although all the supporting paragraphs relate to the thesis, each one deals with one aspect of that thesis. Like any good paragraph, each has its own topic sentence and supporting sentences.

> The **supporting paragraphs** in the body of a composition develop the thesis statement.

Following is the introduction and body of a composition. Notice how each of the supporting paragraphs develops the thesis statement.

CHAPTER 3

---

**MODEL: Introduction and Body of a Composition**

### Running the Whole Show

Starting a business while going to school and leading an active social life takes time! So why do young entrepreneurs do what they do? Besides the obvious—earning money—learning to operate a business is a very broadening experience.

"The experience you gain as an entrepreneur can provide tremendous insights," says Lon Goforth, an official with Entrepreneur America and host of the video, *How to Become a Teenage Entrepreneur*. "You learn more than just one specific job skill. Instead of flipping hamburgers, for example, you might learn about selling, managing, accounting, and other functions."

Taking the path of an entrepreneur can be a great confidence booster, too. "Starting a business is an excellent way to discover self-worth at an early age," says Sarah Riehm, author of *50 Great Businesses for Teens*. "In work, kids learn how to strive for important goals and cope with real problems."

Another plus is that you discover more about your future job interests. "You might find that you enjoy selling, but hate accounting," Goforth says. "If you learn this while in high school, it can help you in choosing the right major in college."

In fact, running a small business can provide great preparation for both college and careers. Some teen entrepreneurs use their experience as a basis for studying business in college, going to work in the corporate sector, or starting new companies later in life.

Others experiment with business, but then go into entirely different fields. Whatever the case, the process teaches skills in areas such as planning, time management, and communication. Perhaps most important, when you're an entrepreneur you become accustomed to thinking and acting independently.

In the following outline of the body of this composition, you can see how the supporting paragraphs develop the thesis statement. Each Roman numeral corresponds to a paragraph in the body.

**Thesis Statement**     Besides the obvious—earning money—learning to operate a business is a very broadening experience.

**Supporting Statements**
  **I.** Teaches more than just one skill
  **II.** Boosts confidence
  **III.** Helps point to future job interests
  **IV.** Prepares for college and work
  **V.** Teaches independence

## ● Practice Your Skills

### Analyzing Supporting Paragraphs

Reread "But Did They Floss?" on pages 106–107. Write the thesis statement. Then develop an outline like the one above. In your outline, use Roman numerals to show the main ideas of each supporting paragraph and the way each idea supports the thesis statement.

## ● Practice Your Skills

### Developing Supporting Ideas

Under each of the following thesis statements, write three ideas that could be developed into three supporting paragraphs for the body of a composition. Write them in the form of the outline above.

**1.** My three favorite movies are each in a very different genre.

**2.** My advice to incoming freshmen involve three rules.

**3.** Here are three rules for training your dog to sit on command.

## ADEQUATE DEVELOPMENT

Readers are looking for information and clear explanations, so provide ample well-chosen details to support your ideas.

### Writing Tip

Check your compositions for **adequate development** and, if necessary, add more information to clarify and enrich your main idea with strong, lively examples, illustrations, and other supporting details.

In the first model below, not enough details are included. In the second, the writer provides specific information, allowing the reader to understand the subject more completely.

### MODEL: Inadequately Developed Paragraph

Miriam Amanda Wallace "Ma" Ferguson was the first female governor of Texas. She was born in Bell County and was called "Ma" because she was a woman with the initials M.A. While running for office as a Democrat, she told voters that they would get "two for the price of one" because her husband had been governor but was impeached. She was the second female United States governor as Nellie Ross of Wyoming was the first.

### MODEL: Adequately Developed Paragraph

Miriam Amanda Wallace "Ma" Ferguson was the first female governor of Texas. She was born in Bell County, Texas, in 1875 and was elected to office in 1925 after her husband, then-governor James Ferguson, was removed from office. Ferguson acquired the nickname "Ma" based on the initials *M. A.* and because *ma* was a term used for married women during that time. While running for office as a Democrat, she told voters that she would seek her husband's advice if elected, thus offering them "two governors for the price of one." A popular campaign slogan of the time read "Me for Ma, and I Ain't Got a Durned Thing Against Pa." As governor, Ferguson tackled some of the tougher issues of the day, including taking a firm stand against the Ku Klux Klan.

*Checking for Adequate Development*

Reread the introduction and body of the composition about teen entrepreneurs (page 113). Make a paragraph-by-paragraph listing of all the supporting details used. Then write a sentence or two evaluating the development of this composition. Is it adequate? Are enough specific details offered? Is anything missing?

## LOGICAL DEVELOPMENT

The ideas you developed to support your thesis statement are called claims.

**Claims** are statements asserted to be true.

In *Running the Whole Show* the claims are:

- Young entrepreneurs can learn many different job skills.
- Entrepreneurship can boost confidence.
- You can discover more about your future job interests.
- It can prepare a young person for college.

Examples are then given to support the claims made, as in the chart below.

| CLAIMS | EXAMPLES |
|---|---|
| Young entrepreneurs can learn many different job skills. | You might learn about selling, managing, and other areas of a job. |
| Being a young entrepreneur can boost confidence. | You learn that you can achieve important goals and successfully cope with real problems. |
| You can discover more about future job interests. | You learn what aspects of a career you enjoy and which you don't, which can point you in the right direction. |

Simply providing examples for claims, however, does not support your assertion that they are true. You need to go further and provide a warrant for each claim.

A **warrant** is a statement that explains how an example serves as evidence for a claim.

Warrants often use the word "because," as in the following example.

| CLAIMS, EXAMPLES, AND WARRANTS | |
| --- | --- |
| Claim | Being a young entrepreneur can boost confidence. |
| Example | Young entrepreneurs often achieve success in their businesses and cope successfully with real problems. |
| Warrant | Because young entrepreneurs often achieve success in solving problems, their confidence is boosted. |

## PROJECT PREP    *Drafting*    *Body Paragraphs*

Following the plan you developed with your writing group, draft the body paragraphs of your essay. Be sure to provide adequate development, and support each claim with evidence and a warrant that explains how the example illustrates the claim. You might want to make a chart like the one below to help you keep track of your claims, examples, and warrants.

| | Topic sentence (claim) | Example | Warrant |
| --- | --- | --- | --- |
| First body paragraph | | | |
| Second body paragraph | | | |
| Third body paragraph | | | |

# Think Critically

## Making Valid Inferences

In addition to providing warrants for your claims, you also need to make sure that your conclusions or inferences are valid. An inference is **valid** if it follows logically from the claims. For example, suppose you make these claims:

> **Claim:** All teenagers benefit from having a part-time job.
>
> **Claim:** Ashton Nicholls is sixteen years old.
>
> **Valid Inference:** Ashton would benefit from having a part-time job.

That inference is valid because the first claim asserts that all teenagers benefit from having a part-time job. In that case, because Ashton is a teenager, he would benefit from having a part-time job.

Suppose, however, that you make these claims:

> **Claim:** All teenagers benefit from having a part-time job.
>
> **Claim:** Lola has a part-time job.
>
> **Invalid Inference:** Lola is a teenager.

This inference is invalid because it does not follow logically from the claims. The original claim is that all teenagers benefit from having a part-time job, not that *only* teenagers benefit from having a part-time job. Just because Lola has part-time job does not logically lead to the inference that she is a teenager.

## Thinking Practice

Read each set of claims and the inference that follows them and determine if the inference is valid or invalid. If it is invalid, write a valid inference.

1. **Claim:** Teenagers have more car accidents than older people.
   **Claim:** Teenagers exhibit riskier behaviors than older people.
   **Inference:** The legal age to drive should be raised.
2. **Claim:** Teenagers are more likely to use text messaging than their grandparents.
   **Claim:** Nia is a teenager.
   **Inference:** Nia is more likely to use text messaging than her grandmother.

# 4 Unity, Coherence, and Emphasis

In a composition with **unity,** all the supporting paragraphs relate directly to the main idea in the thesis statement. If a composition lacks unity, readers will experience detours and dead-ends that take away from the impact of the main idea.

In a composition with **coherence,** one idea flows logically to the next. Well-planned, logical organization is the most important element of coherence. Within that structure, transitional words and phrases should help readers follow the logical progression of ideas.

### Strategies for Achieving Coherence

- Double-check your organization to make sure each detail fits logically into your method of organization.
- Use transitional words and phrases. See charts with transitions on pages 5, 95, and 300.
- Every now and then repeat key words.
- Use similar words or phrases in place of key words.
- Use pronouns in place of key words.

**Emphasis,** another important quality of a composition, helps readers recognize your most important ideas. You can show emphasis by writing more about one idea, by discussing it first, or by using transitional words and phrases to highlight it.

John Nobel's essay "But Did They Floss?" on pages 106–107 shows all three of these qualities. It has unity because the supporting paragraph describes the evidence that indicates archaic Homo sapiens used toothpicks. It has coherence because each sentence is followed by one that supplies further information that builds on the main idea. Finally, Nobel creates emphasis in his conclusion with a clever quote from a professor of anthropology that supports the main idea of the essay.

Check your compositions for the qualities of **unity,** **coherence,** and **emphasis.**

CHAPTER 3

# The Power of Language ⚡

## Parallelism: The Power of 3s

You don't want your compositions to plod along, one sentence trudging after the other. You want your composition to take flight, each sentence soaring and expanding on the previous one. You want your composition to include grammatical options—as Virginia Woolf so elegantly demonstrates in her informative and heartfelt lecture found in *A Room of One's Own*. To make her points emphatically, Woolf employs **parallelism**: the same kind of word or group of words, grammatically speaking, in a series of three or more. Read the following sentences aloud. Notice the impact of the three action verbs and the whirlwind of participial phrases that follow them:

> He had, it seemed, a taste for the theatre; he began by holding horses at the stage door. Very soon he got work in the theatre, became a successful actor, and lived at the hub of the universe, meeting everybody, knowing everybody, practicing his art on the boards, exercising his wits in the streets, and even getting access to the palace of the queen.

Next read the description below, which also uses parallelism to create an image that makes a powerful point.

> Meanwhile his extraordinarily gifted sister, let us suppose, remained at home. She was as adventurous, as imaginative, as agog to see the world as he was. But she was not sent to school.

The strong statements, presented in a rush of parallel constructions describing the gifted sister, become poignant with the following abrupt sentence: *But she was not sent to school.*

## Try It Yourself

1. Write a sentence about your topic that uses parallelism to create a positive image of a person, object, or event.
2. Write a sentence about your topic that uses parallelism to create a negative effect concerning a person, object, or event.

Use the resulting sentences in your draft if you can, and try creating other similar sentences. You can always add more details with phrases when you revise.

### Punctuation Tip

**Use a comma** to separate parallel constructions **in a series.**

## Practice Your Skills

### Testing Coherence with a Flow Chart

One way to test the coherence of your composition is to picture the paragraphs within it as a series of connected boxes. The lines connecting the boxes will remind you to use appropriate transitions.

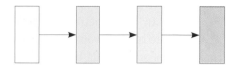

Complete a flow chart for the composition "Running the Whole Show" (pages 113–114). Use each box to show connected ideas in the supporting paragraphs.

## Practice Your Skills

### Analyzing Unity, Coherence, and Emphasis

Reread the introduction and the body of the composition on young entrepreneurs. Then write answers to the following questions.

**1.** How do the body paragraphs help the composition achieve unity?

**2.** What transitions in the body paragraphs link each paragraph to the previous one?

**3.** What key term is repeated in the fourth body paragraph to help link it back to the previous one?

**4.** What phrase in the final body paragraph helps both the coherence and the emphasis of this composition?

**5.** How would you evaluate the unity, coherence, and emphasis of this composition? Evaluate each quality in a separate sentence.

---

**PROJECT PREP** *Evaluating* **Reviewing Drafts**

Bring your expanded draft to your writing group. For each paper, think about how effectively the author makes claims, includes examples, ties examples and claims together through warrants, and draws valid inferences. Also evaluate one another's latest drafts for unity, coherence, and emphasis. Note suggestions your partners make for your writing and make revisions as you see fit.

**TIME OUT TO REFLECT**

What have you learned in this chapter about writing longer compositions? When reviewing the qualities of good compositions, did you recognize your problem areas? What are your strengths as a writer? What would you like to improve? Does your essay accomplish its purpose, consider the audience, and suit the occasion and genre? Now is the time to make your revisions.

# ⑤ Conclusion of a Composition

You have grabbed your readers' attention with your introduction and held their interest with the body of your composition. In your conclusion you add the tag line—a memorable phrase or statement that leaves a deep impression—before letting your readers go.

The **conclusion** completes the composition and reinforces the thesis statement.

On page 111 you read the introduction to a newspaper column by Anna Quindlen about her happiness at her son's reading. Following is her conclusion.

## MODEL: Conclusion of a Composition

You had only to see this boy's face when he said "I finished it!" to know that something had made an indelible mark upon him. I walked him back upstairs with a fresh book, my copy of *A Wrinkle in Time,* Madeleine L'Engle's unforgettable story of children who travel through time and space to save their father from the forces of evil. Now when I leave the room, he is reading by the pinpoint of his little reading light, the ship of his mind moving through high seas with the help of my compass. Just before I close the door, I catch a glimpse of the making of myself and the making of him, sharing some of the same timber. And I am a happy woman.

—Anna Quindlen, "Enough Bookshelves"

Like many good conclusions, Quindlen's conclusion returns to an image or idea from the introduction. Referring back to the introduction helps a reader feel the experience has been completed.

## PROJECT PREP Drafting Conclusion

Based on the feedback from your writing group, revise the introduction and body of your essay and add a strong conclusion. Submit your draft to your teacher as well as your writing group members for review.

# The Language of Power  *Run-ons*

**Power Rule:** Use the best conjunction and/or punctuation for the meaning when connecting two sentences. Revise run-on sentences. (See pages 736–738.)

**See It in Action**  A run-on sentence is the incorrect joining of two complete sentences. When this mistake is made with a comma between the sentences, it is called a **comma splice.**

> **Comma Splice**   Researchers considered whether the grooves could have been the result of tooth decay, dietary grit or stripping and processing fibers in making domestic goods, "none of these, however, really fits the evidence," *Nature* reported.

"Researchers considered whether the grooves could have been the result of tooth decay, dietary grit or stripping and processing fibers in making domestic goods" is a complete thought, an independent clause. It can stand alone as a sentence. The same is true for "'none of these, however, really fits the evidence,' *Nature* reported."

> **Corrected**   Researchers considered whether the grooves could have been the result of tooth decay, dietary grit or stripping and processing fibers in making domestic goods. "None of these, however, really fits the evidence," *Nature* reported.

In some cases it may be better to put a subordinating conjunction before one sentence to make it and the ideas it contains subordinate to the other clause.

> **Corrected**   **Although** researchers considered whether the grooves could have been the result of tooth decay, dietary grit or stripping and processing fibers in making domestic goods, "none of these . . . really fits the evidence," *Nature* reported.

**Remember It**  Record this rule and examples in the Power Rule section of your Personalized Editing Checklist.

**Use It**  Read through your project and check your sentences for comma splices or other run-ons. Combine sentences by making one clause dependent on the other or separate the incorrectly joined sentences into two separate sentences.

# Using a Six-Trait Rubric    Compositions

| Ideas | **4** The text conveys an interesting idea with abundant supporting details and is well chosen for the purpose and audience. | **3** The text conveys a clear idea with ample details and suits the purpose and audience. | **2** The text conveys a main idea with some supporting details and suits the purpose and audience. | **1** The text does not convey a main idea and fails to suit the purpose and audience. |
|---|---|---|---|---|
| Organization | **4** The organization is clear with abundant transitions. | **3** A few ideas seem out of place or transitions are missing. | **2** Many ideas seem out of place and transitions are missing. | **1** The organization is unclear and hard to follow. |
| Voice | **4** The voice sounds natural, engaging, and personal. | **3** The voice sounds natural and personal. | **2** The voice sounds mostly unnatural with a few exceptions. | **1** The voice sounds mostly unnatural. |
| Word Choice | **4** Words are specific, powerful, and precise. | **3** Words are specific and some words are powerful and precise. | **2** Some words are overly general. | **1** Most words are overly general. |
| Sentence Fluency | **4** Varied sentences flow smoothly. | **3** Most sentences are varied and flow smoothly. | **2** Some sentences are varied but some are choppy. | **1** Sentences are not varied and are choppy. |
| Conventions | **4** Punctuation, usage, and spelling are correct. The Power Rules are all followed. | **3** Punctuation, usage, and spelling are mainly correct and Power Rules are all followed. | **2** Some punctuation, usage, and spelling are incorrect but all Power Rules are followed. | **1** There are many errors and at least one failure to follow a Power Rule. |

## PROJECT PREP    Revising and Editing    *Final Draft*

Based on the feedback from your writing group and teacher, prepare a final, polished version of your essay. You might exchange papers with a writing partner for one final critique before you consider it done. When you are satisfied with your essay, publish it to an appropriate place. For instance, you might find places on the Internet where stereotyping, misconceptions, and particular groups of people are discussed, and post your essay as part of this wider conversation about this issue.

# In the Media

## Visual Compositions

Like a written composition, a visual composition contains elements that contribute to the whole. Also like a written composition, visual compositions convey meanings, attitudes, and tones. "Read" this photograph of UNIVAC I, the first commercial computer produced in the United States.

Write a paragraph answering these questions about the photograph.

### QUESTIONS FOR ANALYZING A PHOTOGRAPH

- What feeling does this photograph give you about how people once worked with computers?
- How do line, shape, color, and texture in the photograph contribute to your understanding of this image?
- What is the tone of this photo? What visual elements convey the tone?
- What attitude does this photograph convey about this era as compared to today?

## Media Activity

Bring in pictures from magazines that convey a message about computer culture today. Explain how the elements of design contribute to the message the pictures convey.

# Writing Lab

## Project Corner

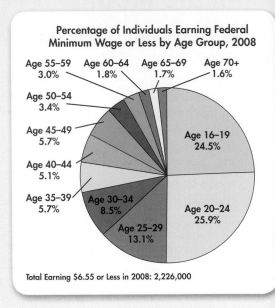

**Percentage of Individuals Earning Federal Minimum Wage or Less by Age Group, 2008**

Age 55–59 3.0%
Age 60–64 1.8%
Age 65–69 1.7%
Age 70+ 1.6%
Age 50–54 3.4%
Age 45–49 5.7%
Age 40–44 5.1%
Age 35–39 5.7%
Age 30–34 8.5%
Age 25–29 13.1%
Age 20–24 25.9%
Age 16–19 24.5%

Total Earning $6.55 or Less in 2008: 2,226,000

## Interpret Graphics
### Translate from Graphic to Print

Look at the pie chart, which represents the various age groups earning minimum wage (about $7.25 per hour in most states) in the United States in 2008. You can see that the largest group includes those people who are between the ages of 20 and 24. What is the next largest group? Which group is the smallest? **Write a paragraph** interpreting the information in this chart.

## Speak and Listen Panel Discussion

Meet with other students who have written on the same instance of historical prejudice or bias that you've written about. **Plan and present a panel discussion** in which you share with your class the facts of these historical events. Also address the issue of how people today can start to outline ways to create a more humane world. (See pages 584–586 for more on panel discussion.)

## Reflect Make a Difference

Think about the biases and prejudices you have learned about based on the discussions you have been in and the papers your classmates have written. What have you learned from this inquiry? Is there anything one person can do to eliminate prejudice? **Write a reflection** on the subject and share it with your class.

## Experiment Change Genres

Use what you have learned while writing your essay to **create another literary or artistic work.** For instance, Virginia Woolf gave a lecture about gender bias. Perhaps a poem, short story, graphic novel, painting, collage, or drawing would serve the subject equally well.

# In Academic Areas
## Library Instructions

1. You have been asked to contribute to the orientation guide for incoming freshmen. Your job is to inform students about important aspects of the school library. **Write a short overview** of the library in second-person point of view and instructions about how to check out books. Classify your details in order of importance. (You can find information on writing instructions on pages 562–564.)

# In the Workplace Descriptive Blog

2. As an explorer and writer who has just returned to the States after having ascended Mount Everest, you want to share your experience with others. You decide to write a blog that gives your readers an understanding of what it is like to trek to the top of the world's tallest mountain. In your blog you plan to include your feelings of triumph upon reaching the pinnacle as well as the fears you experienced along the way—and perhaps inspire others to visit foreign lands. Research Mount Everest and what conditions at the top are like. Then **write a blog entry** imagining you were there yourself and describing what you see and feel. (You can find information on writing descriptive essays on pages 154–177.)

# Timed Writing 🕐 Persuasive Letter

3. Your favorite professional sports team is considering a move to another state. Fan loyalty is fading and the city refuses to fund the construction of a new sports arena that the team needs in order to generate more revenue. Write a persuasive letter to the editor of your local newspaper explaining why you think the city government should or should not support the building of a new sports arena. You have 20 minute to complete your work.

**Before You Write** Consider the following questions: What is the subject? What is the occasion? Who is the audience? What is the purpose?

Include a strong thesis statement and an introduction that grabs the reader's attention. Make sure your arguments are developed in a coherent manner and that you acknowledge opposing viewpoints. Use transitions to connect ideas.

**After You Write** Revise your work to be sure it accomplished its purpose. Then evaluate your work using the six-trait evaluation form on page 124.

# Unit 2

# Purposes of Writing

Every time you sit down to write, you ask and answer fundamental questions: What is my writing purpose? Will I write to describe, inform, persuade, analyze, entertain, or reflect? Who are my readers? What tone and style will spark their interest? With those questions answered, you begin to set your writing in motion. With your best thinking, you may soon find yourself in a force field where one idea after another crackles with energy.

*Words set things in motion. I've seen them doing it. Words set up atmospheres, electrical fields, charges.* — Toni Cade Bambara

# CHAPTER **4**

# Personal Writing

**A** **personal narrative** expresses the writer's personal point of view on a subject drawn from the writer's own experience.

The moments of insight we all have are excellent subjects for narratives of expression and reflection. The power of narration is the story it tells and the effect it has on listeners and readers. Here are just a few examples.

- **Prospective college students write brief autobiographies** that tell about their personal and academic achievements and hopes for the future.

- **Writers use a single real or imagined event** as the seed of a poem, short story, or entire novel.

- **Artists, performers, and politicians write their memoirs** as a way to keep their names and deeds alive.

- **Parents write or recount family stories** so that children become familiar with the family's heritage and history.

- **People of all walks of life keep journals** to remind themselves of what they have done with their lives—and often of what they still want to do.

- **Friends exchange e-mails** to share experiences that are surprising, unusual, or deeply affecting.

## Writing Project *Personal Narrative*

***Surprise!*** *Write a personal narrative about a time when someone surprised you by behaving against the expectation you had formed about his or her group.*

***Think Through Writing*** Sometimes people are surprised by the behavior of members of other groups. Write about an experience you once had in which you had assumed that people in a particular group were all the same in some way, then learned that one or more people in the group were different from what you had expected.

**Talk About It**  In your writing group, discuss the ways in which people may underestimate or misunderstand those who are different from themselves, and how such assumptions affect both groups as they make their way in the world.

**Read About It**  The following personal narrative by Gary Soto relates his experience of attending a classical music performance, where he and his wife sat with working class people in a remote balcony of the hall. Compare his account of the surprise he felt at the sophistication of these people's music appreciation with your own narrative of the time you were surprised by the behavior of someone about whom you had formed limiting assumptions.

## MODEL: Personal Narrative Writing

# The Concert

*Gary Soto*

Once in Mexico City and tired of its noise and rushed people, my wife and I flew to Oaxaca, a city known for its pottery, weavings, and the nearby ruins of Monte Alban and Mitla. We stayed in a hotel whose courtyard was sheltered by a huge skylight that let in a hazy, almost silver light. For two days we took buses to the ruins, bought Mexican toys, and walked from one end of the town to the other in search of out-of-the-way shops.

On our last night we went to hear the National Symphony. I bought low-priced tickets, but when we tried to sit on the ground floor, a portly usher pointed us to the stairwell. We climbed to the next landing where another usher told us to keep climbing by rolling his eyes toward *el paraiso*—the gallery of cheap seats. We climbed two more flights, laughing that we were going to end up on the roof with the pigeons. An unsmiling usher handed us programs as we stepped to the door. We looked around, amazed at the gray, well-painted boxes that were our seats. There were no crushed velvet chairs with ornate wooden arms, no elegant men and women with perfect teeth. Most were Indians and *campesinos*,[1] and a few university students holding hands, heads pressed together in love.

*In the first paragraph, Soto sets up a contrast between Mexico City and Oaxaca. This contrast provides a setting for the story he wants to tell.*

*Contrasting the laughing by his wife and himself with the unsmiling face of the usher helps Soto set the tone. Listening to music in the upper seats is serious.*

---

1  **campesino:** Peasant.

I led Carolyn to the boxes in the front row against the rail and together we looked far down where the others sat. Their rumblings rose like heat. They fanned themselves and smiled wide enough for us to see their teeth. We watched them until an old man touched my shoulder, said *con permiso*[2] and took small steps to get past me to the box on our left. When he sat down I smiled at him as I wanted to be friendly. But he didn't look at me. He took out a pair of glasses from his breast pocket. They were broken, taped together at the bridge. I looked away, embarrassed to see that he was poor, but stole a glance when the program began: I saw his coat, slack and full from wear, and his pants with oily spots. His shoes were rope sandals. His tie was short, like a withered arm. I watched his face in profile that showed a knot of tape protruding from his glasses, a profile that went unchanged as it looked down at the symphony.

I listened but felt little as the violins tugged and pulled and scratched through an hour of performance. When the music stopped and the conductor turned around, moon-faced and trying to hide his happiness by holding back a grin, I craned my neck over the rail and watched the *elegantes*[3] applaud and smile at one another. We applauded, too, and looked around, smiling. We were busy with an excitement that lit our eyes. But while the *elegantes* got up to take drinks and stand in the foyer under torches, those around us leaned against the wall to smoke and talk in whispers. A group of young men played cards and, in a sudden win, laughed so hard that the usher came over to quiet them down.

We stayed for the second half—something by Haydn—but no matter how hard I tried to study the movements of musicians and conductor on his carpeted box, I couldn't help but look around the room at the Indians and *campesinos* whose faces, turned in profile in the half-lit shadows, held an instinctive awareness of the music. They would scratch a cheek or an elbow, speak quietly to one another, and sometimes squirm on the boxes. But most were attentive. It amazed me. I had never known the poor to appreciate such music, and I had lived among the poor since I was a child. These field laborers and rug weavers listened

---

Soto uses a short, direct sentence that begins with "But" to establish the contrast between himself and the old man.

Note the order of details that Soto takes in about the old man: he starts with his suit, moves down to his shoes, and then back up, finishing with his glasses.

Again, Soto starts a sentence with "But" to indicate that he is describing a contrast between two types of people.

---

2 **con permiso**: Excuse me. (Spanish)
3 **elegantes**: Elegant or stylish people. (Spanish)

to music that was not part of their lives, music written to titillate the aristocrats who wanted so much to rise above the dirty faces of the poor. The poor sat on the fifth tier on painted boxes, bodies leaning in the direction of the music that couldn't arrive fast enough to meet their lives.

When the concert ended, the old man next to me stood up and asked for permission to pass. I pinched my knees together, and Carolyn stood up. She sat back down and together, heads touching like lovers, we looked down to the first floor where the *elegantes* chatted with drinks and fluttery fans, and shook each other's hands as if celebrating their wealth.

After a while we got up and, with *campesinos* who were talking about a recently read book, descended the four flights to the ground.

> The basic organization of this essay is chronological, from the start of the trip to Oaxaca to the end of the concert.

> The final paragraph provides a short but strong conclusion. By noting that the *campesinos* were discussing a book, Soto repeats his main point about how serious they were about culture.

**Respond in Writing** Respond to Gary Soto's essay about his experience of learning of the sophisticated musical tastes of the Indians and *campesinos* at the National Symphony concert. What do he and his wife learn by sitting in the balcony at the performance? What did you learn from reading about it?

**Develop Your Own Ideas** Work with your classmates to develop ideas to assist you in understanding how limiting assumptions affect your ability to navigate the world in a fair and compassionate way.

**Small Groups:** In your writing group, use a graphic organizer like the following to outline the issues you have written about. Think more about how unfair assumptions or stereotypes form and how you can become more sensitive to other people's lives.

| Your unfair assumption (stereotype) | How you came to believe something that you later learned was untrue about a group of people | What happened to give you a more complex view of people from this group | How you were affected by this realization |
|---|---|---|---|
| | | | |

*Whole Class:* Make a master chart of all of the ideas generated by the small groups, and use these ideas for further discussion of stereotypes and how they affect both the people being stereotyped and those who do the stereotyping.

***Write About It*** You will next write a narrative about an experience you have had with stereotypes about a group of people. Your may choose from any of the following possible topics, forms, and audiences.

| Possible Topics and Examples | Possible Audiences | Possible Forms |
| --- | --- | --- |
| • a stereotype you held about people in a particular social or economic class<br><br>• a stereotype you held about people in a particular social group in school<br><br>• a stereotype you held about people in a region or country<br><br>• a stereotype you held about a group of people identified by gender, age, or other characteristic | • other people who share this stereotype<br><br>• the people of whom you held the stereotype<br><br>• people in your school who need to know more about the effects of this stereotype<br><br>• people outside school who need to know more about the effects of this stereotype | • a letter to a public forum<br><br>• a letter of apology<br><br>• a proposal for a change in school rules<br><br>• a narrative posted to a Web board about stereotyping |

## ① Getting the Subject Right

Gary Soto's "The Concert" is a narrative of expression and reflection. In the context of narrating a real-life event, he tells the reader how it changed him. Turning points—of whatever kind—are ideal subjects for this kind of writing.

The subject of a personal narrative may grow out of one of life's big events, such as a graduation, or out of a seemingly minor event, such as a camping trip or a rock concert. Following is the first part of an excerpt from a personal narrative Hal Borland wrote about a simple, common experience—yet one that had much significance for him.

> ### MODEL: Subject of a Personal Narrative
>
> I suspect that a midsummer dawn is so special because so few people are up and trying to manage or improve it. It is a tremendous happening in which [humans have] no part except as an occasional fortunate witness. And it happens with neither haste nor confusion. The stars aren't hooked to a switch that turns them all off at once. The birds don't bounce out of bed and immediately start singing in unison. Darkness doesn't rise like a theatrical curtain and reveal the sun crouched like a sprinter ready to race across the sky.
>
> I was up at four o'clock the other morning to go fishing before breakfast. First streaks of light were in the sky and the lesser stars had begun to dim when I got up, but I brewed a pot of coffee, had a first cup, filled a vacuum bottle, gathered bait and gear, and still had only half-light when I cast off my boat. By then the first birds were wakening and uttering first sleepy calls. But I went almost half a mile up the river before they really began to sing.
>
> I had boated three fish before the full light of dawn, and even then the sun hadn't risen. Time was so deliberate that when I looked at my watch I thought it had stopped. So I sat and watched and listened, and it was like seeing the earth emerge from the ancient mists. I was alone with creation; I and the birds who were in full voice now, a vast chorus of sheer celebration.
>
> —Hal Borland, "Summer and Belief"

The preceding excerpt has three important characteristics of a personal narrative. First, the writer draws on a personal experience that was important to him. Second, he uses the pronoun *I,* which makes the telling more vivid and personal. Finally, he uses conversational style, as if he were sitting in your living room, talking personally to you.

## DRAWING ON PERSONAL EXPERIENCE

Hal Borland's essay may have grown out of random observations that he had made in his journal. You will find your journal to be a rich source of possible subjects, such as experiences you have written about repeatedly, the feelings that you expressed about those experiences, and observations of people, places, or objects. In addition to using your journal, try clustering. Then explore the following sources.

| SOURCES OF SUBJECTS FOR PERSONAL NARRATIVES | |
| --- | --- |
| photograph albums | school newspapers |
| letters from friends | souvenirs from vacations |
| family stories | school yearbooks |
| scrapbooks and old journals | items in your desk |

## EXPLORING THE MEANING OF AN EXPERIENCE

A personal narrative should express a main idea that you may state directly or you may simply imply. Either way, the main idea of the personal narrative will evolve from the meaning, or significance, that the experience had for you.

In the continuation of Hal Borland's essay about a summer dawn, notice how he explores the meaning of his experience.

### MODEL: Expressing the Meaning of an Experience

And at last came the silence, the hush—not a birdsong, not a rustled leaf. It was a kind of reverence, as though everything was awaiting the daily miracle. It lasted until the first ray of sunlight lit the treetops. Then the silence ended. The birds began to sing again, a vast jubilation. The sun had risen. A new day had begun. But it would be still another hour or two, until diurnal human beings were up and stirring, before the . . . haste would start all over again. Meanwhile, I had witnessed the deliberation of the dawn.

That is what I mean by perfection. Everything is right, at dawn. Nothing is hurried. Everything necessary to the day's beginning is in order and happening on its own schedule. Time is reduced to its true, eternal dimensions.

—Hal Borland, "Summer and Belief"

As Borland makes clear, dawn is significant to him because it reveals the perfection that he sees in the natural world. He expresses this meaning directly in sentences like "That is what I mean by perfection. Everything is right, at dawn." However, he also expresses the meaning indirectly through details such as "The birds began to sing again. . . . The sun had risen." The simplicity of such details work through the reader's senses to convey meaning.

● **Practice Your Skills**

*Finding the Main Idea*

Look back at "The Concert." In your own words, write the main idea of Soto's personal narrative.

**PROJECT PREP** *Prewriting* *Main Idea and Meaning*

1. Determining the main idea of an essay with a view toward writing one of your own is not always simple. It can be easier, however, if you talk it over with a classmate or two. For example, explain how you deduced the main idea of "The Concert" and compare it with the process others used. Then mention the subject and possible main idea of your personal narrative—and ask for input from your partners. Be sure to ask questions and/or "say back" what you believe your peers are suggesting to be sure your understanding is clear.

2. Explore the meaning of the experience you are writing about in your personal narrative. Freewriting can help you discover its significance.

**TIME OUT TO REFLECT**

Now you have thought about and determined the subject and main idea you wish to convey in your personal narrative. What was it about this experience that made you decide on this subject and main idea? Record your answer in your Learning Log.

# Think Critically

## Interpreting

When you select an experience for a personal narrative, you may know that the experience was important, but you may not know why. To figure out why, you need to interpret that experience. **Interpreting** involves first recalling your feelings and impressions at the time, then completing a checklist like the following.

 **Checklist for Interpreting Experience**

**Experience:** I was reprimanded by my new boss, which angered me until I realized she was right.

*This experience is important to me now because it*

✓ helped me see something in a new way.

✓ changed the way I felt about someone.

changed the way I felt about myself.

*I will always remember this experience because it*

strongly affected my emotions.

✓ gave me new knowledge or understanding.

had important consequences.

*This experience is worth writing about because*

it will be familiar to many readers.

it is unique or extraordinary.

✓ writing will help me to understand it better.

**Interpretation:** This experience helped me learn to delay judgments about people until I have learned more about them.

## Thinking Practice

Select one of the following experiences or one of your own and interpret that experience by using the checklist above. Then write a statement that interprets the experience.

**1.** an incident in which your opinion of a person changed

**2.** an incident that taught you about leadership

# ② Refining Your Subject

When you have decided on a subject and its meaning for your personal narrative, think about your writing purpose and your audience.

## CONSIDERING YOUR PURPOSE

Usually your purpose in a personal narrative is to express your thoughts and feelings in a way that entertains readers. To achieve this purpose, you may use narrative, descriptive, or informative writing. For example, if you were writing about helping to renovate a state park, your paragraphs might have the specific aims shown in the following box.

*You may wish to consult pages 98–105 on writing paragraphs for different purposes.*

| PURPOSE IN PERSONAL NARRATIVES | |
|---|---|
| **Overall Purpose:** to express how the experience of renovating a state park teaches the value of teamwork | |
| **Specific Aims** | **Kinds of Paragraphs** |
| to describe the conditions of the park before work was started | descriptive |
| to explain the process of renovating a campsite and the reasons why this effort requires cooperation | informative |
| to tell an anecdote about how teamwork achieved a goal | narrative |

## CONSIDERING YOUR AUDIENCE

Give special consideration to your audience when writing a personal narrative. For instance, suppose you are planning to write about several funny and interesting relatives at your family reunion. You might develop the narrative by using anecdotes. For example, do not simply tell readers that Uncle Bob is hilarious. Instead, include a story that shows his sense of humor and tells readers some of the funny things he has said and done. In using this strategy, you will have considered your audience and shaped your writing to suit that audience.

**PROJECT PREP** *Prewriting* **Purpose and Audience**

Evaluate the main idea statement for your personal narrative to be sure that it still accurately summarizes the meaning of the experience for you. Then add a statement about the purpose of the narrative and the audience to whom it will be directed. Save these statements for later use.

# ③ Developing and Organizing Details

## SELECTING DETAILS

Details are the lifeblood of a personal narrative because they make the experience seem truly compelling. The following strategies will help you make a list of vivid details.

| STRATEGIES FOR DEVELOPING DETAILS | |
|---|---|
| **Events** | Close your eyes and visualize the experience that you are writing about. Then write down the details as you "see" them. |
| **People** | Visualize each person that you are writing about. Start by visualizing the head of each person and slowly move down to the feet. |
| **Places** | Visualize the places you are describing. Start at the left side of the setting and visualize slowly to the right. |
| **Feelings** | Imagine once again undergoing the experience that you are writing about. Focus on your feelings and thoughts as you move through the experience. |

After making your list of details, make a check mark next to those that you will include when you write the first draft of your personal narrative.

### Guidelines for Selecting Details

- Choose details appropriate for your purpose and audience.
- Use factual details to provide background information.
- Use vivid descriptive and sensory details to bring your experience to life.

In the following excerpt, Annie Dillard describes a creek that has overflowed because of a hurricane. She has carefully selected details to develop her main idea—that the flood has transformed what was once a peaceful and quiet setting.

## MODEL: Details in a Personal Narrative

That morning I'm standing at my kitchen window. Tinker Creek is out of its four-foot banks, way out, and it's still coming. The high creek doesn't look like our creek. Our creek splashes transparently over a jumble of rocks; the high creek obliterates everything in flat opacity. It looks like somebody else's creek that has usurped or eaten our creek and is roving frantically to escape, big and ugly, like a blacksnake caught in a kitchen drawer. The color is foul, a rusty cream. Water that has picked up clay soil looks worse than other muddy waters, because the particles of clay are so fine; they spread out and cloud the water so that you can't see light through even an inch of it in a drinking glass.

—Annie Dillard, *Pilgrim at Tinker Creek*

● **Practice Your Skills**

*Identifying Vivid Details*

Analyze the model paragraph on a flooded creek for details that are so vivid that you can visualize the scene in an instant. List the writer's carefully selected details and comparisons that make the scene immediate and real.

## ORGANIZING DETAILS

The overall organization of personal narratives is often **developmental order,** in which one idea grows out of the previous idea and leads into the following one. Within this pattern of organization, you may also use narrative, descriptive, and informative writing. To organize details using these kinds of writing, use the following types of organization.

| ORGANIZING DETAILS | | |
|---|---|---|
| **Kind of Writing** | **Kind of Details** | **Type of Order** |
| Narrative | events in a story from beginning to end | chronological order |
| Descriptive | details to help readers visualize a person, object, or scene | spatial order (left to right, top to bottom, far to near, etc.) |
| Informative | background details and details explaining the meaning of a particular experience | order of importance (most to least important or least to most important) |

Personal narratives are more informal in structure than informative or persuasive essays. Still, they need a clear organization so that readers can follow the flow of ideas without effort.

**PROJECT PREP** *Prewriting* **Details**

Look back over the list of details you chose to include in your personal narrative. Decide on an organization for your ideas, keeping in mind your purpose and the kinds of writing that help convey your specific aims in individual paragraphs (pages 5–6 and 98–105).

# The Power of Language⚡

## Absolutes: Zooming In

Many of the details provided by Soto about the characters and actions in "The Concert" come in phrases—groups of words that do not have subjects and verbs. Some of the phrases that add information about specific words are almost a sentence, but not quite.  They begin with a noun as "subject," which is followed by a modifier, often one beginning with an action word that ends in -*ing*.  Writers use such **absolute phrases** to zoom in with details about a person or persons.

> The girl rushed across the stage.  Her long hair was streaming behind her.

These two sentences can be combined, with the second becoming an absolute phrase:

> The girl rushed across the stage, her long hair streaming behind her.

Instead of two short, choppy sentences, this one makes a main statement about the girl and then zooms in with an absolute that describes a detail of her appearance.

The following examples from  "The Concert" show how absolute phrases can come in the middle or the end of a sentence.

> She sat back down and together, heads touching like lovers, we looked down to the first floor.

> The poor sat on the fifth tier on painted boxes, bodies leaning in the direction of the music.

## Try It Yourself

Write sentences similar to each of the three examples above, using an absolute phrase in a different position in each sentence. Use commas as they are used in the examples.

### Punctuation Tip

Use one **comma** after an absolute phrase **at the beginning** of a sentence.

Use **two commas** to enclose an absolute phrase **in the middle** of a sentence.

Use one comma or a dash to separate an absolute phrase from the rest of the sentence when it appears **at the end**.

# Personal Writing  Drafting

Since personal narratives are less formal than other kinds of writing, they are usually written from the first-person point of view and they do not have a formal thesis statement. Like all compositions, however, a personal narrative should have a clear main or controlling idea. It should include an attention-getting introduction, a well-organized body, and a striking conclusion.

##  Drafting the Introduction

In a personal narrative, you will be writing about a subject that may not be important or relevant to readers at first glance. Therefore, your goal in the introduction is to make an immediate impact on your readers. Following are some strategies for beginning your work.

 **Ways to Begin a Personal Narrative**

- Begin with a startling statement that catches readers by surprise, as Eudora Welty begins her essay "A Sweet Devouring."

  When I used to ask my mother which we were, rich or poor, she refused to tell me. I was nine years old and of course what I was dying to hear was that we were poor.

- Begin with a statement that promises interesting things to follow, as John Updike introduces his essay "Central Park."

  On the afternoon of the first day of spring, when the gutters were still heaped high with Monday's snow but the sky itself was swept clean, we put on our galoshes and walked up the sunny side of Fifth Avenue to Central Park.

- Begin with an interesting detail related to the setting, as N. Scott Momaday does in "A Kiowa Grandmother."

  A single knoll rises out of the plain in Oklahoma, north and west of the Wichita Range.

## CREATING A TONE

In addition to building interest, your introduction should establish the **tone,** which is your attitude toward the subject. To choose an appropriate tone, think about the effect the subject had on you. If it made you laugh, for example, you would use a humorous tone. Personal narratives have a variety of tones, as the following excerpts show.

**MODEL: Alarmed Tone**

There is something uneasy in the Los Angeles air this afternoon, some unnatural stillness, some tension. What it means is that tonight a Santa Ana will begin to blow, a hot wind from the northeast whining down through the Cajon and San Gorgonio Passes, blowing up sandstorms out along Route 66, drying the hills and the nerves to the flash point. For a few days now we will see smoke back in the canyons, and hear sirens in the night. I have neither heard nor read that a Santa Ana is due, but I know it, and almost everyone I have seen today knows it too. We know it because we feel it. The baby frets. The maid sulks. I rekindle a waning argument with the telephone company, then cut my losses and lie down, given over to whatever it is in the air.

—Joan Didion, "Los Angeles Notebook"

Didion creates a tone of alarm through phrases such as "something uneasy," "unnatural stillness," and "sirens in the night." Notice how another writer creates a different tone.

**MODEL: Reflective Tone**

The sound of the sea is the most time-effacing sound there is. The centuries roll in a cloud and the earth becomes green again when you listen, with eyes shut, to the sea—a young green time when the water and the land were just getting acquainted and had known each other for only a few billion years and the mollusks were just beginning to dip and creep in the shallows; and now man the invertebrate, under his ribbed umbrella . . . pulls on his Polaroid glasses to stop and glare and stretches out his long brown body at ease upon a towel on the warm sand and listens.

—E. B. White, "On a Florida Key"

E. B. White's details such as "the earth becomes green again when you listen, with eyes shut, to the sea" create a reflective tone.

● **Practice Your Skills**

*Generating Sensory Details*

Identify specific words and details that Gary Soto used in "The Concert" to create a reflective and affectionate tone for each sense: sight, sound, touch, smell, and taste. For some senses you may not find words or details.

**PROJECT PREP** *Drafting* *Working with Peers*

Bring your draft to your writing group. Evaluate one another's introduction for impact and tone.

# ② Drafting the Body

Once you have written an introduction that piques the interest of your readers, move on to draft the body of your essay, including the details that you selected earlier in your planning.

## How to Draft the Body

- Make sure that each supporting paragraph has a topic sentence that supports the main idea.
- Follow a logical order of ideas and details.
- Use transitions between sentences and paragraphs to give your narrative coherence.
- If you discover new ideas and details as you write, go back and make changes in those sections of the narrative that are affected by the new insights or details.

As you draft the body of your essay, note that you should narrate the experience as if it were a story, with events arranged in chronological order. Remember, however, that descriptive details will be especially important in establishing and maintaining its tone. In the model that follows, writer Agatha Christie uses description to help the reader visualize her first concept of the famous fictional detective, Hercule Poirot.

## MODEL: Body of a Personal Narrative

Sure enough, next day, when I was sitting in a tram, I saw just what I wanted: *a man with a black beard, sitting next to an elderly lady who was chatting like a magpie.* I didn't think I'd have *her,* but I thought *he* would do admirably. Sitting a little way beyond them was a large, hearty woman, talking loudly about spring bulbs. I liked the look of her too. Perhaps I could incorporate her? I took them all three off the tram with me to work upon—and walked up Barton Road muttering to myself.

—Agatha Christie, *Agatha Christie: An Autobiography*

## PROJECT PREP · Drafting · Setting Up

In your writing group, consider how writers build a "set up" so their main point will be clear, as Soto does at the beginning of "The Concert." In a narrative about a fallen stereotype, for example, examine the way each writer set up the realization that things were different from what he or she assumed. What were the assumptions about the other group, and on what were they based? What was the prior relationship between the author and the group of people? How has the author presented this relationship and the accompanying assumptions? Help each author to provide a clear account of the set of expectations that would be changed during the course of the narrative.

# ③ Drafting the Conclusion

The conclusion of your personal narrative should leave the readers with a memorable impression of the personal experience or insight that serves as your subject. The following strategies will help you write a striking conclusion.

## How to End a Personal Narrative

- Summarize the body or restate the main idea in new words.
- Add an insight that shows a new or deeper understanding of the experience.
- Add a striking new detail or memorable image.
- Refer to ideas in the introduction to bring your narrative full circle.
- Appeal to your readers' emotions.

The following paragraph concludes the E. B. White piece from which you read a paragraph on page 144. The conclusion adds a new insight that reveals a further understanding of his subject.

> ## MODEL: Conclusion of a Personal Narrative
>
> The sea answers all questions, and always in the same way; for when you read in the papers the interminable discussions and the bickering and the prognostications and the turmoil, the disagreements and the fateful decisions and agreements and the plans and the programs and the threats and the counter threats, then you close your eyes and the sea dispatches one more big roller in the unbroken line since the beginning of the world and it combs and breaks and returns foaming and saying: "So soon?"
>
> —E. B. White, "On a Florida Key"

In your reading experiences, you may have felt that what makes a strong conclusion was a bit of a mystery, but using the strategies listed above should help you craft your own.

## PROJECT PREP  Drafting  *Presenting the Event*

In your writing group, focus on each writer's presentation of the event that triggered a new understanding. How clearly is this event described? Do you as readers follow the event easily as a result of the author's vivid descriptions? For each author, help to identify ways in which the transforming event unfolded and what happened in its aftermath to cause a change in thinking on the part of the author.

# In the Media

## Personal Narratives

Personal narratives are everywhere in the media. They range from celebrity anecdotes and poignant human interest stories to the sometimes terrifying accounts related by victims of war and natural disasters.

In the visual media, narratives range from 2- or 3-minute stories on the nightly news to 20-minute segments on newsmagazines and 50-minute documentaries. In the print media, newspapers have more coverage than a story on the nightly news but not as much as a magazine. Narratives on the Internet, a mix of visual and print presentations, are often comparable to those in newspapers, but they can be supplemented with related links. Some of the most interesting Internet narratives are found in newsgroups or blogs where members share their experiences.

Regardless of the medium, concise expression enhances the telling of the tale. Details make a personal narrative compelling, but rambling thoughts can lose even the most interested audience. Each word should have a purpose.

## Media Activity

Choose three media forms to explore for personal narratives. After identifying a good example from each form, prepare an analysis by answering these questions.

### QUESTIONS FOR ANALYZING PERSONAL NARRATIVES

- What are the subjects? In which medium and where in the medium did you find each one?
- What was the writer's or speaker's purpose? What do you think was the motive of the producer or publisher?
- How are the narratives alike and different? Does the medium explain some of their differences? If so, how?
- Has the writer shaped the narrative to fit the medium? Why or why not? Has an interviewer or reporter influenced the delivery of the narrative?
- Is each narrative rich in detail but concise in expression?

### editing ☆

Make the following passage more concise and therefore more compelling by cutting out needless words and phrases.

> There we were driving high up on a remote mountain road, and night was closing in, snow picking up, and we were really anxious to get home, when we rounded a curve and saw the wounded deer in our headlights.

**CHAPTER 4**

After you have drafted your personal narrative, put it aside for a few days so that you will be able to reread it with a fresh eye. When you review it, read it aloud to yourself and ask yourself whether it sounds lively. Do you hear your personality in it? Do your feelings about the subject come through? Revise your draft with the goal of making it as fresh and natural sounding as possible. The following box shows some common problems with first drafts and ways to fix them.

## STRATEGIES FOR REVISING PERSONAL NARRATIVES

| Problem | Strategy |
| --- | --- |
| The essay is too short, general, or vague. | Find more details. Visualize again the people, places, things, or experiences you are writing about. |
| The tone is inconsistent. | Revise parts of the personal narrative that stray from the tone set in the introduction. |
| The essay sounds too stiff and formal. | Replace formal or technical words with everyday vocabulary. |

### Evaluation Checklist for Revising

✓ Does your introduction capture the reader's interest? (pages 143–144)

✓ Have you held the reader's interest to the end? (pages 143–146)

✓ Does your feeling about your subject come through? (pages 135–139)

✓ Does your ending give the reader a sense of completion? (page 146)

## PROJECT PREP  *Revising*  *Strategies and Checklist*

Evaluate your personal narrative by asking yourself whether it is adequately developed and natural sounding. Decide whether your feelings will come across to your readers. Then revise your personal narrative using the strategies and checklist above as guides. Save your revised draft for later use.

You revised your personal narrative to make it as fresh and natural sounding as possible. You also checked for adequate development and the clarity of the feelings you are trying to express. Now you are ready to edit for grammar, usage, and mechanics.

# The Language of Power *Verb Tense*

**Power Rule:** Use a consistent verb tense except when a change is clearly necessary. (See pages 762–776.)

**See It in Action** The following passage from "The Concert" is easy to follow because the verb tenses are consistent. The words in bold type are all past-tense verbs. The passage would be confusing if the author had shifted from past tense to present tense.

> I **led** Carolyn to the boxes in the front row against the rail and together we **looked** far down where the others sat. Their rumblings **rose** like heat. They **fanned** themselves and **smiled** wide enough for us to see their teeth. We **watched** them until an old man **touched** my shoulder, **said** *con permiso* and **took** small steps to get past me to the box on our left.

In special cases, a shift in verb tense is necessary. In the following sentence from "The Concert," Soto uses different tenses to make clear what happened in the past and is over, and what happened in the past but remains true in the present.

> We **sat, mesmerized,** listening to the music. We **are always drawn** to the music of Haydn.

**Remember It** Record this rule and example in the Power Rule section of your Personalized Editing Checklist.

**Use It** Read through your personal narrative to make sure you have used consistent verb tenses, except when—as explained—a tense shift is clearly necessary. Highlight or underline verbs to help you keep track of tenses as you edit.

## PROJECT PREP  *Revising*  *Teacher Comments*

Ask your teacher for comments on your draft. Based on this feedback, produce a new draft in which you take into account the suggestions you have received and incorporate them into your narrative.

## Using a Six-Trait Rubric — Personal Narratives

Use an evaluation form like the one below to measure a personal narrative.

| Ideas | **4** The topic and details convey the experience powerfully to the intended audience and fulfill the intended purpose. | **3** The topic and details convey the experience to the intended audience and fulfill the intended purpose. | **2** The topic and details do not clearly convey the experience to the intended audience or fulfill the intended purpose. | **1** The topic and details do not convey the experience and fail to address the audience and fulfill the purpose. |
|---|---|---|---|---|
| Organization | **4** The introduction, body, and conclusion fulfill their purposes. | **3** The organization is mostly clear, but a few ideas seem out of place or transitions are missing. | **2** Many ideas seem out of place and transitions are missing. | **1** The organization is unclear. The narrative does not present, develop, and interpret the experience. |
| Voice | **4** The voice sounds natural, engaging, and personal. | **3** The voice sounds natural and personal. | **2** The voice sounds mostly unnatural with exceptions. | **1** The voice sounds mostly unnatural. |
| Word Choice | **4** Words are vivid, specific, and rich in sensory images. | **3** Words are specific and some appeal to the senses. | **2** Some words are overly general. | **1** Most words are overly general. |
| Sentence Fluency | **4** Varied sentences flow smoothly. Devices that promote coherence are used effectively. | **3** Most of the sentences are varied and smoothly flowing. Transitions help coherence. | **2** Some sentence patterns are not varied and some sentences are choppy. Few transitions are present. | **1** Sentences are not varied and are choppy. There are very few transitions and little coherence. |
| Conventions | **4** Punctuation, usage, and spelling are correct. | **3** There are only a few errors in punctuation, usage, and spelling. | **2** There are several errors in punctuation, usage, and spelling. | **1** There are many errors and at least one failure to follow a Power Rule. |

## PROJECT PREP — Evaluating — Using a Rubric

Produce a final version of your story, using correct grammar, spelling, and punctuation.

# Personal Writing   Publishing

The writing process is complete when you share your writing with others. You may want to share your personal narrative with someone who was part of your experience or who may have an interest in it.

CHAPTER 4

## PROJECT PREP   Publishing   *Final Draft*

Work with a writing partner to exchange papers and read one another's narratives for clarity, insight, and form. After providing and receiving feedback, produce a polished draft that you publish in an appropriate form. You might, for instance, find an Internet site that combats stereotyping. If it allows readers to upload narratives, you might add your story to the collection.

**TIME OUT TO REFLECT**

How have your narrative skills improved? Take out a narrative piece you wrote earlier in the school year, and compare it with your current work. Have you improved in your use of details and in the structure of your sentences? Is there anything that you did better in the earlier piece? In which areas do you think you have made the most progress? In which areas do you still need improvement? Record your answers to these questions in the Learning Log section of your journal.

# Writing Lab

## Project Corner

### Get Creative Write a Poem

**Rewrite your personal narrative or a part of it as a poem.** Consider a variety of poetic forms. Compose a poem in free verse or use traditional forms that include rhyme and meter. Consider modeling your poem on an example of a narrative poem or ballad that you have read or heard.

### Write a Sequel Follow It Up

Choose a story written by another member of your writing group and **write a sequel**—that is, a story that takes place following the events of the narrative. The sequel should follow clearly from the narrative on which it is based.

### Speak and Listen Reflect and Apply

With your classmates, **discuss the issues of stereotyping** that have arisen during the writing and discussion of the narratives. What have you learned from this experience? How, if at all, will you act differently in the future? What might the class do to address issues of stereotyping in the school?

### Change Perspectives
### Another Point of View

How would your narrative be told if the speaker were a different character in the story? **Rewrite your narrative** from a different perspective, considering how someone else might see, interpret, and describe the events of the story.

# In Everyday Life
## Narrative Essay

1. The editor of the school newspaper has selected you to write an essay for a special edition of the paper. The purpose of the special edition is to prepare freshmen for starting high school by including personal narratives by the seasoned seniors. **Write a narrative essay** using a friendly tone describing a memorable experience from your first week of high school.

# In the Workplace Narrative Report

2. You are a policeman who has received a call from a concerned citizen about a man in the park who is dressed in black and wearing white makeup. When you arrive at the scene you immediately recognize that the man in question is a mime. **Write a narrative report** for the police chief describing what happened when you responded to the call. Choose details appropriate for your purpose and audience. Provide background information and use vivid descriptive and sensory details to bring your experience to life.

# Timed Writing ⏱ Thrilling Report

3. You have finished writing several college entrance essays and have only one more to write. So far, your essays have been about people you admire, world problems that concern you, and the contributions you think you can make to society. You are extremely relieved to read the final question: Look back at your life so far. What have you done that has thrilled you? Write a personal narrative describing the most exciting experience in your life with such vivid detail that the people on the admissions committee will feel as if they have experienced it too. You have 30 minutes to complete your work. (For help budgeting time, see pages 37 and 493.)

**Before You Write** Consider the following questions: What is the subject? What is the occasion? Who is the audience? What is the purpose?

**After You Write** Evaluate your work using the six-trait evaluation form on page 150.

# CHAPTER **5**

# Descriptive Writing

**D**escriptive writing creates a well-developed verbal picture of a person, object, or scene.

You can find description and observation in all of the following.

- **Novels, stories, and poems describe settings, characters, and objects** as part of creating a believable fictional world.

- **Orators arguing for solutions to social problems provide specific, vivid, moving descriptions** of those problems' effects.

- **Soldiers in the field must report local conditions** accurately to their commanders.

- **Radio announcers describe sports events** so clearly that a listener can visualize the play-by-play.

- **Students at college describe life in the dorms, classes, and new friends** in letters, e-mails, and phone calls to their families.

## Writing Project Procedural

***Step by Step*** *Explain clearly and in vivid detail how to do something that interests you.*

***Think Through Writing*** Describe a process for how to do something, such as cook a meal, plant a tree, design a Web page, or complete another activity that interests you. Assume that the person to whom you are explaining this process is completely unfamiliar with the task. For now, don't worry about grammar, punctuation, or spelling; focus instead on getting your ideas out on paper.

***Talk About It*** In your writing group, discuss the writing you have done. What details has each author included to help the reader understand the process?

***Read About It*** In the following passage, author Chang-rae Lee describes watching his mother cook. As you read, absorb the descriptions with each of your senses. See if you can follow along and imagine replicating the process.

# Coming Home Again

*Chang-rae Lee*

When I was six or seven years old, I used to watch my mother as she prepared our favorite meals. It was one of my daily pleasures. She shooed me away in the beginning, telling me that the kitchen wasn't my place, and adding, in her half-proud, half-deprecating way, that her kind of work would only serve to weaken me. "Go out and play with your friends," she'd snap in Korean, "or better yet, do your reading and homework." She knew that I had already done both, and that as the evening approached there was no place to go but her small and tidy kitchen, from which the clatter of her mixing bowls and pans would ring through the house.

I would enter the kitchen quietly and stand beside her, my chin lodging upon the point of her hip. Peering through the crook of her arm, I beheld the movements of her hands. For kalbi,[1] she would take up a butchered short rib in her narrow hand, the flinty bone shaped like a section of an airplane wing and deeply embedded in gristle and flesh, and with the point of her knife cut so that the bone fell away, though not completely, leaving it connected to the meat by the barest opaque layer of tendon. Then she methodically butterflied the flesh, cutting and unfolding, repeating the action until the meat lay out on her board, glistening and ready for seasoning. She scored it diagonally, then sifted sugar into the crevices with her pinched fingers, gently rubbing in the crystals. The sugar would tenderize as well as sweeten the meat. She did this with each rib, and then set them all aside in a large shallow bowl. She minced a half-dozen cloves of garlic, a stub of gingerroot, sliced up a few scallions, and spread it all over the meat. She wiped her hands and took out a bottle of sesame oil, and, after pausing for a moment, streamed the dark oil in two swift circles around the bowl. After adding a few splashes of soy sauce, she thrust her hands in and kneaded the flesh, careful not to dislodge the bones. I asked her why

---

1  **kalbi:** Korean barbecued ribs

The introduction creates an overall impression as the reader learns that watching his mother cook was one of the author's "daily pleasures."

Sounds help bring the scene to life.

The process of preparing kalbi is described in exact detail with very specific language.

Such specific verbs as "butterflied" and adjectives as "glistening" make the scene easy to picture.

These details appeal to the senses of smell and taste.

CHAPTER 5

it mattered that they remain connected. "The meat needs the bone nearby," she said, "to borrow its richness." She wiped her hands clean of the marinade, except for her little finger, which she would flick with her tongue from time to time, because she knew that the flavor of a good dish developed not at once but in stages.

Whenever I cook, I find myself working just as she would, readying the ingredients—a mash of garlic, a julienne of red peppers, fantails of shrimp—and piling them in little mounds about the cutting surface. My mother never left me any recipes, but this is how I learned to make her food, each dish coming not from a list or a card but from the aromatic spread of a board.

**Respond in Writing** Respond to Lee's essay about food preparation. How does he help readers envision his mother's food preparation process?

**Develop Your Own Descriptive Ideas** Work with your classmates to develop ideas that will help you describe a process clearly.

**Small Groups:** In your writing group, make an organizer like the one below, leaving plenty of room in each cell to catalog the information each writer might include in his or her process description.

| Writer | Setting in which the activity takes place | Sequence of actions necessary | Reasons for taking each action in order | Details within the sequence of actions | Sensory details to explain the process |
|---|---|---|---|---|---|
| Writer 1 Topic: | | | | | |
| Writer 2 Topic: | | | | | |
| Writer 3 Topic: | | | | | |

*Whole Class:* Share your organizer with the other writing groups. Identify some of the most important types of information for describing a process and make a list of them that the whole class can refer to as each student writes his or her process description.

*Write About It* You will next write a vivid explanation of a process you know how to do well. These are your goals:

- You will clearly state you purpose and support your viewpoint on the topic with facts and details.

- You will use an appropriate organizational structure and formatting techniques such as headings, graphics, and white space to make your text easy to follow.

- You will include some relevant questions that will engage your readers and address their potential problems and misunderstandings. If you include technical information, it will be accurate and presented in accessible language.

The following chart provides possible topics, audiences, and forms for your writing.

| Possible Topics | Possible Audiences | Possible Forms |
|---|---|---|
| • how to prepare a meal<br>• how to play a musical instrument<br>• how to execute a maneuver in a particular sport<br>• how to repair a problem with a car<br>• how to make or construct something | • people who are completely unfamiliar with the process you are explaining<br>• experts in the process you are explaining<br>• people who want to learn how to do what you are explaining<br>• people who are evaluating your knowledge | • a user's manual<br>• a set of instructions<br>• an instructional video<br>• a letter explaining your hobby to a friend<br>• a reflective essay on how you learned to do something |

In Chang-rae Lee's writing, you have read rich sensory detail about a subject the author knows intimately. Description is not always found in the obvious places, however, such as in the details of cooking traditional food. Description has a place in many kinds of writing, including narrative, expository, persuasive, and expressive writing.

When you are writing a descriptive essay, you should have three major sections just as you do when writing a descriptive paragraph.

## Structuring a Descriptive Essay

- In the **introduction,** capture the reader's interest, introduce the subject, and suggest or imply an overall impression of the subject that you wish to convey.
- In the **body of supporting paragraphs,** present vivid details, especially sensory details.
- In the **conclusion,** reinforce the overall impression and tie the essay together, possibly leading the reader to further thought.

## ❶ Specific Details and Sensory Words

You may be familiar with the literary adage "Show, don't tell." This means that you should use strong, specific details and words that appeal to the senses in order to make the reader feel that he or she is actually seeing, hearing, and feeling the things you describe. A description is not merely a list; it is a re-creation of a part of life.

## Writing Tip

Use **specific details** and **sensory words** to bring your description to life.

One reason "Coming Home Again" is so richly descriptive is that Chang-rae Lee's observations show his attitudes about his subject. The selection is not an impersonal account of someone cutting up meat and vegetables; it is a description of the author's mother preparing meals the author has loved since childhood. Readers can sense how important the subject is to Lee and can participate in Lee's experience because they may have had similar life experiences.

The fundamental reason Lee's descriptive writing succeeds, however, is because its physical details are specific, vivid, accurate, and imaginatively worded. Some of these details are listed on the chart below.

| SPECIFIC SENSORY DETAILS | |
|---|---|
| Sights | small, tidy kitchen; the shape of a beef bone; the glisten of meat; dark oil swirling in circles in a bowl; sight of mother's arms moving; mounds of ingredients on cutting board |
| Sounds | clatter of mixing bowls and pans |
| Smells | "aromatic spread" including garlic, ginger, shrimp |
| Taste | sweetness of sugared meat; flavor of marinade |
| Feelings | child's chin lodging on mother's hip; her rubbing of sugar into meat |

● **Practice Your Skills**

*Analyzing a Descriptive Essay*

Answer the following questions about "Coming Home Again."

**1.** What constitutes the beginning, or introduction, of the essay?

**2.** What constitutes the body of the essay?

**3.** What constitutes the conclusion of the essay?

**4.** What overall impression does the essay convey?

**5.** List six or more details that convey or imply the overall impression.

**6.** Find one or more examples in which the writer uses a comparison, either stated or implied, to enrich a description.

**7.** How would you describe the organizational pattern of this essay? What is the underlying logic connecting one paragraph to the next?

**8.** By means of a description of food, what is the author saying about human life?

---

**PROJECT PREP** *Prewriting* *Focusing Your Subject*

Review your initial writing and focus on what you will choose for your subject, audience, and form or genre. For the descriptive process project, for example, review what you wrote before you read "Coming Home Again" and review the chart of project possibilities on page 157. Is the writing you began suitable for developing further in this project? If not, what might you write about instead? For which audience are you writing, and what form will your final text take? Write a few sentences focusing your subject and identifying your audience and the form you will write in.

# ② Figurative Language

A figure of speech, also called a **trope** or a play on words, can add extra flavor to a description. Think of tropes as seasonings added to a dish of food in just the right proportion. The most familiar types of tropes are imagery, similes, and metaphors. Others include personification, onomatopoeia, oxymoron, hyperbole, irony, analogies, and symbolism. Chang-rae Lee uses figurative language sparingly, applying a subtle effect at carefully chosen points. The following are some examples from "Coming Home Again."

| | |
|---|---|
| **Imagery** | "the barest opaque layer of tendon" |
| **Simile** | "the flinty bone shaped like a section of an airplane wing" |
| **Personification** | "The meat needs the bone nearby . . . to borrow its richness." |
| **Onomatopoeia** | "snap"; "clatter"; "flick" |
| **Hyperbole** | "There was no place to go but her small and tidy kitchen." |
| **Symbolism** | Food is often a symbol of love, the warmth of family life, and nostalgia for home. |

*You can learn more about tropes on pages 51–53, and 326.*

Writing Tip

Use **figurative language** and **comparisons** to bring your description to life.

## ● Practice Your Skills

### Composing Figurative Language

Have a conversation with a partner about memories of food such as those in "Coming Home Again." Write down three details from the conversation. They may come from your recollections, your partner's, or both. For each detail, write a descriptive sentence containing a figure of speech.

## ● Practice Your Skills

### *Finding Similarities Using a Comparison Cluster*

You are already familiar with clustering as a strategy for developing ideas. A special kind of cluster diagram can not only develop figurative comparisons, but also show you how to analyze the things being compared. To make a comparison cluster, follow this procedure:

- In the center of a piece of paper, write the object for which you want to find a comparison. Circle it.

- Surround the circled word or phrase with words or phrases that come to mind as possible comparisons, such as *snow* and *happiness* in the cluster below. Be spontaneous at this point; write down anything that comes to mind, whether or not you understand the comparison and no matter how weird it seems.

- Focus on each word or phrase in turn, and try to think of how it is similar to the circled word or phrase. Draw a connecting line, and on that line, write a brief description of the similarity.

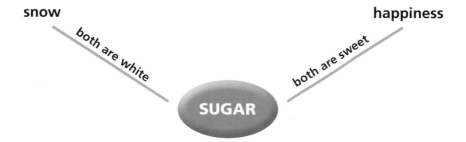

- If you have trouble thinking of a point of similarity, leave the connecting line blank so that you might fill it in later. If you are certain there is no similarity, write an X on the connecting line.

- Add at least three possible comparisons for "sugar" on the diagram above. Then make a comparison cluster for a detail from your recollections of food—other than sugar, of course.

---

### PROJECT PREP *Prewriting* *Using Tropes*

In your writing group, focus attention on each author's opportunities to use figurative language. Are there comparisons the author could make that would clarify, illustrate, or illuminate any part of the process? Help the author identify areas that would benefit from figurative language and other tropes that would help readers follow the explanation of the process and be able to go through it on their own.

Prewriting is often the first thinking that a writer does, but it can continue throughout the other stages of the writing process as well. The fact that you have made a plan and begun to draft does not mean that you should stop thinking about your subject or evaluating your approach. In addition, although the prefix *pre-* suggests that prewriting is done before putting pen to paper, remember that many aspects of prewriting, such as listing, free writing, clustering, charting, and outlining, are best done on paper.

## ① Purpose, Subject, and Audience

### PURPOSE

When you think of descriptive writing, you probably think first of literature: poems, stories, and novels all rely on description of the sights, sounds, and emotions of life. Descriptive writing, however, is also found in informative and persuasive writing. If your purpose is to explain how to do something, it is helpful to describe the actions and objects involved. If your purpose is to persuade the reader to think or feel a certain way, you will be better able to rouse those responses if your arguments include descriptions that appeal to emotion. Consider your purpose and how descriptive writing fits with that purpose.

### SUBJECT

Chang-rae Lee chose to describe a subject that was important to him. His subject was not a major event in world history and perhaps not even in his own life, even though it had a powerful emotional impact on the author. The scale of the event is not the crucial factor in determining whether a subject is worth describing. What is important is that the author is able to transmit the impact of the subject to the reader.

The following guidelines will help you choose a subject for your descriptive essay.

### Guidelines for Choosing a Subject

- Ask yourself, "How interested am I in this subject?" If you are not very interested in your subject, your reader is probably not going to be, either.
- Ask yourself, "How well do I know this subject?" For your descriptive essay, select a subject that you know thoroughly and in detail.
- Ask yourself, "Does this subject have the potential for rich descriptive detail?"

Of the three questions, the first is the most important. If you know only a little bit about a subject, you can learn more by doing research, provided your interest is strong. If you are at first unaware of how your subject offers potentially rich descriptive detail, a deeper knowledge of the subject will probably make you aware of it.

## AUDIENCE

If Lee had been describing his mother's preparation of food for an audience of professional chefs, he probably would have presented details with different vocabulary. The readers for whom you are writing should influence how you write. The level of vocabulary you choose should be geared to your intended readership, and so should the length and complexity of your sentences. You should also think about whether your audience already knows a great deal about your subject. This will affect the amount of background material you need to provide.

The following questions will help you refine your style so that it suits the occasion and your audience and purpose.

### Questions for Analyzing an Audience

- How much, if anything, does my audience already know about my subject?
- What background information, if any, must I include if my description is to be clear, concise, and meaningful for this particular audience?
- How does my audience feel about my subject? Should I expect to encounter any biases, and if so, how can I organize my essay in order to neutralize or disarm them?
- What tone and what kind of vocabulary would be best in order to bridge any gap between my view of the subject and my audience's view?

### ● Practice Your Skills

*Identifying Your Audience*

Identify four possible audiences for each of the following descriptive subjects.

**Example**     a mountain

**Audiences**     geologists, mountain climbers, artists, people who have never seen a mountain

**1.** a lamp          **3.** a family

**2.** a superhighway     **4.** a blueprint for a building

### PROJECT PREP   *Prewriting*   *Audience*

In your writing group, play the role of an audience for each author's description of a process. First ask the author what audience he or she is writing for. Read with that audience in mind. Does the author take your needs into account? Help each author include details and language that help the intended audience follow the explanation.

# ② Creating an Overall Impression

As rich in detail as "Coming Home Again" is, it is also an excellent example of selective detail. Lee does not describe everything he saw, heard, felt, smelled, and tasted while watching his mother prepare food. Imagine the kinds of things that might have been left out of this description: the phone rings, the cook turns on the stove, the narrator's eyes stray to the refrigerator and he feels hungry for a snack. . . . One of the most important skills of descriptive writing is selecting, or filtering, details: knowing what to put in and what to leave out.

Writers intuitively have personal criteria for filtering details in or out of a given composition. To develop a sense of the relative value of details, you should have in mind an overall impression you wish to convey to the reader. You can then filter in any material that contributes to the desired impression and filter out any material that does not. Different readers may receive different impressions from the same text, but the writer should always have a clear vision in mind.

## ● Practice Your Skills

### *Identifying Overall Impressions*

Reread "Coming Home Again" and answer the following questions.

1. What is the overall impression Lee was trying to convey in "Coming Home Again"?
2. What phrases or passages introduce this overall impression in the introduction to the essay?
3. What phrases or passages sustain this overall impression in the body of the essay?
4. What phrases or passages carry this overall impression into the conclusion of the essay?
5. Did you derive any different or conflicting impressions from the essay? If so, what were those impressions and how did you get them?

---

### PROJECT PREP  *Prewriting*  *Setting and Impression*

In your writing group, focus your attention on the setting in which the process being described takes place. The process might occur in a kitchen, a sewing room, a garage, a batting cage, or other location. What overall impression of the setting do you want to create? What details about the setting are important to include to create and support that impression and to aid in the description of the process? Help each author provide a detailed and relevant account of the setting so that readers are aware of their surroundings as they go through the process.

# 3 Developing a Description

Bearing in mind your intended audience and the overall impression you want to make, you can begin to work with the details you intend to include in your descriptive essay. Use the strategies below.

## Strategies for Developing a Description

- List sensory images you associate with your subject—as many images as possible. Make a chart like the one on page 159 if you wish.
- Brainstorm figurative comparisons and other kinds of tropes that come to mind in association with your subject and your sensory images.
- If background information would significantly help provide a basis of knowledge for your readers, find the relevant facts and data. Do research if necessary.
- Draw a picture (or a map, if appropriate) as a prewriting tool to clarify your mental image of your subject.
- For each detail, ask yourself whether it fits with the overall impression you wish to make; filter out those details that do not fit.

## Practice Your Skills

### Filtering Details

Look at the following list of details for a descriptive essay about a city. Write the ones that do not seem to fit the overall impression. Explain why you think they do not fit.

**Overall Impression**    inspiring, active, civilized, beautiful

**Details**
- skyline lit up at night
- boats in the harbor tooting their horns
- cockroaches running through apartment buildings in the dark
- nannies wheeling babies to a park
- two cab drivers who have crashed their taxis, arguing loudly
- women and men in a wide array of clothing, walking briskly to work or other destinations
- the scent of roasting chestnuts from a street vendor's cart wafting toward the museum steps
- steam surging up from an open manhole as a utility crew makes repairs
- a jackhammer drilling into the pavement

- from a wheelchair basketball tournament, the cheers of fans and the whistle of a referee
- pigeons, picking at a loaf of bread that dropped from a delivery truck, scattering at the approach of a bus
- an ambulance stuck in a traffic jam, impatiently sounding its siren
- diners in an elegant restaurant bringing forkfuls of delicious food to their mouths

## PROJECT PREP *Prewriting* *Filtering Details*

1. In your writing group, develop an overall impression of the scene shown in this photo. Then brainstorm a list of details about it. Review the details to decide which, if any, should be filtered out because they do not support the overall impression.

2. Help each author determine if any of the details in his or her description are unnecessary or distracting. What could each author eliminate from the description so that 1) readers can focus on what is important and necessary, and 2) the overall impression is supported?

# Think Critically

## Observing

If a machine observed a woman preparing a meal, the machine's observations would be **objective.** "Human cuts meat. Smaller human watches. Humans talk." Human beings are not like machines. Our personal responses influence our observations and make them **subjective.**

Although Chang-rae Lee makes few explicit statements of his feelings in the selection, his choices of words are subjective and often enable a reader to infer his attitudes. The following chart shows some objective facts Lee observes about his subject and some of the subjective "spins" he (or the reader) puts on those facts.

| OBJECTIVE DETAILS | SUBJECTIVE DETAILS |
|---|---|
| He watches his mother cook. | Watching her cook "was one of my daily pleasures." |
| His mother tries to shoo him out of the kitchen. | Her tone is "half-proud, half-deprecating." |
| As an adult, he cooks Korean food without recipes. | His Korean cooking is a loving legacy from his mother that comes "from the aromatic spread of a board." |

If you compare the two kinds of details, you can see that the objective ones would be verified by any impartial onlooker. The subjective details, which interpret the experience rather than merely report it, are what make Lee's descriptive essay touching, personal, and revealing.

## Thinking Practice

Make a chart like the one above to record objective and subjective observations of your school. Compare your work to that of a classmate.

# ④ Organizing a Description

The organizational plan for a descriptive essay should depend on your purpose and on the nature of your details. The following chart shows some possible patterns of organization. Your essay may require using one or more of these patterns. Chang-rae Lee had at least two purposes in "Coming Home Again": to describe a scene from his childhood and to explain how his mother cooked dinner. You too may find that you need to shift from one type of order to another as you develop your essay.

| WRITING PURPOSE | KINDS OF DETAILS | TYPE OF ORDER |
|---|---|---|
| to **describe** a person, place, object, or scene | sensory details | spatial (pages 94–95) |
| to **recreate** an event | sensory details, events | chronological (pages 94–95) |
| to **explain** a process or show how something works | sensory and factual details, steps in a process, how parts work together | sequential (pages 256–259) |
| to **persuade** | sensory and factual details, examples, reasons | order of importance (pages 94–95) |
| to **reflect** | sensory and factual details, interpretations | developmental (pages 94–95) |

## ● Practice Your Skills

### Organizing a Description

Review the list of details describing a city on pages 165–166. Decide on an appropriate organizational pattern for them and make a rough outline showing the order in which you would present them. Exclude any details that would work against your desired overall impression. Conclude by writing a sentence or two explaining your choices.

**PROJECT PREP** *Prewriting* *Organizing Details*

Review your filtered list of details and think through how best to arrange them. Refer back to the graphic organizer your group compiled (see page 156) for further thoughts about organization. Arrange your ideas in a logical order, and share your plan with your writing group. Be open to ideas they have for improving the organization of your process description.

# The Power of Language ⚡

## Adverbial Clauses: Scene Setters

Throughout your school years, you have been using adverbial clauses in both speech and writing. You create such clauses by putting a subordinating word like *when, if, because, until, while, since, as,* or *although* in front of a sentence (see pages 718–730). To avoid fragments, you then attach the subordinate clause to an independent clause, forming a complex sentence. The following example is constructed from a sentence in "Coming Home Again."

| | |
|---|---|
| **Simple Sentence** | I was six or seven years old. |
| **Adverbial Clause** | When I was six or seven years old … |
| **Complex Sentence** | When I was six or seven years old, I used to watch my mother … |

Here is another example from "Coming Home Again."

> After adding a few splashes of soy sauce, she thrust her hands in and kneaded the flesh.

Adverbial clauses add power to writing and speaking in part because they do such a good job of setting the scene for the rest of the sentence. They also show the relative importance of ideas, with the idea in the independent clause carrying the most weight. There are two adverbial clauses in the example below from "Coming Home Again."

> Whenever I cook, I find myself working just as she would. …

## Try It Yourself

1. Write a sentence with one or more adverbial clauses that describes a reason you need to do something.
2. Write two or more sentences with adverbial clauses that tell when something happened in your topic.

If you can, use these sentences in your draft and add other descriptive clauses as you draft your descriptive piece. Later, as you revise, see if there are other places where you can use clauses like these.

### Punctuation Tip

When a subordinating clause comes at the **beginning of a sentence**, **set it off** from the rest of the sentence **with a comma**. (See page 721.)

# Descriptive Writing

Some writers feel freest when drafting because they can let their pens flow or their fingers fly over the keyboard, secure in the knowledge that they can cross out, add to, or rephrase things later. Even those writers, however, no doubt have a sense of direction during drafting. By this point you should have a fairly clear, if flexible, idea of what you want to describe. You should also know the light in which you wish to present your description and the general shape it will take. Additionally, keeping your audience in mind will help you stay on course.

**HERE'S HOW** **Tips for Drafting a Description**

- Find a "hook" to arouse the reader's interest during the introduction; try out several possible beginnings if necessary.
- Suggest or imply your overall impression early on to unify the essay; this impression should be conveyed through your choices of details and words.
- Follow your outline, but be prepared to improvise changes in response to inspiration.
- Use fresh, vivid, descriptive sensory words and images.
- Use appropriate transitions to carry through your organizational plan (pages 5 and 95).
- Draft a strong conclusion, perhaps referring back to earlier ideas or leaving the reader with an intriguing thought.

## PROJECT PREP  Drafting  *Pulling It All Together*

Based on all the recent feedback from your writing group, write a new draft of your description of a process, using the preceding tips. Make sure your description is clear and easy for a reader to follow. Use transitions and sentence variety, including complex sentences with adverbial clauses, to keep your draft flowing smoothly.

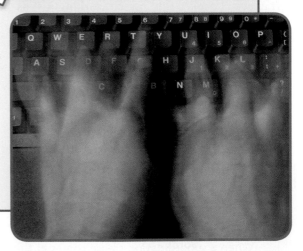

The revising stage is your chance to sift through what you have thought and planned and written, separating the things that work from the things that do not. You should revise for both style and content, and on both the micro-level (the level of individual words and details) and the macro-level (the level of concept and organization).

 ## Evaluation Checklist for Revising

### Checking Your Introduction

✓ Does your introduction seize the reader's attention? (pages 108–112 and 158)

✓ Does the introduction give a sense of your subject and purpose? (pages 108–112 and 158)

✓ Does your introduction set a tone that is appropriate for your subject and audience? (pages 108–112 and 158)

✓ Does your introduction provide necessary background information for your audience? (pages 108–112 and 158)

### Checking Your Body Paragraphs

✓ Have you supported your overall impression with suitable details? (pages 113–118 and 158–159)

✓ Did you include specific, well-chosen sensory words and details, and have you avoided generalities? (pages 47–48 and 158–159)

✓ Is each paragraph within the body well-developed, with a clear main idea and adequate supporting details? (pages 90–92 and 113–118)

✓ Did you use figurative language effectively? (pages 51–54, 160–161, and 217)

✓ Did you move logically from one paragraph to the next in a clear order and with helpful transitions? (pages 5 and 94–95)

### Checking Your Conclusion

✓ Does the conclusion reinforce the overall impression? (pages 122–123 and 158)

✓ Do you refer back to an idea in your introduction to give a sense of completion to your essay? (pages 122–123 and 158)

✓ Did you end with a memorable phrase or image that might linger in the reader's mind? (pages 122–123 and 158)

### Checking Your Essay Overall

✓ Is your essay adequately developed with supporting details, or do parts seem skimpy? (pages 87–91 and 113–118)

✓ Does your essay fulfill its purpose with unity and coherence? (pages 93–96 and 119)

### Checking Your Words and Sentences

✓ Are your words specific and lively, and do they appeal to several senses? (pages 47–48 and 158–159)

✓ Are your sentences varied? (pages 59–66)

After you have used the evaluation checklist to make revisions, you can move into the editing stage. As always when editing, pay special attention to the power rules.

## The Language of **Power**  *Negatives*

**Power Rule:** Use only one negative form for a single negative idea. (See pages 866–867.)

**See It in Action** In casual language someone may say "My mother never left me no recipes." In writing, though, using more than one negative like that would take attention away from the subject and focus it on the mistake instead, unless the double negative is being used to help create a character. In "Coming Home Again," Lee's conventional use of negatives allows the reader to stay focused on the thought.

> My mother never left me any recipes, but this is how I learned to make her food, each dish not coming from a list or a card but from the aromatic spread of a board.

In a similar way, only one negative should be used at the end of this sentence:

> . . . and adding, in her half-proud, half-deprecating way, that her kind of work would never serve to strengthen me. (not *wouldn't never*)

**Remember It** Record this rule and examples in the Power Rule section of your Personalized Editing Checklist. Note that other expressions with double negatives should also be avoided, such as "couldn't hardly" and "can't scarcely."

**Use It** Read through your descriptive essay and put a checkmark by each negative. Review each sentence to make sure you have not mistakenly used more than one negative for a single negative idea.

---

**PROJECT PREP** **Rethinking** *Revising and Editing*

Exchange drafts with a writing partner. Provide feedback to help each other write the clearest account possible. If at any point you have trouble following the process, alert your writing partner and suggest ways to make the explanation clearer. After that, check one another's paper for errors in spelling, grammar, usage, and mechanics. After making corrections, evaluate your description using the rubric on the next page.

# Using a Six-Trait Rubric **Descriptive Writing**

Evaluate your work using the six-trait rubric below.

| Ideas | **4** The text conveys an overall impression with abundant vivid details and is well chosen for the purpose and audience. | **3** The text conveys an overall impression with ample details and suits the purpose and audience. | **2** The text conveys an overall impression with some vivid details and suits the purpose and audience. | **1** The text does not convey an overall impression and fails to suit the purpose and audience. |
|---|---|---|---|---|
| **Organization** | **4** The organization is clear with abundant transitions. | **3** A few ideas seem out of place or transitions are missing. | **2** Many ideas seem out of place and transitions are missing. | **1** The organization is unclear and hard to follow. |
| **Voice** | **4** The voice sounds natural, engaging, and personal. | **3** The voice sounds natural and personal. | **2** The voice sounds mostly unnatural with a few exceptions. | **1** The voice sounds mostly unnatural. |
| **Word Choice** | **4** Words are specific and powerful, rich in sensory images. | **3** Words are specific and some words appeal to the senses. | **2** Some words are overly general. | **1** Most words are overly general. |
| **Sentence Fluency** | **4** Varied sentences flow smoothly. | **3** Most sentences are varied and flow smoothly. | **2** Some sentences are varied but some are choppy. | **1** Sentences are not varied and are choppy. |
| **Conventions** | **4** Punctuation, usage, and spelling are correct. The Power Rules are all followed. | **3** Punctuation, usage, and spelling are mainly correct and Power Rules are all followed. | **2** Some punctuation, usage, and spelling are incorrect but all Power Rules are followed. | **1** There are many errors and at least one failure to follow a Power Rule. |

**PROJECT PREP** *Polishing* **Using Peer Feedback**

Based on the feedback from your writing partner, make any changes that would improve your process description.

Make your writing available to interested readers by publishing it in an appropriate format of your choice. Consider the following possible forms of publication for your descriptive essay—and try to think up some others as well, perhaps by collaborating with one or more partners.

## HERE'S HOW  Publishing Options for Descriptive Writing

- Include your essay in a class anthology.
- Send your descriptive essay as an e-mail to a friend who shares an interest in your subject.
- Create a bulletin board to display the essays from your class. Enhance the essays with illustrations.
- Submit your descriptive piece to a magazine or other periodical that publishes student writing, such as your school literary magazine.
- Conduct an oral reading in your classroom.

## PROJECT PREP  Publishing  Genre

Meet with your writing group and discuss the possible forms the descriptive process papers might take. The chart of project possibilities lists these four:

- a user's manual
- a set of instructions
- an instructional video
- a letter explaining your hobby to a friend

Discuss the requirements of each genre or form. For example, what unique features should a user's manual have that a letter to a friend may not have? After coming to an understanding about the characteristics of your chosen genre, prepare a final copy for publication. Connect with your chosen audience and share your work.

**TIME OUT TO REFLECT** As a reader, what are your feelings about descriptive writing? Have your feelings changed as a result of working on this chapter, and if so, how? As a writer, do you like writing descriptions more, less, or the same as before you worked on this chapter? As you go on to college or to the world of work in the near future, what kinds of writing do you expect to do, and how might descriptive writing be part of that? Record your thoughts in the Learning Log section of your journal.

# In the Media

## Photo Essay

The photo essay is a composition form that combines visual art and text. Though it has existed for more than a century, the form has come into its own only in the past fifty years. The text for a photograph might be as short as one sentence or stretch to a page or more. The essay as a whole covers one subject, and the photographs may be sequenced logically, narratively, or intuitively, even if explaining the sequence would be difficult.

## Media Activity

Look for visually striking subjects in your everyday life. Go to new places in search of photogenic subjects. Take many photographs of your subject, in black-and-white or color. As you work, investigate such elements as light and shadow, composition, camera angle, focus, and cropping. Include at least six photographs in your finished photo essay. If you do not have access to a camera, make detailed drawings instead.

The text may contain a description of the picture, but the most compelling text will be your responses to the picture. Bind your photographs and texts in a scrapbook, thinking carefully about the visual relation of photo to text. Give your photo essay a title, and present the work in class. Then discuss the following questions.

### QUESTIONS FOR EVALUATING YOUR PHOTO ESSAY

- How do the text and pictures enhance or detract from each other?
- Who is your audience? What ideas might someone get from your work? How might those ideas differ from what you intended?
- What were the problems and pleasures of creating a photo essay? How did your ideas about photography or descriptive writing change?

# Writing Lab

## Project Corner

### **M**ake It Real Instructional Manual

If you did not choose the form of an instructional manual for your process description, **rewrite it now in that format,** complete with diagrams, pictures, and other graphics that illustrate aspects of the process. If you did choose this format, rewrite your manual as a letter. (See pages 531–538 for more on letter writing.)

### **M**ake a Video Film Yourself

Film yourself going through the process so that you **produce a video instructional guide**, complete with a commentary that helps viewers learn the process. (See pages 454–455 and 596–601 for information on creating a video documentary.)

### **R**esearch It Dig Deeper

**Find out more about the process you have described** by gathering information from sources and putting together a research report that provides more extensive information about the process. (See pages 393–453 for information on gathering information from sources and creating a research report.)

### **C**onduct an Interview Get Feedback

After asking someone to learn the process you wrote about by reading your composition, **conduct an interview** with that person in which you ask what was easy and difficult, and what could have been made easier with clearer instructions. (See pages 393–394 on conducting interviews.)

# In Everyday Life
## A Descriptive Friendly Letter

1. Bart, your penpal, is a genius. He skipped middle school, high school, and college and went right to work for NASA. Bart has no idea what high school is like. He has never walked the halls between classes and never had a high school locker. ***Write a letter*** to Bart describing what he might observe at the hallway lockers between classes. Create an overall impression with sensory details and figurative language, using vivid words and avoiding clichés.

# In the Workplace Descriptive E-mail

2. You work for an elevator company installing computer terminals in the elevators of skyscrapers so that passengers can check their e-mail on their long rides up. You love your job, but the music piped into the elevators drives you crazy. ***Write an e-mail message*** to your boss describing the elevator music and the type of music you would rather hear. Be sure to use both objective and subjective details in your description. (You can find information on writing e-mail on pages 534, 566, and 609–611.)

# Timed Writing ⏲ Letter to the Future

3. You have been chosen as a student representative for the Time Capsule Committee to write a letter to a teenager living in the future describing some aspect of your everyday life. Write a letter to a teenager living 1000 years from now, describing your daily observations on your way to school. Consider what background information you must include for your particular audience. Use specific details, sensory words, figurative language, and comparisons in your letter. You have 20 minutes to complete your work. (For help budgeting time, see pages 37 and 493.)

***Before You Write*** Consider the following questions: What is the situation? What is the occasion? Who is the audience? What is the purpose?

***After You Write*** Evaluate your work using the six-trait evaluation rubric on page 173.

# CHAPTER 6

# Creative Writing

**T**he power of creating is everywhere, within everyone. Yet the way in which it is expressed by each individual is unique.

Here are some of the ways in which creative stories, plays, and poems enrich the world.

- **People send poems on greeting cards** for almost every conceivable occasion, from birthdays to illnesses, and even for no reason at all.

- **People give books of fiction or poetry as gifts** to those they care about.

- **Workers on breaks,** or waiting for transportation, or sitting in vehicles, read stories in print or online to keep their minds active.

- **People all over the world are familiar with famous fictional characters**—from Hamlet to Luke Skywalker—and allude to them in conversation.

- **Science fiction helps people speculate** about—and thus begin planning for—the future of our society, our species, our planet.

- **Millions of people throughout the world** spend hours per day engrossed in fictional drama on television.

## Writing Project  Story, Scene, and Poem

*Something Special  Write a story about characters who have a very special relationship. When you are done, write the same story as a play or poem.*

*Think Through Writing*  Think of a special relationship that you have. It could be a friendship, a romance, a platonic relationship, a unique relationship with an older or younger person, a relationship with an animal, or any other relationship that is important to you. It could be a current relationship or one from your past. Write about this relationship, considering what makes it special.

*Talk About It*  In your writing group, discuss the relationships you have written about. What is the basis for the relationships? What qualities characterize them? How do people sustain them?

**Read About It** In the following story, author Vladimir Nabokov describes a relationship from his past with a young girl. Although it is autobiographical, it has the features of a literary short story. Think about his account of this relationship in the context of what you and your classmates have written about. When you read for a second time, think about the characters' relationships to one another.

> **MODEL: Autobiographical Story**

# First Love

*Vladimir Nabokov*

She would be ten in November, I had been ten in April. Attention was drawn to a jagged bit of violet mussel shell upon which she had stepped with the bare sole of her narrow long-toed foot. No, I was not English. Her greenish eyes seemed flecked with the overflow of the freckles that covered her sharp-featured face. She wore what might now be termed a playsuit consisting of a blue jersey with rolled-up sleeves and blue knitted shorts. I had taken her at first for a boy and then had been puzzled by the bracelet on her thin wrist and the cork-screw brown curls dangling from under her sailor cap.

She spoke in birdlike bursts of rapid twitter, mixing governess English and Parisian French. Two years before, on the same *plage,*[1] I had been much attached to Zina, the lovely, sun-tanned, bad-tempered little daughter of a Serbian naturopath[2]—she had, I remember (absurdly, for she and I were only eight at the time), a *grain de beauté*[3] on her apricot skin just below the heart, and there was a horrible collection of chamber pots, full and half-full, and one with surface bubbles, on the floor of the hall in her family's boardinghouse lodgings which I visited early one morning to be given by her, as she was being dressed, a dead hummingbird moth found by the cat. But when I met Colette, I knew at once that this was the real thing. Colette seemed to me so much stranger than all my other chance playmates at Biarritz! I somehow acquired the feeling that she was less happy than I, less loved. A bruise on her delicate, downy forearm gave rise to awful conjectures. "He pinches as bad as my mummy," she said, speaking of a crab. I evolved various schemes to save her from her parents, who were *"des bourgeois de Paris"*[4] as I heard somebody tell my mother with a slight shrug. I interpreted the disdain in my own fashion, as I knew that those people had come all the way from Paris in their blue-and-yellow

---

1 *plage:* Beach. (French)
2 **naturopath:** A believer in a system of natural remedies to fight disease.
3 *grain de beauté:* Beauty mark. (French)
4 *des bourgeois de Paris:* Middle-class Parisians. (French)

limousine (a fashionable adventure in those days) but had drably sent Colette with her dog and governess by an ordinary coach-train. The dog was a female fox terrier with bells on her collar and a most waggly behind. From sheer exuberance, she would lap up salt water out of Colette's toy pail. I remembered the pail, the sunset, and the lighthouse pictured on that pail, but I cannot recall the dog's name, and this bothers me.

During the two months of our stay at Biarritz, my passion for Colette all but surpassed my passion for Cleopatra. Since my parents were not keen to meet hers, I saw her only on the beach; but I thought of her constantly. If I noticed she had been crying, I felt a surge of helpless anguish that brought tears to my own eyes. I could not destroy the mosquitoes that had left their bites on her frail neck, but I could, and did, have a successful fistfight with a red-haired boy who had been rude to her. She used to give me warm handfuls of hard candy. One day, as we were bending together over a starfish, and Colette's ringlets were tickling my ear, she suddenly turned toward me and kissed me on the cheek. So great was my emotion that all I could think of saying was, "You little monkey."

I had a gold coin that I assumed would pay for our elopement. Where did I want to take her? Spain? America? The mountains above Pau? *"Là-bas, là-bas, dans la montagne,"*[5] as I had heard Carmen sing at the opera. One strange night, I lay awake, listening to the recurrent thud of the ocean and planning our flight. The ocean seemed to rise and grope in the darkness and then heavily fall on its face.

Of our actual getaway, I have little to report. My memory retains a glimpse of her obediently putting on rope-soled canvas shoes, on the lee side of a flapping tent, while I stuffed a folding butterfly net into a brown-paper bag. The next glimpse is of our evading pursuit by entering a pitch-dark *cinéma* near the Casino (which, of course, was absolutely out of bounds). There we sat, holding hands across the dog, which now and then gently jingled in Colette's lap, and were shown a jerky, drizzly, but highly exciting bullfight at St. Sébastian. My final glimpse is of myself being led along the promenade by Linderovski.[6] His long legs move with a kind of ominous briskness and I can see the muscles of his grimly set jaw working under the tight skin. My bespectacled brother, aged nine, whom he happens to hold with his other hand, keeps trotting out forward to peer at me with awed curiosity, like a little owl.

Among the trivial souvenirs acquired at Biarritz before leaving, my favorite was not the small bull of black stone and not the sonorous sea-

---

5  *Là-bas, là-bas, dans la montagne:* Far away, far away, on the mountain. (French)
6  **Linderovski:** The boy's tutor.

shell but something which now seems almost symbolic – a meerschaum[7] penholder . . . with a tiny peephole of crystal in its ornamental part. One held it quite close to one's eye, screwing up the other, and when one had got rid of the shimmer of one's own lashes, a miraculous photographic view of the bay and of the line of the cliffs ending in a lighthouse could be seen inside.

And now a delightful thing happens. The process of recreating that pen holder and the microcosm in its eyelet stimulates my memory to one last effort. I try again to recall the name of Collette's dog – and, triumphantly, along those remote beaches, over the glossy evening sands of the past, where each footprint slowly fills up with sunset water, here it comes, here it comes, echoing and vibrating: Floss, Floss, Floss!

---

7 **meershaum:** A clay-like substance often used to make the bowls of pipes.

***Respond in Writing*** Respond to Vladimir Nabokov's story about the narrator's first love. What characterizes this relationship? Do you think it will last? Why or why not?

***Develop Your Ideas*** Work with your classmates to develop ideas that you might incorporate into a short story centered on a key relationship.

***Small Groups:*** Vladimir Nabokov, in addition to being an author of fiction, was a distinguished lepidopterist, or butterfly researcher. He achieved fame for his study of South American Blue butterflies, for which he created elaborate taxonomies. The taxonomies provide detailed categories for plants and animals into Kingdom, Phylum, Class, Order, Family, Genus, and Species. This classifying requires a keen eye for detail in order to provide the clearest distinctions from one creature to another.

In your writing group, consider the sorts of details that would help you provide readers with a clear picture of the images you write about in your short story about a relationship. Make a story organizer like the one on the next page to help think of possible details for each author's story in each of the following categories. Leave plenty of room in the right-hand column for details.

| Story Organizer | |
|---|---|
| Setting | |
| Narrator | |
| Characters in special relationship | |
| Plot and events of story | |
| Outcome or resolution | |

**Whole Class:** Make a master chart of all of the ideas generated by the small groups to share possible characters, settings, and plot directions for a short story about a special relationship.

**Write About It** You will next write a story about a special relationship. It could be based on real events, or it could be entirely fictional. The following chart lists possible topics, audiences, and forms from which to choose.

| Possible Topics | Possible Audiences | Possible Forms |
|---|---|---|
| • a relationship between the narrator and a special friend or loved one<br><br>• a relationship between people other than the narrator<br><br>• a relationship between a person and an animal<br><br>• a relationship between two animals | • judges of a fiction-writing contest<br><br>• the person the story Is based on<br><br>• other creative writers<br><br>• other teenagers | • a short story<br><br>• a song<br><br>• a poem<br><br>• a graphic novel<br><br>• an animation |

# Analyzing a Short Story

Think about the stories that you have enjoyed reading. What aroused your curiosity and kept your interest?

Short stories are born in the author's imagination. The characters and events can be realistic or fanciful, ordinary or extraordinary. The events all revolve around a conflict faced by the main character. Just how the character deals with this conflict provides the story with its interest and suspense.

> A **short story** is a well-developed fictional account of characters resolving a conflict or problem.

## ELEMENTS OF A SHORT STORY

All short stories have three main sections: a beginning, a middle, and an end. Usually in the beginning of a story, the writer provides all the necessary background information that readers will need to understand and to enjoy the story. For example, readers will find out where the story takes place, who the main characters are, and what problem, or **conflict,** the main character has to solve or overcome. The middle of the story then develops the plot; that is, the writer relates—usually chronologically—what happens to the characters as a result of the conflict and how the characters react to those events. The ending of the story tells the outcome or shows the **resolution** of the central conflict.

*For information about how the elements of a short story contribute to its meaning, turn to pages 327–328.*

---

**PROJECT PREP** *Analyzing* **Story Elements**

Write answers to the following questions about *First Love*.

1. What is the plot of the story? Briefly outline the main events.

2. Who are the characters in the story? Which one is the main character, and how do you know that?

3. What is the setting? Describe it in a few sentences.

4. From what point of view is the story told? How do you think that point of view affects the story?

5. What do you think the theme of the story is? Express the theme in a few sentences in your own words.

---

# Writing a Short Story

To create an effective short story, play, or poem, you need to encourage and direct your imagination. The prewriting strategies that follow can help move the creative process along as you plan the conflict, theme, characters, setting, point of view, and plot of your story. Treat the strategies as suggestions only, and feel free to move back and forth among the techniques, selecting and adding, as you work your way through them.

## 1 Choosing a Conflict or Problem

What will your story be about? All short stories are based on a **central conflict** or problem. Therefore, deciding what your story will be about actually means deciding what the main conflict or problem will be.

A story can revolve around any kind of conflict, as dramatic as a disabled spaceship or as ordinary as a misplaced homework assignment. Usually the conflict builds between the main character and some other force in the story. The following chart summarizes and gives examples of the most common kinds of conflicts that are at the center of short stories.

| TYPES OF CONFLICT | |
| --- | --- |
| **Between the main character and another character** | A son objects to his mother's limits on his use of her car. |
| **Between the main character and a natural force** | An inexperienced surfer faces unusually rough surf. |
| **Between forces or feelings inside the main character** | A student is torn between her desire to go to college and the need to help support her family. |

You might begin your search for story ideas by brainstorming lists of familiar conflicts or problems, such as those relating to friendships, family situations, school activities, and other areas of your life. Also review your journal, which—if you record thoughts and observations regularly—can be a rich source of ideas. Discuss story ideas with others. A comment from someone else may ignite your imagination.

As you search for story ideas, remember that dramatic stories do not always require extraordinary conflicts. If the events are well told, a search for a lost book can be as absorbing as a search for a lost planet. Also, hold on to your sense of humor. Problems and their solutions do not always have to be serious.

Review your list of ideas and put a check next to the conflicts that inspire an interesting character or plot. Then choose one you think you would enjoy writing about.

## ● Practice Your Skills

### Listing Familiar Conflicts

Brainstorm a list for each question below, and save your list in your writing folder.

1. What personal values of yours are different from those of a friend or a relative? What conflicts has this caused?
2. If you were writing a situation comedy for television called "Senior Year," what situations might you use for some of the episodes?
3. When has humor helped you or someone else deal with a problem?
4. What sorts of problems have been caused by the weather, a power failure, illness, or some other event beyond your control?
5. When have you had to struggle to fulfill a dream?

## PROJECT PREP *Prewriting* Conflict

Review the writing you did in response to the prompt on pages 181–182 and identify the conflict in your story. Share your rough draft and your ideas with your writing group. Together, think through the conflict in each group member's story. For each author, discuss possible tensions that could contribute to the development of his or her story.

## ② Choosing a Theme

When you write a story, you may want to leave the reader with some message, idea, or question. The main idea you want to plant in the reader's mind is called the **theme.** Usually you imply the theme, rather than state it directly. You arrange the details so that your reader can infer your message. In the following excerpt from "The Doll's House," Katherine Mansfield centers the conflict on a young girl's desire to reach out to some poorer children, though her family and friends disapprove. Rooted in this conflict is the theme, which is that the differences between social classes can lead to cruelty. Like many writers Mansfield does not state her theme directly but leaves clues for the reader to infer it. In the following excerpt, notice how Mansfield implies the theme.

### MODEL: Implied Theme

"Hullo," she said to the passing Kelveys.

They were so astounded that they stopped. Lil gave her silly smile. Our Else started.

"You can come see our doll's house if you want to," said Kezia, and she dragged one toe on the ground. But at that Lil turned red and shook her head quickly.

"Why not?" asked Kezia.

Lil gasped, then she said, "Your ma told our ma you wasn't to speak to us."

"Oh, well," said Kezia. She didn't know what to reply.

— Katherine Mansfield, "The Doll's House"

Before you write a story, think about the theme or comment you want your story to express, such as a comment about growing up. The theme should be an idea you care about, as well as one that fits your story.

### ● Practice Your Skills

#### *Generating Story Themes*

Choose three conflicts from your work on the previous Practice Your Skills activity. First freewrite about each to generate possible story themes; then choose a suitable theme for each. Write a statement expressing each theme.

### PROJECT PREP   *Prewriting*   Theme

For each author in your writing group, discuss possible themes that might be emphasized in his or her story. What is the "message" that your story could suggest? How could this message follow from the characters' engagement with the primary tension of the story? Give each author suggestions on how to develop a theme to guide the action in the story.

# ③ Sketching Characters

Every story has one or more **main characters** who deal with the central problem. To develop each character, freewrite, brainstorm, or cluster around a detail or idea. Go on to sketch the characters fully if you are to bring them to life. Effective characters are individual and often quirky, like people themselves, not tired stereotypes of people. Use the diagram to help you develop complex and non-stereotypical character sketches.

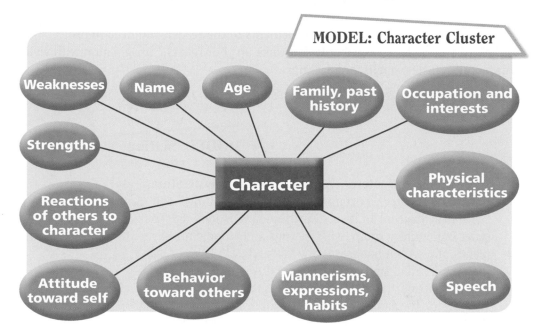

**MODEL: Character Cluster**

- Weaknesses
- Name
- Age
- Family, past history
- Occupation and interests
- Strengths
- Reactions of others to character
- **Character**
- Physical characteristics
- Attitude toward self
- Behavior toward others
- Mannerisms, expressions, habits
- Speech

## ● Practice Your Skills

### Sketching Characters

Use the details below to sketch two characters. Freewrite about one detail and brainstorm about the second. Then complete a character cluster for each.

**1.** a person with a high-pitched, squeaky voice

**2.** a person who is an ambitious young musician

---

**PROJECT PREP** *Prewriting* **Sketching Characters**

In your writing group, discuss the possible characters that could populate each author's story. For each main character, consider the details that could be included to make their relationship seem real and special. Make suggestions to each author on how to develop each character so that readers can relate to them and feel empathy for their situation.

# 4 Framing Your Story

Your story is well on its way with a conflict, theme, and characters. Now frame your story with a meaningful setting and the appropriate point of view.

## CREATING A SETTING

The setting is the time and place in which the story occurs. However, it is more than a physical location; it is also an atmosphere and **mood** that provide a suitable framework for the events. In order to convey these elements to the reader, you need to use description, especially sensory words that wake up your readers' imagination with vivid sights, sounds, tastes, smells, and feelings.

*You can learn more about description on pages 100–101 and 154–177.*

> ### MODEL: Setting
>
> The room that afternoon was full of such shy creatures, lights and shadows, curtains blowing, petals falling—things that never happen, so it seems, if someone is looking. The quiet old country room, with its rugs and stone chimney pieces, its sunken bookcases and red and gold lacquer cabinets, was full of such nocturnal creatures. . . .
>
> But, outside, the looking glass reflected the hall table, the sunflowers, the garden path so accurately and so fixedly that they seemed held there in their reality unescapably. It was a strange contrast—all changing here, all stillness there. One could not help looking from one to the other.
>
> —Virginia Woolf, "The Lady in the Looking Glass: A Reflection"

This "strange contrast," as well as the mirror itself, provides an appropriate framework for a story in which the main character herself seems to move into another person—as caught, of course, by the mirror.

> ### Writing Tip
>
> Match the **setting** of your story to the action, mood, and characters' feelings.

# CHOOSING A POINT OF VIEW

Every story has a **narrator**—the person who tells the story. When you choose the narrator, you decide not only who will relate the events but also through whose eyes, or from whose **point of view,** the reader will see them. Once you choose a point of view, use it consistently throughout the story. Otherwise your story will be confusing. The following chart outlines the choices you have for point of view.

| POINT OF VIEW | NARRATOR |
|---|---|
| First-Person | • Observes or participates in the action personally.<br>• Tells personal observations and thoughts.<br>• Uses first-person pronouns. |
| Third-Person Limited | • Observes one character who participates in the action.<br>• Tells the words, actions, and feelings of the character and observations about him or her.<br>• Uses third-person pronouns. |
| Third-Person Omniscient ("All Knowing") | • Observes but does not participate in the action.<br>• Tells the words, actions, and feelings of all the characters as well as observations about them.<br>• Uses third-person pronouns. |

The **first-person point of view** allows the reader to view the events from inside the mind of one of the characters. This adds a personal tone to the story, as in the following example.

> **First-Person**    **I** closed the door softly, wondering if anyone had seen **me.**

When you choose **the third-person limited** point of view, your story has a less personal tone. Yet this point of view allows you to give the reader more information.

> **Third-Person Limited**    **Eva** closed the door softly, wondering if anyone had seen **her. She** did not even realize that **she** had held **her** breath all the way down the stairs.

The **third-person omniscient** point of view balances the impersonal disadvantage with the advantage of letting the reader know the thoughts of all the characters.

> **Third-Person Omniscient**    **Eva** closed the door softly, wondering if anyone had seen **her.** A block away **David** waited anxiously, hoping that **she** would come.

## ● Practice Your Skills

### *Using Different Points of View*

The following summary of events can be told in a story of just a few paragraphs. Write three versions of the story, choosing a different point of view each time: (1) the first-person as Leon, (2) the third-person limited as Mr. Gomez, and (3) the third-person omniscient.

> Leon and three other high school seniors have been performing as a rock group since eighth grade. They audition for a local variety show, but lose to another group. Discouraged, they decide to disband after graduation. Then Mr. Gomez, one of the judges, invites them to perform at his club.

### PROJECT PREP *Prewriting* *Narrator*

In your writing group, consider who will tell each author's story. Is it best told by one of the characters or by an outsider? What does the narrator know and not know? How does the narrator's perspective help the story to unfold? Help each author identify a narrator and to consider that speaker's point of view on the situation and how that speaker would present the events of the story.

# 5 Outlining the Story

Always prepare an informal outline of the important elements of your story to make sure that the parts fit together. Include the following headings in your outline.

| STORY OUTLINE | |
|---|---|
| Title | Choose a title with some mystery to make readers eager to read on. |
| Setting | Indicate the mood you want and key details of the setting. |
| Characters | List the characters and include brief descriptions. |
| Conflict | Identify the source of the conflict. |
| Plot | List the events, one by one, in order of presentation. |
| Resolution | Tell the outcome for each character. |

**Title** Although the title appears first in the outline, you may want to choose it last. Select a title that fits the subject and mood and will arouse the reader's interest.

**Setting** Choose a suitable backdrop for the events of your story and describe it briefly in your outline.

**Characters** Write a brief description of each character, starting with the main character.

**Conflict** Add a sentence or two telling about the conflict or problem that the main character will have to face. See pages 184–185.

**Plot** Next in the outline of the story is the series of events, or plot. Most plots begin with an incident that triggers the conflict. Then, as the plot progresses, the conflict becomes more and more involved until it reaches a critical point, or climax. After that the conflict is resolved. In your outline, list the events in the order in which you will relate them, such as **chronological order.**

**Resolution** To complete your outline, write the resolution—the way the conflict or problem is settled. Tie up the events of the story in a way that will satisfy the reader.

## PROJECT PREP  *Prewriting*  *Plot*

In your writing group, discuss possible plot outlines for your short story. What might happen with the relationship as a result of the characters' experience of a tension? How does the setting of the story contribute problems and possibilities to the relationship? Through what actions could the theme of the story be realized? How will the story be resolved? Help each author lay out a plot outline to guide his or her writing.

# Think Critically

## Implying

By **implying** information, a writer can captivate and involve readers, forcing them to make inferences and draw conclusions, as Katherine Mansfield does in the following excerpt from "The Singing Lesson."

> This little ritual of the flower . . . was as much part of the lesson as opening the piano. But this morning . . . Miss Meadows totally ignored the chrysanthemum, made no reply to her [Mary's] greeting, but said in a voice of ice, "Page fourteen, please . . ."

Through specific details Katherine Mansfield implies that Miss Meadows is not in a good mood. First, Miss Meadows acknowledges neither the flower nor Mary's kind gesture. Second, she continues to direct her class "in a voice of ice."

A chart like the one below can help you imply unstated facts or conclusions. On the left, list events, settings, or character traits for your story, and on the right, list details to imply those elements.

| TRAIT | DETAILS |
|---|---|
| considerate | fearful of awakening sister, uses hallway light to guide her, creeps softly into room |
| EVENT | DETAILS |
| graduation | field of blue and gold ribbons, applause fills the stadium, tasseled caps tossed in the air |

## Thinking Practice

Write a passage that implies a setting, event, or character trait from your story or use any of the following suggestions.

1. **traits:** kindness, dishonesty, perseverance
2. **settings:** an amusement park, a university, a mall
3. **events:** a track meet, a job interview, a car accident

# The Power of Language ⚡

## Adjectives and Adjectival Phrases:
## Modifiers Come Lately

Adjectives can come after the word they modify (see pages 631–634), and so can a variety of phrases—groups of words (see pages 688 and 695). Here are some examples from "First Love," by Vladimir Nabokov (pages 179–181).

> I had been much attracted to Zina, the lovely sun-tanned, bad-tempered little daughter of a Serbian naturopath.

> There was a horrible collection of chamber pots, full and half-full, and one with surface bubbles.

> There we sat, holding hands across the dog.

## Try It Yourself

Write sentences imitating the structure of each of these sentences. If you can, add various kinds of descriptive phrases as you draft your short story. Then later, see if there are other places where you might add details in phrases like these.

### Punctuation Tip

When modifiers "come lately" within a sentence, they are enclosed in commas or dashes.

> Zina, lovely and sun-tanned, was the daughter of a Serbian naturopath.

When modifiers "come lately" at the end of a sentence, they are preceded by a comma or dash.

> There we sat, holding hands across the dog.

When modifiers do not come lately, but instead come before the noun they describe, they are followed by a comma.

> From sheer exuberance, she would lap up salt water out of Colette's toy pail.

Your goal in drafting a story is to produce a workable narrative that can be shaped and polished into a solid story. As you draft your story, you can use a variety of types of writing, including narration, description, and expository writing.

*You can learn more about these types of writing on pages 98–103, 130–177, and 224–273.*

## DRAFTING THE BEGINNING

As the following examples demonstrate, you can open a story in many different ways.

### STARTING A STORY

| Method | Example |
| --- | --- |
| Dialogue | "They say he's worth a million," Lucia said.<br><br>—Graham Greene, "Across the Bridge" |
| Introduction of the Character | With despair—cold, sharp despair—buried deep in her heart like a wicked knife, Miss Meadows, in cap and gown and carrying a little baton, trod the cold corridors that led to the music hall.<br><br>—Katherine Mansfield, "The Singing Lesson" |
| Descriptive Details | North Richmond Street, being blind [dead end], was a quiet street except at the hour when the Christian Brothers' School set the boys free.<br><br>—James Joyce, "Araby" |
| Narrative Details | Toward the end of her day in London Mrs. Drover went round to her shut-up house to look for several things she wanted to take away.<br><br>—Elizabeth Bowen, "The Demon Lover" |
| General Statement | People should not leave looking glasses hanging in their rooms any more than they should leave open checkbooks or letters confessing to some hideous crime.<br><br>—Virginia Woolf, "The Lady in the Looking Glass: A Reflection" |

Each of these openings sets up a situation that makes the reader curious. Think of a question you have about each. Use your opening sentences, like these sentences, to hook your reader. Then give further details to keep the reader engaged.

### Guidelines for Beginning a Story

- Set the time and place and establish the mood or tone with sensory details.
- Introduce the main character or characters.
- Provide needed background information.
- Set the plot in motion with a triggering event.
- Establish the conflict or problem.

## DRAFTING THE MIDDLE

As you draft the middle portion of your story, connect the events so that they flow naturally. Transitions, such as *the next day* and *a week later,* help tie events together and show the passage of time. Also try to make every event add to the development and extension of the story until the climax of the plot is reached.

### Building Suspense

As you work your way up to the high point in the story, build suspense by using the following strategies.

### Strategies for Building Suspense

- Plant clues. Hint at something that will not be revealed until later.
- Give characters a secret that plays a role in the plot.
- Have characters work against a time deadline so the reader wonders, "Will they make it?"
- Keep readers off balance by presenting the unexpected at times. Though unexpected, the event or development you introduce should not be so far-fetched that readers might say, "Oh, that could never happen."
- Pace the story so there are mini-climaxes and then let-downs during the rise to the real high point of the story.

### Developing Characters

As you develop your characters, give details that tell how they look, what they think, and how they behave. Notice in the following excerpts how much livelier the version with the dialogue is.

| Narrative | They stopped talking when they heard a noise. |
| Dialogue | "Shhh!" hissed Elena. "I just heard something!" |

### Enhancing the Plot

The following devices will help you enrich and enhance your plot.

| DEVICES FOR ENHANCING THE PLOT | |
| --- | --- |
| Flashback | an event from the past that interrupts the chronological order |
| Foreshadowing | clues that help the reader anticipate what is to come |
| Story Within a Story | a story that is told during the telling of another story |
| Subplot | a secondary plot line that reinforces the main plot line |
| Juxtaposition | placing two normally unrelated events, characters, or words next to one another to create a surprise effect |

If you include a flashback, use one of these two methods.

**Showing a Flashback with Spacing**

As Ben walked along the beach, his eyes followed the gulls, but his thoughts were far away.

\*\*\*\*

"Ben, wake up! Are you up, Ben?" That day had begun like every other school day, with his mother's voice.

**Showing a Flashback with Narrative**

As Ben walked along the beach, his eyes followed the gulls, but his thoughts were on that day almost a year ago. It had begun like every other school day, with his mother's voice.

The following chart summarizes some of the strategies for drafting the middle of a story.

## Guidelines for Drafting the Middle of a Story

- Relate the events either chronologically or with flashbacks.
- Use transitions to connect the events smoothly and clearly.
- Build suspense to keep your readers interested.
- Use dialogue to make your characters vivid.
- Use devices such as flashbacks and foreshadowing to enhance the plot

## DRAFTING THE ENDING

A story ending does not need to be positive or happy, nor does it need to solve every problem. It does, however, need to bring the story to a close by tying the events together.

## Guidelines for Ending a Story

- Resolve the conflict and complete the action of the plot.
- Use dialogue, action, or description to show, not just tell, what happens.
- Leave the reader feeling satisfied.

---

**PROJECT PREP** Drafting *Dialogue and Plot Techniques*

After you review all your prewriting about character, setting, plot, and narrator, write the first draft of the short story you have been developing. Work in dialogue that sounds realistic and that advances the plot. Build suspense, and try using some devices from the chart above to enhance your plot and make it more gripping. Use peer conferencing to test your ideas or to get help with trouble spots. Keep writing until you have a workable first draft.

"I have never thought of myself as a good writer . . ." claimed James A. Michener, "but I'm one of the world's great rewriters." For many writers the revising stage can be the most productive of all.

## IMPROVING PLOT

Not every sequence of events is a plot. Compare the following two sets of sequences and notice how they are different.

| | |
|---|---|
| **Events** | Mark got dressed. He went for a walk. He walked to the bank. He returned two hours later. |
| **Plot** | Nervously Mark got dressed. He walked to the bank for a job interview. The bank was being robbed. Mark ran for the police. He was a hero. He did not get the job. |

In the first sequence, the events are related only chronologically. In the second sequence, every event relates to Mark's job interview. One event leads naturally to the next in a pattern of rising action. To tighten your plot, ask yourself the following questions.

### Guidelines for Improving the Plot

- Are events arranged chronologically, except for flashbacks?
- Are flashbacks easily recognizable?
- Are transitions used to help tie events together and to show the passage of time?
- Does every event revolve around the central conflict?
- Is each event clearly linked to the events before and after?
- Did you use a range of strategies to enhance the plot?
- Does each event add to the tension and build to the climax?
- Does the resolution tie up the events convincingly?

### ● Practice Your Skills

*Improving a Plot*

Think of an event that could be added to the plot of "First Love" that would make sense in relation to what Vladimir Nabokov has already written. Then decide whether you think your proposed plot addition would improve the story, weaken the story, or keep its quality unchanged. Explain your reasoning.

CHAPTER 6

## IMPROVING CHARACTERIZATION

Bland, predictable characters mean that even the most exciting of plots will be dull. As you revise, look for ways to make your characters real, complex, and engaging. Be sure you avoid stereotyped characters—let your characters do and say the unexpected sometimes. Read the following excerpt and try to identify the techniques D. H. Lawrence uses to draw the picture of a woman so bitter and disappointed that she finds it hard to feel love.

### MODEL: Characterization

There was a woman who was beautiful, who started with all the advantages, yet she had no luck. She married for love, and the love turned to dust. She had bonny children, yet she felt they had been thrust upon her, and she could not love them. They looked at her coldly, as if they were finding fault with her. . . . Everybody else said of her: "She is such a good mother. She adores her children." Only she herself, and her children themselves, knew it was not so. . . .

"Mother," said the boy Paul one day, "why don't we keep a car of our own? Why do we always use uncle's, or else a taxi?"

"Because we're the poor members of the family," said the mother.

"But why *are* we, Mother?"

"Well—I suppose," she said slowly and bitterly, "it's because your father has no luck."

—D. H. Lawrence, "The Rocking-Horse Winner"

Following are characterization techniques that Lawrence and other writers use. Look for places to apply them in your own story.

### Guidelines for Improving Characterization

- Add natural-sounding dialogue that fits the personality.
- Add descriptive details about appearance and behavior.
- Show how the character acts and reacts in a unique, nonstereotyped way.
- Show how others react to the character.

## ● Practice Your Skills

*Improving Characterization*

Write a scene for a story starring one of the characters you sketched on page 187. Then revise the scene to improve the characterization.

## IMPROVING STYLE

Style refers to the way you use words and sentences. Your style may be simple and spare or lush and complex or somewhere in between. The choice depends upon your personal preference and the needs of your story. Every style, however, demands skillful use of language—the right word connected to the right word to form the right sentence.

The right words at the right time help create the tone you want for your story. **Tone** is the writer's attitude toward his or her characters and subject. Tone can also refer to the attitude one character has about another. Word choice and sentence structure help determine tone.

Carefully chosen words also help you create the **mood** you intend for your story. (See pages 188 and 210). The mood is the atmosphere you want to create with the details you choose.

Go over your story for style, reading it aloud and listening to the rhythm and flow of the words. As you do, keep in mind the questions listed below.

### Guidelines for Improving Characterization

- Does your style fit the theme, events, and characters?
- Is the style appropriate for your audience?
- Do your words and sentences fit the style and the characters?
- Does the language fit the tone? Is the tone consistent throughout the story?
- Does the language fit the mood of the story?
- Have you maintained the style consistently?
- Are your words vivid and precise?
- Have you varied the length and the structure of your sentences?
- Have you used such tropes as figurative language and such schemes as parallelism to add interest and power to your style?

### ● Practice Your Skills

**Improving Style**

Revise again the character sketch you wrote for the previous activity, improving its style using the guidelines above.

*editing*

A strong story has nothing in it that does not contribute in some way to its meaning and power. As you revise, eliminate any unnecessary element you find—a word, a phrase, a sentence, or a whole passage.

# USING AN EVALUATION CHECKLIST FOR REVISING

The following checklist will help you remember basic points to look for as you revise a short story.

## Evaluation Checklist for Revising

✓ Does your beginning capture attention and present the conflict, setting, and main characters? (pages 194–195)

✓ In the middle do you present events chronologically or through flashbacks? Do all events relate to the conflict and build to a climax? Do transitions connect the events and show the passage of time? (pages 195–197)

✓ Is your resolution fitting and satisfying? (page 197)

✓ Do you use dialogue and description? (pages 192, 194, and 199)

✓ Do you use sensory details that define the mood or tone? (pages 188–189, 191, and 200)

✓ Is the theme clearly implied? (pages 186 and 192)

✓ Is the point of view consistent? (pages 189–190)

---

**PROJECT PREP** *Revising* *Teacher and Peers*

Share your story with your writing group. At the same time, submit your draft to your teacher, if you are directed to do so. Use your peers' and teacher's comments and the preceding guidelines to revise your story.

In the editing stage, the writer produces error-free writing that shows accurate spelling and correct use of the conventions of punctuation and capitalization as well as control over grammatical elements such as subject-verb agreements, pronoun-antecedent agreement, verb forms, and parallelism. Putting your work aside long enough to give you some distance will help you see these instances. You may want to use the checklist on pages 30 and 201 as you edit.

## The Language of Power  *Pronouns*

**Power Rule:** Use subject forms of pronouns in subject position. (See pages 790–801.)

**See It in Action** When do you use *who* and when *whom*? Nabokov demonstrates:

> I could not destroy the mosquitoes that had left their bites on her frail neck, but I could, and did, have a successful fistfight with a red-haired boy who had been rude to her. (use *who* when the pronoun is used as a subject)
>
> My bespectacled brother, aged nine, whom he happens to hold with his other hand, keeps trotting out forward to peer at me with awed curiosity, like a little owl. (use *whom* when the pronoun is used as a object)

When it's not obvious, you can test for whether *who* or *whom* is needed by inverting the whole construction (highlighted in the examples above and below) and replacing *who* or *whom* with one of the more familiar pronouns, *I* (subject) or *me* (object). For example, you would never say *He happens to hold I,* so you can be sure that the subject form (*who*) is incorrect. The same rules apply to *whoever* and *whomever*.

> We have a surprise for whoever finishes first.
> We have a surprise for whomever she designates.

**Remember It** Record this rule and example in the Power Rule section of your Personalized Editing Checklist.

**Use It** Check the pronouns in your story. Make sure you have used subject and object forms appropriately unless you are using non-mainstream forms to show character. Pay special attention to *who, whom, whoever,* and *whomever*.

## PUBLISHING

In the publishing stage, the writer makes a final copy to share with his or her intended audience. You may also decide to read your story aloud to family members or friends. If your school has a literary magazine, consider submitting your story to it.

### Page Design

Look through some literary anthologies you have or your school may have and notice the design elements on the pages. Find a style you like and consider adapting it for the publication of your story.

One common design element in literature is the **pull quote** or **callout**—a quote pulled out of the story itself and put into the margin in larger type to add visual interest to the page and to call attention to an important part, as shown below. Consider adding pull quotes to your story when you prepare the final copy.

and sweeper, at the rate of one dollar a week. He had a little desk to himself, but he did not use it much. Upon inspection, the drawer exhibited a great array of the shells of various sorts of nuts. Indeed, to this quickwitted youth the whole noble science of the law was contained in a nutshell. Not the least among the employments of Ginger Nut, as well as one which he discharged with the most **alacrity**, was his duty as cake and apple purveyor[22] for Turkey and Nippers. Copying law papers being proverbially a dry, husky sort of business, my two scriveners were fain to moisten their mouths very often with Spitzenbergs to be had at the numerous stalls nigh the Custom House and Post Office. Also, they sent Ginger Nut very frequently for that peculiar cake—small, flat, round, and very spicy after which he had been named by them. Of a cold morning, when business was but dull, Turkey would gobble up scores of these cakes, as if they were mere wafers—indeed they sell them at the rate of six or eight for a penny—the scrape of his pen blending with the crunching of the crisp particles in his mouth. Of all the fiery afternoon blunders and flurried rashnesses of Turkey, was his once moistening a ginger-cake between his lips, and clapping it on to a mortgage for a seal. I came within an ace of dismissing him then. But he **mollified** me by making an oriental bow and saying—"With submission, sir, it was generous of me to find you in[23] stationery on my own account."

Now my original business—that of a conveyancer and title hunter, and drawer-up of **recondite** documents of all sorts—was considerably increased by receiving the master's office. There was now great work for scriveners. Not only must I push the clerks already with me, but I must have additional help. In

**alacrity:** quickness; alertness

*I* can see that figure now—pallidly neat, pitiably respectable, incurably forlorn! It was Bartleby.

**mollified:** pleased; gratified

**recondite:** obscure; scholarly

---

## PROJECT PREP  Publishing  *Sharing Your Work*

Exchange your new draft with a writing partner, and read one another's stories with a critical eye. Help each author in two ways: to provide good detail for the characters, setting, tensions, plot, and resolution; and to help the author polish the grammar, spelling, and punctuation. Use this feedback and the rubric on the next page to help you produce a final version of your story. Publish in the form you chose (see page 182) or another appropriate medium. Your class, for instance, might develop an online anthology of stories about relationships to share with other readers on the Internet.

# Using a Six-Trait Rubric

Use the rubric below to assess your own or another's story.

| Ideas | **4** The plot, setting, characters, and dialogue are original and creative. | **3** The plot, setting, characters, and dialogue are effective. | **2** Most aspects of the plot, setting, characters, and dialogue are effective. | **1** Most aspects of the plot, setting, characters, and dialogue are ineffective. |
|---|---|---|---|---|
| **Organization** | **4** The organization is clear with abundant transitions. | **3** A few events or ideas seem out of place or transitions are missing. | **2** Many events seem out of place and transitions are missing. | **1** The order of events is unclear and hard to follow. |
| **Voice** | **4** The narrator's voice sounds natural and the point of view is effective. | **3** The narrator's voice sounds mostly natural and the point of view is effective. | **2** The narrator's voice sounds unnatural at times and the point of view seems forced. | **1** The narrator's voice sounds mostly unnatural and the point of view is forced and ineffective. |
| **Word Choice** | **4** Specific words and sensory images help readers picture characters and setting. | **3** Words are specific and some words appeal to the senses to help readers picture characters and setting. | **2** Some words are overly general and do not bring characters or setting into focus. | **1** Most words are overly general and do not bring characters or setting into focus. |
| **Sentence Fluency** | **4** Varied sentences flow smoothly and dialogue reflects characters. | **3** Most sentences are varied and flow smoothly, and dialogue reflects characters. | **2** Some sentences are choppy and dialogue seems forced. | **1** Sentences are choppy and not varied, and dialogue seems forced or is missing. |
| **Conventions** | **4** Conventions are correct and Power Rules are followed except for effect. | **3** Conventions are mainly correct and Power Rules are followed except for effect. | **2** Some conventions are incorrect but Power Rules are followed except for effect. | **1** There are many errors and at least one accidental failure to follow a Power Rule. |

# Writing a Play or Screenplay

Plays and screenplays are forms of writing which are intended to be performed by actors. The story of a play or a screenplay is told through dialogue—the words that the actors say—as well as action.

A **play** is a piece of writing containing action that can be presented live on a stage by actors. A **screenplay** is a piece of writing containing action that can be presented on film.

William Shakespeare's *Romeo and Juliet* is so important in Western culture that you probably know something about it even if you have never read or seen the play. Romeo and Juliet, teens from enemy clans in Verona, Italy, meet at a dance and fall in love at first sight, opposing the wills of their families with tragic results.

The scene that follows is from the movie script *Shakespeare in Love,* a comic portrayal of what twenty-something playwright William Shakespeare may have been like at the time he was writing his great love story. In the movie young Shakespeare is stuck with writer's block as he tries to write *Romeo and Juliet.* Meanwhile, a wealthy young woman named Viola has her heart set on becoming an actor. Shakespeare and Viola fall in love, and theater and love reflect each other.

In the scene that follows, Viola is presented at the palace and the Queen tartly questions her about their shared interest. To solve a disagreement about whether plays can truly present love, the Queen proposes a wager—which will involve Shakespeare.

**MODEL: Movie Script**

*(Angle on The Queen.)*

*(The Lord In Waiting has presented Viola. Viola speaks from a frozen curtsey.)*

**Viola:** Your Majesty.

**Queen:** Stand up straight, girl.

*(Viola straightens. The Queen examines her.)*

**Queen:** I have seen you. You are the one who comes to all the plays— at Whitehall, at Richmond.

**Viola:** *(agreeing)*

Your Majesty.

**Queen:** What do you love so much?

**Viola:** Your Majesty . . .

**Queen:** Speak out! I know who I am. Do you love stories of kings and queens? Feats of arms? Or is it courtly love?

**Viola:** I love theatre. To have stories acted for me by a company of fellows is indeed—

**Queen:** *(interrupting)*

They are not acted for you, they are acted for me.

*(Viola remains silent, in apology. Angle on Will. He is watching and listening. He has never seen the Queen so close. He is fascinated.)*

**Queen:** *(Cont'd.)*

And—?

**Viola:** And I love poetry above all.

**Queen:** Above Lord Wessex?

*(She looks over Viola's shoulder and Viola realizes Wessex has moved up behind her. Wessex bows.)*

**Queen:** *(Cont'd.) (to Wessex)*

My lord—when you cannot find your wife you had better look for her at the playhouse.

*(The courtiers titter at her pleasantry.)*

**Queen:** *(Cont'd.)*

But playwrights teach nothing about love, they make it pretty, they make it comical, or they make it lust. They cannot make it true.

**Viola:** *(blurts)*

Oh, but they can!

*(She has forgotten herself. The courtiers gasp. The Queen considers her. Wessex looks furious. Will is touched.)*

**Viola:** *(Cont'd.)*

I mean . . . Your Majesty, they do not, they have not, but I believe there is one who can—

**Wessex:** Lady Viola is . . . young in the world. Your Majesty is wise in it. Nature and truth are the very enemies of playacting. I'll wager my fortune.

**Queen:** I thought you were here because you had none.

*(Titters again. Wessex could kill somebody.)*

**Queen:** *(Cont'd.)*

*(by way of dismissing him)*

Well, no one will take your wager, it seems.

**Will:** Fifty pounds!

*(Shock and horror. Queen Elizabeth is the only person amused.)*

**Queen:** Fifty pounds! A very worthy sum on a very worthy question. Can a play show us the very truth and nature of love? I bear witness to the wager, and will be the judge of it as occasion arises.

*(which wins a scatter of applause. She gathers her skirts and stands.)*

I have not seen anything to settle it yet.

*(She moves away, everybody bowing and scraping.)*

So—the fireworks will be soothing after the excitements of Lady Viola's audience.

## FINDING IDEAS FOR PLAYS

You will be writing a screenplay scene—a linked series of camera shots that tells a small part of the story of your imaginary movie. As in a stage play or a short story, you should build your screenplay idea out of the building blocks of characters who are involved in a compelling conflict, or problem. Their struggles with the problem take them through a series of connected actions—a plot. Your scene will capture the characters at one important point in their involvement with the conflict.

To find ideas for a screenplay, use the tried-and-true methods that you have used to generate ideas for short stories, and in earlier grades perhaps for stage scenes. Question yourself about your life, the lives of people around you, and lives you have only heard about or dreamed about. Reread your journal notes in search of concepts. Freewrite about events that have seemed dramatic. Make cluster diagrams for characters you know, or imagine, who seem larger than life.

In addition, many successful movie concepts are combinations of previous movie concepts. Return to your journal entry describing movies you have seen, and try to build on it using the following tips.

*To find out more about characterization, conflict, and plot turn to pages 184–201.*

**Tips for Developing Screenplay Ideas**

- Describe each of your ideas in a single sentence, to help you pinpoint the dramatic essence of the concept. Focus on the sentence as a way of tinkering with the concept.
- Take an existing movie concept and add a twist; for example, "Young Will Shakespeare trades places with his rival Christopher Marlowe, and the two geniuses live out each others' lives and deaths."
- Splice together the ideas for two different movies, using the pattern "Movie A Meets Movie B"; for example, "*Shakespeare in Love* Meets *Robin Hood*" or "*Shakespeare in Love* Meets *The Hunchback of Notre Dame*."

● **Practice Your Skills**

*Finding Ideas for a Scene through Freewriting in Your Journal*

Freewrite a response to each question below. Save your work.

1. Who is the most "larger-than-life" person you know, and why do you characterize this person that way?
2. At times, have you said to yourself, "My life is like the movies"? Describe one or more moments that might fit that description.
3. What news events during your lifetime have seemed most dramatic? Freewrite your strongest impressions of the events.
4. If you could live in another world, or in the future, what would it be like?

● **Practice Your Skills**

*Finding Ideas for a Scene by Building on Previous Ideas*

Return to the list of movie concepts in your journal entry. Select one of them, and add a twist or variation that would make it an essentially different movie.

## CRAFTING A THEME

A play or screenplay should have a theme, just as a story does. The theme is the message, or main idea, you want the audience to take away. The theme can be explicit, stated directly, or implicit, not stated directly so that the audience infers the message. In the scene from *Shakespeare in Love,* the queen directly states one message the movie raises, "Can a play show us the very truth and nature of love?" The theme of the play *Romeo and Juliet,* which the movie *Shakespeare in Love* revolves around, is implicit and based in the idea that "True love sees beyond the prejudices of one's upbringing." Think about the theme you want to convey in your screenplay, and keep it in mind as you write.

## DEVELOPING CHARACTERS

In movies, characterizations are fleshed out by actors; the personality of a movie star can drastically affect the nature of a role. The screenplay writer gets "first crack" at the characterization, however, by writing the character's dialogue and giving the character actions to perform. A published screenplay may not contain a capsule sketch or description of the characters; for example, the screenplay of *Shakespeare in Love* does not contain an actual description of Shakespeare, because the physical appearance of the actor is the only description needed. As a writer, however, you might want to compose a brief sketch of each character for your own use.

● **Practice Your Skills**

*Sketching Characters*

Complete two of the following exercises.

**1.** Write a concise, vivid, one-paragraph sketch of the person you named as the most larger-than-life figure you know.

**2.** Write a character sketch based on yourself, using the same format.

**3.** Write a character sketch of a public figure you admire, using the same format.

**4.** Write a character sketch of a public figure you do not admire, using the same format.

## CREATING A SETTING

In contrast to the settings of traditional plays, which are limited by the need to fit them on a stage, the settings of movies can change from shot to shot. A movie may show Mount Everest in one frame, and the quiet midwestern home of an Everest climber in the next frame. It can show imaginary settings that are created digitally or by means of special effects. The action of a movie may occur on a sound stage in front of artificial scenery, or scenes may be shot on location—in real places. Many movies use both location shots and studio scenery.

Your biggest problem in planning a screenplay setting might be that of limiting your settings to a manageable scope. In real movie productions, money is the major limiting factor: to shoot scenes in too many different locations may cost too much. In addition, an audience may be confused by excessive changes in setting. Although your screenplay scene will not involve planning a budget, try to keep in mind a realistic evaluation of the number of settings the scene can accommodate.

## ESTABLISHING TONE AND MOOD

**Tone** is the attitude the writer has toward his or her subject. The music and visuals of a movie contribute greatly to the tone. Before a single line of dialogue is spoken, the music and visuals used in the opening credits can establish a serious or comical, admiring or critical, joyful or sad tone. **Mood** is the atmosphere the audience draws from the details of the music and visuals of setting and characters. Tone and mood influence one another and are often closely intertwined. What kind of music would best be used with your scene to establish the tone and mood? What visuals would convey the tone and mood and fit with the music? Include notes about both music and visuals in your screenplay scene.

## WRITING DIALOGUE

Although dialogue is important in movies, the typical movie contains much less dialogue than the typical play. In a movie, visuals—camera shots of characters, settings, or actions—are often more important than dialogue. Many screenplay writers (and directors, who often participate in revising screenplays) take pride in keeping dialogue to a minimum, having characters speak only what cannot be said in pictures. Playwrights and fiction writers who attempt screenplays often find that their biggest challenge is to cut the dialogue, leaving only what is absolutely needed in order to express a scene.

● **Practice Your Skills**

*Writing Screen Dialogue*

Follow the steps listed below.

**1.** Imagine a conversation between the person you named as larger-than-life and one other character. Take a couple of minutes to imagine a discussion.

**2.** Write down the conversation as completely as you can. Include at least five separate speeches per character.

**3.** Now cut as much of the talk as you can without losing the essential point of the discussion.

## WRITING CAMERA DIRECTIONS

In the texts of plays, there are stage directions that describe actions: they are usually found in italics. Screenplays also include directions that tell what the camera shows. The fact that a movie camera can show a scene from a number of possible angles, at various distances, makes camera directions vital. For example, a camera direction in *Shakespeare in Love* specifies, "high angle on audience and stage"—the camera shows the audience and stage from above. Also, because cameras can show closeups, stage directions in screenplays sometimes specify gestures that would be too small for a stage play.

In a screenplay, each new passage of directions represents a new **camera shot,** not just a gesture by an actor. The change in camera placement is the crucial factor that makes a direction necessary. (See pages 599–600 for more on camera angles and shots.)

Screenplays differ in how specifically they describe camera shots. One screenplay might give each shot a number and describe it in technical terms, such as, *"50. closeup on the Sheriff's face. He looks determined. cut to—51. closeup on the Sheriff's hand gripping his six-gun."* Another screenplay may simply name the setting and the time of day or night. The technicalities of camera placement are left to the director and the cinematographer.

Unless you already know a great deal about camera placement, you will probably want to use the simpler method in your own screenplay. However, this does not alter the fact that descriptions of visuals will be as important in your screenplay as the dialogue will be. It may happen that at times, you describe several camera shots without any dialogue at all.

### ● Practice Your Skills

*Writing Camera Directions*

> Return to the shorter version of the dialogue that you wrote in the previous activity. Now divide the conversation into at least three separate camera shots. Write directions for each shot, using the simpler format shown in *Shakespeare in Love.*

# Using a Rubric for a Screenplay

Use the rubric below as a guide to revising a dramatic scene.

| | | | | |
|---|---|---|---|---|
| **Dramatic Elements** | **4** The plot, setting, characters, and dialogue are original and creative. The theme is meaningful. | **3** The plot, setting, characters, and dialogue are effective. The theme is clear. | **2** Most aspects of the plot, setting, characters, and dialogue are effective, but the theme is unclear. | **1** Most aspects of the plot, setting, characters, and dialogue are ineffective. The theme is unclear. |
| **Stage Directions** | **4** The stage directions clearly indicate actions and states of mind and add depth and subtlety. | **3** The stage directions indicate actions and states of mind. | **2** The stage directions indicate actions but do not go deeper. | **1** There are few if any stage directions. |
| **Mood and Tone** | **4** The scene establishes a mood effectively and the mood is appropriate to the theme. The tone enhances the mood and theme. | **3** The scene establishes a mood effectively and the mood is appropriate to the theme. The tone reflects the mood and theme. | **2** The scene establishes a mood but some of the details included don't seem related to that mood. The tone is not clearly tied to the mood and theme. | **1** The mood and tone are hard to identify. |

## PROJECT PREP  Changing Genre  *From Story to Screenplay*

Use the short story you developed and rework it as a screenplay. Use the suggestions on subjects, characters, setting, dialogue, and camera directions to help you create it. Write a first draft that includes both dialogue and action. Convey an explicit or implicit theme. Then, evaluate your scene using the rubric above. Revise for both content and cinematic touches that occur to you. Make a final copy, using the same screenplay format used in *Shakespeare in Love,* for interested readers, classmates, friends, and relatives. Publication of a screenplay usually implies making it into a film; however, screenplays are also published in book form.

# Writing a Poem

Dig deeply into your feelings, and you may discover not a story waiting to be written, but a poem. Poems are usually more tightly structured than stories, and poems use words not only to express feelings, but also to "paint pictures" and produce "a kind of music." In this section you will be guided as you express your creativity through poetry.

**Poetry** is a form of writing that encourages the expression of feelings through sound, images, and other imaginative uses of language.

## 1 Finding Ideas for Poems

Poetry is not reserved for lofty or romantic subjects such as patriotism, the soaring of an eagle, or a great love. In fact, any subject can be poetic. W. D. Snodgrass wrote "Lobsters in the Window," and Pablo Neruda wrote "Ode to My Socks."

To find an idea for a poem, then, you need not look for an imaginative subject. Instead, look for an imaginative response to a subject by searching inside yourself. For example, what does a traffic jam make you think of? How does it feel to sleep late on a weekend morning? What comes to mind when you look at a particular picture? What do you associate with the color orange? Concentrate on your impressions and sensations as you dig into your thoughts.

Filling out a chart might help you launch some ideas. Begin by listing some general subject areas and then brainstorm or list examples for each one. Use your journal as well as your memory as a source of examples. The following beginning of a chart may be used as a guide.

| IDEA CHART | |
|---|---|
| Events | birthday, football touchdown, first moon landing |
| Scenes | streets after a rain, bus stop, surface of Venus |
| Sensations (Smells) | fish frying, shampooed hair, air after a rainstorm |

Look over the ideas on your chart and start exploring the most promising ones. Use free-writing, brainstorming, clustering, questioning, and any other technique that will prod your imagination and encourage ideas and images to flow freely.

● **Practice Your Skills**

*Charting to Find Ideas for a Poem*

Use item 1 and four others to create a chart like the one on page 213. List at least ten examples for each subject. Keep your chart.

**1.** some personal values       **6.** sensations: sounds

**2.** world events              **7.** sensations: textures

**3.** busy scenes               **8.** sensations: tastes

**4.** peaceful scenes           **9.** emotions

**5.** sensations: smells        **10.** hopes and dreams

● **Practice Your Skills**

*Focusing to Find Ideas for a Poem*

Write your responses to the questions below. Focus on the sensations, emotions, images, and impressions that come to mind.

**1.** What does a spider bring to mind?

**2.** Why does a hot shower feel good?

**3.** What do you associate with the color yellow?

**4.** What thoughts do you have about free speech?

*Drawing on Poetic Tradition to Find Ideas for a Poem*

In addition to exploring your own feelings and experiences, explore the world of poetry to find ideas for a poem. In your writing group, brainstorm a list of poems that you have read in school or on your own. Discuss what forms you are familiar with, such as sonnets, ballads, limericks, haiku, or free verse. Consider what subjects are treated in each of these forms. Then freewrite a list of subjects that you might consider for different forms. Save your work.

**PROJECT PREP** *Drafting* **Poem**

In your writing group, discuss ways to take your story about a special relationship and rewrite it as a poem. What would you need to eliminate in order to make the fiction poetic? Give one another suggestions on how to use poetic conventions and forms to present the relationship. Based on this discussion, write a first draft of a poem about a special relationship.

# ② Using Poetic Conventions

Poets use the sounds of words as well as their meanings to achieve an effect. The following chart shows the major sound devices or **schemes** you can use when you write a poem. In a scheme, words retain their literal meaning, but they are placed in an order that points to a meaning or emphasis.

| SOUND DEVICES | |
|---|---|
| **Onomatopoeia** | Use of words whose sounds suggest their meaning:<br>*snap, howl, hiss, whine, creak, murmur* |
| **Alliteration** | Repetition of a consonant sound at the beginning of a series of words:<br>And in the **pr**etty **p**ool the **p**ike stalks<br><div align="right">—Stevie Smith, "Pretty"</div> |
| **Consonance** | Repetition of a consonant sound or sounds with different vowel sounds, usually in the middle or at the end of words:<br>And whe**re** the wat**er** had dri**pp**ed<br>**fr**om the ta**p** . . .<br><div align="right">—D. H. Lawrence, "Snake"</div> |
| **Assonance** | Repetition of a vowel sound within words:<br>And r**a**diant r**ai**ndrops c**ou**ching in c**oo**l fl**ow**ers . . .<br><div align="right">—Rupert Brooke, "The Great Lover"</div> |
| **Repetition** | Repetition of a word or phrase:<br>**We are the hollow men**<br>**We are the stuffed men** . . .<br>Remember us—if at all—not as lost<br>Violent souls, but only<br>**As the hollow men**<br>**The stuffed men.**<br><div align="right">—T. S. Eliot, "The Hollow Men"</div> |
| **Rhyme** | Repetition of accented syllables with the same vowel and consonant sounds:<br>I was angry with my **friend:**<br>I told my wrath, my wrath did **end.**<br>I was angry with my **foe:**<br>I told it not, my wrath did **grow.**<br><div align="right">—William Blake, "A Poison Tree"</div> |

Before you compose a poem, you may want to compile a word-and-phrase list from which you can draw as you write. Begin by listing words and phrases associated with your subject. Then, for each item on your list, think of words and phrases associated with it by sound or by meaning. You can keep an eye and ear out for sound patterns by speaking words aloud as you work. Although you will not include all the listed items in your poem, creating the list will help you focus and identify sound patterns.

## RHYTHM AND METER

A basic part of the sound of a poem is its **rhythm**—the beat created by the arrangement of accented and unaccented syllables. Sense the rhythm as you read the lines below, with different marks for accented and unaccented syllables.

> Tiger, Tiger, burning bright
>
> In the forests of the night . . .
>
> —William Blake, "The Tiger"

The rhythm of poetry is usually more regular than that of prose, shaping its effect and providing a musical quality. When the rhythm follows a strict pattern, as it does in Blake's lines above, it is called **meter.** The most common meter in English is a line of five accented syllables called **iambic pentameter** shown in the following example.

> When in disgrace with fortune and men's eyes . . .
>
> —William Shakespeare, Sonnet 29

Not all poems follow a strict meter. Some are written in **free verse,** with a freely moving rhythm that flows from the rhythm of the words. Sometimes the rhythm will emerge naturally as you write a poem; other times you will want to plan the pattern of syllables. Experiment with your subject. A single phrase or image may set the rhythm for an entire poem.

● **Practice Your Skills**

### *Developing Sound Devices for a Poem*

Using item 1 and two others for ideas, find three subjects for a poem. For each subject develop word lists and sound devices as suggested above.

**1.** values you do not admire

**2.** music

**3.** big moments in sports

**4.** someone you would like to meet

**5.** something you fear

Poetry should appeal to the mind's eye as well as to the ear. Poets use the following major conventions, or **tropes**, to paint pictures with words.

## FIGURATIVE LANGUAGE

**Imagery**
Use of concrete details to create a picture and appeal to the senses.
> And now a gusty shower wraps
> The grimy scraps
> Of withered leaves about your feet . . .
> > —T. S. Eliot, "Preludes"

**Simile**
Comparison between unlike things, using *like* or *as*.
> She walks in beauty like the night . . .
> > —Lord Byron, "She Walks in Beauty"

**Metaphor**
Implied comparison between unlike things.
> Life's but a walking shadow, a poor player
> That struts and frets his hour upon the stage . . .
> > —William Shakespeare, *Macbeth*

**Personification**
Giving human qualities to something nonhuman.
> As Earth stirs in her winter sleep . . .
> > —Robert Graves, "She Tells Her Love While Half Asleep"

**Hyperbole**
Use of exaggeration or overstatement.
> Our hands were firmly cemented . . .
> > —John Donne, "The Ecstasy"

**Oxymoron**
Use of opposite or contradictory terms, such as *joyful misery, living death, dark snow.*
> Beautiful tyrant! fiend angelical!
> > —William Shakespeare, *Romeo and Juliet*

**Symbol**
Use of one thing to stand for another, as the sea journey mentioned below stands for death.
> And may there be no moaning of the bar,[1]
> When I put out to sea . . .
> > —Alfred, Lord Tennyson, "Crossing the Bar"

---

1 sandbar

Once you have chosen the subject of your poem, find related images, figures of speech, and symbols by closing your eyes and focusing on different aspects of your subject. Put all your senses to work as you dig into your imagination. If you want to take a few notes, try not to interrupt the flow of your thoughts and feelings too much. Then, after your mind has traveled for a while, brainstorm or freewrite. Promising ideas are bound to emerge.

● **Practice Your Skills**

*Developing Figurative Language for Poems*

Return to the sound devices you developed. Now use the techniques described above to explore figurative language for each of the three subjects. Save your notes.

**PROJECT PREP** *Revising* *Poetic Conventions*

In your writing group, discuss ways to improve the use of poetic conventions such as sound devices, rhythm, and meter of each author's poem. Also help each author develop ways to include figurative language in his or her poetic account of a special relationship.

# ③ Choosing a Form

Most poems have a pattern of sound and rhythm, plus a visual arrangement of words. These patterns help to hold the reader's attention and to strengthen the effect of the poem. The pattern of rhyme, rhythm, and lines determines the form of a poem. At times you may wait for the details of form to reveal themselves as you work. At other times you will decide on these elements in advance.

## WRITING A RHYMED POEM

A rhymed poem usually has a tighter structure than an unrhymed poem does. The pattern of rhyme, or **rhyme scheme,** can be shown by letters of the alphabet, each letter standing for a different rhyme. Notice in the following two poems that the rhyme scheme does not dictate a particular meter. The first poem has four accents per line, for example, while the second poem, following, has five.

> Had we but world enough, and **time,**     *a*
> This coyness lady were no **crime.**     *a*
> We would sit down, and think which **way**     *b*
> To walk, and pass our long love's **day.**     *b*
>
> Andrew Marvell, "To His Coy Mistress"
>
> It is a beauteous evening, calm and **free,**     *a*
> The holy time is quiet as a **Nun**     *b*
> Breathless with adoration; the broad **sun**     *b*
> Is sinking down in its **tranquility.**     *a*
>
> William Wordsworth, "It is a Beauteous Evening,<br>Calm and Free"

Lines with similar rhyme schemes and rhythms can be grouped into **stanzas,** as in the poem below, which has yet another rhyme scheme. As you read it, notice the **half rhymes,** which are words that have similar but not identical sounds *(plow/furrow, falling/stumbling)*. The poem is "Follower" by Seamus Heaney.

> My father worked with a horse **plow,**     *a*
> His shoulders globed like a full sail **strung**     *b*
> Between the shafts and the **furrow.**     *a*
> The horses strained at his clicking **tongue.** . . .     *b*
>
> I was a nuisance, tripping, **falling,**     *c*
> Yapping always. But **today**     *d*
> It is my father who keeps **stumbling**     *c*
> Behind me, and will not go **away.**     *d*

As the poet, you decide what rhyme scheme to use, if any. Try a few alternatives and then choose the one that works best for you.

## WRITING FREE VERSE

**Free verse** is verse that does not have a strict meter. Instead, the rhythm flows freely from the natural beats of the spoken language. Lines and stanzas, if any, may vary in length. If there is rhyme, it is usually irregular, as in the following excerpt from the poem "Snake" by D. H. Lawrence.

### Snake

A snake came to my water trough
On a hot, hot day, and I in pajamas for the heat,
To drink there.

In the deep, strange-scented shade of the great dark carob tree
I came down the steps with my pitcher
And must wait, must stand and wait, for there he was at the
    trough before me.

He reached down from a fissure in the earth-wall in the gloom
And trailed his yellow-brown slackness soft-bellied
    down, over the edge of the stone trough
And rested his throat upon the stone bottom,
And where the water had dripped from the tap, in a small
    clearness,
He sipped with his straight mouth,
Softly drank through his straight gums, into his slack long body.
Silently.

—D. H. Lawrence

## PROJECT PREP   *Revising*   *Form*

In your writing group, discuss the possible poetic forms that each author's poem could take. Consider what you know about poetic traditions within different forms such as sonnets, ballads, or free verse. Which ones might be most appropriate for a poem about a special relationship? Provide one another suggestions on how to produce that form using the content you have developed so far. Then write a poem that takes into account the content you have developed in light of the poetic techniques you have reviewed in this chapter.

# In the Media

## An Interactive Poem

Poems once existed primarily on paper. Before that, poems existed only orally. In our time, poems exist in both those ways and in cyberspace. A poem on the screen, however, can acquire extra dimensions. The development of the World Wide Web has made poetry interactive. Hyperlinks may lead to any of the following:

- A biography of and interviews with the author
- Other works by the poet
- Explanations of difficult concepts, plus additional background material
- The author's portrait
- A recording of the author reading the poem
- A discussion group among readers

## Media Activity

Plan and create an interactive version either of Shakespeare's "Shall I Compare Thee to a Summer's Day?" or of a poem you wrote for this chapter. Specify how you would use the interactive features described above—and add any other features you can imagine. After finishing your creation, discuss the following questions.

### QUESTIONS FOR ANALYZING INTERACTIVE POETRY

- How much access to the Internet does the average American have?
- How might the audiences for printed poetry and interactive poetry be different or similar?
- If you were a poet, would you want your poem to be available online or only on paper? Explain.
- What is the difference in impact between "Shall I Compare Thee to A Summer's Day" on paper and online?
- Can the extra features of online poetry affect a poem's meaning? If so, how, and is it a good thing?
- Do you think the existence of interactive media might change the way poets write? If so, how, and if not, why not?

# Writing Lab

## Project Corner

### Get Dramatic
**Act It Out**

Using the dramatic scripts developed in this chapter, **produce a short play** based on one of your writing group members' stories. Either perform it live for an audience or film it and show it on a screen.

### Look Into the Future
**Write a Sequel**

**Write a sequel** to one of the stories produced by someone in your writing group. Based on what you know from the original story, what might happen next?

### Change Perspectives Point of View

**Rewrite your story about a special relationship from a different character's perspective.** What would a different character know and not know compared to the original narrator? In what ways would a different character relate the same events?

### Get Visual Storyboard It

**Use the dramatic script you have produced as the basis for a storyboard** that could serve as the basis for a television show. What events would you feature? From what perspective would you draw them? How would the storyboard feature key events around which to build a story? (See page 597 for more information on storyboards.)

# In the Workplace Humorous Poem for a Greeting Card

1. You have been hired at the greeting card company because you have a knack for poetry. Your first assignment is to create a rhyming poem, from ten to twenty lines long, that expresses sympathy for someone's first parking ticket. **Write the poem using a humorous tone** and at least one instance of onomatopoeia. (You can find information on writing poems on pages 213–221.)

# For Oral Communication Informal Bedtime Story

2. The last time you babysat for your seven-year-old cousin Mack, he was a complete terror and refused to go to sleep until you told him a bedtime story. You have to babysit again tomorrow night. This time you will be ready for him. Your idea for a story involves a little boy named Mack and all that befalls him on one dark night. **Prepare the story you will tell to Mack.** Arrange the events chronologically, create tension, and build the story to an effective resolution to tie the events together.

# Timed Writing 🕐 Short Story

3. Sally was walking home from her job at the tire factory on a cold and rainy evening. Coming toward her, beside the bridge, was a young man with a bright and happy face and his nose in the air. His clothes were new and fashionable, and he seemed to completely ignore Sally. Just then Sally heard a cry of help coming from the river below the bridge. Two young boys in a canoe were heading for the dangerous whitewater falls! Sally and the young man looked at each other. They knew they had to help.

Write a short story about what happens next in this scene. You have 25 minutes to complete your work. (For help budgeting time, see pages 37 and 493.)

**Before You Write** Prewrite to develop additional details and vivid descriptions about the scene and the characters involved. Use figurative language and sensory words. Be sure to choose an appropriate point of view and to tie each step in the plot together coherently. Also be sure to consider your purpose, occasion, and audience for the story.

**After You Write** Evaluate your work using the six-trait evaluation rubric on page 204.

# Expository Writing

**E**xpository writing presents information or offers an explanation or analysis. Expository writing that looks at the parts of a subject in relation to the whole is called **analytical writing.**

Writing is one way to explore subjects and learn about the world. When the purpose is to explain or provide information about a subject, the piece is expository writing. Following are just a few of the many uses of expository writing in daily life.

- **Research scientists inform their colleagues** of the latest discoveries in their fields.

- **Journalists inform the public** and provide commentary in newspapers and periodicals about current and past events.

- **Anthropologists explain the customs** of diverse cultures in professional journals and popular magazines.

- **Investigative reporters expose corruption** at home and abroad.

- **Business analysts write annual reports** to inform board members and stockholders about the performance of their investments.

- **College applicants write of their accomplishments** and qualifications in essays accompanying college admission applications.

## Writing Project — *Analytical*

*Act of Conscience  Write an analytical essay about an act of conscience by completing the following project.*

*Think Through Writing*  An act of conscience is a brave act taken when someone feels that there is a widespread wrong that must be challenged and changed. It can be local, as when someone protests an unfair rule in work or school, or historical, as when colonial Americans protested the British taxation without representation by throwing tea into the Boston harbor. Write about a time when you either engaged in an act of conscience, observed an act of conscience, or learned about an act of conscience by reading or following the news. What was the problem being contested? How was the protest undertaken? What was the outcome of the protest? Do you agree with the protesters in contesting this problem the way they did?

**Talk About It** In your writing group, discuss the topic you have chosen. What sorts of problems lead to an act of conscience to solve them? At what point do you believe that an act of conscience is an appropriate response to a perceived wrong?

**Read About It** The following text was written by Coretta Scott King in 1969, two years after her husband Martin Luther King, Jr., had been killed. It concerns the Montgomery, Alabama bus boycott initiated by Rosa Parks, who refused to give up her seat on a bus to a white passenger. She was arrested for violating the state's law requiring black passengers to sit in the back of the bus and yield their seats to whites.

**MODEL: Expository Text**

From

# My Life with Martin Luther King, Jr.

*Coretta Scott King*

Of all the facts of segregation in Montgomery, the most degrading were the rules of the Montgomery City Bus Lines. This Northern-owned corporation outdid the South itself. Although seventy percent of its passengers were black, it treated them like cattle—worse than that, for nobody insults a cow. The first seats on all buses were reserved for whites. Even if they were unoccupied and the rear seats crowded, Negroes would have to stand at the back in case some whites might get aboard; and if the front seats happened to be occupied and more white people boarded the bus, black people seated in the rear were forced to get up and give them their seats. Furthermore—and I don't think Northerners ever realized this—Negroes had to pay their fares at the front of the bus, get off, and walk to the rear door to board again. Sometimes the bus would drive off without them after they had paid their fare. This would happen to elderly people or pregnant women, in bad weather or good, and was considered a great joke by drivers.

On December 1, 1955, Mrs. Rosa Parks, a forty-two-year-old seamstress whom my husband aptly described

From the very first sentence, the focus of this passage is clear. King goes on to provide detailed background information on conditions in Montgomery, Alabama.

as "a charming person with a radiant personality," boarded a bus to go home after a long day working and shopping. The bus was crowded, and Mrs. Parks found a seat at the beginning of the Negro section. At the next stop more whites got on. The driver ordered Mrs. Parks to give her seat to a white man who boarded; this meant that she would have to stand all the way home. Rosa Parks was not in a revolutionary frame of mind. She had not planned to do what she did. Her cup had run over. As she said later, "I was just plain tired, and my feet hurt." So she sat there, refusing to get up. The driver called a policeman, who arrested her and took her to the courthouse. From there Mrs. Parks called E.D. Nixon, who came down and signed a bail bond for her.

> Although informational writing, this text is also a narrative, and this event is the triggering action that sets all the rest of the events in motion.

Mr. Nixon was a fiery Alabamian. He was a Pullman porter who had been active in A. Philip Randolph's Brotherhood of Sleeping Car Porters and in civil-rights activities. Suddenly he also had had enough; suddenly, it seemed, almost every Negro in Montgomery had had enough. It was spontaneous combustion. Phones began ringing all over the Negro section of the city. The Women's Political Council suggested a one-day boycott of the buses as a protest. E.D. Nixon courageously agreed to organize it.

> The term "spontaneous combustion" creates a metaphor for the great force and intensity of the civil rights movement.

The first we knew about it was when Mr. Nixon called my husband early in the morning of Friday, December 2. He had already talked to Ralph Abernathy. After describing the incident, Mr. Nixon said, "We have taken this type of thing too long. I feel the time has come to boycott the buses. It's the only way to make the white folks see that we will not take this sort of thing any longer."

> As the events unfold, King adds insights into how the people involved were feeling and the meaning the actions had.

Martin agreed with him and offered the Dexter Avenue Church as a meeting place. After much telephoning, a meeting of black ministers and civic leaders was arranged for that evening. Martin said later that as he approached his church Friday evening, he was nervously wondering how many leaders would really turn up. To his delight, Martin found over forty people, representing every segment of Negro life, crowded into the large meeting room at Dexter. There were doctors, lawyers, businessmen, federal-government employees, union leaders, and a great many ministers.

. . . After a stormy session, one thing was clear: however much they differed on details, everyone was unanimously for a boycott. It was set for Monday, December 5. Committees were organized; all the ministers present promised to urge their congregations to take part. Several thousand leaflets were printed on the church mimeograph machine describing the reasons for the boycott and urging all Negroes not to ride buses "to work, to town, to school, or anyplace on Monday, December 5." Everyone was asked to come to a mass meeting at the Holt Street Baptist Church on Monday evening for further instructions. . . .

Saturday was a busy day for Martin and the other members of the committee. They hustled around town talking with other leaders, arranging with the Negro-owned taxi companies for special bulk fares and with the owners of private automobiles to get the people to and from work. I could do little to help because Yoki was only two weeks old, and my physician, Dr. W. D. Pettus, who was very careful, advised me to stay in for a month. However, I was kept busy answering the telephone, which rang continuously, and coordinating from that central point the many messages and arrangements.

Our greatest concern was how we were going to reach the fifty thousand black people of Montgomery, no matter how hard we worked. The white press, in an outraged exposé, spread the word for us in a way that would have been impossible with only our resources.

King sets up the background for the anecdote that explains how the movement got publicity from an unlikely source.

As it happened, a white woman found one of our leaflets, which her Negro maid had left in the kitchen. The irate woman immediately telephoned the newspapers to let the white community know what the blacks were up to. We laughed a lot about this, and Martin later said that we owed them a great debt.

On Sunday morning, from their pulpits, almost every Negro minister in town urged people to honor the boycott.

Martin came home late Sunday night and began to read the morning paper. The long articles about the proposed boycott accused the NAACP of planting Mrs. Parks on the bus—she had been a volunteer secretary for the Montgomery chapter—and likened the boycott to the tactics of the White Citizens' Councils. This upset Martin. That awesome conscience of his began to gnaw at him, and he wondered if he were doing the right thing. Alone in his study, he struggled with the question of whether the boycott method was basically unchristian. Certainly it could be used for unethical ends. But, as he said, "We are using it to give birth to freedom . . . and to urge men to comply with the law of the land. Our concern was not to put the bus company out of business, but to put justice in business." He recalled Thoreau's words, "We can no longer lend our cooperation to an evil system," and he thought, "He who accepts evil without protesting against it is really cooperating with it." Later Martin wrote, "From this moment on I conceived of our movement as an act of massive noncooperation. From then on I rarely used the word *boycott*."

> At the time King wrote this, the word "awesome" had not lost its power to evoke greatness. Note also her use of the subjunctive mood of the verb, showing his uncertainty (he wondered if he "were" doing the right thing).

Serene after his inner struggle, Martin joined me in our sitting room. We wanted to get to bed early, but Yoki began crying and the telephone kept ringing. Between interruptions we sat together talking about the prospects for the success of the protest. We were both filled with doubt. Attempted boycotts had failed in Montgomery and other cities. Because of changing times and tempers, this one seemed to have a better chance, but it was still a slender hope. We finally decided that if the boycott was 60 percent effective we would be doing all right, and we would be satisfied to have made a good start.

A little after midnight we finally went to bed, but at five-thirty the next morning we were up and dressed again. The first bus was due at 6 o'clock at the bus stop just outside our house. We had coffee and toast in the kitchen; then I went into the living room to watch. Right on time, the bus came, headlights blazing through the December darkness, all lit up inside. I shouted, "Martin! Martin, come quickly!" He ran in and stood beside me, his face lit with excitement. There was not one person on that usually crowded bus!

> This homey detail helps make the scene very vivid.

We stood together waiting for the next bus. It was empty too, and this was the most heavily traveled line in the whole city. Bus after empty bus paused at the stop and moved on. We were so excited we could hardly speak coherently. Finally Martin said, "I'm going to take the car and see what's happening in other places in the city."

He picked up Ralph Abernathy, and they cruised together around the city. Martin told me about it when he got home. Everywhere it was the same. A few white people and maybe one or two blacks in otherwise empty buses. Martin and Ralph saw extraordinary sights—the sidewalks crowded with men and women trudging to work; the students of Alabama State College walking or thumbing rides; taxi cabs with people clustered in them. Some of our people rode mules; others went in horse-drawn buggies. But most of them were walking, some making a round trip of as much as twelve miles. Martin later wrote, "As I watched them I knew that there is nothing more majestic than the determined courage of individuals willing to suffer and sacrifice for their freedom and dignity."

The specificity of the details makes this final scene powerful and memorable.

***Respond in Writing*** Write freely about Coretta Scott King's account of Rosa Park's arrest and the boycott that followed. Do you think that Parks' response was appropriate to the problem she identified? What other options might she have pursued to address what she believed to be a wrong?

***Develop Your Own Ideas*** Work with your classmates to develop ideas that you might use to write about how and why people undertake acts of conscience.

*Small Groups:* In your small group, discuss the writing you have done. Answer the following questions to help think of possible details for each author's expository text in each of the following categories.

- What is the setting of the situation, including the circumstances that brought about the act of conscience?

- What sort of people were responsible for the problem being contested, and how did they act?

- What form of protest was undertaken? What other options were available, and did the protester take the best course of action?

- What events comprised the protest? Was the scale of the protest appropriate to the situation?

- What was the outcome of the protest? Was the protest worth the risk and effort?

*Whole Class:* Make a master chart of all of the ideas generated by the small groups about when acts of conscience are appropriate, what their appropriate scale should be, and what sorts of outcomes they produce.

*Write About It* You will next write an analytical essay about an act of conscience, with attention to the events that caused it and the outcome of the protest. The following chart shows possibilities for the project.

| Possible Topics | Possible Audiences | Possible Forms |
| --- | --- | --- |
| • a protest initiated by you against something in your immediate world<br><br>• a protest you have witnessed but that did not necessarily involve you<br><br>• a protest you are familiar with through your following of current events<br><br>• a protest from history you are familiar with, based on your reading and watching of documentary or historical films | • other teens who would be inspired by your act of conscience<br><br>• readers who would benefit from understanding how, when, and why protests are undertaken<br><br>• readers who believe that young people should never question authority<br><br>• readers who would benefit from a better understanding of world history | • an essay<br><br>• a blog<br><br>• a newspaper article<br><br>• an entry in a historical volume |

The selection from Mrs. King's book is an excellent example of writing that informs about a historical event. An expository essay can take many forms, but its main purpose is to set forth an explanation, to analyze a subject, or to communicate information.

# 1 Getting the Subject Right

As you know by now, you begin the prewriting stage with the search for an idea and end it by shaping that idea into an organized plan for an essay. Your initial step in writing an expository essay, therefore, is to discover possible subjects by using prewriting strategies.

## DISCOVERING AND CHOOSING A SUBJECT

How can the seniors raise money to defray the cost of the senior class trip? What do birds do when it rains? What strategy do you use to get a good seat at a baseball game? Why was George Washington an effective president? How has popular music changed in the last five years? Possible subjects for an expository essay, such as these, are limited only by your own interests and knowledge.

Countless ideas for subjects are inside your head right now. The task is to bring them to the surface by letting your mind relax or by asking yourself some probing questions. Start by using the strategies discussed in Chapter 1 on pages 13–14: taking an inventory of your interests, freewriting, and using your journal. Ask yourself questions about your interests and skills. You can also skim books and magazines and search the Internet. Another idea is to look over your textbooks and class notes for possible topics.

## LIMITING AND FOCUSING A SUBJECT

The following guidelines will help you choose a subject from the many ideas you gather.

 **Guidelines for Choosing a Subject**

- Choose a subject that you would enjoy writing about.
- Choose a subject that you know enough about to develop adequately in a short essay.
- Consider your **audience.** Who will be reading your work? What subject would be appropriate for and interesting to them?
- Consider your writing **purpose.** What subject will best fulfill your purpose?
- Consider the **occasion.** What subject would be right for the occasion of your writing?

Your next step is to make sure that your subject is narrow enough to be covered adequately in a short essay. The following questions will help you limit your subject.

## Questions for Limiting a Subject

- What aspect of my subject do I want to explain?
- How can I narrow it even further?
- What do my readers need to know to understand my subject?
- What insight can I draw from my subject?
- How might I express my main idea in one sentence?

Suppose you chose a subject you had read about in psychology class and had found fascinating: a boy who was discovered living in the wild in Aveyron, France, in the early 1800s. The answers to the five questions for limiting a subject might look like the following.

- I want to explain what happened to the wild boy after he was discovered.

- I can explain how the wild boy was educated.

- Because my readers probably have not heard of the wild boy, they will need some background information.

- Finding the wild boy gave scientists a chance to study how heredity and environment influence human development.

- Work with the wild boy has led to new ideas in education and psychology.

## PROJECT PREP  *Prewriting*  *Subject*

Based on the discussions you have had with your classmates and your preliminary writing, limit and focus your subject. Use the five questions in the chart above to help you articulate your thoughts. Share your answers with your writing group and listen to the feedback. Make any changes in your answers that seem reasonable.

# ❷ Exploring and Refining the Subject

## GATHERING INFORMATION

Next gather information that will help you explain your subject, researching primary and secondary sources in magazines, newspapers, the Internet, and other sources. Evaluate each source for validity, reliability, and relevance. (See pages 299 and 396–398.) Your goal is to accumulate enough well-chosen details to provide substantial evidence for your thesis and to cover your subject effectively. The specific types of details you select will often indicate the method of development to use. (See pages 90 and 256–273.)

Also gather information about all relevant perspectives on your subject and on the views and information contradicting your thesis statement and the evidence presented for it. Analyzing these and addressing them in your text will strengthen your own position by anticipating and answering readers' concerns. (See page 436.) The following notes are on the subject of the wild boy of Aveyron. They are not, however, arranged in any logical order.

CHAPTER 7

| | |
|---|---|
| **Limited Subject** | Education of the wild boy of Aveyron |
| **Facts and Examples as Details** | • doctor's name was Jean-Marc-Gaspard Itard |
| | • François Truffaut made a movie about the boy |
| | • Itard named the boy Victor |
| | • found in France in 1800, age twelve |
| | • had 23 scars on him |
| | • couldn't talk; trotted instead of walked |
| | • learned how to fetch water and say *milk* |
| | • had a nice smile |
| | • expressed only joy and sorrow at first |
| | • Itard saw to the boy's needs before educating him |
| | • insensitive to heat and cold and some sounds |
| | • responded only to sounds related to foods |
| | • hard to imagine how boy survived by himself |
| | • Itard played games with him to develop thinking powers; games Victor was most interested in involved food |
| | • work with Victor helped Itard develop ideas about how to teach deaf people |
| | • educator Maria Montessori was influenced by Itard's work |

# Think Critically

## Constructing Analogies

An effective device for explaining unfamiliar ideas or processes in an expository or persuasive essay is an analogy. An **analogy** is an extended comparison that uses a familiar object to explain something abstract or unfamiliar by pointing out similarities between the two things. For example, suppose you want to explain the process of interviewing for a job by comparing it to advertising a new car. To think through the analogy, make a chart like the following. Begin by writing your idea for the analogy (interviewing for a job *is like* advertising a new car) at the top of the chart. Then list parallel processes on both sides of your chart.

| ANALOGY CHART | |
|---|---|
| **Interviewing for a Job** | **Advertising a New Car** |
| Make experience and qualifications clear | Make features of car (comfort, reliability) apparent |
| Make best appearance by dressing neatly, combing hair, polishing shoes | Present product attractively by using good photography in beautiful surroundings |
| Emphasize what you can do for employer: do quality work, solve problems | Emphasize what new car can do for consumer: provide comfortable transportation, communicate an image |

## Thinking Practice

Choose one of the following analogies or make up your own. Then make a chart like the one above to help you draw parallels between the abstract concept and the familiar concept.

1. success is like mountain climbing
2. fear is like a virus
3. friendship is like a mirror

# DEVELOPING A WORKING THESIS

At this point you need to pull together all the information you have gathered and identify a main idea that grows out of connections and patterns you see in the information. This main idea is called the **working thesis.** Later, as you develop your expository essay, you will refine your working thesis into a polished thesis statement.

## Steps for Developing a Working Thesis

- Review your prewriting notes and the questions you answered to limit your subject.
- Express your main idea.
- Look closely at your notes to see that your working thesis covers all of your information and ideas.

Using the steps above, you might develop the following working thesis about the wild boy of Aveyron.

**Working Thesis** — The methods Dr. Itard used to help the wild boy had an influence on education and psychology.

Once you have a working thesis, go over your list of details and check off only those that fit within the thesis. These are the details that you will use in your essay. Given the working thesis above, you would *not* use the following details about the wild boy of Aveyron.

- François Truffaut made a movie about the boy
- hard to imagine how boy survived by himself

Irrelevant details such as these, no matter how interesting, can detract from the unity of your essay if you include them in the body. Hold them in reserve, however, for you may be able to use them to enliven your introduction or conclusion.

## PROJECT PREP  *Prewriting*  *Working Thesis*

In your writing group, discuss how the answers to the five questions on page 232 might point to a working thesis and help one another develop a working thesis. On your own, review your preliminary writing and delete any details that do not seem directly related to your working thesis. Save them for reconsideration when you draft your introduction and conclusion.

# ③ Organizing Your Essay

The final step in prewriting involves the arranging of your ideas in a logical order. The thoughts that occurred to you as you generated details now need to be grouped into categories and arranged in an order that the reader can easily follow. Many writers use a two-step process to create an outline for their essay: (1) grouping supporting details into categories and (2) arranging those categories in a logical order with letters and numbers. Other writers use a less formal graphic organizer to get their ideas in order.

## GROUPING SUPPORTING DETAILS INTO CATEGORIES

Scan your list of supporting details, asking yourself what each detail might have in common with the other details. Try to create three to five main categories into which most of your details will fit. Details that do not easily fit into one of your main categories may be usable in the introduction or conclusion of your essay. The following categories have been created from the notes about the wild boy of Aveyron.

**MODEL: Grouping Details**

**Itard's methods and successes in helping Victor**

- Itard made sure boy's needs were met before educating him
- Itard played games with him to develop thinking powers; games Victor most interested in involved food
- learned how to fetch water and how to say *milk*

**How Itard's work influenced later educational practices**

- work with Victor helped Itard develop ideas about how to teach deaf people
- educator Maria Montessori was influenced by Itard's work

**Boy's state when found**

- had 23 scars on him
- trotted instead of walked
- had a nice smile
- expressed only joy and sorrow at first
- couldn't talk
- insensitive to heat and cold and some sounds
- responded only to sounds related to foods

## ARRANGING CATEGORIES IN LOGICAL ORDER

The categories you create when you group your supporting details are the main topics that you will use to support your thesis statement. Your next step is to arrange these topics in a logical order. If your essay presents steps in a process or uses an incident to explain something, chronological order is probably best. If your essay analyzes an object, spatial order might be the most logical. If your essay focuses on the similarities and differences between two items, the method of comparison and contrast would be the best. Otherwise you will probably want to use either order of importance or developmental order, the most common arrangements for informative essays.

The most logical organization for the main topics about the wild boy is developmental order. If a Roman numeral is assigned to each category, a simple outline for the body of this essay would appear as follows.

### MODEL: Simple Outline

**I.** Boy's state when found

**II.** Itard's methods and successes in helping Victor

**III.** Itard's influence on later educational practices

Notice that the wording of the third main topic is different from the wording on page 236. The change was made so that the three main topics would be expressed in **parallel form.** The main topics and each group of subtopics in an outline should always be parallel expressions.

After your simple outline is complete, you continue the outlining process by arranging the items within each category in a logical order. These items, called **subtopics,** are assigned capital letters. As you build your outline, you may add new ideas as you think of them, provided there is a logical place for them in your outline.

The following is an appropriate outline for an informative essay about the wild boy of Aveyron. Notice the indentation of the topics.

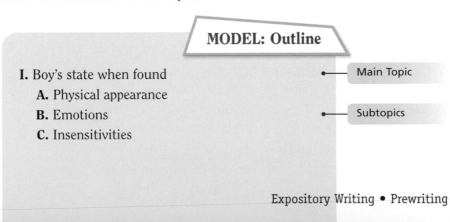

### MODEL: Outline

**I.** Boy's state when found — Main Topic
  **A.** Physical appearance
  **B.** Emotions — Subtopics
  **C.** Insensitivities

II. Itard's methods and successes in helping Victor ●——— Main Topic
    A. First step: meeting boy's needs
    B. Second step: developing boy's sensitivities ●——— Subtopics
    C. Third step: playing thinking games
    D. Fourth step: teaching language and chores

III. Itard's influence on later educational practices ●——— Main Topic
    A. Idea of good learning environment
    B. Education for deaf ●——— Subtopics
    C. Influence on Montessori

Your final step in outlining is to add any necessary supporting points under the subtopics. These **supporting points** are assigned Arabic numerals. If your supporting points can be broken down even further, use lowercase letters to list the details.

### MODEL: Outline Form

I. (Main topic)
    A. (Subtopic)
        1. (Supporting point)
        2. (Supporting point)
           a. (Detail)
           b. (Detail)
    B. (Subtopic)
        1. (Supporting point)
        (etc.)

**Writing Tip**

Organize your notes in an outline that shows how you will cover the **main topics, subtopics, and supporting points** of your subject; or develop a **graphic organizer** of a different sort to help you organize your ideas.

Following is the final outline for the essay on the wild boy of Aveyron.

### MODEL: Final Outline

I. Boy's state when found
    A. Physical appearance
        1. Scars
        2. Method of walking
    B. Emotions
        1. Smile
        2. Expression of only joy or sorrow

**C.** Insensitivities

    **1.** Heat and cold

    **2.** Certain sounds

        **a.** Failure to take notice of speech

        **b.** Ready notice of sounds relating to food

**II.** Itard's methods and successes in helping Victor

    **A.** First step: meeting boy's needs

    **B.** Second step: developing boy's sensitivities

    **C.** Third step: playing thinking games

    **D.** Fourth step: teaching civilized ways

        **1.** Language

        **2.** Chores

**III.** Itard's influence on later educational practices

    **A.** Idea of good learning environment

    **B.** Education for deaf and developmentally challenged

    **C.** Influence on Montessori

A less formal way to organize your thoughts is in a graphic organizer such as the following.

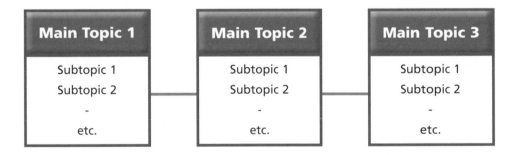

**PROJECT PREP** *Prewriting* *Organizing*

In your writing group, help each author develop a logical sequence for the presentation of information and events. If the story is told chronologically, are the events described in a logical order? If a different way of sequencing information is taken, is it followed consistently throughout the account?

# In the Media
## News Coverage

Your understanding of the world is as complete or as limited as your sources of information. Different people can have widely divergent views about the same event if they are relying on different media for their information. Consider, for example, the coverage of a single event across the media.

If you read about the event in the **newspaper,** you will not have up-to-the minute results. You will have to rely on descriptive writing and one or two photos to provide you with a visual sense of the event. Your knowledge will consist primarily of highlights, selected quotes, and statistics. The event is frozen in time as a succession of great moments.

If you listen on the **radio,** you will have no visual connection with the event. You must rely on the descriptive powers of the commentators to bring the event to life before your mind's eye. Your imagination fills in the blanks. Unlike the newspaper, however, the radio may offer real-time coverage, periodically interrupted by advertisements.

The **Internet** combines advantages of the newspaper and radio, and adds the dimension of interactivity. E-mail or live discussions, links to related stories, and multimedia content are among the features offered by this medium.

The **television** viewer can follow coverage of the event. The viewer sees what the camera is focused on. The viewer also hears live commentary and learns about the background of the event through special features and interviews. Commercials are a regular feature.

## Media Activity

Form four groups in your class. Choose an ongoing news event, such as an effort by Congress to pass controversial legislation. Group leaders draw lots to see which group will follow the event in a particular medium. Discuss the event the next day, keeping the following questions in mind: What do the different media have in common? On what particular points did they differ? To what extent does one's choice of media dictate one's sense of reality?

*editing* ⭐

Because space is such a premium in newspapers, reporters and editors need to be very word conscious. Revise the following wordy statement as a newspaper editor might.

The protesters took to the street as they marched down the boulevard toward the state capitol buiding in their march to protest cutbacks in spending at the schools of the state.

# The Power of Language ⚡

## Participial Phrases: Getting into the Action

Modifiers can help make your meaning come alive and at the same time create appealing sentence variety. For example, consider participial phrases (including present particples, which end in *–ing,* and past participles, which often end in *–ed* or *–en).* These modifiers describe a person, thing, or action. (See pages 694–696.) Coretta Scott King could have written about Rosa Parks:

So she sat there. She refused to give up.

Instead, she chose to express those ideas more fluently and in a way that added a sense of action to the past tense by using a present participial phrase.

So she sat there, refusing to give up.

Here's another example that uses two participial phrases to help suggest the bustle of activity preceding the Montgomery bus boycott.

They hustled around town talking with other leaders, arranging with the Negro-owned taxi companies for special bulk fares.

Here's an example that uses both a present and a past participle to head up the phrase.

To his delight, Martin found over forty people, representing every segment of Negro life, crowded into the large meeting room at Dexter.

## Try It Yourself

On your project topic, write one sentence with a present participial phrase at the end. Add a second participial phrase to create a sentence like the second example above. Write a third sentence that uses both a present participial phrase and a past participial phrase. As you draft and later revise your expository composition, look for opportunities to add participial phrases to highlight the action.

### Punctuation Tip

**Separate nonessential participial phrases** from the main part of the sentence **with a comma.** (You can learn more about essential and nonessential elements on pages 954–956). If the phrase comes **in the middle** of the sentence, enclose it **in two commas.**

Using your outline and other prewriting notes, you are ready to draft your essay, which should include an introduction with a thesis statement, a body of supporting paragraphs, and a conclusion.

## 1 Drafting the Thesis Statement

Even if your essay does not begin with your thesis, you should refine your working thesis first to keep your main idea in focus.

### HERE'S HOW Steps for Drafting Your Thesis

- Review your outline and revise your working thesis so that it covers all of your main topics.
- Avoid expressions that weaken your thesis, such as "In this paper I will . . ." or "This essay will be about."

Review the prewriting notes and the outline on the wild boy of Aveyron on pages 233 and 236–239. Then study the problems in the following thesis statements.

| | |
|---|---|
| **Weak Thesis Statement** | When he was first captured in 1800, the wild boy of Aveyron was very different from a normal child. (too narrow: does not cover boy's education and the influence of Itard's work) |
| **Weak Thesis Statement** | Wild children exist in both fiction and fact. (too general: does not even mention the wild boy of Aveyron) |
| **Weak Thesis Statement** | This essay will be about the wild boy of Aveyron. (focuses reader's attention on the essay instead of on the wild boy) |

In contrast, the thesis statement below is specific and covers all the supporting details.

| | |
|---|---|
| **Strong Thesis Statement** | Dr. Itard's methods in attempting to civilize the wild boy from Aveyron led to new developments in education and psychology that people take for granted today. |

### PROJECT PREP Drafting *Thesis Statement*

In your writing group, help each author evaluate his or her working thesis statement and develop it into a strong thesis statement that will cover all the supporting details.

# ② Drafting the Introduction

The introduction is the place to state your subject and thesis and to set the tone for the entire essay. The tone may be direct, reflective, casual, bitter, comic, joyous.

The **tone** of the essay is the author's attitude toward his or her subject and audience.

### Strategies for Introductions to Expository Essays

- Relate an incident that shows how you became interested in your subject or that tells a dramatic story related to your subject.
- Give some background information.
- Cite an example that catches the reader's attention.
- Present something startling—an usual quote, a vivid description, something that captures the imagination and stirs the feelings of your readers.
- Establish the tone.

## MODEL: Introduction Using Personal Incident

I remember, to start with, that day in Sacramento, in a California now nearly thirty years past, when I first entered a classroom—able to understand about fifty stray English words. The third of four children, I had been preceded by my older brother and sister to a neighborhood school. Neither of them, however, had revealed very much about their classroom experiences. They left each morning and returned each afternoon, always together, speaking Spanish as they climbed the five steps to the porch. Their mysterious books, wrapped in brown shopping bag paper, remained on the table next to the door, closed firmly behind them.

—Richard Rodriguez, *Aria: A Memoir of a Bilingual Childhood*

## MODEL: Introduction Using Background Information

For almost three-quarters of a century, James Van DerZee has with rare artistry compiled a sweeping photographic survey of a way of life among black people of eastern America, particularly Harlem, that is unique and irreplaceable. It is both an historical record of value and an achievement of disciplined and feeling art. Van DerZee is only now beginning to be recognized as one of the notable photographers of middle-class people of the country.

—Clarissa K. Wittenberg, *Smithsonian*

## MODEL: Introduction Using Attention-Grabbing Example

With his 47-pound bow drawn taut, a carbon graphite arrow held close to his cheek and EEG wires flowing from his scalp to monitor his brain, Rick McKinney seemed to be gazing absently at the majesty of Pikes Peak towering above the U.S. Olympic Training Center in Colorado Springs. Suddenly, he released the arrow and hit a perfect bull's eye that stood 98.6 yards downrange. Dr. Daniel Landers, an exercise scientist from Arizona State University, looked up from his EEG monitor, smiled and nodded with approval. McKinney had really not been thinking during the shot; the left side of his brain had shown diminished electrical activity.

—Lee Torrey, *How Science Creates Winners*

When you write your introduction, you may need to revise your thesis statement to make it work with the other sentences. Notice in the following introduction about the wild boy that the thesis statement has been reworked to fit smoothly into the introduction.

## MODEL: Introduction of an Expository Essay

The idea of a child's growing up away from humans has turned up again and again in popular tales. Edgar Rice Burroughs's Tarzan and Rudyard Kipling's Mowgli the wolf boy are two famous examples. Wild children turn up in fact as well as in fiction, although there is no evidence that any were raised by animals. One of the most interesting factual cases is that of the wild boy of Aveyron, France. The doctor who worked with the boy after he was captured in 1800 was Jean Marc Gaspard Itard. The young doctor's methods in trying to civilize the boy, whom he named Victor, led to new ideas in education and psychology—ideas that people take for granted today.

Revised thesis statement

## PROJECT PREP  Drafting  *Introduction*

Draft an opening. In your writing group, read each paper with attention to:
- the clarity of the stated or implied thesis
- elements in the opening paragraph that grab the reader's interest
- the appropriateness of the tone

# ③ Drafting the Body

Follow your outline or graphic organizer when you draft the body of your expository text. Each main topic, with some or all of the subtopics and supporting points, will become at least one paragraph. If you have a number of supporting details, you may need two or more paragraphs to cover each topic adequately.

## Guidelines for Adequately Developing an Essay

- Include enough relevant and substantial evidence to develop your thesis statement fully.
- Include information on all relevant perspectives.
- Include an analysis of views and information that contradict the thesis statement and the evidence presented for it.
- Include enough information to present each topic and subtopic fully.
- Use well-chosen details and precise language.

## LOGICAL DEVELOPMENT

The ideas you developed to support your thesis statement are claims.

**Claims** are statements asserted to be true.

In the opening reading by Coretta Scott King, two of the claims are:

- The segregation rules of the Montgomery City Bus Lines were degrading.
- There is nothing more majestic than the determined courage of individuals willing to suffer and sacrifice for their freedom and dignity.

King develops these claims with supporting information and examples.

| CLAIMS | SUPPORTING DETAILS |
|---|---|
| The segregation rules of the Montgomery City Bus Lines were degrading. | The first seats on all buses were reserved for whites. Even if they were unoccupied and the rear seats crowded, Negroes would have to stand at the back in case some whites might get aboard; and if the front seats happened to be occupied and more white people boarded the bus, black people seated in the rear were forced to get up and give them their seats. Negroes had to pay their fares at the front of the bus, get off, and walk to the rear door to board again. Sometimes the bus would drive off without them after they had paid their fare. |

There is nothing more majestic than the determined courage of individuals willing to suffer and sacrifice for their freedom and dignity.

The sidewalks crowded with men and women trudging to work; the students of Alabama State College walking or thumbing rides; taxi cabs with people clustered in them. Some of our people rode mules; others went in horse-drawn buggies. But most of them were walking, some making a round trip of as much as twelve miles.

Examples alone, however, do not support your assertion that your claims are true. Each claim must be back up by a warrant.

A **warrant** is a statement that explains how an example serves as evidence for a claim.

Warrants often uses the word "because," as in the following example:

| Claim | The Montogomery Bus Lines rules were the most degrading. |
| Information | African Americans had to stand even if no whites were on board, just to leave room for them if they should board. |
| Warrant | Because African Americans had to stand at the back of buses just *in case* a white person might board, the Montgomery Bus Line segregation rules were degrading. |

*Valid Inferences* In addition to providing warrants for your claims, you also need to make sure that your conclusions or inferences are valid.

An inference is **valid** if it follows logically from the claims. For example, suppose you make these claims:

| Claim | Having to stand on a bus *in case* others board is degrading. |
| Claim | Rules required African Americans in Montgomery, Alabama to stand on the bus *in case* whites might board. |
| Valid Inference | The rules requiring African Americans to stand *in case* whites might board were degrading. |

That inference is valid because the second claim just gives a specific example of a general truth stated in the first claim.

In the following circumstance, however, the inference would not be valid.

| | |
|---|---|
| Claim | Having to stand on a bus *in case* others board is degrading. |
| Claim | Andre had to stand on the bus during rush hour because it was packed with passengers. |
| Invalid Inference | It was degrading for Andre to stand on the bus. |

This inference is invalid because it does not follow logically from the claims. The original claim is that having to stand when there are empty seats is degrading. Just because Andre had to stand does not logically lead to the inference that his experience was degrading.

**Coherence** As you move from point to point in your draft, you will need to supply transitions to connect your thoughts within and between paragraphs to achieve coherence.

> **Coherence** is the quality that makes each sentence or paragraph seem related to the one before.

Following are some other ways you can achieve coherence.

*You can learn more about transitions and coherence on pages 5 and 94–96.*

### Strategies for Achieving Coherence

- Repeat a key word from an earlier sentence.
- Repeat an idea from an earlier sentence using new words.
- Use a pronoun in place of a word used earlier.

The following is a draft of the second body paragraph from the outline on the wild boy of Aveyron on pages 237–239. Notice how each point of the outline has been fleshed out into complete sentences and paragraphs. The transitions are in **bold** type.

### MODEL: Body Paragraph of an Expository Essay

Itard's first step in educating Victor was attending to his needs and desires. He gave Victor the foods he liked (mainly vegetables), plenty of rest, privacy, and exercise. **Then** he began developing the boy's sensitivities, such as those of sight and hearing, for Itard believed that no attempt to teach him to talk would succeed unless he was first sensitive to sound. **Next** he tried to play games with Victor to stretch the boy's mental powers. He **soon** learned that only when food was involved did Victor

— From II in Outline

pay any attention. To motivate Victor, Itard devised a game in which Victor would find a chestnut under one of three inverted cups. When he **finally** began teaching Victor to speak and read, **however,** Itard met with very little success. **After** years the only words Victor learned were *milk* and *Oh God,* the latter expression having been picked up by imitating his caretaker, Madame Guérin. Victor never learned to read. He did, **however,** learn some simple chores, including fetching water and sawing wood. He never became what most people would consider a normal person, although he did respond to the affectionate concern of those around him.

## PROJECT PREP  Drafting  *Body Paragraphs*

Using the guidelines on the preceding pages, draft the body of your analytical essay. Choose your supporting details carefully. Provide smooth transitions from your introduction to the body and between each body paragraph. Monitor how well you are addressing your purpose and audience and if the tone is appropriate.

For the text about an act of conscience (pages 224–230), you may want to create a chart like the one below to help you keep track of your claims and warrants.

|  | Topic sentence | Examples/ information | Warrant |
|---|---|---|---|
| 1st body paragraph |  |  |  |
| 2nd body paragraph |  |  |  |
| etc. |  |  |  |

In your writing group, read each author's account. On the topic of an act of conscience, pay attention to how the author has developed the events. Is the evidence relevant and substantial? Are the details well chosen? Do you get a complete picture of the nature of the conflict: what the problem is, how it is protested, and how the protest works out? Has the author considered all relevant positions on the subject? Has the author analyzed information and views that contradict the thesis statement and the evidence presented for it? Has the author provided paragraph breaks appropriately so that each new topic has its own distinct presentation? Once you have drafted the body paragraphs, give some thought to a title that will raise a reader's interest. It may be words from the body of the essay or a headline-type phrase. Discuss your thoughts with your group.

**Drafting the Conclusion**

The conclusion provides a good opportunity to express whatever insight your subject has inspired. One or a combination of the following may be an effective way to end an expository essay.

 **Strategies for Concluding an Expository Essay**

- Talk about a lesson learned from the subject.
- Refer to ideas in the introduction to bring the essay full circle.
- State your personal reaction to the subject.
- Draw a conclusion from the details in the body of your work.
- Relate an incident supporting your thesis or conclusion.
- Ask a question that leaves the reader thinking.
- Appeal to the reader's emotions.

The closing to the essay about Victor draws a conclusion based on the supporting details in the body. The last sentence, often called a **clincher** because it fixes the message firmly in the reader's mind, provides a strong ending.

**MODEL: Conclusion of an Expository Essay**

After Itard stopped working with Victor, the French government paid for Victor's care for the rest of his life. He never fit into normal society. Itard concluded that the early years of human life are precious periods of learning; and if a child is deprived of a human environment during those years, full learning can never take place. Although scientists and psychologists are still debating the influences of heredity and environment, Itard drew his own conclusion. It is human society—civilization—that makes us what we are, and no amount of inborn humanity could make up for the loss of companionship that Victor endured in the wild.

Clincher sentence

Now add an appropriate title to your draft. Whether words from the essay, a headline, or a summary phrase, a title should appeal to a reader and pique interest.

**PROJECT PREP**  *Conclusion*

Using the strategies above, draft the conclusion of your expository text. Then, in your writing group, read each author's conclusion and evaluate its effectiveness. Help each author provide a conclusion that presents a clear resolution and leaves a strong impression in the reader's mind. Review each title for effectiveness and appeal.

Leave enough time to put your draft away for a while so you can revise it with a clear mind. Ask yourself as you revise, "Will my readers understand exactly what I mean?"

## CHECKING FOR UNITY, COHERENCE, AND EMPHASIS

In a unified expository essay, the paragraphs work together to develop a single thesis. The topic sentence of each supporting paragraph relates directly to the thesis, creating **external coherence,** and each sentence within a paragraph relates directly to the topic sentence, creating **internal coherence.** As you revise, watch for and delete stray ideas.

Also be on the alert for transitional words and phrases to keep your work coherent. Look for ways to improve the organization and flow of ideas. Your writing should guide your reader along a logical path of thought.

As you revise, check for appropriate emphasis. **Emphasis** is the quality in essays that makes the most important points stand out clearly in the reader's mind. You can achieve the proper emphasis by devoting more space to the most important ideas, by using transitional words and phrases to indicate relative importance, and by repeating the most important points.

**Writing Tip**

A good essay has **unity, coherence,** and **emphasis.**

## STRATEGIES FOR REVISING

Use the following strategies to improve your draft.

| REVISION STRATEGIES | |
|---|---|
| Adding | Add supporting details such as facts, examples, and incidents to explain your ideas more completely. |
| Deleting | Delete unnecessary words, phrases, and ideas that stray from your thesis statement. |
| Substituting | Substitute vivid words for ordinary words and specific details for general ones. |
| Rearranging | If your order is weak, rearrange sections or ideas and revise transitions to make the order clear. |

# USING AN EVALUATION CHECKLIST

An evaluation checklist like the one that follows can help you keep track of what you are looking for and what you have completed.

 **Evaluation Checklist for Revising**

### Checking Your Text as a Whole

✓ Does the introduction set the tone and capture attention? (pages 243–244)

✓ Does the thesis statement make your main idea clear? (page 242)

✓ Is your idea well developed, with substantial, relevant evidence and well-chosen details? (pages 245–248)

✓ Did you include information on all relevant perspectives, including an analysis of views and information that contradict the thesis statement and the evidence presented for it? (pages 233, 245, and 248)

✓ Does your essay have unity? Does the topic sentence of each paragraph relate directly to the thesis statement? (pages 88–89 and 250)

✓ Are the paragraphs arranged in a logical order? (pages 237–239)

✓ Do transitions smoothly connect the paragraphs? (pages 247–248 and 250)

✓ Did you use the techniques for achieving coherence between paragraphs? (pages 247–248 and 250)

✓ Did you devote the most space to the most important ideas? (page 250)

✓ Did you repeat key ideas to show their importance? (pages 247 and 250)

✓ Do you have a strong concluding paragraph? (page 249)

✓ Did you add a title? (page 251)

✓ Did you maintain a consistent tone throughout? (pages 243–244)

### Checking Your Paragraphs

✓ Does each paragraph have a topic sentence? (pages 88–89 and 250)

✓ Is each paragraph unified and coherent? (pages 93–96)

### Checking Your Sentences and Words

✓ Are your sentences varied, clear, and concise? (pages 59–72)

✓ Did you use specific words and sensory words? (pages 47–48 and 158–159)

✓ Did you include figurative language and other tropes? (pages 51–54 and 160–161)

✓ Did you use parallelism and other schemes? (pages 77, 120, and 301)

## PROJECT PREP *Revising* *Second Draft*

Based on the feedback from your writing group and from your teacher if you have it, produce a new draft of your text. In addition to all of the issues raised during your writing group discussions, make an effort to polish the grammar, spelling, and punctuation in this draft.

Your Personalized Editing Checklist will help you avoid the errors you are prone to make. As always, watch for the Power Rules.

## The Language of Power — *Of v. Have*

**Power Rule:** Use the contraction *'ve (not of)* when the correct word is *have,* or use the full word *have.*

**See It in Action** Confusing *have* for *of* is understandable because when spoken they often sound the same. In writing, however, using *of* instead of *have* or *'ve* would detract from the message by calling attention to an error. Notice the correct use of *have* in the following sentence from *My Life with Martin Luther King, Jr.*

> We finally decided that if the boycott was 60 percent effective we would be doing all right, and we would be satisfied to *have* made a good start.

**Remember It** Record this rule and example in the Power Rule section of your Personalized Editing Checklist.

**Use It** Read through your essay and look for each instance of *can, could, will, would, shall, should, may, might, must.* If *of* follows it, change it to *'ve* or *have.*

After revising and editing the final draft of your essay you are ready to share it.

### Publishing Options for Expository Writing

- a formal essay (see pages 33–34 for proper manuscript form)
- a magazine or newsletter article (see pages 82 and 86)
- a speech (see page 578 for a guide for presenting speeches)
- an electronic presentation (see pages 589–595 for using presentation software)
- a media presentation (see pages 596–601 for a guide for creating video presentations)

### PROJECT PREP — Polish and Share / Final Draft

Exchange your new draft with a writing partner and review one another's writing. Provide any final suggestions. Publish your finished writing through an appropriate medium.

# Using a Six-Trait Rubric  Expository Writing

Use the following rubric to evaluate your own or another's expository text.

| Ideas | **4** The topic, focus, and details convey information powerfully with valid inferences. | **3** The text conveys information, using valid inferences. | **2** Some aspects of the topic are not clear and/or well developed. | **1** Most aspects are not clear and/or well developed. |
|---|---|---|---|---|
| Organization | **4** The organization is clear and easy to follow. Transitions provide coherence. | **3** The organization is clear, but a few ideas seem out of place or disconnected. | **2** Many ideas seem out of place and transitions are missing. | **1** The organization is unclear and hard to follow. |
| Voice | **4** The voice sounds natural and knowledgeable and is appropriate for the audience. | **3** The voice sounds mostly natural and knowledgeable and is right for the audience. | **2** The voice sounds a bit unnatural and does not seem right for the audience. | **1** The voice sounds mostly unnatural or is inappropriate for the audience. |
| Word Choice | **4** Words are specific and figures of speech are used. | **3** Words are vivid and specific. | **2** Some words are overly general. | **1** Most words are overly general. |
| Sentence Fluency | **4** Varied sentences flow smoothly. Sentences vary in structure and length. | **3** Most of the sentences are varied and flow smoothly. | **2** Some sentence patterns are not varied and some sentences are choppy. | **1** Sentences are not varied and are choppy. |
| Conventions | **4** Punctuation, usage, and spelling are correct and all Power Rules are followed. | **3** There are only a few errors in punctuation, usage, and spelling and no Power Rule errors. | **2** There are several errors in punctuation, usage, and spelling and no Power Rule errors. | **1** There are many errors in punctuation, usage, and spelling and at least one Power Rule error. |

**TIME OUT TO REFLECT**

Compare your process of writing this expository text with the way you wrote earlier. In what ways have you improved your writing? What strategies have helped you do a better job of planning, drafting, and revising, such as setting a draft aside for a few days? Record your responses in your Learning Log.

# Writing Lab

## Project Corner

### Speak and Listen
### Make a Group Presentation

In your writing groups, discuss the following quote by former Supreme Court Justice Robert H. Jackson:

"It is not the function of the government to keep the citizen from falling into error; it is the function of the citizen to keep the government from falling into error."

Then, using examples from your expository texts or other examples you know of from history or current affairs, **make a presentation** to the rest of the class supporting or refuting that statement. Decide how you are going to divide up the presentation and run through it before delivering it so your presentation can be as smooth as possible.

### Read and Reflect Read Protest Literature

In small groups, **read and discuss a set of protest literature texts,** such as Thoreau's *Civil Disobedience,* Martin Luther King's *Letter from a Birmingham Jail, The Use and Need of the Life of Carrie A. Nation,* and other texts. Consider their arguments in light of those that you and your classmates have written, and consider the role of acts of conscience In society. **Write a reflection** expressing your insights.

### Show It Create a Multimedia Presentation

**Produce a multimedia presentation** based on the protest you have described, synthesizing images, graphics, and sounds from various media sources to reflect information from multiple points of view. Depict the problem, the protest, and the outcome. Be as creative as you can. Consider the specific audience to which you want to appeal and show your presentation to it.

# In Everyday Life
## Informative Letter

**Apply and Assess**

1. You lived in a peaceful neighborhood until a rock star moved into the house next door. Swarms of fans camp outside on the street, and he practices with his band until 2 a.m. **Write a letter to the rock star** explaining some of the problems you have with his behavior. Inform him of how you think he should behave as a considerate neighbor. (You can find information on writing letters on pages 531–538.)

# In Academic Areas Informative E-mail

2. As a scientist who specializes in animal behavior, you observe and record all activities of two chimpanzees, looking for ways they mimic human behavior. You have come to the conclusion that sometimes the chimps appear to be laughing at you. **Write an e-mail** to a colleague, informing him or her of your observations. Include a thesis statement that expresses the main idea clearly. (You can find information on writing e-mail on pages 534, 566, and 609–611.)

# Timed Writing 🕐 Letter to the Board of Education

3. Your history teacher is developing a virtual reality device that will create animated holograms of famous figures and events in history to make her lectures more interesting for her students. As a student representative, write a letter to the board of education about the device, informing the board of the educational benefits and requesting that it increase the funding for her project. You have 20 minutes to complete your work. (For help budgeting time, see pages 37 and 493.)

**Before You Write** Consider the following questions: What is the situation? What is the occasion? Who is the audience? What is the purpose?

Develop a thesis statement around which you can select and organize your details in a logical order. Decide whether the ideas should be organized in chronological order, spatial order, order of importance, or developmental order. Use transitional words and phrases to achieve coherence.

**After You Write** Evaluate your work using the six-trait evaluation form on page 253.

CHAPTER 7

# Expository Writing Workshops

When you want to convey information, choose the organizational model and method of development best suited to what you want to write. In a longer expository text, you may use a number of different methods for dfferent parts of your composition. The following workshops will help you decide how best to gather and present the information you want to convey.

##  How-To, or Procedural, Texts

A **procedural text** gives step-by-step instructions for making or doing something.

A process is a sequence of steps by which something is made or done. Procedural texts often appear in directions, user manuals, and handbooks. (See pages 562–564 for procedural texts related to the workplace and college.)

> ### MODEL: Procedural Text from a Handbook on Car Care
>
> ## Changing the Oil
>
> Changing the oil every 3,000 miles can add years of life to your car. To change the oil, you will need oil, a new oil filter, a basin, an oil filter wrench, and a wrench sized to fit your car's oil drain plug.
>
> - First check your owner's manual for the amount of oil and type of oil filter for your car. Place the basin under the oil drain plug and remove the plug with a wrench. When all the oil has drained—it will take about 20 minutes—replace the drain plug and tighten it with the wrench.
>
> - Next, locate the oil filter at the side or bottom of the engine and remove it with the oil filter wrench. Before you insert the new filter, use your finger to apply a layer of oil on the rubber gasket around the filter. Now screw the new filter onto the engine by hand until tight. (Using the filter wrench to tighten the oil filter can cause damage.)
>
> - Then locate and remove the oil filter cap on top of the engine and add the required number of quarts of oil. Replace the cap and check for leaks around the drain plug and oil filter. Tighten them if needed. Finally, use the dipstick to check the oil level and add more oil if necessary.

You can use a graphic organizer to help you organize your information for a procedural text. The chain links in this organizer represent transitions between steps.

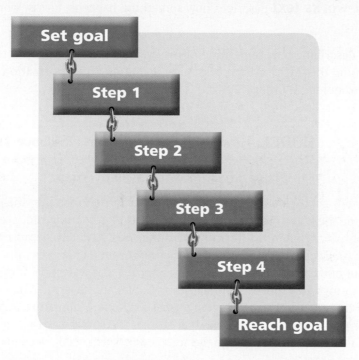

## QuickGuide for Writing Procedural Texts

→ Make a list of ingredients or materials needed, and a second list of the steps to follow, written in the correct order.

→ Use transitions such as *first, next, then, finally* to keep the order of steps clear.

→ Use formatting structures such as bullet points, boldface, or numbers.

→ Clearly state your purpose and fully support your viewpoint on the topic with facts and details.

→ Include relevant questions to engage readers and address their potential problems and misunderstandings.

→ Make sure that technical information is accurate and expressed in accessible language

## ● Create Real-World Texts

1. Write a set of instructions for an eighth or ninth grader on how to study for a test.

2. Write the steps for a young sibling on how to make breakfast.

3. Compose an e-mail to a friend describing the steps involved in using the computer to burn a CD or post a blog.

# ❷ How-It-Works Texts

A **how-it-works text** describes how something happens, forms, works, or is put together.

When you are describing how something forms, happens, works, or is put together, you are explaining the stages in a process or an operation. The information is usually arranged in chronological order.

**MODEL: How-It-Works Text from a Science Textbook**

## How Springs Arise and Form

Springs get their start when rain and melting snow seep into the ground. For a time the water remains there, filtering through the soil into layers and layers of rock, being purified naturally as it flows. Eventually, because this *groundwater* is lighter in weight than the rock around it, it rises until it finds a way out of the earth, where it becomes a *spring*. The water that forms the largest springs first collects in underground caves and caverns. When it finally reaches the surface, the spring often gushes forth like a miniature waterfall. In other places, trickles of groundwater seep in a leisurely way through their natural filters. When they rise to the surface they form small, deep pools of fresh, clear water.

Use the graphic organizer below to help you organize a how-it-works text. The arrows in this organizer represent transitions between steps.

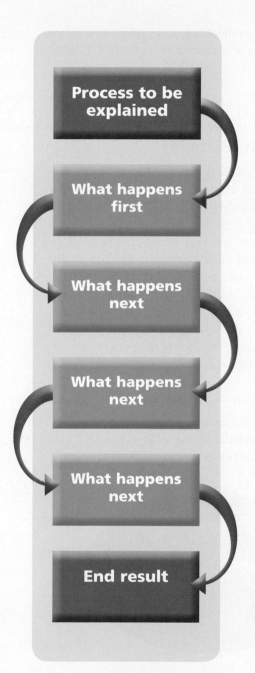

Process to be explained

What happens first

What happens next

What happens next

What happens next

End result

## QuickGuide for Writing How-It-Works Texts

→ List the steps or stages involved and put them in chronological order.

→ Use transitions such as *eventually, first, when, finally* to keep the order of steps clear.

→ Use appropriate formatting structures that explain or show how, such as illustrations or diagrams.

→ Clearly state your purpose and fully support your viewpoint on the topic with facts and details.

→ Include relevant questions to engage readers and address their potential problems and misunderstandings.

→ Make sure that technical information is accurate and expressed in accessible language.

## ● Create Real-World Texts

1. Write about a natural phenomenon you have observed or read about and explain how it happens.

2. Choose a manufactured item that interests you; research it and explain how it works.

3. Explain the logistics of a presidential election to a foreign-exchange student living with your family.

# ③ Compare-and-Contrast Texts

A **compare-and-contrast text** examines the similarities and differences between two subjects.

This type of paragraph will help you interpret, understand, and explain two related subjects or events (such as made-for-TV movies and movies made for the theater).

**MODEL: Compare-and-Contrast Text from a Book about Dogs**

## Boxers and St. Bernards

Dog breeds are often classified by the way people use them. The boxer and the St. Bernard, for example, are both working dogs; both are medium-to-large animals, and both are trained to help people. Yet there are interesting differences between them. The boxer was bred in Germany and was crossed with the bulldog during the 1800s. The St. Bernard, however, was developed during the 1600s by monks at the abbey of Saint Bernard in the Swiss Alps. Boxers normally weigh 60 to 75 pounds and stand 21 to 24 inches tall at the shoulder. In contrast, St. Bernards weigh from 165 to 200 pounds and stand 26 to 30 inches tall at the shoulder. Boxers make excellent companions for children and are often used as seeing-eye or hearing-ear dogs. St. Bernards, on the other hand, are best known as rescue dogs for people lost in the mountains; they also make excellent watchdogs.

Use a Venn diagram to list the similarities and differences between two subjects. In the area where the ovals overlap, note the characteristics the two subjects have in common. In the outer parts of the ovals, note the characteristics that are different.

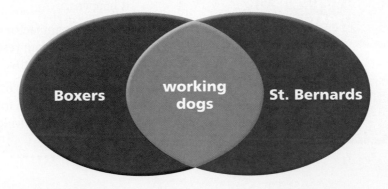

Boxers — working dogs — St. Bernards

# ORGANIZING COMPARISON AND CONTRAST

You can choose one of two patterns for organizing your information. In one pattern, called the **AABB pattern,** you include all that you have to say about subject A before you discuss subject B. You can discuss subject A in one paragraph and subject B in another paragraph, or you can explain both in the two halves of the same paragraph. In one section of the essay about Civil War generals Robert E. Lee and Ulysses S. Grant, the historian Bruce Catton uses this *AABB* pattern.

## MODEL: AABB Pattern of Organization

**(A) Lee** was tidewater Virginia, and in his background were family, culture, and tradition . . . the age of chivalry transplanted to a New World which was making its own legends and its own myths. **(A) He** embodied a way of life that had come down through the age of knighthood and the English country squire. . . . **(A) Lee** stood for the feeling that it was somehow of advantage to human society to have a pronounced inequality in the social structure. There should be a leisure class, backed by ownership of land; in turn, society itself should be keyed to the land as the chief source of wealth and influence. It would bring forth (according to this ideal) a class of men with a strong sense of obligation to the community; men who lived not to gain advantage for themselves, but to meet the solemn obligations which had been laid on them by the very fact that they were privileged.

**(B) Grant,** the son of a tanner on the Western frontier, was everything Lee was not. **(B) He** had come up the hard way and embodied nothing in particular except the eternal toughness and sinewy fiber of the men who grew up beyond the mountains. **(B) He** was one of a body of men who owed reverence and obeisance to no one, who were self-reliant to a fault, who cared hardly anything for the past but who had a sharp eye for the future. These frontier men . . . stood for democracy, not from any reasoned conclusion about the proper ordering of human society, but simply because they had grown up in the middle of democracy and knew how it worked. . . . No man was born to anything, except perhaps to a chance to show how far he could rise. Life was competition.

—Bruce Catton, *Grant and Lee: A Study in Contrasts*

The second way to organize a comparison and contrast essay is to use the **ABAB pattern.** In this pattern you point out one similarity or one difference between subject A and subject B and then go on to another similarity or difference. For instance, if you are contrasting travel by airplane and travel by car, you might start with one difference: the amount of time it takes to travel long distances. In a sentence or two, you would state that for long distances, travel by airplane is faster. Then you would go on to another difference: the expense. Later in his essay on Grant and Lee, Bruce Catton shifts to this ABAB pattern of organization.

## MODEL: ABAB Pattern of Organization

Yet it was not all contrast, after all. Different as they were—in background, in personality, in underlying aspiration—these two great soldiers had much in common. . . . Each man had, to begin with, the great virtue of utter tenacity and fidelity. **(A) Lee** hung on in the trenches at Petersburg after hope itself had died. **(B) Grant** fought his way down the Mississippi Valley in spite of acute personal discouragement and profound military handicaps. In each man there was an indomitable quality . . . the born fighter's refusal to give up as long as he can still remain on his feet and lift his two fists. Daring and resourcefulness they had, too; the ability to think faster and move faster than the enemy. These were the qualities which gave **(A) Lee** the dazzling campaigns of Second Manassas and Chancellorsville and won Vicksburg for **(B) Grant.**

—Bruce Catton,
*Grant and Lee:*
*A Study in Contrasts*

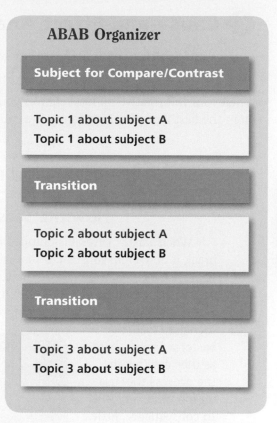

**AABB Organizer**

**Subject for Compare/Contrast**

Topic 1 about subject A
Topic 2 about subject A
Topic 3 about subject A

**Transition**

Topic 1 about subject B
Topic 2 about subject B
Topic 3 about subject B

**ABAB Organizer**

**Subject for Compare/Contrast**

Topic 1 about subject A
Topic 1 about subject B

**Transition**

Topic 2 about subject A
Topic 2 about subject B

**Transition**

Topic 3 about subject A
Topic 3 about subject B

## QuickGuide for Writing Compare-and-Contrast Texts

→ Choose two subjects and make a list of their similarities and differences. Use a Venn diagram to organize your ideas.

→ Choose an organizational pattern using either the AABB pattern or ABAB pattern.

→ Use transitions such as *similarly, in contrast, like, however,* to make the similarities and differences clear.

→ Include a clear introduction and conclusion.

## ● Create Real-World Texts

**1.** Compare and contrast race relations in your experience with race relations in the 1960s.

**2.** Compare and contrast the job opportunities open to a young person today as opposed to the job opportunities open to a young person of your grandparents' generation.

**3.** You've narrowed down your choice of colleges to two. Write a comparison and contrast text to help you make a decision about which one to attend.

# 4 Cause-and-Effect Analysis Texts

A **cause-and-effect text** explains why actions or situations (causes) produce certain results (effects).

When your informative subject requires you to explain *why* something happened, very often the best type of writing to use is a cause-and-effect paragraph.

---

**MODEL: Cause-and-Effect Text from a Science Magazine**

## How the Seas Become Polluted

When waste material is dumped into the sea, natural bacteria regularly break it down into substances that will not harm the fish or plants. But what happens when too much waste matter accumulates? The natural bacteria in the sea attempt to cope with the influx, but they cannot keep up with the amount of waste. As a result, the water grows dirtier and dirtier. Fighting the increased load, the bacteria work as hard as they can, but in the process they use up too much oxygen. In consequence, little of the precious gas is left for the fish and plants, and eventually they die. Their remains add even more waste matter to the water. Finally, the oxygen is used up. That is when, in the waste area, the sea itself "dies," choked by pollution.

---

In a graphic organizer, such as the one that follows, you can develop and organize a cause-and-effect text. You can start with the cause and explain the effects or start with the effect and explain the causes.

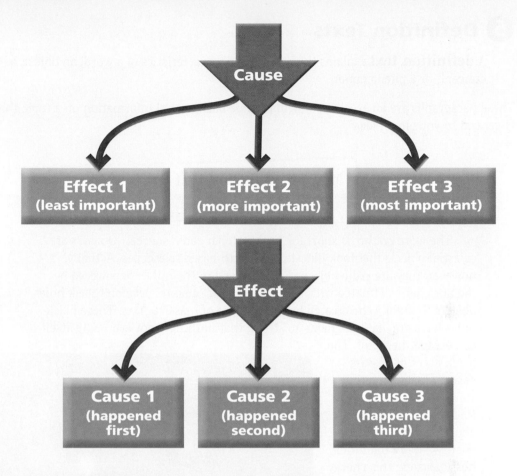

## QuickGuide for Writing Cause-and-Effect Texts

→ Choose an effect you want to analyze and identify the cause(s) of the effect.

→ Conduct research to gather information and verify your analysis.

→ Put the information in a logical order, and identify the event as a chain of causes and effects or as a cause with multiple effects or an effect with multiple causes.

→ Include a clear introduction and conclusion.

## ● Create Real-World Texts

**1.** Analyze the causes and effects of a serious wildfire or forest fire. Make posters to raise awareness of what students can do to prevent such fires.

**2.** Explain and interpret the causes and effects of a boycott, such as the bus boycott described by Coretta Scott King in *My Life with Martin Luther King, Jr.*

**3.** For your world history class, explain why the Silk Road came into being and the effects it had on European life.

# 5 Definition Texts

A **definition text** explains the nature and characteristics of a word, an object, a concept, or a phenomenon.

These paragraphs are an excellent way to provide background information on a topic that is central to your main idea.

## MODEL: Definition Text from an Encyclopedia

### What Is a Quasar?

The word *quasar* is short for "quasi-stellar radio source." Quasars are celestial objects that look like stars to Earth-based telescopes. Actually, however, they are radio objects—phenomena in the universe powered by radiant energy. Situated within "host galaxies," quasars develop "black holes," objects thought to be created by the collapse of massive stars. These black holes have gravitational fields so strong that nothing—not even light itself—can escape their pull. The black holes of quasars devour dust, gas, and stars from the host, and in the process produce enormous amounts of energy—more than their host galaxies. This energy accounts for their star-like brightness. Little else is known about quasars. It is hoped that Cygnus A, a new quasar discovered only 600 million light-years from Earth, virtually in Earth's backyard, will increase our knowledge of these mysterious entities.

A graphic organizer like the one on the following page can help you develop a definition text.

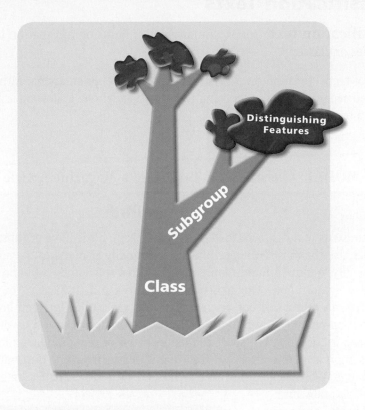

Distinguishing Features

Subgroup

Class

## QuickGuide for Writing Definition Texts

→ Research and list the qualities of the subject you want to define. Decide on an order to present the information.

→ Make sure your topic is narrow enough to define clearly. Then use everyday language to present the information for readers unfamiliar with the topic.

→ Include three basic parts: the subject you are defining, the class it belongs in, and the characteristics that make it different from other members of that class.

→ Include a clear introduction and conclusion.

## ● Create Real-World Texts

**1.** Define an aspect of your family heritage, such as a custom or an article of clothing worn for a certain holiday.

**2.** Define *democracy* or choose another concept from your social studies textbook to define.

**3.** Define *postmodernism* and how it appears in literature.

# ⑥ Classification Texts

A **classification text** groups similar types of items of information into separate categories or classes.

These kinds of texts are common in writing about natural phenomena. Although each class is treated separately, the parts come together as a whole. Following is an example of a classification text.

## MODEL: Classification Text from a Magazine Article on Birds

### Common Birds

Hundreds of birds form the class *aves,* or true birds. Five groups, however, are the most familiar. Pigeons are equally at home in the suburbs and the city. About 12 inches long, pigeons are a soft, sandy buff and sing a mellow "kooo-krooo." Cuckoos nest in pastures and orchards, grow to 12 inches, and are a soft buff or gray. Cuckoos are named for their song, a clear "cu-cu-cu-cu." Hummingbirds live in suburban parks and gardens. They are only 3 inches long but sport exquisite shades of red, orange, and green. Their song is a mere twitter, but their name comes from the humming of their wings. Woodpeckers nest in tree holes. From 7 to 9 inches long, they have black-and-white barred backs, and some wear black, red, or white caps. Their call is a loud "churr" or "chuck-chuck." Perching birds are a group of 60 common types of birds, such as sparrows and robins. They live in city parks, grasslands, and forests, and each has its own colors, markings, and call. Although each group is distinct, all enrich our lives with the sight of fluttering wings and the sound of birdsong.

The following graphic organizer can help you develop a classification text. Identify each category and the examples and descriptive details that help explain its characteristics.

**Topic:** _____

| | |
|---|---|
| **Category:** | |
| **Ideas & Information** | |
| **Category:** | |
| **Ideas & Information** | |
| **Category:** | |
| **Ideas & Information** | |

**Concluding Idea:** _____

## QuickGuide for Writing Classification Texts

→ Make a list of all the classes in a group and what they have in common.

→ Then identify the specific characteristics of each class and list these in a graphic organizer or chart.

→ Use transitions such as *similarly, all, although, each,* to make the common characteristics and specific characteristics clear.

→ Include a clear introduction and conclusion.

## ● Create Real-World Texts

1. Write a classification paragraph for a second grader about sports for kids that are played with a ball.

2. Write an e-mail to a pen pal in a different country classifying a group of animals that live near your home, such as birds, mammals, or reptiles.

3. Write notes for a museum tour of Native American cultures from the west coast of the United States to the eastern forests.

# 7 Analysis Texts

An **analysis text** examines a person, place, thing, or idea by breaking it into parts and showing how, together, they make a whole.

One common use of the analysis text is artistic or literary analysis, in which a work of art is examined in detail. The following is an example of an analysis text.

> ## MODEL: Analysis Text from a Web Site about Artistic Techniques
>
> ### A Pointillist Masterpiece
>
> The painting *Sunday Afternoon on the Island of La Grande Jatte* by French painter Georges Seurat is an example of the technique of *pointillism*. Unlike the Impressionist painters who strove to capture what the eye sees at a glance, Seurat, a post-impressionist, used a more controlled, scientific approach. Instead of brushstrokes, he composed the painting using tiny dots of color side by side. The color of each dot contrasts sharply with that of the one next to it. Yet when the painting is seen from a distance, the colors seem to blend into one another. Painting with dots, however, also forces the artist to simplify his figures. As a result, the couples on their Sunday outing look more like robots than real people. The shadowed and sunlit grass, the leaves on the trees, and even the water all resemble elements of a newspaper photo under high magnification. Despite these drawbacks, Seurat's canvas remains a triumph of color and light—and a joy to the eye.

A graphic organizer, like the one on the following page, can help you develop an analysis text.

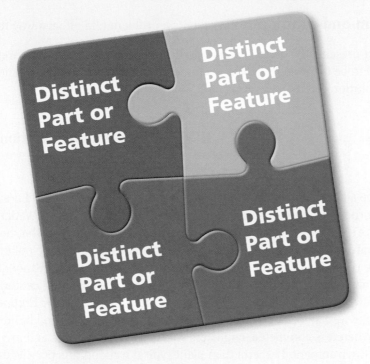

Distinct Part or Feature
Distinct Part or Feature
Distinct Part or Feature
Distinct Part or Feature

## QuickGuide for Writing an Analysis Text

→ Choose an object, an idea, or a profession and freewrite to capture some of its elements.

→ Organize the parts of the whole to analyze in a graphic organizer.

→ Use transitions such as *unlike, instead, yet, as a result* to show the relationships of ideas or parts.

→ Include a clear introduction and conclusion.

## ● Create Real-World Texts

1. Explain what it takes to become an engineer, musician, or pilot for an article on future careers.

2. Select a work of art you enjoy, either visual or literary, and examine it in detail for an arts magazine.

3. Explain how you are getting ready for life beyond high school. Analyze your preparations and explain how they fit together.

# 8 Problem-and-Solution Texts

A **problem-and-solution text** presents a problem and offers a way to solve it.

This type of text presents the details of a problem and outlines the steps that were followed or are proposed to be followed in finding a solution. The following is an example of a problem-and-solution text.

**MODEL: Problem-and-Solution Text**

## Engineering the Wetlands

We've all heard it before. A developer wants to destroy a wetland area to build another shopping center. Should this be allowed to happen? Wetlands are nature's way of preventing floods and recharging the aquifers that hold groundwater. Microorganisms in the wetlands break down organic pollutants, while the roots of wetland plants hold the soil and slow erosion. Although environmentalists would immediately lobby against the shopping center, there may be a way to placate both parties in the dispute. The solution? Engineer an artificial wetland. Suppose the shopping center is approved and building begins. When it is completed, engineers survey an adjacent area and prepare the soil. Environmental experts then plant typical wetland greenery. Water may be added until the new plants take hold. Finally, after the next big rain, runoff will flow into the artificial wetland, and nature can take over from there.

The following graphic organizer can help you organize a problem-and-solution text. Alter the graphic organizer to fit the specific problem and possible solutions to consider.

| Problem: | |
|---|---|
| **Causes** | |
| **Possible or attempted solutions** | |
| **Problems with those solutions** | |
| **Solution** | |
| **Why it will work** | |

## QuickGuide for Writing Problem-and-Solution Texts

→ Identify problems in several areas, choose one that appeals to you, and brainstorm or research a solution.

→ Analyze alternate solutions and show why they did not or would not work.

→ Use a graphic organizer to help you put your ideas into a logical order.

→ Use transitions to guide your reader through the parts of the problem or alternate solutions.

→ Include a clear introduction and conclusion.

## ● Create Real-World Texts

1. Write about how early school starts in the morning and the problem this causes for teenagers. Suggest a reasonable solution to present to the school board.

2. Your little brother is not supposed to ride his skateboard on the sidewalks or in the street, but he and many of his friends do, risking an accident. Write a letter to the editor of your local newspaper proposing a solution.

# Writing to Persuade

**P**ersuasive writing states an opinion and uses facts, reasons, and examples to convince readers to accept that opinion and/or take a specific action.

The following examples show ways people in different positions and professions use persuasive writing to influence others.

- **The school debate team persuades the audience** that it is more important to spend limited public funds on libraries than on parks.

- **A local newspaper columnist writes an editorial** about the environmental dangers of clearing land to build malls and parking lots.

- **You convince a neighborhood business to hire you** as a part-time worker.

- **A doctor explains the results of physical exams and tests** to persuade a patient to follow a new course of treatment.

- **A critic writes a rave review** that convinces crowds that they should flock to the theater to see a new play or hear a new band.

- **A community group** persuades their city council representative to upgrade Internet services in the neighborhood branch library.

## Writing Project — Argumentative

***Tech Talk*** *Write an argumentative essay about the effect on society of a specific technology.*

***Think Through Writing*** Each era has its own technological innovations. Even the pencil was once regarded as a new and exciting technology. In the 21st century, most technology is assumed to be electronic: new computer capabilities, new video streams, new telephone applications, new ways to interact online. While many people embrace new technologies, others fear that some technologies will create problems for humanity.

Write about a technology with which you are familiar, and take a position on its value to humanity. Will people benefit from, or be harmed by, this technology?

Consider as many issues as possible in your view of whether or not this technology will contribute to the progress of civilization.

**Talk About It** In your writing group, discuss the writing you have done. What technology did each author consider? What perspective did he or she take? What is the overall consensus on the role of technology in advancing civilization?

**Read About It** The following persuasive essay offers the opinion of a college professor who has strong beliefs about the value of Internet research. Follow his argument and decide whether he presents it effectively. What points does he make? Are they logical? Does he persuade you to accept his point of view?

## No Computer Can Hold the Past

*Robert Darnton*

Does the Internet help college students learn? Enthusiasts proclaim that it has made a world of information available to any freshman with a computer. Skeptics warn that cyberspace is so full of junk that research in it will never amount to anything more than garbage collecting.

As a college teacher who has just started a program for publishing historical monographs on the Web, I concede that the skeptics have a case. But the problem with doing research on the Internet is not about garbage. It's that, by doing all their homework on the Internet, students may develop a misunderstanding of research itself and even of the subjects they are studying.

Historical research takes place in libraries and archives, but it is not a straightforward process of retrieving information. You may open a box of manuscripts and confront information in the form of letters or diaries or memos. But this raw material isn't raw at all. It's cooked. Every document embodies some rhetorical convention, argues for some hidden agenda, must be read between the lines and related to all the surrounding documents.

Moreover, most documents never make it into archives—they didn't 100 years ago and they don't today, when government agencies shred, erase, or discard most of the material they produce. And far from taking place primarily in governments, history happens to everyone.

Darnton clearly lays out the opposing views on his subject in the introduction.

This statement offers a concession to the skeptics, with whom he ultimately disagrees.

The thesis statement is the final sentence of the introduction. It presents a more subtle position than either of the earlier positions Darnton identifies.

The argument begins building here, with background information.

Darnton uses figurative language here, extending the metaphor suggested by "raw" to an idea of "cooked" information.

Unfortunately for historians, the vast majority of humans have disappeared into the past, without leaving a trace of their existence. What remains amounts to nothing more than a tiny fragment of human experience, even though the components of that fragment could fill so many archival boxes that you couldn't get through a statistically significant sample of them if you read for centuries. How can you assemble a few pieces into a meaningful picture of the past?

The task seems daunting, yet our students arrive in class with the illusion that we've got history pretty well under control. It's in books, they think: hard facts bound between hard covers, and now we're making it all available online. How can we teach them that history is an interpretive science, not a body of facts; that it involves argument from evidence, not mere information; that it has no bottom line but is, by its very nature, bottomless?

To help students understand the nature of historical knowledge, we assign them research papers. Most of them will never open a box of manuscripts, but all of them can try to find a path of their own through printed sources scattered in a library. By studying texts and relating texts to one another, they can appreciate the tenuousness as well as the rigor involved in the attempt to make sense of the past. But instead of reading for meaning in books, many students search for information on the Internet.

Of course, the Internet can open up bibliographical pathways and can even provide digitized versions of primary sources. But no digitized text can duplicate the original—its handwriting or typography, its layout, its paper and all the paratextual clues to its meaning. We read the front page of a newspaper as if it were a map of yesterday's events. We gauge the importance of each article by the size of its headline, its position (lead story on the right, off-lead on the left, lighter fare below the fold) and by whatever photographs or sidebars may accompany it. If we merely read the article in isolation on a screen, we would miss the context that shapes its meaning.

Digitizers often dump texts onto the Internet without considering their quality as sources, and students often fail to read those texts critically. Instead, they scan them

This body paragraph offers another key supporting point, that most humans leave no record of their experience. What role does that idea play in building Darnton's argument?

In this body paragraph the background information in the preceding paragraphs is connected directly to the thesis statement.

Darnton makes an important distinction that ties back to the thesis statement.

This statement is another concession, even though Darnton does not exactly disagree.

Darnton uses the rhetorical scheme of analogy here, comparing how people read newspaper stories in the context of other stories, just as historians must read primary sources in context.

with search engines, locate key words, jump in at any point and cobble passages together by computerized cutting and pasting.

"Where do you find history?" I imagine asking the students of the future.

"On the Web," they answer.

"How do you get at it?"

"By surfing."

"What method will you use to write your paper?"

"Access, download, hyperlink and printout."

Such thoughts touch off Luddite[1] fantasies: smash all the computers and leave the Internet to drown in the ocean of its own junk. But that way madness lies, and my students have taught me that, if handled with care, the Internet can be an effective tool.

Last semester, I directed a student who was writing a research paper in Paris. After consulting me by e-mail, she followed the leads I gave her by logging on to French library catalogues. She located the relevant sources, read them, e-mailed drafts to me, rewrote extensively and got a well-earned A.

> Darnton provides a specific example of the Internet used as an effective tool.

The Web can provide a way to publish research in fields where the monograph has become an endangered species, owing to the costs of publishing conventional books. The American Historical Association, with a grant from the Andrew W. Mellon Foundation, is sponsoring a program, Gutenberg-e, to publish dissertations—not by dumping them unedited on the Internet but by reworking them into electronic books of the highest quality with skilled editors at Columbia University Press.

Instead of turning our backs on cyberspace, we need to take control of it—to set standards, develop quality controls and direct traffic. Our students will learn to navigate the Internet successfully if we set up warning signals and teach them to obey: "Proceed with caution. Danger lies ahead."

> The concluding paragraph reinforces the thesis statement but does not simply restate it. It ends with strong words.

---

1  **Luddite:** One who is opposed to technological change. The word comes from the name of textile workers in 19th century England who destroyed machinery they thought would eliminate their jobs.

**Respond in Writing** Identify in writing exactly what Darnton's position is. What, if anything, does he persuade you of, and why?

**Develop Your Own Idea Bank** Work with your classmates to develop ideas you might use to persuade readers of the effect of certain technology.

*Small Groups:* In your small group, discuss the writing you have done. Answer the following questions to help think of possible details for each author's argument.

| Questions for Developing Ideas |
| --- |
| • What is the technology discussed in the essay? |
| • What new capabilities do people have when they use this technology? |
| • In what areas of life is the technology designed to make human life better? |
| • What are the potential problems that might follow from development of and dependence on this technology? |
| • What are the potential benefits? |
| • What is the range of opinions about this technology? |
| • What is the overall conclusion about the consequences of the development and expanded use of this technology? |

*Whole Class:* Make a master chart of all of the ideas generated by the small groups for each question to see how different members of the class wrote about different technologies and what they mean to the future of civilization.

**Write About It** You will next write a persuasive piece in which you argue about the effects of a given technology on the quality of life in society. You might use any of the following possible topics, audiences, and forms for your writing.

| Possible Topics | Possible Audiences | Possible Forms |
| --- | --- | --- |
| • a biological technology, such as developing clones | • people who might use this technology | • a blog |
| • a computer technology, such as robots | • people who might fear this technology | • a letter |
| • a communications technology, such as a telephone that is a full-featured computer | • lawmakers | • an opinion column |
| • a gaming technology, such as a device that can play games with new capacities and speeds | • researchers | • a magazine article |
| | • people who might be harmed by this technology | |

A persuasive essay is like other essays in its structure but not in its substance. The core of a persuasive essay lies in its arguments—the logical presentation of facts designed to move the reader to believe or act in a certain way.

## 1 Structure

Like other kinds of essays, a persuasive essay is made up of three parts—an introduction, a body of paragraphs, and a conclusion. The following chart shows how to structure a persuasive essay effectively.

**HERE'S HOW**

### Structuring a Persuasive Essay

- In the introduction, present the issue and your position on the issue, which is expressed in a clear thesis statement.
- In the body of supporting paragraphs, present facts, reasons, statistics, incidents, examples, the testimony of experts, and other kinds of evidence to support your opinion.
- In the conclusion, provide a strong summary or closing that drives home your position.

Persuasion is a powerful tool and carries responsibility. Accuracy, fairness, and careful reasoning are the substance of responsible argumentation. A strong persuasive text

- presents information on the complete range of relevant perspectives and represents divergent views accurately and honestly, not a limited and distorted slice of the issue;

- incorporates complexities and discrepancies in information from multiple sources while anticipating and refuting counter-arguments, recognizing that matters worth arguing about are usually layered with complexities and characterized by disagreement among responsible thinkers;

- demonstrates an awareness and anticipation of audience response that is reflected in different levels of formality, style, and tone, acknowledging respect for the intelligence and ethics of the audience; and

- considers the validity and reliability of all primary and secondary sources, knowing that not all information sources are equally objective.

The following two editorials from *USA TODAY* were posted on a blog on the newspaper's Web site on September 24, 2009. The first was written by a *USA TODAY* editor. The second is a citizen's response to it. Both are about how federal money from the Airport Improvement Program, which provides grants to public-use airports, should be spent.

## Our view on taxing air travelers: Ticket taxes get diverted to fund tiny airfields

Thanks to Congress and the small-plane lobby, big airports lose out.

Every frequent flier knows how irritating air travel can be these days: long lines, cramped seats, extra fees for just about everything, and assorted government charges that drive up the cost of a typical $250 roundtrip ticket by 16%.

What most passengers don't realize, however, is that a wildly disproportionate amount of taxes they're paying for airport improvements goes to more than 2,800 fields across the USA that they'll never use. Unless, of course, they fly on the private planes that these small fields serve.

Since the Airport Improvement Program began in 1982, $15 billion—about a third of the money collected for the program—has gone to the smaller airfields with no scheduled passenger flights, according to a USA TODAY analysis published last week. By contrast, the nation's 30 largest airports, which enplaned more than 500 million passengers last year alone, got about $13 billion.

How to explain such a senseless allocation of taxes? It's the same two words responsible for earmarks[1] and other political distortions: Congress and lobbying.

At the start of this decade, Congress reworked the airport program to steer more money to the 2,834 smaller fields, which handle only "general aviation." How it happened is easy to understand. Private pilots with their own planes, and corporations that own jets, make up one of the most formidable lobbies in Washington. Just about every lawmaker has scores of pilots in his district, and many lawmakers have been frequent fliers on private planes. From 2001 to 2006, lawmakers took 2,154 trips on corporate jets, according to a study by Political Money Line, an independent research group.

This flow of forced largesse[2] from commercial air passengers brings business and services to small towns and helps connect rural areas with the rest of the country. Some small airports help relieve congestion at nearby

---

1 **earmarks:** Funds set aside for a specific project.
2 **largesse:** Great generosity.

**Thesis Statement**

This paragraph appeals to the reader's ethics or sense of fairness and right and wrong. The word "wildly" adds a strong emotion to the sentence.

The chief source of information, the USA TODAY analysis, is identified here, and facts from it are presented.

The argument offers an explanation of how the law came about and refers to a statistic from an independent (and theoretically unbiased) research report.

This paragraph anticipates a counter-argument that would focus on the importance of the small airports.

bigger airports. But it would be hard to find fliers who wouldn't rather keep their money or see it spent to improve the airports they use.

Besides, USA TODAY's analysis found that half of the small fields are within 20 miles of another private-aviation airport, making many redundant. And in seven states analyzed, 90% of the private-aviation airports operate at less than one-third capacity. For example, the Williamsburg-Whitley County Airport in Kentucky—built with $11 million in federal funds and boasting a 5,500-foot lighted runway and colonial-style terminal—sees just two or three flights a day.

The powerful groups that represent private pilots (the Aircraft Owners and Pilots Association has been dubbed "the NRA[3] of the air") argue that commercial airports have other sources of federal funds, which they do, and that the nation's small airfields are akin to the nation's highway and road system, which is just silly. Virtually everyone in the nation drives a car, rides in cars or buses as a passenger, or benefits from products moved on the nation's highways. That's not the case with private-aviation airfields, where projects are financed mostly by taxes on passengers who never set foot in them.

We don't argue that this network is unnecessary. The Airport Improvement Program, however, wasn't intended to be a piggy bank for the small-plane lobby. Air passengers shouldn't have their pockets picked to fund an extravagance that benefits a select few.

_____

3  **NRA:** National Rifle Association, known for its powerful pro-gun lobby.

## Opposing view: Small airports benefit all

*Craig Fuller*

Surveys tell us people view general aviation as an important part of our national transportation system. But, we also know GA is not well understood. It comprises all flying except scheduled airlines and the military. That means law enforcement, firefighting, air ambulance, search-and-rescue, traffic reporting, package

> One specific and very dramatic example is offered as supporting evidence that the money to small airports may not be well spent.

> The comparison to the NRA is potentially insulting and appeals to strong emotions about gun control.

> The editorial here is expressing the relative value of ideas, agreeing with the argument that commercial airports have other federal funding sources but calling the comparison to the nation's highways "just silly," far from neutral language.

> The term "piggy bank" is another word with a negative connotation.

> This author also refers to information gathered from a theoretically unbiased source, although he does not name the actual surveys.

delivery and more fit under the "general aviation" banner. In short, GA provides services that millions of Americans and thousands of American businesses rely on every day.

Just as highways crisscross the nation, serving small towns and big cities, so the nation's more than 5,000 public-use airports link communities of all sizes. Commercial air carriers serve fewer than 150 of those airports. That's like having a highway system that connects only the country's 150 largest cities.

Just as every driver pays taxes that fund road maintenance and development, so every person who flies pays taxes to maintain the airport and air traffic control system. You might never drive to the tens of thousands of small communities served by our national highway system, and you might never visit thousands of small airports that make up our aviation system. But because those roads, and airports, serve the public good, we all pay a share for their maintenance.

Many public-use airports, large and small, are eligible to receive federal funding for infrastructure maintenance and improvement. In fiscal 2007, GA airports that received federal grants got an average of $750,000 each. That same year, commercial air carrier airports that received funding got an average of $5.5 million each—more than seven times the amount awarded to smaller fields.

Small airports create jobs and development opportunities, attract businesses and allow them to grow. In fact, GA is responsible for creating some 1.2 million jobs and contributing $150 billion annually to America's economy.

And general aviation airports relieve congestion and reduce delays at the big airline airports. Without them, thousands more flights would crowd into already overburdened airports, slowing traffic, increasing delays and adding to security lines.

A robust general aviation system is a valuable national asset and vital transportation link serving millions of Americans every day. Let's keep it that way.

—Craig L. Fuller, president and CEO of the Aircraft Owners and Pilots Association.

The author does indeed use the example the original editorial said the opposing view would present, but he then turns it to downplay the importance of the largest airports.

The author evaluates the relative value of facts by referring to the total federal funding large airports get rather than just the funds from the Airport Improvement Act.

This paragraph appeals to readers' sense of fairness by pointing out the economic value of small airports. It may also appeal to readers' fears of job loss if the airports are not supported.

The newspaper published Craig Fuller's information in part to help readers understand both Fuller's credentials for responding and also any possible bias he may have.

## Practice Your Skills

### Considering a Range of Views

Based on these two editorials and any additional research you do, form a position on the subject of the Airport Improvement Program and the way it distributes funds. Then write a few paragraphs that

- consider the complete range of relevant perspectives on the topic of Airport Improvement Fund spending and represent divergent views honestly and accurately;

- incorporate complexities and discrepancies in information from different sources while anticipating and refuting counter-arguments; and

- consider the validity and reliability of all sources.

Share your paragraphs with a partner and discuss how honest and accurate you were, how successful was your anticipation and refutation of counter-arguments, and how careful was your analysis of the validity and reliability of sources of information.

---

### PROJECT PREP  Planning  To-Do List

Based on the work you completed in the previous activity, think through the tasks you will need to accomplish to complete your argumentative essay. For example, on the project about the effects of a certain technology, what strategies can you use to locate a range of relevant perspectives on the subject? Will you conduct a survey? conduct research in the library or online? interview people who can give you your information? How will you know what counter-arguments to anticipate and how to refute them? Create a "to-do" list for your persuasive text that will serve as a roadmap for your project. Share your list with your writing group members and compare notes. Begin gathering information. Consider the validity, reliability, and relevance of the primary and secondary sources you find and choose those that will provide the strongest evidence for your essay.

# ❷ Facts and Opinions

Every persuasive essay includes both facts and opinions. The soundness of the essay hangs on the writer's awareness of the difference between the two: facts can be proven true while opinions cannot.

A **fact** is a statement that can be proved.

An **opinion** is a judgment that cannot be proved.

Opinions cannot be proved, but some can at least be supported with convincing evidence.

An **arguable proposition** is an opinion that can be backed up with facts.

Arguable propositions, as their name implies, can be argued. Opinions that express only personal preferences, on the other hand, are not worth arguing, for there are no facts to support them.

| | |
|---|---|
| **Arguable Proposition** | The performers' waiting room should be painted green. (Experiments have provided evidence that green has a calming effect.) |
| **Preference** | Green is a prettier color than blue. (No facts are available to back up this statement.) |

Opinions need to be supported by facts, not by other opinions. As a writer, be sure to back up every opinion with facts. As a reader, be on your guard for unsupported opinions and for opinions offered up as facts. Remember that only arguable propositions form a solid basis for a persuasive essay.

## ● Practice Your Skills

### *Identifying Arguable Propositions*

Identify each statement as an arguable proposition or a preference.

1. Airplane rides are more exciting than train rides.
2. There should be more rigorous training for flight mechanics in order to improve airline safety.
3. Aircraft of the future will be controlled by computers.
4. An airplane takeoff is the most thrilling sight there is.
5. Air traffic controllers should have more frequent rest periods in order to perform more effectively.
6. After a number of flights, flying loses its excitement and becomes monotonous.

## ● Practice Your Skills

### *Supporting Opinions with Facts*

Write one fact that, if verified, you would accept as evidence to back up each of the following arguable propositions.

**Example**         The guitar is one of the most versatile of musical instruments.

**Possible Answer**   The guitar is used in playing folk, classical, and rock music.

1. Too much television watching can have a harmful effect on performance in school.
2. Raising fines can help keep people from speeding.
3. Americans should consume more fruits and vegetables.
4. Electrical appliances should not be used near water.
5. New sources of energy should be developed.
6. On hot days joggers should run only in the morning.
7. Using a computer makes writing easier and more fun.
8. Police work has become increasingly dangerous.
9. Eva Ramirez is a better candidate than Nelson Gooden.
10. The minimum age for a driver's license should be eighteen.

## ● Practice Your Skills

### *Analyzing Persuasive Writing*

In a newspaper or other publication, choose an editorial or some other piece of persuasive writing. List the opinions and facts you find in the text. Then identify each opinion as either a preference or an arguable proposition. Finally, write a paragraph explaining the argument presented and expressing your opinion of its soundness, using the arguable propositions to support your analysis. Save your work for later use.

## PROJECT PREP  *Planning*  *First Steps*

Review your to-do list and identify the first steps you will take in carrying out your plan. As you proceed, be alert to the thesis statements you encounter as you gather the range of relevant perspectives on your subject. Which are appropriate for a persuasive text, and which might just express preference? Begin to think about the kinds of thesis statements you might develop. For example, you might assert that new video game capabilities make gaming more fun but also so engrossing that young people develop few other areas of interest and the development of their social skills is inhibited. Discuss your possible propositions with your writing group and evaluate the extent to which each author has grounds to substantiate them in his or her essay.

# ③ Appeals to Reason

Facts by themselves do not form a solid argument. What do the facts mean? Why are they relevant? How do they fit together? Interpreting facts in these ways to construct an argument requires reasoning power, or logic.

**Logic** is clear, organized thinking that leads to a reasonable conclusion. You can reach conclusions through inductive reasoning and deductive reasoning. One way to persuade your audience is to appeal to their reason with your clear thinking. In rhetoric, appealing to logic or reason is called **logos.**

## INDUCTIVE REASONING AND GENERALIZATIONS

**Inductive reasoning** is a formal term for something that you do quite naturally, that is, use known facts to make a generalization. A **generalization** is a statement about a group of things based on observations about a few items in that group.

**Writing Tip**

Use inductive reasoning to form a generalization based on known facts about particulars.

The following chain of thoughts about naval officers shows inductive reasoning.

| | |
|---|---|
| **Specific Fact** | A fleet admiral is the highest officer in the navy. |
| **Specific Fact** | A fleet admiral wears one large gold stripe and four smaller gold stripes. |
| **Specific Fact** | An admiral is lower in rank than a fleet admiral. |
| **Specific Fact** | An admiral wears one large gold stripe and three smaller gold stripes. |
| **General Conclusion** | The rank of naval officers can probably be detected by the number of gold stripes on their uniforms. |

Notice the word *probably* in the general conclusion. The conclusions reached by the inductive method should always be qualified or limited in some way. They should be open to new evidence. Suppose, for example, you learned these new facts about navy uniforms.

| | |
|---|---|
| **New Fact** | A commodore wears one two-inch gold stripe. |
| **New Fact** | An ensign wears one half-inch gold stripe. |
| **New Fact** | A commodore has a much higher rank than an ensign. |

The first conclusion equated rank with the number of gold stripes. However, if both a commodore and an ensign wear just one stripe, that conclusion cannot hold. The conclusion, however, can be revised to accommodate the new facts, as follows:

**Revised Conclusion**     The rank of navy officers can probably be detected by the number and size of the gold stripes on their uniforms.

**Hasty Generalizations**  Beware of **hasty generalizations**—generalizations that are too broad. The writer of the following paragraph attempts to use inductive reasoning but arrives at a conclusion too hastily. The hasty generalization is highlighted.

## MODEL: Hasty Generalization

If you dislike hot weather, you need to avoid not only the obvious places in the South and Southwest, but also a more surprising "hot spot" in the Northeast. I have visited Boston three times, and every time I have been there the temperature has been 90 degrees or above. My first visit took place in late spring 2005. On the day I arrived, the mercury reached 95 degrees. I was there again in the summer of 2007 when the temperature hit 98 degrees. In September 2009, I passed through Boston again, and the temperature reached 91 degrees. Heat haters, beware! Boston is one of the hottest cities in the nation.

The writer bases the generalization on only three days over a four-year period. In addition, the writer fails to compare Boston's temperatures with those of other cities. The hasty generalization could have been avoided by using the following guidelines.

**Avoiding Hasty Generalizations**

- Examine a sufficient number of facts and examples.
- Be sure your examples are representative of the whole group.
- Check reliable authorities to confirm the generalization.
- Be able to explain any exceptions.
- Limit the generalization by using words like *some, many, most.*
- Avoid words like *all, complete, always, never, none.*

*Using Inductive Reasoning*

Read each set of facts below. Then write a generalization based on the facts.

**Facts**         Two weeks ago my new computer froze. On the day it
froze, the weather was very hot and humid. Yesterday, on
a hot and humid day, my computer froze again.

**Generalization**    High temperature and high humidity sometimes cause a
computer to freeze.

1. **Facts:** At my brother's college, my cousin's college, and my friend's
college, more students major in business than in liberal arts.
2. **Facts:** When the Chicago White Sox meet the Toronto Blue Jays in
Chicago, "The Star-Spangled Banner" is played before "O Canada." When
the Chicago White Sox meet the Toronto Blue Jays in Toronto, "O Canada"
is played before "The Star-Spangled Banner."

## DEDUCTIVE REASONING

While induction moves from the particular to the general, deduction moves from
the general to the particular. In **deductive reasoning,** you begin with a general
statement and then apply it to a particular case. The following chain of thoughts
illustrates the deductive process.

**Generalization**    No mail is delivered on legal holidays.

**Particular**        Today is a legal holiday.

**Conclusion**        Therefore, no mail will be delivered today.

Use deductive reasoning to prove that what is true about a group (general) will be true
about an individual member of that group (particular).

The steps in the deductive process can be expressed in a three-part statement called a
**syllogism.** Each part of the syllogism has a name.

**Major Premise**     All members of the jazz band are seniors.

**Minor Premise**     Kristin is a member of the jazz band.

**Conclusion**        Therefore, Kristin is a senior.

In the following example, on the other hand, the conclusion is not logical even if both of
the premises are true.

| Major Premise | All members of the jazz band are seniors. |
|---|---|
| Minor Premise | Kristin is a senior. |
| Conclusion | Therefore, Kristin is a member of the jazz band. |

The fact that Kristin belongs to the larger group, seniors, does not guarantee that she belongs to the smaller group, the jazz band. The conclusion is illogical, or **invalid.**

A syllogism is *sound* if the premises are true. A syllogism is *valid* if the reasoning is logical.

### ● Practice Your Skills

*Recognizing Flaws in Deductive Reasoning*

Each syllogism below is unsound or invalid. Write *unsound* if the premises are not true. Write *invalid* if the reasoning is illogical.

**1.** All late papers will be given failing grades.

Bill's paper was given a failing grade.

Therefore, Bill's paper was late.

**2.** All southern states begin with the letter M.

Florida is a southern state.

Therefore, Florida begins with the letter M.

**3.** All four-legged animals are cows.

My cat is a four-legged animal.

Therefore, my cat is a cow.

### ● Practice Your Skills

*Using Deductive Reasoning*

Study the following example of deductive reasoning. Then supply the logical conclusion for each of the following sets of premises.

| Example | All city officials live within the city boundaries. Sal Savetti is a city official. |
|---|---|
| Answer | Therefore, Sal Savetti lives within the city boundaries. |

**1.** All Triple Crown winners have won the Kentucky Derby. Seattle Slew was a Triple Crown winner.

**2.** All bowling team members must have a minimum average of 175. Carlos is a bowling team member.

**3.** All of the fruit in this basket is either apples or oranges. This piece of fruit from the basket is not an apple.

**4.** All Marx brothers movies are comedies. *A Day at the Races* is a Marx brothers movie.

**5.** The seniors do not have to come to school this Thursday and Friday. Jonathan is a senior.

## COMBINING INDUCTIVE AND DEDUCTIVE REASONING

The arguments in a persuasive essay are not neatly arranged in three-part syllogisms. Actual reasoning normally involves a back-and-forth process of induction and deduction. For example, a writer may gather evidence in order to draw a general conclusion (induction) and then use that conclusion as the premise of a syllogism (deduction).

| | |
|---|---|
| **Evidence** | Scientific studies have shown that walking, running, and swimming benefit the heart and lungs. |
| **Conclusion** | Aerobic exercises benefit the body. |
| **Major Premise** | Aerobic exercises benefit the body. |
| **Minor Premise** | Dancing is an aerobic exercise. |
| **Conclusion** | Therefore, dancing benefits the body. |

One famous example of combining inductive and deductive reasoning is the Declaration of Independence. This document can be viewed as an essay that sought to persuade Great Britain and the rest of the world that the American colonies were justified in severing their ties with the British Crown. As you read the following excerpt from the Declaration of Independence, use the side labels to help you follow the reasoning.

---

**MODEL: Combining Inductive and Deductive Reasoning**

### Declaration of Independence

We hold these truths to be self-evident, that all men are created equal, that they are endowed by their Creator with certain unalienable Rights, that among these are Life, Liberty and the pursuit of Happiness. That to secure these rights, Governments are instituted among Men, deriving their just powers from the consent of the governed. That whenever any form of Government becomes destructive of these ends, it is the ●——— Major Premise Right of the People to alter or to abolish it, and to institute new Government. . . .

Such has been the patient sufferance of these Colonies; and such is now the necessity which constrains them to alter their former Systems of Government. The history of the present King of Great Britain is a history of repeated injuries and usurpations, all having in direct object the establishment of an absolute Tyranny over these States. To prove this, let Facts be submitted to a candid world. . . .

**Minor Premise of a Syllogism**

He has refused his Assent to Laws, the most wholesome and necessary for the public good.

He has combined with others to subject us to a jurisdiction foreign to our constitution, and unacknowledged by our laws; giving his Assent to their Acts of pretended Legislation:

For quartering large bodies of armed troops among us:

For protecting them, by a mock Trial, from punishment for any Murders which they should commit on the Inhabitants of these States:

**Facts Supporting Minor Premise**

For cutting off our Trade with all parts of the world:

For imposing Taxes on us without our Consent:

For depriving us in many cases, of the benefits of Trial by Jury.

In every stage of these Oppressions We Have Petitioned for Redress in the most humble terms:

Our repeated Petitions have been answered only by repeated injury. A Prince, whose character is thus marked by every act which may define a Tyrant, is unfit to be the ruler of a free people. . . . We, therefore, the Representatives of the United States of America, in General Congress, Assembled, appealing to the Supreme Judge of the world for the rectitude of our intentions, do, in the Name, and by Authority of the good People of these Colonies, solemnly publish and declare, That these United Colonies are, and of Right ought to be Free and Independent States. . . .

**Conclusion**

CHAPTER 8

The Declaration of Independence is based on a deduction that can be expressed in the following syllogism.

| Major Premise | When a government violates natural rights, the people have a right and duty to abolish it. |
| Minor Premise | The British Crown violated the natural rights of the colonists. |
| Conclusion | Therefore, the colonists have a right and duty to break their ties with Great Britain. |

Inductive reasoning also plays its part. The minor premise—that Great Britain violated the colonists' rights—is a generalization based on specific facts presented about the behavior of the king.

● **Practice Your Skills**

*Analyzing Persuasive Writing*

Continue the analysis of the selection you began on page 285. Complete a chart that lists any facts or evidence, generalizations, major premise, minor premise, and conclusion you find in the text. Then write an additional paragraph that discusses inductive and deductive reasoning as well as the soundness of the reasoning and the conclusion.

**PROJECT PREP** *Planning* **Appeals to Reason**

Return to the possible propositions you developed and discussed with your writing group. What reasoning strategies would you use to develop your argument? Where, for example, might you use deductive reasoning, and where inductive reasoning? Discuss these questions with your writing group and help each author come up with some possible reasoning strategies.

**Appeals to Emotions and Ethical Beliefs**

In addition to appealing to reason, effective persuasive writers make appropriate appeals to the emotions and ethical beliefs of their readers.

Thomas Jefferson appealed to more than just the reasoning power of the colonists when he wrote the Declaration of Independence. Look at the emotional words he used.

| EMOTIONAL WORDS: BRITAIN | | EMOTIONAL WORDS: COLONIES |
|---|---|---|
| • injuries | • mock trial | • wholesome |
| • usurpations | • murder | • public good |
| • absolute tyranny | • imposing | • humble |
| | • depriving | • free people |
| • refused | • oppressions | • rectititude |

Using emotional language is one way to **appeal to emotions.** Another is to provide examples that create sympathy, such as the story of a sick child in a poor family in an argument that health care needs to be reformed. In rhetoric, an appeal to emotions is called **pathos.** Some appeals to emotion are effective and appropriate. Going too far, however, can weaken your argument by making it seem that you may not have enough substance to appeal to reason.

Jefferson also understood the power of appealing to a "higher power," the system of **ethical beliefs** that guide the course of a citizen's behavior.

> We hold these truths to be self-evident, that all men are created equal, that they are endowed by their Creator with certain unalienable Rights, that among these are Life, Liberty and the pursuit of Happiness. That to secure these rights, Governments are instituted among Men, deriving their just powers from the consent of the governed. That whenever any form of Government becomes destructive of these ends, it is the Right of the People to alter or to abolish it, and to institute new Government. . . .

This paragraph lays out the principles of Enlightenment thought about government. The words reflecting the appeal to ethical beliefs are highlighted.

**PROJECT PREP** *Planning* **Appeals to Emotions and Ethics**

In your writing group, help each author think of two possible audiences for his or her persuasive text. Then discuss the appeals each author might make to both the emotions of each audience and their ethical beliefs. Keep notes of these ideas.

# In the Media

## A Political Campaign

There's a tight race for mayor in your city. The hot issue in the election is new development in the downtown area. Incumbent mayor Anita Rodriguez favors large-scale development, arguing that more businesses downtown will make more tax money available for social services. Her closest challenger, Sam Silver, a local business owner, believes a more moderate development makes sense. He's afraid an overdeveloped downtown will result in empty storefronts and traffic problems. The third candidate, Florence Channing, is a minister. She believes that a more run-down part of town should be redeveloped first to give residents in that community a share in the benefits of new development.

How will the candidates persuade enough people to vote for them so that they can carry through on the positions they have taken? Form a group to choose one of the candidates and plan a political media campaign.

## Steps for Planning a Political Campaign

- Decide which of your candidate's qualities you want to highlight.
- Determine what group of voters would be most likely to support your candidate.
- Determine what campaign events you want your candidate to take part in.
- Think of effective slogans and/or graphics to use on a campaign poster.
- Sketch out a newspaper ad including graphics and text.
- Write scripts for a 15-second radio ad and a 30-second television ad for your candidate. Decide what kinds of stations to play them on and explain your reasons.
- List three themes for your candidate to focus on in televised debates. What advice would you give about how to talk about the opponents? Why?

After each group has made its presentation, compare campaigns. What do they have in common? What was memorable about each? What kind of relationship was there between the candidate's position and his or her campaign slogan and other media products?

The prewriting stage is the most critical in the development of a persuasive essay. Take time to prepare and organize your arguments thoroughly. The more carefully you think through your position, the more forcefully you will be able to present it. In the prewriting stage, you will choose your subject, develop your thesis, and gather and organize your evidence.

## ① Purpose, Subject, and Thesis Statement

### PURPOSE

As you prepare to write a persuasive essay of your own, always keep your purpose in sight. Your efforts at every stage are directed at finding a means of convincing the reader to think a certain way or to act a certain way. Clear, logical arguments, appropriate appeals to emotions and ethical beliefs, and a strong, consistent approach to your position are your most effective tools.

### CHOOSING A SUBJECT

The world is full of opinions, but not every opinion makes a good subject for a persuasive essay. Only certain issues will stir your thoughts and your emotions. Furthermore, of the many opinions you hold, only some will be arguable propositions. Others, such as a liking for apples over pears, would be difficult to defend. Only an issue that you care about and that you can support makes an appropriate subject for a persuasive essay.

Try to be more aware of the controversial issues all around you—in the newspapers, on TV, in your school, and in your home. Notice matters about which you can say, "I think" or "I believe." Brainstorm or freewrite answers to questions such as "What do I care about?" When you have accumulated a list of possible subjects, use the following guidelines to help you choose among them.

 **Guidelines for Choosing a Subject**

- Choose an issue that has at least two sides.
- Choose an issue that you feel strongly about.
- Choose an issue for which there is an audience whose belief or behavior you would like to influence.
- Choose an issue that has a position you can support with facts, examples, and reasons.

# DEVELOPING A CLEAR THESIS STATEMENT

Once you have selected a subject, you should develop a thesis statement. Often the statement will be a recommendation that includes a word such as *should, ought,* or *must.* Stay away from statements of fact or preference, for they do not make suitable thesis statements for a persuasive essay.

> **Fact**        In some areas wolves are near extinction.
>
> **Preference**    I am horrified by the killing of wolves.
>
> **Thesis**       Laws protecting wolves must be strengthened.

After you write your thesis, ask yourself the following questions. If your thesis does not meet all of these guidelines, you should rethink your position or look for a more appropriate issue.

## Guidelines for Developing a Thesis Statement

- Can you state the thesis simply in one sentence?
- Is the statement either a judgment or a recommendation rather than a fact or a preference?
- Is the point of view debatable as you have expressed it? Can you think of any opposing arguments?
- Is the thesis statement based on logical reasons?

## ● Practice Your Skills

### *Identifying Suitable and Unsuitable Thesis Statements*

Write whether each statement is suitable or unsuitable for a persuasive essay and why.

1. Despite its potential for education, television has developed into a negative influence.
2. Our society is becoming too dependent on computers.
3. We must learn to make better use of the sun for energy.
4. The incidence of violent crime in our nation is horrifying.
5. We must all learn to respect one another more.

**PROJECT PREP**   *Prewriting*   *Focusing Your Subject*

Given your previous discussions with your writing group, choose the topic you would most like to write about and focus your subject clearly enough so that you can develop an effective thesis statement for it. Share it with your writing group to be sure it accomplishes the purposes of a thesis statement and represents an arguable proposition.

**Knowing Your Audience**

To prepare the most effective argument possible, you need to know where your readers stand on the issue. If you are addressing readers who agree with your position, but whom you wish to persuade to take action, you would make appeals that reinforce your shared beliefs and focus on the need for action. If you are addressing readers who disagree with you, however, you will need to make stronger appeals to convince them, and you will need to know the reasoning, emotions, and ethical beliefs they have that led them to their opposing positions. Anticipating your audience's response to your argument will also affect the level of formality, tone, and style that you use. Use a worksheet like the following to help you understand your audience, anticipate their questions and concerns, and devise ways to address those concerns persuasively.

## AUDIENCE WORKSHEET

| | | | |
|---|---|---|---|
| **Range of Positions** | (describe the extremes of the position and the various positions that lie between them) | | |
| **Where My Audience Stands** | (identify where on the spectrum your audience is) | | |
| **Understanding Their Position** | **Their Reasoning** (study their arguments) | **Their Emotions** (put yourself in their position and try to feel as they do) | **Their Ethical Beliefs** (understand the higher principles that guide their lives) |
| **How I Can Address Their Position (Counter-arguments)** | **Appeals to Reason** (identify any flaws in their thinking) | **Appeals to Emotions** (try to find common emotional ground) | **Appeals to Ethical Beliefs** (respect their beliefs and work within them) |
| **What I Concede** | (identify the areas where your audience disagrees with you but has a good point that you accept) | | |

**PROJECT PREP** *Prewriting* *Choosing and Analyzing Audience*

Choose the audience you wish to address in your persuasive text (see the project possibilities chart on page 278 for ideas) and create and complete a worksheet like the one above to understand your audience thoroughly. Consider the different levels of formality, tone, and style you might use depending on how you think the audience will respond to your argument.

# ③ Developing an Argument

With your audience in mind, list arguments they might find convincing and then search for the appropriate evidence. You will want to find information on the complete range of relevant perspectives so that you can anticipate and refute counter-arguments that oppose your position. Your evidence will normally take the form of facts, examples, incidents, reasoning, and expert opinions. This needed information can be found in library reference material, books, magazines, newspapers, personal interviews, and your own experience. Once you have collected evidence and evaluated it, use the following guidelines to help you build an argument.

## Guidelines for Developing an Argument

- List all positions in your prewriting notes and be prepared to represent them honestly and accurately and address the opposing views.
- To support your opinion, use facts and refer to well-respected experts and authorities who support your opinion.
- If the opposing view has a good point, admit it. Conceding a point in this way will strengthen your credibility.
- Use logical reasoning, both deductive and inductive, to pull your evidence together and draw conclusions from it.
- Express your arguments in polite and reasonable language.

## ● Practice Your Skills

### Listing Pros and Cons

For each of the following thesis statements, list three facts, examples, incidents, or personal experiences that support the statement and three that oppose it. Save your notes in case you want to develop your own pros and cons later.

**1.** A greater percentage of our tax money should go to improving education.

**2.** We should make our holidays less commercial.

**3.** Speed limits on all highways should be raised to 75 miles per hour.

**4.** For many people a college education is the most important investment for the future.

---

**PROJECT PREP** *Prewriting* *Developing an Argument*

With your writing group, talk through the arguments you can make for a persuasive position. Your classmates may see a flaw in reasoning that you missed or may be able to suggest additional points. After your discussion, write notes summarizing what you verbalized. Follow up on research you began earlier, and finish gathering information.

# Think Critically

## Evaluating Evidence and Sources

When you write to analyze and persuade, you make your argument convincing by presenting evidence that strongly supports your opinions. When you choose facts, examples, incidents, statistics, and expert opinions, you use the skill of evaluating to judge the strength of each to support your position. To evaluate a piece of evidence, use the following criteria.

- Is evidence clearly relevant to the thesis and up to date?
- Is the source of the evidence reliable?
- Is the evidence unbiased and objective?

Suppose, for example, that you are arguing in favor of allowing seventeen-year-olds in your state to vote in primary elections. The following chart shows how you could evaluate evidence on this issue.

| EVIDENCE | EVALUATION |
|---|---|
| Polls show that seventeen-year-olds are as knowledgeable as eighteen-year-olds. | Supports thesis—explains logical reason to extend vote to seventeen-year-olds. |
| A low percentage of eighteen-year-olds turn out to vote. | Does not support thesis—evidence focuses on eighteen-year-olds. |
| Seventeen-year-olds claim that such a law will encourage civic awareness. | Does not support thesis—source of evidence may be biased and not objective. |

You also need to evaluate the validity, reliability, and relevance of the primary and secondary sources you use for your evidence. (See pages 396–398 for more on evaluating sources.) When you draft, demonstrate the consideration you gave to the validity of sources by identifying why they can be trusted or what their limitations might be.

## Thinking Practice

Choose one of the arguable propositions below or one based on an issue that is important to you. Think of relevant facts. Then make a chart like the one above to evaluate the evidence for your position.

1. Leash laws should be strictly enforced in public parks.
2. Public libraries should be open longer hours.
3. Good personal grooming is essential to obtaining a job.

# 4 Organizing an Argument

After you have gathered the information you need to build your argument, you should organize your ideas in a logical way that is appropriate to your purpose, audience, and context.

For example, if your **purpose** is to convince people that your solution to a problem is the best one, you would probably structure your text following a problem-solution pattern. (See pages 272–273.) Or maybe you want to structure your text like a comparison-contrast text, alternating opposing views with your views and showing why yours are stronger. (See pages 260–263.) If your **audience** is policymakers deciding on funding for a new law, you might want to intersperse personal stories from citizens with your hard evidence in support of your view. If your **context** is that you are responding to a magazine article you read via a letter to the editor, you would probably want to follow the structure of other letters to the editor you have read. There is no one "right" way to organize a persuasive text. The right way is the way that takes your purpose, audience, and context into account.

Many persuasive essays use order of importance or developmental order. Spatial order and chronological order do not usually serve the persuasive purpose as well. Whatever organization you choose, use transitions like the following to guide the reader through your arguments.

### TRANSITIONS FOR CONCESSION OR CONTRAST

| | | |
|---|---|---|
| although | despite | even though |
| admittedly | nevertheless | still |
| however | nonetheless | while it is true that |

---

**PROJECT PREP** *Prewriting* *Organizing an Argument*

Using your notes from discussions and the information you have gathered, sketch out an organizational plan for your persuasive text. Then, in your writing group, focus your attention on each author's plan for sequencing the major claims of the argument, presenting evidence, and anticipating and refuting counter-arguments. If any points seem out of synch, help the author figure out if the point should be included in the final version of the essay or whether it should be revised, moved, or discarded.

# The Power of Language

## Parallelism: The Power of 3s

A **parallel structure** is one in which three or more ideas are expressed in the same grammatical form. Parallelism helps readers understand related ideas. In the following example from "No Computer Can Hold the Past" by Robert Darnton (pages 275–277), three parallel clauses are separated by semicolons. The spacing in the sentence is altered so you can see the parallelism clearly.

> How can we teach them
>
> that history is an interpretive science, not a body of facts;
>
> that it involves argument from evidence, not mere information;
>
> that it has no bottom line but is, by its very nature, bottomless?

Parallelism can not only emphasize the relationship of ideas; it can also help generate them. The pattern of gerund phrases in the second sentence below from a speech by President George W. Bush gives rise to new ideas.

> We have seen the state of our Union in the endurance of rescuers, working past exhaustion. We've seen the unfurling of flags, the lighting of candles, the giving of blood, the saying of prayers—in English, Hebrew, and Arabic.

## Try It Yourself

1. Write a sentence on your topic that uses parallelism as the first example does.
2. Write a sentence with at least four parallel gerund phrases like the second example.

If you can, use these sentences in your draft to make comparisons of related ideas. When you revise, you can look for even more places to add parallelism.

**Punctuation Tip**

When using parallel clauses that contain internal commas, separate the clauses with semicolons. (See pages 976–977.)

If you have been thorough during the prewriting stage, then drafting should essentially involve putting your prewriting notes together in fluent sentences.

### Drafting an Argument

- Introduce your subject in a way that makes your thesis clear and that captures attention.
- Present various forms of support (facts, reasons, common sense, expert opinions).
- Represent the complete range of relevant perspectives accurately and honestly.
- Demonstrate that you considered the validity and reliability of the sources you used.
- Use carefully crafted language to move audiences who are either neutral or opposed.
- Use an appropriate level of formality, tone, and style for your audience.

Begin by writing your thesis, which you may want to refine. Then write an introduction that includes the thesis. Because your introduction will explain your subject and state your position, you must capture the reader's attention. Make the reader both aware of the importance of the subject and interested in what you have to say.

Next draft the body of the essay, devoting one or more paragraphs to each main topic in your outline. In addition to presenting your own supporting evidence, anticipate and refute counter-arguments; concede points where appropriate. Also remember to add transitions to guide the reader. Finally, write a concluding paragraph that summarizes your argument and, if appropriate, urges the reader to take action.

## USING PERSUASIVE RHETORIC

In general you will be more persuasive if the tone of your essay is calm and reasonable. Inflamed, emotional language may persuade your reader not to support your proposition.

| | |
|---|---|
| **Inflamed** | Nasty, unruly dogs are terrorizing decent citizens. |
| **Reasonable** | We need a leash law to discourage pet owners from allowing their animals to run free. |

If you choose your words carefully, you can make effective use of **persuasive rhetoric**—language with strong positive or negative connotations that appeals to the reader's emotions. Be sure to support your statements with facts.

| | |
|---|---|
| **Persuasive Rhetoric** | Tens of thousands of our precious young people are killed or maimed each year by drunk drivers. |

## ● Practice Your Skills

### Using Persuasive Rhetoric

Rewrite each sentence below using calm, persuasive rhetoric to replace inflammatory, emotionally charged words and expressions.

1. The swindling scoundrels on the city council ought to be run out of town.
2. The airlines must inspect and repair their rattletraps to prevent millions of innocent travelers from being mangled and mutilated in fiery crashes.
3. The riffraff who foul our roadways and rivers should be forced to live in their own trash.

## ESTABLISHING BELIEVABILITY

In addition to appealing to the ethical beliefs of your readers, you also need to present yourself as a trustworthy and ethical person worthy of believing. In rhetoric, the credibility of the author is called **ethos.** As you draft, be aware of the voice you are using and how you can demonstrate your ethical standards.

---

### PROJECT PREP  Drafting  *Organizing an Argument*

Draft your persuasive text, following the plan you made and the guidelines on these pages. Then meet with your writing group for the following activities:

1. Focus your attention on each author's introductory paragraph. Has the writer taken the guiding proposition and developed it into a clear thesis statement? Does the remainder of the introductory paragraph extend the thrust of the thesis statement? On the technology topic, help each author clarify the thesis statement and focus the introductory paragraph of the essay on the specific effects of the target technology.

2. Next help each author develop body paragraphs so that each paragraph is centered on a specific claim that is related to the paper's thesis statement. For each claim, consider whether the examples offered are based on solid evidence such as facts, and help each author evaluate the evidence offered.

3. For each body paragraph, help each author explain why each example illustrates the claim on which the paragraph is centered; such statements are known as *warrants* and often include a word such as *because*. (See pages 116–117 and 245–246 for more on claims and warrants.)

4. Focus attention on the rhetoric used in the draft. Is it crafted carefully to be persuasive? If not, how can it be improved?

5. Discuss how believable each author seems. What accounts for that? If an author needs to come across as more believable, what can he or she do to achieve that?

6. Discuss how effectively each author concluded his or her persuasive text.

---

No matter how carefully you have prepared and drafted your essay it can still benefit from revising. You may need to bolster your opening, strengthen your arguments, refine your language, or add evidence. Review your essay several times, focusing on a different aspect each time. However, reserve at least one reading to check your logic, looking especially for the fallacies discussed below.

## ① Eliminating Logical Fallacies

A **fallacy** is a flaw in reasoning like the hasty generalization and the faulty syllogism discussed on pages 287–289. The following six fallacies also merit special attention, since they often surface in a poorly reasoned argument.

### ATTACKING THE PERSON INSTEAD OF THE ISSUE

This fallacy is often called *argumentum ad hominem,* which is Latin for "argument against the man." Writers who commit this fallacy target the character of their opponent instead of the real issue.

| | |
|---|---|
| **Ad Hominem Fallacy** | Senator Moreland has missed every important vote this year. How could his new bill have any merit? |
| **Ad Hominem Fallacy** | Don't vote for Marla Firth. She's just a housewife. |

Although Moreland's voting record may be irresponsible, his new bill may have merit. Just because Firth is a housewife does not mean her political positions are unworthy.

### EITHER-OR/IF-THEN FALLACIES

Writers guilty of these fallacies assume that there are only two sides to an issue; they ignore other viewpoints. Notice how the following issues are limited to two choices.

| | |
|---|---|
| **Either-Or Fallacy** | Either we stop using nuclear power for energy or we face certain disaster. |
| **If-Then Fallacy** | If you are against the new social center, then you are against the young people of our town. |

In the first example, "certain disaster" might be averted by better nuclear waste management. In the second example, the plans for the social center might be faulty. Between the two extreme positions on most issues lie a number of valid viewpoints.

# THE FALLACY OF NON SEQUITUR

In Latin, the words *non sequitur* mean "It does not follow." You have already seen in syllogisms (pages 288–289) some examples of conclusions that do not necessarily follow from the evidence. Most non sequiturs are the result of illogical deductive thinking.

**Non Sequiturs**     My sister liked this book; therefore, it must be good.

John's car was more expensive than mine; he must be richer than I am.

Like the fallacy of either-or, the non sequitur can neglect possible alternatives. Judgments about the quality of books vary greatly, and your sister's taste may not match your own. John may have gone into serious debt to buy an expensive car.

## CONFUSING CHRONOLOGY WITH CAUSE AND EFFECT

This fallacy assumes that whatever happens after an event was caused by that event.

**Cause-Effect**     On my birthday I wished that I would win something. That week I won two concert tickets in a raffle. Wishing really works!

The roof collapsed today because of yesterday's snowfall.

In the first example, only coincidence relates the two events. In the second example, the snowfall may have contributed to the collapse of the roof, but it may not have been the only cause. If the roof had been sound, it probably could have withstood the snowfall. Such errors in reasoning often result from failing to consider more than one cause.

## FALSE ANALOGIES

An **analogy** is a comparison between two things that are alike in significant ways. A **false analogy** attempts to compare two things that are not enough alike to be logically compared.

**False Analogy**     The phone company's discontinuation of my service was unfair, since even a criminal gets one phone call.

There are no logical grounds for comparing the situation of a free citizen who has not paid his or her telephone bill with that of a person arrested for a crime.

## BEGGING THE QUESTION

A writer who "begs the question" builds an argument on an unproved assumption.

> **Begging the Question**
>
> That unethical doctor should not be allowed to practice medicine.
>
> George Bernard Shaw was a great playwright because he wrote a number of superb plays.

In the first example, the writer bases the conclusion on the unproved assumption that the doctor is unethical. The second sentence provides an example of **circular reasoning.** All the sentence says is that Shaw was a great playwright because he was a great playwright.

## ● Practice Your Skills

### Identifying Fallacies

Write the letter for the fallacy committed in each statement.

**A.** attacking the person instead of the issue

**B.** either-or/if-then

**C.** non sequitur

**D.** confusing chronology with cause and effect

**E.** false analogy

**F.** begging the question

1. Either you allow the hunting of wolves, or you end up with slaughtered farm animals.
2. The dog is barking; someone must have rung the doorbell.
3. The sun reappeared after the cave dwellers chanted a hymn during the eclipse. The chanting must have caused the sun to reappear.
4. I didn't hear Jennifer's speech, but I know I disagree with it. She's always so disorganized!
5. These unnecessary taxes are a burden on taxpayers.
6. Just as a car needs gasoline to keep running, a hospital needs volunteers.
7. If you don't clean your room, then you obviously do not care what people think about you.

**PROJECT PREP** *Evaluating* *Logical Fallacies*

In your writing group, read each author's essay for logical fallacies of the sort reviewed above. If an author uses a fallacious means of reasoning, point it out and suggest alternative ways to substantiate the point.

# ❷ Avoiding Propaganda Techniques

As you listen to or read the literal meanings of words, pay attention to any hidden purposes or motives behind those words. Also attend carefully for the writer's point of view or bias. What is the intent of a commercial, an editorial, or a political speech? **Propaganda** misrepresents or distorts information or presents opinions as if they were facts. Do not confuse propaganda with persuasion. In persuasion the writer uses facts, evidence, and logical arguments to promote a viewpoint. In propaganda, on the other hand, the writer uses emotional language, exaggeration, and sometimes scare tactics to win people over.

## BANDWAGON APPEALS

The **bandwagon appeal** tries to get you to do or think the same thing as everyone else. Often bandwagon appeals are used in advertising to make customers feel inadequate if they do not buy a certain product. These appeals are used in politics to make potential voters feel that they must support a particular candidate or risk being out of step with everyone else.

> Rosemary Filippo has the support of all our city workers. She has the support of the young, the middle-aged, and the seniors. Rosemary Filippo has the support of all the people! Doesn't she deserve your support too?

## TESTIMONIALS

A famous person's endorsement of a product is called a **testimonial.** A testimonial, however, can be misleading because it often suggests that because the famous person uses the product or endorses it, the product is so good that everyone else should also use it. A testimonial may suggest that using the product will give you the same success as the famous person endorsing it. The following testimonials are misleading for both of these reasons.

> I'm Jeff Strong. I hope you liked my last movie, *Muscle Head*. When I auditioned for the movie I wore my InvisiVision contact lenses. Glasses are a bother when I am doing all those action shots. So get yourself some InvisiVision lenses if you want to be a star!

> I'm Dunk Hooper, basketball player of the year. I rely on more than sheer leaping power for my high-altitude hoopitorial acrobatics. I wear Hiptop Footflyers with the "energy booster" heel. Try Footflyers and you too will enjoy life above the rim.

## GLITTERING GENERALITIES

Careless thinking about general ideas can lead to a reasoning problem called **glittering generalities.** These are words and phrases most people associate with virtue and goodness that are used intentionally to trick people into feeling positively about a subject.

Here are some words that typically stir positive feelings in people.

| | | |
|---|---|---|
| Democracy | Family | Motherhood |
| Values | Moral | Education |

When one of these words is attached to a controversial idea, chances are the writer or speaker is trying to force you to evoke your positive attitude toward this idea. For example, suppose a politician says, "This new law is a threat to the liberty we cherish." He or she presumes you value liberty and will oppose the new law rather than surrender your freedom.

When you recognize a glittering generality, sometimes called a "virtue word," slash through it by asking yourself these questions, recommended by the Institute for Propaganda Analysis.

### Recognizing Glittering Generalities

- What does the virtue word really mean?
- Does the idea in question have any legitimate connection with the real meaning of the word?
- Is an idea that does not serve my best interests being "sold" to me merely by its being given a name that I like?
- Leaving the virtue word out of consideration, what are the merits of the idea itself?

### ● Practice Your Skills

*Analyzing a Glittering Generality*

Analyze the following glittering generality by writing answers to the four questions above.

> "Unrestricted Internet access in the schools threatens the very foundation of the American family."

### PROJECT PREP   *Evaluating*   *Propaganda Techniques*

In your writing group, review each author's essay to identify any glittering generalities, bandwagon appeals, or other means of spurious argumentation. If authors employ such methods, help them see the problem and make the point in a more logically responsible way.

**Using a Revision Checklist**

Use the following checklist to go over your persuasive text one more time.

 **Evaluation Checklist for Revising**

*Checking Your Introduction*

✓ Is the thesis statement clear and based on logical reasons? (pages 279 and 296)

✓ Does the introduction capture attention? (page 302)

*Checking Your Body Paragraphs*

✓ Does each paragraph have a topic sentence? (pages 88–89)

✓ Is each paragraph unified and coherent? (pages 93–96 and 119)

✓ Have you consistently used an organizing structure appropriate for your purpose, audience, and context? (page 300)

✓ Have you supported your main points? (pages 298 and 302)

✓ Have you evaluated your evidence and sources and demonstrated that you have done so? (pages 298–299 and 396–397)

✓ Have you presented the whole range of relevant perspectives and accurately and honestly worded opposing views? (pages 279 and 300)

✓ Have you anticipated and refuted counter-arguments? (pages 279, 297–298, and 436)

✓ Did you concede a point if appropriate? (pages 297–298, 300, and 302)

✓ Did you avoid logical fallacies? (pages 304–306)

*Checking Your Conclusion*

✓ Does your conclusion summarize the main points? (pages 279 and 302)

✓ Do you restate your thesis forcefully? (page 279)

✓ Have you asked your reader to take some action, if that was your purpose? (pages 297 and 302)

*Checking Your Words and Sentences*

✓ Does your level of formality, tone, and style reflect the audience's anticipated response? (pages 279 and 297)

✓ Have you used carefully crafted language to move a neutral or opposed audience? (pages 300–303)

✓ Did you use rhetorical language appropriately? (pages 51–54)

✓ Are your emotional appeals, if any, sincere and restrained? (page 293)

**PROJECT PREP**  *Using Feedback*

Based on feedback from your writing group, use the checklist to revise your essay. In this draft, also make sure that you use proper spelling, grammar, and punctuation so that your readers respect you as an articulate and erudite person whose views cannot be ignored.

As you edit your persuasive essay, watch for spelling errors, such as the use of *right* for *write* or *capitol* for *capital*. If you are using a word-processing program, you can use the Spell Check feature, but remember that it will not catch usage errors. Go back over quoted material to check on the spellings of the names of people and organizations. Then check your punctuation. As you work, refer to your Personalized Editing Checklist to avoid the kinds of errors you have made before. Ask someone else to do a quick reading of your work.

# The Language of Power    *Agreement*

**Power Rule:**  Use verbs that agree with the subject. (See pages 826–853.)

**See It in Action**  In some sentence constructions, you may have trouble identifying the subject, or the subject may be separated from the verb. These constructions are often the source of mistakes in agreement. In the following example from "No Computer Can Hold the Past" by Robert Darnton, the subject is *What remains*.

> What remains amounts to nothing more than a tiny fragment of human experience…

Since the word *remains* can be a noun or a verb, it can be misunderstood as a plural subject that would call for the use of the verb *amount*. You might understand the proper construction Darnton used by substituting "is left" for the word *remains*.

Separated subjects and verbs can also be tricky. In the following example, the singular subject *amount* is separated from the verb by a prepositional phrase that contains many plural items, possibly tempting a writer to use a plural verb.

> The vast amount of public records, private letters, and everyday documents makes the historian's task endless.

**Remember It**  Record this rule and example in the Power Rule section of your Personalized Editing Checklist.

**Use It**  Read your persuasive text looking only for the subject and verb in each sentence and making sure they agree. Try ignoring any phrases that separate the subject and verb to help you check for agreement.

Let your solid evidence and skillful appeals carry the day in your persuasive text, and avoid such weakening filler phrases as "In my opinion," "I believe," "as far as I can see." Edit your essay one more time to eliminate these wasteful and ineffective terms.

## PUBLISHING

You might publish your persuasive essay by reading it aloud to your classmates, sharing it with your family, making a recording of it, or placing the printed version in a collection of essays written by the class.

You might send it to a local or regional newspaper, to a teen magazine, or to a magazine that deals specifically with the issue you wrote about. Reference books from your library or media center can explain how to go about submitting a manuscript to a magazine or to a publishing company. The Internet also provides many publishing opportunities—Web pages, wikis, blogs, and more. Whatever method you choose, keep a copy of the essay for yourself.

## POWER PRESENTATIONS

Consider how images, graphics, and sound might add to the persuasive power of your argumentative text. You can include visuals, sound, and text using presentation software to create a persuasive essay that will make a strong impression and effectively represent and synthesize multiple viewpoints.

Presentation software is easy to use and can produce some powerful effects. For example, when presenting different points of view, you might use juxtaposition—placing slides that emphasize different viewpoints next to each other for contrast. Here are some other points to keep in mind as you prepare an audience-friendly persuasive presentation.

### Tips for Creating Effective Multimedia Presentations

**Content**

1. Keep it simple. Keep text to a minimum.
2. Include only the most important information.
3. Limit the number of bullet points per slide. Three or four should be the maximum.

**Images and Video**

4. Make sure the images and video support your key points.
5. Do not use graphics just as decoration.
6. Limit the number of words you use.

### Language

7. Use parallel language. For example, if the first bullet point is a complete sentence, the second should be too.

### Fonts

8. Heavy fonts are easier to read from a distance than light ones.

9. Keep the font size large enough to be seen easily at the back of the room.

10. Use only two font styles per presentation.

**PROJECT PREP** Editing and Publishing *Final Form*

Exchange papers with a writing partner, and read each other's essays with a critical eye. Provide any feedback that would help your partner produce an error-free text. Then publish your finished essay through an appropriate medium. You might, for instance, find a technology discussion board on the Internet and submit your essay to the discussion. Other possibilities included in the chart on page 278 are

- a blog
- a letter
- a newspaper opinion column
- a magazine article

If you have chosen one of these, discuss how its format would make different requirements on the writer and make any necessary adjustments before publishing.

**TIME OUT TO REFLECT**

Evaluate your persuasive text in writing using the rubric on the next page. Think about other persuasive texts you have written. Do you think they would have received about the same evaluation? Have you learned anything about writing persuasion since the last time? Answer these questions and keep them, with your evaluation record, in your writing portfolio.

# Using a Six-Trait Rubric **Persuasive Writing**

Use the rubric below to evaluate the effectiveness of your persuasive text.

| | | | | |
|---|---|---|---|---|
| **Ideas** | **4** The thesis statement is clear. Evidence is solid and there are no logical fallacies. Rebuttals are effective. | **3** The thesis statement is clear. Most evidence is solid and there are no logical fallacies. Some rebuttals are effective. | **2** The thesis statement could be clearer. Some evidence is solid, but there is one logical fallacy. Rebuttals are weak. | **1** The thesis statement is missing or unclear. Some evidence is solid, but there are logical fallacies. No rebuttals are offered. |
| **Organization** | **4** The organization is clear and suitable to the purpose, audience, and context. Transitions are abundant. | **3** A few ideas seem out of place or transitions are missing, but overall the organization suits the purpose, audience, and context. | **2** Many ideas seem out of place and transitions are missing; the organization could be more appropriate. | **1** The organization is unclear and hard to follow. |
| **Voice** | **4** The voice sounds natural, engaging, and believable. | **3** The voice sounds natural and engaging. | **2** The voice sounds mostly natural but is weak. | **1** The voice sounds mostly unnatural and is weak. |
| **Word Choice** | **4** Words are specific and powerful. Language is respectful and carefully crafted. | **3** Words are specific and language is respectful. | **2** Some words are too general and/or emotional. | **1** Most words are overly general and emotional. |
| **Sentence Fluency** | **4** Varied sentences flow smoothly. | **3** Most sentences are varied and flow smoothly. | **2** Some sentence are varied but some are choppy. | **1** Sentences are not varied and are choppy. |
| **Conventions** | **4** Punctuation, usage, and spelling are correct. The Power Rules are all followed. | **3** Punctuation, usage, and spelling are mainly correct and Power Rules are all followed. | **2** Some punctuation, usage, and spelling are incorrect but all Power Rules are followed. | **1** There are many errors and at least one failure to follow a Power Rule. |

# Writing Lab

## Project Corner

### Speak and Listen
### Oral Presentation

Think through a typical day. How many times do you use electronic technology? What types do you use everyday? Use your imagination to describe a day without technology. What would your life be like, in real, concrete terms, without the technology you usually use? **Prepare an oral presentation describing a day in such a life.** Practice your presentation before delivering it to the class, and be creative in how you will use gestures, vocal changes, and movement to make your points.

### Change Genres Write Science Fiction

**Write a science fiction short story** about the technology you have written about. Rather than explaining Its consequences logically, illustrate these consequences through the actions of your characters. Develop an engaging plot and use dialogue.

### Get Technical Make a Multimedia Presentation

**Create a multimedia presentation** using the very technology you choose as the subject of your presentation. For example, give a power presentation about presentation software, make a video about making videos, write and record a song for YouTube about YouTube, or think of any of your own ideas for a presentation. Be sure you have a focused point to make in your presentation.

# In Everyday Life
## Persuasive E-mail

1. You have just moved into a tiny one-room apartment when you receive a letter from a friend who says she is coming to visit. She plans to bring along her Saint Bernard, three cats, and her pet emu and would like to stay for six weeks. ***Write an e-mail*** convincing your friend that she should not stay with you. Make sure you have a thesis statement and support your thesis with facts and opinions. (You can find information on writing e-mails on pages 534, 566, and 609–611.)

# For Oral Communication Persuasive Speech

2. The city council in your town is considering banning skateboarders from the city parks. You love skateboarding and are upset about the prospect of skateboarders being banned. ***Prepare a persuasive speech*** to be delivered to the city council at their next meeting supporting your view that skateboarding should be allowed in city parks. Remember to acknowledge opposing views and to avoid making hasty generalizations. (You can find information on writing speeches on pages 574–576.)

# Timed Writing ⏱ Letter to the School Board

3. At the high school you attend a group of students who are upset by the performance of the soccer team have been circulating a petition to have the name of the team changed to the Weasels. The soccer team has been named the Lions for over thirty years, and you do not see any good reason for changing it, whether the team wins or not. Write a letter to the school board convincing them not to change the name of the soccer team. Remember to have a thesis statement and to support your thesis statement with reasons, facts, and examples. Make appropriate appeals to the board members' emotions and ethical beliefs. You have 20 minutes to complete your work. (For help budgeting time, see pages 37 and 493.)

***Before You Write*** Consider the following questions: What is the situation? What is the occasion? Who is the audience? What is the purpose?

***After You Write*** Evaluate your work using the six-trait evaluation form on page 313.

## CHAPTER 9

# Writing About Literature

**A** **literary analysis** presents an interpretation of a work of literature and supports that interpretation with appropriate responses, details, quotations, and commentaries.

Here are some examples of how the skills of thinking, writing, and speaking about literature are used both in school and in life.

- **Students read and analyze passages from works of literature for college admissions tests,** standardized tests, and class tests.

- **An innovative theater group decides to perform a well-known play as a musical.** They transform the dialogue into songs and include interpretive dance numbers to express certain scenes.

- **A group forms a club to read and discuss books** as well as to share experiences and to socialize.

- **An Internet entertainment magazine previews one chapter of an author's upcoming memoir.** Readers are invited to chat online with the author about the experiences she relates in the book.

## Writing Project *Interpretive Response*

*Literary Analysis* *Analyze a literary work and write an interpretation of it using quotations from the work.*

*Think Through Writing* Think about a short story, novel, play, or poem that you like, and write about why you think that the author wrote it. What is the point of the literary work?

*Talk About It* In your writing group, discuss the writing you have done. What kinds of points did people identify for literature that they like?

*Read About It* In the following short story, the narrator recalls a man named Mr. Gessler who put quality above everything else. Read the story first for enjoyment. As you read it a second time, consider how you bring your own experience, whether similar or vastly different, to the short story. How would you begin to write a literary analysis of this short story?

# Quality

*John Galsworthy*

I knew him from the days of my extreme youth, because he made my father's boots; inhabiting with his elder brother two little shops let into one, in a small by-street—now no more, but then most fashionably placed in the West End.

That tenement had a certain quiet distinction; there was no sign upon its face that he made for any of the Royal Family—merely his own German name of Gessler Brothers; and in the window a few pairs of boots. I remember that it always troubled me to account for those unvarying boots in the window, for he made only what was ordered, reaching nothing down, and it seemed so inconceivable that what he made could ever have failed to fit. Had he bought them to put there? That, too, seemed inconceivable. He would never have tolerated in his house leather on which he had not worked himself. Besides, they were too beautiful—the pair of pumps, so inexpressibly slim, the patent leathers with cloth tops, making water come into one's mouth, the tall brown riding-boots with marvelous sooty glow, as if, though new, they had been worn a hundred years. Those pairs would only have been made by one who saw before him the Soul of Boot—so truly were they prototypes, incarnating the very spirit of all footwear. These thoughts, of course, came to me later, though even when I was promoted to him, at the age of perhaps fourteen, some inkling haunted me of the dignity of himself and brother. For to make boots—such boots as he made—seemed to me then, and still seems to me, mysterious and wonderful.

I remember well my shy remark, one day, while stretching out to him my youthful foot:

"Isn't it awfully hard to do, Mr. Gessler?"

And his answer, given with a sudden smile from out of the sardonic redness of his beard: "Id is an Ardt!"

Himself, he was a little as if made of leather, with his yellow crinkly face, and crinkly reddish hair and beard, and neat folds slanting down his cheeks to the corners of his mouth, and his guttural and one-toned voice; for leather is a sardonic substance, and stiff and slow of purpose. And that was the character of his face, save that his eyes, which were gray-blue, had in them the simple gravity of one secretly possessed by the Ideal. His elder brother was so very like him—though watery, paler in every way, with a great industry—that sometimes in early days I was not quite sure of him until the interview was over. Then I knew that it was he, if the words, "I will ask my brudder," had not been spoken, and that, if they had, it was the elder brother.

When one grew old and wild and ran up bills, one somehow never ran them up with Gessler Brothers. It would not have seemed becoming to go in there and stretch out one's foot to that blue iron-spectacled face, owing him for more than—say—two pairs, just the comfortable reassurance that one was still his client.

For it was not possible to go to him very often—his boots lasted terribly, having something beyond the temporary—some, as it were, essence of boot— stitched into them.

One went in, not as into most shops, in the mood of: "Please serve me, and let me go!" but restfully, as one enters a church; and, sitting on the single wooden chair, waited—for there was never anybody there. Soon—over the top edge of that sort of well—rather dark, and smelling soothingly of leather—which formed the shop, there would be seen his face, or that of his elder brother, peering down. A guttural sound, and the tip-tap of bast slippers beating the narrow wooden stairs, and he would stand before one without coat, a little bent, in leather apron, with sleeves turned back, blinking—as if awakened from some dream of boots, or like an owl surprised in daylight and annoyed at this interruption.

And I would say: "How do you do, Mr. Gessler? Could you make me a pair of Russia leather boots?"

Without a word he would leave me, retiring whence he came, or into the other portion of the shop, and I would continue to rest in the wooden chair, inhaling the incense of his trade. Soon he would come back, holding in his thin, veined hand a piece of gold-brown leather. With eyes fixed on it, he would remark: "What a beaudiful biece!" When I, too, had admired it, he would speak again. "When do you wand dem?" And I would answer: "Oh! As soon as conveniently can." And he would say: "Tomorrow fordnighd?" Or if he were his elder brother: "I will ask my brudder!"

Then I would murmur: "Thank you! Good-morning, Mr. Gessler." "Goot-morning!" he would reply, still looking at the leather in his hand. And as I moved to the door, I would hear the tip-tap of his bast slippers restoring him, up the stairs, to his dream of boots. But if it were some new kind of foot-gear that he had not yet made me, then indeed he would observe ceremony—divesting me of my boot and holding it long in his hand, looking at it with eyes at once critical and loving, as if recalling the glow with which he had created it, and rebuking the way in which one had disorganized this masterpiece. Then, placing my foot on a piece of paper, he would two or three times tickle the outer edges with a pencil and pass his nervous fingers over my toes, feeling himself into the heart of my requirements.

I cannot forget that day on which I had occasion to say to him: "Mr. Gessler, that last pair of town walking-boots creaked, you know."

He looked at me for a time without replying, as if expecting me to withdraw or qualify the statement, then said:

"Id shouldn't 'ave greaked."

"It did, I'm afraid."

"You goddem wed before dey found demselves?"

"I don't think so."

At that he lowered his eyes, as if hunting for memory of those boots, and I felt sorry I had mentioned this grave thing.

"Zend dem back!" he said; "I will look at dem."

A feeling of compassion for my creaking boots surged up in me, so well could I imagine the sorrowful long curiosity of regard which he would bend on them.

"Zome boods," he said slowly, "are bad from birdt. If I can do noding wid dem, I dake dem off your bill."

Once (once only) I went absent-mindedly into his shop, in a pair of boots bought in an emergency at some large firm's. He took my order without showing me any leather, and I could feel his eyes penetrating the inferior integument[1] of my foot. At last he said:

"Dose are nod my boods."

The tone was not one of anger, nor of sorrow, not even of contempt, but there was in it something quiet that froze the blood. He put his hand down and pressed a finger on the place where the left boot, endeavoring to be fashionable, was not quite comfortable.

"Id 'urds you dere," he said. "Dose big virms 'ave no self-respect. Drash!" And then, as if something had given way within him, he spoke long and

---

1 **integument:** Covering.

bitterly. It was the only time I ever heard him discuss the conditions and hardships of his trade.

"Dey get id all," he said, "dey get id by adverdisement, nod by work. Dey dake id away from us, who lofe our boods. Id gomes to this—bresently I haf no work. Every year id gets less—you will see." And looking at his lined face I saw things I had never noticed before, bitter things and bitter struggle—and what a lot of gray hairs there seemed suddenly in his red beard!

As best I could, I explained the circumstances of the purchase of those ill-omened boots. But his face and voice made a so deep impression that during the next few minutes I ordered many pairs! Nemesis fell! They lasted more terribly than ever. And I was not able conscientiously to go to him for nearly two years.

When at last I went I was surprised that outside one of the two little windows of his shop another name was painted, also that of a bootmaker—making, of course, for the Royal Family. The old familiar boots, no longer in dignified isolation, were huddled in the single window. Inside, the now contracted well of the one little shop was more scented and darker than ever. And it was longer than usual, too, before a face peered down, and the tip-tap of the bast slippers began. At last he stood before me, and, gazing through those rusty iron spectacles, said:

"Mr.—, isn'd id?"

"Ah! Mr. Gessler," I stammered, "but your boots are really too good, you know! See, these are quite decent still!" And I stretched out to him my foot. He looked at it.

"Yes," he said, "beople do nod wand good boods, id seems."

To get away from his reproachful eyes and voice I hastily remarked: "What have you done to your shop?"

He answered quietly: "Id was too exbensif. Do you wand some boods?"

I ordered three pairs, though I had only wanted two, and quickly left. I had, I know not quite what feeling of being part, in his mind, of a conspiracy against him; or not perhaps so much against him as against his idea of boot. One does not, I suppose, care to feel like that; for it was again many months before my next visit to his shop, paid I remember, with the feeling: "Oh! well, I can't leave the old boy—so here goes! Perhaps it'll be his elder brother!"

For his elder brother, I knew, had not character enough to reproach me, even dumbly.

And, to my relief, in the shop there did appear to be his elder brother, handling a piece of leather.

"Well, Mr. Gessler," I said, "how are you?"

He came close, and peered at me.

"I am breddy well," he said slowly; "but my elder brudder is dead."

And I saw that it was indeed himself—but how aged and wan! And never before had I heard him mention his brother. Much shocked, I murmured: "Oh! I am sorry!"

"Yes," he answered, "he was a good man, he made a good bood; but he is dead." And he touched the top of his head, where the hair had suddenly gone as thin as it had been on that of his poor brother, to indicate, I suppose, the cause of death. "He could nod ged over losing de oder shop. Do you wand any boods?" And he held up the leather in his hand: "Id's a beaudiful biece."

I ordered several pairs. It was very long before they came—but they were better than ever. One simply could not wear them out. And soon after that I went abroad.

It was over a year before I was again in London. And the first shop I went to was my old friend's. I had left a man of sixty, I came back to find one of seventy-five, pinched and worn and tremulous, who genuinely, this time, did not at first know me.

"Oh! Mr. Gessler," I said, sick at heart; "how splendid your boots are! See, I've been wearing this pair nearly all the time I've been abroad; and they're not half worn out, are they?"

He looked long at my boots—a pair of Russia leather, and his face seemed to regain its steadiness. Putting his hand on my instep, he said:

"Do dey vid you here? I 'ad drouble wid dat bair, I remember."

I assured him that they had fitted beautifully.

"Do you wand any boods?" he said. "I can make dem quickly; id is a slack dime."

I answered: "Please, please! I want boots all round—every kind!"

"I will make a vresh model. Your food must be bigger." And with utter slowness, he traced round my foot, and felt my toes, only once looking up to say:

"Did I dell you my brudder was dead?"

To watch him was quite painful, so feeble had he grown; I was glad to get away.

I had given those boots up, when one evening they came. Opening the parcel, I set the four pairs out in a row. Then one by one I tried them on. There was no doubt about it. In shape and fit, in finish and quality of leather, they were the best he had ever made me. And in the mouth of one of the town walking-boots I found his bill. The amount was the same as usual, but it gave me quite a shock. He had never before sent it in until quarter day. I flew downstairs and wrote a check, and posted it at once with my own hand.

A week later, passing the little street, I thought I would go in and tell him how splendidly the new boots fitted. But when I came to where his shop had been, his name was gone. Still there, in the window, were the slim pumps, the patent leathers with cloth tops, the sooty riding-boots.

I went in, very much disturbed. In the two little shops—again made in one—was a young man with an English face.

"Mr. Gessler in?" I said.

He gave me a strange, ingratiating look.

"No, sir," he said, "no. But we can attend to anything with pleasure. We've taken the shop over. You've seen our name, no doubt, next door. We make for some very good people."

"Yes, yes," I said, "but Mr. Gessler?"

"Oh!" he answered; "dead."

"Dead! But I only received these boots from him last Wednesday week."

"Ah!" he said; "a shockin' go. Poor old man starved 'imself."

"Good God!"

"Slow starvation, the doctor called it! You see he went to work in such a way! Would keep the shop on; wouldn't have a soul touch his boots except himself. When he got an order, it took him such a time. People won't wait. He lost everybody. And there he'd sit, goin' on and on—I will say that for him—not a man in London made a better boot! But look at the competition! He never advertised! Would 'ave the best leather, too, and do it all 'imself. Well, there it is. What could you expect with his ideas?"

"But starvation—!"

"That may be a bit flowery, as the sayin' is but I know myself he was sittin' over his boots day and night, to the very last. You see, I used to watch him. Never gave 'imself time to eat; never had a penny in the house. All went in rent and leather. How he lived so long I don't know. He regular let his fire go out. He was a character. But he made good boots."

"Yes," I said, "he made good boots."

**Respond in Writing** What do you think is the point of the story? What is its theme? What evidence in the text makes you think so?

**Develop Your Own Ideas** Work with your classmates to develop ideas that you might use in writing a literary analysis, an argument in which you try to persuade other people how to interpret a work of literature.

*Small Groups:* In your small group, discuss the writing you have done. Use the following graphic organizer to help think of possible details for each author's description in each of the following categories.

| Overall Meaning: What do you think is the point of the story? | |
|---|---|
| **Literary Elements** | **Examples of Evidence in the Story** |
| Who is the narrator in the story? Are the speaker and author the same? If not, what effect does the choice of narrator have on the story? | |
| How do the plot and dialogue express the point of the story? | |
| What is the setting of the story? How does the setting affect your understanding of the point of the story? | |
| How does the story's ending affect your understanding of the point of the story? Does the ending change the story's meaning to you? If so, how and why? | |

*Whole Class:* Make a master chart of all of the ideas generated by the small groups to see how different members of the class interpreted the story's meaning and how the author crafted the story to help imply that meaning.

**Write About It** You will next write a literary interpretation of "Quality" by John Galsworthy. You may choose from any of the following possible topics, audiences, and forms.

| Possible Topics | Possible Audiences | Possible Forms |
|---|---|---|
| • the story's meaning with a focus on the narrator's actions<br>• the story's meaning with a focus on Mr. Gessler's actions<br>• the story's meaning with a focus on the relationship between the narrator and Mr. Gessler | • university English professors<br>• other short story authors<br>• people who don't understand the story<br>• your friends | • an essay<br>• a blog<br>• a letter |

# Responding to Literature

"To read without reflecting is like eating without digesting," declares Sir Francis Bacon in his essay "Of Studies." A work of literature that is read but not considered in a thoughtful manner is as ineffectual as a meal that is eaten but not digested. The story or play or poem fulfills its purpose when you, the reader, respond to the work—personalize, analyze, and evaluate it—and determine the significance of the work for yourself and for other readers.

The structure of a literary analysis is shown in the following chart. As you will see, it has the same basic structure as other kinds of essays.

| STRUCTURE OF A LITERARY ANALYSIS | |
|---|---|
| Title | Identifies which aspect of the work the writer will focus on |
| Introduction | Names the author and the work<br>Contains a thesis statement expressing an interpretation of some aspect of the work |
| Body | Supports the thesis statement with responses, quotations from the work and from respected sources, and commentary |
| Conclusion | Summarizes, clarifies, or adds an insight to the thesis statement |

The meaning of a literary work is not found on the pages alone. Part of its meaning is to be found in you—in the experiences and knowledge you bring to whatever you read.

In this way, reading is a two-way process. The author makes a statement and you respond. Because your background, knowledge, and experiences are unique, the meaning of a work will also be unique to you. To uncover that meaning, you look inside yourself as you read— to become aware of your reactions and the reasons for them.

## 1 Responding from Personal Experience

Reading sets up a special relationship between you and the writer. An author's words can leap off the page into your mind and memory, where they take on a meaning that is special to you. Your response will not always be positive, however; you may even feel annoyed, confused, or uninterested. Both negative and positive responses serve as starting points for expressing your ideas about a work of literature.

The strategies below will help you identify feelings and memories that can enrich your reading. When you use these strategies, record your responses in your journal.

## Personal Response Strategies

1. Freewrite answers to the following questions:

   **a.** Which character do you identify with most closely? Why? How do your feelings about that character change?

   **b.** How do certain characters remind you of people you know?

   **c.** Would you behave the same way as certain characters?

   **d.** How are plot situations like or unlike situations in your life?

   **e.** What feelings does the work evoke? How did it move you? Why?

2. Write a personal response statement that explains what the work means to you. Use any form that allows you to express your response comfortably.

3. In small discussion groups, share your reactions to the questions in item 1 above. Listen carefully to the reactions of others; compare and contrast them with your own. Be open to other points of view that may convince you of a new way to look at the work. Later, write freely about how and why the discussion affected your ideas.

● **Practice Your Skills**

> *Responding from Personal Experience*
>
> Answer the following questions about John Galsworthy's "Quality" on pages 317–322.
>
> **1.** Do you see yourself in any character? Why or why not?
>
> **2.** How would you feel if you were the narrator? How would you behave?
>
> **3.** Which character reminds you of someone you know? How?
>
> **4.** Do the events in the story remind you of anything in your own life? How was your experience similar? Different?

---

**PROJECT PREP** *Responding* **Personal Experience**

In your writing group, discuss your response from personal experience to "Quality." Based on these responses, what sense do you make of the story? Discuss the various ideas your writing group members have and be open to changing your mind if a group member's ideas seem valid.

---

# ② Responding from Literary Knowledge

When you respond to literature on the basis of your literary knowledge, you analyze the elements—the characteristics—of a literary work. The way you approach a work will depend on the type of work it is—fiction, poetry, or drama. Although each type has its own set of elements, there is much that overlaps. For example, plot is critical in fiction, but it is also important in drama.

The following charts list the main elements of fiction, poetry, and drama. These include such rhetorical devices as **tropes** (nonliteral language such as metaphors, similes, and personification) and **schemes** (artful arrangements of words, such as parallelism, alliteration, or repetition). Since drama shares many of the same elements as fiction, the elements listed under drama pertain only to the reading of a dramatic work.

## ELEMENTS OF LITERATURE

### FICTION

| | |
|---|---|
| **Plot** | events that lead up to a **climax,** or high point, and resolve the central **conflict** or explain the outcome |
| **Setting** | when and where the story takes place |
| **Characters** | people in the story whose thoughts and actions move the events forward |
| **Dialogue** | conversations among characters that reveal personalities, actions, and **motivations,** or reasons characters behave as they do |
| **Tone** | the author's attitude toward the events and the characters |
| **Mood** | the prevalent feeling or **atmosphere** in a piece of literature |
| **Irony** | the occurrence of the opposite of what is expected; can be verbal, dramatic, or situational |
| **Point of View** | the "voice" telling the story: **first person** *(I)* or **third person** *(she* or *he)* |
| **Theme** | the main idea or message of the story |

### POETRY

| | |
|---|---|
| **Persona** | the person whose "voice" is saying the poem |
| **Meter** | the pattern of stressed and unstressed syllables in each line |
| **Rhyme Scheme** | the pattern of rhymed sounds in a poem, or at the end of each line |
| **Sound Devices** | ways in which sounds are used to create certain effects, such as **onomatopoeia** *(You can read about sound devices on pages 215–216.)* |

| POETRY | |
|---|---|
| **Figures of Speech** | imaginative language, such as similes and metaphors<br>*(You can read about figures of speech on pages 51–54, 160–161, and 216–218.)* |
| **Imagery** | expressions that appeal to the senses |
| **Symbols** | objects or events that stand for other things |
| **Allusions** | references to persons or events in literature or in the past |
| **Shape** | the way a poem looks on the printed page, which may contribute to the poem's overall meaning |
| **Theme** | the overall feeling or underlying meaning of the poem |

| DRAMA | |
|---|---|
| **Setting** | the time and place of the action; lighting and the stage sets, as described in the stage directions |
| **Characters** | the people who participate in the action of the play |
| **Plot** | the story of the play divided into acts and scenes and developed through the characters' words and actions |
| **Theme** | the meaning of a play, revealed through the setting and the characters' words and actions |

## How Literary Elements Contribute to Meaning

Each genre's literary elements contribute to a work's meaning. When you analyze a work, you break it down into these elements. In poetry, for example, you examine stylistic and rhetorical devices such as the rhyme scheme, figures of speech, and other elements that contribute to the meaning of a poem. The following groups of questions will help you explore the meaning of a short story or a novel, a poem, or a play.

### Questions for Finding Meaning in Fiction

**Plot**

- What is the significance of each main event in the development of the plot? How does each event in the plot affect the main characters?
- Which details in the plot reveal the central conflict?
- What do the climax and the ending reveal about the theme?

**Setting**

- How does the setting contribute to the tone or mood of the story? How do details of the setting help define the characters?
- Which details of the setting are most important in the development of the plot? How do these details relate to the theme?

**Characters**

- How do the characters relate to their setting?
- How does each character contribute to the plot development?
- How are the characters revealed by their thoughts, actions, words, or others' actions toward them?
- How does the point of view of the story affect the characterizations?
- What does the point of view contribute to the theme?

**Theme**

- What passages and details in the story best express the main theme? What other story elements contribute to the meaning?
- How does the author communicate the theme through the development of setting, characters, and plot?
- Does this theme have meaning for you? What else have you read that has a similar theme?

## Questions for Finding Meaning in Poetry

- What is the poet's persona? How does the persona relate to the subject, mood, and theme of the poem?
- How does the meter affect the rhythm of the poem? How does that rhythm express the mood?
- How does the rhyme scheme affect the expression of thoughts and feelings?
- If the poet uses sound devices like alliteration and onomatopoeia, what sounds do you hear in the poem? What images do those sound devices create in your mind?
- What images do the figures of speech create? What feelings do those images suggest?
- How does the shape of the poem relate to the subject, mood, or theme?
- What effect does the poem have on you? How does the poem achieve its effect?
- What feeling, theme, or message does the poem express? What meaning does the poem have for you?

## Questions for Finding Meaning in Drama

- What details of setting and character do the stage directions emphasize? How do those details add to the impact of the play?
- What are the key relationships among the characters? How do those relationships reveal the central conflict? What changes in the relationships help resolve the conflict?
- How does the dialogue advance the plot? What plot developments occur with each change of act and scene?
- What subject and theme are treated in the play? What in the play has meaning for you?

# EVALUATING A LITERARY WORK

As you build your evaluating skills, you will gain an increased appreciation not only of literature but also of the techniques that go into its creation. Because there are different standards of evaluation, you may find it helpful to know the following criteria by which great literature—a **classic**—is usually judged.

**SOME CHARACTERISTICS OF GREAT LITERATURE**

- Explores great themes in human nature and the human experience that many people can identify with—such as growing up, family life, personal struggles, or war
- Expresses universal values—such as truth or hope—to which people from many different backgrounds and cultures can relate
- Conveys a timeless message that remains true for many generations of readers
- Presents vivid impressions of characters, settings, and situations that many generations of readers can treasure

If a literary work you are reading is not regarded as a classic, you can apply other standards of evaluation. For example, when you are making judgments about a work, use the questions below to help you evaluate it.

**Questions for Evaluating Literature**

- How effectively does the writing achieve the purpose?
- How vividly and believably are the characters, settings, dialogue, actions, and feelings portrayed?
- In fiction, how well structured is the plot? Does it contain a satisfying resolution of the central conflict?
- How strongly did you react to the work?
- Did you identify with a character, situation, or feeling?
- Did the work evoke any memories or emotions?
- Did the work have meaning for you? Will you remember anything about it a year from now?

## ● Practice Your Skills

*Responding from Literary Knowledge*

Answer the following questions about "Quality" on pages 317–322.

**1.** What is the central conflict? What are the key events? How is the story finally resolved?

**2.** Describe the main setting. How does it create a suitable backdrop for the events? What does it add to the story?

3. Describe the tone. What is the author's approach to the events and characters?

4. Describe the mood of the story. How do the characters reflect the mood?

5. Describe the main character, Mr. Gessler. How does the narrator feel about him?

6. How would you describe the narrator? What is his impact on the story?

7. From what point of view is the story told? How might it have been different if told from a different point of view?

8. What is the underlying theme of the story?

9. How well does the author convey the theme through the characters and plot?

10. Do the characters, dialogue, and plot seem believable? How vividly are the setting and the feelings portrayed?

11. How do the different elements fit together? How do they convey meaning?

12. What is the meaning for you? Was your response to the story positive or negative? Why?

**PROJECT PREP** *Responding* *Literary Knowledge*

In your writing group, discuss your written responses from literary knowledge to "Quality." Use this discussion to further your understanding of the story so that you can write a strong interpretive essay about it.

# Think Critically

## Making Inferences

When you write about literature, you will find that there are a variety of elements about which to write. For example, from the story "Quality" you could focus on the motivation of the bootmaker, Mr. Gessler. But to figure out the bootmaker's motivation, you would have to make **inferences.** That is, you would have to make reasonable guesses about his motivation, basing your guesses on clues in the story.

A reliable method of making inferences is to recall and apply your own experience. Suppose you read in a story, "The man's dark eyebrows gathered in a frown." In your own experience, you have seen people gather their eyebrows together in a frown. You can thus infer that the character is displeased.

The following chart shows how you can make inferences about the motivation of the bootmaker in "Quality."

| INFERENCE CHART | |
|---|---|
| Type of Clue | Clue |
| Description of the character | "Himself, he was a little as if made of leather, with his yellow crinkly face, and crinkly reddish hair and beard. . . ." |
| Statements about the character | ". . . he would stand before one without coat, a little bent . . . blinking—as if awakened from some dream of boots" |
| Character's own words | "Zome boots," he said slowly, "are bad from birdt. If I can do noding wid dem, I dake dem off you bill." |
| Other characters' words | "He was a character. But, he made good boots. . ." |
| Inference | Mr. Gessler was a bootmaker who was concerned with the art of making perfect boots, not with the business of selling boots. |

## Thinking Practice

Make an inference chart like the one above to explain the motivation of the narrator in "Quality."

## ❶ Choosing and Limiting a Subject

Unless you have been assigned a subject by your teacher, you will have a wide choice of possible subjects. To narrow the choice, first determine what subjects appeal to you personally. Ask yourself the following questions to locate ideas that spark your interest.

### Questions for Choosing a Subject

- What parts of the work puzzle me? What would I like to understand better?
- What parts of the work do I find moving? Surprising? Disappointing? Why do they have that effect on me?
- What details or images made a strong impression on me? What do they contribute to the overall work?
- With which character do I most identify? Why?
- How do the characters differ from one another? What motivates each one?
- What does the work "say" to me? What message does it convey? What insight or understanding have I gained from it?
- What other works does this remind me of? How are the works similar? How are they different?

### SYNTHESIZING PERSONAL AND LITERARY RESPONSES

A helpful process as you search for a topic is to **synthesize,** or combine, your personal and literary responses. First, zero in on some strong personal reaction. For example, suppose that the story "Quality" brought to mind an older relative who frequently talks about how things were better in the past. To make this idea for a subject more specific, you need to synthesize your personal response with your literary response to the story. To do so, think about the elements of the story that have to do with the change of values from past to present. Some elements from "Quality" related to this theme are as follows:

- Mr. Gessler carefully crafts each boot, showing his respect for bootmaking as an art. (characterization)
- Mr. Gessler looks as if he is made of leather. (rhetorical device—symbolism)
- Mr. Gessler loses business because he doesn't advertise. (plot)
- Mr. Gessler's brother dies of disappointment over the loss of business. (plot)
- Mr. Gessler says, "beople do nod wand good boods, id seems." (dialogue)

This process might lead you to this subject for a literary essay: the effects of a change in society's values. To develop that subject, you would analyze how the "change of values" theme is dramatized through several elements of the story.

For a literary analysis, you can assume you are writing for an audience familiar with the work, usually your classmates or teacher.

## LIMITING A SUBJECT

You will need a subject narrow enough to handle adequately in an essay. The first step in limiting your subject is to decide on your approach. Do you want to focus on content by analyzing one or more elements of the work, or do you want to focus on the author's presentation, analyzing some aspect of the writing style or technique?

The following model is an abbreviated version of the steps the writer went through to narrow the subject of an essay on the story "Quality."

| | |
|---|---|
| **Too General** | How the theme is carried out |
| **Ask** | What do I want to say about how the theme is carried out? |
| **Possible Answer** | The author uses the decline of the bootmaker to portray the ways in which changes in society can affect individuals within it. |
| **Limited Subject** | The writer uses the failure and death of the old bootmaker to show how a society changes and how these changes affect people whose abilities are less relevant and useful in the new circumstances. |

● **Practice Your Skills**

**Limiting Subjects**

Narrow each of the following broad subjects to a suitably limited subject for a literary analysis of the story "Quality."

| | |
|---|---|
| **Example** | setting |
| **Limited Subject** | how the writer uses details about the shop to help portray the bootmaker |

**1.** honesty     **3.** dialogue     **5.** tone

**2.** the narrator     **4.** the bootmaker

**PROJECT PREP** *Prewriting* *Limiting a Subject*

In your writing group, discuss how you might limit your interpretive topic for your essay on "Quality" or another literary work.

# ② Developing a Thesis

A literary analysis is based on a **thesis,** or proposition, that states your interpretation of some aspect of a piece of literature. Because you bring your own experiences and reactions to a work, your interpretation will most likely be different from the interpretation of another reviewer. Your task is to defend your proposition by presenting evidence that will convince the reader that your interpretation is valid.

A literary analysis, then, is not just a collection of hasty and careless reactions to a work nor a simple summary of the literal meaning but rather a carefully reasoned set of arguments. All of your arguments, if they relate to and support the limited subject you have chosen, can be refined to a concise statement that states your interpretation clearly—that is your thesis.

Once you have limited your subject, you are well on the way toward stating your thesis. In fact, if your limited subject is clear and specific, all you may have to do is rephrase it as a sentence. If you need to narrow your thesis further, you can use a technique like the one used for your limited subject. Keep asking yourself, "What exactly do I want to say about the subject as it relates to this story?" until you arrive at a statement that you can defend convincingly.

The thesis you develop in the prewriting stage is a **working thesis** only. It should be clear and specific enough to guide your thoughts, but it can be revised and even rewritten as you move deeper into your process of writing. For an essay on the story "Quality," one writer moved from the limited subject to the thesis shown below.

**Limited Subject**     How the author uses the decline of the bootmaker to help portray the decline of standards in society

**Thesis**     In the short story "Quality," John Galsworthy uses the decline of a skilled bootmaker to show the general decline of standards in society.

---

**PROJECT PREP** *Prewriting* *Working Thesis*

In your writing group, revisit the thesis statement that you drafted earlier in your interpretive process. Based on the discussions you have had, consider whether or not you need to revise this thesis statement so that it will serve as the major thrust of the interpretive essay you write. Then, in consultation with your writing group, draft an introductory paragraph for your essay. In the introduction, you might begin by stating your thesis and then explaining it briefly. Have other members of your writing group read your thesis statement and provide suggestions on how you could sharpen it so that it provides a clear focus for your essay.

# In the Media

## The Art of Parody

The process of defining your thesis statement is one way in which writing a literary analysis helps deepen your understanding of a creative work. Another technique for exploring a work of art is to create a parody, or spoof. Parodies are funny only if they capture the essence of the original.

In the classic 1957 Swedish film by Ingmar Bergman called *The Seventh Seal,* a dejected knight returns from the Crusades in search of life's meaning. Death arrives in the form of the Grim Reaper, but the knight stalls him with a game of chess. The movie is a dark, haunting mystery.

Thirty-four years later, the film *Bill and Ted's Bogus Journey* included a parody of *The Seventh Seal*. When Bill and Ted meet the "Reaper Dude," they challenge him to a game of Battleship™ and note that "he has a lot to learn about sportsmanship."

## Media Activity

Working with a partner, choose a well-known work of entertainment to parody. One way to make your choice is to think about memorable characters with memorable flaws. For example, Hamlet's memorable flaw, among others, is his inability to make decisions. A parody of Hamlet might be a scene in which he is *almost* ready to commit murder but he just cannot make up his mind.

Another way to choose a subject for a parody is to think of someone with a very distinctive style and to imagine how that artist would present someone else's work. For example, what would a movie version of Hamlet look like if it were created by the people at Pixar or directed by Spike Lee?

When you have chosen your subject, consider the specific audience to which you want to appeal. Refer to *Electronic Publishing,* pages 589–603, to produce your audio or video parody. Invite friends and family to an evening at school for a showing of the parody and follow-up discussion.

## ③ Gathering Evidence

As you read, you automatically gather details and fit them into a pattern in your mind. It is this pattern that allows you to make sense of what you read and that helps you form an impression of a work. The first time you read "Quality," whether or not you were aware of it, you were already noting details that led you to your thesis. Now you need to return to the story to collect those details and gather others that can back up your thesis. Dialogue, description, events, thoughts, stylistic or rhetorical devices—anything you find in the story can be used as evidence.

### Gathering Details for a Literary Analysis

- Scan the work, looking for quotations and other details that support your interpretation. Details can include events, descriptions, and any other ingredients of the work.
- Write each detail on a commentary card. If it is a quotation, indicate who said it and write the page number on which it appears. If it is from a reference work, write the source. (In drama, note the act and scene; in poetry, the line number.)
- Add a note telling how the detail supports your interpretation.
- Use a separate card or piece of paper for each detail.

## USING COMMENTARY CARDS

Beginning below, you can see some commentary cards for an essay on the story "Quality." The commentary cards appear on the right. On the left are the portions of the story from which the notes were made. The details were chosen by the writer to support the thesis that Galsworthy uses the physical decline of the bootmaker to show the decline of standards in society.

### MODEL: Gathering Evidence

I knew him from the days of my extreme youth, because he made my father's boots; inhabiting with his elder brother two little shops let into one, in a small by-street—now no more, but then most fashionably placed in the West End.

"Id 'urds you dere," he said. "Dose big virms 'ave no self-respect. Drash!" And then, as if something had given way within him, he spoke long and bitterly. It was the only time I ever heard him discuss the conditions and hardships of his trade.

1. Bootmaker combined two little shops into one. In early days the shop was "most fashionably placed" and "had a certain quiet distinction." (p. 317)

—Shows bootmaker was successful

2.a. Bootmaker sees poor quality of other boots. Speaks bitterly about big firms taking business away from craftsmen—"Every year id gets less..."

—bootmaker (p. 320)

"Dey get id all," he said, "dey get id by adverdisement, nod by work. Dey dake id away from us, who lofe our boods. Id gomes to this—bresently I haf no work. Every year id gets less—you will see."

And looking at his lined face I saw things I had never noticed before, bitter things and bitter struggle—and what a lot of gray hairs there seemed suddenly in his red beard!

As best I could, I explained the circumstances of the purchase of those ill-omened boots. But his face and voice made a so deep impression that during the next few minutes I ordered many pairs!

It was over a year before I was again in London. And the first shop I went to was my old friend's. I had left a man of sixty, I came back to find one of seventy-five, pinched and worn and tremulous, who genuinely, this time, did not at first know me.

"That may be a bit flowery, as the sayin' is, but I know myself he was sittin' over his boots day and night, to the very last. Never gave 'imself time to eat; never had a penny in the house. All went in rent and leather. How he lived so long I don't know. He regular let his fire go out."

2.b. Shows bootmaker bitter about changing standards and what's going to happen

3. Narrator sees bitterness and first signs of decline: "and what a lot of gray hairs there seemed suddenly in his red beard!" (p.320) Bitterness showing; physical decline starting; affects narrator.

4. Next visit more than a year later. "I had left a man of sixty, I came back to find one of seventy-five, pinched and worn and tremulous,..." (narrator, p.321)—Had declined terribly.

5. "...he was sittin' over his boots day and night, to the very last..." (new owner, p. 322)

—Bootmaker used his last bit of energy to keep up his high standards

## PROJECT PREP — *Prewriting* — Gathering Evidence

In your writing group, discuss the details of the story that led you to your interpretation. Identify ambiguities, nuances, and complexities that you may wish to explore further. Use the following triple-entry organizer to help you sort the details into categories. These categories will then serve as the basis for the body paragraphs of your essay.

| Category | Details from the text (including quotes) | Possible meaning of the details in light of the paper's thesis |
|---|---|---|
| Sample: Mr. Gessler's success in bootmaking | | |

**Organizing Details into an Outline**

Once you have the details to support the thesis of your essay, you need to organize them. Your method of organization will depend on the nature of your thesis.

| PRIMARY METHODS OF ORGANIZATION | |
|---|---|
| **Thesis** | **Method** |
| changes in a character over time | chronological order (pages 94–95, and 191) |
| similarities and differences between the characters or comparison of the two different works | comparison and contrast: AABB or the ABAB pattern of development (pages 261–263) |
| analysis of a character's motivation or the significance of the setting | order of importance (pages 94–95) |
| conclusions about the theme | developmental order (pages 94–95) |

After choosing a method of organization, arrange your details in an outline you can. use to guide your writing. The following formal outline was prepared for a literary analysis about the short story "Quality." To suit the thesis, the writer arranged the ideas chronologically.

**Thesis**      In the short story "Quality," John Galsworthy uses the decline of a skilled bootmaker to show the general decline of standards in society.

**MODEL: Outline**

**I.** Successful bootmaker        • — Main Topic
    **A.** Combined two shops into one    • — Subtopics
    **B.** Located in fashionable neighborhood
    **C.** Considered bootmaking "an Ardt"

**II.** First sign of decline        • — Main Topic
    **A.** Narrator wearing low-quality boots    • — Subtopics
    **B.** Big firms taking business away
    **C.** Bootmaker beginning to age

**III.** Two years later        • — Main Topic
    **A.** Narrator's return to shop    • — Subtopics
    **B.** Shop's division

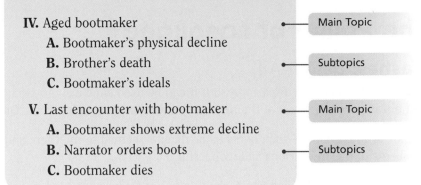

**IV.** Aged bootmaker — Main Topic
    **A.** Bootmaker's physical decline
    **B.** Brother's death — Subtopics
    **C.** Bootmaker's ideals

**V.** Last encounter with bootmaker — Main Topic
    **A.** Bootmaker shows extreme decline
    **B.** Narrator orders boots — Subtopics
    **C.** Bootmaker dies

If you have taken notes on a story but have difficulty fitting those notes into an outline, mapping the story's meaning can be a helpful intermediate step. A **meaning map** plots a story's main events in sequence, along with other major elements such as setting and characters. Each element is linked to a statement about what that element contributes to the thesis about the story. This map can help make clear which topics to emphasize as major topics and which ones should be subtopics.

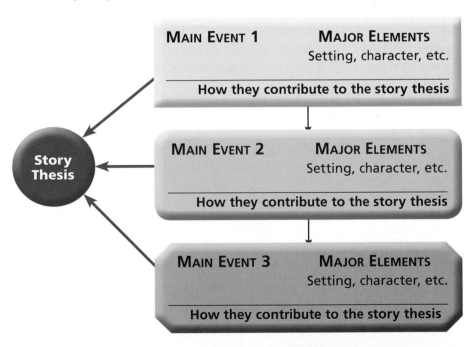

**PROJECT PREP** *Prewriting* *Outline*

Make a meaning map for "Quality" or another literary work. Group the major details into categories or main topics, and decide on an appropriate topic order. Develop an outline based on the graphic organizer and meaning map you have constructed.

# The Power of Language⚡

## Dashes: Dash It All

The dash should be used sparingly, but it can be used effectively to separate words and phrases from the rest of the sentence, as in these examples from "Quality":

> For to make boots—such boots as he made—seemed to me then, and still seems to me, mysterious and wonderful.

> And looking at his lined face I saw things I had never noticed before, bitter things and bitter struggle—and what a lot of gray hairs there seemed suddenly in his red beard!

Two dashes can be used to separate a phrase in the middle of a sentence, as in the first example, or one dash can be used to separate a phrase at the end of a sentence, as in the second example. A dash at the end can be used for dramatic effect, when you want to emphasize the last phrase.

Here are two more examples of dashes in "Quality." Dashes can often be used in the same places where commas would work, or parentheses. As you read these examples, imagine the dashes replaced with commas or parentheses, and then read again with the dashes restored. What nuances and subtleties of meaning do the dashes convey?

> One went in, not as into most shops, in the mood of: "Please serve me, and let me go!" but restfully, as one enters a church; and, sitting on the single wooden chair, waited—for there was never anybody there. Soon—over the top edge of that sort of well—rather dark, and smelling soothingly of leather—which formed the shop, there would be seen his face, or that of his elder brother, peering down.

> I ordered several pairs. It was very long before they came—but they were better than ever.

## Try It Yourself

Write two sentences similar to any of the examples on this page on the topic chosen for your literary analysis. In one, use dashes in the middle of a sentence. In the other, use a dash at the end of the sentence for dramatic effect.

> ### Punctuation Tip
>
> To create a dash on the computer, type two hyphens, with no space before and none after. The computer may convert these to the kind of dash you see in published writing, which is a single line known technically as an *em dash*.

**CHAPTER 9**

## 1 The First Draft

Use the following guidelines to help you draft your literary analysis.

### Guidelines for Drafting a Literary Analysis

- Do not retell the story. You can assume that your readers have read the work you are analyzing.
- Keep yourself and your feelings out of the essay. Use the third-person point of view and avoid *I*.
- Use the present tense to discuss the work. (For example, write, "The character **is** respected at first . . ." or "In the third stanza, the poet **speaks** about . . .")
- In the introduction, identify the title of the work and the author.
- Revise your thesis statement as needed and work it into the introduction as smoothly as possible.
- In the body of your essay, present your supporting details in a clearly organized form.
- Put each topic into its own paragraph. Use transitions to show how one detail relates to another.
- In the conclusion, draw together your details to reinforce the main idea of your essay. You may want to restate the thesis in a slightly different form.
- Throughout your essay, embed direct quotations from the work to strengthen the points you want to make.
- Add a title that suggests the focus of your essay.

### USING QUOTATIONS

When you planned your essay, you took notes to use as evidence to support your thesis. When you draft your essay, you should work this evidence into your essay as convincingly as possible. One way to do so is to quote directly from the work.

> Use **direct quotations** from the work to support your points and provide evidence that strengthens your position.

You should not just drop the quotations randomly into your essay. Instead, work them smoothly into your writing and punctuate them correctly.

**CHAPTER 9**

## Guidelines for Using Direct Quotations

- Always enclose direct quotations in quotation marks.
- Follow the examples below when writing quotations in different positions in the sentence. Notice that quotations in the middle or end of a sentence are not ordinarily capitalized.

| | |
|---|---|
| **Begins Sentence** | "The old familiar boots, no longer in dignified isolation," were added to the pile of shoes in the window (320). |
| **Interrupts Sentence** | Noting their low quality, "**h**e spoke long and bitterly" about big firms (319–320). The bootmaker is shockingly "aged and wan," with thinning hair (321). |
| **Ends Sentence** | The shop has "an air of distinction" (317). |

- Use ellipsis—a series of three dots ( . . . )—to show that words have been left out of a quotation.

  His "hair had suddenly . . . gone wan and thin" (321).

- If the quotation is five lines or longer, set it off by itself, without quotation marks. Indent on both sides and leave space above and below it.

  > It was over a year before I was again in London. And the first shop I went to was my old friend's. I had left a man of sixty, I came back to find one of seventy-five, pinched and worn and tremulous, who genuinely, this time, did not at first know me. (321)

- After each quotation cite the page number of the source in parentheses. The citation should precede punctuation marks such as periods, commas, colons, and semicolons. For plays or long poems, also give the act and scene of the play or part of the poem, plus line numbers.

You can also use indirect quotations in your analysis. **Indirect quotations** are not set in quotation marks, but often you will want to cite a page number with these as well.

| | |
|---|---|
| **Indirect Quotation** | Shocked at the news of Mr. Gessler's death, the narrator exclaims that he only received new boots from him last Wednesday (322). |

In addition to using quotations in your analysis, you include commentary on them to make sure that readers understand why the quotation supports a particular point.

You can use the following sample of a literary analysis as a model.

# A Double Decline in Quality

Title: Identifies focus

In "Quality" John Galsworthy tells the story of an aging bootmaker in a changing society. After spending his life making boots of the highest quality, Mr. Gessler cannot fit into a world that cares more about doing things quickly than well. Through the physical decline of the bootmaker, Galsworthy shows the decline of standards in society.

Introduction: Identifies author and title

Thesis Statement

At the beginning of the story, Mr. Gessler is a respected craftsman. He is successful enough to have combined two little shops into one, which is "most fashionably placed" and has "a certain quiet distinction" (317). The young narrator is impressed by the dignity of the bootmaker and the wonder of his craft. "For to make boots—such boots as he made—seemed to me then, and still seems to me, mysterious and wonderful" (317). To Mr. Gessler bootmaking is "an Ardt" (317), and he is completely devoted to that art. The joy of working with a beautiful piece of leather and shaping it into a perfect boot—that is his entire life.

First body paragraph: Describes Mr. Gessler as a respected bootmaker

For a while people appear to appreciate Mr. Gessler and the remarkable boots he creates. However, the first sign of decline comes when the narrator enters the shop wearing boots bought somewhere else. "Dose are nod my boods" (319), the bootmaker recognizes immediately. Noting their low quality "he spoke long and bitterly" (319–320) about big firms who use advertising, not quality, to take business away from real craftsmen. He predicts what is happening: "Id gomes to this—bresently I haf no work. Every year id gets less—you will see" (320). As Mr. Gessler gives his bitter speech, the narrator notices "what a lot of gray hairs there seemed suddenly in his red beard" (320). The bootmaker is beginning his decline, along with the standards he holds so high.

Second body paragraph: Uses specific details to show signs of decline

Two years later the narrator returns and is surprised to see that the shop has been divided. "And it was longer than usual, too, before a face peered down" and the bootmaker appeared (320). Things are obviously getting worse, and "beople do nod wand good boods, id seems" (320).

Third body paragraph: Offers details to show decline

The decline continues. When the narrator visits the shop again many months later, he finds the bootmaker shockingly "aged and wan" (321), and his "hair had suddenly gone . . . thin" (321). Mr. Gessler has lost his brother and half his shop, and he is obviously falling apart physically. Still, he

Fourth body paragraph: Shows how declining quality affects bootmaker physically takes joy in a beautiful piece of leather and fashions boots that "were better than ever" (321). The struggle to hold on to his ideals is aging him, but he is not giving them up.

It is more than a year before the narrator returns, and this time the bootmaker's decline is extreme.

> It was over a year before I was again in London. And the first shop I went to was my old friend's. I had left a man of sixty, I came back to find one of seventy-five, pinched and worn and tremulous, who genuinely, this time, did not at first know me. (321)

*Fifth body paragraph: Sets up direct quotation to emphasize decline*

The narrator orders boots and hurries away, for "To watch him was quite painful, so feeble had he grown" (321). When the boots finally arrive, however, "they were the best he had ever made me" (322). The bootmaker seems to have used up his last bit of energy, "sittin' over his boots day and night, to the very last" (322), for then he died.

At the end of the story, the new young bootmaker explains that even though "not a man in London made a better boot" (322), there is no place in the modern world for someone who does all his own work, who takes time to do a job right, who insists on the best leather, and who never advertises for customers. The old bootmaker himself knows he no longer fits in a changed world, and so he leaves it. Do his precious values die with him? Galsworthy seems to say that they do.

*Conclusion: Wraps up the main idea*

## PROJECT PREP  *Drafting*  *First Draft*

1. Draft the body paragraphs of your essay. Each body paragraph and its topic sentence should be built on one of the categories from your graphic organizer. For each paragraph, state an interpretive claim in the form of a topic sentence. You might say, for instance, that "Over the course of the story, Mr. Gessler's business methods increasingly work to his disadvantage."

2. The details you gathered will serve as your supporting evidence. For example: "Early on he conducts business by establishing close relationships with his customers. But as time goes by, he has difficulty competing with businesses that advertise."

3. Provide a warrant to show how these examples support the topic sentence. (See pages 116–117 and 246.) For example, "Mr. Gessler's business principles of working slowly and carefully, put him at a disadvantage with sellers who provide faster service and more choices."

4. Then provide a concluding paragraph in which you explain how the evidence you have provided demonstrates the thesis statement from the essay's introduction.

# ② The Second Draft

When you have your first draft completed, you have the basics in place for an interpretive essay. Now, though, you can begin the process of "stepping it up," of taking it to a new level of analysis and criticism.

### Guidelines for a Close Critical Analysis

- Look closely at the aesthetic effects of an author's use of **stylistic or rhetorical devices.**
- Identify and analyze **ambiguities, nuances,** and **complexities** within the text.
- Anticipate and respond to **readers' questions** and **contradictory interpretations.**

## ANALYZING AESTHETIC EFFECTS OF STYLE AND RHETORIC

When you analyze the aesthetic effects of style and rhetorical devices, you zoom in on the artistic effect of micro-level aspects of the text. In the following excerpt, literary critic Michael D. C. Drout argues that J.R.R. Tolkien's *The Lord of the Rings* is worthy of serious literary study in part because it draws on literary tradition. He argues that the language and style in *The Return of the King* (RK) echoes that of Shakespeare's *King Lear.*

> ### MODEL: Analysis of Style
>
> We begin our analysis with a subtle literary reference to *King Lear* that connects triangularly the Lord of the Nazgûl, Denethor, and Shakespeare's mad King. This reference is the Lord of the Nazgûl's threat "Come not between the Nazgûl and his prey" which echoes King Lear's "Come not between the dragon and his wrath" (I, i, 122). The two passages are syntactically identical, relying on the fronting of the verb "come" in order to delete the dummy morpheme "do". . . . While it is true that the Lear passage and the RK passage do not mean identical things (the Nazgûl is talking about something physical; Lear is more metaphorical), the similarity is significant: the passages can be transformed from one to another with the mere substitution of two nouns, one of these being the substitution of one monster for another (Nazgûl for dragon). This reference, then, connects the Lord of the Nazgûl to Lear and invokes . . . the greater, "more echoic" context of the referenced literary tradition, creating a set of interconnecting references that can tell readers more about the characters involved than is explicit in the narrative. These links also provide some hints that can be used to understand better the complex interplay of ideas (aesthetic, political, moral, and religious) in *The Lord of the Rings*.

CHAPTER 9

## ANALYZING AMBIGUITIES, NUANCES, AND COMPLEXITIES

When you analyze a work of literature for subtleties and complexities, you are often "reading between the lines," looking for double meanings and puzzling impressions. Consider the short story "Araby" by James Joyce, for example. It begins this way, describing the poor neighborhood in which the narrator, a young boy, grew up:

> North Richmond Street, being blind, was a quiet street except at the hour when the Christian Brothers' School set the boys free. An uninhabited house of two stories stood at the blind end, detached from its neighbors in a square ground. The other houses on the street, conscious of decent lives within them, gazed at one another with brown imperturbable faces.

A "blind" is a dead-end street, and that literal meaning, at first, seems to account for its use. However, as the paragraph unfolds, the word is repeated, and the houses are personified, given the ability to gaze at one another. This second and third reference to sight begins to suggest that there are ambiguities involved in that language use. As the story continues to unfold, the boy describes his childhood in ways that suggest its innocence, until he becomes infatuated with his friend's sister, who evokes images —imagined sights—of romance and gallantry, of an ideal world. By the end, however, the boy is disillusioned: "Gazing up into the darkness I saw myself as a creature driven and derided by vanity; and my eyes burned with anguish and anger." No longer "blind," as he was in his innocent childhood, and no longer buoyed by his imaginings, the boy sees with new eyes the poverty and dreariness of his life. The nuances and complexities of the sight imagery help create a powerful effect.

## ADDRESSING CONFLICTING INTERPRETATIONS

As in any argument, anticipating questions and challenges is an important part of presenting a convincing case. Notice how differing interpretations are addressed in the following excerpt from an analysis of the meaning of *Heart of Darkness* which appeared in a special issue of *Journal of Maritime Law & Commerce* called "Admiralty Law in Popular Culture" (2000).

## MODEL: Addressing Differing Interpretations

What is the lesson of *Heart of Darkness*? What meaning does the novella convey? As with almost all enduring literary works, no simple answers are available for these questions. Most certainly the work is symbolic, the symbolism is multifaceted, and the meaning is plural. One critic has seen the story as an allegory of the soul's travels through purgatory and hell to salvation, comparable to the quest for the Holy Grail or to the journey in Dante's *Inferno*.[1] Another critic has interpreted the story as a comment on the agony of writing fiction,[2] and still another has suggested it is about the incompleteness of self-knowledge, both for Marlow and in general.[3]

> Introduces various interpretations, with references to their sources

For purposes of this special issue of the Journal, it might be best to focus on what Eloise Knapp Hay calls "the solid soil of the story."[4] To wit: a tale about a man employed by a European company to pilot a steamer up the Congo River to reach the company's best acquirer of African ivory. Although his thoughts do not control the interpretive enterprise, Conrad's own words seem to point to this kind of interpretation. Before the episodes of the story began appearing in *Blackwood's Magazine*, Conrad wrote to its editor to say the tale was about the "criminality of inefficiency and pure selfishness when tackling the civilizing work in Africa."[5]

> Turns away from other interpretations for the sake of his purpose and audience

> Admits that Conrad's thoughts do not prove anything about interpretation, but points out that Conrad himself articulated a view on imperialism which, in the critic's opinion, the text supports

1. Lillian Feder, "Marlow's Descent into Hell," *Nineteenth-Century Fiction* 9.4 (1955): 289, 292.

2. Louis J. Halle, "Joseph Conrad: An Enigma Decoded," *Saturday Rev. Lit.* (May 22, 1948): 7–8.

3. Morton Zabel, *Youth: A Narrative*, Introduction (1959).

4. Eloise Knapp Hay, *The Political Novels of Joseph Conrad: A Critical Study* (Chicago: University of Chicago Press, 1963), 110.

5. W. Blackburn, (Ed.) *Letters to William Blackwood* (Durham, NC: Duke University Press, 1958), 37.

In the following passage from a literary analysis of Joseph Conrad's *Heart of Darkness*, student Griffin Burns identifies nuance, derives meaning from Conrad's stylistic choices, and also addresses the complex relationship between the Europeans and the Africans.

**STUDENT MODEL:** *Close Critical Analysis*

Morals, the ideals which the group holds to be "right" and acceptable, can offer a clear view of a culture's social progress and refinement. It is through this medium that Conrad chooses to make many of his comparisons between the wild and the established. For example, he writes that "… the pilgrims [European traders] buried something in a muddy hole" (Conrad 170). Mr. Kurtz, the officer who had just returned from a long term in Africa, is buried without grief, and by referring to his resting place as a "muddy hole," Conrad reveals the pilgrims' distaste for the repentant man. Additionally, Conrad manages to say more using less through the lack of funeral or rites given to the important ivory-hunter's burial. The pilgrims are juvenile, caught up in their greed for ivory and social rank, so drastically that they let the meaningful death go with disregard. Meanwhile, the eulogy the natives had written offers a passionate explanation of their desertion: "From the depths of the woods went out such a tremulous and prolonged wail of mournful fear and utter despair as may be imagined to follow the flight of the last hope from the earth" (Conrad 145). The sheer number of adjectives describing the parting of Kurtz from the jungle, compared to those used, or rather not used, by the pilgrims, shows the natives' greater expressed love and devotion. The free souls of the jungle seem vastly more capable of heartfelt morality and progressed love towards a soul than the begrudging and juvenile kin to the deceased.

> Burns picks up a nuance of the text: the rough burial of Kurtz suggests a roughness of emotion on the part of the pilgrims.

> Burns uses the number of adjectives, a stylistic choice, to draw meaning about the two groups, the Europeans and the Africans.

**PROJECT PREP** Drafting *Second Draft*

1. Read the relevant portions of the work you are analyzing again. Look closely for stylistic and rhetorical techniques that support your interpretation. Look for and explain in the framework of your interpretation any nuances, ambiguities, and complexities you see.

2. Ask members of your writing group to challenge your interpretation. Note their questions and concerns with your approach and analysis. Prepare a second draft of your critical essay that addresses the closer look you took as well as your partners' concerns.

# Writing a Literary Analysis  Revising

Rework your draft until you are reasonably satisfied. Then do not look at it for a day or two so that you can return to it with a critical eye. If possible, give your draft to another student to read and comment on in the meantime. Then use your peer's suggestions and the checklist below to make your revisions.

## Evaluation Checklist for Revising: Whole Essay

✓ Do you have a strong introduction that identifies the author and the work you will discuss? (page 324)

✓ Does your introduction contain a clearly worded thesis? (page 334)

✓ Does the body of your essay provide ample details from the work and commentary on them to support your thesis? (pages 324, 341, and 344)

✓ Does your essay examine the aesthetic effects of an author's use of stylistic or rhetorical devices? (page 345)

✓ Does your essay identify and analyze ambiguities, nuances, and complexities within the text? (page 345)

✓ Does your essay anticipate and respond to readers' questions and contradictory interpretations? (pages 345–348)

✓ Have you quoted from the work to strengthen your points? (pages 341–344)

✓ Are your major points organized in a clear, appropriate way? (pages 338–339)

✓ Does your conclusion synthesize the details in the body of the essay and reinforce the thesis statement? (pages 324, 341, and 344)

✓ As a whole, does your essay show unity and coherence? (pages 93–96 and 119)

✓ Would any part of your essay be improved if you **elaborated** by adding details, **deleted** unnecessary or irrelevant parts, **substituted** better examples or details, or **rearranged** any parts? (pages 24 and 250)

✓ Do you have an interesting and appropriate title? (pages 324 and 341)

**Evaluation Checklist for Revising: Paragraphs, Sentences, and Words**

*Checking Your Paragraphs*

&check; Does each paragraph have a topic sentence? (pages 88–89)

&check; Is each paragraph unified and coherent? (pages 93–96)

*Checking Your Sentences and Words*

&check; Are your sentences varied and concise? (pages 59–72)

&check; Are your words specific and lively? (pages 47–57)

&check; Have you used language precisely to express subtle shades of meaning? (pages 47–48)

*Checking Your Tropes and Schemes*

&check; Have you used such tropes as metaphors, similes, analogies, hyperbole, understatement, rhetorical questions, and irony to express complex thoughts clearly? (pages 326–327)

&check; Have you used such schemes as parallelism, antithesis, inverted word order, repetition, and reversed structure to add emphasis and clarity? (pages 326–327)

Literary analysis can become complex. Take special care to keep your words and sentences as crisp as possible. Revise the following sentence to make it less dense and easier to read.

> Through imagery, Joyce paints a dismal picture of the poor, impoverished neighborhood in which the narrator grew up, choosing images that suggest dreariness and a dismal view, with a darkening sky.

**PROJECT PREP** *Revising* *Alone and with Peers*

When you have completed your second draft, use the checklists on these pages to revise it to the very best of your ability, until you feel proud of what you have written. Then share it with your writing group. In your writing group, help each author provide a clear thesis statement in the introduction, a series of body paragraphs that are guided by a topic sentence and supported with warranted evidence, and a conclusion that explains how your examples demonstrate the plausibility of your thesis statement. Also help each author "step it up" to analyze the aesthetic effects of Galsworthy's use of stylistic or rhetorical devices; to identify and analyze nuances, ambiguities, and complexities; and to anticipate and respond to readers' questions or conflicting interpretations.

Although you probably began the writing process with the rules of grammar in mind, take time at this stage to edit your work for grammar, spelling, mechanics, and usage. Pay special attention to the participial phrases in your essay. Make sure you have used and punctuated them correctly.

## The Language of **Power** *Fragments*

**Power Rule:** Use sentence fragments only the way professional writers do, after the sentence they refer to and usually to emphasize a point. Fix all sentence fragments that occur before the sentence they refer to and ones that occur in the middle of a sentence. (See pages 661–663.)

**See It in Action** Writers try to make their characters sound real. For this reason, they use many techniques that are not always appropriate in formal writing, as the following passage from "Quality" shows:

> When I, too, had admired it, he would speak again. "When do you wand dem?" And I would answer: "Oh! As soon as conveniently can."

Unconventional spellings and sentence fragments breathe life into dialogue, but they distract readers of a formal paper unless they are used carefully for emphasis.

**Remember It** Record this rule and examples in the Power Rule section of your Personalized Editing Checklist.

**Use It** As you edit your paper, make sure that your style is appropriate for the purpose of your paper and avoid unintended sentence fragments in formal writing.

## PROJECT PREP **Editing** *Checking for Conventions*

Read through your essay with your concentration focused on conventions: grammar, spelling, usage, and mechanics. Refer to your Personalized Editing Checklist for errors you are prone to making. Check for sentence fragments. Use proofreading marks or your word processor to make corrections. Then use the rubric on the following page for a final evaluation before making a neat, polished copy.

CHAPTER 9

| Ideas | 4 The thesis statement is clear. Evidence and inferences are solid. The analysis goes beyond mere summary and addresses subtleties of meaning. | 3 The thesis statement is clear. Most evidence and inferences are solid. The analysis goes beyond mere summary and addresses subtleties. | 2 The thesis statement could be clearer. Some evidence and inferences are solid, but there is too much simple summary. | 1 The thesis statement is missing or unclear. There is little evidence and few inferences, and ideas rarely go beyond summary. |
|---|---|---|---|---|
| Organization | 4 The organization is clear with abundant support and abundant transitions. | 3 Support is abundant but a few ideas seem out of place or transitions are missing. | 2 More details are needed. Many ideas seem out of place and transitions are missing. | 1 The development of the body is inadeqaute and the organization is unclear and hard to follow. |
| Voice | 4 The voice sounds natural, engaging, and forceful. | 3 The voice sounds natural and engaging. | 2 The voice sounds mostly natural but is weak. | 1 The voice sounds mostly unnatural and is weak. |
| Word Choice | 4 Words are specific and powerful. Language is sophisticated. | 3 Words are specific and language is appropriate. | 2 Some words are too general and/or inappropriate. | 1 Most words are overly general and inappropriate for the purpose and audience. |
| Sentence Fluency | 4 Varied sentences flow smoothly. Schemes add elegance. | 3 Most sentences are varied and flow smoothly. Some schemes are used. | 2 Some sentence are varied but some are choppy. | 1 Sentences are not varied and are choppy. |
| Conventions | 4 Punctuation, usage, and spelling are correct. Quotes are handled correctly. The Power Rules are all followed. | 3 Punctuation, usage, and spelling are mainly correct and Power Rules are all followed. | 2 Some punctuation, usage, and spelling are incorrect but all Power Rules are followed. | 1 There are many errors and at least one failure to follow a Power Rule. |

# Writing a Literary Analysis  *Publishing*

Publishing a literary analysis is a way to fulfill your writing purpose—to have readers read and reflect upon your work. Find out whether your school's literary magazine includes works of analysis, and, if so, submit yours for publication. Be sure to follow any guidelines the magazine has about presentation for submitted works. Save a copy of your literary analysis in your portfolio.

## PROJECT PREP  *Publishing*  *Connecting with Readers*

1. For the chapter project, you were free to choose among three types of publications for your literary analysis: an essay (the most common medium for writing of this type); a blog (an increasingly popular way to share ideas about literature); and a letter (some people exchange letters or e-mails to share their understanding of literary works, much as people discuss works in a book group). In your writing group, discuss ways in which a blog and a letter would require different treatment from a writer. After the discussion with your writing group, make any changes that would be fitting for the medium you chose and make an effort to connect your literary analysis with one or more readers.

2. Entering your literary analysis in a competition is one great way to share your work with others. For information on literary contests, write to the National Council of Teachers of English, 1111 Kenyon Road, Urbana, IL 61801. Be sure to follow standard manuscript form and follow any specific entry rules for the competition.

3. You may also want to have a literary conference. A literary conference is an interactive way to share opinions and discuss responses. With other interested students and teachers, find a suitable room in which to gather and read aloud your works of literary analysis. Follow each reading with questions and discussion. If you cannot meet in person, meet via Internet in a safe space you can create for a private conference. Distribute a list of the e-mail addresses of all participants, and begin the conference by e-mailing a paper to everyone on the list. All readers may respond, with the result that a lively discussion is likely to follow.

**TIME OUT TO REFLECT**

You have reached the last year of high school and this was possibly the last time you will write a literary analysis in high school. Write a brief "history" of your progress as a literary critic. What were some of the biggest challenges you faced? What aspects of writing literary analysis come fairly easily to you? Save your reflection as an entry in your writing portfolio.

# Writing Lab

## Project Corner

### Speak and Listen Debate

**Organize a debate** with your classmates on the notion of "progress." Is there such a thing? How does progress affect those whose skills and beliefs are better suited to a prior era? What do people need to do to adapt to a changing world? If you feel that the world isn't improving as it changes, why do you feel that way, and how can you convince others? Form teams and develop arguments on both sides. Research debate formats, collectively decide how to organize your debate, and hold a debate in your class.

### Read Further Theme Study

Read other literature concerned with the notion of progress, such as William Faulkner's "The Bear," Thomas Berger's *Little Big Man,* Ursula LeGuin's *The Word for World Is Forest,* N. Scott Momaday's *The Way to Rainy Mountain,* and H. G. Wells's *The Time Machine.* How do these authors portray the notion of human progress? How is your view of society affected by the views expressed through these literary works? **Write a critical essay with a clear thesis analyzing this theme** in two or more works.

### Write from a Different Perspective Creative Writing

**Rewrite "Quality"** from the perspective of a different narrator. How would telling the story from Mr. Gessler's point of view affect the story's meaning?

# In the Workplace
## Analytical Memo

1. You work at an advertising agency and your competitors have come up with a new television commercial that everyone in the business is calling a masterpiece. Your boss has asked you to **write a memo** to the entire staff analyzing the commercial and explaining why it is a success. Choose a television commercial you think is especially effective. Pay close attention to any metaphors or allusions it might make. Examine its images and dialogue, relating them to the commercial's meaning. Explain to your audience why you feel the commercial is successful. (You can find information on writing memos on pages 564–566.)

# For Oral Communication Radio Presentation

2. A local radio station sponsors a weekly "You are the DJ" contest. To enter you must submit a playlist of five songs and prepare an introduction to each song explaining why it is significant to you. Think about five songs that hold meaning for you. For each song, **write a personal response** that shares how and why it affects you. Analyze the songs in the way you might analyze a poem. After you have prepared the speech, present it to your class members. (You can find information on oral presentations on pages 574–580.)

# Timed Writing ⏱ Critical Essay for School Newspaper

3. The new principal at your high school is making plans to cut funding for literature classes because he firmly believes that "reading poems, short stories, and plays is nothing but plain entertainment." You agree that reading literature is entertaining, but you believe that it serves a greater purpose as well. Explain this in an essay for the school newspaper. Find a short story, poem, or play that has special meaning to you. Responding from personal experience, write an essay for the school newspaper that explains how and why the short story, poem, or play has special meaning for you. Also explain what you have learned from the work. You have 30 minutes to complete your work.

**Before You Write** Consider the following questions: What is the situation? What is the occasion? Who is the audience? What is the purpose?

**After You Write** Evaluate your work using the six-trait evaluation rubric on page 352.

# Unit 3

# Research and Report Writing

The research process is indeed a journey through alleys of information, leading you on occasion to blind alleys and frustrating dead ends. This unit offers step-by-step guidance for taking such a journey. It will help you choose a reachable destination, create a detailed map, gather information, summarize findings, and draw valid conclusions. You will learn to strengthen the venture by evaluating each element along the way. In short, you will learn to proceed with purpose and discipline, and to welcome the occasional blind alley for what it is—an inevitable and at times illuminating part of the process.

*Research is the process of going up alleys to see if they are blind.*

—Marston Bates

# CHAPTER **10**

# Summaries and Abstracts

**A** **summary** is a concise condensation of a longer piece of writing, covering only the main points of the original.

Here are some examples of how the skills of summarizing are used in school, in the workplace, and in everyday life.

- **A student summarizes a book** she has just read for a literature assignment.

- **A movie critic writes a summary of the new blockbuster movie** that will open in theaters over the weekend.

- **A campaign worker prepares summaries of relevant newspaper articles** for the gubernatorial candidate to read before speaking at the campaign rally.

- **A classmate summarizes his recent spring-break trip** in an e-mail to his grandmother who had helped him finance the get-away.

- **A nurse summarizes a patient's medical history** for his medical chart.

- **A reporter summarizes a breaking news story** for the newspaper's Web site.

## Writing Project  Summary

**News Brief** *Write a summary of a news story about a topic that interests you.*

**Think Through Writing** Think of a news story you find interesting. It could concern sports, politics, entertainment, weird news, or any other story that you know of and are fascinated by. Write a brief description of this event, capturing the key details and explaining enough so that others get the gist of the story.

**Talk About It** In your writing group, discuss the news story you have selected. What sorts of information should you include in the summary? What else might be included, without including too much?

**Read About It** The following original piece of writing tells about a mathematical invention that most people take for granted. The summary that follows highlights the main points of the article.

*From*

# Charles Babbage: Father of the Computer

*Dan Halacy*

## Original

John Napier was a sixteenth-century Scottish mathematician whose neighbors feared he was a magician practicing the black arts. Fearful that Spain would invade the British Isles, he drew plans for all manner of strange defenses, from solar mirrors for burning ships at a distance to submarines and primitive tanks. However, his true fame rests on two great mathematical inventions: the decimal point and logarithms.

> The first sentence states the topic and a fact that will catch the interest of readers.

Today mathematicians take for granted these handy exponents of numbers that make it possible to multiply and divide by simple addition and subtraction. In Napier's day calculations were done laboriously in the old-fashioned way, and he fretted many hours over the time such arithmetic took. . . . In 1594, the thought struck Napier that all numbers could be written in exponential form, or as powers of a certain base number. For instance, 4 is $2^2$ and 8 is $2^3$. This alone is not startling, but Napier saw beyond it to a simple way of multiplying 4 times 8 without really multiplying. $2^2$ plus $2^3$ equaled $2^5$ in Napier's new arithmetic, and $2^5$ equals 32, the same as the product of 4 times 8.

> The words *for instance* introduce a specific example of the general statement in the previous sentence.

The same principle applies to exponents of all numbers, although there was a fantastic amount of work involved in computing these exponents extensively. In fact, it was not until 1614, twenty years after his revelation of the basic idea, that Napier published his logarithm tables. The result was something like the introduction of the electronic computer in our time. Logarithms drastically reduced the amount of work involved in mathematics and relieved scientists, particularly astronomers, from a great burden of mental drudgery.

> Comparing the impact of logarithms to that of computers helps modern readers understand the significance of logarithms.

# Summary

John Napier, an eccentric Scottish mathematician of the sixteenth century, invented the decimal point and logarithms. Napier was concerned about the time-consuming calculations needed to multiply and divide. In 1594, Napier realized that if numbers were expressed with exponents, the simpler tasks of addition and subtraction could be used instead of multiplication and division, with the same results. Twenty years of work followed this discovery. When Napier finally published his logarithm tables in 1614, the time savings were similar to the efficiency offered by electronic computers in the present age.

A short, simple sentence between two longer, more complex sentences provides variety in the writing.

**Respond in Writing**  Respond to this story and summary of Napier's mathematical discoveries. What is gained and lost when going from the full story to the summary? Of what value is the summary to readers?

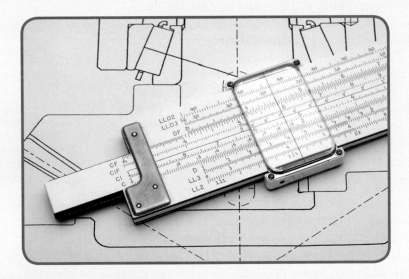

**Develop Your Own Ideas**  Work with your classmates to develop ideas that you might incorporate into a summary of a story from the news.

**Small Groups:**  In your small group, discuss the writing you have done so far. Make a copy of a graphic organizer similar to the one on the next page to help you organize your thoughts. In the center oval, write the main point of the story. On each line extending from the middle, add an important point. Use more than four lines if necessary.

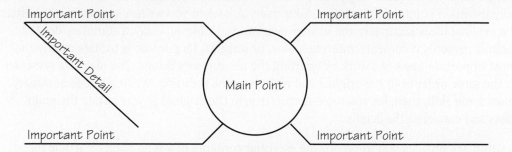

Important Point

Important Point

Important Detail

Main Point

Important Point

Important Point

***Whole Class:*** Share with the rest of the class the graphic organizer your group developed. Discuss and make a chart showing what they have in common.

***Write About It*** You will next write a summary of a news event. You may choose from any of the following possible topics, audiences, and forms for your summary.

| Possible Topics | Possible Audiences | Possible Forms |
|---|---|---|
| • a story concerning a celebrity <br><br> • a story about a political development <br><br> • a story about a military situation <br><br> • a story about a sports-related person <br><br> • a story about a situation in your community | • people with similar interests to yours <br><br> • people who like their news short and sweet <br><br> • people interested in the topic <br><br> • people who like to stay informed about current events | • a blurb for a news index <br><br> • a letter <br><br> • an e-mail message <br><br> • a post to a Web-based bulletin board |

# Understanding Summaries

The summary, often called a **précis,** is a condensation of a longer piece of writing, covering only the main points of the original. Your main task when you write a summary is to restate the original ideas accurately and in your own words. Unlike an essay, a summary does not include personal comments, interpretations, or insights. Its purpose is to state clearly the most important ideas of a work by omitting the unnecessary details. The ideas are presented in the same order as in the original and with the same meaning. Writing a good summary takes some skill, then, for you must remain true to the original as you restate the main ideas and condense the details.

A summary enables you to record the essential contents of a long book or article for future reference. A summary should be thorough but brief. You can refer to a summary to refresh your memory and you can use it as a source for your own essay when writing about another author's ideas. Writing summaries is a way of thinking about what you have read. The following chart shows the essential features of a good summary.

### Features of a Summary

- A summary is usually no more than one-third the length of the original.
- A summary states the main ideas of the original, including only the most vital details.
- A summary presents the main ideas in the same order as the original.
- A summary states the main ideas of the original in the summary writer's own words.

### Analyzing a Summary

Review the original writing about John Napier on page 359 and the summary that follows it. Then write answers to these questions.

**1.** Is the summary no longer than one-third the length of the original? To how many sentences is the first paragraph in the original reduced in the summary?

**2.** What two details about Napier from the first paragraph are omitted in the summary? What adjective in the summary sums up those omitted details?

**3.** The second paragraph in the original is reduced to how many sentences in the summary?

**4.** Is the specific example in the third paragraph of the original retained in the summary?

**5.** Are all the dates from the original in the summary?

**6.** Consider your answers to questions 2, 4, and 5. What is the difference between the details omitted in the summary and those retained?

**7.** What detail about the effect of the logarithm tables has been left out of the summary?

**8.** How are the main ideas ordered in the summary?

---

**PROJECT PREP** *Analyzing* **Key Points**

Based on the discussions you have had with your classmates, make notes about what you want to include in your summary. For a summary of a news story, include information about the people in the story, the actions each took, and the results.

To write a concise summary you should first learn how to identify the main ideas of a piece and how to restate them in your own words. During the prewriting stage you will practice these skills as you follow the steps for writing a formal summary.

## PREPARING TO WRITE A SUMMARY

In writing, you begin with a main idea and then add details. When writing a summary, however, you begin with a detailed composition and reduce it to its main ideas by omitting details. The following list will prepare you to write a summary.

### Preparing to Write a Summary

- Read the original work to get the main idea.
- Read the work again, writing down unfamiliar words.
- Write a synonym or a simple definition for each unfamiliar word.
- Write down the main ideas in the order in which they are presented.
- Determine the length of the original, in words, lines, or pages.

## RECOGNIZING MAIN IDEAS

After you understand the selection, you can move on to distinguishing between main ideas and supporting ideas. To find the main idea, ask, "Which idea is more general than all the others?" The sentence expressing the most general idea will be the topic sentence of a paragraph or the thesis statement of an essay. Sometimes, however, the main idea will be implied, not stated. In such cases, compose a statement of your own that expresses the main idea. Study these examples.

**MODEL: Main Idea Stated**

### Weight-Lifting Goals

Despite its apparent simplicity, or perhaps because of it, people have different ideas about what the sport of weight lifting should be. Some confine themselves to seeing how many pounds they can lift. Others feel that strength should be combined with speed. Still others think that what's most important is not what they lift but how their muscles look after they lift it.

—William F. Allman, "Weight Lifting: Inside the Pumphouse"

The main idea of the preceding paragraph is stated directly in the first sentence, or topic sentence. Now look for the implied main idea in the paragraph that follows.

## Teenagers and Gulls

An outsider might look at a group of teenagers standing in front of a school and see only a confused and apparently random grouping of individuals. This interpretation, however, would be misleading, just as misleading as it would be to describe a colony of herring gulls as a bunch of birds. The gullery is, in reality, a highly structured society with leaders and followers, defined territories, and a whole host of subtle but very powerful symbols that keep each gull in its place. It is the same with the teenagers standing in front of their school. Generally everybody in the group knows who the leaders are, and a careful observer might be able to spot the leaders by the particular confidence in the way that they walk or stand and by the way others in the group act toward them.

—Daniel Cohen, *Human Nature, Animal Nature: The Biology of Human Behavior*

In the preceding paragraph there is no stated idea that is more general than the others. The main idea is quite clear, nevertheless, and could be expressed as follows: However random they may seem, certain groups of people, like certain groups of animals, are highly structured. All the other sentences support this idea.

### Writing Tip

Find the **main idea** in a passage by identifying the most general statement or by expressing an **implied main idea** in your own words.

## Practice Your Skills

### Recognizing Main Ideas

Write the main idea of each paragraph that follows. If the main idea is implied, write your own sentence expressing the idea.

**1.** Some of the most important movies to come from postwar Europe were the Neo-Realist films from Italy. These films show life as it is lived, not as film studios imagine it to be. They show the streets, the houses, the vital everyday people of a struggling world; they neglect glamour, fancy houses and clothes, and movie stars. They argue against poverty, unemployment, inadequate housing, and the moral chaos caused by the war; and they offer realistic approaches, if not solutions, to realistic problems. The postwar Neo-Realist movement was short-lived, but it contributed some film masterpieces and left a distinct influence on future film-making.

**2.** The producer works closely in the selection of actors and actresses, and he or she makes sure that the length of their contracts fits the overall shooting schedule. He or she goes over the shooting script (the screenplay broken down into shots, scenes, and locations) to plan indoor sound-stage settings and outdoor shooting locations. The locations must be scouted for such all-important variables as weather, geography, local facilities, transportation, and accessibility. The shooting schedule must be planned around another set of variables, which includes shooting "out of continuity" (in other words, a film in which the last scene might be shot before the first) and weather (when the script calls for sun, the schedule must be planned for a time of year when the sun is likely to shine). When the movie is completed, the producer is in charge of selling it to distributors, of planning advertising and publicity, and of other agreements, such as sales to television. If the film is successful at the box office, the producer takes a large share of the profits. If it wins awards, such as the Academy Award for the best picture, it is the producer, not the director, who receives it.

**3.** Movie photography is the responsibility of two people: the director of photography and the camera operator. The director of photography (also called the cinematographer) attends the story conference and plans the shots to be filmed in consultation with the director, writer, and other members of the unit. The camera operator is the person responsible for overseeing the lighting and operating the camera used in shooting the film. In many films the two roles are performed by the same person.

**4.** When Harrison Ford gets into a fight in *Raiders of the Lost Ark* (1981), the chances are that he is not in the fight at all but that a "double" is performing for him. Stunt performers act as doubles for actors and actresses when the action called for in the script is dangerous. Other stunt performers are experts at various sports or at driving fast cars or at falling off horses without getting hurt. Great skill is used in photographing these performers so that the audience sees their work but not their faces. When the film is edited, we are fooled into thinking that the stars of a picture are also excellent skiers or boxers or motorcyclists.

—Preceding Excerpts by Richard Meran Barsam from *In the Dark: A Primer for the Movies*

**PROJECT PREP** *Prewriting* *Main Ideas*

In your writing group, focus on each author's account of the key ideas in the original. Help each author to identify the main ideas to include in a summary while removing details that are of lesser importance.

# The Power of Language ⚡

## Wordiness: Less Is More

When you write a summary or abstract, use as few words as possible to express your point clearly. The following sentence is taken from Dan Halacy's writing about John Napier.

> In fact, it was not until 1614, twenty years after his revelation of the basic idea, that Napier published his logarithm tables.

To trim this sentence of the least essential information, ask yourself, "What is important to remember?" The following summary sentence eliminates wordiness and concisely states the facts.

> Napier published his logarithm tables in 1614.

You can use a number of "Power of Language" strategies you have learned, especially appositives, absolutes, and participial phrases, to isolate and express the most important ideas. In the following example, the revised version uses an appositive and saves 49 words.

**Original**   John Napier was a sixteenth-century Scottish mathematician whose neighbors feared he was a magician practicing the black arts. Fearful that Spain would invade the British Isles, he drew plans for all manner of strange defenses, from solar mirrors for burning ships at a distance to submarines and primitive tanks. However, his true fame rests on two great mathematical inventions: the decimal point and logarithms.

**Revised**   John Napier, an eccentric Scottish mathematician of the sixteenth century, invented the decimal point and logarithms.

## Try It Yourself

Write one sentence of your summary using an appositive (pages 61 and 691–692), another using an absolute (page 142), and a third using a participial phrase (pages 241 and 694–696) to condense information effectively.

> ### Punctuation Tip
>
> If you summarize information in an **appositive in the middle** of a sentence, **enclose the appositive in commas.** If it appears **at the end** of a sentence, **separate it** from the rest of the sentence **with a comma. Separate certain introductory elements,** including absolutes and participial phrases, from the rest of the sentence **with a comma.**

CHAPTER 10

Once you understand all the main ideas of a selection, you are ready to write the first draft of your summary. The draft should include all the important ideas of the original, restated in your own words and presented in a shortened form.

## CONDENSING

To **condense** means to shorten the information in a passage. You can do this by eliminating repetitious ideas, examples, and descriptions. You can also combine ideas and reduce long phrases and clauses into shorter expressions. The following passage and its summary show how these techniques are applied. The sentences in both the original passage and the summary are numbered for easy reference.

> MODEL: Condensing

### Mount Rushmore

### Original

**(1)** Rushmore got a great deal of free publicity in 1934 when the Hearst newspapers sponsored a contest for a six-hundred-word history to be carved on Mount Rushmore. **(2)** An inscription had been part of Gutzon Borglum's design for a long time. **(3)** At one point he had asked [President] Coolidge to write the inscription, but he and Coolidge disagreed over the wording, so nothing came of that. **(4)** Eight hundred thousand entries were submitted in the Hearst contest, and many cash prizes were given. **(5)** No entries were ever used because eventually Gutzon abandoned the inscription idea in favor of a great Hall of Records to be cut in the stone of the canyon behind the faces. **(6)** Gutzon felt that records carved or placed in a room in the mountain would last much longer than any identifying inscription on the surface of the mountain.

### Summary

**(1)** In 1934, the Hearst newspapers sponsored a contest for an inscription to be carved on Mount Rushmore, which had been part of artist Gutzon Borglum's original plan. **(2)** Eight hundred thousand people responded. **(3)** Although many won cash prizes, their inscriptions were abandoned when Borglum decided to carve a room into the stone, which would last longer than an outdoor inscription.

The following chart shows how the sentences from the original paragraph were condensed in the summary.

| ORIGINAL SENTENCE | SUMMARY SENTENCE |
|---|---|
| 1 and 2 $\longrightarrow$ | 1 (main idea) |
| 3 $\longrightarrow$ | omitted (unnecessary detail) |
| 4 $\longrightarrow$ | 2 |
| 5 and 6 $\longrightarrow$ | 3 |

### Writing Tip

**Condense** information by omitting repetition and unnecessary details and by combining ideas from two or more sentences into one sentence. Present the main ideas and the important supporting details in the same order as the original.

## Practice Your Skills

*Condensing*

Condense each of the following paragraphs to no more than two sentences.

**1.** Writers exclaim over the coast of Maine so often that their descriptions lose meaning. "Rugged," "rockbound," and "pineclad" generally fail to stir up any visions of this northeastern shore. Yet the Maine coast is all of them and much more, too. It is a splendid part of the country—shaped and hammered by vast natural forces, softened by forests, haunted by human history. People cannot visit these coves and harbors without falling hopelessly in love with the feeling of morning fog burning off under a warm sun, the scent of pine needles in the cool shade of the forest, the taste of wild blueberries, the muffled thunder of waves, the crisp hue of sunset on a cool evening. The best example of the 3,478-mile Maine coast (including the islands) is Acadia National Park, which became the first great park in the East.

**2.** During the last Ice Age, this shoreline was pressed down by the huge weight of ice and snow. Glaciers scraped the rocky land, smoothed the hills, cracked loose rock away from parent ledges. The result is a sunken coast where what were once valleys are now sounds and inlets, where little granite islands jut from the ocean, where tumbled boulders clog the shore. Most of Maine is like this: Acadia typifies it. For here rise the heights of Mount Desert Island, the round-sculptured remnants of the pre-Ice Age mountain ridge. Its tallest summit is the highest point in the United States that overlooks the Atlantic, and one of the first to catch the rising sun's rays.

**3.** A deep, narrow sound cuts Mount Desert Island almost in two: Somes Sound, the only true fjord on the New England coast. On either side the hills rise, covered with tough, stunted pine and spruce and rich with wildflowers. Cadillac Mountain, 1,530 feet, marks the high point. Below it spreads Frenchman Bay and the old summer resort of Bar Harbor.

**4.** The history of Mount Desert Island portrays a long struggle for ownership. Samuel de Champlain, a French explorer, discovered the island and named it L'Isle des Monts Deserts (the Isle of Bare Mountains). A French colony, later founded on the island, was taken over by English colonists from Virginia. Subsequently, the island was owned privately by several British and French aristocrats including Antoine de la Cadillac, who founded the city of Detroit, and Sir Francis Bernard, the last English governor of Massachusetts. After the Revolutionary War the land was sold to settlers in Maine. By 1900, Mount Desert Island was discovered by thousands of summer visitors.

**5.** Acadia was donated to the Federal government by the summer residents (once called "rusticaters" by the locals) who, between them, owned most of Mount Desert Island. That's why the park boundaries are strangely uneven— they follow the property lines. Most of the 48-square-mile park lies on Mount Desert Island; some is across Frenchman Bay on the Schoodic Peninsula; some occupies part of the Isle au Haut, an offshore island southwest of Mount Desert. All these park lands contain choice elements of scenery. Fresh-water ponds and lakes gleam among the dark evergreens on Mount Desert. Trout, salmon, and bass flirt with the angler, while salt-water fishing invites visitors to brave the gray Atlantic in chartered vessels.

—Paul Jensen, *National Parks*

## PARAPHRASING

Another valuable technique when summarizing material is **paraphrasing**—that is, using your own words to express the main ideas and essential details. One technique for paraphrasing information is to use synonyms to replace the original words. A second method is to vary the sentence structure of the original.

> ### Writing Tip
> **Paraphrase,** or restate ideas in your own words, by using synonyms and varying the sentence structure of the original.

The following paraphrase shows you how an idea can be stated in different words.

| | |
|---|---|
| **Original** | Portuguese writer José Saramago was awarded the Nobel Prize for Literature in 1998 for imaginative, compassionate, and ironic parables. |
| **Paraphrase** | For the creative, sensitive and paradoxical stories he has given the world, Portuguese writer José Saramago was presented with the Nobel Prize for Literature in 1998. |

## ● Practice Your Skills

### *Paraphrasing*

Read the following passage about the camel. Then paraphrase each sentence in the excerpt by using synonyms and by varying sentence structure. Look up unfamiliar words in a dictionary.

(1) The camel has long had a reputation for being able to go for long periods of time without drinking any water. (2) Ancient writers believed that the camel had some mysterious internal water reservoir—a story that was told for so many centuries that it came to be believed. (3) No such reservoir, however, has ever been found. (4) Nevertheless, the camel is remarkably suited to getting along well on a minimum of water.

(5) Even in the Sahara's dry summer, when little natural food is available, camels can go for a week or more without water and for ten days without food. (6) Camels accomplish this feat by drawing on water from their body tissues and on water produced chemically as a breakdown product of fat. (7) The camel's hump contains up to 50 pounds of fat, which is accumulated when food and water are plentiful. (8) As the fat is used up to supply the camel's energy needs, about 1.1 pounds of water are produced for every pound of fat used up. (9) This is made possible because hydrogen is given off as a by-product in the breakdown of fat. (10) Oxygen from breathing is then combined with the hydrogen to produce water.

(11) With the help of this water-producing system, a camel can function well for a good many days, even when carrying a load. (12) When water is again available, the camel gulps down as much as 25 gallons at one time to compensate for the water lost during the period of deprivation.

—William C. Vergara, *Science in the World Around Us*

---

**PROJECT PREP**

Write a first draft of your summary and share it with your writing group. Help each author to eliminate unnecessary words and streamline the presentation of the events of the story.

# Think Critically

## Evaluating

When you plan a party, you do not invite everyone you know. Instead, you select people who know one another and who fit the occasion for the party. When you pack for a trip, you likewise do not take everything you own. Instead, you select only those things that will meet your needs on the trip. In each case you select items by **evaluating,** or judging, them according to a particular set of criteria, or standards. This is the procedure you should follow when you select ideas to include in a summary.

As you gain practice in writing summaries, you are likely to develop criteria of your own. The list below, however, will help you get started evaluating the relative importance of ideas. If you find you answer *yes* to one or more of the questions, you will probably want to include the idea in your summary.

### Evaluating Ideas to Include in a Summary

1. Does the idea support the main thesis of the work?
2. Is the idea needed for the reader to understand the work? Does the thesis become unclear if the idea is omitted?
3. Does the idea provide new information, rather than repetitious information?
4. Is the idea necessary to the understanding of another idea, rather than just helpful or interesting as an example or anecdote?
5. Is the idea needed as a logical bridge connecting other ideas?
6. Summing up the work in your mind, do you find yourself including the idea?

## Thinking Practice

Use the criteria in the chart above to help you write and evaluate a short summary from an article of your choosing.

As you revise your summary, check for accuracy and conciseness. Reread the original to make sure you have represented the ideas accurately. Also try to reduce your summary to the fewest words possible. The following checklist will help you.

### Evaluation Checklist for Revising

✓ Compare your summary to the original. Are the ideas presented accurately? (page 362)

✓ Are the ideas in your summary presented in the same order as they appear in the original? (pages 362, 364, and 369)

✓ Is your summary no more than one-third the length of the original? If it is too long, condense your work further by using the strategies discussed on pages 368–371.

✓ Did you use your own words and vary the sentence structure of the original? (pages 362, 368, and 370–371)

✓ Did you use transitions and other connecting devices to make your summary flow smoothly? (pages 94–95)

## ● Practice Your Skills

### Checking a Summary for Accuracy

Use the checklist above to revise the following first draft of a summary. The original piece, which you will need to refer to as you revise, is on page 365.

> A group of teenagers in front of a school is as confused and random a group as a colony of herring gulls. Everybody in the group knows who the leaders are, and outsiders can spot the leaders by their confidence and the way others act toward them. Both are organized groups—with directors and followers, their own turf, and private signals.

### PROJECT PREP **Revising** *Writing Smoothly*

Get feedback from your writing group about ways to make your summary flow more smoothly. Combine or divide sentences and use transitions so that each idea leads smoothly into the one that follows it.

**CHAPTER 10**

In the editing stage you will tighten up your summary and check to make sure that it communicates neither too much nor too little. Monitor your work for clarity, grammatical correctness, and logical consistency.

## The Language of Power *Sound-Alikes*

***Power Rule:*** For sound-alikes and certain words that sound almost alike, choose the word with your intended meaning. (See pages 874–903.)

***See It in Action*** It is easy to confuse two words that are pronounced alike but have different meanings, such as *base*, as in military base, and *bass*, as in string bass. The following sentences from Dan Halacy's writing use homophones correctly.

| | |
|---|---|
| **Base and Bass** | The thought struck Napier that all numbers could be written…as powers of a certain **base** number. |
| **Principle and Principal** | The same **principle** applies to exponents of all numbers. |
| **Great and Grate** | Logarithms…relieved scientists, particularly astronomers, from a **great** burden of mental drudgery. |

Some words sound almost alike and are easily misused, such as *affect/effect, envelop/envelope, comprise/compose, allusion/illusion, emigrate/immigrate,* and *lightening/lightning.* If you are unsure about a word choice, use a dictionary to confirm a word's meaning and usage.

***Remember It*** Record this rule and these examples in the Power Rule section of your Personalized Editing Checklist.

***Use It*** Read through your project topic and look for homophones and words that sound almost like another word. Check to see that you have chosen and used the word with your intended meaning.

It is always a good idea to cut out wordiness in your writing, but this is especially true when writing a summary. In the following sentence, eliminate the words that are unnecessary for a concise summary of the idea. Then write a summary statement of the idea in the sentence.

> Logarithms drastically reduced the amount of laborious time and mental drudgery involved in mathematical computation at the time.

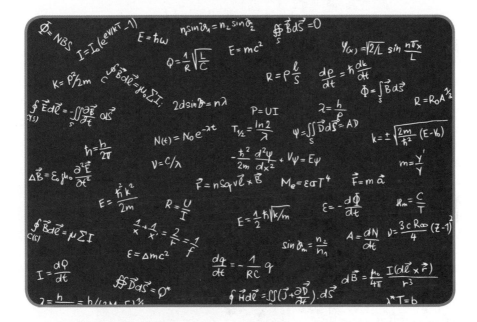

**PROJECT PREP** *Editing and Publishing* *Final Version*

Exchange your summary with a writing partner and check the grammar, spelling, and punctuation used in each other's summary. Prepare a final, polished version of your summary. Publish it through an appropriate medium. For a summary of news events, for example, you might submit it to your school newspaper for a "news briefs" section in which events are summarized.

# In the Media

## Media Presentations

When you write summaries and abstracts, you condense your material to suit a special purpose. Media presentations, however, are often condensed simply because there is not enough time to cover the story in detail. Some high-profile news events preempt regular programming, but for the most part news stories have to fit in whatever time is allotted for the news broadcast.

To make the stories fit, editors must cut back the information and resources they have. They may have only 30 seconds of air time to tell a story. They may have 10 minutes or more of video on the story, and 5 minutes of interviews. They have to cut what doesn't fit and try their best to present balanced coverage.

## Media Activity

As an exercise in judging the impact of editing on broadcast media, watch the evening news tonight. Have a stopwatch or clock nearby. When you see a story that interests you, note the time it begins. Listen closely to the story and take notes. At the end of the story, note the time and estimate how long the entire story lasted.

Now, use your imagination to ask yourself these questions: If there had been twice as long to air the story, what might have been included that was not? Would an additional person or two have been interviewed? What might they have said? Would those originally interviewed have added or clarified something that would have given a different slant to the story? What additional video clips might have been used? Write up your speculations in a paragraph.

# Writing an Abstract

When you must make your way through vast seas of information, abstracts can serve as helpful guides. Whether you are looking for a good book to read for a research paper or simply making plans for the weekend, abstracts can save time and prevent wild-goose chases.

> An **abstract** is a very condensed summary that communicates the essential content of a work in as few words as possible.

Abstracts appear in several formats and serve many purposes. A typical scientific or scholarly abstract tells the purpose of a study, how it was conducted, the findings, and conclusions. Abstracts in various fields of study compile volumes of print and electronic information. Such **informative abstracts** seldom exceed 350 words, but contain enough detail for the reader to grasp the essential information without reading the full article.

**Writing Tip**

Read **abstracts** when compiling a list of sources to read for a research project.

You are probably more familiar with **indicative abstracts,** which give a summary of an article, book, play, or movie in no more than two or three sentences. The entries that you find in annotated bibliographies, the content descriptions that appear in Internet search results, the synopses that appear in the table of contents of a journal, as well as the one- to two-line book and movie reviews from a newspaper or magazine are examples of indicative abstracts. Both informative and indicative abstracts usually include the title, the author's name, a general statement of content, and publication information.

**MODEL: Abstract**

*Avatar* (2009) A wheelchair-bound soldier, played by Sam Worthington, takes on the avatar of the blue-skinned Na'vi (the creatures who live on the alien moon of Pandora) in an effort to help infiltrate Pandora and secure a mineral the Earth requires for survival. Soon, however, Worthington's Jake Sully finds himself falling in love with Neytiri, played by Zoe Saldana, and siding with the Na'vi in their fight against humans.

—Review from *At the Movies with Peter Travers*

**PROJECT PREP**  *Drafting* *Abstract*

Try your hand at writing an abstract of your summary. First write an informative abstract. Then condense it even more to write an indicative abstract of two sentences.

# Writing Lab

## Project Corner

### Speak and Listen
### Design a Magazine

Discuss with your classmates the stories you have summarized. What sorts of interests characterize you and your classmates? What do these interests tell you about yourselves as a group? Based on these comments, **describe a new magazine** that you think would appeal to your class.

### Research It
### Expand on Your Summary

Conduct further research into the events you have summarized. **Develop a broader picture** of the events, including more details about the events, greater background on the events, and a variety of perspectives from various news sources.

### Experiment
### Put It Online

**Make a Web version** of your summary, complete with links to longer versions of the story, news video clips, related stories, and other extensions of your summary.

# In Everyday Life
## Chapter Summary

1. You have an important test next week that covers material from four chapters of your textbook. A large part of your semester grade depends on how well you perform on this test. You have decided to review one chapter at a time. **Write a summary** of one of the chapters in a textbook from a course you are currently taking. Make sure the ideas in the chapter are presented accurately. The summary should be no more than one-third the length of the book's chapter. (You can find information on writing summaries on pages 364–376.)

# In the Workplace News Summary

2. You are a reporter for a Web site that presents breaking news. This week you have been sent to cover storm preparations in a small coastal town that's directly in the path of an approaching hurricane. **Prepare a summary** of what the town's residents are doing to get ready for this possible deadly storm. (Find information on storm preparedness in your library or online.) Keep the summary concise and interesting. Avoid repetition and unnecessary details. Use transitions and other connecting devices to make your summary flow smoothly. (You can find information on preparing summaries on pages 364–376.)

# Timed Writing 🕐 Game Show Bio

3. You have been chosen to be a contestant on a game show specializing in trivia questions and answers. This is a once-in-a-lifetime chance for fame and fortune. At the start of each show, the host reads thirty-second biographies of the contestants. Write a short summary of your life to give to the show's producers. You have 15 minutes to complete your work. (For help budgeting time, see pages 37 and 493.)

**Before You Write** Consider the following questions: What is the situation? What is the occasion? Who is the audience? What is the purpose?

Include the important events in your life. Keep the summary concise, entertaining, and interesting to appeal to the show's audience. It can take no more than thirty seconds to read your summary.

**After You Write** Ask a family member to review your biography. Discuss with your family member why you included some details but left others out.

# Research: Planning and Gathering Information

**R**esearch reports are a genre of writing based on information drawn from books, periodicals, interviews, and media resources including Internet or other online sources.

Research reports are valuable means for communicating information to multiple audiences not only about literature and the sciences, but also about daily life. Here are some examples of situations in which research reports play important roles.

- **Librarians consult data from research reports,** in print and online, to determine the appropriate age groups for new reference texts.

- **Physicians use pharmacology studies** to determine whether a patient would benefit from a particular medication.

- **College admissions officers review** standardized tests results, essays, and high-school records to decide whether students will be successful at their institution.

- **Attorneys review rulings in previous legal cases** and gather new evidence in order to argue their clients' cases effectively.

- **A reporter writes a news article** on the latest Internet developments.

## Writing Project  *Research Report*

***What's New?*** *Plan and gather information for a research report on a recent development in technology.*

***Think Through Writing*** In the minute it takes you to read this page, 20 hours of video will be uploaded to the YouTube site by people just like you—anyone who has a video file and access to the Internet. Further, the most popular Internet encyclopedia, Wikipedia, will get edited hundreds of times each hour, again by people like you—anyone can edit a Wikipedia article, or post one to begin with. So not only is the technology always changing and making such phenomena possible, but also the very nature of who supplies the content is changing.

What about the new technology that surrounds you holds special interests for you? Maybe you are especially interested in video games, or cell phone applications, or even how to exericse via a game station. What can you tell others about recent developments in technology? What more do you want to learn about them? Brainstorm about topics related to technology that you can research and write meaningfully about. Write down everything that comes to mind about the topics.

**Talk About It** In your writing group, discuss the topics you have identified. Which topics would be interesting to pursue through research? Which topics would have enough written about them to serve as a good research subject? Which topics would interest your intended audience? Which topics might be trimmed from the list for any reason?

**Read About It** The Wikipedia entry that follows explains the history of YouTube. Think about the sorts of information that the authors include to help people learn more about this phenomenon. Also think about who has provided the information and steps you can take to evaluate its accuracy.

## MODEL: Research Report

*From Wikipedia, the free encyclopedia*
*(as it existed on January 11, 2010 )*

# History of YouTube

YouTube was founded by Chad Hurley, Steve Chen and Jawed Karim, who were all early employees of PayPal.[1] Prior to PayPal, Hurley studied design at Indiana University of Pennsylvania. Chen and Karim studied computer science together at the University of Illinois at Urbana-Champaign.[2] The domain name "YouTube.com" was activated on February 15, 2005,[3] and the website was developed over the subsequent months. The creators offered the public a preview of the site in May 2005, six months before YouTube made its official debut. Like many technology startups, YouTube was started as an angel-funded enterprise from a makeshift office in a garage. In November 2005, venture firm Sequoia Capital invested an initial $3.5 million;[4] additionally, Roelof Botha, partner of the firm and former CFO of PayPal, joined the YouTube board of directors. In April 2006, Sequoia put an additional $8 million into the

The content in Wikipedia, like some other online content, changes frequently.

One characteristic of online research articles is that they contain numerous links to topics referred to in the article.

The footnotes are linked to the text.

company, which had experienced huge popular growth within its first few months.[5]

During the summer of 2006, YouTube was one of the fastest growing websites on the Web,[6] and was ranked the 5th most popular website on Alexa, far out pacing even MySpace's rate of growth.[7]

> What kinds of sources have been used to back up the facts in this article?

According to a July 16, 2006 survey, 100 million video clips are viewed daily on YouTube, with an additional 65,000 new videos uploaded every 24 hours. The website averages nearly 20 million visitors per month, according to Nielsen/NetRatings,[8] where around 44% are female, 56% male, and the 12- to 17-year-old age group is dominant.[9] YouTube's pre-eminence in the online video market is substantial. According to the website Hitwise. com, YouTube commands up to 64% of the UK online video market.[10]

> The first section of this article is an overview of YouTube's history, organized chronologically.

On October 9, 2006, it was announced that the company would be purchased by Google for US$1.65 billion in stock. The purchase agreement between Google and YouTube came after YouTube presented three agreements with media companies in an attempt to escape the threat of copyright-infringement lawsuits. YouTube will continue operating independently, with its co-founders and 67 employees working within the company.[11] The deal to acquire YouTube closed on November 13, and was, at the time, Google's second largest acquisition.[12] Google's February 7th, 2007 SEC filing revealed the breakdown of profits for YouTube's investors after the sale to Google. At the time of reporting Sequoia Capital's shares were valued at more than $442 million, Chad Hurley's at more than $345 million, Steve Chen's at more than $326 million, and Jawed Karim's at more than $64 million.[13] [edit]

> Throughout the article, there are links for editing. Editing is very easy, and Wikipedia provides an easy tutorial as well as a "sandbox" where people can try out their new editing "toys" before actually posting to the article.

**Contents** [hide]
[edit]

> After a general overview, Wikipedia articles have a list of links that take a user to other parts of the article.

### Press coverage

Time featured a YouTube screen with a large mirror as its annual 'Person of the Year', citing user-created media such as YouTube's, and featuring the site's originators along with several content creators. The Wall Street Journal and New York Times have also reviewed posted content on YouTube, and its effects upon corporate communications and recruitment in 2006. PC World Magazine named YouTube the 9th of the Top 10 Best Products of 2006.[14] In 2007, both Sports Illustrated and Dime Magazine featured stellar reviews of a basketball highlight video entitled, *The Ultimate Pistol Pete Maravich MIX*.[15] Because of its acquisition by Google, it is sometimes referred to as "GooTube."[15] [edit]

Because editing is so easy, anyone can do it, including people who have incorrect information.

### Economy of YouTube

Before being purchased by Google, YouTube declared that its business model was advertisement-based, making 15 million dollars per month. Some industry commentators have speculated that YouTube's running costs—specifically the bandwidth required—may be as high as 5 to 6 million USD per month,[16] thereby fueling criticisms that the company, like many Internet startups, did not have a viably implemented business model. Advertisements were launched on the site beginning in March 2006. In April, YouTube started using Google AdSense[citation needed]. YouTube subsequently stopped using AdSense but has resumed in local regions.

Wikipedia strives to be neutral and will point out when something seems biased or when it needs a citation to back it up.

Advertising is YouTube's central mechanism for gaining revenue. This issue has also been taken up in scientific analysis. Don Tapscott and Anthony D. Williams argue in their book Wikinomics that YouTube is an example for an economy that is based on mass collaboration and makes use of the Internet. "Whether your business is closer to Boeing or P&G, or more like YouTube or flickr, there are vast pools of external talent that you can tap with the right approach. Companies that adopt these models can drive important changes in their industries and rewrite the rules of competition;"[17] "new business models for open content will not come from traditional media establishments, but from companies such as Google, Yahoo, and YouTube. This new generation of companies is not burned by the legacies that inhibit the publishing incumbents, so they can be much more agile in responding to customer demands. More important, they understand that you don't need to control the quantity and destiny of bits if they can provide compelling venues in which people build communities around sharing and remixing content. Free content is just the lure on which they layer revenue from advertising and premium services"[18].

Tapscott and Williams argue that it is important for new media companies to find ways to make a profit with the help of peer-produced content. The new Internet economy that they term Wikinomics would be based on the principles of openness, peering, sharing, and acting globally. Companies could make use of these principles in order to gain profit with the help of Web 2.0 applications: "Companies can design and assemble products with their customers, and in some cases customers can do the majority of the value creation"[19] . Tapscott and Williams argue that the outcome will be an economic democracy.

There are other views in the debate that agree with Tapscott and Williams that it is increasingly based on harnessing open source/content, networking, sharing, and peering, but they argue that the result is not an economic democracy, but a subtle form and deepening of exploitation, in which labour costs are reduced by Internet-based global outsourcing.

The second view is e.g. taken by Christian Fuchs in his book "Internet and Society". He argues that YouTube is an example of a business model that is based on combining the gift with the commodity. The first is free, the second yields profit. The novel aspect of this business strategy is that it combines what seems at first to be different, the gift and the commodity. YouTube would give free access to its users, the more users, the more profit it can potentially make because it can in principle increase advertisement rates and will gain further interest of advertisers.[20] YouTube would sell its audience that it gains by free access to its advertising customers.[21]

"Commodified Internet spaces are always profit oriented, but the goods they provide are not necessarily exchange value and market oriented; in some cases (such as Google, Yahoo, MySpace, YouTube, Netscape), free

Sometimes the writing or styling of an article needs polishing.

goods or platforms are provided as gifts in order to drive up the number of users so that high advertisement rates can be charged in order to achieve profit."[22]

In June, 2009, BusinessWeek reported that, according to a report by San Francisco-based IT consulting company RampRate, YouTube was far closer to profitability than previous reports, including the April, 2009, projection by investment bank Credit Suisse estimating YouTube would lose as much as $470 million in 2009.[23] RampRate's report pegged that number at no more than $174 million[24]. [edit]

### References

1. ^ Graham, Jefferson (2005-11-21). "Video websites pop up, invite postings" (in English). *USA Today.* Gannett Co. Inc. Retrieved on 2006-07-28.

2. ^ University of Illinois Department of Computer Science (2006). "YouTube: Sharing Digital Camera Videos"

3. ^ "Info for YouTube.com" (in English). *Alexa.com.* Amazon.com. 2006-07-26. Retrieved on 2006-07-26.

4. ^ Woolley, Scott (2006-03-13). "Raw and Random" (in English). *Forbes.com* (Forbes). Retrieved on 2006-07-28.

5. ^ Sequoia invests 11.5 million total in YouTube, accessed July 7, 2006

6. ^ "YouTube Fastest Growing Website" Advertising Age

7. ^ "Info for YouTube.com" (in English). *Alexa.com.* Amazon.com. 2006-07-26. Retrieved on 2006-07-26.

8. ^ "YouTube serves up 100 million videos a day online" (in English). *USA Today* (Gannett Co. Inc.). 2006-07-16. Retrieved on 2006-07-28.

9. ^ "YouTube U.S. Web Traffic Grows 17 Percent Week Over Week, According to Nielsen//Netratings" (in English) (Press Release). *Netratings,* Inc. Nielsen Media Research. 2006-07-21. Retrieved on 2006-09-12.

10. ^ "Google pays the price to capture online video zeitgeist" (in English). *www.Eurekastreet.com.au* (Jesuit Communications.). 2006-10-17. Retrieved on 2006-10-18.

The article draws on a variety of established information sources.

11. ^ "Google to buy YouTube for $1.65 billion". October 9, 2006. Retrieved on 2006-10-09.

12. ^ "Google closes $A2b YouTube deal". *theage.com.au.* 2006-11-14. Retrieved on 2007-03-03.

13. ^ http://logicbank.com/2007/02/09/google-sec-filing-reveals-youtube-investors-win-big/

14. ^ Stafford, Alan (2006-05-31). "The 100 Best Products of 2006". PC World. Retrieved on 2007-03-03.

15. ^ a b "GooTube: Google buys YouTube". Boing Boing. 2006-10-09. Retrieved on 2007-03-04.

16. ^ http://willy.boerland.com/myblog/youtube_bandwidth_usage_25_petabytes_per_month]. *Forbes.* April 27, 2006.

17. ^ Tapscott, Don and Anthony D. Williams. 2007. Wikinomics: How Mass Collaboration Changes Everything. New York: Penguin. p. 270.

18. ^ Tapscott, Don and Anthony D. Williams. 2007. Wikinomics: How Mass Collaboration Changes Everything. New York: Penguin. p. 271sq.

19. ^ Tapscott, Don and Anthony D. Williams. 2007. Wikinomics: How Mass Collaboration Changes Everything. New York: Penguin. p. 289sq.

20. ^ Christian Fuchs (sociologist)|Christian Fuchs (2008) Internet and Society. Social Theory in the Information Age. New York: Routledge.

21. ^ Christian Fuchs (sociologist)|Christian Fuchs (2008) Internet and Society. Social Theory in the Information Age. New York: Routledge. p. 181.

22. ^ Christian Fuchs (sociologist)|Christian Fuchs (2008) Internet and Society. Social Theory in the Information Age. New York: Routledge. p. 181.

23. ^ http://newteevee.com/2009/04/03/analyst-youtube-could-lose-470m-this-year/

24. ^ http://www.businessweek.com/the_thread/techbeat/archives/2009/06/maybe_google_is.html

**External links** [edit]

The History of YouTube at YouTube

**Respond in Writing** In your journal, write about the Wikipedia entry on YouTube. What did you learn? If you were to edit this entry, what kinds of information would you add? What would you delete?

**Develop Your Own Data** Brainstorm with your classmates to come up with ideas about which topics would be the most interesting to investigate.

**Small Groups:** In small groups, use the following graphic organizer to identify the sorts of information you might use to investigate topics related to new developments in technology.

| Why does this topic interest you? | What do you already know about the topic? | What do you need or want to know about the topic? | What kinds of evidence do you need to answer any questions? | Where can you find this kind of evidence? |
|---|---|---|---|---|
| | | | | |

**Whole Class:** Make a master chart of all of the ideas generated by the small groups to get a broader idea of how each author might go about researching his or her topic.

**Write About It** You will next write a research report in which you inquire into a question that extends your knowledge and understanding of a recent development in technology. Your report should be of sufficient length and complexity to address the topic fully. You may choose from any of the following topics, audiences, and forms.

| Possible Topics | Audiences | Possible Forms |
|---|---|---|
| • the history of how the new technology came into being<br><br>• the range of opinion available on the new technology<br><br>• aspects of the new technology with which you are unfamiliar<br><br>• the impact of the new technology on society<br><br>• the qualities of the new technology that draw you to it, and why | • people who are interested in your topic<br><br>• people who are unfamiliar with your topic<br><br>• people who would like to educate others about your topic<br><br>• people In a doctor's office waiting room looking to kill time | • a blog entry<br><br>• a post to a Web-based discussion board<br><br>• a formal report<br><br>• a letter<br><br>• a Wikipedia entry |

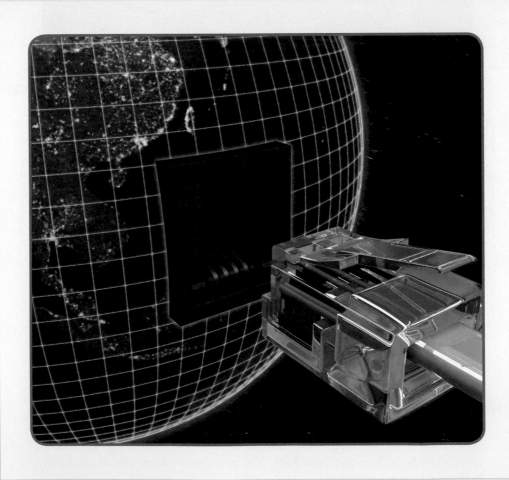

# Writing a Research Report | Planning

When you write research reports, you draw on many different skills. For example, you will do background reading to find information in books, magazines, and electronic media—using your reference and study skills. As you gather information and take notes, you use the skills of summarizing and paraphrasing. Finally, since the purpose of a research report is to convey information, you will use your expository writing skills to present the information clearly and concisely.

Your main goals in the first stages of a research report are to choose your subject and then gather information. As you collect information, keep track of notes from different sources. Index cards, paper clips, rubber bands, and a folder with pockets will make your job easier. Keep track of any Internet sources you consult by creating a bookmark folder for your report topic. Store your information in a secured part of a hard drive if you are not using your own computer for this work.

## 1 Choosing and Limiting a Subject

Subjects for a research report can come from many sources. There are two fundamental places to look for ideas for major research topics. One is inside you—your experiences and thoughts. The other is outside—the classes you take, the books you enjoy, the news stories you read, either in print or online. Brainstorming and consulting with teachers and peers are other good ways to explore possible research topics. (You can learn more about brainstorming on page 18.)

After you have explored your thoughts and experiences, use the following guidelines to help you choose one idea as a subject.

### Guidelines for Choosing a Research Subject

- Choose a subject you want to know more about.
- Choose a subject that will interest your audience.
- Choose a subject that can be adequately covered in a research report of about 2,000 words (or seven typed pages).
- Choose a subject for which there is enough information from a variety of sources in the library or media center.

To see if sufficient information exists for your subject, check the computer catalog and online databases in the library or media center. If you cannot find at least two books, two magazine articles, and one online source for your subject, you should probably choose another one.

**_Limiting a Subject_** When you are satisfied that you can find enough information, your next step is to limit your major research topic and give it a clear focus. Even a complex, multi-faceted topic must be focused so that it can be covered adequately in a certain amount of space. The subject of black holes in space, for example, is broad enough to fill a whole book. Within that broad topic, though, are more specific subjects such as "how Albert Einstein's work predicted the possibility of black holes" or "how astronomers search for black holes," that are suitably limited.

One way to limit your subject is to ask yourself a series of "what about" questions. Each question helps you focus on a more specific aspect of the broader subject. The following model shows how to use "what about" questions to narrow down the broad subject of computers.

> ### Writing Tip
>
> Limit your subject by asking, "What about [the subject]?" until you can express the focus of your research report in a phrase or partial sentence.

**EXAMPLE: Limiting a Research Subject**

| | |
|---|---|
| **Broad Subject** | Computers |
| **First Question** | *What about* computers? |
| **More Limited** | how computers help people with disabilities |
| **Second Question** | *What about* computers and people with disabilities? |
| **More Limited** | how computers help people with disabilities in communication, vision, and motion |
| **Third Question** | *What about* computers' helping with communication, vision, and motion? |
| **Suitably Limited** | the latest developments and successes in ways computers help people with disabilities in communication, vision, and motion |

Continue your "what about" questions until your answer is a phrase. This statement will keep you focused as you work through the stages of the research and writing process. Asking "what about" questions is the first step toward developing a major research question.

One helpful way to limit a subject is by using a graphic organizer like the one below. In this modified cluster diagram, the broad subject, computers, appears in the middle, and the answers to your "what about" questions fill each area as you limit the subject even further.

How computers help people with disabilities

Recent developments and successes helping people with disabilities

**Computers**

Helping people with communication, vision, and motion disabilities

Recent developments helping people with communication, vision, and motion disabilities

## PROJECT PREP  *Prewriting*    *Finding a Research Topic*

Review your journal notes on a possible research subject, and consider what you brainstormed and discussed with your classmates. Identify those topics that would be most appropriate for a research report—the project topic. You may want to review recent newspaper or magazine articles for other subject ideas. Once you have a list of at least five possible subjects, use the criteria on page 389 to help you select one major research topic. After you choose one, use a graphic organizer to limit it until your final choice is one that is focused and manageable. Save your work for later use.

## ② Developing Research Questions

After you have limited your subject, decide what you already know about it. Then formulate a major research question to address the major research topic. This question will guide you as you gather your research information. By summarizing your questions into one major research question, you can focus your efforts and thoughts. The chart below shows how this questioning process works.

Continue to suppose you are writing a research report on computers. You might ask the following questions. They will lead you to your major research question, the question that will guide your research and writing. The **major research question** is the broad question you seek to answer. The other questions address only part of the topic.

| FORMULATING A MAJOR RESEARCH QUESTION | |
|---|---|
| **Limited Subject:** | What are recent computer developments that help the disabled? |
| **Focus Questions** | **Possible Answers** |
| **What do I already know about this subject** | I saw a documentary about how young people with autism could express themselves using a computer. |
| **What More Do I Want to Find Out?** | Are there different kinds of computers for different disabilities? How do computers help people who have lost their ability to speak or have never been able to speak? In what ways do computers help people who are blind "see"? How do they help them read and write? How do computers help people who have limited mobility or are paralyzed? What tasks do they help them perform? What are the costs of this technology? What are the benefits? |
| **Major Research Question** | What are recent computer developments that help people with language, vision, and motion disabilities? |

### PROJECT PREP  *Prewriting*  *Formulating a Major Research Question*

1. With your topic selected, generate with your group a list of facts you already know about your subject and a list of questions you would like to answer through your research. Help one another ask questions that are appropriate to the topic, that may be answered through research, and that are limited enough to be answered in 5–10 pages.

2. When you have exhausted the questions, discuss each writer's list and help each writer come up with a major research question that encompasses all the other questions. Write your major research question clearly, since that is what will guide your research. Formulate a plan for your in in-depth research on your multi-faceted topic question and sketch out a rough research plan. Remember, you can modify your question as needed.

## 1 Finding Relevant Sources

With your major research question in mind, you can formulate and follow a plan for answering them. The following strategies will help you gather evidence from experts on your topic and from texts written for informed audiences in the field.

### Strategies for Gathering Information

- Consult a general reference work such as an encyclopedia or handbook either in print or online to get an overview of your subject. Make note of any sources that are listed at the ends of relevant entries.

- In the library or media center, do a subject search in the online catalog for books on your subject.

- Consult the library's online databases to find magazine and newspaper articles on your subject.

- Use a search engine to do a keyword search on the Internet for Web sites and other online resources for your subject. Note the exact addresses of sites that you think will be useful.

- For research on past events or federal policies, consult microfiche or microfilm databases to identify articles and government documents that may not be available in print or online.

- Use a variety of primary sources (firsthand accounts, documents, or physical objects written or created during the time under study) and secondary sources (information that interprets and analyzes primary sources) to explore your subject in depth, especially if your subject is about an historic figure or event.

- Make a list of all the sources you find. For each one, record the author, title, copyright year, name and location of the publisher, and call number or Internet address, if there is one. If your source is a magazine or newspaper, record the name and date of the publication, the author, the title, and the location (section and page numbers) of the article. If you found a source through a library database note the name of the database with the other information.

- Assign each source a number to identify it in your notes.

***Conducting an Interview*** In some cases, you may need to do some original research to gather information that's not available in printed or online sources. If you know of one or more experts who can contribute valuable information to your report, make an appointment to interview them, either in person or by telephone. The following steps will help you prepare for an interview and conduct it productively.

## Steps for Conducting an Interview

- Prepare at least five specific questions to ask the person you are interviewing.
- Go to the interview with your questions in hand, either in a notebook, or on index cards. Take pencils, pens, and a note pad for taking notes. Bring a small recorder if you have one.
- If you are taking notes quickly, summarize the main ideas in your own words.
- Listen for important details and interesting phrases that you might be able to quote in your report. Be sure to write these quotes word for word and indicate them with opening and closing quotation marks.
- If you need extra time to write your notes, politely ask the interviewee to wait for a few moments while you finish writing.
- If you are recording the interview, be sure to take some notes in your own words at the same time, in case anything goes wrong with the recorder. If you have time to record comments word for word, be sure to use quotation marks.
- Right after the interview, write any details you may not have had time to record.
- Thank the person for agreeing to the interview. Offer to share your finished report.

## ● Practice Your Skills

### *Gathering Information*

Using resources in the library or media center, list five sources written for informed audiences for each of the subjects below. At least two should be magazine articles, and one should be an online source. Include all the information named in the **Strategies for Gathering Information** chart on page 393.

**1.** violence on television

**2.** pros and cons of nuclear power plants

**3.** new energy-efficient car designs

## ● Practice Your Skills

### *Conducting an Interview*

Interview a classmate in preparation for a research report on the future plans of today's high school graduates. Follow the **Steps for Conducting an Interview** above. Paraphrase the interview, including quotations.

## PROJECT PREP  *Prewriting*  *Gathering Information*

Follow the research plan to gather evidence from experts on your topic and from texts written for informed audiences in the field. Begin to collect relevant and substantial information on your subject by reading appropriate sources, watching appropriate media programming, and/or interviewing people with knowledge on your topic. Take notes on information that you might include in your research report.

# Think Critically

## Analyzing a Subject

Breaking something down into its various parts is usually the best way to understand it—whether it is a car, a story, or an idea. When you carry out the process systematically, you are **analyzing.** As you prepare to write a research report, stop to analyze your complex, multi-facted topic. Ask yourself how you can break it down into smaller parts. To open your mind and help you analyze the subject, try a cluster. Below, for example, is a cluster made by a student preparing a research report on computers.

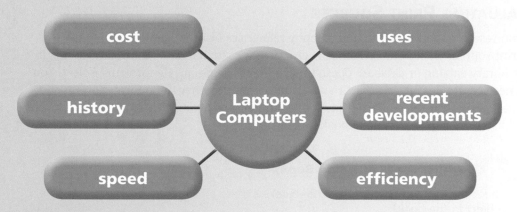

Once you have identified the major parts of a subject, you can use them to limit the subject and also point out specific directions for your research.

## Thinking Practice

Make a cluster to analyze the main parts of your research report, and use it to limit your subject and decide on specific aspects of your topic you should investigate. Remember that your report must be of sufficient length and complexity to adequately address the topic.

# ② Evaluating Sources

As you begin to search for information about your subject, remember that not all sources you find are equally reliable. Depending on how you have limited your topic, many sources will not be useful for your research purpose. Before you use a source, you should evaluate it using this criteria: All sources should be relevant to the topic and objective. The information should relate directly to your limited subject. The author should be a credible expert on the subject. Information should be current and written for informed audiences in the field. If the subject is debatable, your report should present all relevant perspectives and identify major issues and debates on the subject.

## EVALUATING PRINT SOURCES

As you research, you may find bibliography references or other citations that lead you to print sources. Just because someone else cited a particular source or because it is in your library catalog or database doesn't mean that it's appropriate for your project. You still need to decide if it's relevant to your subject and whether the information is valid, accurate, up to date, and appropriate to the kind of report you are writing. The following checklists can help you evaluate books and articles.

 **Checklist for Evaluating Books**

✓ Check the table of contents and the index. Is there information on your limited subject in the book?

✓ What is the publication date? If the subject requires the most up-to-date information, such as recent medical findings, then avoid books that are more than a few years old.

✓ What are the author's credentials? Read the book jacket, online catalog entries, or a biographical reference work to get information about the author.

✓ Is the author a recognized expert? See if other people frequently cite this author.

✓ Is there anything in the author's background or associations that might suggest a biased viewpoint?

✓ Who is the publisher? Major publishers, including university presses and government agencies review what they publish and are likely to be reputable sources.

 **Checklist for Evaluating Print Articles**

✓ Does the article contain specific information on your limited subject?

✓ When was the article published? If your subject requires the most up-to-date information, then avoid publications that are more than a few years old.

✓ Who is the author? What are his or her credentials? You can find these in a note at the beginning or end of the article.

✓ Does the magazine or newspaper appeal to a special interest group that may have a biased viewpoint on your subject? For example, a magazine called *Conserving Energy* would probably try to persuade people to rely less on automobiles. A periodical called *Highways and Byways*, on the other hand, might try to boost tourism by encouraging people to use their automobiles for long trips.

# EVALUATING ONLINE SOURCES

When you check out a book from the library, a librarian or a committee of educators has already evaluated the book to make sure it's a reliable source of information, but remember, no one owns or regulates the Internet. Just because you read something online, doesn't mean it's true. How can you tell the difference? This checklist will help you evaluate an online source.

### Checklist for Evaluating Internet Sources

✓ Start by identifying the top-level domain name. Is the site maintained by a for-profit company (.com) that might be trying to sell something? Is it an educational institution (.edu) which tends to be more reliable, or an independent organization (.org)? If it is an organization, is it one whose name you recognize or is it one that you have never heard of before? Be aware that ".org" sites are often owned by nonprofit organizations that may support a particular cause.

✓ If the Web site contains an article, is it signed? If it is not signed, you should be skeptical of its credibility. If you do not recognize the author's name, you can send a question to a newsgroup or e-mail list server asking if anyone else knows something about this person. You can also do a Web search using the author's name as the keyword to get more information.

✓ Does it use reasonable and sufficient facts and examples to make its points? Is it free from obvious errors?

✓ Is the site well designed and organized? Do the language and graphics avoid sensationalism?

✓ Has the site been recently updated? Is the information still current? Look for a date on the main Web page indicating the last time it was updated.

✓ Is the site rated by a reputable group for the quality of its content? You can find recommendations for reliable Web sites at ipl2 (Internet Public Library) <http://www.ipl.org/>.

*You can learn more about using the Internet for research on pages 421–423.*

After using the preceding checklists to evaluate books, articles, and online sources, use only those primary and secondary sources that are valid, reliable, and relevant. Search for information on all relevant perspectives on your topic  Five to ten reliable sources should supply you with enough information to build a strong research report.

● **Practice Your Skills**

*Evaluating Sources*

Each of the following sources for a report on consumer safety suffers from one of the weaknesses listed below. Write the weakness that applies to each source.

A.   probably outdated

B.   probably biased

C.   lacks strong author credentials

D.   does not relate to subject

1. "Unnecessary Safety Controls Will Raise Prices," article in *Toymaker's Trade*, written by Lara Scranton, director of public relations at Smile-a-While Toy Company, published in 2008.
2. "Consumer Price Index Holds Steady," article in *Today* magazine, written by Manuel Garcia, chief economist at Central State Bank, published in 2009.
3. *Consumer Rights and Safety*, book published in 1973, written by William Stepanian, researcher in the Office of Consumer Affairs in the state of Illinois.
4. "The Need for Warning Labels," article in *Your House*, written in 2009 by Helene Mayer, a magazine writer who writes a column on fashion tips.
5. "Harmful Additives," pamphlet published in 2009 by Nature-Foods Industries, written by Kyle Gardner, Executive Vice President of Nature-Foods Industries.

---

**PROJECT PREP** *Prewriting* **Evaluating Sources**

In your writing group or with a research partner, discuss the sources you have found to locate verifiable facts for your research. For each writer, make a source evaluation chart like the one below. When you have completed such a chart for each writer, help one another decide which sources are valid, reliable, and relevant, and which are not, and focus your research using the reliable sources.

| Evaluation Chart for Research Sources | | | | | | |
|---|---|---|---|---|---|---|
| Source title | Reputable name? | Well designed? | Authors named? | Bias? | Date published? | Original language? |
| 1 | | | | | | |
| 2 | | | | | | |
| 3 | | | | | | |

# In the Media

## Multiple Media Identities: Check Us Out Online

In addition to their primary medium, most large media corporations also have an extensive presence on the World Wide Web. The following are just a few examples.

**Magazines**

*Discover Magazine*         http://discovermagazine.com
*Time Magazine*             http://www.time.com/time

**Newspapers**

*The Washington Post*       http://www.washingtonpost.com
*The New York Times*        http://www.nytimes.com

**Television**

The Discovery Channel       http://dsc.discovery.com
NBC News                    http://www.msnbc.msn.com
PBS                         http://www.pbs.org

**Radio**

National Public Radio       http://www.npr.org

## Media Activity

Each of the examples above would be worth using in research projects in its original medium. To find out what extra value, if any, the online presence adds, choose two of the references above and carefully research their Web sites. Write a paragraph for each one comparing the kinds of information available in the original and online versions and offering an opinion on the value of the Internet material.

The research guide questions you developed earlier will help you locate relevant information in each source. As you take notes on that information, keep the following guidelines in mind.

## HERE'S HOW  Taking Notes

- Write the identifying number of each source in the upper right-hand corner of the note card.
- Write the topic of the note in the upper left-hand corner of your card.
- On each card, include only notes that relate to a single topic, which will usually correspond with a guide question.
- Include only information that answers a guide question.
- If necessary, revise your questions to be more specific or to cover different aspects of your subject.
- Clip together all cards from the same source.

The following paragraphs are from a *Discover* magazine article found through an online database. The source has been assigned the identifying number 10. Read the excerpt and compare it with the sample note card that follows.

### Writing Tip

The goals of note taking are to summarize main points in your own words and record quotations that you might use in your research report.

### MODEL: Taking Notes on a Source

It is a stiflingly hot summer day in Atlanta. Scientist and physician Philip Kennedy has a packed schedule, so he suggests that I interview him while he drives to the tiny town of Bowdon, Georgia, just east of the Alabama line. It's a journey he takes every Memorial Day to a small cemetery.

We park behind the red brick Sandy Flat Baptist Church. The sun is blazing overhead, the glare from the white gravel parking lot almost blinding. But Kennedy knows exactly where he's going. He quickly walks through the simple graves carpeted by carefully tended grass, then stops and bends down. Visibly moved by private thoughts, the scientist touches a simple headstone and leaves beside it a tribute he wrote for the man buried here, a man he calls a hero.

Johnny Ray, who died on this date six years ago, was Kennedy's patient, his research subject, and the world's first human cyborg, fitted with brain implants that allowed him to communicate directly with a computer.

Kennedy is the chief scientist of Neural Signals, a company he founded in 1987 to develop a brain-computer interface, or BCI, though he prefers the term "neural prosthetics."

By any name, the devices created by Kennedy and a handful of others can decode the conscious intentions conveyed by neural signals. For those who are missing a leg or who have a broken spine, the signals can control computers, wheelchairs, and prosthetic limbs. For those suffering from "locked-in syndrome," their bodies so immobilized by catastrophic disorders like amyotrophic lateral sclerosis (ALS) or brain stem stroke that they are unable to speak or communicate their needs, the devices can translate neural signals to spell out words on a computer screen. Spoken language through a voice synthesizer is coming soon.

—Sherry Baker, *Discover*

## Sample Note Card

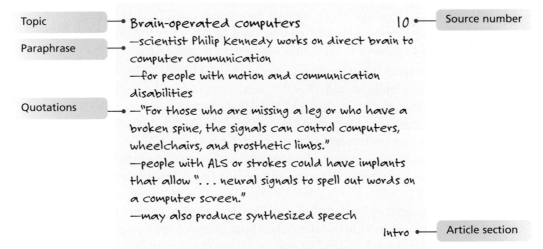

Topic • **Brain-operated computers**    10 •— Source number

Paraphrase •—scientist Philip Kennedy works on direct brain to computer communication
—for people with motion and communication disabilities

Quotations •—"For those who are missing a leg or who have a broken spine, the signals can control computers, wheelchairs, and prosthetic limbs."
—people with ALS or strokes could have implants that allow ". . . neural signals to spell out words on a computer screen."
—may also produce synthesized speech

Intro •— Article section

● **Pratice Your Skills**

*Taking Notes*

Take notes on the following excerpt about Stonehenge, the ancient arrangement of stones in England through which one can observe celestial activities. The excerpt is from the first two pages of an article "New Light on Stonehenge," written by Dan Jones, which appeared in *Smithsonian Magazine* October 2008 and found at <http://www.smithsonianmag.com/>. Assume that the work has the identifying number 3.

The Druids arrived around 4 P.M. . . . With the pounding of the drum growing louder, the retinue approached the outer circle of massive stone trilithons[1]—each made up of two huge pillars capped by a stone lintel[2]—and passed through them to the inner circle. Here they were greeted by Timothy Darvill, 50, professor of archaeology at Bournemouth University, and Geoffrey Wainwright, 70, president of the Society of Antiquaries of London.

For two weeks, the pair had been leading the first excavation in 44 years of the inner circle of Stonehenge—the best-known and most mysterious megalithic[3] monument in the world. . . . [W]hile other experts have speculated that Stonehenge was a prehistoric observatory or a royal burial ground, Darvill and Wainwright are intent on proving it was primarily a sacred place of healing, where the sick came to be cured and the injured and infirm restored.

Darvill and Wainwright's theory rests, almost literally, on bluestones— unexceptional igneous[4] rocks, such as dolerite and rhyolite—so called because they take on a bluish hue when wet or cut. Over the centuries, legends have endowed these stones with mystical properties. . . .

We now know that Stonehenge was in the making for at least 400 years. The first phase, built around 3000 B.C., was a simple circular earthwork enclosure similar to many "henges" (sacred enclosures typically comprising a circular bank and a ditch) found throughout the British Isles. Around 2800 B.C., timber posts were erected within the enclosure. Again, such posts are not unusual—Woodhenge, for example, which once consisted of tall posts arranged in a series of six concentric oval rings, lies only a few miles to the east.

Archaeologists have long believed that Stonehenge began to take on its modern form two centuries later, when large stones were brought to the site in the third and final stage of its construction. The first to be put in place were the 80 or so bluestones, which were arranged in a double circle with an

1. A trilithon is a grouping of three rocks in which two tall pillar rocks are connected at the top by a third that spans the distance between them.
2. A lintel is a horizontal beam or stone that rests over an opening such as a doorway.
3. Made of very large stones by prehistoric cultures.
4. Formed by volcanic action.

entrance facing northeast. "Their arrival is when Stonehenge was transformed from a quite ordinary and typical monument into something unusual," says Andrew Fitzpatrick of Wessex Archaeology, a nonprofit organization based in Salisbury.

The importance of the bluestones is underscored by the immense effort involved in moving them a long distance—some were as long as ten feet and weighed four tons. Geological studies in the 1920s determined that they came from the Preseli Mountains in southwest Wales, 140 miles from Stonehenge. Some geologists have argued that glaciers moved the stones, but most experts now believe that humans undertook the momentous task.

## PROJECT PREP *Prewriting* *Taking Notes*

Continue to follow your research plan and gather evidence in reliable sources that will help you answer your research questions, taking notes when you find information that you can use in your report. Focus your efforts on gathering evidence from texts written for informed audiences. Use the above procedures for using note cards, computer technology, and other tools for conducting your research. Paraphrase, summarize, and quote from your sources as you take notes.

# Writing Lab

## Project Corner

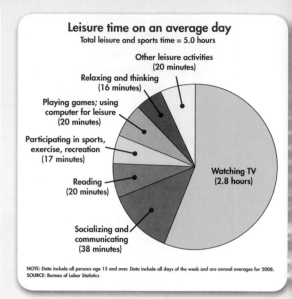

**Leisure time on an average day**
Total leisure and sports time = 5.0 hours

Other leisure activities (20 minutes)
Relaxing and thinking (16 minutes)
Playing games; using computer for leisure (20 minutes)
Participating in sports, exercise, recreation (17 minutes)
Reading (20 minutes)
Socializing and communicating (38 minutes)
Watching TV (2.8 hours)

NOTE: Data include all persons age 15 and over. Data include all days of the week and are annual averages for 2008.
SOURCE: Bureau of Labor Statistics

## Think Critically
### Take Stock

With your writing group, **evaluate your progress** so far in working on your research project. You may want to consider such questions as:

- Is my topic genuinely interesting to me?

- Is my major research question open enough to allow room for me to adapt it to new evidence? Have I identified a variety of reliable sources?

- Do my notes contain enough information so that I do not need to find the source and page number again when I am drafting?

- Do my notes summarize and paraphrase in my own words?

If you answer "no" to any of these questions, rethink your topic and adjust your research accordingly. (For more on researching see pages 380–457.)

## Chart It Interpret From Visual to Print

The pie chart on this page indicates favorite American pastimes. **Interpret this chart** by writing a paragraph explaining the numbers. Then write your opinion about what these numbers indicate.

## Speak and Listen Conduct an Interview

Not all sources for reports are found in the library or online. People themselves are often good sources, and you can find out what they know related to your subject by conducting an interview. Think of a person you know who might be able to offer you helpful information about your topic, or direct you to someone else who can. **Set up and conduct an interview to gain information.** Take notes (or, with your interviewee's permission, record the interview) so you will remember what was said. (For more on interviewing see pages 393–394.)

# In the Workplace
## Research Music History

1. You work as a talent manager, booking concerts for many successful musicians. You must convince the owner of the local concert hall that the 1930s boogie-woogie piano style is a direct ancestor of rock and roll and that there is a market for this music. ***Research the history of boogie-woogie*** and its performers. Find at least five reliable sources and take notes for a report you will write in the future to persuade the concert hall owner to book a boogie-woogie concert.

# In Spoken Communication
## Plan a Career Day Speech

2. Your class is hosting a career day designed to broaden students' ideas about possible professions. You are asked to speak for three minutes on a career that you find interesting. ***Develop a research plan*** for your speech. Use "what about" questions to help you limit your topic and develop a series of guide questions to help you plan your research. Find reliable sources from the library and online that will provide answers to your questions. Consider interviewing someone who works in the profession. Take notes on the information you find.

# Timed Writing 🕐 Research Movies

3. You and your friends watch a lot of movies on DVD and at the movie theater. You enjoy talking about them and sharing your reactions. Recently, a teacher at school suggested that you and your friends create a guide to help other moviegoers choose what films to see. You think this is a great idea—perhaps you could even start your own movie-review television show or create a film-guide Web site for teenagers. As a first step, choose four films that you would like to review. Research your choices in magazines, newspapers, or on the Internet to list where to find the film, the principal cast, and the director. You have 20 minutes in the library or media center to complete your research.

   ***Before You Write*** Consider the following questions: What is the situation? What is the occasion? Who is the audience? What is the purpose?

   ***After You Write*** Evaluate your work by evaluating your sources as outlined on pages 396–398.

# Research **Companion**

It may be impossible to know everything, but almost anything worth knowing can be found in your library or media center. Libraries contain, preserve, and provide access to knowledge that has survived since the advent of the written word. However, when embarking on the glorious quest for knowledge, it is advisable to take a compass. Research skills are a precision instrument to help you find exactly what you seek. With so many avenues of research to explore, applying your reference skills can be an enjoyable part of the writing process, and an exciting way to expand your knowledge about any subject imaginable.

## Using the Library or Media Center

In the past, when people thought about the library, they mostly thought of it as a place to find books. Today, however, most libraries operate as media centers where, in addition to books, you can find magazines, newspapers, and a wide range of reference materials in print, online, or in electronic formats. In addition to printed materials, libraries and media centers also carry nonprint materials, such as audio recordings, video documentaries, downloadable audio books and electronic books, photographic archives, and computers that provide access to the Internet, online databases, and the World Wide Web. The library or media center is the best place to learn how to use reference materials and become a better researcher. Understanding the library's arrangement and the wide variety of resources available will help you efficiently locate the materials you need.

### LIBRARY OR MEDIA CENTER ARRANGEMENT

For many years the most popular system of organizing books was the **Dewey decimal system.** As library collections grew to include more than 30,000 titles, another system became necessary. As a result, the **Library of Congress system,** which can be used to classify millions of books, was developed. Today large libraries, such as those at colleges and universities, use the Library of Congress system.

***Dewey Decimal System*** Most school libraries and media centers use the Dewey decimal system. In this system, works of fiction, such as short stories and novels, are kept separate from nonfiction works. Works of fiction are arranged alphabetically by the authors' last names. These books can also be marked with the letters *F* or *Fic*. When searching for works of fiction, remember the following guidelines.

## Guidelines for Finding Fiction

- Two-part names are alphabetized by the first part of the name. (**De** Soto, **O'Connor**, **Van** Buren)
- Names beginning with **Mc** or **St.** are alphabetized as if they began with **Mac** or **Saint**.
- Books by authors with the same last name are alphabetized by the authors' first names.
- Books by the same author are alphabetized by the first important word in the title.
- Numbers in titles are alphabetized as if they were written out. (40,000 = forty thousand)

In the Dewey decimal classification system, nonfiction books are assigned a number according to their subjects, as shown in the following chart.

| DEWEY DECIMAL SYSTEM | |
| --- | --- |
| 000–099 | General Works (reference books) |
| 100–199 | Philosophy and Psychology |
| 200–299 | Religion |
| 300–399 | Social Sciences (law, education, economics) |
| 400–499 | Languages |
| 500–599 | Natural Sciences (math, biology, chemistry) |
| 600–699 | Technology (medicine, inventions) |
| 700–799 | Arts (painting, music, theater) |
| 800–899 | Literature |
| 900–999 | Geography and History (including biography and travel) |

For each main subject area, there are ten smaller divisions. The following subdivisions show how the main subject Literature (800–899) is classified by number.

| 800–899 LITERATURE | | | |
| --- | --- | --- | --- |
| 800–809 | General | 850–859 | Italian |
| 810–819 | American | 860–869 | Spanish |
| 820–829 | English | 870–879 | Latin |
| 830–839 | German | 880–889 | Greek |
| 840–849 | French | 890–899 | Other |

These subdivisions are divided further with the use of decimal points and other identifying symbols. The shelves are also marked with numbers so that books can be easily located.

The numbers identifying a book make up the **call number.** Every book has a different call number. In addition to the call number, some books carry a special label to show the section of the library in which they are shelved.

The following chart shows some special labels.

| CATEGORIES | SPECIAL LABELS |
| --- | --- |
| Easy Reading | E |
| Juvenile Books | J or X |
| Young Adult | YA |
| Reference Works | R or REF |

***Biographies and Autobiographies*** Biographies and autobiographies are often in a section of their own and marked with a *B* or *92* (a shortened form of 920 in the Dewey decimal system). They are arranged in alphabetical order according to the name of the person they are about. Books about the same person are further arranged according to the author's last name.

● **Develop Research Skills**

### *Using the Dewey Decimal System*

Using the list of classifications on page 407, write the subject numbers for each book. If the title is marked with an asterisk (*), also write the subdivision listed on page 407.

| Example | *Shakespeare's Imagery\** |
| --- | --- |
| Answer | 800–899, 820–829 |

**1.** *This Chemical Age*
**2.** *Anglo-Saxon Riddles\**
**3.** *Drawing Portraits*
**4.** *New Church Programs for the Aging*
**5.** *Basic Principles of Geometry*
**6.** *Twentieth-Century French Literature\**
**7.** *The British Empire before the American Revolution*
**8.** *Guide to Philosophy*
**9.** *Greek Lyric Poetry\**
**10.** *Principles of Political Economy*

***The Library of Congress System*** This system differs from the Dewey decimal system in two main ways: it uses letters to identify subjects rather than numbers; and works of fiction and nonfiction are grouped together. The letters correspond to 20 main subject areas, rather than the 10 designated by the Dewey decimal system. The chart below outlines the 20 subject categories found in the Library of Congress system.

| LIBRARY OF CONGRESS SYSTEM | |
|---|---|
| A General works | M Music |
| B Philosophy, religion | N Fine Arts |
| C Sciences of history | P Language and literature |
| D Non-American history and travel | Q Science |
| E American history | R Medicine |
| F U.S. local history | S Agriculture |
| G Geography, anthropology | T Technology |
| H Social sciences | U Military science |
| J Political science | V Naval science |
| L Education | Z Library science |

These 20 main categories can be further divided by using a second letter. QB, for example, refers to the general category of science, with a focus on astronomy. Further subdivisions are made by using numbers and letters.

## ● Develop Research Skills

### *Using the Library of Congress System*

Copy the book titles from the previous **Develop Research Skills** activity. Then, referring to the classification chart for the Library of Congress, write the first letter of the call number for each book.

**Example**     *Shakespeare's Imagery*

**Answer**     P

## THE LIBRARY CATALOG

Most libraries and media centers store records of their holdings in an **online catalog.** Computer systems can vary from library to library, but generally the search methods are the same. To search the listings in an online catalog, you select a category to search—author, title, or subject. Authors' names are written last name first; for most titles, the words *A, An,* and *The* are omitted at the beginning of a title; and for subjects, searchers must enter the exact words for each category.

On some systems, you can execute a keyword search, just as you would on an Internet search engine. A keyword search can sort through the library's collections by both title and subject headings simultaneously. The computer can tell you whether the book you seek is available or—if it has been checked out—when it is due back. By using the Web to search other library databases, the librarian can also tell you if the book is available elsewhere.

If your book is in the catalog, the computer displays an entry similar to that in the following example. Hypertext links enable you to move back and forth between sections of the catalog.

### ONLINE CATALOG RECORD

**The crucible**
   Miller, Arthur, 1915–2005

| | |
|---|---|
| **Personal Author:** | Miller, Arthur, 1915–2005 |
| **Title:** | The crucible/Arthur Miller. |
| **Publication info:** | New York: Viking Penguin, c1981. |
| **Physical descrip:** | 152 p.; 20 cm. |
| **Subject term:** | Witchcraft–Massachusetts–Salem–Drama. |
| **Geographic term:** | Salem (Mass.)–History–Colonial period, ca. 1600–1775–Drama. |

You may also find a simpler record of the book that may appear as follows. This type of catalog entry tells you where you can find the book in the library. It may also include a brief summary of the book.

### ITEM INFORMATION ENTRY

**The crucible**
   Miller, Arthur, 1915–2005

Here, especially for high school students, is an analysis and summary of Arthur Miller's famous play. Titles in the Literature Made Easy Series analyze novels and plays found in most school curricula. More than mere plot summaries, these books explain themes, analyze characters, and discuss each author's unique writing read more . . .

| | |
|---|---|
| **Publisher:** | Viking Penguin, |
| **Pub date:** | c1981. |
| **Pages:** | 152 p.; |
| **ISBN:** | 0140481389 |
| **Item info:** | 1 copy available at Columbia Public Library. |
| **A Look Inside:** | |
| **Holdings** | |

| Columbia Public Library | Copies | | Material | Location |
|---|---|---|---|---|
| 812.52 MIL | 1 | | Paperback | Non-Fiction |

## Strategies for Using an Online Catalog

Think about what you already know that can limit your search. A title or author search will always give you more focused results than a subject search. If you are doing a subject search, find a way to limit the category, either by year or by subcategory.

### Searching by Author's Name

- If the last name is common, type the author's complete last name followed by a comma and a space and the author's first initial or complete first name.
- Omit all accent and punctuation marks in the author's name.
- For compound names, try variations in placement of the parts:

    **von karajan herbert** or **karajan herbert von**

### Searching by Title

- If the title is long, type only the first few words. Omit capitalization, punctuation, accent marks, and articles.

    **bell for adano**
    **grapes of wrath**
    **plains trains and automobiles**

- If you are unsure of the correct form of a word, try variations such as

    spelling out or inserting spaces between initials and abbreviations,
    entering numbers as words,
    using an ampersand (&) for *and,* or
    spelling hyphenated words as one or two words.

### Searching by Subject

- Omit commas, parentheses, and capitalization.
- Broad categories can be divided into subcategories to make your search more specific.
- If you don't know the correct subject heading, find at least one source relevant to your topic by doing a title or keyword search. Use one or more of the subject headings listed there for additional searches.

### Searching by Keyword

- Searching with a single word such as *Shakespeare* will find that word anywhere in the entry: in the title, author, subject, or descriptive notes.
- A phrase such as *space travel* finds entries containing the words *space* and *travel.* To search for *space travel* as a phrase, type *space and travel,* or *space adj travel* (adj = adjacent).
- An open search will look anywhere in the entry for your word. You can limit your keyword searches to specific search fields (either author, title, or subject) by doing an advanced search and selecting the appropriate field.

● **Develop Research Skills**

*Searching Online Catalogs*

Write what you would type into the online catalog to search for each of the following.

1. the life and times of Emilio Zapata
2. the books of Mark Twain
3. the skills of rollerblading
4. Sherlock Holmes stories
5. a history of writing

6. the castles of Germany
7. the poems of Nikki Giovanni
8. Mayan calendars
9. bicycling through France
10. falconry in India

## PARTS OF A BOOK

The first step in the research process is to find sources that can help you with your project. Once you find several sources, you need to spend some time looking through them to see if they have any information that you can use. Books have features that can make finding this information easier, if you know how to use the parts of a book effectively.

### INFORMATION FOUND IN PARTS OF A BOOK

| PART | INFORMATION |
|---|---|
| Title Page | shows the full title, author's name, publisher, place of publication |
| Copyright Page | gives the date of first publication and of any revised editions |
| Table of Contents | lists chapter or section titles in the book and their starting page numbers |
| Introduction | gives an overview of the author's ideas in each chapter and in relation to the work that other writers have done on the subject |
| Appendix | gives additional information on subjects in the book; charts, graphs, and maps are sometimes included here |
| Bibliography | lists sources that the author used to write the book, including title and copyright information on related topics |
| Index | lists topics that are mentioned in the book and gives the page numbers where these topics can be found |

*Using the Parts of a Book*

Write the part of the book you would use to find each of the following items of information.

**1.** a chart or graph with additional information

**2.** the name and location of the publisher

**3.** the title of a specific chapter

**4.** the name and publication information for a source used by the author

**5.** the year of publication

**6.** definition of a difficult or technical word

**7.** a specific topic or person mentioned in the book

**8.** the author's explanation of the book's contents

# Using Print and Nonprint Reference Materials

In most libraries and media centers, reference materials are kept in a separate room or area. Since these materials cannot be removed from the media center, a study area is usually provided.

Now libraries and media centers are also often the best way to find the most authoritative online reference sources. Most libraries subscribe to **online databases** that can be accessed through computers in the library. Often, anyone with a library card may use a home computer to search the databases through the library's Web site. These databases provide a wealth of reliable information that is not usually available for free just by searching on the Internet. Some databases are especially designed for high school students. Following is a review of the kinds of reference materials you may find most helpful.

## PRINT AND ELECTRONIC REFERENCES

- general and specialized encyclopedias

- general and specialized dictionaries

- atlases, almanacs, and yearbooks

- specialized biographical and literary references

- online databases and indexes of periodicals (including magazines, newspapers, and journals)

- microfilm and microfiche files of periodicals and government documents

- computers with access to the Internet and World Wide Web

- audio recordings and video documentaries

- vertical file of print material

## PERIODICALS—MAGAZINES AND NEWSPAPERS

Periodicals, including magazines and journals, are excellent sources for current information. The periodical reading room in the library or media center should have the most recent print issues of all the periodicals to which the library subscribes. You can usually search for periodical titles in the library's online catalog but you cannot search for individual articles. The entry will describe the extent of the library's holdings. For example, a library may keep two months of a daily newspaper and two years of weekly or monthly magazines.

By subscribing to online databases, libraries can now offer people access to a wider variety of periodicals than they would have space for in the library. Databases may cover general interest periodicals, scholarly journals, or periodicals covering specialized fields such as business or health. A librarian or media specialist can help you determine which databases are best for your particular research project. You can search in a database using keywords as you would with an Internet search engine. Database entries provide an abstract or short summary of the article so you can decide if it is useful to read the full text. Full text is available for many articles from the 1990s onward. These full text articles can be downloaded or printed. Many databases allow you to save your search results in folders for future reference.

*You can learn more about searching with keywords on pages 411 and 422.*

***Newspapers*** Newspapers are valuable sources of current and historical information. Some online databases contain only newspapers and others combine newspapers and magazines. Some even include radio and television news transcripts. Many databases allow you to limit your search to specific dates or even specific periodical titles. While most databases focus on articles from the 1990s to the present, some include references to articles from earlier periods. The *Historical New York Times* database offers full text articles back to the newspaper's first issue in 1851.

Most major newspapers now have Web sites and electronic databases where you can view current issues and search for archived articles. The following examples are only a few of the many available online.

| | |
|---|---|
| *The Chicago Tribune* | http://www.chicago.tribune.com |
| *The Dallas Morning News* | http://www.dallasnews.com |
| *The Los Angeles Times* | http://www.latimes.com |
| *The Miami Herald* | http://www.herald.com |
| *The New York Times* | http://www.nytimes.com |

By going directly to the Web, you can also search databases that locate and access the home pages of newspapers from every state in the United States and many countries around the world. Both of the following sites list hundreds of newspapers by location (country and state) and by subject (business, arts and entertainment, trade journals, or college papers).

**ipl2 (Internet Public Library)**    http://www.ipl.org/div/news

**Newspapers Online!**    http://www.newspapers.com

Remember: always read the guidelines at the home page for each newspaper. Recent articles are usually available free of charge, but you may have to pay a fee to download and print an archived article.

*Older Periodicals*  To save space, many libraries store older issues of some magazines and newspapers as photographic reproductions of print pages on rolls and sheets of film. **Microform** holdings may be included in the library's online catalog or may have a separate catalog or list in the microform area of the library or media center. **Microfilm** (rolls) or **microfiche** (sheets) are stored in filing cabinets and can be viewed easily on special projectors. Newspapers, for example, are arranged in file drawers alphabetically by keywords in their titles. The holdings for each newspaper are then filed chronologically by date. For example, if you wanted to know what happened in Houston, Texas, on New Year's Eve in the year you were born, you could go to the file cabinets and get the roll of film for the *Houston Chronicle* on that day in that year. Check with a librarian to see if there are indexes for any of the newspapers to help you locate articles on specific topics.

Researchers looking for older magazine articles not covered in online databases may use *The Readers' Guide to Periodical Literature,* an index of articles, short stories, and poems published in a large number of magazines and journals. Articles are indexed by date, author, and subject. Libraries may subscribe to print or online versions of the *Readers' Guide*. A search of the library's catalog will tell you which issues of the guide are available in your library and whether they are in print or electronic form. Once you know the name of the magazine or journal you want you will need to check the library's catalog to see if that specific periodical is available.

## ENCYCLOPEDIAS

Encyclopedias provide basic information on just about every subject imaginable. The information in most encyclopedias is arranged alphabetically by subject in multiple volumes. Some encyclopedias have a comprehensive index, either as a separate volume or at the back of the last volume. This index will help you find out quickly if your subject is covered, and under what headings. If it is not covered, it might suggest other subjects to look up. At the end of each encyclopedia article, you might also find a listing of additional topics to reference.

Online encyclopedias are arranged in the same manner as printed encyclopedias—alphabetically, but there are no guide words or indexes. Instead, in order to find information on a particular subject, you enter the subject in a search box. The best online encyclopedias are the ones available through your library's databases. Beware of open source encyclopedias that have unsigned articles that can be changed without being reviewed by an expert.

| Print and Online | Through libraries and media centers:<br>*Encyclopaedia Britannica*<br>*World Book Encyclopedia*<br>*Encyclopedia Americana*<br>*Grolier Multimedia Encyclopedia* |
| Online | Reliable free encyclopedia:<br>*Columbia Encyclopedia* http://www.bartleby.com/65/ |

**Specialized Encyclopedias** Specialized encyclopedias focus on a variety of specific subjects, from auto racing to weaving. Because they concentrate on a specific subject, these encyclopedias provide more in-depth information than general encyclopedias do. These can also be found in the reference section of the library. Specialized encyclopedias online let you search for information by subject and connect to other Web sites on your topic through hyperlinks. The online *Encyclopedia Smithsonian,* for example, covers topics in physical sciences, social sciences, and U.S. and natural history.

Following are some specialized encyclopedias.

| Print | *World Sports Encyclopedia*<br>*Encyclopedia of Mythology*<br>*International Wildlife Encyclopedia*<br>*Encyclopedia of American Facts and Dates*<br>*The International Encyclopedia of the Social Sciences* |
| Online | *Encyclopedia Smithsonian*<br>http://www.si.edu/Encyclopedia_SI/default.htm<br>A collection of almost 50 different encyclopedias<br>http://www.encyclopedia.com |

## BIOGRAPHICAL REFERENCES

Information about famous historical figures can be found in encyclopedias. To find information about contemporary personalities, you may need to use other biographical references. For example, *Who's Who, Who's Who in America*, and *Who's Who of American Women* have biographical sketches on people in popular culture that are not always found in an encyclopedia.

Many libraries subscribe to one or more biographical databases that contain information from a variety of published sources including books and magazine articles and that may have links to reliable Web sites with information on the person. Some biographical resources focus on the lives of women and African Americans in U.S. history, and some multimedia or online resources contain film clips and audio recordings of important historical events.

| | |
|---|---|
| Print | *Current Biography* |
| | *Who's Who in America* |
| | *Merriam-Webster's Biographical Dictionary* |
| | *Dictionary of American Biography* |
| | *American Men and Women of Science* |
| Online | *Distinguished Women of Past and Present* |
| | http://www.distinguishedwomen.com |
| | *Encyclopaedia Britannica Guide to Black History* |
| | http://search.eb.com/blackhistory/ |

## REFERENCES ABOUT LANGUAGE AND LITERATURE

The following reference works, which are usually shelved with the general works of the same type, provide information about language and literature.

| | |
|---|---|
| Specialized Dictionaries | *Dictionary of Literary Terms* |
| | *Brewer's Dictionary of Phrase and Fable* |
| Specialized Encyclopedias | *Reader's Encyclopedia of American Literature* |
| | *Encyclopedia of American-Indian Literature* |
| Biographical References | *Contemporary Authors* |
| | *American Authors 1600–1900* |
| | *Contemporary Poets* |
| | *Notable African American Writers* |

Handbooks, or companions, are another kind of literary references. Some handbooks give plot summaries or describe characters. Others explain literary terms or give information about authors.

Books of quotations tell you the source of a particular quotation. These books also list complete quotations as well as other quotations on the same subject.

Indexes are useful for finding a particular poem, short story, or play. An index such as *Granger's Index to Poetry* lists the books that contain the particular selection you are looking for. The *Gale Literary Index* contains information about authors and their major works.

Comprehensive online databases combine many of these literary references into a convenient resource that you can search by author, title, subject, or keyword. You may find complete works along with biographical information and literary criticism. A database likely contains information from hundreds of sources on thousands of authors. Ask your librarian what your library provides.

| Print | *The Reader's Encyclopedia* |
|---|---|
| | *The Oxford Companion to American Literature* |
| | *The Oxford Companion to English Literature* |
| | *Bartlett's Familiar Quotations* |
| | *The Oxford Dictionary of Quotations* |
| | *Granger's Index to Poetry* |
| | *Short Story Index* |
| Online | *About.com: Classic Literature* http://classiclit.about.com/ |
| | *Gale Literary Index* http://www.galenet.com/servlet/LitIndex |
| | *Bartlett's Familiar Quotations* http://www.bartleby.com/100 |
| | *The Quotations Page* http://www.quotationspage.com/ |

● **Develop Research Skills**

*Using Literary References*

Write the name of one source listed on page 417 that you could use to answer each question.

**1.** In what year did Leo Tolstoy write *War and Peace*?

**2.** Where could you find a short story called "Flowering Judas" by Katherine Anne Porter?

**3.** What American novelists were at work during the Civil War period?

**4.** Which poem begins, "The time you won your town the race"?

**5.** What does the term *picaresque* mean in literature?

## ATLASES

Besides being a book of maps, an atlas usually contains information about the location of continents, countries, cities, mountains, lakes, and other geographical features and regions. Some atlases, however, also have information about population, climate, natural resources, industries, and transportation. Historical atlases show maps of the world during different moments in history. Some online resources from the United States Geological Survey incorporate satellite imagery to let you examine the geography of the United States by state and by region.

| Print | *Goode's World Atlas* |
| | *The Times Atlas of the World* |
| | *The World Book Atlas* |
| | *Hammond Odyssey World Atlas* |
| | *Rand McNally International World Atlas* |
| | *The National Geographic Atlas of the World* |
| | *Rand McNally Atlas of World History* |
| Online | *National Atlas of the United States* http://www-atlas.usgs.gov/ |

## ALMANACS AND YEARBOOKS

Almanacs are generally published each year and contain up-to-date facts and statistical information such as: population, weather, government, and business. Almanacs also provide historical facts and geographic information. *The Old Farmer's Almanac* provides weather and seasonal information.

| Print | *Information Please Almanac* |
| | *World Almanac and Book of Facts* |
| | *Guinness Book of World Records* |
| Online | *The Old Farmer's Almanac,* http://www.almanac.com |
| | *Infoplease* http://www.infoplease.com/ |

## SPECIALIZED DICTIONARIES

When you do research on a specialized subject, you often encounter a word that you do not recognize. You will find that specialized dictionaries can be very helpful. These dictionaries provide information about the vocabulary used in specific fields of study, like medicine, music, and computer science. Often, you can find online sources of dictionaries in several languages.

| Print | *Harvard Dictionary of Music* |
| | *Concise Dictionary of American History* |
| | *Merriam-Webster's Geographical Dictionary* |
| Online | Medical, legal, and multilingual dictionaries and a style guide http://dictionary.reference.com/ |
| | *Strunk's Elements of Style* http://www.bartleby.com/141/ |

**Books of Synonyms** Another type of dictionary, called a **thesaurus,** features synonyms (different words with the same meanings) and antonyms (words with opposite meanings). This resource is especially helpful if you are looking for a specific word or if you want to vary your word usage and build your vocabulary. Many Web browsers, online databases, and word processing software programs include dictionary and thesaurus features.

| Print | *Roget's 21st Century Thesaurus in Dictionary Form* |
|-------|-----------------------------------------------------|
|       | *Merriam-Webster Dictionary of Synonyms and Antonyms* |
|       | *Oxford American Writer's Thesaurus* |
| Online | *Roget's Thesaurus* http://thesaurus.reference.com/ |
|        | *Merriam-Webster Dictionary and Thesaurus* http://www.merriam-webster.com/ |

## OTHER REFERENCE MATERIALS

Most libraries and media centers have a variety of printed materials that are not found in bound form. They also have other nonprint resources such as audio recordings and video documentaries that contain information that cannot be conveyed in print form.

***Vertical Files*** Libraries often store pamphlets, catalogs, and newspaper clippings alphabetically in a filing cabinet called the vertical file. Materials are stored in folders in file cabinets and arranged alphabetically by subject.

***Government Documents and Historical Records*** References stored on microforms may include government documents from state and federal agencies and original, historic records and papers. Libraries may also subscribe to databases that provide access to some government documents or historical records. Many government Web sites also provide access to such documents. Two useful sites for federal government documents are <http://usasearch.gov/> and <http://www.gpoaccess.gov/>.

### ● Develop Research Skills

#### *Using Specialized References*

Write one kind of reference work, other than a general encyclopedia, which would contain information about each of the following.

**1.** newspaper articles about space shuttles

**2.** information about a senator's life

**3.** how ocean currents affect climate

**4.** pamphlet on obtaining a lifesaver's certificate

**5.** the meaning of the computer term *interface*

**6.** the highest mountain peak in the Himalayas

**7.** synonyms for the word *imagination*

**8.** pamphlets on windsurfing or board sailing

**9.** magazine articles about job opportunities in Alaska

**10.** college and university catalogs

# Using the Internet for Research

The Information Superhighway could be the best research partner you've ever had. It's fast, vast, and always available. But like any other highway, if you don't know your way around, it can also be confusing and frustrating. This is particularly true of the Internet because the sheer volume of information can be intimidating.

This section will explore ways to help you search the Web effectively. Be patient. It takes time to learn how to navigate the Net and zero in on the information you need. The best thing to do is practice early and often. Don't wait until the night before your paper is due to learn how to do research on the Internet!

## GETTING STARTED

Just as there are several different ways to get to your home or school, there are many different ways to arrive at the information you're looking for on the Internet.

**Internet Public Library** Perhaps the best place to start your search for reliable information on the Web is to go to ipl2, the Internet Public Library site <http://www.ipl.org/>. This virtual reference library provides links to Web sites that have been reviewed and recommended by librarians. The home page is organized with links to sections much like those at your local library or media center. There is even a special section for teens. Clicking on the links that relate to your subject will take you to a list of suggested resources.

**Search Bar** Another good first step is your browser's search bar. You can usually customize your browser by adding the search tools you use most often to the drop down menu. Some of these tools, sometimes referred to as **search engines,** include:

- AltaVista—http://www.altavista.com/
- Ask—http://www.ask.com/
- Bing—http://www.bing.com/
- Google—http://www.google.com/
- Lycos—http://www.lycos.com/
- Yahoo!—http://www.yahoo.com/

**Metasearch engines** search and organize results from several search engines at one time. Following are a few examples:

- Clusty—http://clusty.com/
- Dogpile—http://www.dogpile.com/
- Ixquick Metasearch—http://ixquick.com/

Search services usually list broad categories of subjects, plus they may offer other features such as "Random Links" or "Top 25 Sites," and customization options. Each one also has a search field. Type in a **keyword,** a word or short phrase that describes your area of interest. Then click Search or press the Enter key on your keyboard. Seconds later a list of Web sites known as "hits" will be displayed containing the word you specified in the search field. Scroll through the list and click the page you wish to view.

The tricky part about doing a search on the Internet is that a single keyword may yield a hundred or more sites. Plus, you may find many topics you don't need. For example, suppose you are writing a science paper about the planet Saturn. If you type the word *Saturn* into the search field, you'll turn up some articles about the planet, but you'll also get articles about NASA's Saturn rockets and Saturn, the automobile company.

## SEARCH SMART

Listed below are a few pointers on how to narrow your search, save time, and search smart on the Net. Many popular search engines use their own advanced methods and not all of the following strategies will work with all search engines.

### Guidelines for Smart Searching

- The keyword or words that you enter have a lot to do with the accuracy of your search. Focus your search by adding the word "and" or the + sign followed by another descriptive word. For example, try "Saturn" again, but this time, add "Saturn + space." Adding a third word, "Saturn + space + rings" will narrow the field even more.

- On the other hand, you can limit unwanted results by specifying information that you do *not* want the search engine to find. If you type "dolphins not football," you will get Web sites about the animal that lives in the ocean rather than the football team that uses Miami as its home base.

- Specify geographical areas using the word "near" between keywords as in "islands near Florida." This lets you focus on specific regions.

- To broaden your search, add the word "or" between keywords. For example, "sailboats or catamarans."

- Help the search engine recognize familiar phrases by putting words that go together in quotes such as "Tom and Jerry" or "bacon and eggs."

- Sometimes the site you come up with is in the ballpark of what you are searching for, but it is not exactly what you need. Skim the text quickly anyway. It may give you ideas for more accurate keywords. There might also be links listed to other sites that are just the right resource you need.

- Try out different search engines. Each service uses slightly different methods of searching, so you may get different results using the same keywords.

- Check the spelling of the keywords you are using. A misspelled word can send a search engine in the wrong direction. Also, be careful how you use capital letters. By typing the word *Gold,* some search services will only bring up articles that include the word with a capital *G.*

*You can learn more about evaluating online sources on pages 397–399.*

## SAVING A SITE FOR LATER

You may want to keep a list handy of favorite Web sites or sites you are currently using in a project. This will save you time because you can just click on the name of the site in your list and return to that page without having to retype the URL.

Different browsers have different names for this feature. For example, AOL's Netscape calls it **My Links,** Mozilla's Firefox calls it a **bookmark,** while Microsoft's Internet Explorer calls it **favorites.**

## INTERNET + MEDIA CENTER = INFORMATION POWERHOUSE

Although the Internet is a limitless treasure chest of information, remember that it's not cataloged. It can be tricky to locate the information you need, and sometimes that information is not reliable. The library is a well-organized storehouse of knowledge, but it has more limited resources. If you use the Internet *and* your local media center, you've got everything you need to create well-researched articles, reports, and papers.

### Using the Internet and Media Center

**Use the Internet to**

- get great ideas for topics to write about;
- gather information about your topic from companies, colleges and universities, and professional organizations;
- connect with recognized experts in your field of interest;
- connect with other people who are interested in the same subject and who can put you in touch with other sources.

**Use the Media Center to**

- find reliable sources of information either in print or online;
- get background information on your topic;
- cross-check the accuracy and credibility of online information and authors.

# Research: Synthesizing, Organizing, and Presenting

**L**ike a hiker, when you are putting together a research report you need to plan your trip and gather your gear before starting the journey. In the previous chapter you have done just that. You have

- chosen and limited a subject
- posed a major research question
- formulated a research plan
- followed the plan to find sources in your library and media center
- evaluated those sources
- taken notes

The activities in this chapter will take you through the rest of the process of preparing a research report.

## Writing Project   *Research Report*

***What's New?  Complete a research report on a recent development in technology.***

***Review***  Now that you have followed your research plan and gathered the evidence you need, you are prepared to draft, revise, edit, and publish your research report on a recent change in technology. As you work on and complete your report, you may wish to modify or revise your major research question so that it is aligned with the emphasis of your inquiry.

# Writing a Research Report  Synthesizing

To prevent your report from being a mere collection of facts, you need to synthesize what you have learned to develop your own insights. To **synthesize** means to merge together information from different sources and your own experience and understanding. The following diagram shows the steps you can take to synthesize information.

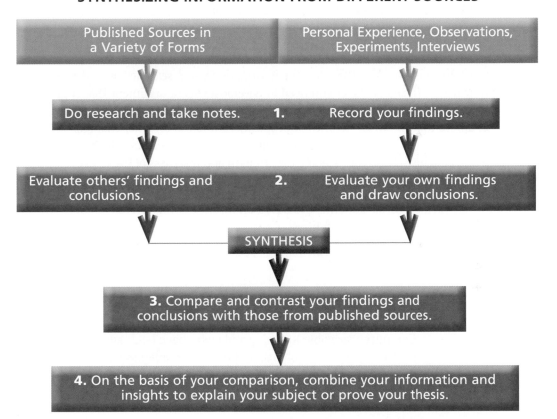

## SYNTHESIZING INFORMATION FROM DIFFERENT SOURCES

| Published Sources in a Variety of Forms | Personal Experience, Observations, Experiments, Interviews |
|---|---|
| Do research and take notes. **1.** | Record your findings. |
| Evaluate others' findings and conclusions. **2.** | Evaluate your own findings and draw conclusions. |

SYNTHESIS

**3.** Compare and contrast your findings and conclusions with those from published sources.

**4.** On the basis of your comparison, combine your information and insights to explain your subject or prove your thesis.

---

**PROJECT PREP** *Prewriting* *Synthesis*

Review your research question and all the notes you took as you conducted research. Follow the steps in the diagram above to synthesize the information, beginning with step 2. Write a brief paragraph evaluating the findings and conclusions of others. Write a second brief paragraph evaluating your own views on the subject. Then complete steps 3 and 4. Write a few sentences explaining how you combined the various sources of information to build the understanding you now have.

## 1 Developing a Working Thesis

Before you formulate your working thesis, review your major research question and notes. A **working thesis statement** should express the main idea and reflect the purpose of your report. See if you have modified your major research question or want to refocus your report. A working thesis is a tentative proposition; you can revise it as needed if you discover more information that you want to include in your research report.

In a research paper, as in a critical essay, you may frame your thesis as a statement that you intend to prove is true. You then give the information you researched as evidence to support your thesis. In such a paper you need to develop a cogent argument that supports your personal opinion rather than simply restate existing information. In developing your argument, differentiate between theories or propositions and the evidence that supports those theories. These theories may come from the experts you consult or reflect your own inferences and conclusions. As you evaluate the strength and weakness of the evidence, you will be able to argue for or against a particular thesis.

The following working thesis statement is based on information gathered about computers helping people with disabilities.

*You may wish to review how to develop an argument in persuasive writing on pages 298–299.*

---

**MODEL: Working Thesis Statement**

Computers are able to help people who have language problems, vision problems, and motion problems related to paralysis and loss of limb.

---

**PROJECT PREP** *Prewriting* *Working Thesis*

In your writing group, help each author develop a working thesis statement. Work on crafting a statement that reflects a personal opinion that the writer can provide arguments to support. Discard statements that are so broad or self-evident that they would not need support, as well as statements that are so narrow that finding supportive arguments will be too difficult.

## ② Organizing Your Notes

Your working thesis statement and your guide
questions are all you need to help you sort your note
cards containing relevant and accurate information
into categories. These categories should reflect the
central ideas, concepts, and themes of your report.
Notice, for example, that the following categories
on the subject of computers helping people with
disabilities are directly related to the questions that
guided the research. Some questions have been left
out, however, to control the length of the report.


**Writing Tip**

Group your notes
into three or more
main categories
of information.

**Category 1**  How computers help those with language disabilities

**Category 2**  How computers help those with vision-related problems

**Category 3**  How computers help those with paralysis or loss of limb

**Category 4**  Computer costs versus benefits

Group your notes into three or more main categories of information. After you arrange
your note cards by category, clip the cards in each group together. If some notes do
not fit a category, put them into a separate group for possible use in your introduction
or conclusion.

---

**PROJECT PREP** *Prewriting* **Organizing Notes**

Using the guide questions that you wrote earlier, create three
or more categories of information for your research report, as
suggested by the sub-questions you generated for your major
research question. Check to see that the categories reflect the
central ideas, concepts, and themes of your planned report.
Then sort the note cards into these categories and clip each
group together. Include only note cards that contain relevant
and accurate information. Clip notes separately that do not fit
into your categories. Save your work for later use.

# ❸ Outlining

Your final prewriting step is to organize your notes into an outline. As the basis for your outline, use the categories into which you grouped your notes. Then look over your notes to determine the overall organization of the details in the report. If your subject is a historical event, **chronological order** may be appropriate. If you intend to describe something, **spatial order** may be suitable. However, the two most common methods of organizing research reports are **order of importance** and **developmental order.**

Plan the outline of your research report by deciding on a method of organization and by assigning your categories accordingly. Before you develop a formal outline you may want to outline your ideas using conceptual maps or timelines. Timelines are especially useful for papers using chronological order. Various conceptual maps such as Venn diagrams or cluster diagrams may help you visualize how your ideas are related.

The following model is the beginning of the outline for the body of a report on computers and disabilities. Notice the parallel phrasing and use of Roman numerals.

*For more information about ordering information, you may want to review pages 94–95, 236–239 and 338–339.*

## MODEL: Categories

I. Computers helping people with language disabilities

II. Computers helping people with vision disabilities

III. Computers helping people with motion disabilities

### Writing Tip

Plan the **outline** of the body of your research report by deciding on a method of organization and assigning categories accordingly, using Roman numerals.

An outline organizes the material for the body of a research report. It should show how you intend to support central ideas, concepts, and themes. The outline above omits one category from the previous page—computer costs versus benefits—because this material will be covered briefly in the conclusion. The writer realized after reviewing her notes that to analyze this category adequately would require a longer report. In fact, this topic could lend itself to a separate report that might have a thesis that argued for or against the benefits of computers for the disabled compared to their costs.

Once you have outlined your main topics, you can use the information on your note cards to add subtopics (listed with capital letters) and supporting points (listed with Arabic numerals).

The following outline can serve as a model for your own outline. Each group of subtopics and supporting points is phrased in parallel form.

**MODEL: Outlining**

Computers are able to help people who have language problems, vision problems, and motion problems related to paralysis and loss of limb. ••—— Working Thesis Statement

I. Computers helping people with language disabilities ••—— Main Topic
   A. Talking word processor ••—— Subtopics
   B. Voice output communication aids
   C. Computer and speech synthesizer

II. Computers helping people with vision disabilities
   A. "Seeing Eye" computers
   B. Reading machines
      1. Scan/read programs ••—— Supporting Points
      2. Screen readers
      3. DAISY format

III. Computers helping people with motion disabilities
   A. Wheelchairs and prosthetic limbs
   B. Voice recognition software
   C. Eye-operated computers
      1. ERICA
      2. VisionKey
   D. Brain-operated computers

**PROJECT PREP**   *Prewriting*   *Outline*

Write an outline for your own research report. Write your working thesis statement at the top of the page. Next, organize your note cards into categories and arrange those categories using a conceptual map or timeline. Then develop a formal outline based on the categories you created. As you fill in subtopics and supporting points from your notes, check the form of your outline. Save your work for later use.

# The Power of Language

## Fluency: Let It Flow

You have learned how to add content and detail to your sentences, and to use grammatical options to add style and voice to your writing. But fluency involves still more. When you write a research report about a complicated topic, you will naturally tend to have longer, more complicated sentences than if you were writing a simpler composition. You can add variety to a report like this by using short, simple sentences to state main points or emphasize conclusions. Your goal is to avoid a monotonous style. A smoothly written research report will include a mixture of long and short sentences. Compare these two passages.

> Where do you go when you want to do research for your report on public attitudes toward technology, but the library is closed? The Internet can help you, particularly if it is too late at night to conduct a phone survey.

> Where do you go when you want to do research for your report on public attitudes toward technology, but the library is closed and it is too late at night to take a phone survey? The Internet can help.

Note that in the example above, the writer also uses different sentence types for variety. The first is a question, an interrogative sentence. The second is declarative.

Using a mix of simple, compound, complex, and compound-complex is another good way to achieve flow, as is varying the way you begin sentences.

## Try It Yourself

Write a passage of about five sentences on your project topic. Include sentences of varying length and type and begin your sentences in varied ways.

### Punctuation Tip

Use a comma after certain introductory elements in a sentence. (See pages 946–947.)

## ① Revising a Working Thesis

Once you have synthesized, or pulled together, your research to form an outline, you should use that outline as the basis of your first draft. As you draft, you want to flesh out your outline, adding an introduction and conclusion and working the results of your research into the flow of your report. You will begin by drafting a focused thesis statement.

A clear, well-worded thesis statement expresses your main idea and serves as a guiding beacon to help you keep on track as you write your first draft. Therefore, before you start to write, evaluate your working thesis to ensure that it covers all the topics in your outline—and only those topics. You may have to try two or three times before your working thesis is focused. The following guidelines will help you revise your working thesis statement.

**Guidelines for Revising a Thesis Statement**

- A thesis statement should make the main point of your research report clear to a reader.
- A thesis statement should be broad enough to cover all the main topics listed in your outline.
- A thesis statement should be narrow enough to cover only the topics listed in your outline.
- A thesis statement should fit smoothly into your introduction.

Suppose you are doing research on the subject of animals' natural camouflage and have come up with the following main topics.

**MODEL: Nature's Camouflage**

   **I.** Creatures with spots resembling eyes that appear threatening to would-be predators

  **II.** Creatures with coloration that matches the environment

 **III.** Creatures with coloration that changes with the seasons

CHAPTER 12

You might then start with the following working thesis.

## MODEL: Working Thesis Statement

Many creatures find some protection from predators through coloration that blends into the environment.

The preceding thesis is too narrow because it fails to include the category of creatures with eyespots, whose camouflage does not blend into the environment but instead makes the creature appear threatening. A simple revision, however, can broaden the thesis.

## MODEL: Revised Thesis Statement

Many creatures adopt a disguise that helps protect them from predators.

## PROJECT PREP  Drafting  *Refining Thesis Statement*

1. Using the guidelines on page 431, consider the working thesis statement that you wrote at the top of your outline and revise it if it needs to be better aligned with the contents of the outline. Be sure that the thesis statement covers all the information you have gathered in your research.

2. Using this refined thesis, then, each author should draft an introductory paragraph that states and briefly develops the statement. This paragraph will provide the focus for the body paragraphs that follow. Save your work for later use.

# ❷ Using Sources

Supporting your thesis with the words and ideas of experts will give authority to your report. Using a variety of authoritative sources rather than relying too much on a single source also strengthens your report. Failure to give credit for borrowed words, ideas, and facts is a serious offense, called **plagiarism.** Therefore, give credit for any borrowed material with parenthetical notes or footnotes. A list of works cited (similar to a bibliography) must appear at the end of your report. The following techniques will help you work borrowed material smoothly into your report.

## Tips for Using Sources

• Use a quotation to finish a sentence you have started.

| | |
|---|---|
| **Example** | People with ALS or severe strokes may soon have brain implants that allow them to "translate neural signals to spell out words on a computer screen" (Baker). |

• Quote a whole sentence.

| | |
|---|---|
| **Example** | "Had Stephen Hawking lived a century ago, many of his thoughts on the universe would never have been recorded" (Williams). |

• Quote just a few words.

| | |
|---|---|
| **Example** | Screen readers translate everything on a computer screen to speech or a "refreshable" Braille display (Alliance for Technology Access 243). |

• Quote five or more lines from your source. Start the quotation on a new line after skipping two lines and indenting ten spaces. Single-space the quoted lines. End the sentence that introduces the quotation with a colon. Do not use quotation marks.

| | |
|---|---|
| **Example** | Here's how computer technology helped Cameron Clapp after he lost both legs in an accident: |
| | Because of the severity of his injuries, a prosthetist told Clapp that he'd be confined to a wheelchair. But after consulting other amputees, his family found Hanger Prosthetics and Orthotics, who fitted him with computerized prosthetic legs that restore mobility. Expected to struggle just to walk, he stunned clinicians by running three months after his fitting. ("Life without Limits") |

• Paraphrase and summarize information from a source.

As you read the relevant sources on your topic, you likely encountered both factual information and complex inferences made by the experts. Perhaps you began to make such inferences yourself. It is important to separate facts and inferences as you organize the information from your sources so that you can accurately include the material in your report. You must give citations for borrowed facts and inferences.

Remember that the ideas you develop to support your thesis statement are claims that you intend to support by providing relevant and substantial evidence in the form of examples and logical arguments. Warrants are statements that explain how an example supports a claim. Inferences you make must follow logically from your claims to be valid.

*You can learn more about making valid inferences on pages 118 and 246–247.*

● **Practice Your Skills**

### *Using Sources*

Read the following excerpt about the movements of the continents and use it as a source to complete the assignment that follows.

## Earth's Next Supercontinent

Geologists now suspect that the movements of the Earth's continents are cyclical, and that every 500 to 700 million years they clump together. Unfolding over a period three times as long as it takes our solar system to orbit the center of the galaxy, this is one of nature's grandest patterns. So what drives this cycle, and what will life be like next time the continents meet?

The continents move because of circulation in the Earth's mantle beneath the seven major tectonic plates. Where the plates meet, one is forced below the other in a process called subduction. This pulls apart the crust at the other side of the plate, allowing new molten rock to well up to the surface to fill the gap. This process means that oceanic crust is constantly being created and destroyed, but because the continents are made from less dense rock than the heavier and thinner oceanic crust that forms the ocean floor, they ride higher in the mantle and escape subduction.

As a result, the continents hold their shape for hundreds of millions of years as they glide slowly around the planet. Inevitably, though, continents collide, and sometimes clump together to form a supercontinent. . . .

Right now, we are halfway through a cycle. The Pacific is gradually closing, as oceanic crust sinks into subduction zones in the north Pacific, while the Mid-Atlantic Ridge is feeding out new ocean floor as the Americas move apart from Europe and Africa. Africa is moving northward, heading for the southern coast of Europe, while Australia is also on its way north towards south-east Asia. The continents are moving at about 15 millimetres [millimeters] per year—similar to the speed your fingernails grow.

—Caroline Williams, *New Scientist* (20 Oct. 2007)

1. Write a sentence about the cyclical movement of the continents. End your sentence with a quotation.

2. Write three sentences about what is happening in different regions now. One sentence should be a direct quotation.

3. Write a paragraph about why the continents move. Include an extended quotation of at least five lines. Be sure to indent and space the quoted lines correctly. Remember that quotation marks are not necessary.

4. Write a sentence about the rate at which the continents are moving, quoting just a few words from the source.

5. Write a paraphrase of the third paragraph.

## PROJECT PREP  Drafting  *Using Sources*

1. Practice summarizing, paraphrasing, and using quotations from your note cards for your research report. Clearly indicate inferences made by other authors and jot down your own inferences from quoted or paraphrased material. Share your work with a partner and exchange suggestions.

2. In your writing group, help each author to prepare for writing the body paragraphs of the report. Each body paragraph should be organized around one of your research questions or a major category in the outline and should include a topic sentence/claim, at least one illustration, and a warrant explaining how the illustration demonstrates the claim.

# Think Critically

## Anticipating and Refuting Counter-Arguments

When you research all the relevant perspectives on a topic, there are likely to be complexities and discrepancies in information from multiple sources. In developing a strong argument to support your thesis statement, you should incorporate these complexities and discrepancies in your report. To do this, anticipate the possible counter-arguments or objections to your thesis and related claims. Then think of a way to refute or answer each counter-argument. To try this, create a two-column chart showing a list of counter-arguments and possible refutations.

**Thesis:** Installing Talking ATMs at banks allows the visually impaired to withdraw cash and conduct other banking transactions independently.

| COUNTER-ARGUMENTS | REFUTATIONS |
|---|---|
| 1. These "talking" automated teller machines (ATMs) are too expensive for many banks. | 1. The new machines are actually quite affordable, and the increased volume of transactions will pay for the cost of the machines. |
| 2. ATMS already have Braille on their keys for blind users. | 2. Only about 15 percent of the blind are literate in Braille. |
| 3. Talking ATMs raise privacy and security concerns, as passers-by may hear personal financial information. | 3. With today's Talking ATMs, spoken information can only be heard through special headsets. |

## Thinking Practice 1

With a partner, discuss the complexities and discrepancies you have found in your research. Talk through the various positions until both you and your partner understand them well. Then construct a chart of the counter-arguments, and try to develop a refutation to answer each one.

# Refuting Counter-Arguments Clearly

When you go through an exercise like the one on the previous page, you are anticipating counter-arguments or opposing points of view by imagining what someone might think. When you refute counter-arguments that are possible, but not necessarily ones you have come across in your research, you can do so as follows:

> Some may argue that braille on the keypad should be enough of an accommodation. However, only about 15% of the blind population . . .

This pattern might be represented this way:

| COUNTER-ARGUMENT REFUTATION PATTERN #1 | | | | |
|---|---|---|---|---|
| Opponents | Verb Expressing Uncertainty + that | Their Position | However | Refutation |
| Some | may argue that | braille is enough. | However, | only 15% . . . |

A second pattern covers opposing views you find in your research, not just imagined opposition.

| COUNTER-ARGUMENT REFUTATION PATTERN #2 | | | | |
|---|---|---|---|---|
| Opponents and Source | Present-Tense Verb + that | Their Position | However | Refutation |
| Larson, in his book *Blind Justice* (624), | argues that | talking ATMs pose a privacy threat. | However, | with special headsets . . . |

Other verbs besides *argue* can serve in these patterns. These include *assert, claim, propose, speculate,* and *conclude.* Also note that the source is identified.

You can also use subordination to refute a counter-argument. This pattern is especially useful when conceding a point.

| COUNTER-ARGUMENT REFUTATION PATTERN #3 | | | |
|---|---|---|---|
| Subordinating Conjunction | Assertion of truth + that | Their Position | Refutation |
| While | it is true that | talking ATMs pose a privacy threat, | with special headsets . . . |

# Thinking Practice 2

On your project topic, write three sentences refuting counter-arguments using each of the three patterns shown above. Compare your work with your classmates.

# ③ Studying a Model Draft of a Research Report

Read the following model research report, noticing how each element fits into the whole structure. In addition, notice how research details are worked in and cited. You can see that the writer used a variety of authoritative sources rather than relying too heavily on one source. The Works Cited list is included on pages 441–442. When you write your own report, you will also incorporate words, ideas, and facts from your sources. Each time you use information from a source, write the title, author, and page number in parentheses directly after the detail. Since the following report has been revised and edited, you can use it as a model to work toward as you draft and redraft. As you read, notice how the paper follows the outline on page 429.

Your report may be more complex than this model or have a different purpose. This model analyzes evidence to support the thesis that computers allow people with disabilities to do things that might have seemed impossible. The weight of the evidence supports the author's opinion that the benefits of these computer advances reach beyond those who are disabled.

Certain topics or assignments require that you explore theories held by various scholars in the field. In such a report, differentiate between the theories and the evidence that supports them. Then analyze which evidence is strong and which is weak and use that analysis to build your argument. This model report only briefly summarizes the complex information found in a variety of sources. Sometimes a more detailed analysis of your research is required. Also, often you will find discrepancies in information from various sources. You may be asked to incorporate different perspectives in your argument and to explicitly anticipate and refute counter-arguments. In writing such a research report you would use the formats and strategies of persuasive writing to argue for your thesis. (See pages 274–315).

## MODEL: Research Report

### New Help for People with Disabilities

*Title*

*Introduction*

Computers have proved their usefulness in business, learning, and play. For much of the population, at work and at home, they have made ordinary tasks easier, faster, and often more fun. Computers, however, can do more than make already possible procedures more efficient. For many people with disabilities, computers can make the impossible possible by providing language for those who cannot speak, vision for those who cannot see, and movement for those who cannot move. Such computer advances often have uses far beyond the populations for which they were first designed.

*Thesis Statement*

Laura Meyers developed the first talking word processor in the 1980s to help children with language disabilities communicate. Children could not only see what a letter or word looked like but also hear what it sounded like. Meyers found that using technology allowed the children to "'participate in the natural processes of language learning'" (Peet, par. 1.2). Now there are a variety of Voice Output Communication Aids that help people with speech disabilities to communicate ("What Is a Voice Output Communication Aid?"). For example, in 2009 the Kessler Foundation and O'Brien Technologies planned to introduce Survivor Speech Companion, designed for people recovering from stroke or brain injury. "Speech Companion is a handheld touchscreen device that comes preloaded with a list of places, conversations, and pictures, such as popular phrases, stores, and restaurants" (Robitaille). This device allows the disabled to communicate with others who can carry out their wishes to go to a certain place or have a certain kind of food, for example.

*Body: Main Topic I*

*Borrowed words in quotation marks*

Even regular computers can be equipped with speech synthesizers that imitate the sound of a human voice. A speech synthesizer has allowed world-famous physicist Stephen Hawking to give hundreds of lectures. A victim of the disease amyotrophic lateral sclerosis (ALS), Hawking is unable to talk or to move, except for some fingers on one hand. Using a special software program, Hawking operates his computer by a switch in his right hand to write words and sentences and send them to a speech synthesizer that speaks for him (Business Wire). "Had Stephen Hawking lived a century ago, many of his thoughts on the universe would never have been recorded" (Williams).

Computers are also opening new doors for the visually impaired. GPS systems designed for pedestrians are available for many mobile phones and personal digital assistants. The software is programmed with common landmarks and allows the blind to have step-by-step directions from one place to another (Robitaille). A British company developed UltraCane, which uses sonar technology based on the way bats navigate in the dark. The cane not only detects obstacles at ground level but above the user's path, making it easier to avoid low hanging objects (Hopkins).

*Body: Main Topic II*

*Borrowed facts cited with note*

Devices have also been developed to help people who are blind read. Scan/read programs scan printed material into a computer and then read it aloud through voice software. Some of these programs also include talking dictionaries and may be useful for students with learning disabilities as well as

CHAPTER 12

for those who are blind (Alliance for Technology Access 29). Other devices such as screen readers translate everything on a computer screen to speech or a "refreshable" Braille display. This type of display provides blind users with temporary Braille output so that they can execute commands or read a certain portion of text without embossing the Braille onto paper (Alliance for Technology Access 243, 238).

The digital accessible information system (DAISY) format converts text to voice so users can easily search it. DAISY is the "standard audio file for the blind and is considered superior to MP3 because DAISY uses metadata to find chapter headings, bookmarks, and page numbers" (Robitaille). All these devices show that computerized speech is as useful for people who are blind as it is for those who are language impaired.

Computers have come to the aid of people who are movement-impaired as well. Wheelchairs have been "souped up using microprocessors and sophisticated computer design" for years (Bronson 143). Now computerized prosthetic limbs enable people like Cameron Clapp to leave their wheelchairs behind. Clapp, who became a triple amputee at fifteen after being hit by a train, now competes in triathlons. "I'm constantly setting new goals," Clapp says. "It makes me happy—and it gives others hope" ("Life without Limits").

> Body: Main Topic III

Voice recognition software allows people with movement disabilities, such as cerebral palsy or repetitive motion injuries, to enter text into a computer much faster than the most skilled typists. Many schools now encourage all students to learn to use the software to make their writing process more efficient (Rae-Dupree).

Even people who can neither move nor speak can begin to do things on their own. In the late 1980s, Thomas Hutchinson, professor of biomedical engineering at the University of Virginia developed ERICA, the Eye-gaze Response Interface Computer Aid. "An infrared camera records light from the eye, and the computer indicates which portion of the screen the eye is focused on" (Albrecht 86). The system now allows users to operate computers with just eye movements to do everything from surf the Internet and send emails to play games and speak ("ERICA System"). The VisionKey system allows people to use their eyes to operate computers and other appliances as well as to open doors and windows and turn on the lights (Jorissen).

Philip Kennedy is working on devices that allow the disabled to use their brains alone to communicate with computers. Kennedy and other scientists have discovered that neurons in the brain that signal an intention to move still function, even when the body is not able to act on that signal because of injury or disease. "For those who are missing a leg or have a broken spine, the signals can control computers, wheelchairs, and prosthetic limbs." People with ALS or severe strokes may soon have brain implants that allow them to "translate neural signals to spell out words on a computer screen." Neural signals may produce synthesized speech, too (Baker).

Conclusion

As laws have mandated more accommodations for people with disabilities, the variety of tools to make work and leisure activities more accessible has expanded. Many experts now say that products that are designed with the disabled in mind cost little more than similar products for the able-bodied. Most agree that, "accommodating people with disabilities—whether mild or severe—brings productivity gains to all" (Anthes).

CHAPTER 12

## Works Cited

Albrecht, Lelia. "With Thomas Hutchinson's Marvelous ERICA, a Flick of an Eye Brings Help to the Helpless." *People Weekly* 20 July 1987: 85–86. Print.

Alliance for Technology Access. *Computer Resources for People with Disabilities.* 4th ed. Alameda: Hunter House, 2004. Print.

Anthes, Gary H. "Making IT Accessible." *Computerworld* 28 May 2001: 56–57. *MAS Ultra – School Edition.* Web. 3 Mar. 2009.

Baker, Sherry. "Rise of the Cyborgs." *Discover* Oct. 2008: 50–57. *MAS Ultra – School Edition.* Web. 3 Mar. 2009.

Bronson, Gail. "In the Blink of an Eye." *Forbes* 23 Mar. 1987: 140+. Print.

Business Wire. "A 'New Voice' for Stephen Hawking." *Ride for Life Online.* Ride for Life, 15 Mar. 2004. Web. 18 Mar. 2009.

"ERICA System." *Eyeresponse.com.* Eye Response Technologies, 2009. Web. 11 Mar. 2009.

Hopkins, Brent. "High-Tech Devices Help Disabled Get Back Lives." *Daily News* [Los Angeles] 18 Mar. 2005. *Newspaper Source.* Web. 12 Mar. 2009.

Jorissen, Petra. "A Visit to the Virtual World: Computer-Adaptations for Disabled People." *Disability World.* World Institute on Disability, Apr.–May 2004. Web. 12 Mar. 2009.

"A Life without Limits." *People* 10 Oct. 2005: 88. *MAS Ultra – School Edition.* Web. 12 Mar. 2009.

Peet, William. "Why, How, and For Whom We Need to Use Talking Word Processors." *Drpeet.com.* Interest-Driven Learning, 15 Jan. 2004. Web. 19 Mar. 2009.

Rae-Dupree, Janet. "Let's Talk." *U.S. News & World Report* 12 May 2003: 58–59. *MAS Ultra – School Edition.* Web. 3 Mar. 2009.

Robitaille, Suzanne. "For the Disabled, More Power for Play." *Business Week
Online* 24 Dec. 2008: 23. *MAS Ultra – School Edition.* Web. 3 Mar. 2009.
"What Is a Voice Output Communications Aid?" *Axistive.com.* Axistive, 25 June
2007. Web. 19 Mar. 2009.
Williams, John. "Tech Opens Stephen Hawking's Universe." *Business Week Online.*
McGraw, 20 June 2001. Web. 18 Mar. 2009.

## USING TRANSITIONS

Transitions help you achieve a smooth flow and a logical progression of ideas. Therefore,
in your research report, use transitional words and phrases such as *first, second, most
important*, and *finally*. Other transitional devices are repeated key words or phrases from
earlier sentences or paragraphs and pronouns used in place of nouns from earlier sentences.

*For a list of transitions and more information on using them refer to pages 5, 95, and 300.*

● **Practice Your Skills**

### Recognizing Transitions

Answer the following questions about the research report on computers and
people with disabilities on pages 438–441.

**1.** What transitional word showing contrast prepares readers for the
thesis statement?

**2.** What key word from the thesis statement is repeated in the first
sentence of the second paragraph?

**3.** What transitional word leads into the fourth paragraph?

**4.** What transitional phrases in the sixth paragraph connect the first two
topics of the report?

## PROJECT PREP  Drafting  *First Draft*

1. Based on the plan you have created, write a draft of the body paragraphs of your
paper. Follow your outline to draft the body. As you write, use a variety of rhetorical
strategies to argue for your thesis, and anticipate and refute counter-arguments.
Differentiate between theories and the evidence that supports them. Analyze your
evidence to determine how strong it is. Use the evidence you have gathered to
create a cogent argument that your readers will understand. For each statement
of evidence, identify the source and page number fully enough so that you know
which source you are using.

2. Next, draft your conclusion. It should consider how you have answered your major
research question in the body paragraphs of your paper. Go beyond simply restating
information by providing personal opinions that your research and analysis support.

# Citing Sources

The notes in a research report that show the original sources of borrowed words or ideas are called **citations.** There are thee different types of citations.

| | |
|---|---|
| **Parenthetical Citations** | appear within parentheses directly following the borrowed material in the report itself |
| **Footnotes** | appear at the bottom of the page |
| **Endnotes** | appear on a separate sheet at the end of the report, after the conclusion but before the works-cited page or bibliography |

Use only one type of citation throughout the report. The following guidelines will help you determine which information in your report requires a citation.

## Guidelines for Citing Sources

- Cite the source of a direct quotation. Use direct quotations when the original wording makes the point more clearly.
- Cite the sources of ideas you gained from your research, even when you express the ideas in your own words.
- Cite the sources of figures and statistics that you use.
- Do not cite sources that are common knowledge.

The type of citation you will use is often determined by your subject matter. Standards are set by professional organizations, such as the Modern Language Association (MLA) in the language arts and humanities or the American Psychological Association (APA) in the sciences and social sciences. Scholars in many fields often refer to *The Chicago Manual of Style* (*CMS*) for guidelines. The MLA and the APA both use parenthetical citations. However, the APA style manual is now focused on professionals writing articles for publication. The *CMS* reference-list style of citation uses parenthetical citations that are similar to the APA style. A useful guide to *CMS* for students is Kate Turabian, *A Manual for Writers of Research Papers, Theses, and Dissertations.*

**Writing Tip**

Cite the sources of information you include in your research report by using **parenthetical citations, footnotes,** or **endnotes.** Use only one type of citation throughout the report.

Parenthetical citations, as shown in the model research report on pages 438–441, identify the source briefly in parentheses directly following the borrowed material. This textbook uses the MLA guidelines for parenthetical citations—the preferred way to give credit to your sources. For most literary research papers, you will use the MLA style. Turabian (*CMS*) uses a slightly different style of parenthetical citation that includes the date of publication. (See page 445.)

The *CMS* notes-bibliography style cites sources with endnotes or footnotes. This style calls for a number to be placed directly after the borrowed material. The number refers the reader to the source listed at the bottom, or foot, of the page or at the end of the report. (See pages 445–446.)

## PARENTHETICAL CITATIONS

In a parenthetical citation, you give the reader just enough information in the report itself to identify the source. The reader then refers to the list of works cited at the end for more complete information about sources. The following information provides examples of two different styles of parenthetical citations.

| MLA STYLE GUIDELINES | |
|---|---|
| **Books by One Author** | Give author's last name and a page reference: (Mann 46). |
| **Books by Two or More Authors** | Give both authors' last names and a page reference: (Edwards and Bassett 23). |
| **Articles; Author Named** | Give author's last name and a page reference; omit page number if the article is only one page long: (Bronson 143). |
| **Works by the Same Author** | Give author's last name, title of work, and page reference: (Baker, "Rise of the Cyborgs" 50). |
| **Author Most Recently Named in the Text** | Give only a page number from the source being used: (52). |
| **Articles; Author Unnamed** | Give title of article (full or shortened; omit initial *A, An,* or *The*) and page reference; omit page number if the article is only one page long: ("Life without Limits"). |
| **Articles in a Referene Work; Author Unnamed** | Give title (full or shortened) and page number, unless article is only one page or if it is from an alphabetically arranged encyclopedia: ("Speech Synthesis"). |
| **Online Articles; Author Named** | Give author's last name; include a page or paragraph number only if the online source includes them; do not use page references from a print version of the article: (Peet, par. 1.2). |
| **Online Articles or Web Pages; Author Unnamed** | Give title of article or Web page, as used on the works-cited page: ("What Is a Voice Output Communications Aid?"). |

## TURABIAN (*CHICAGO MANUAL OF STYLE*) GUIDELINES

| | |
|---|---|
| **Books or Articles by One Author** | Give author's last name and date of publication, then a page reference, separated by a comma: (Mann 2005, 82). |
| **Books or Articles by Two Authors** | Give both authors' names and date of publication, and then a page reference (Edwards and Bassett 1999, 38). |
| **Author Most Recently Named in the Text** | Give only the date of the source being used and a page reference (2005, 94). |
| **Article; Author Unnamed** | Use the name of the publication in place of the author, then give the date of publication and page reference; omit page number if the article is on a single page: (*People* 2005). |

No matter which style you use, place parenthetical citations as close as possible to the words or ideas being credited. In order to avoid interrupting the natural flow of the sentence, place the citations at the end of a phrase, a clause, or a sentence. The following guidelines will tell you specifically where to place the citation in relation to punctuation marks.

### The Correct Placement of Parenthetical Citations

- If the citation falls next to a comma or end mark, place the citation before the punctuation mark.
- If the citation accompanies a long quotation that is set off and indented, place the citation after the end mark.
- If the citation falls next to a closing quotation mark, place the citation after the quotation mark but before any end mark.

*See examples in the sample research report on pages 438–441 and in the **Tips for Using Sources** on page 433.*

## FOOTNOTES AND ENDNOTES

Your teacher may ask you to cite your sources in footnotes or endnotes, rather than in parenthetical citations. The correct form for footnotes and endnotes is essentially the same. Both use a superscript, unlike parenthetical citations, which do not require one. A **superscript** is a number above the line in the text, to refer readers to the footnote or endnote with the same number. The superscript comes immediately after the borrowed material. As shown in the following examples, the footnote or endnote entry itself does not begin with a superscript. The following examples will help you write footnotes or endnotes correctly.

The Turabian *Manual* is also a useful guide for footnotes or endnotes. This notes-bibliography style of citations is used primarily in the humanities and some social sciences.

**EXAMPLES: Turabian (*Chicago Manual of Style*)**
**Guidelines for Footnotes and Endnotes**

| | |
|---|---|
| **General Reference Works** | **1.** William T. Verts, "Computer," in *World Book Encyclopedia,* 2009 ed. |
| **Books by One Author** | **2.** William C. Mann, *Smart Technology for Aging, Disability, and Independence* (Hoboken, NJ: Wiley-Interscience, 2005), 46. |
| **Books by Two or More Authors** | **3.** George Edwards and Helen Bassett, *Computers for the Visually Impaired* (New York: Dover, 1999), 23. |
| **Articles in Magazines** | **4.** Sherry Baker, "Rise of the Cyborgs," *Discover,* October 2008, 50. |
| **Articles in Newspapers** | **5.** James Flanigan, "Creating Software That Opens Worlds to the Disabled," *New York Times,* December 18, 2008. |
| **Articles from Online Databases** | **6.** Gary H. Anthes, "Making IT Accessible," *Computerworld,* May 28, 2001, 56, http://search.ebscohost.com/login.aspx?direct=true&db=ulh&AN=4568343&site=src-live (accessed March 3, 2009). |
| **Articles from Web Sites** | **7.** John Williams, "Tech Opens Stephen Hawking's Universe," *Business Week,* June 20, 2001, http://www.businessweek.com/bwdaily/dnflash/jun2001/nf20010620_067.htm (accessed March 18, 2009). |
| **Interviews** | **8.** Dr. Michelle Harper, personal [or telephone] interview by author, March 18, 2009. |

For repeated references, the author's last name and the page number are enough to refer to a work already cited in full. If you have cited more than one work by the author, include a shortened form of the title in the shortened footnote.

| | |
|---|---|
| **Repeated References** | **9.** Mann, 63. |
| | **10.** Baker, "Rise of the Cyborgs," 50. |

# WORKS-CITED PAGE

A **works-cited page** is an alphabetical list of sources cited or mentioned in a research paper. It appears at the end of the report.

The entries in a list of works cited differ from footnotes and endnotes in three main ways. (1) The first line is not indented, but the following lines are. (2) The author's last name is listed first. (3) Periods are used in place of commas, and parentheses are deleted. The entries would be listed alphabetically—according to the first word of the entry—on one or more pages at the end of the report. The entire works-cited list should be double-spaced. The examples below show correct form for the entries in a list of works cited.

### EXAMPLES: MLA Guide to Works-Cited Page

| | |
|---|---|
| **General Reference Works** | Verts, William T. "Computer." *World Book Encyclopedia*. 2009 ed. Print. |
| **Books by One Author** | Mann, William C. *Smart Technology for Aging, Disability, and Independence*. Hoboken: Wiley, 2005. Print. |
| **Books by Two or More Authors** | Edwards, George, and Helen Bassett. *Computers for the Visually Impaired*. New York: Dover, 1999. Print. |
| **Articles; Author Named** | Baker, Sherry. "Rise of the Cyborgs." *Discover* Oct. 2008: 50–57. Print. |
| **Articles; Author Unnamed** | "A Life without Limits." *People* 10 Oct. 2005: 88. Print. |
| **Articles in Newspapers** | Flanigan, James. "Creating Software That Opens Worlds to the Disabled." *New York Times* 18 Dec. 2008: 7. Print. |
| **Interview** | Harper, Michelle. Personal interview. 18 Mar. 2009. |
| **Articles from Online Databases** | Anthes, Gary H. "Making IT Accessible." *Computerworld* 28 May 2001: 56–57. *MAS Ultra – School Edition*. Web. 3 Mar. 2009. |
| **Articles from Web Sites** | Williams, John. "Tech Opens Stephen Hawking's Universe." *Business Week Online*. McGraw, 20 June 2001. Web. 18 Mar. 2009. |

These entries follow the style recommended in the *MLA Handbook for Writers of Research Papers* (7th ed.). The MLA no longer recommends including URLs for most online sources because they change so frequently. If your teacher requires you to include a URL, enclose it in angle brackets, for example <http://www.businessweek.com/bwdaily/dnflash/jun2001/nf20010620_067.htm>, as the last entry in the citation.

Turabian recommends including URLs for most electronic sources. Following are examples for entries in a works-cited page using different styles.

**EXAMPLES: Turabian (*Chicago Manual of Style*)**
**Bibliography Style for Works-Cited Page**

| | |
|---|---|
| **Books by One Author** | Mann, William C. *Smart Technology for Aging, Disability, and Independence.* Hoboken, NJ: Wiley-Interscience, 2005. |
| **Books by Two or More Authors** | Edwards, George, and Helen Bassett. *Computers for the Visually Impaired.* New York: Dover, 1999. |
| **Magazine Articles** | Baker, Sherry. "Rise of the Cyborgs." *Discover,* October 2008. |
| **Articles from Online Databases** | Anthes, Gary H. "Making IT Accessible," *Computerworld,* May 28, 2001. http://search.ebscohost.com/login.aspx?direct=true&db=ulh&AN=4568343&site=src-live (accessed March 3, 2009). |
| **Articles from Web Sites** | Williams, John. "Tech Opens Stephen Hawking's Universe." *Business Week,* June 20, 2001. http://www.businessweek.com/bwdaily/dnflash/jun2001/nf20010620_067.htm (accessed March 18, 2009). |

**EXAMPLES: Turabian (*Chicago Manual of Style*)**
**Reference-List Style for Works-Cited Page**

| | |
|---|---|
| **Books by One Author** | Mann, William C. 2005. *Smart technology for aging, disability, and independence.* Hoboken, NJ: Wiley-Interscience. |
| **Books by Two or More Authors** | Edwards, George, and Helen Bassett. 1999. *Computers for the visually impaired.* New York: Dover. |
| **Magazine Articles** | Baker, Sherry. 2008. Rise of the cyborgs. *Discover,* October. |
| **Articles from Online Databases** | Anthes, Gary H. 2001. Making IT accessible. *Computerworld,* May 28. http://search.ebscohost.com/login.aspx?direct=true&db=ulh&AN=4568343&site=src-live (accessed March 3, 2009). |
| **Articles from Web Sites** | Williams, John. 2001. Tech opens Stephen Hawking's universe. *Business Week,* June 20. http://www.businessweek.com/bwdaily/dnflash/jun2001/nf20010620_067.htm (accessed March 18, 2009). |

Use the Turabian bibliography style with footnotes or endnotes; use the reference-list style with parenthetical citations based on the Turabian style. Whatever style you use, use it consistently for all the citations in your paper.

In addition to or instead of a list of works cited, your teacher may ask you to include a **bibliography** or a list of works consulted. These lists include all of the sources you used to research your subject, whether you cited them in the research report itself.

Your teacher may also ask you to separate primary and secondary sources in your works-cited list or bibliography. Entries would then be alphabetized within each section. Primary sources might include statistics; autobiographies or interviews; historical documents such as letters, diaries, speeches, photographs, or newspaper articles; or works of literature or art. Secondary sources include books and articles written by experts who have analyzed a particular subject. Consult one of the style guides mentioned in this chapter to cite these sources correctly.

## CAPITALIZATION AND PUNCTUATION OF TITLES

Apply the following rules to the works-cited page in your research report.

### Capitalization and Punctuation of Titles

- Capitalize the first word, the last word, and all important words in the titles of books, newspapers, magazines, online references and sources, stories, poems, movies, plays, and other works of art. In Turabian reference-list style only the first word and proper names are capitalized in most titles.

- Italicize the titles of long written or musical works that are published as a single unit—such as books, newspapers, magazines, full-length plays, and long poems—as well as the names of Web sites and online databases.

- Use quotation marks to enclose the titles of chapters, articles, stories, one-act plays, short poems, songs, pages in Web sites, and entries in encyclopedia references either in print or online. Turabian reference-list style does not use quotation marks.

### PROJECT PREP *Drafting* *Citations*

Prepare the list of works cited for your own research report. Place the entries in alphabetical order and follow a format on pages 447–448. Then, using the examples on pages 444–445, put your parenthetical citations in the correct form. If you need more information, refer to the *MLA Handbook for Writers of Research Papers* or other style guide. Save your work for later use.

When you have finished the first draft, try to put the report away for a day or so. Then come back to it with a fresh eye. The following guidelines will help you as you revise.

## Evaluation Checklist for Revising

✓ Does your introduction contain a well-worded thesis statement? (pages 426 and 431–432)

✓ Does your research report support the thesis statement or create a cogent argument? (page 426)

✓ Is your report organized to support central ideas, concepts, and themes? (pages 427–428)

✓ Is your report long enough to address a complex topic? (pages 428 and 438)

✓ Does your report differentiate between theories and the evidence that supports them? (pages 426 and 438)

✓ Have you evaluated the strength and weakness of that evidence in developing your argument? (page 426)

✓ Does your analysis support your personal opinions on the topic? (pages 426 and 438)

✓ Do you use various formats and rhetorical strategies to back the thesis? (page 442)

✓ Does your argument address different perspectives from multiple sources and anticipate and refute counter-arguments? (pages 436 and 438)

✓ Did you use transitional words and phrases? (page 442)

✓ Does your report have unity, coherence, and emphasis? (pages 93–96 and 119)

✓ Does your conclusion add a strong ending? (page 442)

✓ Did you use and cite sources correctly? (pages 433–449)

✓ Did you use a style manual to format written materials and include a title? (pages 443–449)

## PROJECT PREP Revising Strategies

Using the Evaluation Checklist for Revising above, meet with your writing group and review one another's papers. Help each other to meet the standards in the checklist. If appropriate, use feedback from your teacher to revise your draft further.

CHAPTER 12

To make your research clear for your readers, your finished work should always be free of errors in spelling, punctuation, grammar, and mechanics.

## The Language of Power  *Past Tense*

**Power Rule:** Use mainstream past tense verb forms of regular and irregular verbs. (See pages 750–776.)

***See It in Action*** When you write about events that have already happened, use past tense verb forms. You add *–ed* or *–d* to regular verbs to form the past tense. Irregular verbs form their past tense—and past participle—in a variety of ways and memorizing the present, past, and past participle forms may be the best way to get them right all the time. Following are some of the irregular verbs used in the report on computers and disabilities, along with their past-tense form.

| Present Tense | speak | see | give | break |
|---|---|---|---|---|
| Past Tense | spoke | saw | gave | broke |

***Remember It*** Record this rule in the Power Rule section of your Personalized Editing Checklist. Then review pages 752–758 and look for any irregular verbs you may consistently misuse. Write these in your Personalized Editing Checklist in a chart like the one above but including all three forms: present, past, and past participle, as on pages 752–757.

***Use It*** Check through your research report to make sure you have used the mainstream past-tense forms of irregular verbs, especially those that you chose for your chart.

**PROJECT PREP** Editing *Using a Checklist*

Check your work for grammar, usage, mechanics, and spelling. As you edit your research report, refer to your Personalized Editing Checklist. When you are finished, use the rubric on the following page to measure the strength of each of the six traits in your writing.

# Using a Six-Trait Rubric · Research Reports

| | | | | |
|---|---|---|---|---|
| **Ideas** | **4** The text conveys a clear, original thesis statement with abundant supporting details drawn from reliable sources. | **3** The text conveys a thesis statement with ample details from suitable sources. | **2** The text conveys a thesis statement with some supporting details from acceptable sources. | **1** The text does not convey a thesis statement and fails to offer support from research. |
| **Organization** | **4** The organization is clear with abundant transitions. | **3** A few ideas seem out of place or transitions are missing. | **2** Many ideas seem out of place and transitions are missing. | **1** The organization is unclear and hard to follow. |
| **Voice** | **4** The voice sounds engaging and is appropriate for purpose and audience. | **3** The voice sounds natural and is appropriate for purpose and audience. | **2** The voice sounds mostly unnatural with some exceptions. | **1** The voice sounds mostly unnatural. |
| **Word Choice** | **4** Words are specific. All terms are explained or defined. | **3** Words are specific and some terms are explained or defined. | **2** Some words are overly general and some technical terms are not explained. | **1** Most words are overly general. |
| **Sentence Fluency** | **4** Varied sentences flow smoothly. | **3** Most sentences are varied and flow smoothly. | **2** Some sentences are varied but some are choppy. | **1** Sentences are not varied and are choppy. |
| **Conventions** | **4** Punctuation, usage, and spelling are correct. The Power Rules are all followed. Citations are correct. | **3** Punctuation, usage, and spelling are mainly correct and Power Rules are all followed. Citations are correct. | **2** Some punctuation, usage, and spelling are incorrect but all Power Rules are followed. Some citations are incorrect. | **1** There are many errors and at least one failure to follow a Power Rule. Most citations are incorrect or there are no citations. |

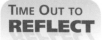

**TIME OUT TO REFLECT**
You will likely have many opportunities to research and write reports in adult life. What tips do you want to remember that will help you write reports in the future? What mistakes would you like to avoid? Record your thoughts in your Learning Log.

# Writing a Research Report  *Publishing*

Always make a neat final copy of your report before sharing your work with others. You may want to submit it to a school, regional, or national publication, or a Web site. You might want to use your computer's desktop publishing features to make a professional version of your work, complete with graphics and photos. Consider these possibilites, as you choose the best way to present your research to the public.

### Publishing Options for Research Reports

• Submit a copy of your report to a Web site that would be interested in the results of your research.

• Present a talk to younger students about what you have learned.

## PROJECT PREP  *Publishing*

Make a neat final copy of your report before sharing your work with others. Use a style manual or the guidelines for standard manuscript form shown on pages 33–35 to prepare the final draft. You may want to post your report to a Web site about your topic. Keep at least one copy of your finished report in your portfolio.

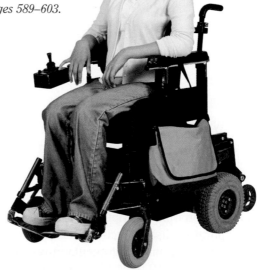

*For more about electronic publishing, see pages 589–603.*

# In the Media

## Documentary

The news media are bombarded with press releases every day. But what about the stories people don't want the press to know about? How do the hidden stories ever get told?

The answer lies in investigative journalism. Sometimes the investigations begin because of a rumor; sometimes they begin because someone calls reporters with a tip. Discovering answers to haunting questions is the basis of investigative work.

One way to stretch your research skills is to help create an investigative documentary. This is a video product that documents evidence previously unknown. Your project does not need to uncover a hidden ill of society or the wrong-doing of a public official—it should just present well-documented answers on a subject of genuine interest to you. The full procedures for planning, producing, and finishing a video are outlined in *Electronic Publishing*, pages 589–603. They require teamwork, so organize a team of at least six students.

## Steps in Making a Documentary

Choosing the subject of your documentary is by far the most important task. Be sure the subject you choose

- is one your group is genuinely interested in
- will hold the interest of your intended audience
- is feasible to document on film
- is feasible to research
- can be covered in no more than 15 minutes

When you have chosen a subject, write a few paragraphs to answer these questions:

- What idea will be communicated through the documentary?
- Who is the intended audience?
- What point of view will be used?
- What evidence will be collected?
- What effect is the documentary expected to have on the audience?

Develop a rough guide, or "treatment," for your documentary. Plan to synthesize information from multiple points of view. Recall what you've learned about incorporating discrepancies and complexities in the information by anticipating and refuting counter-arguments in your documentary.

Finally, assign roles to your team members. These include the following at least:

| | | |
|---|---|---|
| project leader/director | scriptwriters | narrator(s) |
| production manager | equipment manager | photographers |
| video engineer | sound recorders | location coordinator |
| researchers/interviewers | editors | graphic artist (for titles) |

Team members assigned to writing the script should think pictures first and then audio. They may want to work in a two-column format like the one shown below.

| Video | Audio |
|---|---|
| Sam stands at the bank of the river with the fertilizer plant clearly in the background over his left shoulder. He gestures toward the plant then looks down at the river water. | SAM: It is clear that the emissions from the fertilizer plant are largely responsible for the dead fish, the dying vegetation, and the stench that hangs over this once pleasant environment |

The scriptwriters should show the steps in the investigation itself, changing locations as needed, and summarize the results at the end.

When shooting begins, the director shapes the scenes while the equipment manager provides the lighting and other technical needs. Sound recordists and camera persons follow the director's lead. Remember to shoot more than you think you need, since much material is lost in the editing process. Work until you are satisfied that your scenes are in the best possible sequence, and that you have used all the techniques of your visual medium to their best effect. Add music, if appropriate, any necessary voiceovers, and titles.

## Showing and Evaluating

Before deciding you have a final cut, show a preview of your documentary and ask your audience to respond honestly. If necessary, re-edit to make the film more effective based on their reactions.

When you have finished, you might enjoy corresponding electronically with other student groups who have produced their first films.

## Project Corner

### Speak and Listen
#### Present It

Discuss with your classmates what you have learned by conducting research. In addition to the specific information you learned, talk about what you learned about the process of conducting research, evaluating sources, writing, and so on. Using presentation software, **create a slide show** of the major points of your research report and show it to interested parties.

### Collaborate and Create Write a Summary

Work with two other students who wrote on the same topic as you did to **create a summary** of your projects. (See pages 362–376 for help with summarizing.) Figure out the process you will follow to complete the summary, and assign each group member a task. In the summary, use transitions to connect the various parts, and include direct quotes from each paper.

### Experiment
#### Try a Different Form

Review the suggested project forms on page 388. Think about how your project would be different if it were in one of those forms you didn't use or another that you can think of. Choose a part of your project and **recast it in that new form.** What changes would you need to make? Write a brief paragraph explaining those changes.

# In the Workplace
## Persuasive Report

1. Return to the research you conducted on the history of boogie-woogie music (see page 405). *Write a report* based on this research to persuade the owner of a local concert hall to book a concert featuring the boogie-woogie style of music. Formulate a thesis that you will argue for and choose the strongest supporting evidence from your research. You may want to use a conceptual map to organize your ideas before you begin to write. Be sure to cite your sources properly and evaluate your report for unity and coherence. Consider which rhetorical strategies will be most effective in persuading the owner of the concert hall.

# In Spoken Communication Career Day Speech

2. Review the information you found about an interesting career (see page 405). *Prepare a speech* for students attending a career day event at your school. Your purpose is to provide information about the career field and to persuade students to consider going into that field. Include facts and anecdotes that will make the career interesting and appealing. Limit your speech to three minutes in length. Use information from a variety of sources to develop your speech. Then deliver your speech to your classmates.

# Timed Writing 🕐 Movie Review

3. Build on the research you did about films you might like to review (see page 405). Write a brief review of one of the films for your peers. Your review should include a summary of the film's plot and a concise analysis of the film. Support your personal opinion about the film with solid evidence. Include a statement of the criteria you use when deciding whether to recommend a film to others. Organize the information to support the central ideas and themes of your review. You have 25 minutes to complete your work. (For help budgeting time, see pages 37 and 493.)

   *Before You Write* Consider the following questions: What is the subject? What is the occasion? Who is the audience? What is the purpose?

   *After You Write* Evaluate your work using the six-trait rubric on page 452.

# Guide to 21st Century

## School and Workplace Skills

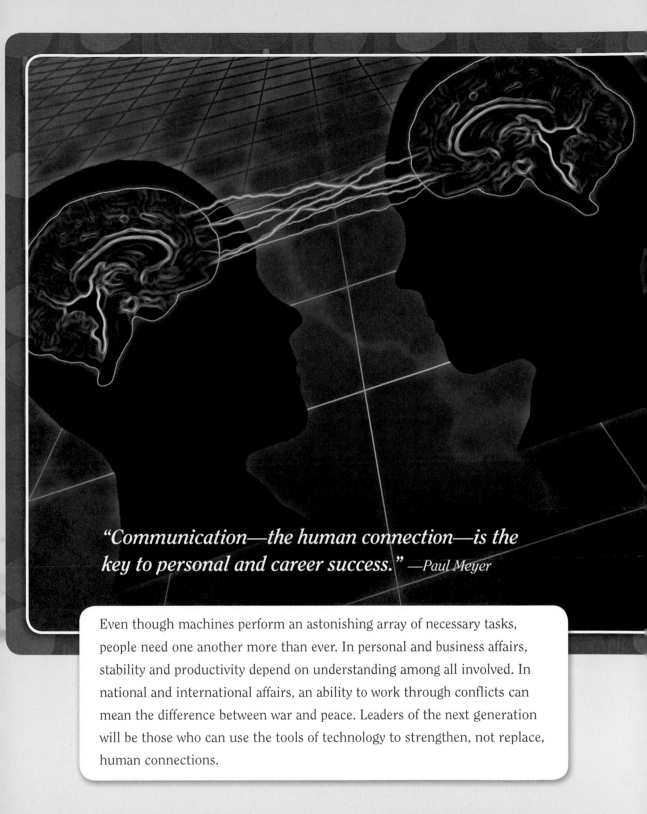

*"Communication—the human connection—is the key to personal and career success."* —Paul Meyer

Even though machines perform an astonishing array of necessary tasks, people need one another more than ever. In personal and business affairs, stability and productivity depend on understanding among all involved. In national and international affairs, an ability to work through conflicts can mean the difference between war and peace. Leaders of the next generation will be those who can use the tools of technology to strengthen, not replace, human connections.

# Critical Thinking and Problem Solving for Academic Success

**21ST CENTURY**

## Essential Skills

In Part I of this guide, you will learn how to apply your **critical thinking** and **problem-solving skills** in order to achieve academic success. These skills will also help you succeed in the workplace.

## 1 Critical Thinking

### USING REASONING

Sound reasoning is essential for every task you perform in school and in the workplace. You frequently use two basic methods of reasoning: deductive and inductive. When you use the **deductive** method, you start with a general concept or theory and support it with, or apply it to, specifics. For instance, you use deductive reasoning when you defend your thesis on an essay test. When you use the **inductive** method, you start with specifics and build to a general point. You use inductive reasoning, for example, when you draw a conclusion based on close reading. Make sure the type of reasoning you use suits the task, and always check for flaws in your logic. (See pages 286–292 and 304–306.)

### ANALYZING OUTCOMES

In your science class, you may be asked to examine how parts of an ecosystem work together. Your history class may examine the economic system, focusing on the factors that led to the global economic decline in 2009. Understanding relationships—between events, factors, or parts of a system—is essential for analyzing outcomes, both their causes and their significance. By analyzing interactions and cause-and-effect relationships, you will gain insight into how systems work.

## EVALUATING AND DRAWING CONCLUSIONS

To think critically, you must do much more than simply comprehend information. You need to analyze and evaluate evidence, claims, and different points of view. (See pages 116–117, 245–246, 299, and 372.) You need to infer, interpret, make connections, and synthesize information. Then you must draw conclusions. (See page 425.) You should also reflect on your learning in order to evaluate your progress, skills, and methods. Learning how to evaluate information effectively and draw logical conclusions will help you make sound judgments and decisions in school and in the workplace.

You can learn more about specific critical thinking skills on the following pages:

| | |
|---|---|
| Comparing, page 54 | Evaluating Evidence and Sources, page 299 |
| Making Valid Inferences, page 118 | Making Inferences, page 331 |
| Interpreting, page 138 | Evaluating, page 372 |
| Observing, page 167 | Analyzing a Subject, page 395 |
| Implying, page 192 | Anticipating and Refuting Counter-Arguments, pages 436–437 |
| Constructing Analogies, page 234 | |

## 2 Developing Solutions

### SOLVING PROBLEMS

Your critical thinking skills—using sound reasoning, analyzing outcomes, evaluating and drawing conclusions—will help you solve problems effectively. Faced with a problem on a test, for example, look for connections between it and other problems you have solved in the past to see if the solution should follow certain conventions. Use reasoning and draw conclusions to determine the correct solution. To solve complex problems, ask questions. Then synthesize and evaluate information and different viewpoints to produce strong, creative solutions. Developing and applying your problem-solving skills in school will prepare you for resolving various types of problems in the workplace.

# A. Learning Study Skills

## Apply Critical Thinking Skills

Independent thinkers know how to distinguish between accurate and inaccurate information. They know how to determine whether an argument is valid or biased and flawed. They draw insightful conclusions and develop creative solutions. They do all this by using their critical thinking skills.

Thinking critically means thinking actively about what you read and hear. It involves asking questions, making connections, analyzing, interpreting, evaluating, and drawing conclusions. When you compare cultural perspectives on an issue or evaluate the reliability of a narrator, you are using your critical thinking skills.

Thinking critically also involves reflecting on your learning. Evaluating the methods you use to study and prepare for assignments and tests will help you identify your strengths. It will also help you determine how you can learn more effectively.

In this section you will develop your study skills. Improving these skills will help you become a better critical thinker and help you succeed academically.

## Developing Effective Study Skills

Good study habits will help you do well on all your daily classroom assignments. The following strategies will help you study more effectively.

### Strategies for Effective Studying

- Choose a study area that is well lighted and free from noise and other distractions.
- Equip your study area with everything you need for reading and writing. You can easily access a dictionary and thesaurus online, but you may want to have print versions of these resources on hand.
- Keep a journal for recording assignments and due dates.
- Allow plenty of time for studying. Begin your assignments early.

# ① Adjusting Reading Rate to Purpose

When you read, keep your purpose in mind. If you are reading a magazine or a story solely for entertainment, you may read at any rate that is comfortable and that allows you to comprehend the material. When you are reading for school assignments or preparing to take a test, however, you need to read more carefully and purposefully. The following techniques will help you match your reading rate to your purpose.

## SCANNING

**Scanning** is reading to get a general impression and to prepare for learning about a subject. To scan, read the title, headings, subheadings, picture captions, words and phrases in boldface or italics, and any focus questions to determine the topic of the reading and the questions to keep in mind.

## SKIMMING

After scanning a chapter, section, or article, quickly skim the introduction, topic sentence and summary sentence of each paragraph, and conclusion. **Skimming** is reading quickly to identify the purpose, thesis, main ideas, and supporting details of a selection.

## CLOSE READING

**Close reading** is used for locating specific information, following the logic of an argument, and for comprehending the meaning and significance of information. It is an essential step for critical thinking. After scanning a selection, you should read it more slowly and carefully. Then apply your critical thinking skills to analyze and interpret information and ideas. Be sure to evaluate points and draw conclusions in order to make judgments and decisions. Pose questions based on your close reading to help you solve problems.

● **Practice Your Skills**

*Choosing a Reading Rate*

List all the reading you have to do in the next week in order to complete assignments and study for tests. For example, you may need to finish a novel, conduct research for a history paper, and review material in your science textbook to prepare for a test. For each item on your list, choose the reading rate(s)—scanning, skimming, or close reading—you will use. For each choice, write one or two sentences explaining your reasons for selecting that strategy.

## ❷ Taking Notes

Note-taking is an important skill for helping you to remember what you read in a textbook or hear in a class. It will also prepare you to engage in critical thinking. Focusing on and recording key information will help you to make connections, evaluate points, and draw conclusions. Three methods for taking notes are the informal outline, the graphic organizer, and the summary.

In an **informal outline,** you use words and phrases to record main ideas and important details. When you study for an objective test, an informal outline will help you easily see important facts and details.

In a **graphic organizer,** words and phrases are arranged in a visual pattern to indicate the relationships between main ideas and supporting details. This is an excellent tool for studying information for an objective test, for preparing an open-ended assessment, or for writing an essay. The visual organizer allows you to see important information and its relationship to other ideas instantly.

In a **summary,** you use sentences to express important ideas in your own words. Summaries are useful in preparing for an essay test because you must think about the information, see relationships among ideas, and state conclusions.

In the following passage from a textbook, the essential information is underlined. Following the passage are examples of notes in the form of an informal outline, a graphic organizer, and a summary.

> **MODEL: Essential Information**
>
> ### Thomas Hardy
>
> Thomas Hardy had two distinct literary careers, the first as a novelist and the second as a poet. His deepening pessimism in *Jude the Obscure,* coupled with the public burning of the book by an Anglican bishop, turned him away from novel writing and toward poetry.
>
> Until the age of fifty-eight, Hardy was known only as a novelist. Among his best-known novels are *The Return of the Native* and *The Mayor of Casterbridge.* These novels show Hardy's pervasive gloominess, yet his rustic characters also reveal an underlying sense of humor. Hardy considered himself a meliorist, one who believes that things tend to improve.
>
> For the last thirty years of his life, Hardy wrote nothing but poetry. His great epic drama, *The Dynasts,* is less well known than his shorter poems, such as "The Man He Killed," "Channel Firing," and "In Time of 'The Breaking of Nations.'" These poems tend to be sad and pessimistic, like his novels, but they also suggest the heroic dignity of humanity's struggle.

**Informal Outline**

**Thomas Hardy**

1. Until age fifty-eight—known only as a novelist
   a. Novels show gloominess but also humor
   b. Meliorism—belief things tend to improve
2. Last thirty years of life—wrote only poetry
   a. Short poems most familiar
   b. Display sadness and pessimism
   c. Reveal heroic dignity of human beings

**Graphic Organizer**

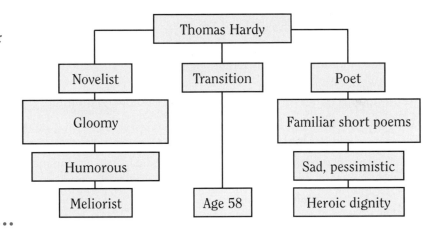

**Summary**

**Thomas Hardy**

Hardy had two different writing careers. He was a novelist until the age of fifty-eight and a poet thereafter. His best-known novels are gloomy but show an underlying humor. Hardy believed that things tend to improve. His short poems, for which he is best known, display sadness and pessimism but also reveal heroic dignity.

## Strategies for Taking Notes

- Label your notes with the title and page numbers of the material you are studying.
- Record only the main ideas and important details.
- Use the titles, headings, subheadings, and words in special type or color to help you select the most important information.
- Use your own words; do not copy word for word.
- Use as few words as possible.

**Informal Outline**

- Use words and phrases.
- Use main ideas for headings.
- List any supporting details under each heading.

**Graphic Organizer**

- Create a logical visual representation.
- Use words and phrases.
- Arrange main ideas and supporting details to show relationships.

**Summary**

- Write complete sentences, using your own words.
- Show the relationships among ideas, using only facts from the material.
- Include only essential information.
- Organize ideas logically.

## Practice Your Skills

*Taking Notes*

Working with two classmates, choose a short reading assignment for one of your classes. Decide who will take notes, who will create a graphic organizer, and who will write a summary. Then take notes on the reading. As a group, compare the outline, graphic organizer, and summary. What are the advantages and drawbacks of each form? Which was the most effective form of note-taking for that particular reading? Why? Write a paragraph in which you reflect on what this activity taught you about the different forms of note-taking.

## ③ Preparing Subject-Area Assignments

You can apply the reading and study strategies you have learned in this chapter to assignments in any subject area.

Mathematics and science textbooks often list rules, formulas, equations, or models. Many of your assignments in math and science will require you to apply these rules or models to solve particular problems. To do so, you will need to use your analytical and computational skills along with sound reasoning and problem-solving strategies.

History, government, and economics classes often emphasize such skills as analyzing and interpreting maps, charts, graphs, chronologies, time lines, documents, and statistical data. In preparing for assignments or tests in these subjects, you should pay special attention to information provided in these formats. Remember to use your critical thinking skills to analyze outcomes and understand how systems work. Analyze and connect the information presented in different formats, and draw conclusions based on this information.

Use the following tips to help you study and prepare assignments for any subject.

## Tips for Preparing Subject-Area Assignments

- Carefully read all directions before beginning any assignment.
- Adjust your reading rate to suit your purpose.
- Take notes on your reading as well as in your classes. If you can write in your copy of the reading material, use the technique of highlighting to help you identify and remember important information, such as names, dates, terms, or facts.
- Be organized. For example, you will find it helpful to keep your reading notes and class notes on the same topic together in your notebook.
- For review purposes, keep a separate list of vocabulary words, key terms and concepts, and rules and equations.
- Keep a running list of questions that arise as you read, listen, or review. Seek answers promptly. If there is anything you do not understand, get help.
- Participate in study groups, following the principles of cooperative learning.
- In preparing for tests, leave ample time for studying. Focus on anticipating and answering the questions that might appear on the test.
- Practice applying what you have learned. Also, practice using the specialized learning aids and skills for a subject area.

# B. Taking Standardized Tests

## *Applying Your Critical Thinking and Problem-Solving Skills*

Applying your critical thinking skills is essential for success. Standardized test questions, such as analogies, require you to use reasoning to arrive at the correct answer. Other types, such as reading comprehension questions, ask you to analyze, infer, interpret, make connections, and draw conclusions. An essay test may ask you to evaluate ideas and give your opinion about a subject.

All types of test questions demand that you use your problem-solving skills. You must determine what a question is asking and how you should arrive at the correct answer. You should decide if a particular question is a familiar type and therefore if the answer should match certain conventions.

Learning to apply your critical thinking and problem-solving skills effectively will help you not only when taking tests but also when completing your daily classroom assignments. It will also prove essential in areas beyond the classroom—in all aspects of your daily life and career.

This section will help you succeed on standardized tests. It will help you become familiar with the kinds of questions you will encounter. Learning test-taking strategies will help you become a better test taker as well.

## Strategies for Taking Standardized Tests

**Standardized tests** measure your skills, progress, and achievement in such a way that the results can be compared with those of other students in the same grade. Standardized tests that measure your verbal or language skills are divided into two broad categories: analogy tests and tests of reading and writing ability. Your best preparation for any standardized test is to work conscientiously in all your school courses, to read widely, and to learn test-taking strategies.

## Strategies for Taking Standardized Tests

- Relax. Concentrate on doing the best you can.
- Read the test questions carefully. Take time to answer sample questions at the beginning of the test to be sure you understand what the test requires.
- Preview the whole test by quickly skimming it. This quick look will give you an overview of the kinds of questions you will be asked and will help you plan your time.
- Plan your time carefully, allotting a certain amount of time for each part of the test. Pace yourself so that you complete sections within the given time frame.
- Read all passages and all questions carefully. Nothing will help you do better on tests than careful reading.
- Answer first the questions you find easiest. Skip those you find hard, coming back to them if you have time.
- Read all choices before you answer. If you are not sure of the answer, eliminate choices that are obviously wrong. Making an educated guess is usually wise, but check the test directions to find out if you will be penalized for guessing. If so, determine when an educated guess is helpful.
- If you have time, check your answers. Look for omissions and careless errors on your answer sheet.

#  Analogies

**Analogy questions** test your skill at figuring out relationships between words. To complete an analogy, you need to use reasoning. The first step is to determine how the two words in the first pair are related. (These words usually appear in capital letters.) The next step is to find the pair of words among the choices with the same relationship.

The punctuation in an analogy question stands for the words *is to* and *as*. The analogy COOK : MEAL :: writer : story would read as follows: *cook is to meal as writer is to story*.

To solve the analogy below, explain to yourself the relationship between the two words in capital letters. You might say, "A finger is part of a hand." Then choose the correct answer.

**FINGER : HAND ::**

(A) author : story      (B) top : bottom

(C) city : state      (D) tea : mug

(E) joke : laughter

(The answer is *(C) city : state* because it contains the only part-to-whole relationship among the choices.)

Sometimes analogies are written in sentence form.

> *Decipher* is to *decode* as *proclaim* is to ■.
>
> (A) influence          (B) acknowledge
>
> (C) announce          (D) annoy
>
> (E) encode
>
> (The first two italicized words are synonyms. Therefore, the correct answer is *(C) announce,* a synonym for *proclaim.*)

Review the common types of analogies in the following chart. In the first step for completing an analogy, determining whether the relationship between the words is one of the familiar, conventional types will make it easier to select the correct answer.

| COMMON TYPES OF ANALOGIES | | | |
|---|---|---|---|
| **Analogy** | **Example** | **Analogy** | **Example** |
| word : synonym | evade : escape | worker : tool | doctor : stethoscope |
| word : antonym | feasible : impossible | worker : product | publisher : book |
| part : whole | caboose : train | item : purpose | bus : transport |
| cause : effect | exercise : fitness | item : category | mosquito : insect |

● **Practice Your Skills**

*Recognizing Analogies*

Using the chart above, write the relationship of the words in each pair in capital letters. Then write the letter of the word pair that has the same relationship.

**1. MAMMAL : VERTEBRATE ::**

    (A) crustacean : snake      (B) money : bank

    (C) fog : precipitation      (D) copper : element

    (E) ore : silver

**2. INSPECT : EXAMINE ::**

    (A) condemn : encourage      (B) cease : begin

    (C) attempt : try      (D) lead : inspire

    (E) inform : confuse

**3. TRIVIAL : IMPORTANT ::**

    (A) windy : wet      (B) patron : client

    (C) lazy : tired      (D) complete : finished

    (E) stale : fresh

**4. EAVES : ROOF ::**

    (A) road : driver     (B) forest : tree

    (C) steps : staircase     (D) germ : bacteria

    (E) pen : ink

**5. PAINTER : BRUSH ::**

    (A) sports : competitor     (B) jeweler : gem

    (C) chisel : stonecutter     (D) shirt : price

    (E) chef : knife

## ● Practice Your Skills

### *Completing Analogies*

Complete each analogy by writing the letter of the word that best completes the sentence.

**1.** *Purpose* is to *intention* as *surplus* is to ▨.

    (A) excess     (B) equipment

    (C) storage     (D) discussion

    (E) determination

**2.** *Heat* is to *expansion* as *wind* is to ▨.

    (A) erosion     (B) donation

    (C) dismissal     (D) air

    (E) temperature

**3.** *Talent* is to *achievement* as *genius* is to ▨.

    (A) innovation     (B) prodigy

    (C) failure     (D) shrewdness

    (E) underachievement

**4.** *Frame* is to *house* as *skeleton* is to ▨.

    (A) skin     (B) ribs

    (C) joint     (D) body

    (E) brain

**5.** *Merge* is to *separate* as *flippant* is to ▨.

    (A) swimming     (B) unbalanced

    (C) talkative     (D) thrown

    (E) respectful

# ➋ Sentence-Completion Tests

**Sentence-completion tests** measure your ability to comprehend what you read and to use context correctly. Each item consists of a sentence with one or more words missing. First read the entire sentence. Then read the answer choices. Use logical reasoning to select the answer that completes the sentence in a way that makes sense.

> Because you failed to meet the April 30 deadline and have since refused to say when or whether you will complete the work, we are forced to ▇ our contract with you.
>
> (A) honor               (B) discuss
>
> (C) terminate       (D) negotiate
>
> (E) extend
>
> (The answer is *(C) terminate.* The rest of the sentence clearly suggests that the contract has not been honored and that the time for negotiating has passed. The other choices do not make sense in the context of the sentence.)

Sentence-completion questions sometimes have two blanks in the same sentence. Find the correct answer in this example.

> Despite ▇ to the contrary, the detective was ▇ that Mrs. Arnold had mislaid her jewels.
>
> (A) suspicions . . . pleased      (B) evidence . . . convinced
>
> (C) feelings . . . certain          (D) confessions . . . depressed
>
> (E) furor . . . surprised
>
> (The answer is *(B) evidence . . . convinced.* The key words that help you determine the answer are *contrary* and *mislaid.* *(C) feelings . . . certain* contains a contradiction, while the other choices do not make sense in the context of the sentence.)

When you answer sentence-completion questions, read the sentence to yourself with the words in place to be sure the answer you've chosen makes sense.

● **Practice Your Skills**

*Completing Sentences*

Write the letter of the word that best completes each of the following sentences.

**1.** Since we had to meet at the station at exactly 2:35 p.m., we decided to  our watches.

(A) synchronize      (B) ignore

(C) wind      (D) consider

(E) hide

**2.** An economist stated that the ▨ of foreign currency could stimulate the small country's economy.

(A) influx      (B) suppression

(C) study      (D) suitability

(E) lack

**3.** The giraffe is ▨, feeding only on plants.

(A) quadruped      (B) hoofed

(C) herbivorous      (D) huge

(E) endangered

**4.** Her acceptance speech was so long that we can print only an ▨ of it in the newspaper.

(A) extension      (B) array

(C) excerpt      (D) overture

(E) understatement

**5.** As a young man, the actor was slim and lithe; however, as the years passed, he became a ▨ character actor.

(A) loose-limbed      (B) portly

(C) well-paid      (D) forgotten

(E) lackluster

*Completing Sentences with Two Blanks*

Write the letter of the pair of words that best completes each of the following sentences.

**1.** The detective claimed that the suspect, in his ▇ to leave the scene, ▇ left a laundry ticket behind.

(A) aversion . . . randomly　　(B) haste . . . inadvertently

(C) anger . . . purposely　　(D) decision . . . foolishly

(E) plot . . . absentmindedly

**2.** Great Britain, with its long coastline and ▇ ports, is one of the leading ▇ nations in the world.

(A) many . . . agricultural　　(B) outstanding . . . industrial

(C) excellent . . . nautical　　(D) crowded . . . financial

(E) overabundant . . . debtor

**3.** When the ▇ was cut to 18 players, Phil was retained despite his ▇ playing.

(A) team . . . superb　　(B) choice . . . exuberant

(C) staff . . . improved　　(D) roster . . . inconsistent

(E) management . . . unsatisfactory

**4.** After a lengthy discussion, the ▇ of the group was that our ▇ affairs should be handled by an accountant.

(A) disagreement . . . legal　　(B) intent . . . basic

(C) equality . . . fund-raising　　(D) action . . . important

(E) consensus . . . budgetary

**5.** We agreed that any ▇ who could play both a teenager and an elderly woman had to be very ▇.

(A) woman . . . elderly　　(B) performer . . . tricky

(C) actress . . . versatile　　(D) stagehand . . . flexible

(E) amateur . . . professional

# ③ Reading Comprehension Tests

**Reading comprehension tests** assess your ability to understand and analyze written passages. The information you need to answer the questions may be either directly stated or implied in the passage. You must use your critical thinking skills to make inferences as you read, analyze and interpret the passage, and then draw conclusions in order to answer the questions. The following strategies will help you answer such questions.

### Strategies for Answering Reading Comprehension Questions

- Begin by skimming the questions that follow the passage so you know what to focus on as you read.
- Read the passage carefully and closely. Notice the main ideas, organization, style, and key words.
- Study all possible answers. Avoid choosing one answer the moment you think it is a reasonable choice.
- Use only the information in the passage when you answer the questions. Do not rely on your own knowledge or ideas on this kind of test.

Most reading comprehension questions focus on one or more of the following characteristics of a written passage.

- **Main Idea** At least one question will usually focus on the central idea of the passage. Remember that the main idea of a passage covers all sections of the passage, not just one section or paragraph.

- **Supporting Details** Questions about supporting details test your ability to identify the statements in the passage that back up the main idea.

- **Implied Meanings** In some passages, not all information is directly stated. Some questions ask you to infer or interpret in order to answer questions about points that the author has merely implied.

- **Tone** Questions on tone require that you interpret or analyze the author's attitude toward the subject.

● **Practice Your Skills**

*Reading for Comprehension*

Read the passage. Then write the letter of the correct answer to each question.

A pebble begins as part of a large rock and often ends up as part of a larger rock. As rocks erode, break away, become fragments, and are transported by water, they become pebbles. Pebbles are generally rounded and smooth, some more so than others. If the rounding and smoothing proceed far enough, the pebbles become gravel or sand. Although pebbles, gravel, and sand all exist independently, they can also form the basis of new rocks.

Pebbles of any size can be bonded together to form either a breccia or a conglomerate. Some rock fragments travel only a short distance by stream or river and thus retain the sharp, angular features of the fragments produced by the original fracturing. If consolidation occurs at this point, the result is a breccia. A breccia is a rock formed by the natural cementing together of sharp, unrounded fragments into a fine-grained matrix.

As the traveling distance of the original eroded rock increases, rounding continues. The bonded rock that is made is called a conglomerate. Many of the pebbles in a conglomerate, unlike those in a breccia, will not have derived from rocks in the immediate vicinity. Some will have been transported long distances, perhaps moved along a seacoast by the action of tides. One famous deposit is in Devon, England. The pebbles in this conglomerate are thought to have come from the rock of the mountains in Brittany, France, and to have been washed to England by the tides.

**1.** The best title for the passage is
   (A) Rocks, Wind, and Waves.
   (B) What Is a Conglomerate?
   (C) A Brief Look at Geology.
   (D) The Life Cycle of Pebbles.
   (E) Pebbles at Devon, England.

**2.** Breccia contains sharp, angular pebbles because
   (A) there was no water to transport the pebbles.
   (B) the water molded the pebbles into that shape.
   (C) the pebbles did not travel far in a stream or river.
   (D) some pebbles are too hard to round off.
   (E) cementing made the pebbles sharp.

**3.** The writer's attitude toward the subject of pebbles is

    (A) impassioned.

    (B) skeptical.

    (C) friendly.

    (D) pessimistic.

    (E) objective.

## THE DOUBLE PASSAGE

Some tests may ask you to read a pair of passages, called the double passage, and then answer questions about each passage individually and about similarities and differences between the two passages. The questions about both passages ask you to compare and contrast such elements as viewpoints, tone, and implied meanings. A short introduction that precedes the passages may help you anticipate the ways in which the passages are similar and different. Questions about double passages require you to use your critical thinking skills in order to make connections and synthesize information.

Both passages are presented first, followed by questions about Passage 1 and then questions about Passage 2. The final questions relate to both passages. You may find it helpful to read Passage 1 first and then immediately answer the questions related only to it. Then read Passage 2 and answer the remaining questions.

● **Practice Your Skills**

*Reading for Double-Passage Comprehension*

The following passages present two views of heroes and heroism. The first passage is from the introduction to a popular book about heroes and heroines in our time. The second is from a book on mythology by Edith Hamilton. Read both passages, and then write the letter of the correct answer to each question.

## Passage 1

In a simple society such as the Greeks' of three thousand years ago, the heroes' world was straightforward and uncomplicated. It was, in the words of Joseph Campbell, a world of "monomyths": it had single goals, definite and clear purposes. The heroes and heroines of that society spoke for and perpetuated humankind's goals and purposes. In more complicated societies, such as our own, heroes and heroines wear many faces because of their numerous responses to the varied needs of individuals, groups of people, and national purposes.

As a society's needs become more complicated, so too do the heroes and heroines; as people become more sophisticated, the heroes and heroines become less modeled on the conventional demigods of the past, less clear-cut and obvious. In a swiftly moving society like America today, heroes and heroines undergo rapid transformation. They frequently develop in ways and for purposes that are not immediately apparent. Twentieth-century American heroes and heroines, existing in a highly technological society and driven by the electronics of mass communication, change quickly. They are often hailed as heroic today and forgotten tomorrow. But though they may disappear rapidly, they serve useful and needed purposes while they endure. So we continue to create heroes and heroines because they can concentrate the power of the people—of a nation—and serve as the driving force for the movement and development of individuals and society.

# Passage 2

The world of Norse mythology is a strange world. Asgard, the home of the gods, is unlike any other heaven men have dreamed of. No radiancy of joy is in it, no assurance of bliss. It is a grave and solemn place, over which hangs the threat of an inevitable doom. The gods know that a day will come when they will be destroyed. Sometime they will meet their enemies and go down beneath them to defeat and death. Asgard will fall in ruins. The cause the forces of good are fighting to defend against the forces of evil is hopeless. Nevertheless, the gods will fight for it to the end.

Necessarily the same is true of humanity. If the gods are finally helpless before evil, men and women must be more so. This is the conception of life which underlies the Norse religion, as somber a conception as the mind of man has ever given birth to. The only sustaining support possible for the human spirit, the one pure unsullied good man can hope to attain, is heroism; and heroism depends on lost causes. The hero can prove what he is only by dying. The power of good is shown not by triumphantly conquering evil, but by continuing to resist evil while facing certain defeat.

1. According to the author of Passage 1, which of the following factors best explains why heroes in Greek society differ from heroes of today?
   (A) lack of monomyths
   (B) mass communication
   (C) technological advancements
   (D) simple versus complicated societies
   (E) development of nations

**2.** In relation to paragraph 1 in Passage 1, the purpose of paragraph 2 is mainly to

(A) define heroes.

(B) trace the development of heroes through the centuries.

(C) contrast contemporary heroes with ancient heroes.

(D) elaborate the point made in sentence 1 in paragraph 1.

(E) illustrate the concept of monomyth.

**3.** According to the author of Passage 2, heroism in Norse mythology is achieved by

(A) overcoming the forces of evil.

(B) triumphing over death.

(C) fighting to the death against forces of evil.

(D) accomplishing great deeds.

(E) mastering godlike powers.

**4.** According to the author of Passage 2, which describes mythology's sphere of influence in Norse culture?

(A) spiritual

(B) social

(C) political

(D) intellectual

(E) artistic

**5.** Which of the following ideas from Passage 1 holds true for the idea of heroism as described in Passage 2?

(A) Heroes undergo rapid transformation.

(B) Heroes may disappear rapidly.

(C) Heroes are not clear-cut and obvious.

(D) Heroes can concentrate the power of a people.

(E) Heroes are varied to reflect cultural diversity.

Objective tests of standard written English assess your knowledge of writing skills. The tests contain passages or sentences with underlined words, phrases, or punctuation. The underlined parts may contain errors in grammar, usage, mechanics, vocabulary, or spelling. These tests ask you to use your problem-solving skills to find each error or to identify the best way to revise a sentence or passage.

## ERROR RECOGNITION

Error-recognition questions test your knowledge of grammar, usage, capitalization, punctuation, word choice, and spelling. A typical test item consists of a sentence with five underlined choices. Four of the choices suggest possible errors in the sentence. The fifth choice states that there is no error. Read the following sentence and identify the error, if there is one.

> The Pacific <u>Ocean</u> is 36,198 feet deep in the Mariana's Trench<u>,</u> even
>     **A**               **B**
>
> deeper <u>then</u> Mount Everest or the mountain K2 <u>is</u> high. <u>No error</u>
>   **C**             **D**   **E**
>
> (The answer is *C*. Standard usage requires *than* instead of *then* in this sentence.)

Sometimes you will find a sentence that contains no error. Be careful, however, before you choose *E (No error)* as the answer. The errors included on this kind of test are often common errors that are hard to notice.

The parts of a sentence that are not underlined are presumed to be correct. You can often use clues in the correct parts to help you identify the error in the sentence.

## ● Practice Your Skills

### *Recognizing Errors in Writing*

Write the letter of the underlined word or punctuation mark that is incorrect. If the sentence contains no error, write *E*.

**(1)** The <u>Reverend</u> William Spooner, <u>who's</u> last name became a common
    **A**       **B**
noun, <u>had</u> <u>an</u> unusual quirk of speech. **(2)** <u>Spooners'</u> quirk was <u>to</u> transpose
  **C** **D**        **A**     **B**
the initial sounds of <u>two</u> or <u>more</u> words. **(3)** <u>There</u> <u>are</u> many examples of <u>his</u>
       **C**  **D**     **A** **B**       **C**
odd<u>,</u> humorous mistakes. **(4)** When Spooner <u>spoke,</u> "a well-oiled bicycle," for
 **D**            **A**        **B**
example, would come out <u>as</u> "a well-boiled icicle"<u>.</u> **(5)** Spooner was an
         **C**         **D**

experienced, <u>knowledgeable</u> teacher <u>who</u> <u>his</u> students liked and respected.
<br>A      B C               D

**(6)** If you <u>was</u> to ask most of his students, they would <u>say</u> he <u>was</u>
<br>    A            B      C  D

unforgettable. **(7)** After all, how could <u>anyone</u> forget a man who said, "Let
<br>          A         B

me sew you to your sheet," when he <u>intends</u> to show you to your <u>seat</u>?
<br>                  C           D

**(8)** Everyone <u>who</u> knew Reverend Spooner <u>had</u> <u>their</u> own story to tell about
<br>      A             B C

<u>him</u>. **(9)** Still, as time went by, the old <u>man's</u> long service at New <u>College</u>,
<br>D                A           B

Oxford, was all but <u>forgotten.</u> **(10)** Spoonerisms, however, are remembered
<br>C      D

to this <u>day</u>, and <u>are</u> the classic examples <u>used</u> in all dictionary definitions of
<br>   A    B            C

the word based on <u>his</u> name.
<br>         D

## SENTENCE CORRECTION

Sentence-correction questions assess your ability to recognize appropriate phrasing. Instead of locating an error in a sentence, you must use your problem-solving skills to select the best way to write the sentence.

In this kind of question, part of the sentence is underlined. Following the sentence are five different ways of writing the underlined part. The first way shown, *(A),* is the same as the underlined part. The other four choices present alternative ways of writing the underlined part. The choices may differ in grammar, usage, capitalization, punctuation, or diction. Consider all answer choices carefully. If there is an error in the original underlined portion, make sure the answer you choose solves the problem. Be sure that the answer you select does not introduce a new error and does not change the meaning of the original sentence. Look at the following example.

We all agreed that the guest lecturer was well informed, articulate, and <u>he had a nice personality.</u>

 (A) he had a nice personality.

 (B) he had a pleasant personality.

 (C) he was likable.

 (D) personable.

 (E) nice personality wise.

(The answer is *(D).* The problem in the original sentence, as well as in choices *(B)* and *(C),* is lack of parallelism. Choice *(E)* is parallel but contains an awkward construction.)

### Correcting Sentences

Write the letter of the best way of phrasing the underlined part of each sentence.

**1.** "Fair is <u>foul, wrote Shakespeare, and</u> foul is fair."
   (A) foul, wrote Shakespeare, and
   (B) foul, "wrote Shakespeare, "and
   (C) foul", wrote Shakespeare, "and
   (D) foul," wrote Shakespeare, "and
   (E) foul," wrote Shakespeare, and

**2.** Each <u>of us in the audience hopes</u> to learn your views on the bond issue.
   (A) of us in the audience hopes
   (B) of we in the audience hopes
   (C) of us in the audience hope
   (D) of we in the audience hope
   (E) member of the audience hope

**3.** The prince, along with all <u>his supporters, were observed coming toward</u> the village.
   (A) his supporters, were observed coming toward
   (B) his supporters were observed, coming toward
   (C) his supporters, was observed coming toward
   (D) his supporters, was observed, coming toward
   (E) his' supporters, was observed coming toward

**4.** Was it Jacqueline who said, <u>Its not too late to get a collar for your puppy?</u>
   (A) Its not too late to get a collar for your puppy?
   (B) "Its not to late to get a collar for your puppy"?
   (C) "It's not too late to get a collar for you're puppy?"
   (D) It's not to late to get a collar for your puppy.
   (E) "It's not too late to get a collar for your puppy"?

**5.** The <u>alarm should of begun</u> ringing by now.
   (A) alarm should of begun
   (B) alarm, it should of begun
   (C) alarm should have begun
   (D) alarm should have began
   (E) alarm should of began

# REVISION-IN-CONTEXT

Revision-in-context questions are based on a brief reading. The questions ask you to choose the best revision of a sentence, a group of sentences, or the essay as a whole. To select the correct answer, use your critical thinking skills to evaluate the relative merits of each choice. You may also be asked to identify the writer's intention. To do so, you will need to analyze the text carefully to determine the writer's purpose.

## ● Practice Your Skills

### Correcting Sentences

Carefully read the passage. Then write the letter of the correct answer to each question.

> **(1)** Recently, a questionnaire was developed that asked people to give their opinions. **(2)** What they were to give their opinions about was the value of leisure time. **(3)** Most people said that their favorite pastime was watching television. **(4)** Commenting on the quality of the <u>shows, however, the programs were not very satisfying.</u> **(5)** Most people felt that their time would be better spent if they pursued physical activities such as sports and athletics. **(6)** They felt such activities would make a noticeable change in the way they felt. **(7)** Unfortunately, they also felt there was little likelihood that they would take up exercise on a regular basis. **(8)** Many people, it seems, are willing to settle for so-so pastimes despite the fact that they know other pastimes might enhance the quality of their lives.

**1.** Which of the following best describes the writer's intention in sentence 8 in relation to the rest of the passage?

   (A) to restate the opening sentence
   (B) to draw a conclusion
   (C) to provide examples
   (D) to contrast active versus passive pastimes
   (E) to offer contradictory evidence

**2.** Which of the following is the best revision of the underlined portion of sentence 4?

(A) shows, however; the programs were not very satisfying.

(B) shows, however the viewers reported that the programs were not very satisfying.

(C) shows, however, the viewers reported that the programs were not very satisfying.

(D) shows; however, the programs were not very satisfying.

(E) shows, however, the viewers reported that, the shows were not very satisfying.

**3.** Which of the following is the best way to combine sentences 1 and 2?

(A) Recently, a questionnaire was developed that asked people to give their opinions, and what they were asked to give their opinions about was the value of leisure time.

(B) Recently, a questionnaire was developed that asked people to give their opinions on the value of leisure time.

(C) Recently, people were asked to give their opinions of leisure time.

(D) Recently, a questionnaire was developed, it asked people to give their opinions on the value of leisure time.

(E) A recent questionnaire developed to ask people to give their opinions on the value of leisure time.

# C. Taking Essay Tests

## *Apply Critical Thinking Skills*

Essay tests are designed to assess both your understanding of important ideas and your critical thinking skills. You will be expected to analyze, connect, and evaluate information and draw conclusions. You may be asked to examine cause-and-effect relationships and analyze outcomes. Some questions may address problems and solutions. Regardless of the type of question you are asked, your essay should show sound reasoning. You must be able to organize your thoughts quickly and express them logically and clearly.

# Doing Your Best on Essay Tests

## 1 Kinds of Essay Questions

Always begin an essay test by carefully reading the instructions for all the questions. Then, as you reread the instructions for your first question, look for key words.

### NARRATIVE, DESCRIPTIVE, AND PERSUASIVE PROMPTS

Following are some sample essay prompts and strategies for responding to them.

### *Narrative Writing Prompt*

Write about a first in your life: first sleepover, first ride on an airplane, first day of school, first date. Tell what happened and what the experience meant to you.

***Analyze the Question*** The key words in this question are "tell what happened." That is your cue that you will be relating a story.

**Sketch Out the Key Parts** You may want to make a chart like the following to be sure that you include all the necessary parts. Refer to the question for the headings in the chart.

| STORY PLANNING SKETCH | |
|---|---|
| The first you chose | |
| What happened leading up to it and during it | |
| How it ended | |
| What it means to you | |

**Use What You Know About Narrative Writing** Think of other narratives you have written and remember their key features: an attention-getting beginning that introduces a conflict; a plot that unfolds chronologically and often includes dialogue; a resolution to the conflict. Draft accordingly.

**Save Time to Revise and Edit** Read over your essay and look for any spots where adding, deleting, rearranging, or substituting would improve your essay. Edit it for correct conventions. Pay special attention to punctuation with dialogue.

## Descriptive Writing Prompt

Think of a musical event you attended that made a strong impression on you. It could be a rock or rap performance, a musical tradition from your culture or one you are familiar with, or your younger sister's 3rd grade band recital. Write a well-organized detailed description of that experience using words that appeal to the senses.

**Analyze the Question** The key words in this question are "detailed description." The directions to use "words that appeal to the senses" is another important item. It sets forth the expectation that you will include vivid sights, sounds, smells, tastes, and feelings.

**Sketch Out the Key Parts** You may want to make a chart like the following to be sure that you include all the necessary parts. Refer to the question for the headings in the chart.

| DESCRIPTION PLANNING SKETCH | |
|---|---|
| Identification of event | |
| Vivid sights | |
| Vivid sounds | |
| Vivid smells, tastes, and feelings | |

**Use What You Know About Descriptive Writing** Call to mind the key features of descriptive writing: a main idea that represents an overall attitude or feeling toward the subject; sensory details that support that overall feeling, often organized spatially; a conclusion that reinforces the main impression of the place. Draft accordingly.

**Save Time to Revise and Edit** Read over your essay and look for any spots where adding, deleting, rearranging, or substituting would improve your essay. Edit it for correct conventions.

### Persuasive Writing Prompt

Your state lawmakers are considering a bill to ban all use of cell phones in cars. Write an essay expressing your views on this subject. Use facts and examples to persuade others.

**Analyze the Question** The key words in this question are "expressing your views" and "persuade." These words tell you that you will be writing a persuasive text to convince people that your opinion is worthwhile.

**Sketch Out the Key Parts** You may want to make a chart like the following to be sure that you include all the necessary parts. Refer to the question for the headings in the chart.

| PERSUASIVE PLANNING SKETCH | |
|---|---|
| **Your position** | |
| **Reason #1** | |
| **Reason #2** | |
| **Reason #3** | |
| **Why the other position is flawed** | |

**Use What You Know About Persuasive Writing** Call to mind the key features of persuasive writing: a main idea that expresses an opinion; facts, examples, reasons, and other supporting details arranged in logical order (often order of importance); a look at why other opinions are not as sound; a conclusion that reinforces your opinion.

**Save Time to Revise and Edit** Read over your essay and look for any spots where adding, deleting, rearranging, or substituting would improve your essay. Edit it for correct conventions.

# EXPOSITORY WRITING PROMPTS

Most of the essay tests you will take will ask you to address an expository writing prompt. Look for the key words such as those listed in the box below. Such key words will tell you precisely what kind of question you are being asked to answer.

| KINDS OF ESSAY QUESTIONS | |
| --- | --- |
| **Analyze** | Separate into parts and examine each part. |
| **Compare** | Point out similarities. |
| **Contrast** | Point out differences. |
| **Define** | Clarify meaning. |
| **Discuss** | Examine in detail. |
| **Evaluate** | Give your opinion. |
| **Explain** | Tell how, what, or why. |
| **Illustrate** | Give examples. |
| **Summarize** | Briefly review main points. |
| **Trace** | Show development or progress. |

As you read a writing prompt, circle key words and underline key phrases in the instructions, as in the following example.

> When Francisco Pizarro first landed in 1531 on the coast of what is now Ecuador, the Inca Empire was larger than any European city of the time. Nevertheless, within only several years, the Spanish were able to destroy this mighty empire. Analyze three possible reasons for the rapid collapse of the Inca Empire. Include specific details to support each point.

## ● Practice Your Skills

### Interpreting Essay Test Questions

Write the key word in each essay question. Then write one sentence that explains what the question asks you to do.

**1.** Explain how carbon-14 is used to date objects.

**2.** Contrast an *ode* and an *elegy*.

**3.** Briefly summarize the plot of *Silas Marner,* a novel by George Eliot.

**4.** Trace the development of a tornado.

**5.** In your own words, define *market economy*.

**6.** How does the working of a gasoline engine compare with that of an electric engine?

**7.** In his *Dictionary of the English Language,* Samuel Johnson defines youth as "the part of life succeeding to childhood and adolescence; the time from fourteen to twenty-eight." Do you agree? Discuss Johnson's definition.

**8.** Briefly evaluate the scientific contributions of lasers.

# ② Writing an Effective Essay Answer

You should apply all that you have learned about the writing process when you write an essay for a test. However, because your time will be restricted in a test situation, you must do some extra planning. You should first decide how much time you will spend on each question and how much time you will devote to each step in the writing process. A general guideline is to allow two minutes for planning and one minute for revising and editing for every five minutes of writing.

## PREWRITING

Because of the limited time in a test situation, you must carefully plan your essay before you write a single word. You should first brainstorm for ideas. Then decide what type of reasoning and organization would be most appropriate. For example, you may want to use deductive reasoning to defend your thesis. You may decide to arrange your ideas in chronological order, developmental order, or the order of importance. To help you organize your answer, create an informal outline or a graphic organizer. Study the following examples.

**Informal Outline**

**Reasons for the Collapse of the Inca Empire**

(thesis statement)

**1.** Reason 1: weapons
   **a.** Spanish: muskets, cross-bows, cannons
   **b.** Incas: spears, slingshots
**2.** Reason 2: transportation
   **a.** Spanish: horses, wheels
   **b.** Incas: on foot
**3.** Reason 3: internal war
   **a.** Murder of half-brother
   **b.** Easy prey
(conclusion)

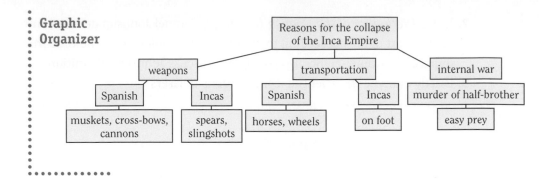

**Graphic Organizer**

Reasons for the collapse of the Inca Empire

weapons — transportation — internal war

Spanish / Incas — Spanish / Incas — murder of half-brother

muskets, cross-bows, cannons — spears, slingshots — horses, wheels — on foot — easy prey

Your next step is to write a thesis statement that expresses the main idea of your essay and covers all of your major supporting ideas. It is often possible to rework the test question to create a thesis statement.

**Essay Question**
When Francisco Pizarro first landed in 1531 on the coast of what is now Ecuador, the Inca Empire was larger than any European city of the time. Nevertheless, within only several years, the Spanish were able to destroy this mighty empire. Analyze three possible reasons for the rapid collapse of the Inca Empire. Include specific details to support each point.

**Thesis Statement**
The Inca Empire rapidly collapsed because the Incas' weapons and mode of transportation were less sophisticated than those of the Spanish and the Incas were torn by civil war.

## DRAFTING

As you write your essay answer, keep the following strategies in mind.

### Strategies for Writing an Essay Answer

- Write an introduction that includes a thesis statement.
- Follow the order of your plan, writing at least one paragraph for each main point.
- Provide adequate support for each main point by using specific facts, examples, and/or other supporting details.
- Be sure your essay contains a logical progression of ideas.
- Be certain your essay has an overall sense of unity.
- Communicate your ideas clearly and effectively.
- End with a strong concluding statement that summarizes your main ideas or brings closure to your essay.
- Write legibly, using Standard English.

In 1531, when Francisco Pizarro arrived in what is now Ecuador, the Inca Empire was larger than any city in Europe. However, the Spanish destroyed the empire in just a few years. The Inca Empire rapidly collapsed because the Incas' weapons and mode of transportation were less sophisticated than those of the Spanish and the Incas were torn by civil war.

**Thesis Statement**

Perhaps the most obvious reason for the collapse of the empire was the discrepancy in the weapons that the Spanish and the Incas used. Having no knowledge of iron, the Incas fought mainly with bronze-edged spears and slingshots. The Spanish returned such attacks with muskets, crossbows, and full-sized cannons.

The Spanish were able to transport themselves, their cannons, and their supplies into the interior of the Inca Empire because they not only had horses, but they also had the use of the wheel. Even though they had built a sophisticated system of roads, the Incas traveled only on foot. They did not have horses, and they could only carry, not pull, things since the wheel was unknown to them.

When Pizarro entered the empire, Atahuallpa had successfully captured the throne from his half-brother. Realizing the threat from the Spanish, Atahuallpa had his half-brother killed. However, shortly afterward, the Spanish killed Atahuallpa himself. As a result, the Incas, greatly divided and lacking a strong leader, became easy prey for the Spanish.

At the time the combination of these three factors was too much for the Incas. Could the course of history have a taken a different turn, however, if someone like Pizarro had come only 20 or 30 years later?

**Concluding Statement**

# REVISING

Leave yourself a few minutes to revise your essay. As you revise, consider these questions.

### Checklist for Revising an Essay Answer

✓ Did you follow the instructions completely?

✓ Did you interpret the question accurately?

✓ Did you begin with a thesis statement?

✓ Did you include facts, examples, or other supporting details?

✓ Did you organize your ideas and examples logically in paragraphs, according to your informal outline or graphic organizer?

✓ Did you use transitions to connect ideas and examples?

✓ Did you end with a strong concluding statement that summarizes your main ideas or brings your essay to a close?

# EDITING

Once you have made any necessary revisions, quickly read your essay to check for mistakes in spelling, usage, or punctuation. To keep your paper as neat as possible, use proofreading symbols to make any corrections.

### Check for the following mistakes:

✓ lack of agreement between subjects and verbs (pages 826–853)

✓ lack of agreement between pronouns and antecedents, especially indefinite pronouns (pages 812–817)

✓ tense shift problems (pages 762–776)

✓ incorrect verb inflections (pages 508 and 517)

✓ incorrect comparative and superlative forms of adjectives and adverbs (page 856)

✓ incorrect capitalization of proper nouns and proper adjectives (pages 913–922)

✓ incorrect use of commas (pages 940–956)

✓ incorrect use of apostrophes (pages 964–973)

✓ incorrect divisions of words at the ends of lines (pages 1002–1003)

# 3 Timed Writing

The more you practice writing within a limited time period, the more confident you will feel when you must complete a timed-writing essay in a test situation.

Time limits can vary from 20 to 60 to 90 minutes, depending upon the purpose and complexity of the task. You might organize your time for a 20-minute essay in this way:

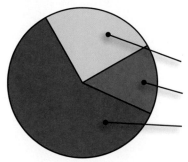

**5 minutes: Brainstorm and organize ideas.**

**3 minutes: Revise your work and edit it for mistakes.**

**12 minutes: Write a draft.**

You will find timed writing prompts on all of the following pages.

## ● Practice Your Skills

### Completing a Timed Writing Assignment

You will have 20 minutes to write an essay on the following topic.

Discuss an important problem in the nation or in the world. Explain why the problem is important. Evaluate solutions that have been proposed or that are in the process of being implemented. You may also present your own ideas for a solution.

Plan time for each stage of the writing process, set a timer, and write your answer.

# Communication and Collaboration

> **Part I** Critical Thinking and Problem Solving for Academic Success
>
> **Part II** Communication and Collaboration
>
> **Part III** Media and Technology

## Essential Skills

In the 21st century, you live and work in a dynamic, global community. In Part II of this guide, you will learn effective communication and collaboration skills. These skills are essential for success, both in school and in the workplace.

##  Communication

### THE PURPOSE OF COMMUNICATION

In all areas of your life, you communicate for a variety of purposes—to inform, instruct, motivate, and persuade, for example. In school, you might motivate other students to reuse and recycle, or you might persuade them to elect you class president. At work, you might inform your boss about your research findings or instruct your colleagues on how to use new software. Having a clear purpose is essential for communicating your ideas successfully in both speech and writing.

### EXPRESSING IDEAS EFFECTIVELY

Regardless of the form you are using to communicate (e-mail, a speech) or the context (a group discussion, a college interview), your goal is to express your thoughts and ideas as effectively as possible. Use words precisely and correctly, and articulate your ideas in a specific, concise manner. Suit your tone to your purpose and audience. Provide valid, relevant support for your ideas, and present information in a logical order. In a speech or presentation, use nonverbal communication skills to help convey your message.

## Using Media and Technology Effectively

Multiple forms of media and technology now exist to help you communicate. You can e-mail, text message, or "tweet" a friend, and apply for a job online. To prepare a speech, you can look up technical terms in an online dictionary and research your subject on the Internet. You can use popular software programs to make a power presentation. To use media and technology effectively, make sure they suit the purpose and context of your communication. They should also help you make a positive impact on your audience by enhancing or facilitating your message.

## Listening Effectively

To listen effectively, you need to do much more than understand what words mean. Your goal is to gain knowledge and determine the speaker's purpose, values, and attitudes. Skillful listeners then evaluate and reflect on the speaker's message, views, and intentions. Listening effectively means listening actively—critically, reflectively, and appreciatively—and remembering what you have heard.

## Communicating in a Diverse World

You probably attend school or work with people from diverse social and cultural backgrounds whose lifestyle, religion, and first language may be different from your own. To communicate effectively in these environments, listen actively in order to understand different traditions, values, and perspectives. Be sure to respect these differences when you express your thoughts and ideas.

## ② Collaboration

### RESPECTING DIVERSITY

In school and in the workplace, you often collaborate with others on diverse teams. Open-mindedness is essential for being an effective team member. Make sure that all team members have an equal opportunity to be heard, and respect and value differences. By doing so, you will help create an environment in which ideas and opinions are freely shared. As a result, team members will benefit from each other's expertise, and you will produce sound, creative solutions.

### ACHIEVING A COMMON GOAL

As a member of a team, you need to cooperate. Often, you may need to resolve conflicting opinions in order to achieve a common goal, whether it is completing a particular task or reaching a decision. Remember to maintain a positive attitude and put the group's needs before your own. Appreciate the merits of diverse viewpoints, and help the group work toward a compromise that all members can accept. Flexibility and openness are essential for successful collaboration.

### SHARING RESPONSIBILITY

For true collaboration to take place, all team members must do their fair share. Complete your assigned tasks, come to meetings prepared, and remain actively engaged in the team's work. Respect the skills, expertise, and efforts of other team members, and provide constructive feedback as necessary. A sense of shared responsibility will lead to a successful collaborative process.

# A. Vocabulary

## Apply Communication Skills

The study of English is the study of words. Whether you are writing an essay, reading Shakespeare's *Macbeth*, or carrying on a conversation, you are dealing with words. It is obvious that the more words you know, the more likely you are to write well and express yourself clearly; however, consider some of the other benefits of having a large vocabulary: many studies have shown that possessing an extensive vocabulary is important to achieving success on standardized tests, in college, and in the workplace.

In this chapter you will see how English developed into a language that is rich and varied. You will also learn strategies for expanding your storehouse of words. Developing your vocabulary will help you become a more effective communicator and a more skillful reader and listener in school and in the workplace.

# Understanding the Development of the English Language

## YESTERDAY, TODAY, AND TOMORROW

English—like Latin, Greek, and many other languages—goes back to a parent language called Indo-European. Although Indo-European was an unwritten prehistoric language, linguists have been able to reconstruct it to some extent. To do so, they have studied words that are similar in several different languages. The following example shows how English is closely connected to Dutch, German, Irish, Latin, and Greek.

| English | brother | German | bruder | Latin | frater |
|---------|---------|--------|--------|-------|--------|
| Dutch | broeder | Irish | brathair | Greek | phrater |

The English that people use today has gone through three principal stages, the first of which began about 1,500 years ago.

## OLD ENGLISH (450–1150)

You have already encountered some Old English with the passage from *Beowulf*. This earliest form of English was the language of three German tribes: the Angles, the Saxons, and the Jutes. These tribes invaded England and then settled there. They seem to have called their language *Englisc* (from *Engle,* "the Angles"). Although the language's vocabulary was extensive, only a small fraction of its words have survived. Among them, however, are some of the most common words in Modern English.

| WORDS FROM OLD ENGLISH | |
|---|---|
| Familiar Objects | horse, cow, meat, stone, earth, home |
| Family Members | father, mother, brother, sister, wife |
| Pronouns | I, you, he, she, we, they, who |
| Numbers | one, two, three, four, five, six, seven |
| Articles | a, an, the |
| Prepositions | in, out, at, by, under, around |

## MIDDLE ENGLISH (1150–1500)

In 1066, the Normans, who came from what is now north-western France, invaded England under the command of William the Conqueror. This invasion, known as the Norman Conquest, had far-reaching effects on the language. For centuries afterward the rulers and the upper classes of England spoke French—the Normans' language— although religious and legal documents continued to be written in Latin. During this period, Old English, French, and Latin gradually became intermixed. Consequently, synonyms for many words came from all three languages. For example, *old* is from Old English, *ancient* is from French, and *venerable* is from Latin.

Geoffrey Chaucer wrote the famous *Canterbury Tales* in Middle English. In this passage one of the travellers, a monk, is telling the story of Holofernes, a powerful and cruel king.

## De Oloferno

Was nevere capitayn under a kyng
That regnes mo putte in subjeccioun,
Ne strenger was in feeld of alle thyng,
As in his tyme, ne gretter of re noun,
Ne moore pompous in heigh presumpcioun
    Than Oloferne, Which Fortune ay kiste
So likerously, and ladde hym up and doun,
Til that his heed was of, er that he wiste.
Nat oonly that this world hadde hum in awe
For lesynge of richesse or libertee,
But he made every man reneyen his lawe.
"Nabugodonosor was god," seyde hee;
    "Noon oother god sholde adoured bee."
Agayns his heeste no wight dar trespace
Save in Bethulia, a strong citee,
Where Eliachim a preest was of that place.
But taak kep of the deth of Oloferne;
Amydde his hoost he dronke lay a nyght,
Withinne his tente, large as is a berne,
And yet, for al his pompe and al his myght,
    Judith, a womman, as he lay upright
Slepynge, his heed of smoot, and from his tente
Ful pryvely she stal from every wight,
And with his heed unto hir toun she wente.

—Geoffrey Chaucer, *The Canterbury Tales*

Here is the same passage, as translated over five hundred years later.

## Holofernes

Was never a captain under a king
That had more kingdoms thrown in subjection,
Nor stronger there was in fields of all things,
As in his time, nor greater of renown,
No one more pompous in high presumption,
Than Holofernes, whom Dame Fortune kissed
So lecherously, and led him up and down

Understanding the Development of the English Language    **499**

Until his head was off before 'twas missed.
Not only did this world hold him in awe
For taking all its wealth and liberty,
But he made every man renounce old law.
"Nebuchadnezzar is your god," said he,
    "And now no other god shall adored be."
Against his order no man dared trespass,
Save in Bethulia, a strong city,
Where Eliachim priest was of that place.
But from the death of Holofernes learn.
Amidst his host he lay drunk, on a night,
Within his tent, as large as is a barn,
And yet, for all his pomp and all his might,
    Judith, a woman, as he lay upright,
Sleeping, smote off his head and from his tent
Stole secretly away from every sight,
And with his head to her own town she went.

— Geoffrey Chaucer, *The Canterbury Tales*

## ● Practice Your Skills

### *Analyzing Language*

With a partner, describe the differences you observe between Middle English and Modern English in the two passages from *The Canterbury Tales*. Be specific, citing particular words and phrases as needed. Also, describe what similarities you see. Note that both the original and the translation conform to ten syllables per line, and that this attention to form helps clarify how certain words are pronounced. When it is your partner's turn to speak, listen carefully and attentively. Ask questions of your partner if you need clarification. Summarize what you have observed and report your findings to the class. Support your findings with specific examples.

## MODERN ENGLISH (1500 TO PRESENT)

By 1500, the assimilation of the contributing languages that formed the basis of English was largely complete. William Shakespeare wrote his great works early in the Modern English period, and more than 200 years later the documents of the American Revolution were written in Modern English. Of course, changes have continued to occur in English since 1500, as more and more cultures contributed words and customs to the language. Today English is a rich, versatile language with choices and variants that are acceptable in different situations and different parts of the country.

Read aloud the opening soliloquy from the play *Richard III,* by William Shakespeare, as it appeared in 1597. Compare the language with Old or Middle English, and notice how much closer this passage is to the English that you are used to speaking.

Now is the winter of our discontent,
Made glorious summer by this sonne of Yorke:
And all the cloudes that lowrd vpon our house,
In the deepe bosome of the Ocean buried.
Now are our browes bound with victorious wreathes,
Our bruised armes hung vp for monuments,
Our sterne alarmes changd to merry meetings,
Our dreadfull marches to delightfull measures.
Grim-visagde warre, hath smoothde his wrinkled front,
    And now in steed of mounting barbed steedes,
To fright the soules of fearefull aduersaries
He capers nimbly in a Ladies chamber,
To the lasciuious pleasing of a loue.
But I that am not shapte for sportiue trickes,
Nor made to court an amorous looking glasse,
I that am rudely stampt and want loues maiesty,
To strut before a wanton ambling Nymph:
I that am curtaild of this faire proportion,
Cheated of feature by dissembling nature,
Deformd, vnfinisht, sent before my time
Into this breathing world fearce halfe made vp,
And that so lamely and vnfashionable,
That dogs barke at me as I halt by them:
Why I in this weake piping time of peace
Haue no delight to passe away the time,
Vnlesse to spie my shadow in the sunne,
And dscant on mine owne deformity.

—William Shakespeare, *Richard III*

## ● Practice Your Skills

### *Analyzing Language*

With a partner, cite specific examples of how Shakespeare's language in the soliliquy above is different from Old English and also how it is different from the English you speak today. Then cite specific examples of how it is linked to Old English and the English you speak. Summarize what you discover and report your findings to the class.

## AMERICAN ENGLISH

Although most of the words in use in the United States today were brought to this country by English settlers, other cultural groups have also contributed—and continue to contribute—words to American English. For instance, the various Native American languages have had a significant influence on place names in the United States—*Omaha, Wichita,* and *Niagara,* for example. Some other English words that come from Native American languages are *succotash, raccoon,* and *opossum.*

In addition, explorers, settlers, and visitors from other countries brought with them their own contributions to American English. For example, the words *Los Angeles* and *tornado* are Spanish, and *opera* and *spaghetti* are Italian. Here are more examples.

| | |
|---|---|
| **Spanish** | breeze, poncho, mustang, alligator, rodeo |
| **French** | cartoon, dentist, liberty, garage, parachute |
| **German** | hamster, nickel, zinc, noodle, waltz |
| **Dutch** | landscape, skipper, cookie, cruise, iceberg |
| **Italian** | zero, candy, magazine, pizza, stanza |
| **African** | Gullah, banjo, banana, dashiki, okra |
| **Chinese** | tea, kowtow, chow, shanghai, typhoon |

The following two passages come from different periods in American history. As you read the selections, look for differences and similarities in vocabulary and sentence structure. The first selection is from President George Washington's First Inaugural Address on April 30, 1789.

### MODEL: Modern English

Fellow Citizens of the Senate and of the House of Representatives: Among the vicissitudes incident to life no event could have filled me with greater anxieties than that of which the notification was transmitted by your order, and received on the fourteenth day of the present month. On the one hand, I was summoned by my country, whose voice I can never hear but with veneration and love, from a retreat which I had chosen with the fondest predilection, and, in my flattering hopes, with an immutable decision, as the asylum of my declining years—a retreat which was rendered every day more necessary as well as more dear to me by the addition of habit to inclination, and of frequent interruptions in my health to the gradual waste committed on it by time. On the other hand, the magnitude and difficulty of the trust to which the voice of my country called me, being sufficient to awaken in the wisest and most experienced of her citizens a distrustful scrutiny into his qualifications, could not but overwhelm with despondence one who (inheriting inferior endowments from nature and unpracticed in the duties of civil administration) ought to be peculiarly conscious of his own deficiencies. In this conflict of emotions all I dare aver is that it has been my faithful study to collect my duty from a just appreciation of every circumstance by which it might be affected. All I dare hope is that if, in executing this task, I have been too much swayed by a grateful remembrance of former instances, or by an affectionate sensibility to this transcendent proof of the confidence of my fellow citizens, and have thence too little consulted my incapacity as well as disinclination for the weighty and untried cares before me, my error will be palliated by the motives which mislead me, and its consequences be judged by my country with some share of the partiality in which they originated.

— George Washington, *First Inaugural Address*

Following is a selection from President Barack Obama's Inaugural Address, given on January 21, 2009.

## MODEL: Modern English

My fellow citizens: I stand here today humbled by the task before us, grateful for the trust you've bestowed, mindful of the sacrifices borne by our ancestors.

. . .

Forty-four Americans have now taken the presidential oath. The words have been spoken during rising tides of prosperity and the still waters of peace. Yet, every so often, the oath is taken amidst gathering clouds and raging storms. At these moments, America has carried on not simply because of the skill or vision of those in high office, but because we, the people, have remained faithful to the ideals of our forebears and true to our founding documents.

So it has been; so it must be with this generation of Americans.

That we are in the midst of crisis is now well understood. Our nation is at war against a far-reaching network of violence and hatred. Our economy is badly weakened, a consequence of greed and irresponsibility on the part of some, but also our collective failure to make hard choices and prepare the nation for a new age. Homes have been lost, jobs shed, businesses shuttered. Our health care is too costly, our schools fail too many—and each day brings further evidence that the ways we use energy strengthen our adversaries and threaten our planet.

These are the indicators of crisis, subject to data and statistics. Less measurable, but no less profound, is a sapping of confidence across our land; a nagging fear that America's decline is inevitable, that the next generation must lower its sights.

Today I say to you that the challenges we face are real. They are serious and they are many. They will not be met easily or in a short span of time. But know this America: They will be met.

. . .

In reaffirming the greatness of our nation we understand that greatness is never a given. It must be earned. Our journey has never been one of short-cuts or settling for less. It has not been the path for the faint-hearted, for those that prefer leisure over work, or seek only the pleasures of riches and fame. Rather, it has been the risk-takers, the doers, the makers of things—some celebrated, but more often men and women obscure in their labor—who have carried us up the long rugged path towards prosperity and freedom.

For us, they packed up their few worldly possessions and traveled across oceans in search of a new life. For us, they toiled in sweatshops, and settled the West, endured the lash of the whip, and plowed the hard earth. For us, they fought and died in places like Concord and Gettysburg, Normandy and Khe Sahn.

Time and again these men and women struggled and sacrificed and worked till their hands were raw so that we might live a better life. They saw America as bigger than the sum of our individual ambitions, greater than all the differences of birth or wealth or faction.

This is the journey we continue today.

— Barack Obama, *Inaugural Address*

## ● Practice Your Skills

### *Analyzing Language*

With a partner, discuss the differences you observe between the words of President Washington and President Obama. Draw conclusions about how English has changed based on your analysis of the similarities and differences between the two selections. Be specific, citing particular words and phrases to support your findings. Organize your ideas in writing to ensure coherence, logical progression, and support. Write a summary of what you observe and report your findings to the class.

**Words with Unusual Origins** Sometimes the names of characters in literature and mythology and the names of real people, places, and historical events become familiar English words. The word *quixotic,* meaning "idealistic to an impractical degree," derives from the name *Don Quixote,* the hero of the seventeeth-century novel *Don Quixote de la*

*Mancha,* by Miguel de Cervantes. Some words have their origins in mythology: *cereal,* for example, comes from *Ceres,* the Roman goddess of the harvest and grain. The *diesel* engine is named for its inventor, Rudolf Diesel. Here are some other words with unusual origins.

| WORD | MEANING | ETYMOLOGY |
| --- | --- | --- |
| malapropism | humorous misuse of a word | from *Mrs. Malaprop,* a character noted for misusing words in Richard Sheridan's 1775 comedy, *The Rivals* |
| Waterloo | decisive or final defeat or setback | from *Waterloo,* Belgium, the scene of Napoleon's defeat in 1815 |
| boycott | refrain from having any dealings with | from Charles *Boycott,* a land agent in Ireland who in 1897 was ostracized for refusing to reduce rents |

## ENGLISH IN THE 21ST CENTURY

No one can say with certainly what the English language will be like in the future. Perhaps it will not have changed very much, or perhaps the influence of new technologies and diverse cultures will make the English we use today as foreign to people in the future as Old English is to us today. One thing is certain to be true: the language will continue to change. As technology erases cultural and geographic borders, English will surely reflect the diversity of influences with which it comes in contact.

***Language of the Digital Revolution*** Computer technologies have added words to our vocabulary from their beginnings. *Virus* is no longer associated only with a living organism; it now has high-tech connotations as well. *Portal, buy, driver,* and *cookie* have also taken on digital definitions. The Internet continues to influence the English language as well. For example, people on social networking sites use the word *friend* as a verb, as well as the related new term *unfriend.* Wireless handheld devices have spawned widespread adoption of shorthand, such as IMHO (in my humble opinion), F2F (face-to-face), and I 1-D-R (I wonder).

## ● Practice Your Skills

### *Analyzing the Influence of Digital Technologies*

With a group of your peers, brainstorm at least five expressions from digital sources, such as Internet shorthand, social networking sites, and terms derived from hand-held technologies. Share your examples with the class. After all the expressions have been shared, discuss the influence of the digital technologies on your own vocabulary and speech.

# Developing Your Word-Search Skills

## USING THE DICTIONARY

The dictionary is a valuable resource tool. As you read, the dictionary can help you understand unfamiliar words. As you write, it can help you make accurate word choices. Whatever your purpose, the dictionary can usually provide the answers.

## INFORMATION IN AN ENTRY

All words listed in the dictionary are called **entry words.** Entry words are printed in heavy type and are broken into syllables to show how the word is divided. In addition to the entry word itself, the dictionary includes the **part of speech** of the word, **other forms** of the word, the **meaning** of the word, the **history** of the word, and often **synonyms and antonyms.** All of this information about each word is called a **main entry.** The following list shows different types of entry words and how they would be listed in the dictionary in alphabetical order.

| | |
|---|---|
| **Single Word** | mercy |
| **Suffix** | –mere |
| **Prefix** | meso– |
| **Compound Word** | mess kit |
| **Abbreviation** | Mrs. |

***Preferred and Variant Spellings*** Some words have more than one correct spelling. The spelling most commonly used, called the **preferred spelling,** is the initial entry word in dark type. Less common spellings, called **variants,** usually follow the preferred spelling, as shown below.

Preferred Spelling ⟶ **caddie** *also,* caddy ⟵ Variant Spelling

## ● Practice Your Skills

### *Finding Preferred Spellings*

The words below have been spelled using the variant spelling. Look up each variant spelling in the dictionary. Write the preferred spelling.

**1.** pilaff

**2.** cooky

**3.** sulphur

**4.** chlorophyl

**5.** dialog

**Division of Words into Syllables** Sometimes when you write an essay or report, you may need to divide a word at the end of a line with a hyphen. The dictionary shows the correct division of syllables for each entry word.

re • sus • ci • tate      ret • i • cence      re • vers • i • ble

**Pronunciation** Following the entry word is the **phonetic spelling** of the word, which shows you how to pronounce the word. All the entry examples in this section are from recent editions of *The American Heritage Dictionary* © by Houghton Mifflin Company.

**in·au·gu·rate** (ĭn-ô′gyə-rāt′) *tr.v.* **-rat·ed, -rat·ing, -rates. 1.** To induct into office by a formal ceremony. **2.** To cause to begin, especially officially or formally: *inaugurate a new immigration policy.* See Synonyms at **begin. 3.** To open or begin use of formally with a ceremony: dedicate: *inaugurate a community center.* [Latin *inaugurāre, inaugurāt-* : *in-,* intensive pref.; see IN−² + *augurāre,* to augur (from *augur,* soothsayer; see **aug-** in Appendix).] —**in·au′gu·ra′tor** *n.*

A chart at the front of the dictionary contains a complete list of phonetic symbols. Most dictionaries also provide a partial pronunciation key at the bottom of every other page. The marks over vowels, called **diacritical marks,** indicate different vowel sounds. The key will tell you how to pronounce a vowel with a diacritical mark. To find out how to pronounce the vowel sound in the last syllable of the word *inaugurate,* for example, you would find the symbol ā in the key. You could then see that this a is pronounced like the *a* in *age.*

Phonetic spellings also show which syllables are stressed. A heavy accent mark, called the **primary stress,** shows which syllable receives the most emphasis. A **secondary stress** indicates a syllable that receives a lesser emphasis.

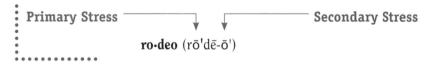

Primary Stress ——————↓   ↓—————— Secondary Stress

**ro·deo** (rō′dē-ō′)

**Parts-of-Speech Label** A dictionary entry will label the parts of speech of the entry word. When a word may be used in several ways, the most common usage of the word is usually listed first. The following abbreviations are used to indicate the parts of speech.

| Part-of-Speech Abbreviations | | | | |
|---|---|---|---|---|
| | *n.* | noun | *v.* | verb |
| | *pron.* | pronoun | *prep.* | preposition |
| | *adj.* | adjective | *conj.* | conjunction |
| | *adv.* | adverb | *interj.* | interjection |

**Multiple Meanings** If a word has more than one meaning, most dictionaries will list the most common meaning first. The meanings may be in historical order, however, with the oldest meaning first.

> **quar·ter** (kwôr′tər) *n.* *Abbr.* **q., qr., quar.** **1.** One of four equal parts. **2.** A coin equal to one fourth of the dollar of the United States and Canada. **3.** One fourth of an hour; 15 minutes. **4. a.** One fourth of a year; three months: *Sales were up in the second quarter.* **b.** An academic term lasting approximately three months. **5.** *Astronomy.* **a.** One fourth of the period of the moon's revolution around Earth. **b.** One of the four phases of the moon: *the first quarter; the third quarter.* **6.** *Sports.* One of four equal periods of playing time into which some games, such as football and basketball, are divided. **7.** One fourth of a yard; nine inches. **8.** One fourth of a mile; two furlongs. **9.** One fourth of a pound; four ounces. **10.** One fourth of a ton; 500 pounds. Used as a measure of grain. **11.** *Chiefly British.* A measure of grain equal to approximately eight bushels. **12. a.** One fourth of a hundredweight; 25 pounds. **b.** One fourth of a British hundredweight; 28 pounds. **13. a.** One of the four major divisions of the compass. **b.** One fourth of the distance between any two of the 32 divisions of the compass. **c.** One of the four major divisions of the horizon as determined by the four major points of the com-

### ● Practice Your Skills

#### Recognizing Multiple Meanings

Use the dictionary entry for the word *quarter,* shown above, to write the part of speech and number of the definition that suits the use of the word *quarter* in each sentence.

**1.** My favorite family restaurant is in the Italian <u>quarter</u> of the city.

**2.** Would you lend me a <u>quarter</u>?

**3.** My grade in physics this <u>quarter</u> should be a B+, giving me an A- for the entire year.

**4.** Duncan Hooper won the basketball game by scoring twenty points in the final <u>quarter</u>.

**5.** Business for the Acme Shoe Company was brisk during the first <u>quarter</u>.

**Inflected Forms** An **inflection** is an ending that changes the form of a word but not its part of speech. Verbs can be inflected with the endings *-ed* or *-ing* to show a change from one principal part to another. Adjectives can be inflected with *-er* or *-est* to show degrees of comparison. Nouns can be inflected by adding *-s* or *-es* to make them plural. Dictionaries usually show these inflected forms only when they are formed irregularly.

**Derived words** are also formed by adding endings, but in such cases the part of speech of the word also changes. For example, adding the suffix *-ly* turns the adjective *hungry* into the adverb *hungrily*. Such derived words are listed at the end of a main entry.

**juic·y** (jōō′sē) *adj.* **-i·er, -i·est. 1.** Full of juice; succulent. **2. a.** Richly interesting: *a juicy mystery novel.* **b.** Racy; titillating: *a juicy bit of gossip.* **3.** Yielding profit; rewarding or gratifying: *a juicy raise; a juicy part in a play.* **—juic′i·ly** *adv.* **—juic′i·ness** *n.*

**Etymologies** The etymology of a word is an explanation of its origin and history. In an etymology, abbreviations are used to stand for the different languages from which a word has developed. Symbols are used to stand for such words as *derived from* (<) or *equal to* (=). A chart at the beginning of the dictionary lists all the abbreviations and symbols used in the etymology of a word. In the following etymology, the most recent source of the word is listed first.

**pre·am·ble** (prē′ăm′bəl, prē-ăm′-) *n.* **1.** A preliminary statement, especially the introduction to a formal document that serves to explain its purpose. **2.** An introductory occurrence or fact; a preliminary. [Middle English, from Old French *preambule*, from Medieval Latin *preambulum*, from neuter of *praeambulus*, walking in front : *prae-*, pre- + *ambulāre*, to walk; see AMBULATE.] **—pre·am′bu·lar′y** (-byə-lĕr′ē) *adj.*

The etymology for the word *preamble* can be translated as follows: The word *preamble* comes from the Middle English, which came from the Old French *preambule. Preambule* came from the Medieval Latin word *preambulum,* which was taken from the Late Latin word *praeambulus,* which meant "walking in front." *Praeambulus* was from the Latin prefix *prae–,* meaning "in front," and *ambulare,* meaning "to walk."

## ● Practice Your Skills

### Tracing Word Origins

Use our dictionary to find the etymology of each word. Then choose one etymology and write its translation. (Use the example of *preamble* as a model.)

**1.** bellicose

**2.** chromosome

**3.** forceps

**4.** geranium

**5.** guitar

**6.** hominy

**7.** menace

**8.** nightmare

**9.** philodendron

**10.** verdict

● **Practice Your Skills**

*Using a Pronunciation Key*

Use the pronunciation key below to sound out each phonetic spelling in the first column. Then write the word in the second column that matches. Also write the phonetic spelling that does not have a match.

| | |
|---|---|
| **1.** kap'–shən | context |
| **2.** kän'–tent | concrete |
| **3.** kap'–tən | captain |
| **4.** kən–tend' | contingent |
| **5.** kən–tin'–jənt | content |
| **6.** kän'–tekst | confide |
| **7.** kän'–krēt | contend |
| **8.** kən–fīd' | |

\ä\ mar \ē\ be \ī\ pie \ə\ about, item

● **Practice Your Skills**

*Practicing Pronunciation*

With a partner, take turns pronouncing the words in the previous activity until you can say them fluently.

# Expanding Your Vocabulary

Learning and understanding new words is valuable to both your reading and your writing. The rest of this chapter will give you some ways to unlock the meanings of unfamiliar words.

## ① Context Clues

The **context** of a word is the sentence, surrounding words, or situation in which the word appears. Usually the context of a word gives clues to meaning rather than an actual definition.

**Restatement**   The sun reached its *zenith,* **or highest point in the sky,** just as we began to eat lunch. (The word *or* introduces an appositive that defines the word *zenith*.)

**Example**   *Symmetry* often contributes to the beauty of architecture, as it does, for example, **in the perfect proportions and balanced forms of the Taj Mahal.** (By using the well-known Taj Mahal as an example, the writer makes clear what is meant by the word *symmetry*.)

**Comparison**   A *prodigy* in music, she was **nearly the equal of Mozart, the composer who wrote a sonata at the age of eight.** (The comparison with Mozart shows that *prodigy* means "a highly talented child.")

**Contrast**   **Mark's customized purple jeep, with a gilt crown for a hood ornament,** is as *gaudy* as Mr. Foster's gray sedan is plain. (The contrast between Mark's car and Mr. Foster's car shows that *gaudy* means just the opposite of plain: "showy, garish, and possibly tasteless.")

**Parallelism**   She was **determined,** he was **iron willed,** and I was equally *resolute.* (The parallel sentence structure suggests that *resolute* is a synonym for *determined* and *iron willed*.)

*Using Context Clues*

Use context clues to help you choose the meaning for the underlined words. Consult the dictionary to check your answers.

**1.** Congress passed a statute, or law, to provide for federal enforcement of the Constitutional amendment.

(A) request       (B) written rule       (C) sculptured likeness

(D) book       (E) statement

**2.** The king decided to abdicate, as King Edward VIII did when he gave up the throne of England in 1936.

(A) relinquish power       (B) be crowned       (C) control

(D) marry       (E) escape

**3.** Amity exists between Switzerland and its neighbors, in contrast to the ill will that exists between some other neighboring nations of the world.

(A) rivalry       (B) hostility       (C) borders

(D) friendship       (E) helplessness

**4.** Inquiring about his son's career, the man naturally took a paternal interest in the boy's success.

(A) brotherly       (B) long-term       (C) fatherly

(D) excessive       (E) mild

**5.** The recent political caucus, unlike those old-time small gatherings, was well reported by the press.

(A) defeat       (B) meeting       (C) campaign

(D) dinner       (E) platform

**6.** A referee should be completely impartial, favoring neither team.

(A) businesslike       (B) enthusiastic       (C) outspoken

(D) cordial       (E) fair

**7.** This is a facsimile, or replica, of a five-hundred-dollar bill issued by the Confederate States of America.

(A) reproduction       (B) variety       (C) counterfeit

(D) bonanza       (E) display

**8.** When the foreman was warned about his laxity, he changed overnight and became a complete perfectionist.

(A) extravagance       (B) appearance       (C) negligence

(D) ignorance       (E) temper

**9.** Although the candidate failed to win a majority of votes in the primary, he did have a sizable <u>plurality</u> over the first runner-up.

(A) loss of votes     (B) excess of votes     (C) celebration

(D) concern     (E) surprise

**10.** Among the other pleasant smells in the village was the <u>savory</u> odor of chili coming from a small café.

(A) appetizing     (B) sturdy     (C) flowery

(D) gracious     (E) rural

## ● Practice Your Skills

### *Practicing Pronunciation*

Use a print or online dictionary to look up the pronunciation of the words in the previous activity. Then in pairs, take turns pronouncing them. Keep practicing until you have the pronunciation just right.

## ② Prefixes, Suffixes, and Roots

Besides using the context of a word, you can use a word's structure, or parts, to find clues to its meaning. These word parts are prefixes, roots, and suffixes. A **root** is the part of a word that carries the basic meaning. A **prefix** is one or more syllables placed in front of the root to modify the meaning of the root or to form a new word. A **suffix** is one or more syllables placed after the root to affect its meaning and often to determine its part of speech.

The English language contains hundreds of roots, prefixes, and suffixes. With a knowledge of even a few examples of each kind of word part, you should be able to make reasonable guesses about the meanings of words that contain these parts. The following examples illustrate how the meaning of each word part contributes to the meaning of the word as a whole.

| WORD PARTS WITH LATIN ORIGINS | | | |
|---|---|---|---|
| Word | Prefix | Root | Suffix |
| abrasive | ab- (away) | -rase- (erase) | -ive (toward action) |
| component | com- (together) | -pon- (put) | -ent (one that performs) |
| inaccessible | in- (not) | -access- (approach) | -ible (capable of) |

## WORD PARTS WITH GREEK ORIGINS

| Word | Prefix | Root | Suffix |
|------|--------|------|--------|
| amorphous | a- (without) | -morph- (form) | -ous (quality of) |
| ejection | e- (out) | -ject- (throw) | -ion (act or process) |
| precedence | pre- (before) | -ced- (go) | -ence (act or process) |

As you can see, the meanings of prefixes, roots, and suffixes seldom give a complete definition of a word. Rather, they give clues to the meaning of a word. Following are dictionary definitions of the previous examples.

**abrasive:** tending to rub or wear away

**component:** simple part or element of a system

**inaccessible:** not capable of being approached

**amorphous:** having no definite form, shapeless

**ejection:** act of throwing out or off from within

**precedence:** act of going before

## PREFIXES

Many prefixes have clear and familiar meanings. The number prefixes, such as *mono-*, *bi-*, and *tri-*, are good examples. Other prefixes, however, have more than one meaning and spelling. The prefix *ad-*, for example, may mean "to" or "toward." It may be spelled *ad-* (adjacent), *ac-* (acquire), or *al-* (allure), depending on the first letter of the root to which it is attached. The following charts show common Latin and Greek prefixes.

## PREFIXES FROM LATIN

| Prefix | Meaning | Example |
|--------|---------|---------|
| ab-, a- | from, away, off | ab + errant: wandering away from the right or normal way |
| ad-, ac-, af-, ag-, al-, ap-, as-, at | to, toward | ad + jacent: nearby<br>ac + quire: get as one's own<br>al + lure: entice by charm<br>as + sure: make certain or safe |
| ante- | forward, in front of, before | ante + chamber: outer room, such as a waiting room |
| bi- | two, occurring twice | bi + lingual: using two languages with equal skill |
| circum- | around, about | circum + navigate: travel completely around |

| | | |
|---|---|---|
| com-, col-, con- | with, together | com + press: squeeze together<br>con + cur: happen together |
| contra- | opposite, against | contra + dict: resist or oppose in argument |
| de- | do the opposite of, remove | de + activate: make inactive or ineffective |
| dis- | opposite of, not | dis + assemble: take apart |
| ex- | out of, outside | ex + clude: shut out |
| in-, il-, im-, ir- | not, in, into | in + animate: not spirited<br>im + press: affect deeply |
| inter- | between, among | inter + stellar: among stars |
| intra- intro- | within, during | intra + venous: within or entering by way of a vein |
| non- | not | non + committal: not giving a clear indication of attitude |
| ob- | against, in the way | ob + stacle: something that stands in the way |
| post- | after, behind | post + script: writing added after a complete work |
| pre- | earlier than, before | pre + determine: decide or establish in advance |
| re- | again, back | re + organize: arrange or systematize again |
| retro- | backward, back, behind | retro + spect: review of past events |
| semi- | half of | semi + circle: half of a circle |
| sub- | beneath, under | sub + plot: secondary series of events in a literary work |
| super- | over and above, more than | super + human: exceeding normal human size, capability |
| trans- | across, beyond, through | trans + atlantic: extending across the Atlantic Ocean |
| ultra- | beyond in space, beyond limits of | ultra + violet: beyond the visible range of violet in the spectrum |
| vice- | one who takes the place of | vice + principal: person who acts in place of the principal |

## PREFIXES FROM GREEK

| Prefix | Meaning | Example |
|--------|---------|---------|
| a-, an- | without, not | a + typical: not regular or usual |
| anti- | against | anti + pathy: dislike, distaste |
| cata-, cat-, cath- | down | cata + comb: underground passageway or tomb |
| dia-, di- | through, across | dia + gonal: extending from one edge of a solid figure to an opposite edge |
| dys- | difficult, impaired | dys + lexia: disturbance of the ability to read |
| epi- | over, after, outer | epi + dermis: outer layer of skin |
| hemi- | half | hemi + sphere: half a sphere |
| hyper- | above, excessive | hyper + tension: above the normal blood pressure range |
| para- | beside, closely related to | para + phrase: restate a text in another form or in other words |
| peri- | all around, surrounding | peri + pheral: relating to the outward bounds of something |
| pro- | earlier than, in front of | pro + logue: introduction to a literary work |
| syn-, sym- | with, at the same time | syn + thesize: combine to from a new, complex product |

● **Practice Your Skills**

### Combining Prefixes and Roots

Use the charts above to find the Latin or Greek prefix with the same meaning as the underlined word. Combine the prefix with the root and write the word.

**Example**    <u>between</u> + cede = act as mediator in a dispute

**Answer**    inter + cede = intercede

**1.** <u>two</u> + lingual = using two languages

**2.** <u>back</u> + active = extending to a prior time or to conditions that existed in the past

**3.** <u>half of</u> + circle = half of a circle

**4.** <u>against</u> + toxin = substance that counteracts poison

**5.** <u>with</u> + league = professional associate

**6.** <u>opposite of</u> + continue = cease to operate or use

**7.** <u>not</u> + fallible = perfect

**8.** <u>before</u> + bellum = existing prior to a war

**9.** <u>around</u> + ference = perimeter of a circle

**10.** <u>excessive</u> + active = excessively energetic

**11.** <u>after</u> + mortem = occurring after death

**12.** <u>beside</u> + graph = distinct division in written composition, often shown by indentation

**13.** <u>again</u> + generate = form or create again

**14.** <u>down</u> + clysm = momentous event marking demolition

**15.** <u>remove</u> + moralize = weaken the morale of

## ● Practice Your Skills

### *Practicing Pronunciation*

Use a print or online dictionary to look up the pronunciation of the answers to the previous activity. Then in pairs, take turns pronouncing each word. Keep practicing until you have the pronunciation just right.

## SUFFIXES

There are two kinds of suffixes: inflectional and derivational. An **inflectional suffix** (or grammatical suffix) changes the number of nouns (*computer, computers*), the possession of nouns (*woman, woman's*), the degree of comparison for modifiers (*soft, softer, softest*), and the form of verbs (*care, cared, caring*). An inflectional suffix does not change the essential meaning of the word or its part of speech.

The **derivational suffix** changes the meaning and very often the part of speech of the word to which it is added. Look at the changes the derivational suffixes make when they are added to the verb *observe*.

| | |
|---|---|
| **Without suffix** | observe (verb) |
| **With -ance** | observance (noun) |
| **With -able** | observable (adjective) |
| **With -ly** | observably (adverb, -ly added to the adjective form) |

Some suffixes form nouns, some form adjectives, some form verbs, and some form adverbs.

## SUFFIXES

| Suffix | Meaning | Example |
|---|---|---|
| -ance, -ence | action, process, quality, state | exist + ence: state or fact of being |
| -ard, -art | one that does to excess | brag + art: one who boasts excessively |
| -cy | action, state, quality | normal + cy: state of being average |
| -dom | state, rank, or condition of | free + dom: state of having liberty or independence |
| -er, -or | one who is, does, makes | retail + er: one who sells directly to customers |
| -ion | act, process, result, state | react + ion: act of responding |
| -ism | act, state, or characteristic of | critic + ism: act of evaluating |
| -ity | state, quality degree | moral + ity: doctrine or system of correct conduct |
| -ness | state, quality | brisk + ness: state of being keenly alert and lively |
| -ure | act, process, function | post + ure: position or bearing of the body |
| -able, -ible | capable of, fit | expend + able: capable of being consumed by use |
| -al | characterized by, relating to | tradition + al: relating to the handing down of customs |
| -en | belonging to, made of | earth + en: soil or made of clay |
| -ful | full of, having the qualities of | master + ful: having the skill of a qualified worker |
| -ic | having the character of | hero + ic: being courageous and daring |
| -ish | characteristic of, inclined to | clown + ish: having characteristics of a clown |
| -less | not having, lacking | purpose + less: lacking goals |
| -ly | like in appearance, manner, or nature | friend + ly: in the nature of a friend |
| -ory | of, relating to, producing | transit + ory: of brief duration |
| -ous | full of, having the qualities of, marked by | clamor + ous: marked by a confused din or outcry |
| -some | characterized by action or quality | burden + some: characterized by being a heavy load to bear |
| -ate | act on, cause to become, influence | captive + ate: influence by special charm |

A. Vocabulary

| -en | cause to be or have | height + en: cause to have increased amount or degree of |
| -fy, -ify | make, form into, invest with | spec + ify: make clear and state explicitly |
| -ize | become like, cause to be | character + ize: cause to be a distinguishing trait of |

Some suffixes can form more than one part of speech. The suffix *-ate*, for example, can be used to form verbs (*activate*), nouns (*candidate*), and adjectives (*temperate*).

● **Practice Your Skills**

### Adding Suffixes to Words

Write the suffix that has the same meaning as the underlined word or words. Then write the complete word.

**Example**     category + <u>cause to be</u> = classify

**Answer**     category + ize = categorize

**1.** zeal + <u>full of</u> = full of eagerness and enthusiasm

**2.** convention + <u>characterized by</u> = relating to established customs

**3.** survey + <u>doer</u> = one who measures tracts of land

**4.** complicate + <u>act of</u> = act of making complex or difficult

**5.** serf + <u>state of</u> = state of being in a servile class in the feudal system

**6.** amalgam + <u>act on</u> = merge into a single body

**7.** lag + <u>one who does to excess</u> = one who lingers too much

**8.** flavor + <u>full of</u> = full of pleasant taste

**9.** pleasure + <u>capable of</u> = capable of gratifying

**10.** daunt + <u>not having</u> = having no fear

**11.** material + <u>cause to be</u> = cause to come into existence

**12.** sheep + <u>characteristic of</u> = resembling a sheep in meekness

**13.** break + <u>capable of</u> = capable of being cracked or smashed

**14.** orate + <u>one who does</u> = one who delivers a formal, elaborate speech

**15.** angel + <u>having the character of</u> = having the goodness of an angel

**16.** enlight + <u>cause to be</u> = cause to receive knowledge

**17.** gull + <u>capable of</u> = capable of being easily deceived or cheated

**18.** tire + <u>characterized by</u> = characterized by being wearisome

**19.** malice + <u>full of</u> = full of spite and ill will

**20.** bounty + <u>full of</u> = characterized by providing abundantly

● **Practice Your Skills**

*Using New Vocabulary*

Use five of the words from the previous activity in a paragraph. Share your sentences with a partner and determine if you have used the words correctly.

## ROOTS

The **root** of a word may be well known in English, or it may be less obvious, having come from Latin or Greek. Sometimes a root may stand alone, as in the word *self*. A root may be combined with a prefix (*retract*), a suffix (*portable*), or even another root (*autograph*). The following charts show some common Latin and Greek roots that are the basic elements of many English words.

| LATIN ROOTS | | |
|---|---|---|
| **Root** | **Meaning** | **Examples** |
| -aqua-, -aqui- | water | aquarium, aqueous |
| -aud- | hear | audience, auditorium |
| -bene- | good, well | benefit, benevolence |
| -cred- | believe | credential, credit |
| -cid- | kill | germicidal, insecticide |
| -fid- | faith, trust | bona fide, infidel |
| -fract-, -frag- | break | fraction, refract, fragile, fragment |
| -grat- | pleasing, thankful | grateful, gratitude, gratuity |
| -loqu- | speak | eloquent, colloquium |
| -mor-, -mort- | death | immortal, mortuary |
| -omni- | all, every | omniscient, omnivorous |
| -ped- | foot | pedestrian, centipede |
| -port- | carry | portable, import |
| -rupt- | break, burst | rupture, interrupt |
| -scrib-, -script- | write | describe, prescribe, inscription, manuscript |
| -sequ- | follow | sequel, subsequent |
| -tort- | twist | distort, tortuous |
| -tract- | draw, pull | traction, retract |
| -vers-, -vert- | turn | invert, subvert, versatile, reverse |
| -vic-, vinc- | conquer | victory, convince, invincible |
| -viv-, -vit- | life, live | survive, vivacious, vitality |

21ST CENTURY

## GREEK ROOTS

| Root | Meaning | Examples |
|---|---|---|
| -anthrop- | man, human | anthropology, anthropomorphic |
| -arch- | rule | monarch, hierarchy |
| -auto- | self | autograph, automobile |
| -biblio- | book | bibliography, bibliophile |
| -bio-, -bi- | life | biology, antibiotic |
| -chrom- | color | chromatic, monochromatic |
| -cosm- | world, order | cosmic, macrocosm |
| -geo- | earth, ground | geography, geology |
| -gram- | drawing, writing | grammatical, program |
| -graph- | write | monograph, typography |
| -log-, -logy- | speech, reason, study, science | catalog, monologue, bacteriology |
| -micro- | small | microfilm, microwave |
| -mono- | one, single | monopoly, monograph |
| -morph- | form | amorphous, morphology |
| -neo- | new | neon, neoclassical |
| -path- | suffering | pathetic, apathy |
| -phon- | sound | phonetic, telephone |
| -pod- | foot | podiatrist, tripod |
| -poly- | many | monopoly, polytechnic |
| -psych- | mind | psychology, psychic |
| -tele- | far off | telescope, telegraph |
| -therm- | heat | thermal, thermometer |

## ● Practice Your Skills

### *Recognizing Latin and Greek Roots*

Write the root of each of the following words. Then use the charts of prefixes, suffixes, and roots to help you write the word's definition. Use the dictionary to check your work.

**Example**     audible

**Answer**     aud—capable of being heard

**1.** disruption

**2.** subscription

**3.** gratify

**4.** convertible

**5.** graphic

**6.** colloquial

**7.** transport

**8.** convivial

**9.** infraction

**10.** sequential

## ● Practice Your Skills

### *Using Roots, Prefixes, and Suffixes*

Using what you have learned in this chapter, write the letter of the phrase closest in meaning to the word in capital letters.

**1. MERITORIOUS**

(A) without value

(B) having worthy qualities

(C) wise

**2. COMPATIBLE**

(A) capable of getting along together

(B) in the manner of a friend

(C) well qualified

**3. EMANCIPATE**

(A) obey a king

(B) cause to become free

(C) win great acclaim

**4. POLYCHROMATIC**

(A) science of color

(B) metal alloy

(C) having many colors

**5. ILLOGICAL**

(A) between reason and knowledge

(B) within reason

(C) not valid, or without skill in reasoning

**6. TRANSITION**

(A) secret underground passage

(B) process of going across from one place to another

(C) loss of credibility

**7. BIPED**

(A) able to walk backward

(B) bicycle

(C) two-footed animal

**8. RETROGRESS**

(A) lack of progress

(B) in need of repairs

(C) go backward

**9. COMMUNICABLE**

(A) capable of being transmitted

(B) full of unnecessary information

(C) condition of being infected

**10. RECOIL**

(A) jump forward suddenly

(B) draw back

(C) lose sight of

## ● Practice Your Skills

### *Using New Vocabulary*

Use five of the capitalized words from the previous activity in a paragraph. Share your sentences with a partner and determine if you have used the words correctly.

# ③ Synonyms and Antonyms

Another way of expanding your vocabulary is to have a thorough understanding of synonyms and antonyms. A **synonym** is a word that has the same or nearly the same meaning as another word. An **antonym** is a word that has the opposite or nearly the opposite meaning as another word.

There are often several synonyms for a word. For instance, among the synonyms for the word *candor* are *sincerity* and *forthrightness*. Notice that these words have slightly different shades of meaning. Dictionary entries often explain the slight differences between synonyms. You have probably also used the specialized dictionary for synonyms called a *thesaurus*. Usually a thesaurus is indexed to help users find the synonyms they need quickly.

● **Practice Your Skills**

*Recognizing Synonyms*

Decide which word is the best synonym of the word in capital letters. Check your answers in a dictionary.

**1. ADAMANT**

(A) skillful        (B) unworthy

(C) unyielding      (D) distressing

(E) faithful

**2. INDICT**

(A) accuse        (B) show

(C) imprison      (D) warn

(E) release

**3. ULTIMATE**

(A) preliminary      (B) substitute

(C) rewarding       (D) eventual

(E) concealed

**4. NOTORIOUS**

(A) legal             (B) fortunate

(C) unfavorably known    (D) unfamiliar

(E) industrious

**5. BESTOW**

(A) discard       (B) give

(C) restore       (D) darken

(E) lackluster

**6. PREDATORY**

(A) entertaining     (B) tragic

(C) corrupt         (D) preying

(E) lackluster

**7. LATERAL**

(A) potential       (B) upward

(C) sluggish        (D) afterward

(E) related to the side

**8. ARBITRATION**

(A) authority       (B) mystery

(C) concern         (D) mediation

(E) treatment

**9. BEGUILE**

(A) deceive         (B) begin

(C) explain         (D) reject

(E) learn

**10. ARABLE**

(A) feathery        (B) fashionable

(C) tillable        (D) windy

(E) livable

## Practice Your Skills

### Recognizing Antonyms

Decide which word is the best antonym of the word in capital letters. Check your answers in a dictionary.

**1. FEASIBLE**

(A) faulty          (B) impossible

(C) impoverished    (D) fatigued

(E) insecure

**2. ACCENTUATE**

(A) de-emphasize    (B) protest

(C) regulate        (D) disagree

(E) relinquish

## 3. ERRONEOUS

(A) mistaken      (B) possible

(C) skillful      (D) tardy

(E) correct

## 4. VULNERABLE

(A) unsusceptible      (B) cheerful

(C) greedy      (D) ridiculous

(E) modest

## 5. EMANCIPATE

(A) forget      (B) strengthen

(C) disallow      (D) enslave

(E) forget

## 6. CYNICAL

(A) soothing      (B) stable

(C) trustful      (D) square

(E) charming

## 7. OBLIQUE

(A) brilliant      (B) questionable

(C) direct      (D) passive

(E) painful

## 8. ALLEVIATE

(A) forget      (B) associate

(C) persuade      (D) improve

(E) aggravate

## 9. HERETIC

(A) villain      (B) conformist

(C) saint      (D) traitor

(E) critic

## 10. EQUILIBRIUM

(A) disapproval      (B) observation

(C) hope      (D) imbalance

(E) high pitch

 **Analogies**

Analogy items require you to identify the relationships between given pairs of words. (See pages 469–471). While many kinds of relationships are used in analogy items, synonyms and antonyms are the most frequent. Consider the following test item.

**HUGE : GIGANTIC ::**

(A) liberate : imprison      (B) noise : clamor

(C) mature : juvenile

To answer this test item, you must first identify the relationship between the two words in capital letters. Those words, *huge* and *gigantic*, are synonyms because they have similar meanings. The next step is to find the other pair of words with the same relationship. Only the words in answer choice *B, noise* and *clamor,* are synonyms. *Liberate* and *imprison* are antonyms, and so are the words *mature* and *juvenile*.

● **Practice Your Skills**

*Understanding Analogies*

Read the first pair of words and determine the relationship between them. Then write the letter of the pair of words that has the same relationship as the first pair. Write synonym or antonym to identify the relationship.

1. **INFINITE : LIMITLESS ::**
   (A) disorganized : orderly      (B) inaccessible : available
   (C) placid : calm

2. **PURGE : CLEANSE ::**
   (A) ornate : plain      (B) privacy : seclusion
   (C) impartial : biased

3. **MALICIOUS : KIND ::**
   (A) gaudy : flashy      (B) harmony : discord
   (C) adage : proverb

4. **AUSPICIOUS : FAVORABLE ::**
   (A) saga : epic      (B) retreat : advance
   (C) savory : bland

5. **LUSTROUS : DULL ::**
   (A) gobble : devour      (B) faultless : perfect
   (C) infallible : unreliable

**6. CRYPT : TOMB ::**

   (A) covetous : desirous      (B) dictate : obey

   (C) fictitious : factual

**7. ORTHODOX : UNCONVENTIONAL ::**

   (A) lament : mourn      (B) trinket : ornament

   (C) acquire : forfeit

**8. SECLUDED : EXPOSED ::**

   (A) parched : wet      (B) paraphrase : reword

   (C) rousing : lively

**9. OBSCURE : OBVIOUS ::**

   (A) brave : dauntless      (B) decrease : maximize

   (C) famous : renowned

**10. TOLERANT : LENIENT ::**

   (A) jovial : merry      (B) inopportune : convenient

   (C) hollow : full

## ● Practice Your Skills

### Using New Vocabulary

Use five of the capitalized words from the previous activity in a paragraph. Share your sentences with a partner and determine if you have used the words correctly.

## ● Practice Your Skills

### Creating Your Own Analogies

Select ten words from your journal. Use a thesaurus or dictionary to come up with a synonym and antonym for each word. You will now have ten pairs of synonyms and ten pairs of antonyms. Use these pairs to create your own analogies. When you are finished, trade with a partner and answer each other's analogies.

 **TIME OUT TO REFLECT**

Look back at an essay you wrote early in the year. How would the vocabulary differ if you were writing the essay now? What vocabulary skills do you need to work on the most? Record your thoughts in the Learning Log section of your journal.

# B. Communication for Careers, Business, and College

## *Apply 21st Century Communication Skills*

As a student, a consumer, and an employee in the 21st century, you can communicate and share information in a number of ways. To communicate effectively, always have a clear purpose in mind and use technology wisely.

# Real-World Communication

## ❶ Communicating for a Purpose

Whether you are writing or speaking, communicating and sharing information can serve a variety of purposes: to inform, instruct, motivate, or persuade, for example. As a consumer, you might write an order letter to inform a company about merchandise you want to buy. As a prospective employee, you have two purposes when you interview for a job—to inform the employer about your skills and experience and to persuade the employer that you are qualified for the position. As a student applying to college, you must complete an application to inform a college about your interests, accomplishments, activities, and personal qualities. Your ultimate purpose is to persuade the school that you have the qualities to succeed there and will make a contribution to the school community.

Whether you are writing a letter or a résumé, filling out an application, or interviewing, you should always keep your purpose in mind. Your goal is to communicate in a clear, concise, focused manner because you want your audience to respond in a positive way.

## ❷ Using Technology to Communicate

Perhaps in the future, people in business will communicate exclusively via e-mail and other forms of electronic communication. Until that time, however, the business letter will remain an effective way to communicate. Writing a letter can be more appropriate than sending an e-mail in certain circumstances. Use these guidelines to determine whether to send a letter or an e-mail.

**Send a letter** in the following circumstances:

- You want to introduce yourself formally or make an impact on your audience by using impressive stationery, for example.

- You are including private, confidential information. E-mail is not a private form of communication; therefore, you should never include confidential information in an e-mail. A recipient can forward an e-mail to others without your knowledge. Also, hackers can break into e-mail systems and steal information.

- You need to have formal documentation of your communication, or you are sending authentic documents.

**Send an e-mail** in the following circumstances:

- You want to communicate quickly with someone.

- You want to send a message, perhaps with accompanying documents, to several people at once.

- You have been instructed by a business or an organization to communicate via e-mail.

## ❸ Characteristics of Effective Real-World Writing

Each situation and each audience requires its unique considerations. Effective real-world writing typically has the characteristics shown below.

### CHARACTERISTICS OF EFFECTIVE EVERYDAY WRITING

- a clearly stated purpose and subject supported by appropriate details

- a formatting structure that enhances readability, including the use of headings, graphics, and white space

- questions that draw readers in and that address their needs

- when necessary, accurate technical information in understandable language

- suitable and clear organizational structure with good supporting details and any necessary documentation

Strive for the above characteristics in your own writing.

# Communication for Careers and Business

Whatever career you decide to pursue, a letter or résumé will often be your first opportunity to communicate information about yourself to a prospective employer. In fact, your letter or résumé may be an important factor in the employer's decision to consider you for the job. To get a favorable response from the receiver, your letter or résumé should state information clearly, purposefully, and thoroughly and should follow an appropriate, standard format. To achieve their purpose, business letters that you write as a consumer should have these qualities as well. In this section, you will learn strategies for writing business letters for a variety of purposes. You will also learn strategies for preparing a résumé and interviewing for a job.

 ## Writing Business Letters

A **business letter** is a formal type of communication. When you write a business letter, your goal is to present yourself in a positive, professional light. Your letter should include a clearly stated purpose, an appropriate organizational structure, and accurate information. Anticipate your reader's potential questions, problems, and misunderstandings, and provide relevant facts and details. Be sure, though, to exclude extraneous information. Check that your vocabulary, tone, and style are appropriate for business communication.

A business letter should be written in an appropriate, customary format that is user-friendly. A commonly used format for a business letter is called the **modified block style.** The heading, closing, and signature are positioned at the right, and the paragraphs are indented.

Neatness is also essential in a business letter. Whenever possible, use a word-processing program to write your business letter. Use white paper 8½-x-11-inches in size. Leave margins at least 1-inch wide.

The following model uses the modified block style. All other sample letters in this chapter use this style. The chart that follows the model explains how to write each part of a business letter.

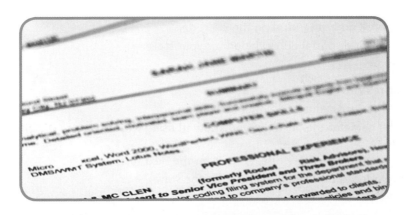

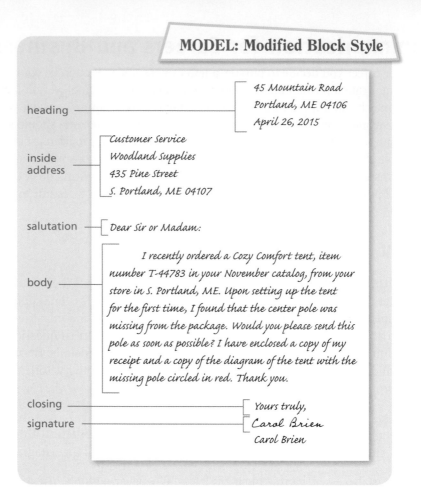

**MODEL: Modified Block Style**

heading —
45 Mountain Road
Portland, ME 04106
April 26, 2015

inside
address —
Customer Service
Woodland Supplies
435 Pine Street
S. Portland, ME 04107

salutation —
Dear Sir or Madam:

body —
I recently ordered a Cozy Comfort tent, item number T-44783 in your November catalog, from your store in S. Portland, ME. Upon setting up the tent for the first time, I found that the center pole was missing from the package. Would you please send this pole as soon as possible? I have enclosed a copy of my receipt and a copy of the diagram of the tent with the missing pole circled in red. Thank you.

closing —
Yours truly,

signature —
Carol Brien
Carol Brien

All business letters have the same six parts: heading, inside address, salutation, body, closing, and signature.

## Parts of a Business Letter

### Heading
- Write your full address, including the ZIP code.
- Use the two-letter postal abbreviation for your state.
- Write the date.

### Inside Address
- Write the receiver's address below the heading.
- Include the name of the person if you know it, using *Mr., Mrs., Ms., Dr.,* or some other title.
- If the person has a business title, write it on the next line.
- Use the two-letter postal abbreviation for the state.

### Salutation

- Start two lines below the inside address.
- Use *Sir* or *Madam* if you do not know the person's name. Otherwise, use the person's last name preceded by *Mr., Mrs., Ms.,* or some other title.
- Use a colon after the salutation.

### Body

- Start two lines below the salutation.
- If the body is only a single paragraph, type it double-space. For longer letters, single-space each paragraph, skipping a line between paragraphs.

### Closing

- Start two lines below the body.
- Line up the closing with the left-hand edge of the heading.
- Use a formal closing such as *Sincerely yours* or *Yours truly* followed by a comma. Capitalize only the first word.

### Signature

- Type (or print, if your letter is handwritten) your full name four or five lines below the closing.
- Sign your full name in the space between the closing and your typed name.

## BUSINESS ENVELOPES

If you use a word-processing program to write your business letter, you should do the same for the envelope. Fold your letter neatly in thirds to fit into a business-sized envelope. Use the format shown below for business letter envelopes.

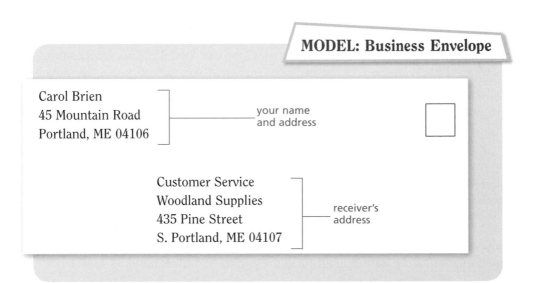

**MODEL: Business Envelope**

Carol Brien
45 Mountain Road
Portland, ME 04106 — your name and address

Customer Service
Woodland Supplies
435 Pine Street
S. Portland, ME 04107 — receiver's address

## BUSINESS E-MAILS

A business letter sent via e-mail should be just as formal as a letter sent by mail. Follow these guidelines when sending a business e-mail.

### Guidelines for Writing a Business E-mail

- Include a formal salutation and closing. Format the body of the letter correctly.
- Use proper grammar and punctuation.
- Check your spelling. (Some e-mail programs have their own spell-check function. Use it.)
- Double-check the person's e-mail address to be sure you have typed it correctly.
- In the subject line of the e-mail, remember to specify the topic you are writing about.

## LETTERS ABOUT EMPLOYMENT

When you apply for a job, you may write a letter to your prospective employer. Your letter should clearly state the job for which you are applying. Anticipate what the employer wants to know about you, and provide relevant, accurate, organized information about your qualifications and experience. Use the appropriate format for a business letter, and be sure your letter is grammatically correct and neat. If the employer requests that you submit a letter by e-mail or via a website, make sure that your letter is still formal and professional.

Include the following information in a letter about employment.

| INFORMATION IN A LETTER ABOUT EMPLOYMENT | |
| --- | --- |
| **Position Sought** | In the first paragraph, state the job you are seeking and how you learned about the opening. |
| **Education** | Include both your age and your grade in school. Emphasize courses you have taken that apply directly to the job you are seeking. |
| **Experience** | State the kinds of work you have done. Although you may not have work experience that relates to the open position, any positions of responsibility you have held, whether paid or unpaid, are valuable work experiences. |
| **References** | Include at least two references, such as a teacher or a former employer, with a mailing address, an e-mail address, or a phone number for each. You should obtain permission in advance from the people you name as references. |
| **Request for an Interview** | In the last paragraph of your letter, ask for an interview. Indicate where and when you can be reached to make an appointment. |

The following employment letter uses the modified block style. Note that it includes information about the position sought and the applicant's education and experience.

72 Helsey Avenue
Vineland, NJ 08360
May 4, 2015

Mr. William Coles
Optima Office Supplies
Vineland, NJ 08360

Dear Mr. Coles:

I would like to apply for the management trainee position advertised in this morning's *Daily Express*. Next week I will graduate with honors from Bodes High School, where I have taken courses in retailing.

For the past three years, I have worked as a part-time salesclerk for the Monroe Computer Center in West Kilmer. Last summer I was a lifeguard at Lenape State Park.

Ms. Toni Armand, owner of the Monroe Computer Center, and Mr. Lance Dooley, staff coordinator at Lenape State Park, have agreed to supply references. Ms. Armand's business phone number is 555-663-3886; Mr. Dooley's is 555-947-2431.

I believe I am qualified for the position you have advertised. I would be pleased to come in for an interview at your convenience. My home telephone number is 555-884-3887.

Very truly yours,

*Michael Paci*

Michael Paci

## Practice Your Skills

### Applying for Employment

Write an employment letter for the following summer job, which has been posted in your school's guidance office. Use your own address and today's date.

### POSITION AVAILABLE

| | |
|---|---|
| **Job title:** | Landscape architect's assistant |
| **Place:** | Lawn & Leaf Landscaping Service, 151 Main Street, Pueblo, CO 81004 |
| **Duties:** | Assist with mowing, pruning, and landscaping tasks; operate mowers; plant shrubs, trees, and garden plants |
| **Hours:** | 8:00 A.M. to 5:00 P.M. Monday through Friday |
| **Salary:** | $7.00/hour |
| **Requirements:** | Person must be dependable, energetic, and conscientious. |
| **Apply to:** | Mr. Paul Petrini |

# ORDER LETTERS

Some catalogs and advertisements include an order blank. If none is available, write a business letter to place an order. Include the order number, price, quantity, and size of the item you want. Make sure the information in your letter is appropriately organized and accurately conveyed. In addition, if you are sending a check or money order (never send cash), identify the amount enclosed in the letter.

**MODEL: Order Letter**

331 Gilgen Avenue N.E.
Missoula, MT 59801
June 30, 2015

Turquoise Treasures
8876 Tuscarawas Avenue
Black Eagle Mountain, MT 59414

Dear Sir or Madam:

    Please send me the following items from your most recent catalog:

| | |
|---|---|
| 1 pair Star Teardrops Earrings, #44781 | $14.95 |
| 1 River of Dawn Necklace, #22801 | $18.95 |
| Shipping and handling | $3.00 |
| | |
| TOTAL | $ 36.90 |

A check for $36.90 is enclosed. Thank you.

      Sincerely,

      *Shirley Mason*

      Shirley Mason

## ● Practice Your Skills

### Placing an Order

Use the modified block style to write a letter ordering the following merchandise from a catalog. Unscramble the information below for the inside address, and write it in the proper order. Use your own name and address and today's date. Organize the order information appropriately, as in the model above.

| | |
|---|---|
| **Inside Address** | Order Department, Bart's Fly Shop, New York, New York, 555 East 55th Street, 10010 |
| **Merchandise** | Six Catchem Rooster Tails, $2.95 each; three Gotcha Spinners, $2.95 each; one 500-yard reel of 30-pound test line, $10.99 |
| **Shipping and handling** | $5.00 |

# LETTERS OF COMPLAINT

If a product or service fails to measure up to its promise, you can write a letter of complaint to try to remedy the problem. Most companies stand behind their goods and services and are willing to make suitable adjustments to solve the problem. If your letter is polite and offers a reasonable solution, chances are it will bring about the desired results. In your letter, try to anticipate the company's questions, and provide relevant facts and details. Use appropriate vocabulary and a courteous, but firm tone. In the following model, notice that the writer suggests a reasonable solution. Notice, too, that the writer includes relevant documentation, in this case a copy of the packing slip.

## MODEL: Letter of Complaint

4544 Canyon Drive
Carson City, NV 89703
June 11, 2015

Adjustments
Keynote Stationers
435 Pine Street
Salt Lake City, UT 84133

Dear Sir or Madam:

    In a letter dated May 15, I ordered several items from your catalog, including a Norman Rockwell poster. On June 9, I received the other merchandise in the mail, but the poster was not in the package.

    Since I have paid in full for the poster, I request an explanation of the missing item as soon as possible. I am enclosing a copy of the packing slip, which shows that the poster was not included. If for some reason the poster is no longer available, please refund my money.

    Thank you very much.

Sincerely,

*Susan Lee*

Susan Lee

## Practice Your Skills

### Making a Complaint

Use the following information to write a letter of complaint. Unscramble the information in the inside address, and write it in the proper order. Use your own name and address and today's date. Remember to recommend a solution and to use a polite tone.

| Inside Address | Rutger's Music Store; Customer Service Department; Ramsey, New Jersey 07446; 465 Washington Street |
|---|---|
| Situation | You ordered several items from a music store, including a Patriot harmonica in the key of G, #471-12, for $15.00. They sent a harmonica in the key of C instead. |

# ② Writing a Résumé

A **résumé** is a summary of your work experience, education, and interests. The purpose of a résumé is to give a prospective employer a brief overview of your qualifications for a job. You will want to update your résumé whenever there is a significant change in your work or school experience.

When you apply for a job, always send a **cover letter** with your résumé. The letter should follow the correct format for a business letter and follow the guidelines for an employment letter (see pages 534–535).

Organize your résumé according to categories of information. The following guidelines and model will help you write your own résumé.

## How to Write a Résumé

### General Form

- Use one sheet of white 8½-x-11-inch paper.
- Use even margins, and leave space between sections.
- Center your name, address, telephone number, and e-mail address at the top of the page.

### Work Experience

- List your most recent job first.
- Include part-time, summer, and volunteer jobs.
- For each job, include the dates you worked, your employer's name, your title, and your primary responsibilities.

### Education

- List the name and address of each school and the years you attended.
- List any related special courses you have taken.

### Skills, Activities, Awards, Interests

- List skills, such as computer literacy or fluency in a foreign language, that relate to the position you are applying for.
- List school or community activities in which you have participated, such as music lessons, volunteer work, or scouting.
- List awards or certificates of merit you have earned.
- Include any relevant hobbies or special interests.

## References

- Give the names and addresses of people who have agreed to give you a recommendation, or write, "Available on request."
- As references, list one previous employer, one teacher or school administrator, and one adult friend. Choose people who can attest positively to your character and abilities. Be sure you obtain permission in advance from the people you list as references.

Read the following résumé. Notice how it uses appropriate formatting structures, such as headings and white space, to present information in a clear, well-organized manner.

**MODEL: Résumé**

CYNTHIA KLEIN
21 Bluebonnet Lane
Odessa, TX 79766
(915) 426-7135
E-mail: cklein@myemail.com

**WORK EXPERIENCE**

| | |
|---|---|
| 2012 to present | Alvis Dance Studio, 945 Main Street, Odessa, TX 79766 |
| | Position: Part-time dance instructor |
| | Responsibilities: Teach ballet to children ages 5 to 12 |
| 2011–2012 | CRM Store, Ravenswood Mall, Odessa, TX 79766 |
| | Position: Cashier |
| | Responsibilities: Rang up purchases at variety store |

**EDUCATION**

| | |
|---|---|
| 2010 to present | Lone Star High School, Fassett Highway, Odessa, TX 79766 |
| | Special Courses: History of Dance, Modern Dance |
| 2007 to 2010 | Nimitz Middle School, 350 Route 17, Odessa, TX 79766 |

| | |
|---|---|
| **SPECIAL SKILLS** | Speak Spanish; Can word process at 80 wpm |
| **ACTIVITIES** | Twelfth grade class president, Drama Club member |
| **AWARDS** | Odessa Fine Arts Achievement Award, 2013 |
| **SPECIAL INTERESTS** | Dance, drama, computers |
| **REFERENCES** | Available on request |

# ③ Interviewing for Employment

When you apply for a job, the employer may ask you to come to a formal interview. The **interview** provides an opportunity for both you and the employer to learn more about whether you are well suited for the job—and vice versa. You will feel more confident during an interview if you prepare for it beforehand.

One way to prepare for an interview is to learn as much as possible about the employer. The more you know about what the employer does and how the business operates, the better able you will be to discuss the job and your qualifications for it. To obtain information about the business, you might talk with people you know who are employed there. If the company has a Web site, review it carefully, and use the Internet to search for other information about the business. In addition, many large companies publish annual reports, which may be available in the library or from the company itself. Information about companies may also be available in business-oriented magazines.

The way you present yourself during an interview may determine whether the employer considers you further for the position. The following strategies will help you interview successfully.

## Strategies for Interviewing

- Prepare a list of questions that you would like to ask the interviewer. Ask questions about the job that display your interest in the business. See the chart on page 541 for specific suggestions.
- Be on time for the interview. If possible, show up a few minutes early in case you need to fill out any paperwork beforehand.
- Present a neat, clean appearance.
- Be polite to the interviewer.
- Make eye contact with the interviewer as you speak.
- Speak clearly and distinctly, and use proper grammar.
- Answer all questions thoroughly and honestly.
- Thank the interviewer for his or her time when the interview is finished.
- Follow up the interview with a letter thanking the interviewer and expressing your interest in the position. Summarize the reasons that you think make you a good candidate for the job.

In most interviews, the interviewer wants you to "fill in" information that may be missing from your job application, letter, or résumé. He or she also wants to get a sense of what kind of person you are—how you speak, how you handle yourself in a conversation, and how clearly you can present information about yourself. Here are some questions you may be asked.

## Questions an Interviewer May Ask You

- How did you find out about this job opening?
- Why did you apply for this job?
- How do your previous experience and education help qualify you for this position?
- What do you study in school and what are your plans for the future?
- What activities do you enjoy in your leisure time?
- What do you expect to earn at this job?
- How many hours can you work a week?
- When can you begin to work?
- Do you have any questions before you leave?

Your answer to the last question should be "Yes." It is important to be interested enough in the position to ask some questions about the job. Remember, you need to find out if the job suits you as much as the interviewer needs to find out if you suit the job. Here are a few suggestions for questions to ask during an interview:

## Questions to Ask an Interviewer

- What exactly would my duties be?
- Who would be my direct supervisor?
- How many hours a week would I be expected to work?
- Are the hours variable? If they are variable, who decides when I would work?
- How much does the job pay and how often are employees paid?
- Are there any benefits that come with this position, such as health insurance, sick pay, or employee discounts?
- Is there room for advancement in this job?
- When will you make a decision about whom you will hire?
- Is there any other information you need?

## ● Practice Your Skills

### Drafting Interview Questions and Responses

Pair up with another student to role-play a job interview. Decide who will play the interviewer and who will be the applicant. The applicant is interviewing for a part-time job at a local sporting goods store that involves checking inventory, stocking shelves, serving as a cashier, helping customers, and record-keeping. Draft five to ten questions for the interview. Then, spend about 15 minutes role-playing the interview. When you are finished, discuss what you learned from this activity.

21ST CENTURY

Communication for Careers and Business   541

# Communication for College

When you communicate for college, you should apply the communication skills you have developed for careers and business. You should have a clearly stated purpose, and information should be precise, accurate, and concise. In written communication, you should use appropriate formatting and organizational structures. Whether you are writing or speaking, your vocabulary, tone, and style should be appropriate for the context and your audience.

In this section, you will learn strategies for writing letters of request to colleges and for completing college applications. Remember to apply these strategies even if you communicate electronically with colleges and submit applications online. You will also learn strategies for interviewing for college admissions.

## 1 Writing Letters to Colleges

There are two kinds of letters you should know how to write when you correspond with colleges. The first is a brief request for information or a catalog from a college or a professional school. If you want specific material, be sure to ask for it. Remember to use the appropriate format for a business letter.

---

**MODEL: Request Letter for Information**

339 Wayland Street, Apt. 14-A
Lubbock, TX 79415
September 6, 2015

Director of Admissions
Grand Canyon College
Phoenix, AZ 85004

Dear Sir or Madam:

    I am a senior at Lubbock High School in Lubbock, Texas. Next fall I plan to attend college with the intention of majoring in early childhood education. I would like to know if Grand Canyon College offers a degree in this field.
    Please send me your current catalog, an application for admission, and any information on available scholarships.
    Thank you very much.

Sincerely yours,

*Joseph Inman*

Joseph Inman

---

The second kind of letter you may write to a college is one requesting an interview. In your letter, you should express your interest in the college and suggest a convenient time for your visit to the campus or your meeting with an interviewer. You can probably find the name of the director of admissions in a college reference book or on the Internet.

## MODEL: Letter Requesting a College Interview

945 Olaf Road
Rochester, MN 55906
August 2, 2015

Mr. Daniel J. Murray
Director of Admissions
Hamline University
St. Paul, MN 55104

Dear Mr. Murray:

Thank you very much for sending me the Hamline University catalog and the application I requested. I would like to learn more about the university before I submit my application. Would it be possible to visit classes for one day during the week of September 14 through 18? If possible, I would like to visit music theory and computer science classes since I hope to major in one of these disciplines.

In addition, I would like to arrange an interview with someone from your office. Please let me know a convenient date and time for my visit. I look forward to visiting Hamline University and learning more about it.

Sincerely yours,

*George Chen*

George Chen

## ● Practice Your Skills

### *Requesting College Information*

Find out the name and address of a college, university, or professional school near you. Consult a current college reference book in your library or guidance office to find the address, or look for the information on the college's Web site. Draft a letter requesting a catalog and an application, following the model on page 542. Use your own name, address, and today's date.

### Requesting an Interview

Find out the name and address of a college, university, or professional school near you. If possible, find out the name of the admissions director by using a college reference book or the Internet. Use the information to draft a letter requesting a college interview, following the model on page 543. Use your own name, address, and today's date.

## 2 Completing College Applications

College admissions officers use applications to learn about your specific qualifications as a prospective student. To give the admissions officer a clear and accurate account of your experiences and accomplishments, you should complete the application carefully and thoroughly. The following strategies may help you.

### Strategies for Completing College Applications

- Read each application thoroughly, including all the directions, before you begin to answer any questions.
- Follow the instructions for submitting an online application carefully. If you are completing a paper application, type or print neatly in dark blue or black ink. Make one or two copies of the application to practice on before you make your final copy.
- Make your responses to questions about work, travel, and awards as concise as possible.
- Be selective about your accomplishments. Stress your most important activities— those you have contributed the most to or learned the most from—instead of simply listing everything you have ever done.
- Make sure to answer every question. Do not leave any blanks. If a question asks about employment experiences and you have not had any, describe volunteer work you have done. If there are questions for which you have no answers, write "N/A" (not applicable).

Many colleges and universities use a common application for undergraduate admission. The common application makes it easier for those who are applying to several colleges at once and ensures that each school will receive the information it needs to review an applicant's qualifications. The first part of this application asks you to provide personal data. You need to read these factual questions carefully and answer them completely and accurately. The second part asks you to make personal statements about who you are as a person and how your activities and experiences have influenced you. These essay questions enable you to demonstrate that you can organize and express your ideas effectively.

## APPLICANT

Legal name _____
Last/Family/Sur  (Enter name **exactly** as it appears on official documents.)   First/Given     Middle (complete)     Jr., etc.

Preferred name, if not first name (choose only one) _____   Former last name(s), if any _____

Birth date _____   ○ Female ○ Male    US Social Security Number, if any _____
        mm/dd/yyyy                                   Optional, unless applying for US Federal financial aid with the FAFSA form

E-mail address _____   IM address _____

Permanent home address _____
              Number & Street                      Apartment #

_____
City/Town          State/Province     Country              ZIP/Postal Code

Permanent home phone (_____) _____   Cell phone (_____) _____
         Area Code                                  Area Code

**If different from above**, please give your current mailing address for all admission correspondence.

Current mailing address _____
              Number & Street                      Apartment #

_____
City/Town          State/Province     Country              ZIP/Postal Code

If your current mailing address is a boarding school, include name of school here: _____

Phone at current mailing address (_____) _____   (from _____ to _____)
              Area Code                          (mm/dd/yyyy)     (mm/dd/yyyy)

## FUTURE PLANS

Your answers to these questions will vary for different colleges.  If the online system did not ask you to answer some of the questions you see in this section, this college chose not to ask that question of its applicants.

College: _____   Deadline: _____
                                                        mm/dd/yyyy

Entry Term:  ○ Fall (Jul–Dec)      ○ Spring (Jan–Jun)

Decision Plan:  ○ Regular Decision       ○ Rolling Admission
                ○ Early Decision         ○ Early Decision II
                ○ Early Action           ○ Early Action II
                ○ Restrictive Early Action  ○ Early Admission
                                            juniors only

Career Interest: _____

Do you intend to apply for need-based financial aid?   ○ Yes ○ No
Do you intend to apply for merit-based scholarships?   ○ Yes ○ No
Do you intend to be a full-time student?               ○ Yes ○ No
Do you intend to enroll in a degree program your first year?  ○ Yes ○ No
Do you intend to live in college housing? _____
Academic Interests: _____
_____

## DEMOGRAPHICS

○ US citizen
○ Dual US citizen
○ US permanent resident visa (Alien registration # _____ )
○ Other citizenship (Visa type _____ )
List any non-US countries of citizenship _____
_____

How many years have you lived in the United States? _____
Place of birth _____
         City/Town          State/Province     Country
First language _____
Primary language spoken at home _____

**Optional** The items with a gray background are optional. No information you provide will be used in a discriminatory manner.

Marital status: _____
US Armed Services veteran?  ○ Yes ○ No

1. Are you Hispanic/Latino?
○ Yes, Hispanic or Latino (including Spain)  ○ No
   Please describe your background _____
2. Regardless of your answer to the prior question, please select one or more of the following ethnicities that best describe you:
○ American Indian or Alaska Native (including all Original Peoples of the Americas)
   Are you Enrolled? ○ Yes ○ No If yes, please enter Tribal Enrollment Number _____
   Please describe your background _____
○ Asian (including Indian subcontinent and Philippines)
   Please describe your background _____
○ Black or African American (including Africa and Caribbean)
   Please describe your background _____
○ Native Hawaiian or Other Pacific Islander (Original Peoples)
   Please describe your background _____
○ White (including Middle Eastern)
   Please describe your background _____

# WRITING

**Short Answer** Please briefly elaborate on one of your extracurricular activities or work experiences in the space below or on an attached sheet (150 words or fewer).

_____

_____

_____

_____

**Personal Essay** Please write an essay (250 words minimum) on a topic of your choice or on one of the options listed below, and attach it to your application before submission. **Please indicate your topic by checking the appropriate box.** This personal essay helps us become acquainted with you as a person and student, apart from courses, grades, test scores, and other objective data. It will also demonstrate your ability to organize your thoughts and express yourself.

○ ① Evaluate a significant experience, achievement, risk you have taken, or ethical dilemma you have faced and its impact on you.

○ ② Discuss some issue of personal, local, national, or international concern and its importance to you.

○ ③ Indicate a person who has had a significant influence on you, and describe that influence.

○ ④ Describe a character in fiction, a historical figure, or a creative work (as in art, music, science, etc.) that has had an influence on you, and explain that influence.

○ ⑤ A range of academic interests, personal perspectives, and life experiences adds much to the educational mix. Given your personal background, describe an experience that illustrates what you would bring to the diversity in a college community, or an encounter that demonstrated the importance of diversity to you.

○ ⑥ Topic of your choice.

## Disciplinary History

① Have you ever been found responsible for a disciplinary violation at any educational institution you have attended from 9th grade (or the international equivalent) forward, whether related to academic misconduct or behavioral misconduct, that resulted in your probation, suspension, removal, dismissal, or expulsion from the institution? ○ Yes ○ No

② Have you ever been convicted of a misdemeanor, felony, or other crime? ○ Yes ○ No

If you answered yes to either or both questions, please attach a separate sheet of paper that gives the approximate date of each incident, explains the circumstances, and reflects on what you learned from the experience.

**Additional Information** If there is any additional information you'd like to provide regarding special circumstances, additional qualifications, etc., please do so in the space below or on an attached sheet.

_____

_____

_____

_____

_____

# SIGNATURE

**Application Fee Payment** If this college requires an application fee, how will you be paying it?

○ Online Payment   ○ Will Mail Payment   ○ Online Fee Waiver Request   ○ Will Mail Fee Waiver Request

## Required Signature

○ *I certify that all information submitted in the admission process—including the application, the personal essay, any supplements, and any other supporting materials—is my own work, factually true, and honestly presented. I authorize all schools attended to release all requested records covered under the FERPA act, and authorize review of my application for the admission program indicated on this form. I understand that I may be subject to a range of possible disciplinary actions, including admission revocation or expulsion, should the information I've certified be false.*

○ *I acknowledge that I have reviewed the application instructions for each college receiving this application. I understand that all offers of admission are conditional, pending receipt of final transcripts showing work comparable in quality to that upon which the offer was based, as well as honorable dismissal from the school. I also affirm that I will send an enrollment deposit (or the equivalent) to only one institution; sending multiple deposits (or the equivalent) may result in the withdrawal of my admission offers from all institutions. [Note: students may send an enrollment deposit (or equivalent) to a second institution where they have been admitted from the waitlist, provided that they inform the first institution that they will no longer be enrolling.]*

Signature ✎ _____ Date _____
                                                                      *mm/dd/yyyy*

The common application is available online at the following address:
https://www.commonapp.org/CommonApp/DownloadForms.aspx

## THE ESSAY

When you write an essay for a college application, apply all that you have learned about effective communication and the writing process. In addition, follow these guidelines.

### Guidelines for Writing a College Application Essay

- Read the directions carefully. Pay special attention to key words that will help you define your purpose and structure your essay.

- Note any requirements for the length of the essay. Some instructions may specify that you write a 250-word or a 500-word essay. Bear in mind that a 250-word essay will be about one and a half typed, double-spaced pages. A 500-word essay will be about three typed, double-spaced pages.

- Begin by brainstorming or freewriting to generate ideas about the topic. Then decide on your focus, write a thesis statement, and brainstorm for supporting details.

- Organize your details in an informal or a modified outline.

- Draft your essay, being sure to include an introduction that states the main idea of your essay, supporting details organized in a logical order and connected by transitions, and a strong conclusion.

- Read your draft and look for ways to improve it. You might ask a teacher, parent, or friend to read your draft and make suggestions.

- Make a final draft of your essay, using the form specified in the directions or standard manuscript form. (See pages 33–34.)

### Practice Your Skills

**Writing a College Application Essay**

Use the guidelines above to draft a 250-word essay on the following topic frequently used in college applications: "Which of your accomplishments are you most proud of and why?" With your teacher's permission, work with a partner to find ways to improve your draft.

## ③ Interviewing for College Admission

Some colleges may request or require an interview. An interview gives a college admissions officer an opportunity to evaluate you firsthand, and it also gives you an opportunity to learn more about the college. As you prepare for an interview, think about what questions you might be asked and how you would answer them. The following are some typical interview questions.

## Questions an Interviewer May Ask

- How has high school been a worthwhile educational experience? How might the experience have been improved?

- What have been your best or favorite subjects in school? Which have given you the most difficulty or been your least favorite?

- How do you spend your time outside of school?

- What was the last book you read that was not required reading in school? Did you enjoy it? Why or why not?

- Have you picked a college major yet? If so, what will it be? Why did you choose it?

- How do you expect to benefit from your college experience?

- How do you imagine your living situation at college? What do you look forward to? What are your concerns?

You should also be ready to ask questions during an interview. In an evaluative interview (as opposed to an informational one), avoid asking questions that cover basic facts about the college. For example, do not ask, "What are the course requirements for freshmen?" The answers to such questions can be readily found in the college's publications or on its Web site. Such questions may point to a lack of interest and initiative.

To ask good questions, prepare for a college interview as you would for a job interview—by doing research. Learn as much as you can about the college by reviewing school brochures, the course catalog, and the college's Web site. Talk to current students or recent graduates whom you know.

Then think of questions that go beyond the basic facts you have learned from your research. Ask specific questions that will give you an in-depth look at an academic department or a campus activity that interests you. Ask qualitative types of questions. For example, you might ask, "What is the atmosphere on campus like?" "How would you describe the relationship between the college and the surrounding community?" "What do you think sets the college apart from other schools with similar profiles?"

Keep in mind that the interviewer will evaluate you not only on the basis of your answers to his or her questions, but also on the types of questions you ask. You want your questions to show that you are a thoughtful, well-prepared, interested applicant.

## ● Practice Your Skills

### Drafting Interview Questions and Responses

Pair up with another student to role-play a college interview. First, each of you should draft five to ten questions that you want to ask. Then, take turns playing the role of the admissions officer, and spend about 15 minutes role-playing each interview. When you are finished, discuss what you learned from this activity.

# C. Communication in the World of Work

## *Apply 21st Century Communication Skills*

Communicating effectively has always been an important skill in the world of work. Now that technology has made the 21st century workforce more mobile as well as more global, good communication skills are even more valuable. You might telecommute to the office each day, submitting reports, proposals, and project files from an office in your home. You might have to send progress reports to your boss who works in the main office in a different state. You might even use videoconferencing to meet with colleagues in a different country. Expressing ideas clearly, directly, and purposefully is essential for making communication effective in all these instances.

In this section you will develop your business communication skills. No matter what you do for a living, it will pay to be a skillful communicator. Communicating well in the workplace will increase your overall effectiveness, make you more valuable to your employers and fellow workers, and often bring you a better salary and position.

# Written Communication at Work

In the world of work, people write for a variety of purposes. They write narrative reports to inform, create proposals to persuade, and draw up procedures to instruct. Employers place a high premium on strong writing skills, and for good reason. Business writing is often read in a hurried, deadline-driven environment, and important decisions are based on the ideas it expresses. More than other writing, business writing needs to achieve clarity almost instantly by using the simplest, most direct ways to convey ideas.

##  Writing Reports

One of the most common forms of writing in the world of work is the report. There are many different kinds of reports. No matter the type, a report should have a clearly stated purpose. It should share key information using formatting and organizational structures appropriate to the purpose, audience, and context.

### INFORMATIONAL REPORTS

**Informational reports** can be invaluable in the workplace because without accurate information, it is impossible to make good decisions. Being able to research effectively and interpret and present information accurately will put you in demand in the world of work. Follow these steps when writing an informational report.

 **Steps for Writing Informational Business Reports**

- Begin by answering three questions:
  1. What are the purpose and objectives of this report?
  2. Who is my audience?
  3. How much time can I realistically spend on preparing the report?
- Gather, evaluate, and synthesize information from a wide variety of sources. Maintain records of your information and sources to ensure that your material is current and accurate.
- Interpret the information to address the specific objectives for the audience and present a clear viewpoint expressed by a main idea statement. Make sure that your viewpoint on the topic is well supported by facts and details.
- Anticipate your audience's questions, needs, and possible misunderstandings, and address these issues in your report.
- Identify relevant questions to pose in your report as you seek collaboration with your fellow employees in finding answers.
- Choose an appropriate organizational structure that will enhance the clarity of your report.
- Convert information from one form to another—from written text to graphics, for example—when this will enhance clarity.

- Present technical information in accessible language. Wikipedia includes the following ways to accomplish this in its guide to contributors: 1) present the easiest parts to understand first, 2) use charts, graphs, or other illustrations, 3) avoid jargon (see page 45), 4) provide clear and concrete examples, and 5) write short sentences with few adjectives but with clear, strong verbs.
- When preparing your first draft, use technology to create appropriate formatting structures, such as headings and white space, that will make your report user friendly.
- Evaluate your report against the initial purpose and objectives. Check that all information is relevant. Cut any extraneous details. Proofread the report for errors in mechanics, grammar, and spelling. Make any necessary revisions.
- Prepare the final report. It should be neat, concise, and uncluttered.

The following case study shows how an employee of a hospital uses these steps to put together an informational report.

## CASE STUDY: EXPANDING PHYSICAL THERAPY

Tony is in charge of the physical therapy unit at a community hospital in a small Midwestern town. His staff includes seven full-time therapists as well as an office clerk. Use of the hospital is increasing, and the board of trustees is considering a major fund-raising campaign to expand the facilities. To help the board make its decision, the head of the hospital asked Tony to prepare a report on whether the hospital should expand its physical therapy unit. She told him that she needed the report in three months.

With his **objective, timeline,** and **audience** clear, Tony was ready to gather the necessary information. He began by collecting information on the existing department. He reviewed time sheets to find out how much overtime therapists had worked in the past year, and he interviewed each therapist.

Then he collected data about the community that might influence the demand for physical therapists in the area that the hospital served. The hospital drew people from a region that included about 35,000 people. Within this region were four large retirement communities and three smaller ones. He spoke with physical therapists at similar-sized hospitals close to his to find out how busy they were. He collected reports on health data for the community from the state and federal government as well as census projections on population growth in the region.

As Tony gathered information, he **organized** it. He recorded information on a laptop, creating separate files for general notes, statistical data, and notes from interviews.

Finally, Tony began to **write** his report. He cut and pasted information from his research into a word-processing program. He created charts as needed. He then proofread the report for spelling and grammatical errors.

When he finished the report, Tony printed out a copy for each board member. He put each report in its own folder with a clear plastic cover. Tony was aware that a professional presentation would make a difference in how his hard work was received.

# Analysis of Demands on the Newburg Community Hospital Physical Therapy Unit

The physical therapy unit of Newburg Community Hospital (NCH) includes seven full-time therapists. This report presents information regarding the current demands upon the staff as well a projected future demands.

## The Need

NCH serves a community of 35,000 people. Nationally, the ratio of physical therapists to the general population is 1 to 3,500. Based on this ratio, our community is large enough to support 10 full-time physical therapists. Furthermore, this region has a higher-than-average number of residents over the age of 65, people who are more likely to use physical therapy services.

## Existing Resources

NCH employs seven full-time physical therapists. As the chart, below shows, staff members worked about 1,000 hours of overtime last year. They report that they often feel rushed to complete appointments so they can squeeze in more patients.

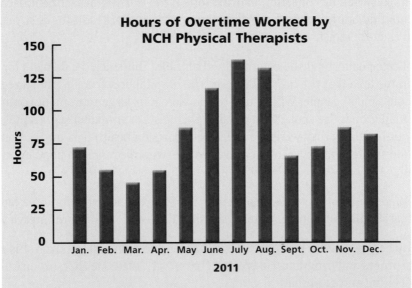

**Hours of Overtime Worked by NCH Physical Therapists**

2011

The four hospitals nearest to NCH are approximately 30 miles away, each in a different direction. Three of these, like NCH, are community-based hospitals. They all report that their physical therapy staffs are busy. To the east is the state university hospital.

This is a large teaching hospital, one that has a large staff of physical therapists. In addition, there are approximately 20 physical therapists that work in retirement communities, for health clubs, or in private practice.

## Limiting Factors

The current physical therapy program uses most of the space allotted to the unit. Any significant expansion of the staff would require an expansion of the space as well.

Tony's report was concise, easy-to-read, and to the point. It included the following features that good reports should have.

### Features of an Informational Business Report

- The purpose is plainly stated in the introduction.
- The scope is precisely outlined.
- The report suits the intended audience.
- Accurate and up-to-date information is presented in a well-organized, logical way.
- Information is conveyed with graphics when they provide greater clarity than text.
- Formatting structures, such as headings, and the page layout simplify quick scanning.
- Ideas are expressed succinctly. (See pages 550–551.)
- The language is accessible and direct. (See page 551.)
- There are no errors in spelling, grammar, usage, and punctuation.

## Practice Your Skills

### Planning an Informational Business Report

You are a meteorologist employed by the state government. Several political leaders have noticed that student absenteeism has increased in each of the past four years. Several people blame the weather for the increase, although they disagree on whether the winters have been colder or warmer. You have been asked to analyze and evaluate the weather data to see if changes in the weather have affected changes in school attendance.

Write a brief description of how you would draft this report. Refer to the steps on pages 550–551 as a guide. State the objectives, audience, and scope for your report. Specify the types of sources you would consult for information. Describe at least one graphic that would improve your presentation.

# USING GRAPHICS

In an increasingly visual world, graphics are a necessary part of communication. Some of the more common types of graphics are tables, charts, graphs, illustrations, and maps. Whatever their type, they usually serve one of the following purposes.

**HERE'S HOW**   **Purpose of Graphics**

- To support an idea in the written text—to prove a point
- To clarify or simplify a complex relationship
- To emphasize an important idea
- To make a report more interesting

**Charts**   One common type of chart is the **organizational chart.** It shows the hierarchy, or levels of authority, of a business or other organization.

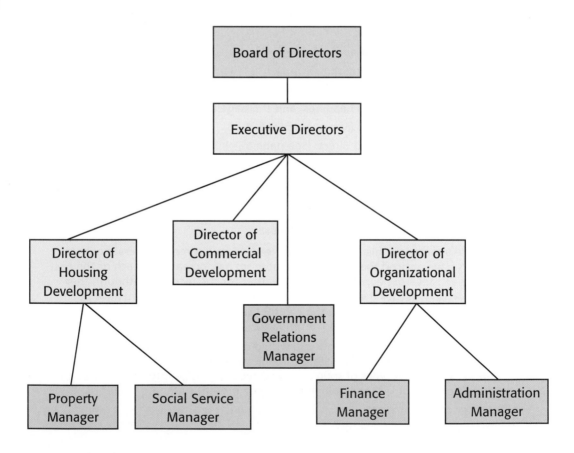

## Practice Your Skills

### *Creating an Organizational Chart*

Create an organizational chart for your school. You might include the school board, principal, teachers, and students.

A **flow chart** is widely used to show how a process works. The following flow chart shows the process one magazine publisher follows to hire a graphics designer.

## HIRING PROCEDURE

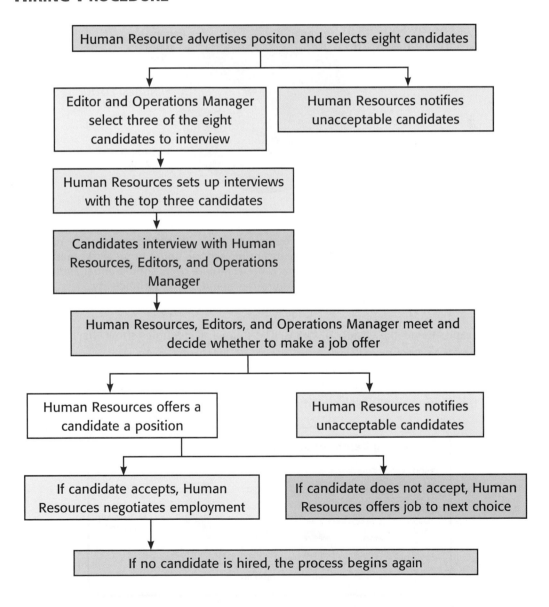

● **Practice Your Skills**

*Creating a Flow Chart*

Create a flow chart showing how you will make decisions about what to do after high school. Include the various options that you are considering and show whether each one leads to other decisions.

A **pie chart** provides an effective way to show how a total amount breaks down into smaller categories, as in the following example of the different energy sources used in the United States in 2007. You can see at a glance that the largest source is petroleum.

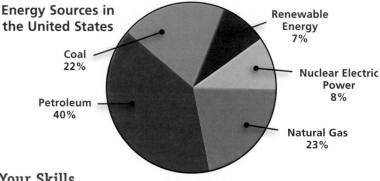

● **Practice Your Skills**

*Creating a Pie Chart*

Make a pie chart that shows how you use your time in a 24-hour period. Some of the categories you might use are attending school, doing homework, reading, eating, and sleeping. In your pie chart, the complete circle should equal 24 hours. Each slice should show how many hours you spend doing each activity.

*Graphs* Graphs come in a variety of forms. The following examples show effective ways to use bar and line graphs.

**Bar graphs** are especially useful for showing comparisons. The following bar graph compares the diving ability of selected marine animals.

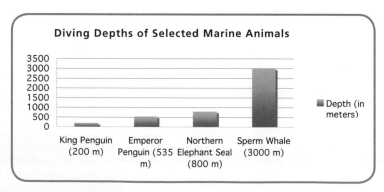

**Line graphs** are effective for showing changes over time. The following line graph shows the changes in carbon monoxide emissions in the United States over an eighteen-year period, according to figures from the Environmental Protection Agency.

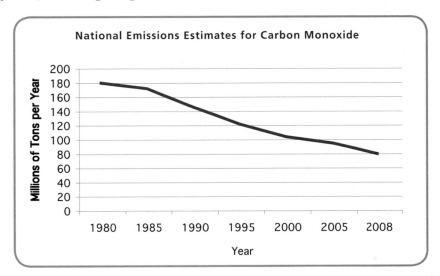

## NARRATIVE REPORTS

Like its counterpart—narrative writing—a business **narrative report** tells what happened during a certain event or situation. A narrative report tells about events in chronological order, using accessible language, facts, and a straightforward style. It is used to report accidents, incidents, and special events.

An employee wrote the following narrative report about staffing a booth in an exhibit room during a convention. The employee's job was to show the company's new products to customers, answer questions, and take orders. Notice that the employee estimates the number of people who visited the booth during each period of the day and analyzes this information.

Daniella and I staffed the company booth during the first day at the national convention. Traffic was heavy when the exhibit room opened at 8:00 a.m. It remained steady until about 10:00 a.m. In those two hours, we had approximately 100 visitors, a rate of 50 per hour. Many of the people we saw were current customers who wanted to see our new products.

Between 10:00 a.m. and 2:00 p.m., the number of visitors fell to about 20 per hour. Traffic at all booths seemed to slow down during this period. During these four hours, many people were attending the keynote speech and eating lunch.

Our biggest rush of visitors came between 4:00 p.m. and 5:00 p.m. In that hour alone, nearly 150 people stopped by. The flow was heavy because many people were visiting the booth next to ours to meet the celebrity spokesperson for the company. Many of these people had almost no knowledge of our company and were pleased to find out that we exist. We had not anticipated the rush and felt overwhelmed.

This report suggests two trends. First, the most important time for speaking with current customers and serious buyers is the beginning of the day. This is the best time for our key salespeople to be available to greet people. Second, we should be prepared for a wave of casual visitors—who are potential new customers—when other booths have special events going on. For such events, we need more people and more brochures.

## Practice Your Skills

### Writing a Narrative Report

Write an account of an incident or event in a form and style suitable for a business report. You may want to write about an event or incident at your job or an event that you participated in as part of an after-school activity.

## PROGRESS REPORTS

Setting and working toward goals will help you stay focused and complete tasks effectively. Writing a **progress report,** which measures your performance against previously set goals and expectations, can help you evaluate whether you are working productively.

The following progress report shows how one paralegal, an assistant in a law firm, monitored and evaluated her achievements. Her employer required progress reports every month.

**MODEL: Progress Report**

**Progress Report: July**

During July, I accomplished the following goals:

- I spent approximately 50 percent of my time researching legal cases relevant to the Grapevine Industries zoning case. I completed the search for relevant cases and have prepared summaries of half of them.

- I spent approximately 30 percent of my time preparing the documents on the interviews that members of our firm conducted in the Anderson disorderly conduct case. This concluded my work on this case.

- I spent approximately 20 percent of my time learning the new legal research software we purchased last month. After reading the documentation, I practiced using the program on the Grapevine case.

- The one goal for the month that I did not accomplish was to conduct training sessions on the new software. At the staff meeting on July 20, we decided to delay the training until next month.

- During August, I expect to accomplish the following goals:

- I should complete the summaries of the cases in the Grapevine dispute by the second Friday of the month.

- I will prepare a written report of my Grapevine research and provide the lead attorneys with an oral summary of it.

- I will schedule and conduct the three training sessions on the new software. Each session will be approximately two hours long.

**Setting Effective Performance Goals** Effective performance goals allow workers to assess themselves and measure the progress of a project. Successful workers set goals that are measurable and achievable, monitor their time accurately, and assess their progress realistically.

**Measurable goals** can be tested against a clear outcome—a specific quantity of work that will be completed by a certain time.

| | |
|---|---|
| **Measurable Goal** | I will send off two job applications by Tuesday. (If you sent two applications by Tuesday, you met your goal. The outcome is easy to measure.) |
| **Nonmeasurable Goal** | I will work on getting a job. (This goal cannot be measured. You have set yourself no time limit, and you have not named a specific task related to getting a job.) |

**Achievable goals** are those with a realistic possibility of being accomplished. Setting unrealistic goals will lead only to failure. If you know, for example, that it usually takes your team two days to prepare an effective power presentation for a client, don't promise to have it completed in one day. Only you will be able to know for sure what is achievable, given your workload. Effective goals should make you reach somewhat beyond your comfort zone, but unrealistic goals are inappropriate.

● **Practice Your Skills**

*Measuring Your Progress*

What is your most pressing project right now? Write three measurable, achievable goals related to that project that you have to accomplish within the next week. At the end of the week, write a progress report measuring your progress against the goals you set.

## ② Writing Proposals

Having accurate information presented in a user-friendly report is the first step in building a sound business. However, the real test of business creativity is how that information is used. A **proposal** takes the business report one step further by recommending a course of action. It presents a clearly stated purpose and viewpoint on a topic and supports this viewpoint with logical reasons, facts, and details.

### PROPOSAL: EXPANDING PHYSICAL THERAPY

After Tony presented his informational report to the head of the hospital, she asked him to add his recommendation to it. Tony developed the following proposal.

## Analysis

Three points stand out in the information.

1. The physical therapy staff of NCH is overworked. The amount of overtime worked by staff members, the shortness of appointments, and the tightness of the schedule all point to the need for more staff.

2. Our region is underserved. In the immediate town and surrounding rural area, many people go to the state university hospital for services that other people receive at NCH.

3. Future use will probably grow. The population in the region is increasing generally, and the elderly population is growing in particular.

## Recommendation

All of the above points suggest that NCH should expand its physical therapy staff. I recommend that NCH hire one person immediately. I estimate from the statistics on overtime and the number of cases that our current patient load would more than pay for an additional therapist. Furthermore, I recommend that we hire two more therapists as soon as the facilities can be expanded.

Tony's proposal, especially alongside his informational report, has all of the following features of a good proposal.

### Features of a Good Proposal

- The proposed actions are clearly stated.
- The information, such as facts and details, that supports the proposed actions is accurate and up-to-date.
- The proposal includes a way to measure the cost against the potential benefits.
- The writer uses an appropriate organizational structure, often arranging ideas in the order of importance.
- Formatting structures, such as headings, enhance the clarity of the presentation of ideas.
- The proposal is written in accessible language and uses an appropriate style and tone.
- The proposal is addressed to the appropriate audience. It anticipates and addresses the reader's potential questions, problems, and misunderstandings.
- The reader understands what he or she is called on to do.

● **Practice Your Skills**

*Writing a Proposal*

> Tony's proposal is only one of many possible responses to the information he collected. Reread his informational report. Then write a counterproposal that uses the same information but presents a different recommendation. You might consider recommendations that do not include three full-time staff people or that use space in different ways. Evaluate your first draft by checking if it has the qualities listed in Features of a Good Proposal. Revise accordingly.

# ③ Writing Procedures and Instructions

Procedures and instructions are two other widely used forms of business writing. (You have already come across this kind of writing on pages 256–257 when you practiced expository writing, specifically when you were asked to describe a process or write a set of expository.) **Procedures** explain which steps are required to complete a job. **Instructions** explain how to complete the necessary steps.

A key difference between procedures and instructions is the scope of the task being described. Procedures often involve several different departments or a number of different employees. Instructions, on the other hand, are more focused. They involve smaller tasks that can be performed by one employee.

You have already seen an example of a procedure represented in a flow chart (page 555). Some procedures are so important, however, that they need to be described in writing. In fact, many companies provide a procedures manual to all employees to make sure that everyone knows and follows the same procedures.

The following model explains how employees are evaluated in one company.

**MODEL: Procedure**

## Employee Evaluation Procedure

Each employee will be evaluated annually, usually in the month of the year in which he or she was hired. The purpose of the evaluation is to help employees increase their value to the company, both by recognizing their strengths and by identifying areas for improvement.

### Step 1 Complete Standard Evaluation Form

The employee and his or her supervisor will each fill out the "Standard Evaluation Form" independently. This form includes a section for numerical ratings and a section for open-ended written responses. This form is available from the Human Resources Office.

### Step 2 Submit Co-workers Names to Human Resources

The employee should submit to the Human Resources Department the names of ten individuals with whom he or she has worked in the past year. These individuals may be at any level in the company. The Human Resources Department will randomly select two of these individuals to complete the "Co-workers Evaluation Form." The Human Resources Office will not release the names of these individuals. It will send copies of the completed forms to both the employee and his or her supervisor.

### Step 3 Meet with Supervisor

The employee and his or her supervisor will meet to review the evaluations each has completed, as well as those by the two co-workers. They should complete a "Final Evaluation Form," which consists of the numerical ratings section of the "Standard Evaluation Form." The two should reach an agreement, to within two points, of how to rate the employee on each item. They should also set goals for the coming year.

### Step 4 Carry Out Plans

During the year the employee should strive to carry out the goals set in the annual review. The employee and his or her supervisor should review these goals periodically throughout the year.

For a routine task, written **instructions** are usually provided to employees. Often experienced workers prepare instructions for workers who are not familiar with a task. Supervisors sometimes write instructions to introduce a new technology or system to the staff. The following instructions tell employees how to request financial assistance for continuing education.

**MODEL: Instructions**

## Instructions for Receiving Continuing Education Money

Syndergaard Industries will pay up to $1,000 per year per employee toward the costs of attending lectures, conferences, or courses that enhance an employee's professional skills. To apply for company support, please follow these instructions.

**1.** Write a brief description of the content of the lecture, conference, or course that you wish to attend, the cost of the program, and the benefit you expect to receive from it. This document should be no more than one page long.

**2.** Give the description to your supervisor and ask for his or her approval. If your supervisor approves, then he or she should sign it and return it to you.

3. Complete a check request form. On this form, indicate the amount requested, to whom the check should be written, and to whom it should be mailed.

4. Send the description, with your supervisor's signature, along with the check request form to the Human Resources Department. Requests should be submitted one month before the program begins. The Human Resources Director may, at his or her discretion, approve payment for programs after they have been completed.

5. After one week, check with the Human Resources Department to see if the check has been mailed.

Well-written instructions and procedures share the following features.

### Features of Good Procedures and Instructions

- They provide all the information necessary to complete a task or procedure.
- They anticipate the reader's questions and potential problems, misunderstandings, and mistakes, and they address these issues.
- They explain unfamiliar terms or describe unfamiliar items.
- They present the steps in their sequential order.
- They use numbering systems, when appropriate, to separate the steps in the process. They may use other formatting structures, such as headings, to make the document user-friendly.
- They describe the task in accessible, concise language.

## ● Practice Your Skills

### Writing Instructions

Write instructions for a task that you know how to do well, but that may be unfamiliar to your classmates. For example, you might explain how to use a desktop publishing program to insert clip art into a report, how to calculate an earned run average, or how to make salsa. Have a classmate evaluate the instructions by checking for the qualities listed in Features of Good Procedures and Instructions. Revise your instructions as necessary, based on your classmate's feedback.

## ④ Writing Memos

A **memo** (short for memorandum) is a brief, somewhat informal communication. It is often used for interoffice communication among employees. The simplicity of its form makes it the universal business communication. It typically begins with the same four headings (shown in boldface type in the following model).

**To:** All members of Local 335
**From:** *Al Levin, Shop Steward*
**Date:** 2/17/15
**Subject:** Meeting on 3/15/15

Please plan to attend a meeting on 3/15/15 at 10:00 A.M. at the Civic Center, Room 118. The purpose is to inform you of some recent changes in the law regarding safety protection on the job.

Thank you.

Business memos are meant to be concise, usually no longer than a single page, but they often contain complex information. Since the recipient probably can't spend much time reading the memo, the message must be unambiguous. A memo should have a clearly stated purpose. Appropriate organizational and formatting structures, such as headings, bullets, and numbers, should be used to present information clearly. Memos should be written in accessible, direct language, and their tone should be polite and professional.

Memos are used for the following purposes.

### Common Purposes for Memos

- To serve as notices or reminders of meetings
- To serve as transmittal sheets accompanying other materials; a transmittal memo should identify the materials being passed along (transmitted) and specify requests for action.

  Attached is my report on the need for physical therapists in our community. Please let me know if there is any additional information that you would like to have.

- To provide a written summary of a conversation in order to document specific agreements

  Thank you for the discussion about improving employee morale. We agreed that, as of 5/1/2015, the time clock will be replaced with the honor system.

- To make a request

  I would like to bring my ten-year-old daughter to work as part of Take Your Child to Work Day next Thursday, November 12. I would appreciate written approval of this request by November 6. Thank you.

- To transmit information about a project, either to fellow workers within a company or to a client or employee working outside the company

Although a memo can serve many purposes, there are times when a phone call or face-to-face conversation is preferable. Everything you put into writing can be read by anyone, even if it is labeled "confidential." If you want to convey privileged information, use the phone or meet with the person face-to-face. Also use the personal approach to resolve differences whenever possible. Human contact often promotes resolution.

## E-MAIL VERSUS PAPER MEMOS

More and more, employees are communicating with one another via e-mail. Since employees tend to receive many e-mails in the course of the day, it is particularly important that you express your ideas clearly, directly, and concisely. Remember to use a formal, professional style when writing a business e-mail.

In memos sent via e-mail, "To," "From," and "Subject" are built into the e-mail format. You can send the same memo to many people, either by adding their e-mail addresses to the "To" entry field or by adding them to the "Cc" (courtesy copy) field.

### ● Practice Your Skills

*Writing an E-mail*

Using an e-mail program, compose a business-style e-mail, giving information about an upcoming school event. Include a description of the event, the time and place, and a brief reason for someone to attend.

### ● Practice Your Skills

*Using Content-Area Vocabulary*

Select three of the terms from this chapter listed below. Write a description of each term along with a scenario in which you might use each form of written communication.

- case study
- organizational chart
- flow chart
- line graph

- narrative report
- instructions
- memo
- e-mail

# Nonwritten Communication at Work

In the 21st century, technology provides an increasing number of options for nonwritten communication in the workplace. Whether you are participating in a teleconference, a videoconference, or a meeting with colleagues in your office, the basic skills required for speaking and listening effectively are the same.

##  Telephone Etiquette

Maybe you've heard the saying "You don't get a second chance to make a first impression." Often a customer's first impression of a company is formed during a telephone conversation. Here are some tips for ensuring that the impression is a good one.

### Tips for Professional Phone Calls

- Speak slowly and clearly. Keep the phone about one and a half inches from your mouth.
- Use a pleasant tone. Vary the pitch of your voice throughout the conversation.
- Listen carefully to the caller's points or questions.
- If you don't know an answer, say something like "That's a good question; let me try to find out the answer for you."
- If the caller has a complaint, apologize for the problem and find some way to provide him or her satisfaction.
- Even if the caller is emotional, remain polite.
- Whenever possible, let the caller end the call. Say, "Thank you for calling," and replace the receiver gently when you hang up.
- Try to answer your calls by the second or third ring.
- Keep writing materials near the phone so you can take a message if you have to. Each message should include the name of the person called, the name and phone number of the caller, the time of the call, a brief summary of the message, and a good time to call back.

## ● Practice Your Skills

### *Role-playing a Telephone Call*

Pair off with a classmate, and role-play a business telephone call. Use your imagination to create a context for the call, including the type of business being called and a specific purpose for the call. Take turns being a slightly rude customer and a polite and professional employee. Be prepared to role-play your call for the rest of the class.

## ❷ Informal Meetings

Teamwork is an essential part of the modern workplace. The team approach helps companies achieve their goals by encouraging employees to collaborate constructively and respectfully. Workplace teams have the following traits.

### Traits of the Team Approach

- All team members understand the goal.
- The structure is flexible enough to permit creative problem solving.
- Mutual respect creates a positive working environment.
- Belonging to a team gives members a sense of identity.
- Team members learn from one another and develop a shared understanding.

Adopting a team approach when you meet informally with your co-workers will help you interact constructively. Sometimes you may have to lead the way; other times you may have to follow another's lead. When you disagree with the ideas of other members, remember that all of you are working toward the same goal. Express your thoughts respectfully and work toward a compromise. A sense of shared responsibility will lead to successful teamwork.

## ❸ Formal Meetings

The team approach is also used for formal meetings. The biggest differences between informal and formal meetings are that formal meetings are structured and have a designated leader.

### LEADING A MEETING

When you lead a meeting, your two most important tasks are to be well prepared and to follow a plan. To lead a meeting effectively, follow these steps.

### Guidelines for Leading a Meeting

- Carefully consider the purpose of the meeting. Decide what you want to accomplish, and then create an agenda (a list of topics to be discussed in order) to ensure that you achieve your purpose. Include as your final item something like "Next Steps." This item is a call for action on the issues that you will have just discussed. Estimate the time needed to discuss each topic.
- Send an advance copy of the agenda to all the people who are expected to attend the meeting. At the top, include a reminder of the meeting's scheduled time and place. You may invite people to propose changes to the agenda. However, you, as the leader, should retain the final authority over the agenda so that the meeting does not become disorganized.

21ST CENTURY

C. Communication in the World of Work

- When the meeting begins, plan to get the discussion started yourself, if necessary. As your co-workers begin participating, make sure that one or two voices do not take over. Call on people who do not volunteer to guarantee that all points of view are expressed. Listen to everyone respectfully, but feel free to politely ask those who are rambling to get to the point. Make sure that participants respond respectfully to each other as well.

- Stick to your time schedule. Move the discussion from point to point even if you have not exhausted the topic.

- Wrap up the meeting with a brief summary of what it accomplished and a preview of next steps. Thank the participants.

## PARTICIPATING IN A MEETING

Meetings at which participants feel like members of a well-functioning team can be stimulating—even fun. Although you should contribute to the meeting by asserting your point of view, remember to be open to the diverse ideas of others. Successful participation in workplace meetings requires good listening skills, flexibility, an open mind, and a genuine commitment to reaching a shared goal.

### Guidelines for Participating in a Meeting

- Think through the issues listed on the meeting agenda ahead of time.
- Bring useful information or documents to the meeting to share with others.
- Respect the time constraints of the meeting, and speak as succinctly as possible.
- Listen attentively and respectfully to the ideas of others.
- Appreciate the diverse viewpoints that people from different backgrounds bring to a problem.
- Compromise when appropriate.

## RECORDING (TAKING NOTES OR MINUTES)

Accurate records must be kept of all business meetings so that the ideas and decisions can be put to use and widely understood. If you are in charge of taking notes (called **minutes** if they are from a very formal meeting), consider using an audio recorder as a backup to your written notes. You can then replay the audiotape to determine if any information is missing from your written notes.

Two skills are especially important when recording a meeting. One is **careful listening** (see pages 580–584). The other is the ability to **summarize** (see pages 364–375). Those skills, along with the following guidelines, will help you take reliable notes. Formal minutes must sometimes follow special guidelines, but these general points still apply.

## Guidelines for Recording a Meeting

- Be thorough.
- Write down word-for-word any formal decisions, votes, resolutions, and so forth.
- Record the name of each speaker as well as the ideas he or she put forward.
- Record only what was said or what happened. Do not add any of your own opinions or observations that were not actually expressed at the meeting.
- Place an icon (perhaps a star or a check) next to items that need action.
- Create a final copy of your notes as soon after the meeting as possible so that the ideas are still fresh in your mind.
- In the beginning of the notes, be sure to include the date of the meeting and a list of all attendees.
- Distribute the notes to everyone who attended the meeting.

## TELECONFERENCES AND VIDEOCONFERENCES

Today many formal business meetings are held using technology so that people in remote sites can attend. A **teleconference** is a meeting in which attendees in different locations participate by using telecommunications equipment. The term often refers to meetings conducted via the telephone. In a **videoconference,** attendees use video technology to "meet" and communicate. When you lead or participate in such a meeting, you should follow the same guidelines you would use if all the attendees were on site. In addition, you may find these tips helpful.

## Guidelines for Teleconferences and Videoconferences

- Before the meeting, check that the telecommunications equipment is working properly. Make sure that all attendees have the information they need to use the technology, such as access codes.
- At the beginning of the meeting, all attendees should be introduced.
- Speak loudly and clearly. If only audio equipment is being used, say your name before you speak, unless the group is small and all attendees can recognize each other's voices.
- At all times, remember that you are communicating with people in remote sites. Make sure that all attendees are engaged in the meeting and have the opportunity to participate. Avoid side conversations with the people sitting next to you.
- Keep background noise to a minimum. For example, avoid rustling papers near speaker phones.
- If documents will be given out at the meeting, make sure these materials are sent in advance to all attendees at remote sites.

# FOCUS GROUPS

One specific kind of formal meeting is the **focus group,** which involves people outside the workplace. Their job is to evaluate products or services or to test new ideas. In fact, many of the television shows you watch, jeans you wear, shampoos you use, and foods you eat were developed with input from focus groups.

## Guidelines for Focus Groups

### Planning

- Identify the purpose of the focus group. What problem are you seeking to solve? What questions do you want answered?

- Invite participants who are qualified to help you achieve your purpose. For example, if you are testing a new line of athletic wear for teenagers, invite high school athletes to the focus group.

- Devote time to the logistics, or the coordination of the details of the project, such as setting the time and place for the focus group and gathering materials. Focus groups should last about an hour and a half. If possible, arrange to have an audio or a video recording made of the event.

- Carefully craft the questions you will ask. Be sure the questions are worded to avoid bias. Pose questions that are open-ended to promote discussion.

- Send a reminder about the meeting to each participant a few days ahead of time.

### Conducting the Meeting

- Introduce yourself and the others conducting the focus group to the participants. Thank everyone for coming. Review the purpose of the meeting, explain that it is being recorded, and ask all present to briefly introduce themselves.

- Ask each question. Follow the general guidelines for running a good meeting by making sure that everyone participates. Keep your own comments brief.

- After all the questions have been addressed, briefly summarize what has been said, thank everyone for coming, and end the meeting on time.

### Following Up

- Having listened objectively to what the participants have said, process the data honestly, even if your favorite idea was unpopular.

- Share the results with the rest of your team. Treat the outcome as one more piece of information to help you shape your business decision.

# Practice Your Skills

## Developing Focus Group Questions

Reread the proposal you wrote about physical therapists (pages 560–561). Imagine that your boss has given her approval for you to test your ideas in a focus group. Copy the following focus group form onto a sheet of paper and complete it.

### FOCUS GROUP MEETING

**Date:** _____

**Time:** _____

**Place:** _____

**Purpose:** _____

**Kinds of Participants:** _____

**Questions**

    1.

    2.

    3.

# Practice Your Skills

## Using Content-Area Vocabulary

Select one of the terms from this chapter listed below. Write a definition of the term along with a scenario in which you might use the form of nonwritten communication.

- informal meeting
- formal meeting
- teleconference
- videoconference
- focus group

# D. Speeches, Presentations, and Discussions

## Apply 21st Century Communication and Collaboration Skills

Communication and collaboration are powerful processes that can expand people's knowledge and bring about change. To communicate successfully, you must express your ideas clearly and forcefully so that your listeners understand and respond to your message. To collaborate constructively, you must freely exchange ideas and share responsibility to achieve a common goal.

For communication and collaboration to be truly effective, they must be based on respect. In the diverse world of the 21st century, you will learn from and work with people from various social and cultural backgrounds who will have different perspectives. Whether you are making a speech, participating in a group discussion, or collaborating with a team to complete a task, respecting varied opinions and values will enrich your understanding and make you a more successful communicator and collaborator.

In this section, you will learn effective strategies for speaking, listening, and collaborating that will help you succeed in school and in the workplace.

## Developing Public Speaking and Presentation Skills

In the course of your academic and professional career, you will probably be called upon to prepare and deliver a speech. In school you might speak to a class, a special-interest group, or a gathering of parents and teachers. In the workplace you might address colleagues at a meeting or a convention. Learning to express your ideas well and to use media and technology effectively will help you deliver a successful speech.

# ① Preparing Your Speech

Preparing a speech is similar to preparing a report or a persuasive essay. In speaking, as in writing, thoughtful, careful preparation will make your final product a success.

## Choosing a Subject to Suit Your Audience and Purpose

Every speech has a main purpose—to inform, instruct, motivate, persuade, or entertain. Most speeches, however, have more than one purpose. For example, a speaker can inform listeners about health risks while trying to persuade them to eat well and exercise regularly.

To deliver a successful speech, you need to match your subject to your purpose and audience. Use these strategies to help you choose a subject that suits your audience and purpose.

### Strategies for Considering Audience and Purpose

- Determine your main purpose. Is it to inform, instruct, motivate, persuade, or entertain? Decide, as well, whether you have more than one purpose.
- Find out the interests of your audience. Then choose a subject that matches your audience's interests and your purpose. For example, asked to deliver a persuasive, entertaining speech at a high school graduation, a speaker might choose to discuss the college experience. However, if that same person were asked to speak at a college graduation, he or she might deliver a persuasive, entertaining speech about personal and professional goals.
- You want your audience to have confidence in you, so choose a subject that you know well or can research thoroughly.

*You can learn more about the specific purposes for written and oral essays on pages 5 and 15.*

## ● Practice Your Skills

### *Determining a Subject that Suits an Audience and Purpose*

1. Write an example of a subject for a informative speech. Your audience is a group of teachers.
2. Write an example of a subject for a persuasive speech. Your audience is a group of U.S. senators.
3. Write an example of a subject for a speech meant to entertain. Your audience is a group of classmates.

# LIMITING A SUBJECT

After you choose an interesting subject, you should limit it so that you can cover it effectively in a given amount of time. To limit your subject, use the following strategies.

## Strategies for Limiting a Subject

- Limit your subject by choosing one aspect of it. For example, for a 20-minute speech about "baseball greats," you could limit the subject to "Babe Ruth: A Great Homerun Hitter and Pitcher."
- Identify what your audience already knows about your subject, and consider what your audience may expect to hear. Then limit your subject to suit your audience's expectations.
- Limit your subject to suit your purpose.

The following examples illustrate three ways to limit the subject of traveling in a foreign country according to the purpose of your speech.

| LIMITING A SUBJECT | |
|---|---|
| **Purpose of Speech** | **Example** |
| to inform | Explain ways to travel cheaply. |
| to persuade | Convince people to visit Mexico. |
| to entertain | Tell about the time you toured Paris, France, in one day. |

## ● Practice Your Skills

### Limiting a Subject

Choose a purpose and an audience. Then limit each subject to be suitable for a 20-minute speech.

**1.** wildlife conservation     **4.** the Olympics

**2.** movies     **5.** careers in technology

**3.** Shakespeare     **6.** the Constitution

# GATHERING AND ORGANIZING INFORMATION

To gather information for an informative speech, follow the same procedures you would use for a written report. List everything you already know about the subject. Then consult several sources, including encyclopedias, books, periodicals, and online materials in the library or media center. In addition, you might interview people who are knowledgeable about the subject. To plan the interview, always make a list of the questions you want to ask.

*You can learn more about gathering and organizing information on pages 224–273.*

**Taking Notes** Take notes on note cards as you do your research. Note cards are the best way to record information because the cards can be easily organized later. If you interview someone, you can take notes or use an audio recorder to record the conversation. You should write down any words from the interview you intend to quote, put them in quotation marks, and get permission from the speaker to use the quotations.

**Collecting Audiovisual Aids** Audiovisual aids, such as maps, pictures, slides, CDs, and DVDs, can add to the impact of your speech. Choose aids that suit the purpose and context of your speech. Make sure the aids will help you communicate your message effectively and will not be distracting. Once you decide on the main points you wish to enhance with the use of audiovisual aids, gather or create these materials as you prepare your speech.

### Strategies for Organizing a Speech

- Arrange your note cards by topics and subtopics.
- Use your note cards to make a detailed outline of your speech.
- Draft an introduction. To capture the interest of your audience, begin your speech with an anecdote, an unusual fact, a question, an interesting quotation, or some other attention-getting device. Present a clear thesis in your introduction. (See pages 110–112.)
- Arrange your ideas in a logical order, and think of the transitions you will use to connect the ideas. (See pages 94–95, 300, and 338–339.)
- Support your points in the body of your speech with valid evidence from reliable sources. Use appropriate appeals to support your claims and argument.
- When defending a point of view, use precise language and appropriate detail.
- Write a conclusion for your speech that summarizes your main ideas. Try to conclude your speech with a memorable sentence or phrase. (See page 122.)

### ● Practice Your Skills

*Gathering and Organizing Information*

Choose and limit a subject for a 20-minute speech in which your purpose is to inform. Write what you know about the subject on note cards. Next, visit the library or media center, and use print and electronic sources to find additional information for at least ten more note cards. Then organize your cards, and write an outline of your speech. Draft an introduction and a conclusion. Prepare any audiovisual aids you will use.

## PRACTICING YOUR SPEECH

Rehearsing your speech will enable you to deliver it with confidence and skill. In most cases you should not write out your speech or memorize it. Instead, use your outline to deliver your speech, or convert your outline into cue cards. Write your main points along with key words or phrases and quotations on separate cards. Remember to arrange your cards in the order in which you will use them. While you are delivering your speech, your cue cards will help you to remember your important points and supporting details. Use the following strategies when practicing your speech.

### Strategies for Practicing a Speech

- Practice in front of a long mirror so that you will be aware of your gestures, posture, and facial expressions.
- Practice looking around the room at an imaginary audience as you speak.
- Practice using your cue cards and any audiovisual aids that are part of your presentation.
- If you plan to use a microphone, practice your technique.
- Time your speech. Add or cut information if necessary. In timing yourself, keep the following rule of thumb in mind: It takes about as much time to give a 20-minute speech as it does to read aloud an 8-page report typed double-space.
- Practice over a period of several days. Your confidence will grow each time you practice, and your nervousness will decrease.

Revise your speech as you practice. Experiment with your word choice, and add or delete information to clarify your main points. Experiment, as well, with different ways to use audiovisual aids. In addition, practice your speech with a classmate or a friend. Your listener's comments will help you improve your speech before you deliver it.

## ● Practice Your Skills

### *Practicing and Revising Your Speech*

Prepare cue cards for your informative speech. Then use the strategies above to practice your speech before a relative, friend, or classmate. Afterward, discuss your speech and revise it, using your listener's comments as a guide.

## ② Delivering Your Speech

The time you spent researching your speech, organizing it, and practicing it will pay off when you deliver it. Just before you begin speaking, you can alleviate any nervousness by reminding yourself that you are now an expert who knows more about your subject than does anyone in your audience. Keep in mind these additional strategies for delivering a speech.

### Strategies for Delivering a Speech

- Have ready all the materials you need, such as your outline or cue cards and audiovisual aids or equipment.
- Make sure that your computer presentation equipment is assembled and running properly.
- Wait until your audience is quiet and settled.
- Relax and breathe deeply before you begin to speak.
- Stand with good posture, your weight evenly divided between both feet. Avoid swaying back and forth.
- Look directly at the members of your audience, not over their heads. Try to make eye contact with people sitting in different parts of the room.
- During your speech, make sure you talk to the audience, not to a particular visual or display.
- Speak slowly, clearly, and loudly enough to be heard. Adjust the pitch and tone of your voice to enhance the communication of your message.
- Strive for good, clear diction.
- Use correct grammar and well-formed sentences.
- Use informal, standard, or technical language appropriate to the purpose, audience, occasion, and subject. Be sure to use respectful language when presenting opposing views.
- Use rhetorical strategies appropriate to the message, whether your purpose is to inform or to persuade.
- Emphasize your main points with appropriate gestures and facial expressions.
- Make sure that everyone in your audience can see your audiovisual aids, such as charts and slides.
- After finishing your speech, take your seat without making comments to the audience.

## ③ Evaluating an Oral Presentation

Evaluating your own speech and being receptive to the comments of others will help you improve your performance when you deliver speeches in the future. In addition, listening carefully to your classmates' speeches and formulating feedback will enhance your understanding of what makes a speech effective. You may find the following **Oral Presentation Evaluation Form** useful for providing feedback.

## ORAL PRESENTATION EVALUATION FORM

**Subject:** _____

**Speaker:** _____ **Date:** _____

**Content:**

Were the subject and purpose of the speech appropriate for the audience?

Was the main point clear?

Were there enough details and examples?

Did all the ideas clearly relate to the subject?

Was the length appropriate (not too long or too short)?

**Organization:**

Did the speech begin with an interesting introduction?

Did the ideas in the body follow a logical order?

Were transitions used between ideas?

Did the conclusion summarize the main points?

**Presentation:**

Did the speaker choose appropriate words?

Was the speech sufficiently loud and clear?

Was the rate appropriate (not too fast or too slow)?

Did the speaker make eye contact with the audience?

Did the speaker use gestures and pauses effectively?

Were cue cards or an outline used effectively?

Were audiovisual aids used effectively?

**Comments:** _____

_____

_____

_____

● **Practice Your Skills**

### Delivering and Evaluating an Informative Speech

Present your informative speech to your classmates. Afterward, complete the Oral Presentation Evaluation Form for your speech at the same time that your classmates are evaluating your presentation. In addition, complete evaluation forms for your classmates' speeches. Use your listeners' suggestions to note ways that you can improve your future speeches.

### Delivering and Evaluating a Persuasive Speech

Because of your recent success in the pet store business, you have the opportunity to move your store to your city's fanciest shopping area. However, some shop owners in that area are unenthusiastic about this move. Prepare a persuasive speech to convince them that your store will be an asset to their businesses. Be sure to present divergent views accurately, and base your position on logical reasons backed by various forms of support. Use language, including rhetorical devices, that is crafted to move your audience. Use audiovisual aids to enhance your message. Present your speech to your classmates. Have them evaluate whether you used effective techniques to make your speech persuasive.

### Delivering and Evaluating an Entertaining Speech

You have been asked to deliver a speech entitled "Highlights of My High School Years" to a group of parents and faculty. Your main purpose is to entertain your audience, but your speech should also be informative. Be sure to include vivid, humorous anecdotes and details along with information that will enlighten your audience about the life of a high school student. Consider how you can use audiovisual aids to make your speech more entertaining. Practice your speech before a friend or family member, and then present it to your classmates. Write a brief assessment of your performance. Were the strategies you used to entertain your audience effective? Why or why not?

# Developing Your Critical Listening Skills

Skillful listening requires you to pay close attention to what you hear. You must comprehend, evaluate, and remember the information. Good listeners engage in critical, appreciative, and reflective listening. They also engage in empathic listening, or listening with feeling. Skills that you have practiced while preparing and presenting a speech will be invaluable to you as you work to develop your critical listening skills.

### Listening Tip

Monitor your understanding as you listen to others. If something is unclear, ask a question to clear it up. You may also want to "say back" what someone has just told you to make sure you are understanding it correctly.

# ① Listening Appreciatively to Presentations and Performances

You may have the opportunity to listen to a reading or a dramatic performance of a literary work. **Oral interpretation** is the performance or expressive reading of a written work. The oral interpreter emphasizes the message through the judicious use of voice and gesture. Pauses and changes in volume, intonation, and pitch can be used to highlight important structural elements in the passage such as rhyme. As a listener, you must judge how successfully the reader has conveyed the intentions, meaning, and style of the work. The following strategies will help you listen appreciatively to oral presentations and performances.

### Strategies for Listening Appreciatively

- Focus your attention on the message of the work.
- Be alert to the expressive power of a pause.
- Observe the use of gestures, voice, and facial expressions to enhance the message.
- Listen for changes in volume, intonation, and pitch used to emphasize important ideas.
- Listen for rhymes and repeated words and sounds.
- Listen for rhetorical strategies and other expressive uses of language.
- Take time to reflect upon the message, and try to experience with empathy the thoughts and feelings being expressed.

You can find many opportunities to practice listening appreciatively. Perhaps your local bookstore hosts readings of original works of prose and poetry by well-known authors. A nearby theater group might be performing a dramatic work that you have read for school. You will get the most out of the experience by developing a listening strategy suited to the speaker's subject and purpose.

## ● Practice Your Skills

### *Listening to Presentations and Performances*

Develop your own strategies for listening to and evaluating the following oral presentations. Identify what you would listen for in each case.

**1.** an actor delivering a monologue from a play

**2.** a poet reading from a collection of poetry

**3.** an author reading a selection from a novel

**4.** a classmate reading Susan B. Anthony's 1873 speech on women's right to vote

● **Practice Your Skills**

*Presenting an Oral Interpretation*

Perform a reading of a scene for your class. Form a small group, and chose a scene from a play that you have read for school. Then follow these steps to prepare and present your oral interpretation.

1. Sit in a circle and read through the scene. Discuss the most important ideas in the scene. Using the five *W*s and *H,* analyze the scene for an understanding of character, purpose, and situation.

2. Prepare a brief introduction to the scene. Then prepare a script of the scene. Highlight the lines that you are to perform. Mark key words that you want to emphasize through gestures, tone, or facial expressions.

3. Rehearse the scene. Try out different readings of your lines until you arrive at the best interpretation. Listen to the other characters as they speak, and respond to them as though you were conducting a real conversation. Use the techniques that you have learned to evaluate your performance and those of your peers.

4. Perform the reading for your classmates. Have them critique your performance, and use their feedback to determine whether you successfully conveyed the meaning of the scene.

## ② Listening to Directions

Throughout a typical day, you will be given many sets of directions to follow, such as those for completing a homework assignment or for performing a task at your job. Always listen carefully to directions from beginning to end. Do not assume you know what the speaker is going to say before he or she finishes giving directions. In addition, follow these strategies.

### Strategies for Listening to Directions

- Write down the directions as the speaker gives them.
- If any part of the directions is unclear, ask specific questions to help you understand the instructions.
- When you finish an assignment, review the directions to make sure you have followed them correctly.

● **Practice Your Skills**

*Following Directions*

Ask someone you know, either a friend or a relative, to give you directions to an unfamiliar place in your area. Use the strategies above, and see if you can accurately repeat or write the directions. Explain in your journal why you think these strategies helped or did not help you to listen to directions more effectively. Are there other strategies you would use in the future to help you follow directions correctly?

# ③ Listening for Information

When you listen for information, you need to comprehend the information well enough so that you can evaluate and apply it. The following strategies will help you listen effectively in order to learn new information.

## Strategies for Listening for Information

- Sit comfortably but stay alert. Try to focus your attention on what the speaker is saying without being distracted by people and noises.
- Determine whether the speaker's purpose is to inform, instruct, motivate, or persuade.
- Listen for verbal cues to identify the speaker's main ideas. Often, for example, a speaker emphasizes important points by using words and phrases such as *most important, also consider, remember that, first,* and *finally.*
- Watch for nonverbal clues, such as gestures, pauses, or changes in the speaking pace. Such clues often signal important points.
- Determine the speaker's values and point of view about the subject. For example, is the speaker expressing positive or negative attitudes or arguing for or against an issue?
- Take notes to organize your thoughts and to help you remember details. Your notes provide a basis for further discussion. You may also want to use your notes to outline the speech or to write a summary of it. If the speech is a course lecture, notes will help you study for a test on the subject.
- Ask clear and relevant questions to monitor and your understanding of ideas.
- Take time to reflect upon what you have heard.

*You can learn more about listening for information on pages 464–466.*

● **Practice Your Skills**

*Listening and Taking Notes*

Form a small group with four or five classmates. One member should present information about a current event in the news to the rest of the group. The listeners should take notes as the information is presented. Afterward, compare the notes each person took. Try to determine why all members recorded certain points and not others.

## LISTENING CRITICALLY

Critical listeners carefully evaluate the information in a speech. They judge whether the information and ideas are valid. Be on the lookout for the following propaganda techniques, which a speaker may use to mislead or manipulate you.

| TECHNIQUE | DEFINITION | FURTHER INFORMATION |
|---|---|---|
| **Confusing Fact and Opinion** | an opinion presented as a fact | To learn more, see page 284. |
| **Bandwagon Appeal** | an invitation to do or think the same thing as everyone else | To learn more, see page 307. |
| **Testimonial** | a statement, usually given by a famous person, that supports a product, candidate, or policy | To learn more, see page 307. |
| **Unproved Generalization** | a generalization based on only one or two facts or examples | To learn more, see pages 286–287. |

● **Practice Your Skills**

*Using Content-Area Vocabulary*

Watch an hour or two of commercial television and keep a log of the commercials, labelling them according to the propaganda techniques listed above.

# Developing Your Group Discussion Skills

**Group discussions** are a way of communicating ideas, exchanging opinions, solving problems, and reaching decisions. Discussions may be formal or informal. You have **informal discussions** with your friends, family, and teachers every day. **Formal discussions,** on the other hand, may have formats and rules that must be followed, and you may have to present information you researched or use evidence to support your opinion. Developing your group discussion skills will help you to present your ideas effectively and to listen thoughtfully to others' ideas.

# ❶ Participating in Group Discussions

Group discussions serve a variety of practical purposes. During the prewriting stage in the writing process, you may brainstorm in a group. You may also use discussion skills to prepare an oral report. As part of a study group, you may discuss assigned readings, help the group to reach an agreement about answers to questions, or prepare for a test.

For a group discussion to be successful, each member must agree with the group's goals. To make a discussion as effective as possible, follow these strategies.

## Strategies for Participating in Group Discussions

- Listen carefully and respond respectfully to others' views.
- Keep an open mind and appreciate diverse perspectives.
- Ask questions to make sure you understand information and others' views.
- Express your ideas clearly. Present examples or evidence to support your ideas.
- Make sure your contributions to the discussion are constructive and relevant to the subject.
- Keep in mind that everyone in the group should have an equal opportunity to speak.
- Give constructive verbal and nonverbal feedback to other members.
- Be flexible and help your group draw a conclusion or reach a consensus.

# ❷ Leading Group Discussions

Sometimes your teacher will lead a discussion and make sure that it does not stray from the agenda. Other times a group appoints its own leader to focus the discussion and keep it on track. Such discussions are called **directed discussions.** If you are chosen to be the leader, or moderator, of a directed discussion group, use the following strategies to help you conduct the discussion effectively.

## Strategies for Leading a Discussion

- Introduce the subject, question, or problem. With the group's help, state the purpose or goal of the discussion.
- Keep the discussion on track to help the group achieve its goals.
- Encourage everyone to participate, and establish a tone of respect. Make sure that everyone has an equal opportunity and equal time to speak.
- Keep a record of the group's main points and decisions, or assign this task to a group member.
- At the end of the discussion, summarize the main points, and restate any conclusions or decisions the group has reached.

● **Practice Your Skills**

*Conducting a Directed Discussion*

Form small groups and conduct a directed discussion. Select a topic relating to careers of interest to the group members. Then establish a goal, and choose a group leader. Set a time limit for the discussion. Afterward assess your participation in the group based on the **Strategies for Participating in Group Discussions.** If you were the leader, evaluate your performance based on the **Strategies for Leading a Discussion.**

## ③ Cooperative Learning

**Cooperative learning** involves working in a group to achieve a learning goal. Each group member takes on a particular task. For example, in a cooperative learning group assigned to deliver a report on France during the Napoleonic era, one student might research Napoleon's rise to power, another might provide information about the French society of the day, and still another might prepare maps and other graphics.

Once the members have fulfilled their individual responsibilities, they coordinate their work to achieve the overall goal of the group. The success of the project depends on the effective collaboration of group members.

### Strategies for Cooperative Learning

- Use the **Strategies for Participating in Group Discussions** (page 585).
- Participate in planning the project and in assigning tasks.
- When you have been given a task, do not let your group down by coming to meetings unprepared.
- Value the contributions of other team members.
- Cooperate with others in the group to resolve conflicts, solve problems, draw conclusions, reach a consensus, and make decisions.
- Help your group achieve its goals by taking your fair share of responsibility for the group's success.

● **Practice Your Skills**

*Organizing a Cooperative Learning Group*

Form a cooperative learning group of three to five members, and plan an oral presentation about a particular current event. First, choose a leader, discuss your goal, and assign tasks. Then gather the necessary information, and coordinate the group members' work. Finally, deliver your presentation to the class, remembering to follow the steps for preparing and delivering an oral presentation.

# Media and Technology

| | |
|---|---|
| **Part I** | Critical Thinking and Problem Solving for Academic Success |
| **Part II** | Communication and Collaboration |
| **Part III** | Media and Technology |

## Essential Skills

You already understand the importance of literacy, or the ability to read and write. In the 21st century, literacy—knowledge of a particular subject or field— in the areas of information, media, and technology is also essential. Part III of this guide will help you develop literacy in these three areas. This knowledge will help you succeed in school and in your future jobs.

### 1 Information Literacy

Today, a tremendous amount of information is available at your fingertips. To acquire information literacy, you must know how to access, manage, evaluate, and use this wealth of information. Learning advanced search strategies will help you locate information efficiently and effectively from a range of relevant print and electronic sources. Evaluating the reliability and validity of sources will help you assess their usefulness. Then you can synthesize information in order to draw conclusions or to solve a problem creatively. Understanding the difference between paraphrasing and plagiarism and knowing how to record bibliographic information will ensure that you use information in an ethical, legal manner. Part III of this guide will help you build your information literacy skills by showing you how to use the Internet to access information.

*You can learn more about information literacy on pages 299 and 406-423.*

## ② Media Literacy

Media messages serve a variety of purposes. They can have a powerful influence on your opinions, values, beliefs, and actions. Part III of this guide will help you develop your media literacy skills by showing you how to use both print and nonprint media to communicate your message. You will learn how to use these media to create effective messages that suit your audience and purpose. You will also learn about the types of tools available for creating media products.

*You can learn more about media literacy on pages 58, 71-72, 125, 147, 175, 221, 240, 294, 335, 376, 399, and 454-455.*

## ③ Technology Literacy

In the 21st century, knowing how to use technology to research, evaluate, and communicate information is essential. You must also know how to use different forms of technology, such as computers and audio and video recorders, to integrate information and create products. Part III of this guide will show you how to use technology effectively to access information and to publish and present your ideas in different media.

*You can learn more about technology literacy on pages 254, 311-312, and 314.*

# A. Electronic Publishing

## Apply Media and Technology Literacy

Everything you may ever have to say or write requires some medium through which you express it and share it with others. The ability to use available media and technology to their fullest potential will enable you to communicate your ideas effectively and to a widespread audience. For now, most academic and workplace communication still depends on print technology. By using that to its full capability, you will prepare yourself for the inevitable improvements and upgrades that will be a feature of communication in the future.

In this section, you will develop your skills in using available technology in your communication.

# Desktop Publishing

The computer is a powerful tool that gives you the ability to create everything from party invitations and banners to newsletters and illustrated reports. Many software programs deliver word-processing and graphic arts capabilities that once belonged only to professional printers and designers. Armed with the knowledge of how to operate your software, you simply need to add some sound research and a healthy helping of creativity to create an exciting paper.

## WORD-PROCESSING MAGIC

Using a standard word-processing program, such as Microsoft Word™, makes all aspects of the writing process easier. Use a word-processing program to

- create an outline
- save multiple versions of your work
- revise your manuscript
- proof your spelling, grammar, and punctuation
- produce a polished final draft document

## USING A SPELL CHECKER

You can use your computer to help you catch spelling errors. One way is to set your Preferences for a wavy red line to appear under words that are misspelled as you type. You can also set your Preferences to correct spelling errors automatically.

A second way to check your spelling is to choose Spelling and Grammar from the Tools menu. Select the text you want to check and let the spell checker run through it looking for errors. While a spell checker can find many errors, it cannot tell you if a correctly spelled word is used correctly. For example, you might have written *The books were over their*. The spell checker will not identify an error here, even though the correct word is *there*, not *their*.

## FASCINATING FONTS

Once your written material is revised and proofed, you can experiment with type as a way to enhance the content of your written message and present it in a reader-friendly format. Different styles of type are called **fonts** or **typefaces**. Most word-processing programs feature more than 30 different choices. You'll find them listed in the Format menu under Font.

Or they may be located on the toolbar at the top left of your screen.

Most fonts fall into one of two categories: **serif** typefaces or **sans serif** typefaces. A serif is a small curve or line added to the end of some of the letter strokes. A typeface that includes these small added curves is called a serif typeface. A font without them is referred to as sans serif, or in other words, without serifs.

Times New Roman is a serif typeface.

Arial is a sans serif typeface.

In general, sans serif fonts have a sharp look and are better for shorter pieces of writing, such as headings and titles. Serif typefaces work well for body copy.

Each typeface, whether serif or sans serif, has a personality of its own and makes a different impression on the reader. Specialized fonts, like the examples in the second paragraph on the next page, are great for unique projects (posters, invitations, and personal correspondence) but less appropriate for writing assignments for school or business.

Since most school writing is considered formal, good font choices include Times New Roman, Arial, Helvetica, or Bookman Antiqua. These type styles are fairly plain. They allow the reader to focus on the meaning of your words instead of being distracted by the way they appear on the page.

With so many fonts to choose from, you may be tempted to include a dozen or so in your document. Be careful! Text printed *in* multiple fonts *can be* EXTREMELY *confusing* to *read*. Remember that the whole idea of using different typefaces is to enhance and clarify your message, not muddle it!

## A SIZABLE CHOICE

Another way to add emphasis to your writing and make it reader-friendly is to adjust the size of the type. Type size is measured in points. One inch is equal to 72 points. Therefore, 72-point type would have letters that measure one inch high. To change the point size of your type, open the Format menu and click Font.

Or use the small number box on the toolbar at the top left side of your screen.

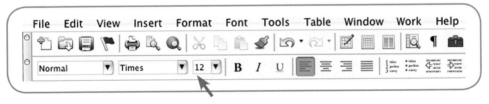

For most school and business writing projects, 10 or 12 points is the best size of type for the main body copy of your text. However, it's very effective to increase the type size for titles, headings, and subheadings to highlight how your information is organized. Another way to add emphasis is to apply a style to the type, such as **bold,** *italics,* or underline. Styles are also found in the Format menu under Font.

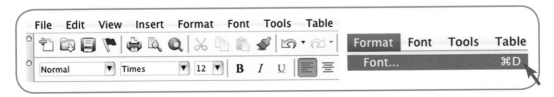

Or look for them—abbreviated as **B** for bold, *I* for italics, and U for underline—in the top center section of the toolbar on your screen.

If you have access to a color printer, you may want to consider using colored type to set your heading apart from the rest of the body copy. Red, blue, or other dark colors work best. Avoid yellow or other light shades that might fade out and be difficult to read.

Use different type sizes, styles, and colors sparingly and consistently throughout your work. In other words, all the body copy should be in one style of type. All the headings should be in another, and so on. Doing so will give your work a unified, polished appearance.

## TEXT FEATURES

Text features such as **bulleted lists** and **numbered lists** are useful ways to organize information and give it a reader-friendly format. If you create pages of text in which information isn't broken up in any way, your readers may lose focus or have trouble identifying your main points. Instead, use bulleted or numbered lists to highlight important information and present it clearly and simply. To create these lists, open the Format menu and click on Bullets and Numbering. You can also click on the numbered or bulleted list on the toolbar at the top right of your screen.

A sidebar is another useful text feature for presenting information. A **sidebar** is a section of text that is placed alongside the main copy. Often the text in a sidebar appears in a box. Use sidebars to present additional, interesting information that relates to your main topic but doesn't belong in the body of your report or paper.

## LAYOUT HELP FROM YOUR COMPUTER

One way to organize the information in your document is to use one of the preset page layouts provided by your word-processing program. All you have to do is write your document using capital letters for main headings and uppercase and lowercase letters for subheadings. Set the headings apart from the body copy by hitting the "return" key. Then open the Format menu and click the Autoformat heading. Your copy will probably look like the illustration on the next page.

You can probably use this automatic, preset format for most of the writing you do in school. You'll also find other options available in the File menu under Page Setup.

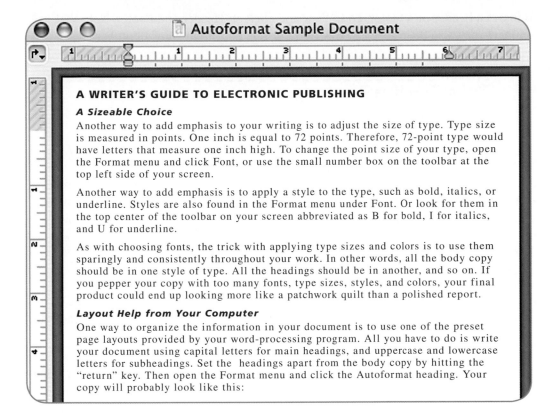

**A WRITER'S GUIDE TO ELECTRONIC PUBLISHING**

*A Sizeable Choice*

Another way to add emphasis to your writing is to adjust the size of type. Type size is measured in points. One inch is equal to 72 points. Therefore, 72-point type would have letters that measure one inch high. To change the point size of your type, open the Format menu and click Font, or use the small number box on the toolbar at the top left side of your screen.

Another way to add emphasis is to apply a style to the type, such as bold, italics, or underline. Styles are also found in the Format menu under Font. Or look for them in the top center of the toolbar on your screen abbreviated as B for bold, I for italics, and U for underline.

As with choosing fonts, the trick with applying type sizes and colors is to use them sparingly and consistently throughout your work. In other words, all the body copy should be in one style of type. All the headings should be in another, and so on. If you pepper your copy with too many fonts, type sizes, styles, and colors, your final product could end up looking more like a patchwork quilt than a polished report.

*Layout Help from Your Computer*

One way to organize the information in your document is to use one of the preset page layouts provided by your word-processing program. All you have to do is write your document using capital letters for main headings, and uppercase and lowercase letters for subheadings. Set the headings apart from the body copy by hitting the "return" key. Then open the Format menu and click the Autoformat heading. Your copy will probably look like this:

Here you can change the margins and add headers, footers, and page numbers. Headers and footers are descriptive titles that automatically appear at the top or bottom of each page without your having to retype them each time. For example, you may wish to add the title of your project and the date as a header or footer to each page.

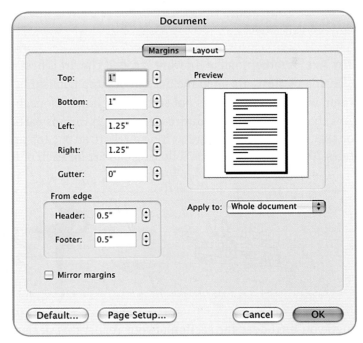

To insert a header or a footer, go to View and click on Header and Footer. Note that page numbers may also be inserted by way of the Insert option on your menu bar.

```
 Header
 Project Title Here ¶
 Date Here ¶
```

## LET'S GET GRAPHIC

The old saying "A picture is worth a thousand words" is particularly true when it comes to spicing up papers and reports. Publishing and presentation software programs (such as Adobe PhotoDeluxe Home Edition™, Macromedia FreeHand™, Microsoft PhotoDraw™, and Microsoft PowerPoint™) give you the ability to include photographs, illustrations, and charts in your work that can express your ideas more clearly and succinctly than words alone.

The key to using graphics effectively is to make sure each one conveys a message of importance. Don't use them just for decoration. Be sure they add something meaningful, or you'll actually detract from your written message.

**Drawings**  Many paint and draw programs allow you to create an illustration or **import** (bring in from another program) one into your document. Drawings can help illustrate concepts that are difficult to describe, such as mechanical parts or procedures. Cartoons can also add a nice touch. If you use them sparingly, they can lighten up an otherwise dry, technical report.

**Clip Art**  Another kind of drawing is called clip art. These simple, black-and-white or color line pictures are often included in desktop publishing or word-processing programs. Pre-drawn clip art usually is not suitable for illustrations, but it does work well as graphic icons that can help guide your reader through various parts of a long report.
For example, suppose you are writing a report on the top arts programs in the United States. You might choose the following clip art for each of the sections:

When you introduce the section of your report that deals with music, you might use the music icon at the large size pictured above. Then, in the headings of all the following sections that deal with music, you might use a smaller version of the icon that looks like this:

𝓜usic 𝓣rends

Using clip art as icons in this manner lets your readers know at a glance which part of the report they are reading.

**Charts and Graphs**   One of the best ways to communicate information about numbers and statistics is by using charts and graphs. Several software programs allow you to create bar graphs, pie charts, and line graphs that can communicate fractions, figures, and comparative measurements much more powerfully than written descriptions.

**Photographs**   With the widespread availability of digital cameras and scanners, adding photos to your project is an easy and effective way to enhance your content. Using a digital camera or a scanner, you can load photos directly into your computer. Another option is to shoot photographs with a regular camera, but when you have them developed, specify that they be returned to you as "pictures on disc," which you can open on your computer screen.

Photographic images are stored as bits of data in an electronic file. Once you have the photos in your computer, you can use a graphics program such as Adobe PhotoDeluxe Home Edition™ to manipulate the images in a variety of ways and create amazing visual effects. You can crop elements out of the photo, add special filters and colors, combine elements of two different pictures into one—the possibilities are endless.

After you have inserted the edited photo into your document, be careful when you print out your final draft. Standard printers often don't reproduce photographs well. You may want to take your document on disc to a professional printing company and have it printed out on a high-resolution printer to make sure you get the best quality.

**Captions and Titles**   While it's true that a single photo can say a great deal, some pictures still need a little explanation in order to have the strongest impact on your reader. Whenever you include an illustration or photograph in a document, also include a simple caption or title for each image.

Add captions in a slightly smaller type size than the body copy and preferably in a sans serif typeface. Use the caption to add information that isn't immediately apparent in the photo. If there are people in the picture, tell readers who they are. If the photo features an odd-looking structure, explain what it is. Be smart with your captions. Don't tell readers the obvious. Give them a reason to read your caption.

**Stand-Alone Graphics** Occasionally you may include well-known graphics or logos in a report. These graphics convey powerful messages on their own and don't require captions. Examples of these logos or symbols include:

# Nonprint Media—Audio and Video

The world we live in is becoming increasingly more multimedia-savvy. Many businesses rely extensively on multimedia presentations to market their products or convey messages to consumers and employees. Exciting opportunities exist for people who can produce clear, concise messages in audio and visual formats.

## PRE-PRODUCTION—PUT IT ON PAPER FIRST

Although the final presentation of your subject material may be an audio recording or a video, your project needs to begin on paper first. When you write down your ideas, you do four things:

- Organize your thoughts.
- Narrow your focus.
- Isolate the main messages.
- Identify possible production problems.

Resist the urge to grab an audio recorder or camcorder and run off to record your project. That's a sure-fire way to create an unorganized mess. Take the time to plan your production.

**Concept Outline** The first task in the writing process is a short, one-page document that describes the basic idea of the project. Ideally this should be three paragraphs—one paragraph each describing the beginning, the middle, and the end. Do not go forward until you have clearly identified these three important parts of your project.

**Brief** Next write one to two pages that describe in detail the point of your project: how it will be used, who the intended audience is, what the purpose is, and what you hope to achieve with the presentation. Do you want your audience to be informed about something? Motivated to do something? Emotionally moved in some way?

**Treatment** The next phase of the writing process fleshes out the ideas you expressed in your outline and brief. The treatment is several pages long. It contains descriptions of the characters, dialogue, and settings and describes the presentation scene by scene. Include in your treatment descriptions of the mood and the tone of your piece. If your project is a video, set the stage by describing the overall look and feel of the production.

**Script**  Once you've completed the first three steps, you are ready to go to script. Everything that is mentioned in the script will wind up in the audio recording or on the screen. Conversely, anything that is left out of the script will likely be overlooked and omitted from the final production. So write this document carefully.

For an audio recording, the script contains all narration, dialogue, music, and sound effects. For a video, it contains all of these elements plus descriptions of the characters, any sets, props, or costumes, plus all camera shots and movements, special visual effects, and onscreen titles or graphic elements. In short the audio script encompasses everything that is heard, and the video script covers everything that is seen and heard.

**Storyboard**  Last, for video productions, it's also helpful to create storyboards—simple frame-by-frame sketches with explanatory notes jotted underneath—that paint a visual picture of what the video will look like from start to finish.

**Pre-production Tasks**  The final stages of pre-production include assembling all the elements you will need before you begin producing your audio recording or video. Here's a general checklist.

 **Pre-Production Checklist**

**Audio Tasks**

✓ Arrange for audio recording equipment

✓ Cast narrator/actors

✓ Find music (secure permission)

✓ Arrange for sound effects

✓ Set up recording schedule

✓ Coordinate all cast and crew

✓ Arrange for transportation if needed

✓ Rehearse all voice talent

**Video Tasks**

✓ Arrange for video equipment (including lighting and sound recording equipment)

✓ Cast narrator/host/actors

✓ Find music (secure permission)

✓ Arrange for sound/visual effects

✓ Set up shooting schedule

✓ Coordinate all cast and crew

✓ Arrange for transportation if needed

✓ Set up shooting locations (secure permission)

✓ Arrange for costumes, props, sets

✓ Arrange for make-up if needed

✓ Rehearse all on-camera talent

**Video Production Schedule**  Tucked into the list of pre-production tasks is "Set up recording/shooting schedule." For a video, this means much more than just deciding what day and time you will begin shooting.

During the video production phase of your project, the idea is to shoot everything that your script calls for in the final production. Often the most efficient way to do this is what is called "out-of-sequence" filming. This means that, rather than shooting scenes sequentially (that is, in the order that they appear in the script), you shoot them in the order that is most convenient. Later you will edit them together in the correct order in post-production.

For example, your video might begin and end in the main character's office. Rather than shoot the first office scene, then move the cast and crew to the next location, then later at the end of the day return to the office, it might be easier to shoot both office scenes back-to-back. This will save a great deal of time and effort involved in moving people, lights, and props back and forth.

Lighting may be a factor in the order in which you shoot your scenes. For example, scenes 3, 4, and 7 may take place in the daytime, and scenes 1, 2, 5, and 6 may take place at night.

To accommodate all of these factors, you will need to plan your shooting schedule carefully. The difference between a smooth shoot day and chaos is a well thought-out shooting schedule.

Last, for video or audio recording, it's also a good idea to assemble your team for a pre-production meeting before you begin. This is your chance to read through the script together, go over time schedules, review responsibilities of each person involved, and answer any questions or discuss potential problems before you begin the production process.

## PRODUCTION

At last, it's production time! There are a number of different formats you can use for audio and video recording. Talk to the AV expert in your school or check with the media center for help in selecting the best format to use. Get tips, as well, for how to use the audio or video equipment to achieve the best results and produce a polished, professional project.

Next, if you are producing a video, think carefully about how you will shoot it. Consider the kinds of camera shots, camera moves, and special effects you will use.

**Camera Shots** To hold the interest of your audience, use a variety of camera shots and angles. Check your local library or media center for good books on camera techniques that describe when and how to use various shots—from long shots to close-ups, from low angles to overhead shots. As a rule, every time you change camera shots, change your angle slightly as well. This way, when the shots are edited together, you can avoid accidentally putting two nearly identical shots side-by-side, which creates an unnerving jarring motion called a "jump cut."

Do some research on framing techniques as well to make sure you frame your subjects properly and avoid cutting people's heads off on the screen.

**Camera Moves** Learn about ways to move the camera in order to keep your audience interested. Three common, but effective camera moves are panning, tracking, and zooming. **Panning** means moving the camera smoothly from one side of the scene to another. Panning works well in an establishing shot to help orient your audience to the setting where the action takes place.

**Tracking** means moving the camera from one place to another in a smooth action as well, but in tracking, the camera parallels the action, such as moving alongside a character as he or she walks down the street. It's called tracking because in professional filmmaking, the camera and the operator are rolled forward or backward on a small set of train tracks alongside the actor or actress.

**Zooming** means moving the camera forward or back, but zooming actually involves moving the lens, rather than the camera. By touching the zoom button, you can focus in on a small detail that you would like to emphasize, or you can pull back to reveal something in the background.

The important factor in any kind of camera move is to keep the action fluid and, in most cases, slow and steady. Also, use camera movement sparingly. You want to keep your audience eager and interested, not dizzy and sick!

**Cuts** Another good way to keep your presentation moving is to use frequent cuts. While the actual cuts will be done during post-production, you need to plan for them in production. Professional filmmakers use the word *coverage* for making sure they have ample choices for shots. You can create coverage for your production by planning shots such as those on the following pages.

Here are three kinds of video shots:

**establishing shot**    This shot sets up where the action of the story will take place. For example, if your story takes place inside an operating room, you might begin with an establishing shot of the outside of the hospital.

**reaction shot**    It's a good idea to get shots of all on-camera talent even if one person does not have any dialogue but is listening to, or reacting to, another character. This gives you the chance to break away from the character who is speaking to show how his or her words are affecting other people in the scene.

**cutaway shot**    The cutaway shot is a shot of something that is not included in the original scene, but is somehow related to it. Cutaways are used to connect two subjects. For example, the first shot may be of a person falling off a boat. The second shot could be a cutaway of a shark swimming deep below the water.

**Special Effects**  If you are adventurous, you may want to try some simple special effects. For instance, dry ice can create smoke effects. You can also have your actors freeze; then stop the camera, remove an object from the set, and restart the camera. This technique will make objects seem to disappear as if by magic. Other effects can be achieved by using false backdrops, colored lights, and filters.

# POST-PRODUCTION—THE MAGIC OF EDITING

Once all of your video recording is complete, it's time to create the final cut—that is, your choice of the shots you wish to keep and the shots you wish to discard. Be choosy and select the footage with only the best composition, lighting, focus, and performances to tell your story.

There are three basic editing techniques:

**in-camera editing**    In this process you edit as you shoot. In other words, you need to shoot all your scenes in the correct sequence and in the proper length that you want them to appear. This is the most difficult editing process because it leaves no margin for error.

**insert editing**    In insert editing you transfer all your footage to a new video. Then you record over any scenes that you don't want with scenes that you do want in the final version.

**assemble editing**    This process involves electronically copying your shots from the original source in your camera onto a new blank source, called the edited master, in the order that you want the shots to appear. This method provides the most creative control.

Consider including effects such as a dissolve from one shot to another instead of an abrupt cut. A *dissolve* is the soft fading of one shot into another. Dissolves are useful when you wish to give the impression that time has passed between two scenes. A long, slow dissolve that comes up from black into a shot, or from a shot down to black, is called a *fade* and is used to open or close a show.

In addition to assembling the program, post-production is the time to add titles to the opening of your program and credits to the end of the show. Computer programs, such as Adobe Premiere™, can help you do this. Some cameras are also equipped to generate titles. If you don't have any electronic means to produce titles, you can always mount your camera on a high tripod and focus it downward on well-lit pages of text and graphics placed on the floor. Then edit the text frames into the program.

Post-production is also the time to add voiceover narration and music. Voiceovers and background music should be recorded separately and then edited into the program on a separate sound track once the entire show is edited together. Video editing programs for your computer, such as Adobe Premiere™, allow you to mix music and voices with your edited video.

After post-production editing, your video production is ready to present to your audience.

# Publishing on the Web

You can become a part of the Web community by building and publishing a Web site of your own.

The Web is a unique medium with distinctive features that make it different from any other form of communication. The Web offers:

- universal access to everyone
- interactive communication
- the ability to use photos, illustrations, animation, sound, and video
- unlimited space
- unlimited branching capabilities
- the ability to link your site with other Web sites

If you are going to publish on the Web, take advantage of all of these features. Your goal should be to make your site interesting enough that visitors will want to stay, explore, and come back to your site again—and that takes thought and planning.

## BACK TO THE DRAWING BOARD

First you need to capture your thoughts and ideas on paper before you publish anything. Start with a one-page summary that states the purpose of your Web site and the audience you hope to attract. Describe in a paragraph the look and feel you think your site will need in order to accomplish this purpose and hold your audience's attention.

Make a list of the content you plan to include in your Web site. Don't forget to consider any graphics, animation, video, or sound you may want to include.

Next go on a Web field trip. Ask your friends and teachers for the URLs of their favorite Web sites. (URL stands for Universal Resource Locator.) Visit these sites, and ask yourself, "Do I like this site? Why or why not?" Determine which sites are visually appealing to you and why. Which sites are easy to navigate and why? Chances are the sites you like best will have clean, easy-to-read layouts, be well written, contain visually stimulating graphic elements, and have intuitive **interfaces** that make it simple to find your way around.

One sure drawback in any Web site is long, uninterrupted blocks of text. Decide how to break up long passages of information into manageable sections. Will there be separate sections for editorial content? news? humor? feedback? Which sections will be updated periodically and how often?

Make a few rough sketches for your site. How do you envision the home page of your site? What will the icons and buttons look like? Then give careful thought to how the pages will connect to each other, starting with the home page. Your plan for connecting the pages is called a **site map**.

Because the Web is an interactive medium, navigation is critical. Decide how users will get from one page to another. Will you put in a navigation bar across the top of the page or down the side? Will there be a top or home page at the beginning of each section?

Once you have planned the content, organized your material into sections, and designed your navigation system, you are ready to begin creating Web pages.

## PUTTING IT ALL TOGETHER

Writing for the Web is different from writing for print. The Web is a fast medium. Keep your messages succinct and to the point. Use short, punchy sentences. Break up your copy with clever subheads. Try not to exceed 500 to 600 words in any single article on any one page.

In order to turn text into Web pages, you need to translate the text into a special language that Web browsers can read. This language code is called HTML—HyperText Markup Language. There are three methods available:

- You can use the Save As HTML feature in the File menu of most word-processing programs.
- You can import your text into a Web-building software program and add the code yourself if you know how.
- You can use a software program such as Adobe PageMill™ that does the work for you. Web-building software programs are referred to as WYSIWYG (pronounced "Wiz-E-Wig"), which stands for "What You See Is What You Get."

Web-building software also allows you to create links to other Web pages using a simple process called **drag and drop**. Be sure to read the directions that come with your software package for complete instructions.

## BLOGS

Blogs (short for weblogs) are a type of Web page. In many ways, they are like online diaries or journals, where "bloggers" post the latest events of their lives and their thoughts and feelings on a wide range of subjects. Some blogs have other purposes, such as to promote community among speakers of certain languages or to influence politics. Among the most popular blogs are those devoted to celebrity news and to animal photos with funny captions. The most popular blog software is free and easy enough to use so that anyone with Web space can build one.

# B. Using the Internet

## Apply Information and Technology Literacy

The "age of information" dawned in the last haf of the 20th century. Success in the 21st century requires the ability to access, evaluate, and wisely use the abundance of information made available by advances in technology. Developing an understanding of the changing technologies and skill in putting them to work for your purposes are key competencies for the rest of your schooling and for your adult life ahead.

In this section, you will develop your skills for understanding and making the most of what the Internet has to offer.

# How Does the Internet Work?

The Internet is made up of thousands of networks all linked together around the globe. Each network consists of a group of computers that are connected to one another to exchange information. If one of these computers or networks fails, the information simply bypasses the disabled system and takes another route through a different network. This rerouting is why the Internet is so valuable to agencies such as the U.S. Department of Defense.

No one "owns" the Internet, nor is it managed in a central place. No agency regulates or censors the information on the Internet. Anyone can publish information on the Internet as he or she wishes.

In fact, the Internet offers such a vast wealth of information and experiences that sometimes it is described as the Information Superhighway. So how do you "get on" this highway? It's easy. Once you have a computer, a modem, and a telephone or cable line, all you need is a connection to the Internet.

## THE CYBERSPACE CONNECTION

A company called an Internet Service Provider (ISP) connects your computer to the Internet. Examples of ISPs that provide direct access are Microsoft

Network, Earthlink, Comcast, and AT&T. You can also get on the Internet indirectly through companies such as America Online (AOL).

ISPs charge a flat monthly fee for their service. Unlike the telephone company, once you pay the monthly ISP fee, there are no long-distance charges for sending or receiving information on the Internet—no matter where your information is coming from, or going to, around the world.

## ALPHABET SOUP—MAKING SENSE OF ALL THOSE LETTERS

Like physical highways, the Information Superhighway has road signs that help you find your way around. Each specific group of information on the World Wide Web is called a **Web site** and has its own unique address. Think of it as a separate street address of a house in your neighborhood. This address is called the URL, which stands for Uniform Resource Locator. It's a kind of shorthand for where the information is located on the Web.

Here's a typical URL: **http://www.perfectionlearning.com.**

All addresses, or URLs, for the World Wide Web begin with **http://.** This stands for HyperText Transfer Protocol and is a programming description of how the information is exchanged.

The next three letters—**www**—let you know you are on the World Wide Web. The next part of the URL—**perfectionlearning**—is the name of the site you want to visit. The last three letters, in this case **com**, indicate that this Web site is sponsored by a **com**mercial company. Here are other common endings of URLs you will find:

- "org" is short for **org**anization, as in http://www.ipl.org, which is the URL of the Web site for the Internet Public Library, ipl2: Information You Can Trust.

- "edu" stands for **edu**cation, as in the Web address for the Virtual Reference Desk, http://thorplus.lib.purdue.edu/reference/index.html, featuring online telephone books, dictionaries, and other reference guides.

- "gov" represents **gov**ernment-sponsored Web sites, such as http://www.whitehouse.gov, the Web site for the White House in Washington, D.C.

To get to a Web site, you use an interface called a **browser**. Two popular browsers are Microsoft Internet Explorer and Mozilla Firefox. A browser is like a blank form where you fill in the information you are looking for. If you know the URL of the Web site you want to explore, all you have to do is type it in the field marked Location, click Enter on your keyboard, and wait for the information to be delivered to your computer screen.

# Basic Internet Terminology

Here are some of the most frequently used words you will hear associated with the Internet.

**address**  The unique code given to information on the Internet. This may also refer to an e-mail address.

**bookmark**  A tool that lets you store your favorite URL addresses, allowing you one-click access to your favorite Web pages without retyping the URL each time.

**browser**  Application software that supplies a graphical interactive interface for searching, finding, viewing, and managing information on the Internet.

**chat**  Real-time conferencing over the Internet.

**cookies**  A general mechanism that some Web sites use both to store and to retrieve information on the visitor's hard drive. Users have the option to refuse or accept cookies.

**cyberspace**  The collective realm of computer-aided communication.

**download**  The transfer of programs or data stored on a remote computer, usually from a server, to a storage device on your personal computer.

**e-mail**  Electronic mail that can be sent all over the world from one computer to another. May also be short for Earth-mail because no paper (and no rainforest acreage) is involved.

**FAQs**  The abbreviation for Frequently Asked Questions. This is usually a great resource to get information when visiting a new Web site.

**flaming**  Using mean or abusive language in cyberspace. Flaming is considered to be in extremely poor taste and may be reported to your ISP.

**FTP**  The abbreviation for File Transfer Protocol. A method of transferring files to and from a computer connected to the Internet.

**home page**  The start-up page of a Web site.

| | |
|---|---|
| **HTML** | The abbreviation for HyperText Markup Language—a "tag" language used to create most Web pages, which your browser interprets to display those pages. Often the last set of letters found at the end of a Web address. |
| **http** | The abbreviation for HyperText Transport Protocol. This is how documents are transferred from the Web site or server to the browsers of individual personal computers. |
| **ISP** | The abbreviation for Internet Service Provider—a company that, for a fee, connects a user's computer to the Internet. |
| **keyword** | A simplified term that serves as subject reference when doing a search. |
| **link** | Short for Hyperlink. A link is a connection between one piece of information and another. |
| **Net** | Short for Internet. |
| **netiquette** | The responsible and considerate way for a user to conduct himself or herself on the Internet. |
| **network** | A system of interconnected computers. |
| **online** | To "be online" means to be connected to the Internet via a live modem connection. |
| **plug-in** | Free application that can be downloaded off the Internet to enhance your browser's capabilities. |
| **real time** | Information received and processed (or displayed) as it happens. |
| **search engine** | A computer program that locates documents based on keywords that the user enters. |
| **server** | A provider of resources, such as a file server. |
| **site** | A specific place on the Internet, usually a set of pages on the World Wide Web. |
| **social network** | An online community of people who share interests and activities, usually based on the Web. |

| | |
|---|---|
| **spam** | Electronic junk mail. |
| **surf** | A casual reference to browsing on the Internet. To "surf the Web" means to spend time discovering and exploring new Web sites. |
| **upload** | The transfer of programs or data from a storage device on your personal computer to another remote computer. |
| **URL** | The abbreviation for Uniform Resource Locator. This is the address for an Internet resource, such as a World Wide Web page. Each Web page has its own unique URL. |
| **Web 2.0** | The so-called second generation of the World Wide Web, which promotes programming that encourages interaction and collaboration. |
| **Web site** | A page of information or a collection of pages that is being electronically published from one of the computers in the World Wide Web. |
| **Wiki** | Technology that holds together a number of user-generated web pages focused on a theme, project, or collaboration. Wikipedia is the most famous example. The word *wiki* means "quick" in Hawaiian. |
| **WWW** | The abbreviation for the World Wide Web. A network of computers within the Internet capable of delivering multimedia content (images, audio, video, and animation) as well as text over communication lines into personal computers all over the globe. |

# Communicating on the Internet

E-mail, mailing lists, and newsgroups are all great ways of exchanging information with other people on the Internet. Here's how to use these useful forms of communication, step-by-step.

## 1 Using E-mail

Any writer who has ever used e-mail in his or her work will agree that sending and receiving electronic messages is one of the most useful ways of gathering information and contacts for writing projects.

Once you open your e-mail program, click on the command that says Compose Mail or New Message. This will open a new blank e-mail similar to the one pictured below. Next, fill in the blanks.

Type the person's e-mail address here. There is no central listing of e-mail addresses. If you don't have the person's address, the easiest way to get it is to call and ask the person for it. You can address an e-mail to one or several people, depending on the number of addresses you type in this space.

Cc stands for courtesy copy. If you type additional e-mail addresses in this area, you can send a copy of the message to other people.

Bcc stands for blind courtesy copy. By typing one or more e-mail addresses here, you can send a copy of the message to others without the original recipient knowing that other people have received the same message. Not all e-mail programs have this feature.

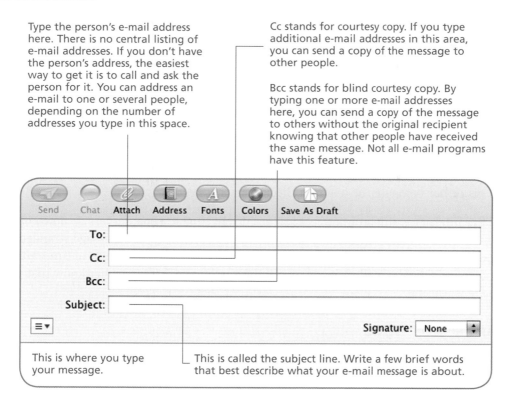

This is where you type your message.

This is called the subject line. Write a few brief words that best describe what your e-mail message is about.

## SAY IT WITH STYLE

Like regular letters, e-mail can assume different tones and styles, depending on to whom you are writing. Usually informal e-mails and instant messages (IMs) to close friends are light, brief, and to the point. In the case of more formal e-mails, such as a request for information from an expert or a museum, keep the following guidelines in mind.

## Guidelines for Writing E-mails

- Make sure your message is clear and concise.
- Use proper grammar and punctuation.
- Check your spelling. (Some e-mail programs have their own spell-check function—use it!)
- Double-check the person's e-mail address to be sure you've typed it correctly.

## ATTACH A LITTLE SOMETHING EXTRA

When you send e-mail, you can also send other information along with your message. These are called **attachments**. Depending on your e-mail program's capabilities, you can attach documents, photos, illustrations—even sound and video files. Click Attach, and then find and double-click on the document or file on your computer that you wish to send.

After you have composed your message and added any attachments you want to include, click the Send button. Your message arrives in the other person's mailbox seconds later, regardless of whether that person lives right next door or on the other side of the world.

## FOLLOW UP

Just because you have sent a message, you shouldn't automatically assume that the other person has received it. Internet Service Providers (ISPs) keep all messages that are sent until the recipient requests them. The person you sent your e-mail to might be away from his or her computer or may not check messages regularly.

Also, the Internet is still an imperfect science. From time to time, servers go down or other "hiccups" in electronic transmissions can occur, leaving your message stranded somewhere in cyberspace. If you don't get a reply in a reasonable amount of time, either resend your original e-mail message or call the person and let him or her know that your message is waiting.

## YOU'VE GOT MAIL

When someone sends you an e-mail message, you have several options:

**Reply** Click Reply, and you can automatically send back a new message without having to retype the person's e-mail address. (Be sure you keep a copy of the sender's e-mail address in your Address Book for future use.)

**Forward** Suppose you receive a message that you would like to share with someone else. Click Forward, and you can send a copy of the message, plus include a few of your own comments, to another person.

**Print** In some instances, you may need to have a paper copy of the e-mail message. For example, if someone e-mails you directions to a party, click Print to take a hard copy of the instructions with you.

**Store** Do you want to keep a message to refer to later? Some e-mail programs allow you to create folders to organize stored messages.

**Delete** You can discard a message you no longer need just by clicking Delete. It's a good idea to throw messages away regularly to keep them from accumulating in your mailbox.

#  Other Online Communication

## Care to Chat?

Another way to communicate online is Internet Relay Chat (IRC), or "chat rooms" for short. Chat rooms focus on a large variety of topics, so it's possible you'll be able to find a chat room where people are discussing the subject you are writing about.

"Chat" is similar to talking on the telephone except, instead of speaking, the people in the chat room type their responses back and forth to each other. As soon as you type your comment, it immediately appears on the computer screen of every person involved in the "conversation." There are also more advanced forms of chat available on the Net, such as video chat and voice chat.

To participate in a chat room, you'll need to invent a nickname for yourself. This name helps to identify who is speaking, yet allows you to remain anonymous. Everyone uses a made-up name in chat rooms (like Zorro, Twinkle, Venus, or Elvis), so don't make the mistake of believing that people really are who their name says they are!

One last word about chat rooms: While they are a great way to meet and communicate with other people, the anonymous nature of a chat room can make people less inhibited than they might otherwise be in person. If you sense that one of the participants in your chat room is responding inappropriately, ask your parents or teacher to step in, or simply sign off.

## Join the Group

Mailing lists and newsgroups are larger discussion forums that can help you get even more information about a specific subject.

**Mailing Lists** To find a directory of available mailing lists, enter "mailing list directory" in a search engine. If you find a mailing list that interests you and wish to subscribe to it, just send a message to the administrative address. You will start to receive messages from the mailing list within a few days.

Remember, mailing lists use e-mail to communicate, so be sure to check your e-mail often because once you subscribe to a list, it's possible to receive dozens of messages in a matter of days.

Another good idea is to read the messages in your new mailing list for a week or so before submitting a message of your own. This will give you a good idea of what has already been discussed so you can be considerate about resubmitting old information.

You can reply to a message any time you wish. However, it doesn't do anyone any good to respond by saying "Yes, I agree." Get in the habit of replying to messages only when you have something important to add. Also, be sure to repeat the original question in your reply so that people understand which message you are responding to.

Be sure that you really want to belong to a mailing list before you subscribe. Unwanted e-mail can be a nuisance. Fortunately, if you change your mind, you can always unsubscribe to mailing lists at any time.

***Newsgroups***  To join a newsgroup, check with your ISP. Service providers frequently list available topics under the heading "Newsgroups." Newsgroups are named with two or more words separated by a period. For example, there is a newsgroup named <u>rec.sport.baseball. college</u>. The first three letters—"rec"—defines the main subject, in this case recreation. Each word that follows—sport, baseball, and college—narrows the scope of the subject to an increasingly more specific area of interest.

As with mailing lists, you can always unsubscribe to newsgroups at any time.

## Mind Your Manners

As in any social setting, there are a few guidelines to follow when you are talking to people online—via e-mail, in a chat room, or in a newsgroup. This conduct is called **netiquette**. The following suggestions will help you be considerate of others in cyberspace.

### E-mail and Chat

- Never use harsh or insulting language. This is called flaming and is considered rude. A continuing argument in which derogatory words are swapped back and forth is called a flamewar. Avoid this situation.

- Type your messages using uppercase and lowercase letters. WRITING IN ALL CAPITAL LETTERS IS DIFFICULT TO READ AND IS REFERRED TO AS "SHOUTING."

- Respect other people's ideas and work. Don't forward a message or attach documents written by someone else without first asking the author's permission.

- Don't send spam. Spamming refers to sending messages to entire lists of people in your address book, on mailing lists, or in newsgroups for the purpose of selling something.

- Respect other people's privacy. The Internet is an enormous public forum, so be careful what you write and post on the Internet that hundreds or thousands of people might see.
- Don't use the Internet to spread rumors or gossip.

### Newgroups

- Read the articles in a newsgroup for 7 to 10 days before posting articles yourself. No one in a newsgroup wants to read the same article twice.
- Make sure the article you are proposing is appropriate to the subject of the newsgroup.
- If you are going to post an article, be sure you express the title clearly in the subject heading so readers will know what the article is about.
- Read the FAQ (Frequently Asked Questions) so you can avoid repeating a question that has already been discussed.

### Cyberbullying

More than half of teenagers recently surveyed reported that they have been the victim of online bullying, also called cyberbullying, or known someone who has been. **Cyberbullying** is the use of such technology as the Internet and cell phones to deliberately hurt or embarrass someone. Cyberbullies often assume fake identities to trick people. They also knowingly spread lies and often post pictures of someone without his or her permission. Cyberbullies can trick their victims into revealing personal information which is then abused.

Victims react in different ways. Some take such reasonable measures as blocking an offending user or refusing to read comments that might be hurtful and deleting them as soon as they arrive. Some seek help from adults, who sometimes help the victim report the problem to the appropriate authorities. Other teens have a more negative and painful reaction. They might withdraw from their usual pastimes and suffer from problems with self-esteem. Or they might get caught up in the negative swirl and try to bully back.

The National Crime Prevention Council (NCPC) makes these suggestions to teens to stop cyberbullying.

- Refuse to pass along cyberbullying messages.
- Tell friends to stop cyberbullying.
- Block communication with cyberbullies.
- Report cyberbullying to a trusted adult.

The NCPC developed a slogan to summarize what to do: "Delete cyberbullying. Don't write it. Don't forward it."

# Unit 4

# Grammar

Every day you set nouns in motion with verbs, add details with modifiers, and join ideas with conjunctions. This working knowledge of English grammar serves you well. Mastery of grammar, however, can help you take the language further. Besides giving you a way to discuss and analyze the language itself, it will help you gain control over the way you construct sentences and paragraphs. It will, as B. J. Chute suggests, act as a rock-solid foundation on which to express your unique ideas.

*Grammar is to a writer what anatomy is to a sculptor, or the scales to a musician. . . . nothing will replace it, and once mastered it will support you like a rock.* —B. J. Chute

# The Parts of Speech

**How can you combine the parts of speech to create vivid and exact sentences?**

## The Parts of Speech: Pretest 1

The following draft paragraph is hard to read because it contains several errors involving parts of speech. Revise the paragraph so that it reads correctly. One of the errors has been corrected as an example.

I ~~got this~~ *have* a friend that waits until the last minutes to study for a test. One time he calls me late the night before a test asks me if he can borrow my notes. "I would help if I could," I says, "but I having to study for the same test." When I tell him he needs to pay more attentive in class. Of course, he gets mad and hung up. The next day he says he was sorry about it. Him and I have geometry together. When I see him daydreaming in class I nudge him awake. He usually thank me with a smile.

# The Parts of Speech: Pretest 2

## Directions

Write the letter of the term that correctly identifies the underlined word in each sentence.

### Realism

(1) Realistic writing emphasizes accuracy <u>of</u> detail. (2) Realism generally concerns <u>itself</u> with common people. (3) A realistic novel <u>is</u> neither moralistic nor preachy. (4) Realism became <u>trendy</u> in the nineteenth century. (5) It may have started <u>earlier</u> with the writings of Defoe and Fielding. (6) In <u>America</u> Howells and James were important realists. (7) French realists include Flaubert <u>and</u> Balzac. (8) An outgrowth of realism was the <u>naturalism</u> of Zola and Dreiser. (9) Naturalists <u>believed</u> in social and economic determinism. (10) Their subjects primarily come from the <u>lowest</u> depths of society.

1. A adjective
   B adverb
   C preposition
   D noun

2. A noun
   B pronoun
   C verb
   D adverb

3. A preposition
   B pronoun
   C verb
   D adverb

4. A adjective
   B adverb
   C preposition
   D noun

5. A adjective
   B adverb
   C preposition
   D noun

6. A adjective
   B adverb
   C preposition
   D proper noun

7. A conjunction
   B interjection
   C preposition
   D adjective

8. A adjective
   B adverb
   C preposition
   D noun

9. A noun
   B pronoun
   C verb
   D adverb

10. A conjunction
    B interjection
    C preposition
    D adjective

Nouns and pronouns are two of the eight parts of speech. The grammatical elements covered in this chapter include all eight parts of speech. Remember, though, that the part of speech of a word can vary depending upon its use in a sentence.

Understanding the function of grammatical elements can help you as a writer. If you know, for example, when a word is a noun and when a word is a verb, then you can diagnose a problem such as incorrect agreement between a subject and a verb as you edit your work.

### THE EIGHT PARTS OF SPEECH

**noun** (names)

**pronoun** (replaces noun)

**verb** (states action or being)

**adjective** (describes, limits)

**adverb** (describes, limits)

**preposition** (relates)

**conjunction** (connects)

**interjection** (expresses strong feeling)

## Nouns

**13 A**   A **noun** is the name of a person, place, thing, or idea.

There are more nouns in our language than any other part of speech. Nouns can be classified in several ways.

## Concrete and Abstract Nouns

**13 A.1**   A **concrete noun** names a person or an object that can actually be seen, touched, tasted, heard, or smelled. An **abstract noun** names qualities, conditions, and ideas that cannot be perceived through the senses.

### CONCRETE AND ABSTRACT NOUNS

| | |
|---|---|
| **Concrete Nouns** | table, feather, lemon, salt, bells, roses |
| **Abstract Nouns** | courage, joy, friendship, loyalty, freedom |

# Common and Proper Nouns

**13 A.2**   A **common noun** names any person, place, or thing. A **proper noun** always begins with a capital letter and names a particular person, place, or thing.

| COMMON AND PROPER NOUNS | |
| --- | --- |
| **Common Nouns** | quarterback, state, city |
| **Proper Nouns** | Sam Levin, New Jersey, Houston |

Some proper nouns, such as *Sam Levin* and *New Jersey*, include more than one word; but they are still considered one noun. *Sam Levin* is one person, and *New Jersey* is one state.

*You can learn about capitalizing proper nouns on pages 913–920.*

# Compound Nouns

**13 A.3**   A **compound noun** is made up of more than one word.

A compound noun can be written as one word, as a hyphenated word, or as two or more separate words. Check a dictionary for the correct, up-to-date form.

| COMPOUND NOUNS | |
| --- | --- |
| **One Word** | peacemaker, falsehood |
| **Hyphenated Word** | sister-in-law, half-truth |
| **Two Words** | life jacket, city hall |

*You can learn about spelling the plural forms of compound nouns on pages 1028–1029.*

# Collective Nouns

**13 A.4**   A **collective noun** names a group of people or things.

Following are some collective nouns.

| COMMON COLLECTIVE NOUNS | | | |
| --- | --- | --- | --- |
| band | congregation | flock | nation |
| class | crew | gang | orchestra |
| colony | crowd | herd | swarm |
| committee | family | league | team |

Some nouns are more colorful and convey meaning more vividly than other nouns. For instance, a noun such as *building* is a general term, but *skyscraper, Empire State Building, factory,* and *hut* are more specific and lively. In your writing, whether formal or informal, use the most precise nouns possible.

*You can learn about spelling plural nouns on pages 1024–1030. You can learn about possessive nouns on pages 964–966.*

● **Practice Your Skills**

*Identifying Nouns*

Write the nouns in the following paragraphs. A date should be considered a noun.

(1) The Eiffel Tower is perhaps the most familiar human-made landmark on Earth. (2) It was designed for the Paris Exposition in 1889. (3) The tower can now accommodate 10,000 visitors annually. (4) Some people, however, go there for publicity, not for enjoyment. (5) A man once climbed 363 steps on stilts, and a stuntman came down the steps on a unicycle.

(6) The tower is repainted every seven years, requiring thousands of gallons of paint. (7) As a part of one cleanup, nearly 1,000 tons of rust and dirt were shaved off. (8) This kind of effort signifies the tremendous pride the city takes in its famous structure—even if only a very small percentage of its visitors are Parisians.

● *Connect to Writing:* **Editing**

*Capitalizing Proper Nouns*

Write each proper noun in the paragraph. Capitalize any proper nouns that are not capitalized.

(1) Distinctive geographical features serve as landmarks across the united states. (2) Each year Carlsbad Caverns attracts crowds of sightseers to new mexico. (3) In Arizona tourists flock to view the grand canyon. (4) Popular for its beaches, florida lures tourists to its swamps and bayous as well. (5) A famous geyser named old faithful draws nature enthusiasts to yellowstone national park. (6) Avid downhill skiers throng the snowy slopes of colorado. (7) Vacationers to Hawaii enjoy waterfalls and volcanoes. (8) Carved into mount rushmore are the faces of four presidents: george washington, thomas Jefferson, abraham lincoln, and theodore roosevelt. (9) Landmarks in America celebrate our nation's natural and historical heritage.

# Pronouns

**13 A.5**  A **pronoun** is a word that takes the place of one or more nouns.

The word the pronoun replaces or refers to is called its **antecedent.** The antecedent of a pronoun can be in the same sentence or in another sentence. In the following examples, an arrow has been drawn from each pronoun to its antecedent.

Stephen wore **his** new jacket to study hall.

Rob and Beth are at the library. **They** have **their** exams tomorrow.

Occasionally the antecedent will follow the pronoun.

"That homework is **mine**," Heather said.

*You can learn more about pronouns and their antecedents on pages 812–820.*

## Personal Pronouns

**Personal pronouns,** the most commonly used type of pronoun, are divided into the following groups.

| PERSONAL PRONOUNS | |
|---|---|
| **First Person** | (the person speaking) |
| **Singular** | I, me, my, mine |
| **Plural** | we, us, our, ours |
| **Second Person** | (the person spoken to) |
| **Singular** | you, your, yours |
| **Plural** | you, your, yours |
| **Third Person** | (the person or thing spoken about) |
| **Singular** | he, him, his, she, her, hers, it, its |
| **Plural** | they, them, their, theirs |

**First Person**  **We** want to publish a study guide.

**Second Person**  Did **you** ever find **your** article?

**Third Person**  **He** told **them** to call **him** if **they** needed more study advice.

# Reflexive and Intensive Pronouns

**Reflexive** and **intensive pronouns** are formed by adding *-self* or *-selves* to personal pronouns.

| REFLEXIVE AND INTENSIVE PRONOUNS | |
|---|---|
| **Singular** | myself, yourself, himself, herself, itself |
| **Plural** | ourselves, yourselves, themselves |

**13 A.6**   A **reflexive pronoun** refers to the noun or pronoun that is the subject of the sentence. It is an essential part of the sentence. An **intensive pronoun** is included in a sentence to add emphasis—or intensity—to a noun or another pronoun.

Because an intensive pronoun is not a necessary part of a sentence, it can be removed without affecting the meaning of the sentence.

| | |
|---|---|
| **Reflexive Pronoun** | Rob taught **himself** to speak French. (*Himself* cannot be removed from the sentence without changing the meaning.) |
| **Intensive Pronoun** | Rob **himself** volunteered to help. (*Himself* can be removed from the sentence. *Rob volunteered to help.*) |

## ● Practice Your Skills

### *Identifying Pronouns and Their Antecedents*

Write the personal, reflexive, or intensive pronoun(s) in each sentence. Then beside each one, write its antecedent.

**(1)** Roberto lost his essay test in the subway when he was going home. **(2)** "Is this essay yours?" Megan asked Roberto the next day. **(3)** Roberto was relieved that Megan had found his test, and he thanked her for returning it. **(4)** Megan told herself that she could do better on the next essay test. **(5)** Roberto told Megan, "I myself have developed a study technique that I could share with you." **(6)** "An essay test is not as difficult if I write a practice answer ahead of time," Roberto said. **(7)** "We should study together for the next test," Megan told Roberto. **(8)** "I will set up a study group with you and Roger," Roberto said to Megan. **(9)** "When I helped Roger study for the last test, he made excellent progress for himself," Roberto continued modestly. **(10)** Megan was glad that she could study with Roberto and Roger, and she was certain that her grades would improve with her hard work.

# Indefinite Pronouns

**13 A.7**   **Indefinite pronouns** often refer to unnamed persons or things and usually do not have specific antecedents.

| COMMON INDEFINITE PRONOUNS | |
|---|---|
| **Singular** | another, anybody, anyone, anything, each, either, everybody, everyone, everything, much, neither, nobody, no one, nothing, one, somebody, someone, something |
| **Plural** | both, few, many, others, several |
| **Singular/Plural** | all, any, more, most, none, some |

**Few** attended the meeting.

**Most** of the teachers did **something** to help **everybody** who failed the midterm.

*You can learn about indefinite pronouns functioning as antecedents on pages 815–817.*

# Demonstrative Pronouns

**13 A.8**   A **demonstrative pronoun** is used to point out a specific person, place, or object in the same sentence or in another sentence.

| DEMONSTRATIVE PRONOUNS | |
|---|---|
| **Singular** | this (points out an object close by) |
| | that (points out an object in the distance) |
| **Plural** | these (points out objects close by) |
| | those (points out objects in the distance) |

**This** is the perfect place for a rest.

Of all the books, **these** were the best.

# Interrogative Pronouns

**13 A.9**   An **interrogative pronoun** is used to ask a question.

| INTERROGATIVE PRONOUNS | | | | |
| --- | --- | --- | --- | --- |
| what | whom | which | whose | who |

**Which** is the best class on filmmaking?

**Who** wrote that screenplay?

**Whose** is better?

## Practice Your Skills

### Identifying Pronouns

Write each pronoun in the following sentences. Beside each pronoun, write what type it is —*personal, reflexive, intensive, indefinite, demonstrative,* or *interrogative.*

**1.** Who is going to lead our study group this week?

**2.** Few attended last week's session.

**3.** We have to do something to increase involvement.

**4.** These should generate a definite interest.

**5.** I will post some of the fliers near the lockers.

**6.** Which of the boxes do you want Krista to take?

**7.** Tell her to take those.

**8.** Whose is this?

**9.** That is Tyrell's drawing, and this is Lee's photograph.

**10.** Either could win an award.

## *Connect to Writing:* Description

### Using Nouns and Pronouns

Just as the Eiffel Tower is a Paris landmark, structures such as the Gateway Arch in St. Louis, Missouri, and the Golden Gate Bridge in San Francisco, California, are landmarks in those cities. You are a travel writer, and you have received an assignment to write about a landmark of your own choosing. Write two paragraphs describing a landmark you have seen, whether it is in your hometown or across the world. Make your descriptions as specific and interesting as possible by using a variety of nouns—concrete nouns, abstract nouns, common nouns, proper nouns, compound nouns, and collective nouns—as well as pronouns.

**13 B** A **verb** is a word that expresses action or a state of being.

A verb is an essential part of a sentence because it tells what the subject does, is, or has.

## ➤ Action Verbs

**13 B.1** An **action verb** tells what action a subject is performing.

Action verbs can show several types of action.

| ACTION VERBS | |
| --- | --- |
| **Physical Action** | drive, march, soar, sing, talk, paint |
| **Mental Action** | believe, think, dream, imagine, wish |
| **Ownership** | have, own, possess, keep, control |

### *When You Speak and Write*

Many action verbs can be used alone to create a one-word action command. These commands can be particularly effective in grabbing a listener's attention.

A drill sergeant tells a soldier: **"March!"**

Your older brother tells you: **"Move!"**

A teacher tells her student: **"Think."**

## Transitive and Intransitive Verbs

**13 B.2** An action verb is **transitive** if it has an object. You can find an object by asking the question *What?* or *Whom?* after the verb. An action verb is **intransitive** if it has no object.

**Transitive**     I **found** a new restaurant. (*Found* what?)

**Intransitive**     We **met** there Friday. (*Met* what or whom?)

Some action verbs may be either transitive or intransitive.

**Transitive**     She **writes** restaurant reviews in her spare time.
**Intransitive**   She often **writes** to me.

*You can learn more about the objects of transitive verbs on page 664.*

● **Practice Your Skills**

### Identifying Transitive and Intransitive Verbs

Write each action verb. Then label each one transitive or intransitive.

1. Rings on the scales of some fish show the age of the fish.
2. The electric eel throws a charge of 600 volts.
3. Rays live on the ocean bottom.
4. The Nile catfish swims upside down.
5. Minnows have teeth in their throat.
6. The female marine catfish hatches her eggs in her mouth.
7. The trout belongs to the salmon family.
8. The flounder changes its color.
9. Some fish thrive in underground streams and caves.
10. Sharks, despite their reputation, rarely attack humans.

# ➤ Verb Phrases

**13 B.3**     A **verb phrase** is a main verb plus one or more helping verbs.

Another name for **helping verb** is **auxiliary verb**.

| COMMON HELPING VERBS | |
|---|---|
| **be** | am, is, are, was, were, be, being, been |
| **have** | has, have, had |
| **do** | do, does, did |
| **Others** | may, might, must, can, could, shall, should, will, would |

In the examples on the next page, the helping verbs are in **bold** type, and the verb phrase is underlined.

Jeff **has been** bringing our food promptly.

You **should have been** notified of the reservations.

A verb phrase is often interrupted by contractions or other words.

Marvin **will** soon apply for that job.

**Have** you always taken the server's suggestions?

I **do**n't want any dessert.

## When You Write

You probably use many contractions in your everyday conversations. When you are writing, though, you need to consider whether contractions are appropriate. The use of contractions depends on your purpose and audience. If you are writing a letter to a friend, contractions are appropriate. If you are writing a research report, you should avoid using contractions. Review a recent research report and edit out inappropriate contractions.

*You can learn more about contractions on pages 971–972.*

*Throughout the rest of this book, the term* verb *will refer to the whole verb phrase.*

## ● Practice Your Skills

### Identifying Verbs

1. Sushi comes from Japan.
2. Some sushi is carefully rolled in a wrapper of very thin, edible seaweed.
3. Sushi consists of raw fish, raw shellfish, and cooked rice.
4. The Japanese have been making sushi for more than a thousand years.
5. Sushi was originally made with salt as a preservative.
6. The fish and salt were aged over several weeks or months.
7. Nowadays, chefs often prepare sushi without the preservative.
8. The sushi is immediately served to the customer.
9. The preparation and display of sushi can be considered an elegant art form.
10. The sushi chef does consider all details of color, texture, and taste.

● *Connect to Writing:* **Revising**

### *Writing Sentences with Verb Phrases*

Each of the sentences below contains a verb phrase. Rewrite the sentence, adding an interrupter so that the meaning of the sentence changes. Underline the verb.

**1.** I have liked that Mexican restaurant.

**2.** We can give our order to the server.

**3.** Our order was sent to the kitchen.

**4.** The server has returned with our water.

**5.** The dish for the chips and salsa has been empty.

## ➤ Linking Verbs

**13 B.4** A **linking verb** links the subject with another word in the sentence. The other word either renames or describes the subject.

A linking verb serves as a bridge between the subject and another word in the sentence.

History **is** my favorite subject. (*Subject* renames the subject *history*.)

This election **has been** exceptionally competitive. (*Competitive* describes the subject *election*.)

The most common linking verbs are the various forms of *be*.

| COMMON FORMS OF *BE* | | | |
|---|---|---|---|
| be | being | would be | had been |
| is | shall be | may be | could have been |
| am | will be | might be | should have been |
| are | can be | must be | will have been |
| was | could be | have been | might have been |
| were | should be | has been | must have been |

Diane **may be** our new class president.

These votes **should have been** anonymous.

The forms of *be* are not always linking verbs. Only a verb that links the subject with another word in the sentence that renames or describes the subject can be a linking verb. In the following examples, the verbs simply make a statement or describe a state of being.

Her running mate **is** here.

She **was** in Memphis on Tuesday.

The campaign buttons **could be** in the box.

They **must have been** there all the time.

Forms of *be* are not the only linking verbs. The verbs in the following box may also be used as linking verbs.

| ADDITIONAL LINKING VERBS | | |
|---|---|---|
| appear | look | sound |
| become | remain | stay |
| feel | seem | taste |
| grow | smell | turn |

Jonathan **became** my campaign manager.
(*Manager* renames the subject *Jonathan*.)

The campaign posters **look** very professional.
(*Professional* describes the subject *posters*.)

Most of the additional linking verbs listed in the box can be linking verbs in some sentences and action verbs in other sentences.

**Linking Verb**    The governor **appeared** weary.
(*Weary* describes the subject *governor*.)

**Action Verb**    The bodyguard **appeared** beside him.
(The verb shows an action performed by the subject *bodyguard*.)

*Subject complements complete the meaning of linking verbs. You can learn more about subject complements on pages 667–670.*

### Identifying Linking Verbs

Write each linking verb. If a sentence does not have a linking verb, write *none*.

1. During the Civil War, Abraham Lincoln was the president of the United States.
2. Lincoln was assassinated while in a theater.
3. Other leaders have been targets for assassins also.
4. Dr. Martin Luther King, Jr., was shot on April 4, 1968.
5. James Earl Ray grew old in prison for that crime.
6. President John F. Kennedy appeared in Texas in November 1963.
7. His assassination seemed a conspiracy to some people.
8. President Ronald Reagan nearly became the victim of John Hinckley.
9. Reagan was whisked away to a hospital and survived.
10. Hinckley had been insane at the time of the crime.

● *Connect to Writing:* **Summary**

### Using Verbs

You are a Web site developer, and you are writing a proposal to the marketing director of a company that specializes in historical memorabilia. You decide to end your proposal by writing a sample page about the era of history that interests you most. For your sample page, write a short summary about your chosen time period. Use verbs to make your sample page as specific and vivid as possible.

**13 C**  **Adjectives** and **adverbs** modify or describe other parts of speech.

Adjectives and adverbs improve the style of sentences by adding vividness and exactness.

**13 C.1**  An **adjective** is a word that modifies a noun or a pronoun.

An adjective answers one of the following questions about a noun or a pronoun.

| ADJECTIVES | | |
|---|---|---|
| **What Kind?** | **fresh** ideas | **plaid** shirt |
| **Which One(s)?** | **red** curtain | **those** few |
| **How Many?** | **six** actors | **many** pages |
| **How Much?** | **extensive** role | **much** publicity |

An adjective may come in one of three places.

**Before a Noun or a Pronoun**   The **young, eager** playwright wrote a script about Homer.

**After a Noun or a Pronoun**   The playwright, **young** and **eager,** wrote a script about Homer.

**After a Linking Verb**   The playwright of the script about Homer was **young** and **eager.**

*You can learn about adjectives that follow linking verbs on page 669.*

CHAPTER 13

## PUNCTUATION WITH TWO ADJECTIVES

Sometimes you will write two adjectives before the noun they describe. If those adjectives are not connected by a conjunction—such as *and* or *or*—you might need to put a comma between them.

To decide if a comma belongs, read the adjectives and add the word *and* between them.

- If the adjectives sound natural, put a comma in to replace *and*.
- If the adjectives do not sound natural with the word *and* between them, do not add a comma.

| | |
|---|---|
| **Comma Needed** | I read a realistic, scary book. |
| | (*Realistic and scary book* reads well.) |
| **No Comma Needed** | It was an unusual mystery story. |
| | (*Unusual and mystery story* does not read well.) |

*You can learn more about using commas to separate adjectives before a noun on pages 942–943.*

## When You Write

A talented writer chooses adjectives that are fresh, vivid, and specific. For example, a **good** steak expresses a general idea, but a **succulent** steak expresses a more specific, vivid idea. A football player's **strong** muscles are one thing, but **Herculean** muscles are another. Go back to a descriptive essay or a piece of creative writing and replace vague adjectives with more specific and vivid adjectives.

# Proper Adjectives

**13 C.2**  Because a **proper adjective** is formed from a proper noun, it begins with a capital letter.

| PROPER ADJECTIVES | |
|---|---|
| **Roman** emperor | **Greek** cuisine |
| **Hawaiian** island | **Shakespearean** play |

*You can learn more about capitalizing proper adjectives on pages 921–922.*

# Compound Adjectives

**13 C.3**  A **compound adjective** is made up of more than one word.

A compound adjective may be one word, a hyphenated word, or two or more separate words. You may need to check a dictionary for the correct form.

| COMPOUND ADJECTIVES | |
|---|---|
| **seaworthy** vessel | **spellbound** audience |
| **long-term** project | **high school** play |

# Articles

**13 C.4**  The words *a, an,* and *the* form a special group of adjectives called **articles.**

The article *a* comes before words starting with a consonant sound; *an* comes before words starting with a vowel sound.

| ARTICLES | | |
|---|---|---|
| **a** comedy | **an** understanding | **the** apple |
| **a** harp | **an** hour | **the** ball |

*You will not be asked to list articles in the exercises in this book.*

## ● Practice Your Skills

### Identifying Adjectives

Write each adjective. Then write the word the adjective modifies.

1. Homer was a famous Greek poet.
2. He told the great story of the Trojan War.
3. Homer also recounted the fantastic adventures of Odysseus in *The Odyssey.*
4. The larger-than-life man lived in a seaside city.
5. An important philosopher of ancient times was Plato.
6. Even today, ambitious scholars choose the study of Platonic philosophy.
7. One of Plato's well-known works is *The Republic.*
8. A Roman writer, Ovid, composed the long poem *Metamorphoses.*
9. *Metamorphoses* includes the romantic story of the handsome Pyramus and the beautiful Thisbe.
10. Nick Bottom and Francis Flute are characters in a Shakespearean play.

*Using Specific Adjectives*

> Work with another student. Ask your partner to look around the room and describe ten things that he or she sees. Write down each description. Then, working together, revise each so that it contains vivid and specific adjectives.

## Other Parts of Speech Used as Adjectives

The same word can be used as a noun in one sentence and as an adjective in another sentence.

| NOUNS USED AS ADJECTIVES | |
|---|---|
| **Nouns** | flower, glass, refrigerator |
| **Adjectives** | **flower** garden, **glass** vase, **refrigerator** door |

Also, the same word may be a pronoun in one sentence and an adjective in another sentence. The words in the box below are adjectives when they come before a noun and modify that noun. They are pronouns when they stand alone.

| WORDS USED AS ADJECTIVES OR PRONOUNS | | | | |
|---|---|---|---|---|
| **Demonstrative** | **Interrogative** | | **Indefinite** | |
| this | what | all | either | neither |
| these | which | another | few | other |
| that | whose | any | many | several |
| those | | both | more | some |
| | | each | most | |

| | |
|---|---|
| **Adjective** | **These** scripts must be yours. |
| **Pronoun** | **These** must be yours. |
| **Adjective** | **Each** actor was given a new costume. |
| **Pronoun** | **Each** of the actors was given a new costume. |

The possessive pronouns *my, your, his, her, its, our,* and *their* are sometimes called **pronominal adjectives** because they answer the adjective question *Which one(s)?*

*Throughout this book, these words will be considered pronouns.*

*Identifying Adjectives*

Write the adjectives in the following paragraph.

**(1)** According to the ancient Greeks, eyes could reveal a personality. **(2)** The Greeks compared the eyes of people to the eyes of various animals. **(3)** Then they attributed the personality traits of those animals to people. **(4)** Lion eyes, for example, are almond-like. **(5)** In a person they signified a sense of fairness, a sense of justice, and leadership skills. **(6)** Monkey eyes are small in relation to the face, but they have large irises. **(7)** The Greeks thought that people with eyes such as these were unpredictable and shy. **(8)** This unusual list of eye types also included the eyes of sheep, horses, wolves, hogs, snakes, and fish.

# ➤ Adverbs

**13 C.5**   An **adverb** is a word that modifies a verb, an adjective, or another adverb.

Although many adverbs end in *-ly,* some do not. Common adverbs that do not end in *-ly* are listed below.

| COMMON ADVERBS | | | |
|---|---|---|---|
| afterward | fast | now | soon |
| again | hard | nowhere | still |
| almost | here | often | straight |
| alone | just | outside | then |
| already | late | perhaps | there |
| also | long | quite | today |
| always | low | rather | tomorrow |
| away | more | seldom | too |
| down | near | so | very |
| even | never | sometimes | well |
| ever | next | somewhat | yesterday |
| far | not (n't) | somewhere | yet |

## Adverbs That Modify Verbs

Adverbs answer the questions *Where? When? How?* and *To what extent?* Notice in the examples on the next page that adverbs that modify verbs modify the whole verb phrase.

| **Where?** | Enrique went **outside.** |
| **When?** | Donna will be swimming **tomorrow.** |
| **How?** | The divers have been competing **fiercely.** |

Be careful not to confuse an adverb that ends in *-ly* with an adjective that ends in *-ly*.

| **Adverb** | Enrique meets **weekly** with his team. (When?) |
| **Adjective** | The **weekly** meeting is a time to plan strategy. (What kind?) |

## *When You Speak*

Sometimes when you are performing an action, another person will use a single adverb to tell you how to do it.

You are carelessly stacking china dishes, and your mother says, *"Carefully."*

You are driving rapidly through a school zone, and your passenger reminds you, *"Slowly."*

You are slowly picking up your clothes, and your dad says, *"Quickly!"*

## Adverbs That Modify Adjectives and Other Adverbs

When adverbs modify adjectives or other adverbs, they usually answer the question *To what extent?* Notice in the following examples that the adverbs that modify the adjectives and the other adverbs come before that word.

| **Modifying an Adjective** | This swimsuit is **too** loose. |
| | The **extremely** hot sand burned the soles of his feet. |
| **Modifying an Adverb** | Sammy moves through the water **very** quickly. |
| | She **almost** always spends the day collecting shells. |

*You can learn about using adjectives and adverbs to show degrees of comparison on pages 856–860.*

*Identifying Adverbs*

Write the adverbs from the sentences below. Then beside each adverb, write the word the adverb modifies.

(1) Enrique always keeps the members of the swim team in stitches. (2) Yesterday, he solemnly asked someone for directions in a fake language. (3) The person listened courteously to him and then walked rapidly in the opposite direction. (4) Another time, he impulsively popped popcorn without the lid on the pan. (5) Popcorn flew crazily around the kitchen, and the dog ran around in circles. (6) When Enrique drove too fast, he irritably paid the fine in pennies. (7) Last week, Enrique secretly started an odd rumor about himself. (8) The rumor evolved radically before it eventually came back to him. (9) He was bored in math class today and carefully wrote his work in Roman numerals. (10) Occasionally, he dresses his little brother and cheerfully sends him to preschool with his clothes on backward.

# Nouns Used as Adverbs

The same word may be used as a noun in one sentence and as an adverb in another sentence.

| | |
|---|---|
| **Noun** | The **outdoors** is the best location for the reptile habitat. |
| **Adverb** | We <u>will move</u> the reptile habitat **outdoors.** (Where?) |
| **Noun** | **Tomorrow** is the day for the lizards' release. |
| **Adverb** | I <u>will release</u> the lizards **tomorrow.** (When?) |

● **Practice Your Skills**

*Identifying Adverbs*

Write the adverbs from the sentences below. Then beside each one, write the word or words each adverb modifies.

1. Southwest deserts appear totally empty of life.
2. Many animals, birds, and insects survive very well in this barren land.
3. An unusually hardy inhabitant of these bleak areas is one type of lizard.
4. This lizard can swiftly skim along the sandy surface and can easily burrow into the sand.

**5.** You have probably watched swimmers at the ocean or a lake on a hot summer day.

**6.** These bathers often run quickly to the water, dive in, and then disappear beneath the surface.

**7.** In the same way, this lizard runs very fast, dives into the sand, and disappears without a trace.

**8.** During the course of this swift run, the lizard may actually fly for a few seconds.

**9.** The body of the lizard is perfectly suited for this incredible stunt.

**10.** During the dive a group of scales cleverly protects the eyes of the lizard.

## ✅ Check Point: Mixed Practice

Divide your paper into two columns. In the first column, write the adverbs in each sentence and the word each adverb modifies. In the second column, write the adjectives and the word each adjective modifies.

**1.** Yesterday, I went to an unusual water park.

**2.** In a huge tank, baby dolphins swam peacefully.

**3.** The older dolphins and their trainers performed daily water shows indoors.

**4.** I most enjoyed the activities available outside.

**5.** A few visitors can swim with the dolphins.

**6.** I was incredibly pleased about this unusual opportunity.

**7.** The trainers carefully gave me several instructions.

**8.** There was a trainer beside me constantly.

**9.** I quickly became friends with a large, happy dolphin. I swam playfully beside him for an hour.

## Connect to Writing: News Story

### Using Adverbs

Imagine that you are a reporter for your local newspaper. You have been asked to cover a high school competition for the readers of the newspaper. You may choose any competition you wish—cheerleading, soccer, football, dance team, tennis, quiz team, or any other. Be sure you use adverbs as you explain the action.

# Other Parts of Speech **Lesson 4**

**13 D** **Prepositions, conjunctions,** and **interjections** are the three remaining parts of speech.

## ➡ Prepositions

**13 D.1** A **preposition** shows the relationship between a noun or a pronoun and another word in the sentence.

In the following examples, the words in **bold** type are prepositions. Notice how the different prepositions change the relationship between the plant and the table.

The plant **on** the table is a geranium.

The plant **beside** the table is a geranium.

The plant **near** the table is a geranium.

Following is a list of common prepositions. Prepositions of two or more words are called **compound prepositions.**

| COMMON PREPOSITIONS | | | | |
|---|---|---|---|---|
| aboard | before | down | off | till |
| about | behind | during | on | to |
| above | below | except | onto | toward |
| across | beneath | for | opposite | under |
| after | beside | from | out | underneath |
| against | besides | in | outside | until |
| along | between | inside | over | up |
| among | beyond | into | past | upon |
| around | but ("except") | like | since | with |
| as | by | near | through | within |
| at | concerning | of | throughout | without |

| COMPOUND PREPOSITIONS | | |
|---|---|---|
| according to | by means of | instead of |
| ahead of | in addition to | in view of |
| apart from | in back of | next to |
| aside from | in front of | on account of |
| as of | in place of | out of |
| because of | in spite of | prior to |

**13 D.2** A preposition is always part of a group of words called a **prepositional phrase.** A prepositional phrase begins with a preposition and ends with a noun or a pronoun called the **object of a preposition.**

One or more modifiers may come between the preposition and its object. The prepositional phrases in the following examples are in **bold** type.

**During history class** we watched a film **about carrier pigeons.**

**On account of the war,** pigeons carried mail **throughout the country.**

## Preposition or Adverb?

The same word may be a preposition in one sentence and an adverb in another sentence. A word is a preposition if it is part of a prepositional phrase. An adverb stands alone.

**Preposition**  I saw the pigeon *outside* the window.

**Adverb**  I saw the pigeon **outside.**

**Preposition**  Professor Reilly speaks well *before* an audience.

**Adverb**  Have you heard this lecture **before?**

*You can learn more about prepositional phrases on pages 684–690.*

*Identifying Prepositional Phrases*

Write the prepositional phrases in the following paragraph. (There are 20 prepositional phrases.)

(1) In a sense the French were the originators of airmail service. (2) During the siege of Paris in the Franco-Prussian War of the 1870s, mail was sent from the capital by balloon, along with hundreds of homing pigeons. (3) Return letters were photo-reduced on thin film, which held an average of 2,500 letters. (4) Then pigeons delivered the letters to the capital. (5) Approximately 300 pigeons carrying the mail were dispatched. (6) Some of these got past the Prussian pigeon snipers. (7) In Paris the messages were enlarged on a projection screen, copied by clerks, and delivered to addresses within the city.

# ➤ Conjunctions

**13 D.3**    A **conjunction** connects words or groups of words.

**Coordinating conjunctions** are single connecting words; **correlative conjunctions** are pairs of connecting words.

| CONJUNCTIONS | | | | |
|---|---|---|---|---|
| **Coordinating** | | | **Correlative** | |
| and | nor | yet | both/and | not only/but also |
| but | or | | either/or | whether/or |
| for | so | | neither/nor | |

Following are some uses of a conjunction.

**Neither** *Marty* **nor** *Lana* has a credit card. (connects nouns)

**Either** *write* her a check **or** *pay* cash. (connects verbs)

That dollar bill is *old* **and** *dirty.* (connects adjectives)

*I can't pay the balance,* **for** *I don't have the money.* (connects sentences)

*A third type of conjunction, the subordinating conjunction, is used to introduce an adverb clause. You can learn about subordinating conjunctions on pages 720–721.*

## Practice Your Skills

### Identifying Conjunctions

Write and label the <u>coordinating</u> and <u>correlative conjunctions</u> in the following paragraphs.

**(1)** Visitors to the Bureau of Engraving and Printing in Washington can buy 150 dollars' worth of United States currency for 75 cents, but there is a catch. **(2)** The money is real, but it has been shredded. **(3)** Every day the bureau shreds not only new, misprinted currency, but also stamps and other items that are not fit for circulation. **(4)** Anyone can take home some souvenir money, for in the bureau's visitor center, machines automatically dispense 75-cent packets of shredded currency.

**(5)** Each of the twelve Federal Reserve district banks is also authorized to dispose of unusable currency, whether it be old, soiled, or worn. **(6)** Residents of Los Angeles can either drop by the district bank or request a delivery. **(7)** For the sum of 83 dollars, the branch will deliver an entire day's output—up to 5,550 pounds—to your door if you live closer than the nearest dump. **(8)** Some of this currency later appears in novelty stores in one form or another.

## *Connect to Writing:* Revising

### Using Conjunctions

Revise the following paragraphs to make them less repetitive and choppy. Use coordinating and correlative conjunctions to join words, phrases, and sentences.

Every year criminals think they have discovered a foolproof way to counterfeit money. They use color copiers. They use scanners. They use high-quality printers. They scrutinize watermarks. They scrutinize paper quality. They scrutinize tiny markings. In 1997, more than 135 million dollars in counterfeit U.S. currency appeared worldwide. Three-fourths of it was discovered. Three-fourths of it was confiscated before it was circulated.

The United States government is well versed in detecting counterfeit money. It issued the first paper currency in 1861. Fewer than five years later, one-third of all notes in circulation were counterfeit. The government created the Secret Service in 1865. Its sole mission was to quell the usage of fake currency. It is part of the U.S. Department of Treasury. It has developed new security features such as inks that change color when viewed from different angles. It has developed new security features such as fine-line printing patterns that are hard for printers and scanners to duplicate.

The Parts of Speech

642

# Interjections

**13 D.4**   An **interjection** is a word that expresses strong feeling or emotion.

Fear, anger, surprise, and happiness are just some of the emotions expressed by interjections. A comma or an exclamation point always separates an interjection from the rest of the sentence, depending on whether strong or mild feeling is being expressed.

**Wow!** This price is unreasonable. (strong feeling)

**Yes,** I will lend you money. (mild feeling)

## Practice Your Skills

### Identifying Interjections

Write the interjections in the sentences below. If there is no interjection, write *none.*

1. Help! I've been robbed.
2. Whew! It could have been worse.
3. The thief wanted my cash but not my credit cards!
4. No, I did not see his face well enough to identify him if I saw him again.
5. Stop! Don't touch my arm there.
6. The thief hit my arm to make me let go of the cash I was holding.
7. Yes, I was standing in line to pay for my candy and gasoline.
8. Oh! I remember a distinctive ring he wore.
9. Come back!
10. Well, I can sketch the ring as I remember it, and I think you'll be able to use the information to catch the thief.

## Connect to Writing: Revising

### Adding Interjections

You can change the intensity of each sentence below by adding an interjection to it. Write each sentence, adding a correctly punctuated interjection.

1. That was my favorite ring.
2. I have to get it back.
3. Wait a minute.
4. I see something shiny on the floor.
5. The thief must have dropped it as he ran away.

# Parts of Speech Review  Lesson 5

A chameleon can change its color to blend with its surroundings. Many words in English are like chameleons. Such words can become different parts of speech, depending on how they are used.

| | |
|---|---|
| **Noun** | The **last** of the books has arrived. |
| **Verb** | The rare book sale will **last** two more days. |
| **Adjective** | The **last** book to sell was by George Eliot. |
| **Adverb** | Her signed edition of *Silas Marner* sold **last.** |

To determine what part of speech a word is, read the sentence carefully. Then ask yourself, *What is each word doing in this sentence?* The following summary of the eight parts of speech will help you determine how a word is used in a sentence.

**Noun**
Is the word naming a person, place, thing, or idea?

The **friendship** between **Silas Marner** and his **neighbor** lasted for many years.

**Pronoun**
Is the word taking the place of a noun?

**Everything they** said about **him** was true.

**Verb**
Is the word either showing action or linking the subject with another word in the sentence?

I **read** the book. It **was** fascinating.

**Adjective**
Is the word modifying a noun or a pronoun? Does it answer the question *What kind? Which one(s)? How many?* or *How much?*

**That large stone** fireplace was very **cozy.**

**Adverb**
Is the word modifying a verb, an adjective, or an adverb? Does it answer the question *How? When? Where?* or *To what extent?*

Baby Eppie was **rather** curious and found

Marner's fireplace **very quickly.**

| | | |
|---|---|---|
| **Preposition** | Is the word showing a relationship between a noun or a pronoun and another word in the sentence? Is it part of a phrase? | |

**By means of** *her determination,* Molly carried Eppie **through** *the snowstorm.*

| | |
|---|---|
| **Conjunction** | Is the word connecting words or groups of words? |

Molly was **either** unconscious **or** dead, **for** she lay motionless in the snow.

| | |
|---|---|
| **Interjection** | Is the word expressing strong feeling? |

**Wow!** Godfrey Cass is really selfish.

## Practice Your Skills

### Identifying Parts of Speech

Write each underlined word in the following paragraph. Beside each one write its part of speech, using these abbreviations.

| | |
|---|---|
| noun = *n.* | adverb = *adv.* |
| pronoun = *pron.* | preposition = *prep.* |
| verb = *v.* | conjunction = *conj.* |
| adjective = *adj.* | interjection = *interj.* |

*Adam Bede,* considered a masterpiece by some, was written by George Eliot and published in 1859. Today this book is still one of the most widely read Victorian novels. Eliot's purpose in telling this story was to show her readers what ordinary life was like. What does that mean? Well, the setting is not any more colorful or the characters any more heroic than readers of her day were likely to find in their own experiences.

## Connect to Speaking and Writing: Vocabulary Review

### Using the Vocabulary of Grammar

With a partner, review the grammar terms introduced in this chapter. (Hint: Important terms are in purple type.) Then quiz each other on the terms until you have them memorized.

## ✅ *Check Point:* Mixed Practice

Write the underlined word in each sentence. Then beside each word, write its part of speech —*noun, pronoun, verb, adjective, adverb, preposition, conjunction,* or *interjection.*

**1.** Where is the <u>party</u> invitation?

**2.** <u>Both</u> girls had seen it on the counter.

**3.** Jack said to come over <u>this</u> afternoon.

**4.** <u>Well</u>, that's a surprise!

**5.** Turn off that <u>loud</u> music.

**6.** At <u>what</u> time did you arrive?

**7.** The <u>rest</u> of my friends are not here yet.

**8.** Will they <u>party</u> all night?

**9.** <u>Oh</u>! I forgot the paper cups.

**10.** Is this <u>well</u> water?

**11.** <u>What</u> is that?

## ● *Connect to Writing:* Letter

### *Using Prepositions, Conjunctions, and Interjections*

Your guidance counselor has invited each student in your class to write her an informal letter describing the ideal job fair. She is interested in your ideas and reactions to different careers, pay rates, work environments, and so on. Take this opportunity to influence the type of job fair you and the other students are provided, and write an expressive letter describing your ideas, opinions, and feelings. Be prepared to identify each preposition, conjunction, and interjection.

## Assess Your Learning

### ▨ Determining Parts of Speech

Write each underlined word. Then beside each word, write its part of speech using the following abbreviations.

| | | |
|---|---|---|
| noun = *n.* | pronoun = *pron.* | verb = *v.* |
| adjective = *adj.* | adverb = *adv.* | preposition = *prep.* |
| conjunction = *conj.* | | |

Aldous Huxley is <u>primarily</u> remembered <u>today</u> <u>as</u> the <u>author</u> of the frightening <u>science-fiction</u> <u>novel</u> *Brave New World.* Huxley <u>began</u> his <u>career</u> as a student of <u>medicine</u>. <u>Temporarily</u> blinded <u>by</u> a <u>disease</u> that affected <u>his</u> eyes, <u>he</u> was unable to practice medicine. His essays <u>and</u> novels, <u>however,</u> reflect his <u>very</u> strong interest <u>in</u> <u>science</u>. Huxley's novels <u>include</u> *Eyeless in Gaza* <u>and</u> *After Many a Summer Dies the Swan.* The <u>lead</u> character in *After Many a Summer Dies the Swan* is a <u>man</u> obsessed <u>with</u> rejuvenation. He <u>discovers</u> that the <u>man</u> who first experimented with <u>rejuvenation</u> is <u>now</u> a <u>200-year-old</u> <u>ape</u>! *Brave New World* is a <u>treatise</u> that studies the effects <u>of</u> scientific progress run amok. <u>Humans</u> created <u>in</u> bottles are trained to be <u>passive</u>. The <u>title</u>, of course, <u>is</u> a phrase <u>from</u> Shakespeare's *The Tempest.*

### ▨ Determining Parts of Speech

Write the underlined word in each sentence. Then, beside each word, write its part of speech using the following abbreviations.

| | | |
|---|---|---|
| noun = *n.* | pronoun = *pron.* | verb = *v.* |
| adjective = *adj.* | adverb = *adv.* | preposition = *prep.* |
| conjunction = *conj.* | | |

**1.** He walked <u>out</u>.

**2.** <u>These</u> are delicious.

**3.** He writes very <u>well</u>.

**4.** Jane has a new <u>cat</u>.

**5.** He <u>leaves</u> at ten.

**6.** Did you see <u>my</u> hat?

**7.** We <u>can</u> tomatoes.

**8.** Finish your banana <u>split</u>.

**9.** Fill the car with <u>gas</u>.

**10.** <u>Both</u> children slept well.

**11.** The <u>gas</u> heater warmed us.

**12.** <u>Cat</u> fur makes me itch.

**13.** I like <u>these</u> songs.

## Understanding Parts of Speech

Write ten sentences that use the following words as the different parts of speech indicated in the parentheses. Then underline each word and label its use in the sentence.

some (pronoun, adjective)

alarm (verb, noun)

either (pronoun, adjective, conjunction)

down (adverb, preposition, adjective)

## Using Parts of Speech

Write a paragraph in which you use each of the eight parts of speech at least once. Write about one of the following topics or one of your choice: someone whose actions you admire or an author whose work you enjoy. Then underline and label one use of each part of speech.

# The Parts of Speech: Posttest

## Directions

Write the letter of the term that correctly identifies the underlined word in each sentence.

**(1)** The Brontë <u>family</u> produced three novelists: Emily, Charlotte, and Anne. **(2)** Charlotte worked as a teacher and governess, <u>but</u> she wrote verse on the side. **(3)** In 1845, she discovered that <u>her</u> sisters Emily and Anne also wrote poetry. **(4)** The sisters collected their <u>poems</u> in a volume, using the pseudonyms Currer, Ellis, and Acton Bell. **(5)** Neither the poems nor Charlotte's first novel <u>was</u> successful. **(6)** However, in 1847, Charlotte's book *Jane Eyre* became very <u>popular</u>. **(7)** *Wuthering Heights,* Emily's one novel, is considered the Brontës' <u>best</u> work. **(8)** <u>My</u>, it is a passionate and inspired work of fiction! **(9)** Anne, the youngest Brontë, is the <u>least</u> famous of the sisters. **(10)** She published two novels <u>before</u> her death in 1849.

**1. A** adjective
   **B** adverb
   **C** preposition
   **D** noun

**2. A** adjective
   **B** adverb
   **C** preposition
   **D** conjunction

**3. A** preposition
   **B** adverb
   **C** pronoun
   **D** noun

**4. A** noun
   **B** pronoun
   **C** verb
   **D** adverb

**5. A** noun
   **B** pronoun
   **C** verb
   **D** adverb

**6. A** conjunction
   **B** interjection
   **C** preposition
   **D** adjective

**7. A** adjective
   **B** adverb
   **C** preposition
   **D** noun

**8. A** conjunction
   **B** interjection
   **C** preposition
   **D** adjective

**9. A** noun
   **B** pronoun
   **C** verb
   **D** adverb

**10. A** conjunction
   **B** interjection
   **C** preposition
   **D** adjective

# Writer's Corner

## Snapshot

**13 A**　A **noun** is the name of a person, place, thing, or idea. (pages 618–620)
A **pronoun** is a word that takes the place of one or more nouns.
(pages 621–624)

**13 B**　A **verb** is a word that expresses action or a state of being. (pages 625-630)

**13 C**　An **adjective** is a word that modifies a noun or pronoun. (pages 631–635)
An **adverb** is a word that modifies a verb, an adjective, or another verb.
(pages 635–638)

**13 D**　A **preposition** shows the relationship between a noun or a pronoun and
another word in the sentence. (pages 639–641) A **conjunction** connects
words or groups of words. (pages 641–642) An **interjection** is a word that
expresses strong feeling or emotion. (page 643)

## Power Rules

 Use standard ways to form **possessive nouns.** Add an *'s* to singular nouns and
plural nouns that don't end in an *s*. Add only an apostrophe to plural nouns
ending in an *s*.  (pages 964–966)

| **Before Editing** | **After Editing** |
| --- | --- |
| I love the *team* new uniforms. | I love the *team's* new uniforms. |
| The *players's* excitement was obvious. | The *players'* excitement was obvious. |

 Use **subject forms of pronouns** in subject position. Use the **object form** when
the pronoun is a direct object, indirect object, or object of a preposition.
(pages 790–801)

| **Before Editing** | **After Editing** |
| --- | --- |
| *Her* and Kylie went to the mall. | *She* and Kylie went to the mall. |
| Juan and *him* met the girls at the mall. | Juan and *he* met the girls at the mall. |
| They wanted to meet with you and *I*. | They wanted to meet with you and *me*. |

## Editing Checklist ✔

Use this checklist when editing your writing.

✓ Did I capitalize proper nouns? Did I use precise and colorful nouns to help my readers visualize the action? (See pages 618–620.)

✓ Did I use pronouns to add fluency to my writing? (See pages 621–624.)

✓ Did I use action verbs to make my writing more lively? (See pages 625–626.)

✓ Did I use adjectives and adverbs to make my sentences more vivid and exact? (See pages 631–638.)

✓ Did I use prepositions and prepositional phrases to show relationships? (See pages 639–641.)

✓ Did I use conjunctions correctly to connect words or groups of words? (See pages 641–642.)

✓ Did I use interjections when appropriate to express strong feelings or emotions? (See page 643.)

## Use the Power ⚡

**Nouns and verbs** are the building blocks of sentences. Using descriptive nouns and powerful verbs will go a long way to making your writing memorable. Adding adjectives and adverbs will help create vivid imagery.

| Plain | Descriptive |
|-------|-------------|
| The raccoon opened the garbage can and ate our table scraps. | The hungry raccoon deftly levered the lid off the garbage can and picked through our table scraps as if he owned the place. |

**Revise** a recent composition by replacing plain nouns with more descriptive nouns and dull verbs with verbs that tell a story.

# The Sentence Base

**How can you use sentences to paint powerful images and tell interesting stories?**

## The Sentence Base: Pretest 1

The following draft of advice on writing college admission essays is hard to read because it contains several errors involving sentence structure. Revise the paragraph so that it reads correctly. The first error has been corrected as an example.

Two important things. ~~They~~ will help you write a strong college admission essay. First, realize that one or several admissions officers. Dedicated, overworked, experienced. Will read your essay. Sentence fragments, poor grammar, and spelling errors. These will destine an essay for the rejection stack. Second, each reader will look for a connection with you through the essay. You can make this connection. By keeping the focus of the essay on the most important topic—you. For example, if you were writing about "An Event That Changed My Life," which do you think is a better statement: "My parents divorced when I was ten. And they spent the next seven years fighting over the house, the furniture, and me" or "I was ten when my parents divorced. And I quickly learned. Responsibility, self-discipline, and dedication"? Is the better sentence. Focuses on the positive qualities in you. Will help make you a successful college student.

# The Sentence Base: Pretest 2

## Directions

Write the letter of the term that correctly identifies the underlined word or words in each sentence.

*The New Yorker* was founded by Harold Ross. **(1)** Among the early contributors to the magazine were <u>Dorothy Parker and E. B. White.</u> **(2)** *The New Yorker* <u>specializes</u> in short fiction, essays, and cartoons. **(3)** After Harold Ross's death, <u>William Shawn</u> became the editor. **(4)** The magazine sometimes <u>carries</u> entire books in installments. **(5)** You <u>should look at a copy someday.</u> **(6)** <u>Ogden Nash</u> and <u>S. J. Perelman</u> contributed to the magazine's reputation for humor. **(7)** Nash <u>wrote</u> light satirical verse and <u>served</u> as an editor for many years. **(8)** His collections of verse include *Everyone But Thee and Me* and *Bed Riddance*. **(9)** East Coast intellectuals were <u>targets</u> of Nash's wit. **(10)** Perelman often used dreadful <u>puns</u> in his satires.

1. A simple subject
   B simple predicate
   C complete subject
   D complete predicate

2. A simple subject
   B simple predicate
   C complete subject
   D complete predicate

3. A simple subject
   B simple predicate
   C compound subject
   D complete predicate

4. A simple subject
   B simple predicate
   C complete subject
   D complete predicate

5. A simple subject
   B simple predicate
   C complete subject
   D complete predicate

6. A compound subject
   B compound verb
   C compound direct object
   D compound predicate nominative

7. A compound subject
   B compound verb
   C compound direct object
   D compound predicate nominative

8. A compound subject
   B compound verb
   C compound direct object
   D compound predicate nominative

9. A direct object
   B indirect object
   C predicate nominative
   D predicate adjective

10. A direct object
    B indirect object
    C predicate nominative
    D predicate adjective

A well-constructed house has a foundation, which holds all the other parts of the house together. Like a house a sentence must also have a foundation. The foundation, or base, of a sentence is composed of a subject, a predicate (verb), and sometimes a complement. All other words in the sentence are added to this foundation.

**14 A**    A **sentence** is a group of words that expresses a complete thought.

A group of words that does not express a complete thought is called a **fragment.** In many cases a group of words is a fragment because it does not have a subject or a predicate.

| Fragment | Sentence |
|---|---|
| Is under the briefcase. | **The script** is under the briefcase. |
| The characters. | The characters **seem real.** |
| Is designing the set. | **Mike** is designing the set. |
| Auditioned for the part. | **She** auditioned for the part. |

To express a complete thought, a group of words must have both a subject and a predicate.

**14 A.1**    A **subject** names the person, place, thing, or idea the sentence is about. The **predicate** tells something about the subject.

| Complete Subject | Complete Predicate |
|---|---|
| My aunt from Alabama | is performing in *Hamlet.* |
| The box on the counter | contains costumes for the actors. |
| The audience | clapped for ten minutes today. |
| The final cast member | took a bow. |

*You can learn more about sentence fragments later in this chapter on pages 661–663.*

## ➤ Simple Subjects and Predicates

**14 A.2**    A **simple subject** is the main word in the complete subject. A **simple predicate,** or **verb,** is the main word or phrase in the complete predicate.

Each complete subject and predicate can be narrowed down to a single word or phrase. In the following examples, the simple subjects and the verbs are in **bold** type.

┌──────complete subject──────┐ ┌─complete predicate─┐
The narrow wooden **stage curved** to the right.

┌─complete subject─┐ ┌──────complete predicate──────┐
Two **reviews** recently **appeared** in the *Chronicle*.

┌──────complete subject──────┐ ┌──────complete predicate──────┐
The **New Globe** in Acton **is raising** money for new seats.

In the last example, *New Globe* is a single proper noun; therefore, both words make up the simple subject. Notice also that the verb phrase *is raising* is considered the verb of the sentence.

Throughout the rest of this book, the term *subject* will refer to a simple subject, and the term *verb* will refer to a simple predicate, which may be a single verb or a verb phrase.

*You can learn more about using verbs on pages 748–787 and about subject-verb agreement on pages 826–853.*

## Finding Subjects and Verbs

To find the subject of an action verb, ask yourself *Who?* or *What?* before the verb. The answer to either question will be the subject of the sentence. In the following examples, each subject is underlined once, and each verb is underlined twice.

Mandy has taken drama classes for two years. (The action verb is *has taken*. Who has taken? The subject is *Mandy*.)

His performance is improving rapidly. (The action verb is *is improving*. What is improving? The subject is *performance*.)

To find the subject of a linking verb, ask yourself, *About whom or what is the statement being made?* When you have answered that question, you will have identified the subject.

My brother is a stagehand at a dinner theater. (The linking verb is *is*. About whom is the statement being made? The subject is *brother*.)

The stage curtains feel exceptionally heavy. (The linking verb is *feel*. About what is the statement being made? The subject is *curtains*.)

*You can learn more about linking verbs on pages 628–630.*

When you look for a subject and a verb, it is often helpful to eliminate all modifiers and all prepositional phrases from the sentence. Remember: *A subject is never part of a prepositional phrase.*

> ~~Numerous~~ masterpieces ~~by Shakespeare~~ are performed ~~throughout England.~~
> (*Masterpieces* is the subject; *are performed* is the verb.)
> ~~His~~ plays can ~~still~~ be seen ~~at the reconstructed Globe Theatre in London.~~
> (*Plays* is the subject; *can be seen* is the verb.)

*You can learn more about modifiers on pages 631–638 and 854–873 and prepositional phrases on pages 639–641 and 684–690.*

● **Practice Your Skills**

### Identifying Subjects and Verbs

Write the subject and the verb in each sentence.

**(1)** William Shakespeare lived from 1564 to 1616. **(2)** At his death this famous playwright left a most unusual will. **(3)** Considerable real-estate holdings in and near Stratford went to his two daughters, Susanna and Judith. **(4)** Shakespeare did, however, make some curious bequests. **(5)** The following line from his will is still confusing many historians. **(6)** "I give unto my Wiffe my 2nd-best bed with the furniture." **(7)** He apparently had just scribbled these words into the will as an additional note. **(8)** His will never mentions his plays. **(9)** This omission has raised serious doubts in some historians' minds. **(10)** The writer of this may not have been the author of the Elizabethan dramas.

## Different Positions of Subjects

When a sentence is in its **natural order,** the subject comes before the verb. For various reasons a sentence may also be written in **inverted order,** with the verb or part of the verb phrase coming before the subject. Subjects in sentences in inverted order are sometimes difficult to find.

**Questions** are often phrased in inverted order. To find the subject and the verb in a question, turn the question around to make a statement.

> **Question**      Have <u>you</u> <u>seen</u> my model of the inner ear?
> **Statement**      <u>You</u> <u>have seen</u> my model of the inner ear.

***There* and *here*** begin sentences that are in inverted order. To find the subject and the verb, place the words in the sentence in their natural order. Sometimes the word *there* or *here* must be dropped before the sentence can be put in its natural order.

**Inverted Order**     Here is your inner-ear model.

**Natural Order**     Your inner-ear model is here.

**Inverted Order**     There will be a test given on the ear.

**Natural Order**     A test will be given on the ear. (Drop *there.*)

**Emphasis and variety** are other reasons for inverted sentences. To create emphasis or variety, you may sometimes deliberately write a sentence in inverted order. To determine the subject and the verb, put the sentence in its natural order.

**Inverted Order**     Throughout the body are innumerable muscle fibers.

**Natural Order**     Innumerable muscle fibers are throughout the body.

**Inverted Order**     Across the gym lay the muscle-building equipment.

**Natural Order**     The muscle-building equipment lay across the gym.

**Understood *you*** is the subject of most commands and requests. Although *you* seldom appears in such sentences, it is still understood to be there. In the following examples, *you* is the understood subject of each sentence.

Smell this fragrant lotion!

(*You* is the understood subject.)

Cathy, breathe deeply.

(*You* is the understood subject even though the person receiving the command is named.)

*You can learn more about subject-verb agreement and inverted order on pages 838–839.*

● **Practice Your Skills**

*Identifying Subjects and Verbs*

Write the subject and the verb in each sentence. If the subject is an understood *you*, write *you* in parentheses.

**1.** Listen to this fascinating information!

**2.** Within the skull is the average three-pound human brain.

**3.** Here is the detailed diagram of the respiratory system.

**4.** Have you studied the respiratory system yet?

**5.** There are millions of tiny air sacs in the lungs.

**6.** Think of this fact at your next mealtime.

**7.** In the food on the table is your supply of vitamins and minerals.

**8.** There are 9,000 taste buds on a person's tongue.

**9.** With increased age comes an inability to hear fewer high-pitched sounds.

**10.** How does the circulatory system transport 680,000 gallons of blood a year?

● *Connect to Writing:* **Drafting**

*Writing Sentences in Inverted Order*

Write two sentences for each type of inverted order sentence: *Questions, There and Here, Emphasis or Variety,* and *Understood You.* Then underline the subjects and circle the verbs.

# ➤ Compound Subjects and Verbs

A sentence can have more than one subject and more than one verb. You can ask yourself the same questions to find compound subjects and verbs as you did to find simple subjects and verbs.

**14 A.3** A **compound subject** is two or more subjects in one sentence that have the same verb and are joined by a conjunction.

The rings and bracelets disappeared suddenly.

Maria, Barry, and Martin searched for the jewels.

**14 A.4** A **compound verb** is two or more verbs that have the same subject and are joined by a conjunction.

You can join the treasure hunt or stay in the cabin.

This map will assist our search and will guarantee success.

A sentence can have both a compound subject and a compound verb.

Paul and his sister had the jewelry and buried it deeply.

Maria and Barry received a treasure map and immediately organized a search party.

*You can find out more about conjunctions on pages 641-642. You can learn about subject-verb agreement with compound subjects on pages 834–836.*

## ● Practice Your Skills

### *Identifying Compound Subjects and Verbs*

Write the subjects and the verbs in the following sentences.

**(1)** Gold and silver in the *Atocha's* hold lay on the bottom of the sea and tempted treasure hunters for centuries. **(2)** In 1622, the ship was bound for Spain but sank in the waters off the Florida coast during a hurricane. **(3)** Because of a second hurricane, other vessels could not rescue the *Atocha's* treasure. **(4)** The position of the ship either was not recorded or was forgotten. **(5)** Eventually, ocean currents covered the ship with sand and hid it from searchers. **(6)** The legend of the *Atocha* and the promise of great wealth brought many treasure hunters to Florida. **(7)** Mel Fisher and his family joined the others and became full-time treasure hunters. **(8)** Mel had once run a chicken farm and then had operated a diving shop. **(9)** He not only had some original ideas about the possible location of the ship but also used clever techniques in the search. **(10)** Both Mel and his family continued their search in the face of many hardships and much scorn.

*Brainstorming for Ideas*

Read the following paragraph to find out what eventually happened to the *Atocha's* treasure. Underline each subject once and each verb twice. Using these subjects and verbs for ideas, brainstorm and list additional subjects and verbs that relate to treasure-hunting. Be sure to include plenty of compound subjects and verbs.

**(1)** Critics constantly laughed at the efforts of the Fishers. **(2)** Finally, in June 1975, Fisher's crew found a cannon from the *Atocha* and silenced the critics. **(3)** The joy of the Fisher party was intense yet brief. **(4)** On the night of July 18, 1975, Fisher's son, his daughter-in-law, and another diver drowned. **(5)** Neither Mel nor his wife stopped work on the project. **(6)** The tragedies would then have been meaningless. **(7)** The two continued and salvaged more and more objects. **(8)** They could not keep all of the treasure. **(9)** The state of Florida claimed a portion of the treasure and held much of it for a long period of time.

## ✔ *Check Point:* **Mixed Practice**

Make two columns. Label one column *Subjects* and the other *Verbs*. Then write the subjects and verbs in each sentence under the appropriate heading.

1. Jamaica is a lush, green island in the Caribbean Sea.
2. There is sparkling clear water surrounding this popular vacation destination.
3. Deep-sea divers and eager swimmers rent boats and buy snorkeling equipment for water recreation.
4. Have you seen the beautiful coral reefs off the coast of Jamaica?
5. Just below the calm surface of the sea grows living coral.
6. Wear a scuba mask for the best view of the coral.
7. Trisha, Jerry, and Ling saw a baby octopus and accidentally frightened it away.
8. Tomorrow I will windsurf, shop, and sunbathe until nightfall.
9. Here are the picture postcards and small souvenirs from our shopping trip.
10. In the early morning hours, enjoy your breakfast and then meet me at the beach for a swim.

# Sentence Fragments — Lesson 2

**14 B**　A **sentence fragment** is a group of words that does not express a complete thought.

To communicate clearly and completely when you write, be sure to check your work for sentence fragments.

**Fragments due to incomplete thoughts** are a common kind of fragment. A fragment that expresses an incomplete thought is often missing a subject or a verb.

| | |
|---|---|
| **Fragment** | Applied to five different colleges. |
| **Corrected** | Jackie applied to five different colleges. <br> (*Jackie* is the subject.) |
| **Fragment** | All of my friends in homeroom. |
| **Corrected** | All of my friends in homeroom graduated. <br> (*Graduated* is the verb.) |

**Fragments due to incorrect punctuation** are another kind of fragment. If you place a period between the parts of a compound verb, you create a fragment. Likewise, if you place a period before a list of items, you create a fragment.

| | |
|---|---|
| **Fragment** | Martin rewrote his application essay five times. And made it stronger each time. |
| **Corrected** | Martin rewrote his application essay five times and made it stronger each time. <br> (*Rewrote* and *made* form a compound verb.) |
| **Fragment** | Sarah consulted many sources for advice. Books, teachers, relatives, and friends. |
| **Corrected** | Sarah consulted many sources for advice: books, teachers, relatives, and friends. <br> (A colon precedes the list of sources.) |

*You can find out about other kinds of sentence fragments on pages 705–706 and 734–735.*

# Ways to Correct Sentence Fragments

You can correct a fragment in one of two ways. You can add words to it to make a complete sentence, or you can attach it to the sentence next to it. Sometimes when you attach a fragment to a sentence next to it, you may have to add or drop words.

| | |
|---|---|
| **Fragment** | Asked her guidance counselor for direction. |
| **Add Words** | Katia asked her guidance counselor for direction. (Who asked for direction? Words are added to complete the sentence.) |
| **Fragment Following a Sentence** | Leon wanted an academic scholarship. Studied diligently all year. |
| **Attach to Previous Sentence** | Leon wanted an academic scholarship and studied diligently all year. (The conjunction *and* is added to connect the fragment to the sentence before it.) |
| **Fragment Preceding a Sentence** | Good grades, social skills, and academic potential. These are all important to the application committee. |
| **Attach to Following Sentence** | Good grades, social skills, and academic potential are all important to the application committee. (*Grades, skills,* and *potential* form a compound subject for the verb *are.*) |

## When You Write

Writers of fiction use sentence fragments to make written dialogue sound more realistic. They know that in daily life, few people speak in complete sentences all the time. Poets often use fragments to focus readers' attention on the thought or idea expressed by the fragment rather than on a complete thought. All formal writing, however, requires complete sentences. An essay, business report, or formal letter free of sentence fragments is the sign of an educated writer. Review a recent piece of formal writing and edit out any sentence fragments you find.

### Identifying Sentence Fragments

Write *F* if the item or part of the item is a sentence fragment. Write *S* if everything in the item is a sentence. Then correct each sentence fragment.

**1.** The most important preparation for college admission. Begins long before you fill out the application.

**2.** Do homework and take thorough notes. In every class.

**3.** Most college freshmen. They wish they had taken high school more seriously.

**4.** Don't forget the value of exercise and sleep.

**5.** Community involvement.

## Power Your Writing: Fluency

Varying the length and structure of your sentences will make your paragraphs flow invitingly. Read the concluding paragraph of "Say It with Flowers," a short story by Toshio Mori, and consider what contributes to its variety and flow:

> On the way out, Teruo remembered our presence. He looked back. "Good-bye, Good luck," he said cheerfully to Tommy and me. He walked out of the shop with his shoulders straight, head high, and whistling. He did not come back to see us again.

You could probably tell that this passage includes sentences of varied lengths. In addition, it has sentences with different structures. The first sentence, for example, begins with an adverbial phrase; the second begins with the subject; the third begins with some dialogue; and the last two begin with the subject.

Look back at one of your own compositions to be sure your writing has fluency.

● *Connect to Writing:* **College Admissions Essay**

### Writing Complete Sentences

The director of admissions of your college of choice has requested that you send a writing sample. Write a short college admission essay about an event that changed your life. Then team up with a writing partner to check for sentence fragments in essays. Help each other correct any fragments you find.

# Complements  Lesson 3

Sometimes a sentence needs more than a subject and a verb to sound complete.

**14 C**  A **complement** is a word or group of words that completes the meaning of a subject or verb.

None of the following sentences, for example, would be complete without the complements in **bold** type.

> Todd wrapped the **gift.**
>
> Dan gave **me flowers.**
>
> Kate has become an **expert** on customs.
>
> The stores are **open.**

There are five kinds of complements. **Direct objects, indirect objects,** and **objective complements** complete the meaning of action verbs. **Predicate nominatives** and **predicate adjectives,** which are called **subject complements,** complete the meaning of linking verbs.

## ➤ Direct Objects and Indirect Objects

**14 C.1**  A **direct object** is a noun or a pronoun that receives the action of the verb.

To find a direct object, ask yourself *What?* or *Whom?* after an action verb. Notice in the third example below that a direct object can be compound.

>          d.o.
> Leo removed the **packages** from his briefcase. (Leo removed what? *Packages* is the direct object.)
>     d.o.
> I drove **Heather** to the airport. (I drove whom? *Heather* is the direct object.)
>       d.o.        d.o.
> Heather will visit **associates** and **clients** in Japan. (Heather will visit whom? *Associates* and *clients* make up the compound direct object.)

Each part of a compound action verb can have its own direct object.

> $\overset{\text{d.o.}}{}$ $\overset{\text{d.o.}}{}$
> Heather focused her **camera** and snapped the **picture.** (*Camera* is the direct
> object of *focused*, and *picture* is the direct object of *snapped*.)

*You can learn more about action verbs and transitive verbs on pages 625–626 and 777.*

**14 C.2**    An **indirect object** is a noun or a pronoun that answers the question *To or for whom?* or *To or for what?* after an action verb.

If a sentence has a direct object, the same sentence may also have an indirect object. To find an indirect object, first find the direct object by asking *What?* or *Whom?* after the action verb. Then ask *To or for whom?* or *To or for what?* after the direct object. An indirect object always comes before a direct object in a sentence.

> $\overset{\text{i.o.}}{}$ $\overset{\text{d.o.}}{}$
> I bought **Paul** a new catcher's mitt.
> (*Mitt* is the direct object of the verb *bought*. I bought a mitt for whom? *Paul* is
> the indirect object. Notice that the indirect object comes before the direct object.)
> $\overset{\text{i.o.}}{}$ $\overset{\text{d.o.}}{}$
> The students gave **Mr. Beacon** tokens of appreciation.
> (*Tokens* is the direct object of the verb *gave*. The students gave tokens to whom?
> *Mr. Beacon* is the indirect object.)

An indirect object may be compound.

> $\overset{\text{i.o.}}{}$ $\overset{\text{i.o.}}{}$ $\overset{\text{d.o.}}{}$
> Sashina Chi is teaching **Lee** and **Kelly** Japanese.
> (*Japanese* is the direct object of the verb *is teaching*. Sashina Chi is teaching
> Japanese *to whom?* *Lee* and *Kelly* make up the compound indirect object.)

Remember that neither a direct object nor an indirect object is ever part of a prepositional phrase.

> $\overset{\text{i.o.}}{}$ $\overset{\text{d.o.}}{}$
> We gave **Roger** an album for his birthday.
> (*Roger* is the indirect object. It comes before the direct object *album* and is not
> part of a prepositional phrase.)

d.o.

We gave an album to Roger for his birthday.

(In this sentence *Roger* is not the indirect object because it follows the direct object *album* and is the object of the preposition *to*.)

*You can learn more about prepositional phrases on pages 639–641 and 684–690.*

## ● Practice Your Skills

### *Identifying Direct and Indirect Objects*

Write the direct and indirect objects in the following sentences. Then beside each one state whether it is a direct object (*d.o.*) or an indirect object (*i.o.*).

**(1)** My Japanese friend Keiko shipped me a collection of herbal teas. **(2)** Last month I gave her a tea service for her birthday. **(3)** Later Keiko recommended a book about gifts to me. **(4)** I read the book with great interest. **(5)** I learned several facts about gift customs in Japanese culture. **(6)** During the year-end gift-giving season, called *O-seibo,* employers treat employees and clients lavishly. **(7)** Department stores stock special sections of appropriate gift items and wrappings. **(8)** Friends, relatives, students, and teachers surprise others with gourmet candy, cookies, and other treats. **(9)** They sometimes send overseas friends souvenir stamps, small pins, or fancy soaps. **(10)** Visitors to Japan should learn the customs about gifts.

# ➤ Objective Complements

**14 C.3**  An **objective complement** is a noun or an adjective that renames or describes the direct object.

To find an objective complement, first find the direct object. Then ask the question *What?* after the direct object. An objective complement will always follow the direct object. Notice the compound objective complement in the third example.

Chin-yau declared the gift **perfect.** (*Gift* is the direct object. Chin-yau declared the gift what? *Perfect* is the objective complement. It follows the direct object and describes it.)

The Chinese consider red a joyful **color** for gift wrap. (*Red* is the direct object. The Chinese consider red what? *Color* is the objective complement. It follows the direct object and renames it.)

The award made Ming **happy** and **proud.** (*Ming* is the direct object. The award made Ming what? The words *happy* and *proud* make up the compound objective complement. These words follow the direct object and describe it.)

## ● Practice Your Skills

### Identifying Complements

Write the complements in the following sentences. Beside each one, write whether it is a *direct object* (*d.o.*), *indirect object* (*i.o.*), or *objective complement* (*o.c.*).

**(1)** The right bouquet will make the recipient happy and appreciative. **(2)** The Spanish consider chrysanthemums a flower of sadness. **(3)** This flower forms floral arrangements for funerals. **(4)** Don't give your girlfriend a chrysanthemum arrangement in Spain. **(5)** In France yellow flowers symbolize infidelity. **(6)** Mexicans use yellow flowers in their "Day of the Dead" events. **(7)** In either country, give loved ones bouquets of flowers in a different color. **(8)** The Japanese comfort the ill with flowers and use flowers at times of death. **(9)** The Japanese also give a future spouse flowers during courtship. **(10)** Like the Spanish, the Japanese use yellow chrysanthemums for funerals.

## ● *Connect to Writing:* Prewriting

### Freewriting for Ideas

You are a member of the committee that organizes activities for International Student Celebration Week. You will not only advise the committee on international gift etiquette, but you will write a feature article on the topic for a small booklet the committee will distribute. To develop ideas for your article, freewrite for ten minutes on anything that comes to mind regarding gifts and etiquette. Then underline and label the complements: *direct object* (d.o.), *indirect object* (i.o.), and *objective complement* (o.c.).

## ➤ Subject Complements

Two kinds of complements, called **subject complements,** complete the meaning of linking verbs.

**14 C.4**  A **predicate nominative** is a noun or a pronoun that follows a linking verb and identifies, renames, or explains the subject.

To find a predicate nominative, first find the subject and the linking verb. Then find the noun or the pronoun that follows the verb and identifies, renames, or explains the subject. Notice in the second example that a predicate nominative can be compound.

p.n.

Bart will become an art **teacher.** (*teacher = Bart*)

p.n.　　p.n.

The winners of the art scholarships are **Bryan** and **Julie.**

(*Bryan* and *Julie = winners*)

p.n.

David was a visiting art **scholar.** (*scholar = David*)

Like other complements, a predicate nominative is never part of a prepositional phrase.

p.n.

Pamela is **one** of the artists at the Colorado Artists' Colony.

(*One* is the predicate nominative. *Artists* is the object of the preposition *of.*)

p.n.

Jeff and Luis were a **couple** of the sculptors there.

(*Couple* is the predicate nominative. *Sculptors* is the object of the preposition *of.*)

## When You Speak

Often when someone asks you a question beginning with *Who is,* he or she wants a predicate nominative for an answer.

"Who is that man?"
"He is the **photographer.**"
"Who is your favorite cartoonist?"
"Scott Adams is my favorite **cartoonist.**

The other subject complement is a predicate adjective.

**14 C.5**   A **predicate adjective** is an adjective that follows a linking verb and modifies the subject.

To find a predicate adjective, first find the subject and the linking verb. Then find an adjective that follows the verb and modifies, or describes, the subject. Notice in the third example that a predicate adjective can be compound.

> p.a.
> That painting was **impressionistic.** (*Impressionistic* describes the subject: *the impressionistic painting.*)
>
> p.a.
> The colors were **vivid.** (*Vivid* describes the subject: *the vivid colors.*)
>
> p.a.        p.a.
> The paints looked **dry** and **lumpy.** (*Dry* and *lumpy* describe the subject: *dry, lumpy paints.*)

Remember that a predicate adjective follows a linking verb and modifies, or describes, the subject. Do not confuse a predicate adjective with a regular adjective.

**Predicate Adjective**   Carlos is **brilliant.** (*Brilliant* describes the subject *Carlos.*)

**Regular Adjective**   Carlos is a **brilliant** sculptor. (*Brilliant* describes the word *sculptor.*)

*You can review lists of linking verbs on page 628–629.*

## ● Practice Your Skills

### Identifying Subject Complements

Write the subject complement in each sentence. Beside it, label it *p.n.* for predicate nominative or *p.a.* for predicate adjective.

**1.** Shelby has become a cartoonist.

**2.** My favorite colors have always been blue and purple.

**3.** *Hue* is another word for *color* or *shade.*

**4.** The silver sequins felt too brittle and fragile.

**5.** My brother is a senior at the Savannah College of Art and Design in Georgia.

**6.** The art museum in my hometown has grown old and drafty.

**7.** After graduation my sister became a graphic artist for a local publisher.

**8.** Woodcarving is a forgotten art form.

**9.** This color scheme seems progressive.

**10.** The foreground appears bright, and the background seems shadowy.

## ✓ *Check Point:* Mixed Practice

Write each complement. Then label each one using the following abbreviations:

direct object = *d.o.*          predicate nominative = *p.n.*
indirect object = *i.o.*        predicate adjective = *p.a.*
objective complement = *o.c.*

1. Mr. Williams gave the class a list of fiction genres.
2. I consider the western a boring category of fiction.
3. I read approximately three mystery novels every month.
4. Two best-selling mystery novelists are Patricia Cornwell and Sue Grafton.
5. The category of science fiction is amazing and exciting.
6. My friend declared Toni Morrison her favorite author of all time.
7. Many bookstores devote special shelves, large posters, and special sales to popular books.
8. Several of my classmates are eager readers and devoted fans of Larry McMurtry's intricate novels about the Southwest.
9. Well-informed bookstore employees show patrons the current favorites in each section of the store.
10. Regular customers often buy themselves a new book and a cup of coffee on the weekend.

## ● *Connect to Speaking and Writing:* Vocabulary Review

### *Using the Vocabulary of Grammar*

With a partner, review the grammar terms introduced in this chapter. (Hint: Important terms are in purple type.) Then quiz each other on the terms until you have them memorized.

# Using Sentence Patterns

Each sentence you write seems unique—like the patterns and shapes of snowflakes. Looking more closely at the sentences you write, however, you will see that each falls into one of six basic sentence patterns. You can vary your writing style by expanding these basic sentence patterns. They can be expanded by adding modifiers or by making the subject, the verb, or any of the complements compound. In this way you create many variations within a particular pattern itself.

**Pattern 1:**   **S-V** (subject-verb)

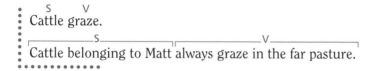

**Pattern 2:**   **S-V-O** (subject-verb-direct object)

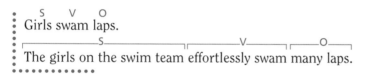

**Pattern 3:**   **S-V-I-O** (subject-verb-indirect object-direct object)

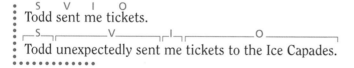

**Pattern 4:**   **S-V-N** (subject-verb-predicate nominative)

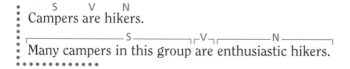

**Pattern 5:** **S-V-A** (subject-verb-predicate adjective)

```
           S      V      A
        Spectators grew restless.
    ┌──────────S──────────┐┌────V────┐┌────A────┐
    The eager spectators suddenly grew very restless.
```

**Pattern 6:** **S-V-O-C** (subject-verb-direct object-objective complement)

```
           S       V     O      C
        Everyone considers Roy trustworthy.
    ┌──────────S──────────┐┌──V──┐┌O┐┌────────C────────┐
    Everyone in my school considers Roy absolutely trustworthy.
```

## ● Practice Your Skills

### *Identifying Sentence Patterns*

Write the sentence pattern for each of the five following sentences.

**1.** Freshly cut hay always smells clean and sweet.

**2.** Many historians consider Harriet Tubman a major personality in United States history.

**3.** The coach of the field hockey team gave each member a certificate of achievement.

**4.** Fallen meteors have been discovered by scientists in various parts of the world.

**5.** The correct answer to the question is the last one.

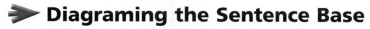

### Diagraming the Sentence Base

A **diagram** is a picture of words. By placing the words of a sentence in a diagram, you can often see the relationship between the parts of a sentence more clearly.

**Subjects and Verbs**  All diagrams begin with a baseline. The subject and the verb go on the baseline but are separated by a vertical line. Capital letters are included in a diagram, but punctuation is not. Notice in the second diagram that compound subjects and verbs are placed on parallel lines. The conjunction joining the subjects or the verbs is placed on a broken line between them.

He is working.

| He | is working |
|---|---|

Lupe and Carl both sang and danced.

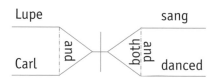

**Inverted Order and Understood Subjects**  An inverted sentence is diagramed like a sentence in natural order. The understood subject *you* is diagramed in the subject position with parentheses around it.

Have you eaten?

| you | Have eaten |
|---|---|

Listen!

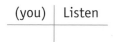

**Adjectives and Adverbs** Adjectives and adverbs are connected by a slanted line to the words they modify. Notice that a conjunction joining two modifiers is placed on a broken line between them. Notice, too, how an adverb that describes another adverb is written parallel to the word it modifies.

Her small but valuable diamond sparkles quite brilliantly.

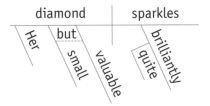

**Note:** Possessive pronouns before nouns, such as *Her* in the example above, are diagramed like adjectives.

## ➤ Complements

All complements except the indirect object are diagramed on the baseline with the subject and the verb.

**Direct Objects** A short vertical line separates a direct object from the verb. Notice in the second example that the parts of a compound direct object are placed on parallel lines. The conjunction is placed on a broken line.

I have already seen that movie.

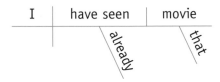

Buy four oranges and six bananas.

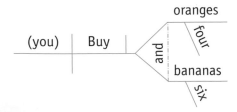

**Indirect Objects** An indirect object is diagramed on a horizontal line that is connected to the verb by a slanted line. Notice in the second example that the parts of a compound indirect object are diagramed on horizontal parallel lines. The conjunction is placed on a broken line between them.

Send them an invitation.

Aunt May bought David and me identical sweaters.

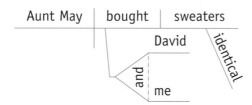

**Objective Complements** Since an objective complement renames or describes the direct object, it is placed to the right of the direct object on the baseline. A slanted line that points toward the direct object separates the two complements. Notice in the second example that a compound objective complement is placed on horizontal parallel lines. The conjunction is placed on a broken line between them.

We named our dog King.

Mom will paint the kitchen yellow or green.

**Subject Complements** A predicate nominative and a predicate adjective are diagramed in exactly the same way. They are placed on the baseline after the verb. A slanted line that points back toward the subject separates a subject complement from the verb. Notice in the second example that a compound subject complement is placed on horizontal parallel lines. The conjunction is placed on a broken line between them.

This camera was a birthday present.

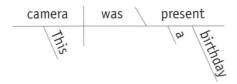

This lecture was not only interesting but also informative.

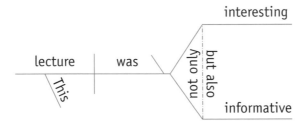

## Practice Your Skills

### *Diagraming Sentences*

Diagram the following sentences or copy them. If you copy them, draw one line under each subject and two lines under each verb. Then label each complement using the following abbreviations.

direct object = *d.o.*                predicate nominative = *p.n.*
indirect object = *i.o.*              predicate adjective = *p.a.*
objective complement = *o.c.*

**1.** Would you be an astronaut?
**2.** The first American astronauts were Abe and Miss Baker.
**3.** These very brave astronauts were monkeys!
**4.** They gave scientists important information.
**5.** Space travel could be safe and reliable.
**6.** The space shuttle has been a really huge success.
**7.** NASA named the first shuttle *Columbia*.
**8.** Shuttles quite often carry many astronauts and large cargo.
**9.** Astronauts now successfully repair satellites.
**10.** Tell us more.

## Assess Your Learning

### Finding Subjects and Verbs

Write the subjects and verbs in the following sentences. If the subject is an understood *you,* write *you* in parentheses.

1. The giant tortoise of the Galápagos Islands may weigh as much as 500 pounds and may live up to 150 years.
2. Here are the balloons and streamers for Leah's birthday party.
3. Did you contact the Better Business Bureau about the problem with your new television set?
4. Most people remember Paul Revere's patriotism but forget his work as a silversmith and engraver.
5. Over the horizon that August day sailed the ships of Columbus's small fleet.
6. Revise your report carefully.
7. There are many inlets and bays along the coast of Nova Scotia.
8. There are more than 200 CDs of classical and popular music in the cabinet.
9. Have you seen the exciting new computers on sale?
10. Brad, take these shirts back to the store for a refund.
11. There is no living descendant of William Shakespeare.
12. Hasn't he answered your letter yet?
13. American Indians do not pay taxes on their land.

### Finding Complements

Write each complement. Then label each one, using the following abbreviations:

direct object = *d.o.*        predicate nominative = *p.n.*
indirect object = *i.o.*        predicate adjective = *p.a.*
objective complement = *o.c.*

1. The Puritans considered buttons a sign of vanity.
2. At first the old trunk in the basement appeared empty.
3. Michelle showed Mom a copy of the yearbook.

**4.** Many early American settlers found the Indians friendly and helpful.

**5.** In Williamsburg, Virginia, we visited several old shops.

**6.** Their grandfather clock is quite old and very valuable.

**7.** James Monroe was the fourth president from Virginia.

**8.** Tell Alma and James that funny story about your uncle.

**9.** From the top of Mount Irazu in Costa Rica, a person can see the Atlantic Ocean and the Pacific Ocean.

**10.** Centuries ago a collection of books was a sign of wealth.

### ■ Using the Sentence Base

Write five sentences that follow the directions below. (The sentences may come in any order.) Write about this topic or a topic of your choice: a trip back in time to a historic event.

Write a sentence that . . .

    **1.** includes a direct object.

    **2.** includes an indirect object.

    **3.** includes a predicate nominative.

    **4.** includes a predicate adjective.

    **5.** includes an objective complement.

Underline each subject once, each verb twice, and label each complement.

# The Sentence Base: Posttest

## Directions

Write the letter of the term that correctly identifies the underlined word or words in each sentence.

(1) The now famous <u>Carl Sandburg</u> was born in 1878 in Galesburg, Illinois. (2) Sandburg <u>served as a soldier during the Spanish-American War</u>. (3) His political beliefs <u>would influence</u> his poetry. (4) <u>Have</u> you <u>read</u> any of his early work? (5) <u>Many of his poems</u> reveal a vision of democracy. (6) Industrial <u>America</u> and American <u>workers</u> are a recurrent theme. (7) Besides free verse Sandburg also wrote <u>biographies</u> and <u>books</u> for children. (8) Sandburg's biography of Lincoln is a remarkable <u>study</u> and a powerful <u>memorial</u> to that great president. (9) *The American Songbag* is a <u>collection</u> of almost 300 folk songs. (10) Sandburg recorded <u>several</u> of the songs himself.

1. **A** simple subject
   **B** simple predicate
   **C** complete subject
   **D** complete predicate

2. **A** simple subject
   **B** simple predicate
   **C** complete subject
   **D** complete predicate

3. **A** simple subject
   **B** simple predicate
   **C** complete subject
   **D** complete predicate

4. **A** simple subject
   **B** simple predicate
   **C** complete subject
   **D** complete predicate

5. **A** simple subject
   **B** simple predicate
   **C** complete subject
   **D** complete predicate

6. **A** compound subject
   **B** compound verb
   **C** compound direct object
   **D** compound predicate nominative

7. **A** compound subject
   **B** compound verb
   **C** compound direct object
   **D** compound predicate nominative

8. **A** compound subject
   **B** compound verb
   **C** compound direct object
   **D** compound predicate nominative

9. **A** direct object
   **B** indirect object
   **C** predicate nominative
   **D** predicate adjective

10. **A** direct object
    **B** indirect object
    **C** predicate nominative
    **D** predicate adjective

## Snapshot

**14 A**  To express a complete thought, a **sentence** must have a **subject** and a **predicate.** (pages 654–660)

**14 B**  A **sentence fragment** is a group of words that does not express a complete thought and may be missing a subject or a verb. (pages 661–663)

**14 C**  A **complement** is a word or group of words that completes the meaning of a subject or verb. (pages 664–670)

## Power Rules

Be sure that **the subject and verb agree.** (pages 826–853)

| Before Editing | After Editing |
| --- | --- |
| The *clouds floats* high above us. | The *clouds float* high above us. |
| The *rain* and the *hail makes* driving dangerous. | The *rain* and the *hail make* driving dangerous. |

Fix **sentence fragments** by adding the missing subject and/or verb or by adding punctuation and/or conjunctions to attach the fragment to another sentence. (pages 661–663)

| Before Editing | After Editing |
| --- | --- |
| *After taking several flying lessons.* Katie was ready to fly solo. | *After taking several flying lessons,* Katie was ready to fly solo. |
| *Good eyesight and excellent judgment.* These are two requirements for all pilots. | *Good eyesight and excellent judgment are* two requirements for all pilots. |

# Editing Checklist

Use this checklist when editing your writing.

✓ Did I write sentences that express complete thoughts? (See pages 654–660.)

✓ Did I correct any sentence fragments? (See pages 661–663.)

✓ Did I put the subject in the correct place in questions and sentences starting with *there* or *here?* (See page 657.)

✓ Did I make my writing more interesting by varying the pattern of my sentences and by using inverted sentences? (See pages 656–658 and 671–672.)

✓ Did I use direct objects and indirect objects to complete the meaning of action verbs? (See pages 664–666.)

✓ Did I use predicate adjectives and predicate nominatives to complete the meaning of linking verbs? (See pages 667–670.)

# Use the Power

**Discuss** with a classmate what you have learned about the sentence base in this chapter. Summarize the most important points, including the six sentence patterns.

**Study** the diagram below. It shows the correct way to diagram this sentence:

Ravi and Rivka wrote Mari a letter.

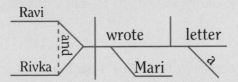

Now diagram this nonsense sentence.

Tifl and Tafl trinsed Tufl a taml.

**Create** two nonsense or imaginative sentences for your partner to diagram. (Use one of the sentence patterns listed on pages 671 and 672.) Go over each other's diagrams and share them with your teacher and classmates.

**Edit** a composition you are working on for fluency. Does it contain a variety of sentence types and sentences of varying lengths?

# Phrases

**How can you use phrases to add variety, clarity, and vitality to your writing?**

## Phrases: Pretest 1

The following draft paragraph about a town council meeting is hard to read because it contains several errors involving phrases. Revise the paragraph so that it reads correctly. The first error has been corrected as an example

    The candidates running ⟨in Centerville⟩ for School Committee held a debate in the town hall. Arriving early, I sat near the stage in a seat. My sister passed out campaign buttons. Spoken with sincerity. The candidate's words stirred the voters. To action. Kathleen Sullivan a former school principal was the best speakers. Instituting change was one of her goals. Ms. Sullivan convinced of the value of school uniforms rallied some teachers to agree. With her point of view. Less convinced the notion of a mandatory dress code did not appeal to some parents and students.

CHAPTER 15

# Phrases: Pretest 2

## Directions

Write the letter of the term that correctly identifies the underlined phrase in each sentence.

**(1)** <u>Growing up in Arkansas,</u> Maya Angelou knew sorrow and hardship from a young age. **(2)** Maya Angelou's autobiographical work, *I Know Why the Caged Bird Sings,* appeared in 1970. **(3)** <u>Triumphing over adversity</u> is a recurring theme in her work. **(4)** It is evident in her collection <u>of poetry</u> *And Still I Rise.* **(5)** <u>Distilling the female and black experience,</u> Angelou writes sensitive, hopeful poetry and prose. **(6)** She prefers <u>raising up</u> to casting down. **(7)** Her optimism has appealed <u>to critics and presidents alike.</u> **(8)** Toni Morrison, <u>an editor and novelist,</u> published three important novels in quick succession. **(9)** *The Bluest Eye, Sula,* and *Song of Solomon* owe some of their color <u>to folklore and myth.</u> **(10)** The experience <u>of black women</u> is Morrison's focus.

1. A prepositional
   B participial
   C gerund
   D infinitive

2. A prepositional
   B participial
   C appositive
   D gerund

3. A prepositional
   B participial
   C gerund
   D infinitive

4. A prepositional
   B participial
   C appositive
   D gerund

5. A prepositional
   B participial
   C gerund
   D infinitive

6. A prepositional
   B participial
   C appositive
   D gerund

7. A prepositional
   B participial
   C gerund
   D infinitive

8. A prepositional
   B participial
   C appositive
   D gerund

9. A prepositional
   B participial
   C gerund
   D infinitive

10. A prepositional
    B participial
    C appositive
    D gerund

# Prepositional Phrases

The subject, the verb, and sometimes a complement are the foundation of a sentence. Once you are familiar with the basic structure of a sentence, you can build on it. In a way, you become an architect. Instead of adding rooms, however, you are adding grammatical elements, such as phrases. The rooms in a house have specific purposes, and their different shapes and sizes make the house interesting and unique.

Similarly, different phrases have different purposes. Some phrases are used to expand or to qualify an idea, while others are used to show relationships between ideas. Using different kinds of phrases will make your writing more varied and more interesting.

**15 A**    A **phrase** is a group of related words that functions as a single part of speech. A phrase does not have a subject or a verb.

In this chapter you will first review prepositional phrases and appositive phrases. Then you will review the three kinds of verbal phrases: participial, gerund, and infinitive. Finally, you will review misplaced and dangling modifiers and phrase fragments.

**15 A.1**    A **prepositional phrase** is a group of words that begins with a preposition and ends with a noun or pronoun called the **object of the preposition.**

The prepositional phrases in the following sentences are in **bold** type.

> **Before midnight** the athlete **from Canton** withdrew **from the competition.**
>
> **In spite of the weather forecast,** all teams are proceeding **with their plans for the outdoor events.**

Prepositional phrases are used like single adjectives and adverbs to modify other words in a sentence.

*You can find a list of prepositions on pages 639–640.*

**Adjectival Phrases**

**15 A.2**   An **adjectival phrase** is a prepositional phrase used to modify a noun or a pronoun.

The following examples show how an adjectival phrase works exactly like a single adjective.

**Single Adjective**      Did you see **that** score?
                          (*That* tells which score.)

**Adjectival Phrase**     Did you see the score **on the scoreboard?**
                          (*On the scoreboard* also tells which score.)

A single adjective and an adjectival phrase answer the same questions: *Which one(s)?* and *What kind?*

**Which one(s)?**         The runner **in the first lane** is Morgan.

**What kind?**            I like athletic events **with music.**

An adjectival phrase usually follows the word it modifies. That word may be the object of a preposition in another prepositional phrase.

Thousands **of athletes of the highest skill** become Olympic competitors.

All **of the winners of the medals for first place** have arrived.

Two adjectival phrases occasionally will modify the same noun or pronoun.

Pick up those programs **of events on the counter.**

## Power Your Writing: Modifiers Come Lately

Vladimir Nabokov is known for vivid imagery and a flowing, textured style. Notice the varied positions of the modifiers in these sentences by the ten-year-old narrator of "First Love."

> **From sheer exuberance,** she would lap up salt water out of Colette's toy pail.
>
> I had been much attracted to Zina, the **lovely, sun-tanned, bad-tempered little** daughter **of a Serbian naturopath.**

Experiment with different locations for your own modifiers.

## Adverbial Phrases

**15 A.3**  An **adverbial phrase** is a prepositional phrase used to modify a verb, an adjective, or an adverb.

An adverbial phrase works exactly like a single adverb. Notice in the following examples that an adverbial phrase, like a single adverb, modifies the whole verb phrase.

**Single Adverb**  The discus throwers will compete **soon.**
(*Soon* tells when the discus throwers will compete.)

**Adverbial Phrase**  The discus throwers will compete **on Friday.**
(*On Friday* also tells when the discus throwers will compete.)

A single adverb and an adverbial phrase answer the same questions: *Where? When? How? To what extent?* or *To what degree?* An adverbial phrase also answers the question *Why?*

**Where?**     I left my sneakers **in my locker.**

**When?**     The practice lasted **until ten o'clock.**

**How?**     I performed the move **according to his instructions.**

**Why?**     **Because of the heavy traffic**, we missed the opening ceremony.

## *When You Write*

Writers use prepositional phrases to add clarity to their writing and to enhance the images in their audience's minds. Sports writers, for example, could not write effective articles without using prepositional phrases to identify the types and locations of games and players. Many questions in a reader's mind will be answered by the prepositional phrases the writer uses.

*Which* baseball player? The player **in left field** caught the fly ball.

*To what extent* did the team practice? The team practiced **until eleven o'clock.**

*Where* did the team play? The team played **at Fenway Park in Boston.**

Revise a recent composition by adding at least three prepositional phrases. Vary the position of these phrases in your sentences.

Fenway Park

Two or more adverbial phrases may modify one verb.

**For the game days,** all the flags were flying **above the stadium.**

**Over the weekend** I put my medals **into the cabinet.**

Although most adverbial phrases modify a verb, some modify adjectives and adverbs.

**Modifying an Adjective**        Coach Margo is kind **to everyone.**

**Modifying an Adverb**        My team arrived late **in the afternoon.**

## PUNCTUATION WITH ADVERBIAL PHRASES

- Do not place a comma after a short introductory adverbial phrase unless it ends in a date or the comma is needed for clarity.

- Place a comma after an adverbial phrase of four or more words or after several introductory phrases.

**No Comma**        **From my seat** I can see the finish line.

**Comma**        **From my seat at the edge of the track,** I can see the finish line.

## When You Speak and Write

When you speak, you pause occasionally so your listeners can better understand you. When you are writing, you use punctuation to indicate these pauses. Since the reader does not have the benefit of listening to you, he or she must rely on your placement of commas to understand your meaning. Sometimes, a comma should be used to avoid confusion. Compare the following sentences.

Behind Peggy Sue sat and watched the competition.

Behind Peggy, Sue sat and watched the competition.

Without the comma, the reader may have to reread the sentence to get the meaning.

Review your use of commas in a recent composition.

## Practice Your Skills

### *Recognizing Prepositional Phrases as Modifiers*

Write the prepositional phrases in the following sentences. Then beside each phrase, write the word it modifies.

1. The first champion of the modern Olympic Games was James Brendan Connolly.
2. In 1896, when he was a 27-year-old undergraduate at Harvard, he read about the revival of the ancient Greek games.
3. At that time Connolly was the triple-jump champion of the United States.
4. Connolly left school and went to Athens in March.
5. Ten American athletes and one trainer spent 16 and a half days on a ship to Naples and another day on a train to Athens.
6. On the following day, the Olympics began with the triple jump.
7. Before his turn Connolly surveyed the mark of the leader on the ground and threw his cap beyond it.
8. He then jumped beyond his cap and became the first champion of the modern Olympics.
9. He later became a journalist and the author of 25 novels.
10. Connolly died in 1957 at age 88.

## Practice Your Skills

### *Identifying Uses of Prepositional Phrases*

Write the prepositional phrases in the following sentences. Then beside each phrase, label it adjectival or adverbial.

1. In 1936, Jesse Owens, a famous track star, beat a horse in the hundred-yard race.
2. During the following year, an Olympic hurdler named Forrest Towns beat a horse in the hundred-yard hurdles.
3. Micki King, a gold-medal winner in the 1972 Olympics, became a diving coach at the U.S. Air Force Academy.
4. Award-winning gymnast Cathy Rigby had a lung ailment during her youth.
5. For six years Hugh Daily played baseball for several major-league teams.
6. As a pitcher he held a long-standing record of 19 strikeouts in a single game.
7. Hugh Daily was a man with only one hand.
8. Fourteen-year-old Nadia Comaneci had seven perfect scores in gymnastics at the Montreal Olympics.
9. She scored the first perfect 10 in the history of Olympic gymnastics.

● *Connect to Writing:* **Revising**

### Using Prepositional Phrases

Make the following sentences more exact by adding an adverbial phrase to each one. Use a comma where needed.

**1.** Stan could see every gymnastic event.

**2.** Sarah could see only the backs of people's heads.

**3.** The competitors stretched and practiced.

**4.** The events would begin in ten minutes.

**5.** The gymnasts exited the floor and waited in an outer hall.

**6.** Mary Lou Retton stood ready to narrate the events for television cameras.

### ✓ *Check Point:* **Mixed Practice**

Write the prepositional phrase or phrases in each sentence and label them adjectival or adverbial.

**1.** Some youngsters under the age of four are learning gymnastics skills.

**2.** Parents take these children to the gym each week.

**3.** They jump on the trampoline.

**4.** On the low balance beam, they walk carefully.

**5.** Their instructors encourage them with words of praise.

**6.** Somersaults are a common sight on the gym floor.

**7.** The older siblings of these young children are often found on the high bars.

**8.** They gather momentum and swing from one bar to the next.

CHAPTER 15

**15 B**    An **appositive** is a noun or a pronoun that identifies or explains another noun or pronoun next to it in the sentence.

An appositive usually follows the word or words it identifies or explains.

> My friend **Bart** is working at an art gallery.
>
> The museum houses an exhibit of sculptures by the French artist **Auguste Rodin.**
>
> I enjoyed my favorite hobby, **sketching.**

**15 B.1**    Most often an appositive is used with modifiers to form an **appositive phrase.**

Note that one or more prepositional phrases may be part of an appositive phrase.

> Chicago, **the Windy City of the Midwest,** is home to the Art Institute of Chicago.
>
> I just bought *Boss,* **a book about Chicago's legendary Mayor Daley.**

---

## PUNCTUATION WITH APPOSITIVES AND APPOSITIVE PHRASES

If an appositive or an appositive phrase contains information essential to the meaning of a sentence, no punctuation is needed.

- Information is essential if it identifies a person, place, or thing.

If an appositive or an appositive phrase contains nonessential information, a comma or commas should be used to separate it from the rest of the sentence.

- Information is nonessential if it can be removed without changing the basic meaning of the sentence. An appositive that follows a proper noun is usually nonessential.

| | |
|---|---|
| **Essential** | The famous artist **Manet** was born in 1832. (No commas are used because Manet is needed to identify which artist.) |
| **Nonessential** | Manet, **a famous French artist,** was born in 1832. (Commas are used because the appositive could be removed from the sentence: *Manet was born in 1832.*) |

### Identifying Appositives and Appositive Phrases

Write each appositive or appositive phrase.

1. Georgia O'Keeffe, an American abstract painter, was famous for her paintings of the desert region of the Southwest.
2. The painting *Sunflowers* is one of van Gogh's most recognized masterpieces.
3. Claude Monet, one of the most well-known impressionist painters, had undergone operations for cataracts when he painted *The Japanese Bridge* around 1923 to 1925.
4. John William Waterhouse painted a picture of the ill-fated woman in Tennyson's poem *The Lady of Shalott.*
5. The Victorian artist William Holman Hunt also painted a scene from *The Lady of Shalott.*
6. Alexandra Nechita, a painter in the abstract cubist style, published a book of her work at age ten.
7. This book, *Outside the Lines,* includes her painting *Variation on the Lion King.*
8. The 1985 Caldecott Award-winning artist, Trina Schart Hyman, received the award for illustrating *Saint George and the Dragon.*
9. The French artist Eugène Delacroix painted a battle scene, *Combat of the Giaour and Hassan,* after becoming inspired by Lord Byron's poem "The Giaour."

● *Connect to Writing:* **Editing**

### Using Commas with Appositive Phrases

Write each sentence, punctuating the appositives or appositive phrases correctly. If a sentence is correct, write **C**.

1. Theodor Seuss Geisel Dr. Seuss was born in 1904 in Springfield, Massachusetts.
2. Dr. Seuss a writer and cartoonist is famous for his rhyming children's books.
3. *And to Think That I Saw It on Mulberry Street* the first of his children's books was published in 1937.
4. *The Cat in the Hat* one of his most famous books was published in 1957.
5. *The Cat in the Hat* a story with only 236 different words was based on a word list for first-grade readers.

Verbals are part of your everyday speech. If you have ever apologized for your *unmade* bed or told someone that you would be ready *to leave* at six o'clock, you have used a verbal.

**15 C**   A **verbal** is a verb form that is used not as a verb, but as a noun, an adjective, or an adverb.

Verbals are verb forms; therefore they usually add action and vitality to your writing. The three kinds of verbals are **participles, gerunds,** and **infinitives.**

## ➤ Participles and Participial Phrases

**15 C.1**   A **participle** is a verb form that is used as an adjective.

Used like an adjective, a participle modifies a noun or a pronoun and answers the adjective question *Which one(s)?* or *What kind?* The participles in the examples below are in **bold** type. An arrow points to the word each participle modifies.

The **rising** sun was reflected on the **frosted** glass of the mayor's limousine.

**Broken** campaign promises are sometimes the downfall of an **elected** official.

There are two kinds of participles: a present participle and a past participle. A **present participle** ends in *–ing,* while a **past participle** has a regular ending of *–ed* or an irregular ending—often *–n, –t,* or *–en.*

| Present Participles | spinn**ing**, shrink**ing**, ring**ing**, winn**ing** |
| --- | --- |
| Past Participles | buri**ed**, defeat**ed**, wor**n**, ben**t**, stol**en** |

Be careful not to confuse a participle used as an adjective and the actual verb in a sentence, which may be in the past tense or part of a verb phrase.

| | |
|---|---|
| **Participle** | The governor's **reserved** seats are in the sixth row of the mezzanine. |
| **Past Tense** | We **reserved** four seats for the senator's speech. |
| **Participle** | The **broken** clock on the mantel in the living room belonged to President Johnson. |
| **Verb Phrase** | During the voter registration, a small table **was broken.** |

## Participial Phrases

Because a participle is a verb form, it may have modifiers and complements. Together these words form a **participial phrase.**

**15 C.2**  A **participial phrase** is a participle with its modifiers and complements—all working together as an adjective.

The following examples show three variations of a participial phrase. As you can see, a participle may be followed by an adverb, a prepositional phrase, or a complement.

| | |
|---|---|
| **Participle with an Adverb** | **Ordered early,** the campaign posters were ready for the rally. |
| **Participle with a Prepositional Phrase** | Our mayor, **speaking to the senior class,** described her path to success. |
| **Participle with a Complement** | Who is that political aide **raising his right hand?** |

The present participle *having* is sometimes followed by a past participle.

> **Having met the senator in person,** I was surprised at how tall she was.

Sometimes an adverb that modifies a participle may come before the participle. The adverb in this position is still part of the participial phrase.

The post-election ball is a grand event ***usually*** **involving bands and caterers.**

***Never*** **having entertained at such a function,** the members of the chorus were nervous.

## PUNCTUATION WITH PARTICIPIAL PHRASES

Always place a comma after an introductory participial phrase.

**Arriving at the White House,** I registered for the tour.

Participial phrases that come in the middle or at the end of a sentence may or may not need commas.

- If the information in a phrase is essential to identify the noun or the pronoun it describes, no commas are needed. (Restrictive phrase)
- If the information is nonessential, commas are needed to separate it from the rest of the sentence. A phrase is nonessential if it contains information that can be removed from the sentence without changing the basic meaning. A phrase that follows a proper noun is usually nonessential. (Nonrestrictive phrase)

| | |
|---|---|
| **Essential** | The FBI agent **guarding the limousine** is Jason Jackson. (No commas are used because the phrase is needed to identify which agent.) |
| **Nonessential** | Jason Jackson, **guarding the limousine,** has twelve years of experience with the FBI. (Commas are used because the phrase can be removed, and the meaning is still clear: *Jason Jackson has twelve years of experience with the FBI.*) |

## ● Practice Your Skills

### *Recognizing Participial Phrases as Modifiers*

Write each participial phrase. Then beside each one, write the word or words it modifies.

1. Winning the confidence of many voters, women have become the mayors of several large cities in the United States.
2. One report identifies some of the women elected mayor in landmark victories.
3. Jane Byrne of Chicago captured the office held by Mayor Richard J. Daley for 21 years until his death.

4. Isabella Cannon, having won the support of young people, became the mayor of Raleigh in a major upset.

5. Having complained unsuccessfully about a dangerous intersection, Janet Gray Hayes ran for mayor of San Jose.

6. Gaining prominence in a nonpartisan campaign, she went on to win the election.

7. Demonstrating her leadership abilities, Mayor Margaret Hance of Phoenix won a second term.

8. Mayor Carole McClellan of Austin, gathering 79 percent of the vote, also won a second term.

9. Effectively governing San Francisco, Dianne Feinstein became nationally prominent.

10. All of these remarkable women led the way for other women entering politics.

Dianne Feinstein

## ● *Connect to Writing and Speaking:* **Expressing an Opinion**

### *Using Participles and Participial Phrases*

Prepare for a class summit on politics. You will have an opportunity to speak your mind on any political issue you choose. You can review the sentences you wrote above to get ideas and to "break the blank page barrier." Write the first draft of your opinion essay to get as many ideas on paper as possible. Then review your writing, looking for opportunities to use participial phrases to help clarify your ideas and to create sentence variety. Finally, prepare the final copy.

**Gerunds and Gerund Phrases**

**15 C.3**    A **gerund** is a verb form used as a noun.

Because a gerund ends in *–ing,* it looks like a present participle. A gerund, however, is used as a noun. The gerunds in the following examples are in **bold** type.

> **Dating** brings out the creativity in some people. (subject)
>
> Kyle and Sasha enjoy **rollerblading.** (direct object)

## Gerund Phrases

Like other verbals, a gerund may be combined with modifiers and complements to form a phrase.

**15 C.4**    A **gerund phrase** is a gerund with its modifiers and complements—all working together as a noun.

A gerund or a gerund phrase may be used in all the ways in which a noun may be used. A gerund may be followed by an adverb, a prepositional phrase, or a complement.

> **Subject**    **Playing tennis** is an enjoyable date.
>
> **Direct Object**    I like **riding on roller coasters.**
>
> **Indirect Object**    My brother gave **writing a love poem** his full attention last Saturday.
>
> **Object of a Preposition**    We drove to the pizza parlor across town without **making a single stop.**
>
> **Predicate Nominative**    Her most enjoyable date was **riding a two-person bicycle.**
>
> **Appositive**    Heather's weekend plan, **applying for jobs for date money,** is admirable.

The possessive form of a noun or a pronoun comes before a gerund and is considered part of the gerund phrase.

> What do you think of ***Eric*'s asking Cindy for a date?**
>
> ***Her* asking Todd out** was surprising.

*You can learn more about possessive nouns and pronouns on pages 801–804 and 964–971.*

### Identifying Gerund Phrases

Write each gerund phrase. Then underline each gerund.

1. We can get good seats for the movie by buying our tickets early.
2. Buying snacks at the concession stand takes time and a great deal of money.
3. I couldn't understand her refusing the buttery popcorn and soda.
4. My creative cousin is capable of planning some very unusual dates.
5. His idea last Saturday was renting a large moving van for the day.
6. Decorating the van's interior like a four-star restaurant was his morning activity.
7. After shopping carefully for ingredients, he cooked a gourmet meal.
8. His date was thrilled with his creating this enjoyable dinner experience.
9. Going to a local bookstore was my most recent memorable date.
10. Our afternoon activity, listening to the children's story hour, was different and fun.

● **Practice Your Skills**

### Determining the Uses of Gerund Phrases

Write each gerund phrase. Then label the use of each one, using the following abbreviations.

| | |
|---|---|
| subject = *subj.* | object of a preposition = *o.p.* |
| direct object = *d.o.* | predicate nominative = *p.n.* |
| indirect object = *i.o.* | appositive = *appos.* |

1. Dancing by the lake is Julie's idea of the perfect evening.
2. Jackie's spontaneous nature welcomes jumping puddles in the rain.
3. Last month Mike surprised his girlfriend by taking her to a fruit orchard.
4. His idea, picking fruit together, was a success.
5. One date I'll never forget was test-driving a new car together.
6. For a sweet evening, give baking cinnamon rolls a try.
7. Two of my friends succeeded in running a marathon together.
8. My bright idea, pretending to be an artist at the beach, was hilarious.

**Distinguishing Between Gerunds and Participles**

Work with a writing partner to brainstorm at least ten gerunds and participles. Use word association to generate words, beginning with the word *dating*. Write down the first *–ing* gerund or participle you think of, and then your writing partner will write down the first *–ing* word that comes to mind. Continue until your combined list totals ten words. Then each of you choose five words and write two sentences for each word. The first sentence should use the word as a gerund. The second sentence should use the word as a participle. Use punctuation where needed. Compare your sentences.

**Using Gerunds and Gerund Phrases**

Your class will write a handbook of dating tips and ideas that will be useful to anyone who is interested in dating. Each student will write one entry for this handbook. Use your prewriting from the preceding exercise to start your first draft. Write a first draft, devoting extra care to using gerunds and gerund phrases. Edit your writing for errors in spelling, punctuation, and grammar. Then prepare the final copy.

# ➤ Infinitives and Infinitive Phrases

**15 C.5**   An **infinitive** is a verb form that usually begins with *to*. It is used as a noun, an adjective, or an adverb.

Infinitives do not look like the other verbals because they usually begin with the word *to*. An infinitive has several forms. The infinitives of *change,* for example, are *to change, to be changing, to have changed, to be changed,* and *to have been changed.* The infinitives in the following examples are in **bold** type.

Pat wanted **to win.** (noun, direct object)

She couldn't think of a story **to write.** (adjective)

The unexpected ideas from Jill were nice **to receive.** (adverb)

Do not confuse a prepositional phrase that begins with *to* with an infinitive. A prepositional phrase ends with a noun or a pronoun; an infinitive ends with a verb form.

**Prepositional Phrase**   Give the book **to me.**

**Infinitive**   When is it time **to read?**

# Infinitive Phrases

An infinitive may be combined with modifiers and complements to form an **infinitive phrase.**

**15 C.6**   An **infinitive phrase** is an infinitive with its modifiers and complements—all working together as a noun, an adjective, or an adverb.

The following examples show how an infinitive phrase may be used as a noun, an adjective, or an adverb. Notice that like other verbals, an infinitive phrase may also take several forms. An infinitive, for example, may be followed by an adverb, a complement, or a prepositional phrase.

| | |
|---|---|
| **Noun** | **To write well** requires patience. (subject) |
| | I tried **to buy two rare books.** (direct object) |
| **Adjective** | These are the fables **to read for tomorrow.** |
| **Adverb** | We printed the story **to create public awareness.** |

Unlike other verbal phrases, an infinitive phrase can have a subject. An infinitive phrase with a subject is called an **infinitive clause.**

┌──────── d.o. ────────┐
Everyone expected **Pat to win the storytelling contest.**

(Pat is the subject of *to win*. The whole infinitive clause is the direct object of *everyone expected*. Everyone expected what?)

┌──────── d.o. ────────┐
We asked **her to distribute the awards.**

(*Her* is the subject of *to distribute*. The subject of an infinitive clause is in the objective case. The whole infinitive clause is the direct object of *we asked*.)

Occasionally the word *to* is dropped when an infinitive follows such verbs as *help, dare, feel, make, let, need, see,* or *watch*. It is, nevertheless, understood to be in the sentence.

We helped **collect** (to collect) **picture books for the preschool.**

The teacher let the children **participate** (to participate) **in story hour.**

## ● Practice Your Skills

### *Identifying Infinitive Phrases*

Write each infinitive or infinitive phrase.

**1.** To be brave from a distance is easy. —*Aesop*

**2.** Aesop created fables to teach people lessons.

**3.** The ant wanted to store food.

**4.** The grasshopper was the one to play all summer.

**5.** The shepherd boy promised to tend sheep.

**6.** He cried "Wolf!" to get a little excitement.

**7.** However, there really was a wolf to fear.

**8.** Later the wolf came to eat the sheep.

**9.** The shepherd boy tried to get help, but no one believed him.

**10.** A runaway slave named Androcles helped pull a thorn from a lion's paw.

● **Practice Your Skills**

### Determining the Uses of Infinitive Phrases

Write the infinitive or infinitive phrases in the following sentences. Then label how each one is used: noun, adjective, or adverb.

1. The fables to read are by Aesop and other Greek storytellers.
2. To credit Aesop with writing all Greek fables has been the tendency.
3. Legend says that Aesop was freed from slavery to become a diplomat for King Croesus.
4. To starve as a free man is better than being a fat slave. —*Aesop*
5. A young wife wants her husband to look more like herself.
6. She plucks out his gray hairs each night to create a younger appearance.
7. The second wife to pluck hairs from the man's head is older.
8. This wife decides to remove all the brown strands.
9. As a result, each wife helps make the husband bald.
10. To bend with the wind is the Reed's wise choice in "The Tree and the Reed."

✔ *Check Point:* **Mixed Practice**

Write the verbal phrases in the following sentences. Then label each one participial, gerund, or infinitive.

1. Born in New York in 1856, Louise Blanchard Bethune is considered the first woman architect.
2. After designing many buildings, she became the first woman to gain membership in the American Institute of Architects.
3. The first American woman to receive the Nobel Peace Prize was Jane Addams.
4. In 1931, she was recognized for establishing a center for social reform in Chicago.
5. The first woman to be pictured on a United States coin in circulation was suffragist Susan B. Anthony.
6. Treasury officials had first considered picturing only a representative female figure such as Miss Liberty.
7. Anthony, appearing later on a one-dollar coin, was selected over Jane Addams and Eleanor Roosevelt.
8. Long before Sarah Walker became the first African American woman millionaire, she supported herself by taking in laundry.

# Misplaced and Dangling Modifiers

**15 D** **Misplaced modifiers** and **dangling modifiers** are common modifier problems that can confuse the meaning of a sentence.

The meaning of a sentence sometimes gets confused because a modifier is placed too far away from the word it describes. When that happens, the modifier appears to describe some other word. Such modifiers are called **misplaced modifiers.** Remember to place phrases used as modifiers as close as possible to the word or words they describe.

**15 D.1** A modifier that is placed too far away from the word it modifies is called a **misplaced modifier.**

| | |
|---|---|
| **Misplaced** | Rob will answer this ad for a gardener **in the _Globe._** |
| **Correct** | Rob will answer this ad **in the _Globe_** for a gardener. |
| **Misplaced** | I found the seedlings **looking through a catalog.** |
| **Correct** | **Looking through a catalog,** I found the seedlings. |

**15 D.2** A **dangling modifier** is a phrase that is used as a modifier but does not describe any word in the sentence.

| | |
|---|---|
| **Dangling** | **To be a good park ranger,** knowledge of animals is needed. |
| | (Knowledge cannot be a good park ranger.) |
| **Correct** | **To be a good park ranger,** you need knowledge of animals. |
| **Dangling** | **Filling the bird feeder,** birds will be attracted to your yard. |
| | (Birds cannot fill the bird feeder.) |
| **Correct** | **Filling the bird feeder,** you will attract birds to your yard. |

## ● Practice Your Skills

### Recognizing Misplaced and Dangling Modifiers

Write the misplaced or dangling modifier in each sentence. If a sentence is correct, write **C.**

**1.** Walking through the nature preserve, we saw many interesting sights.

**2.** Rummaging through the trash can, we saw the raccoon.

**3.** I found the raccoon family cleaning up the area.

**4.** I followed Lisa as she ran around the pond on my bike.

**5.** Booming in the distance, I was startled by the thunder.

**6.** Enjoying the sound of the rain, he fell asleep.

**7.** Trotting through the forest, Kate's ears detected a babbling brook.

**8.** My little brother wanted to play with the baby frogs fascinated by live things in the pond.

**9.** Roaring loudly, Juan took a picture of the lion.

**10.** Rowing steadily, the canoe was brought to the dock.

**11.** Jenny stood on a rock trying to get a good view of the baby birds.

**12.** Having eaten the food, the dish was empty.

**13.** Following the posted rules, we did not attempt to feed any of the animals.

**14.** Stretching to eat leaves on the tree, we could see the tall giraffe.

## ● *Connect to Writing:* Revising

### Correcting Misplaced and Dangling Modifiers

Correct each of the misplaced and dangling modifiers in the previous exercise. Either place the phrase closer to the word it modifies, or add words and change the sentence so the phrase has a noun or a pronoun to modify. Use punctuation where needed.

# Phrase Fragments  Lesson 5

Since a phrase is a group of words that does not have a subject and a verb, it can never express a complete thought. As a result, when a phrase is written as if it were a sentence, it becomes a **phrase fragment.**

**15 E**   A **phrase fragment** is a phrase written as if it were a sentence.

To correct a phrase fragment, add a group of words that contains a subject, a verb, or both; or like the following examples in **bold** type, attach a phrase fragment to a related sentence.

| | |
|---|---|
| **Prepositional Phrase Fragment** | Terry Pratchett is one of the funniest writers. **In the world of fantasy literature.** |
| **Corrected** | Terry Pratchett is one of the funniest writers in the world of fantasy literature. |
| **Appositive Phrase Fragment** | Alice Walker wrote *The Color Purple*. **The 1983 Pulitzer Prize–winning novel.** |
| **Corrected** | Alice Walker wrote *The Color Purple*, the 1983 Pulitzer Prize–winning novel. |
| **Participial Phrase Fragment** | O. Henry produced a story a week for the *World*. **Living in New York City.** |
| **Corrected** | Living in New York City, O. Henry produced a story a week for the *World*. |
| **Gerund Phrase Fragment** | **Winning the Nobel Prize in literature.** This is the dream of many authors. |
| **Corrected** | Winning the Nobel Prize in literature is the dream of many authors. |
| **Infinitive Phrase Fragment** | **To provide facts about authors, works of literature, and literary terms.** This is the primary purpose of a literary encyclopedia. |
| **Corrected** | To provide facts about authors, works of literature, and literary terms is the primary purpose of a literary encyclopedia. |

*You can find information about other types of fragments on pages 661–663 and 734–735.*

If you are like most writers, your first drafts probably contain fragments. That is because many writers think first about subject matter, not accuracy or style. After you have written your first draft, however, you should always edit your work to make sure all your sentences are complete.

## ● Practice Your Skills

### Recognizing Phrase Fragments

Write the phrase fragments in the following paragraph. Then label the use of each one *prepositional, appositive, participial, gerund,* or *infinitive.*

(1) Admired as a great writer. (2) Mark Twain was also an inventor. (3) To make millions on his ideas. (4) This was Twain's hope. (5) Twain predicted innovations such as microfilm, data storage and retrieval, and television. (6) He had great ideas, but he was not a good businessman. (7) He lost $300,000, for example. (8) On an automatic typesetting machine. (9) It had moving parts, but it seldom worked. (10) Numbering 18,000. (11) Twain did make a small profit on one of his ventures. (12) Mark Twain's Self-Pasting Scrapbook. (13) Finally, having lost a fortune. (14) Twain had to earn a living by writing.

## ● *Connect to Writing:* Revising

### Correcting Phrase Fragments

Revise the preceding paragraph on Mark Twain by correcting the phrase fragments. Either add a group of words that contains a subject or a verb or attach the phrase fragment to a related sentence.

## ● *Connect to Writing:* Summarizing

### Using Complete Sentences

You have adopted a pen pal in a retirement home, and you want to include some entertaining information in your next letter to this person. Skim the table of contents of a current almanac or another book of interesting information. (You might also search the Internet.) Find a topic particularly interesting to you, read about it, and take notes. Then write the first draft of a paragraph that summarizes the topic you chose. Remember to put the information into your own words. After you have revised your summary, edit it, correcting any phrase fragments, and prepare the final copy.

### Diagraming Phrases

The way a phrase is used in a sentence determines how and where the phrase is diagramed.

**Prepositional Phrases** An adjectival or an adverbial phrase is connected to the word it modifies. The preposition is placed on a connecting slanted line. The object of a preposition is placed on a horizontal line that is attached to the slanted line. The following example includes two adjectival phrases and one adverbial phrase. Notice that an adjectival phrase can modify the object of the preposition of another phrase.

> The assignment for Mr. Marshard's class in English literature must be completed by tomorrow.

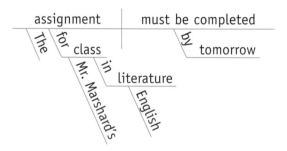

An adverbial phrase that modifies an adjective or an adverb needs an additional horizontal line that is connected to the word modified.

> The two trophies stood close to each other on the mantel.

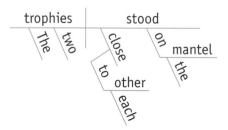

**Appositives and Appositive Phrases** An appositive is diagramed in parentheses next to the word it identifies or explains. Its modifiers are placed directly underneath it.

The appetizer, egg rolls with hot mustard, arrived before a huge meal of several Chinese dishes.

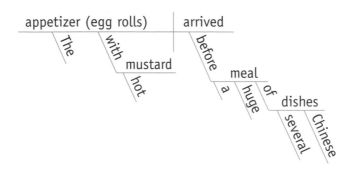

**Participial Phrases** Like an adjective, a participle is always diagramed under the word it modifies. The participle, however, is written in a curve. In the first example below, the participial phrase modifies *Marcy*, the subject of the sentence. In the second example, the participial phrase modifies the direct object *tree*.

Seeing the time on the kitchen clock, Marcy rushed out the door.

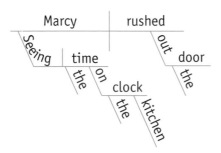

I transplanted the maple tree growing in our backyard.

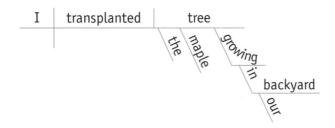

**Gerund Phrases** A gerund phrase is diagramed on a platform in any position in which a noun is diagramed. In the next diagram, the gerund phrase is used as a direct object. In the diagram after that, a gerund phrase is used as a subject, and another gerund phrase is used as the object of a preposition. Notice that the gerund itself curves around a step-like line.

During my summer vacation, I enjoy sitting quietly by the lake.

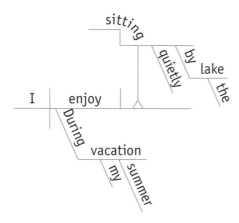

Studying hard is a sure way of guaranteeing a good grade.

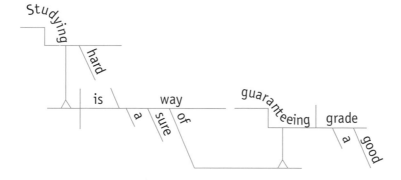

**Infinitive Phrases** An infinitive phrase is diagramed in several ways. In the first example, one infinitive phrase is used as an adjective and one is used as a predicate nominative. In the second example, the infinitive phrase is used as a direct object.

If the *to* of an infinitive is omitted from the sentence, it is diagramed in parentheses.

The only way to have a friend is to be one.    —Emerson

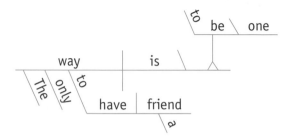

Do you dare interview the mayor?

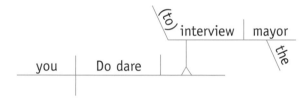

## ● Practice Your Skills

### *Diagraming Phrases*

Diagram the following sentences or copy them. If you copy them, draw one line under each subject and two lines under each verb. Then put parentheses around each phrase and label each one prepositional, appositive, participial, gerund, or infinitive.

**1.** I like to visit my relatives in Tennessee.

**2.** We always go to Opryland in Nashville.

**3.** Buddy, the first dog for the blind, was trained in Nashville.

**4.** Born in Tennessee, Davy Crockett became a national legend.

**5.** You can visit his home by taking a tour through the mountains.

**6.** I liked learning about the real Davy Crockett.

**7.** Arriving in Memphis, we went to Graceland, the home of Elvis Presley.

**8.** To visit his home was my idea.

**9.** We saw his gold records hanging on the walls.

**10.** The best way to travel through Tennessee is by car.

## Assess Your Learning

### Identifying Phrases

Write the phrases in the following sentences. Then label each one prepositional, appositive, participial, gerund, or infinitive.

1. Seaweed sometimes grows to 200 feet in length.
2. At the end of February, Jonathan decided to send in his application.
3. Transporting pollen is the worker bees' job.
4. Meteors, known as shooting stars, may be seen on almost any clear night.
5. Both Cervantes and Shakespeare, two enormously important writers, died on April 23, 1616.
6. Scoring five runs immediately, the Red Sox took command of the game.
7. I enjoy swimming laps every morning.
8. An old game, played since ancient times, is marbles.
9. Do you want to frame your diploma?
10. Running the bases clockwise was the custom during baseball's early years.
11. Joan, my oldest aunt, was an Olympic swimmer and a distance runner.
12. The club's secretary handed me the minutes, printed neatly on bond paper.
13. Dan's father enjoys restoring antique cars.
14. The president, planning an important Cabinet appointment, studied the list of possible candidates.

### ■ Identifying Phrases

Write each phrase in the following paragraph. Then label each phrase prepositional, appositive, participial, gerund, or infinitive.

**Early Will**

**(1)** Little is known about the early life of William Shakespeare, the playwright. **(2)** There are, however, many legends like these. **(3)** Abandoning his family to pursue a more carefree life, Shakespeare became a soldier, lawyer, or teacher. **(4)** Joining an acting troupe, Shakespeare left his home in Stratford-upon-Avon and went to London. **(5)** Shakespeare, having stolen Sir Thomas Lucy's deer, left his birthplace to avoid prosecution. **(6)** Little or no proof exists, though, to support these legends.

### ■ Using Phrases

Write five sentences that follow the directions below. (The sentences may come in any order.) Write about one of the following topics or a topic of your choice: why you enjoy speaking up in class or why you fear public speaking.

Write a sentence that ...

**1.** includes at least two prepositional phrases.

**2.** includes an appositive phrase.

**3.** includes an introductory participial phrase.

**4.** includes a gerund phrase.

**5.** includes an infinitive phrase.

Underline and label each phrase. Then check for correct punctuation in each sentence.

# Phrases: Posttest

## Directions

Write the letter of the term that correctly identifies the underlined phrase in each sentence.

(1) Eugene O'Neill grew up <u>in a theatrical family</u>. (2) Both of his parents, <u>James and Ella</u>, were actors. (3) O'Neill worked as a merchant seaman before tuberculosis forced him <u>to rest and educate himself</u>. (4) <u>Writing twelve one-act plays and two longer works</u> kept him busy for two years. (5) <u>Falling into three main phases</u>, O'Neill's work grew stronger during his life. (6) His early plays feature sailors and their dreams <u>of a better life</u>. (7) *Beyond the Horizon* and *Anna Christie* are his most important plays <u>written before 1921</u>. (8) Both plays won the Pulitzer Prize, <u>an award from the trustees of Columbia University</u>. (9) *The Emperor Jones*, <u>considered America's first expressionist play</u>, owes a lot to Swedish playwright August Strindberg. (10) It marks the beginning <u>of a more experimental phase</u>.

1. **A** prepositional
   **B** participial
   **C** gerund
   **D** infinitive

2. **A** prepositional
   **B** participial
   **C** appositive
   **D** gerund

3. **A** prepositional
   **B** participial
   **C** gerund
   **D** infinitive

4. **A** prepositional
   **B** participial
   **C** appositive
   **D** gerund

5. **A** prepositional
   **B** participial
   **C** gerund
   **D** infinitive

6. **A** prepositional
   **B** participial
   **C** appositive
   **D** gerund

7. **A** prepositional
   **B** participial
   **C** gerund
   **D** infinitive

8. **A** prepositional
   **B** participial
   **C** appositive
   **D** gerund

9. **A** prepositional
   **B** participial
   **C** gerund
   **D** infinitive

10. **A** prepositional
    **B** participial
    **C** appositive
    **D** gerund

# Writer's Corner

## Snapshot

**15 A**  A **phrase** is a group of related words with no subject and verb that functions as a single part of speech. **Adjectival** and **adverbial phrases** are prepositional phrases that modify another part of speech. (pages 684–690)

**15 B**  An **appositive phrase** is a noun or pronoun with modifiers that identifies or explains another noun or pronoun next to it in the sentence. (pages 691–692)

**15 C**  A **verbal** is a verb form used as a noun, adjective, or adverb instead of a verb. The three kinds of verbal phrases are **participial phrases, gerund phrases,** and **infinitive phrases.** (pages 693–702)

**15 D**  A **misplaced modifier** is a phrase placed so far away from the word it modifies that it appears to describe some other word. (page 703) A **dangling modifier** is a phrase that is used as a modifier but does not describe any word in the sentence. (pages 703–704)

**15 E**  A **phrase fragment** is a phrase written as if it were a sentence. (pages 705–706)

## Power Rules

Fix **phrase fragments** by adding words to turn the phrase into a sentence or by attaching the phrase to an existing sentence. (pages 705–706)

| **Before Editing** | **After Editing** |
| --- | --- |
| Sal set a new record last week. *The best high jumper in the district.* | Sal *is* the best high jumper in the district. He set a new record last week. |
| *Babysitting for her cousins.* Micah earned enough money to buy a bike. | *Babysitting for her cousins,* Micah earned enough money to buy a bike. |

# Editing Checklist

Use this checklist when editing your writing.

✓ Did I use different kinds of prepositional phrases to vary my sentences? (See pages 684–690.)

✓ Did I use appositive phrases to clarify nouns and pronouns? (See pages 691–692.)

✓ Did I use commas to set off nonessential and introductory phrases? (See pages 688, 691, and 695.)

✓ Did I use participial, gerund, and infinitive phrases to add action and liveliness to my writing? (See pages 693–702.)

✓ Did I place all of my modifiers close to the word or words they are describing? (See pages 703–704.)

✓ Did I make sure all my sentences are complete thoughts? (See pages 705–706.)

# Use the Power

**Think of phrases** as the colors on a painter's palette. Just as an artist uses colors to bring a painting to life, add phrases to sentences to make your writing vivid and colorful.

Looking behind, the thief, a hardened criminal, tripped on the stairs in the foyer before dropping the jewelry and deciding to give himself up.

**Revise** a recent composition by adding at least three phrases, remembering that appositive phrases add detail and that verbal phrases can add action.

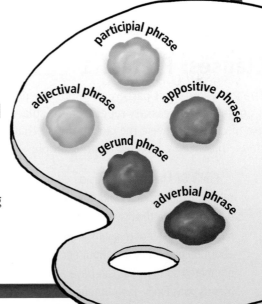

# Clauses

**How can you use clauses to express subtle and precise meaning?**

## Clauses: Pretest 1

The following draft paragraph about the poet Emily Dickinson is hard to read because it contains unnecessary repetition, misplaced clauses, and other problems involving the use of clauses. Revise the paragraph so that it reads more smoothly. The first misplaced clause has been corrected as an example.

Emily Dickinson was considered a recluse in her later life. This intelligent woman seemed to like neighborhood children whose poems fascinate millions of readers. When she wanted to give them sweets. The poet would tie the treats to a string. that she lowered from her window. The poems which she wrote throughout her life are about nature. They are about religion. They are about personal emotions. Her poems do not have titles. They are numbered so that they can have an order. Mabel Todd lived near the Dickinsons. She became friends with Emily. Even though they didn't meet face to face. The friendship was established through notes. It was established through poems and flowers, too. What is amazing is that Todd did finally sit in the same room with Dickinson, that occasion was the poet's funeral.

## Clauses: Pretest 2

### Directions

Write the letter of the term that correctly identifies each sentence or underlined part of a sentence.

(1) Aesop, who lived from 620 to 560 B.C., was a writer of fables. (2) We can infer from Aristotle's descriptions that Aesop was a freed slave, but little else is known about him. (3) Some scholars doubt that he ever lived. (4) His fables exist, however, and fortunately they have been passed down to us. (5) Some fables attributed to Aesop appear on Egyptian papyri dated 1000 years before his birth. (6) <u>What we know as Aesop's *Fables*</u> certainly includes tales from older sources. (7) The translators <u>who collected the fables</u> added other stories they knew. (8) <u>Some stories may have originated in Asia</u>, and others may come from Africa. (9) Do you know <u>what a fable is</u>? (10) A fable is a story <u>that illustrates a moral</u>.

1. **A** simple sentence
   **B** compound sentence
   **C** complex sentence
   **D** compound-complex sentence

2. **A** simple sentence
   **B** compound sentence
   **C** complex sentence
   **D** compound-complex sentence

3. **A** simple sentence
   **B** compound sentence
   **C** complex sentence
   **D** compound-complex sentence

4. **A** simple sentence
   **B** compound sentence
   **C** complex sentence
   **D** compound-complex sentence

5. **A** simple sentence
   **B** compound sentence
   **C** complex sentence
   **D** compound-complex sentence

6. **A** independent clause
   **B** adverbial clause
   **C** adjectival clause
   **D** noun clause

7. **A** independent clause
   **B** adverbial clause
   **C** adjectival clause
   **D** noun clause

8. **A** independent clause
   **B** adverbial clause
   **C** adjectival clause
   **D** noun clause

9. **A** independent clause
   **B** adverbial clause
   **C** adjectival clause
   **D** noun clause

10. **A** independent clause
    **B** adverbial clause
    **C** adjectival clause
    **D** noun clause

You could paint a landscape with just one color, but it would be a dull, unrealistic picture when you finished. You could also write only simple sentences in essays, reports, and letters. People would understand you but, like the picture painted in one color, your writing would be a dull, unrealistic representation of ordinary speech.

You can add color and interest to your writing by varying the structure of your sentences. One way to do this is to include various combinations of clauses within your sentences.

**16 A**    A **clause** is a group of words within a sentence that has a subject and a verb.

Clauses are either independent or subordinate. An **independent clause** makes sense alone. A **subordinate clause** does not make sense alone.

**16 A.1**    An **independent (main) clause** can usually stand alone as a sentence because it expresses a complete thought.

When an independent clause stands alone, it is called a sentence. When it appears in a sentence with another clause, it is called a **clause.** In the following examples, each subject is underlined once, and each verb is underlined twice. Notice that each independent clause can stand alone as a separate sentence.

> ┌──independent clause──┐    ┌──────independent clause──────┐
> Greg waited a long time, but his new saddle never arrived.
> ┌────── sentence ──────┐ ┌────── sentence ──────┐
> Greg waited a long time. His new saddle never arrived.

**16 A.2**    A **subordinate (dependent) clause** cannot stand alone as a sentence because it does not express a complete thought.

A subordinate clause has a subject and a verb; nevertheless, it does not express a complete thought. It can never stand alone as a sentence. A subordinate clause is dependent upon an independent clause to complete its meaning.

┌──subordinate clause ──┐ ┌─independent clause─┐
When we attended the rodeo, we sat in the bleachers.
┌──independent clause ──┐┌─subordinate clause─┐
We found some red paint that matches the barn.
┌──────independent clause──────┐┌────subordinate clause────┐
Nobody at the livestock show knew that you were a newcomer.

## ● Practice Your Skills

### Differentiating Between Independent and Subordinate Clauses

Label each underlined clause *I* for independent or *S* for subordinate.

**1.** We had an enjoyable weekend when we spent two days on Lloyd's farm.

**2.** Before the sun came up, we had eaten a huge breakfast.

**3.** Jeremy helped milk several cows, and Tamara spread grain for the chickens.

**4.** I slowly drove the tractor to the barn, but Steven attached the tractor's trailer.

**5.** After we loaded the trailer with bales of hay, we hauled the load into the pasture.

**6.** I wasn't afraid of the cows until one of them lumbered toward me.

**16 B** **A subordinate clause** can function as an adverb, an adjective, or a noun.

Like phrases, subordinate clauses can function as adverbs, adjectives, or nouns. The difference between them is that a clause has a subject and a verb but a phrase does not.

## ➤ Adverbial Clauses

**16 B.1** An **adverbial clause** is a subordinate clause that is used as an adverb to modify a verb, an adjective, or an adverb.

An **adverbial clause** is used just like a single adverb or an adverbial phrase. In the following examples, the single adverb, the adverbial phrase, and the adverbial clause all modify the verb *arrived*.

| | |
|---|---|
| **Single Adverb** | The hockey team arrived **early.** |
| **Adverbial Phrase** | The hockey team arrived **at five o'clock.** |
| **Adverbial Clause** | The hockey team arrived **before the rink opened.** |

In addition to the questions *How? When? Where? How much?* and *To what extent?,* adverbial clauses also answer the questions *Under what condition?* and *Why?* Although most adverbial clauses modify verbs, some modify adjectives and adverbs.

| | |
|---|---|
| **Modifying a Verb** | **After the snow stopped,** we organized a snowball war. (The clause answers *When?*) |
| **Modifying an Adjective** | Some ice sports are faster **than others are.** (The clause answers *How much?*) |
| **Modifying an Adverb** | The snow was piled higher **than I had ever seen before.** (The clause answers *To what extent?*) |

## Subordinating Conjunctions

An adverbial clause usually begins with a **subordinating conjunction.** Notice in the following list such words as *after, before, since,* and *until;* these words can also be used as prepositions. Notice also that subordinating conjunctions can be more than one word, such as *even though.*

## COMMON SUBORDINATING CONJUNCTIONS

| | | | |
|---|---|---|---|
| after | as soon as | in order that | until |
| although | as though | since | when |
| as | because | so that | whenever |
| as far as | before | than | where |
| as if | even though | though | wherever |
| as long as | if | unless | while |

An adverbial clause that describes a verb modifies the whole verb phrase.

You may watch the team's photo session **as long as you are quiet.**

**When you get your hockey equipment,** you must call me.

The goalie, **after he blocked the puck,** was lying on the ice.

## PUNCTUATION WITH ADVERBIAL CLAUSES

Place a comma after an adverbial clause that comes at the beginning of a sentence.

**Since the country roads were icy,** I drove at a slow and safe speed.

When an adverbial clause interrupts an independent clause, set it off with commas.

The crowd, **after they had enjoyed the exciting game,** applauded the winners.

When an adverbial clause follows an independent clause, no comma is needed.

We hurried out of the arena **before the parking lot became congested.**

## When You Write

Use subordinating conjunctions to show a clear relationship between two ideas.

| | |
|---|---|
| **Unclear** | I worked all summer. I did not get the scholarship. |
| **Clear** | I worked all summer **because** I did not get the scholarship. |

Check over a recent composition to be sure the relationship between your ideas is clear so that the reader does not have to guess.

● **Practice Your Skills**

*Recognizing Adverbial Clauses as Modifiers*

Write each adverbial clause. Then beside it write the word or words the adverbial clause modifies.

1. When a thunderstorm strikes on a hot day, hail may fall.
2. We splashed through puddles after the storm ended.
3. We went back inside so that we could find our umbrellas.
4. After the snowstorm ended, we shoveled the walk and the driveway.
5. As soon as you build the snowman, call me.
6. We left for the ice-skating lesson later than we had planned.
7. We can share the snowboard if each of us pays half.
8. Put the snow chains on your tires after you read the directions.
9. Because Cheryl wanted skis, she worked at the sports store until she saved enough money.
10. Before she skied down the steep hill, she watched the more experienced skiers.

● *Connect to Writing:* **Editing**

*Punctuating Adverbial Clauses*

Write the following sentences, adding a comma or commas where needed. If no comma is needed, write **C** for correct.

1. When the thunderstorm began we ran for shelter.
2. We stayed beneath the trees as long as the rain continued.
3. All day long the downhill skiing champion walked as though she had injured her leg.
4. Because Judy practiced faithfully she did well in the figure skating competition.
5. John after he completed his bachelor's degree in architecture started an ice arena design company.
6. He worked on a design for an Olympic-sized ice arena until he was satisfied with every detail.
7. Even though we were cold we played hockey on the frozen lake for an hour.
8. The mayor of Denver left after he had cut the ribbon at the opening of the new ski resort.
9. I placed a cover over my car so that the hail could not damage the paint.
10. Even though I had taken this precaution the hail dented the bumper.

# Elliptical Clauses

Words in an adverbial clause are sometimes omitted to streamline a sentence and to prevent unnecessary repetition. Even though the words are omitted, they are still understood to be there.

**16 B.2**    An adverbial clause in which words are missing is called an **elliptical clause.**

Notice in the following examples that the elliptical clauses begin with *than* or *as* and are missing only the verb.

> Alvin visits the zoo more often **than I.**
>
> (The completed elliptical clause reads "than I *do*.")
>
> A hippopotamus may be as heavy **as a medium-sized truck.**
>
> (The completed elliptical clause reads "as a medium-sized truck *is*.")

Sometimes the subject and the verb, or just part of the verb phrase, may be omitted in an elliptical clause.

> I collected more donations to the wildlife fund this weekend **than last weekend.**
>
> (The completed elliptical clause reads "than *I collected* last weekend.")
>
> **When sighted,** the zebra had already begun to run.
>
> (The completed elliptical clause reads "When *it was* sighted.")

*You can learn more about using the correct case of a pronoun in an elliptical clause on pages 808–809.*

## When You Write

You may more easily remember what an elliptical clause is if you are familiar with using the mark of punctuation called the *ellipses*. An **ellipses** is a series of three dots that indicates where the writer has omitted words, usually in a quotation. Just as an **elliptical clause** omits words that the reader understands to be there, an ellipses indicates an omission of words that the reader understands to be in the original.

*Recognizing Elliptical Clauses*

Write each elliptical clause and then complete it.

**1.** At five and a half feet tall, the black rhinoceros is as tall as many people.
**2.** The white rhinoceros stands about six inches shorter than the black rhino.
**3.** Most rhinoceroses are taller than the hippopotamus.
**4.** The hippopotamus weighs the same as the rhinoceros.
**5.** When told that the rhinoceros is not a meat-eater, many people are surprised.

● *Connect to Writing:* **Prewriting**

*Freewriting Using Adverbial Clauses*

Many species of animals and plants become extinct every year. Here is a list of a few of the animals that are endangered:

| | | |
|---|---|---|
| black rhinoceros | Idaho spring snail | Florida manatee |
| gorilla | Kirtland's warbler | woodland caribou |
| Amazon River dolphin | brown pelican | Wyoming toad |
| Asian elephant | California condor | pallid sturgeon |
| Hawaiian monk seal | Peruvian penguin | |
| short-tailed albatross | king salmon | |

For ten minutes freewrite about endangered species. Write your thoughts, feelings, questions, and ideas. If you run out of ideas, look over the list of subordinating conjunctions on page 721, and write the first clause that comes to mind.

# ➤ Adjectival Clauses

**16 B.3**  An **adjectival clause** is a subordinate clause that is used as an adjective to modify a noun or a pronoun.

An **adjectival clause** is used just like a single adjective or an adjectival phrase. In the following examples, the single adjective, the adjectival phrase, and the adjectival clause all modify *fire*.

| | |
|---|---|
| **Single Adjective** | The **intense** fire destroyed the building. |
| **Adjectival Phrase** | The fire **with billowing flames and thick smoke** destroyed the building. |
| **Adjectival Clause** | The fire, **which raged out of control,** destroyed the building. |

Like a single adjective, an adjectival clause answers the question *Which one(s)?* or *What kind?*

| | |
|---|---|
| **Which One(s)?** | The firefighters **who volunteered their time last night** became heroes. |
| **What Kind?** | They saved a historic building **that was constructed of valuable hardwoods.** |

## Relative Pronouns

An adjectival clause usually begins with a relative pronoun. A **relative pronoun** relates an adjectival clause to its antecedent. The **relative adverbs** *where* and *when* also introduce adjectival clauses.

| RELATIVE PRONOUNS | | | | |
|---|---|---|---|---|
| who | whom | whose | which | that |

Lakeview's firefighters, **who sponsor a fundraiser each summer,** have not raised enough money for new hoses.

Charles Daly moved here from Miami, **where he had worked as a mechanic at a fire station.**

The relative pronoun *that* is sometimes omitted from an adjectival clause; nevertheless, it is still understood to be in the clause.

Playing with matches is something **everyone should avoid.**

(**That** *everyone should avoid* is the complete adjectival clause.)

*Recognizing Adjectival Clauses as Modifiers*

Write each adjectival clause. Then beside it write the word it modifies.

1. Firefighting is a dangerous job that requires a commitment to public service.
2. Fire hoses, which carry 2,000 gallons of water per minute, will test the user's strength and dexterity.
3. Fire hydrants, where firefighters access critical water supplies, must never be blocked by parked cars.
4. Firefighters, who often carry unconscious people down stairs, must develop strong muscles.
5. Their coworkers, whom they trust with their lives every day, often become close friends for many years.
6. Did you hear about the conference that will update us on firefighting technology?
7. These conferences, workshops, and seminars are events every firefighter should attend.
8. Jerry, whose high school diploma hangs on the wall, passed the firefighter's examination.
9. Some colleges offer fire science programs, which attract many firefighters who are already on the job.

# Functions of a Relative Pronoun

A relative pronoun functions in several ways in a sentence. It usually introduces an adjectival clause and refers to another noun or pronoun in the sentence. A relative pronoun also has a function within the adjectival clause itself. It can be used as a subject, direct object, or object of a preposition. A relative pronoun can also show possession.

| | |
|---|---|
| **Subject** | Robert Frost, **who read a poem at President Kennedy's inauguration,** lived from 1874 to 1963. (*Who* is the subject of *read*.) |
| **Direct Object** | The poems **you like** were written by Emily Dickinson. (The understood relative pronoun *that* is the direct object of *like: you like that . . . .*) |
| **Object of a Preposition** | The volume **in which I found Frost's biography** is quite interesting. (*Which* is the object of the preposition *in*.) |
| **Possession** | Carl Sandburg is an American poet **whose father emigrated from Sweden.** (*Whose* shows possession of *father*.) |

## PUNCTUATION WITH ADJECTIVAL CLAUSES

No punctuation is used with an adjectival clause that contains information essential to identify a person, place, or thing in the sentence.

A comma or commas, however, should set off an adjectival clause that is nonessential.

- A clause is nonessential if it can be removed from the sentence without changing the basic meaning of the sentence.
- An adjectival clause is usually nonessential if it modifies a proper noun.

The relative pronoun *that* usually begins an essential (restrictive) clause, and *which* often begins a nonessential (nonrestrictive) clause.

| | |
|---|---|
| **Essential** | The author **who was Poet Laureate of the United States from 1993 to 1994** was Rita Dove. (No commas are used because the clause is needed to identify which author.) |
| | Here is the book of love poems **that received all the notoriety.** |
| **Nonessential** | Rita Dove, **who was Poet Laureate of the United States from 1993 to 1994,** received the Heinz Award in the Arts and Humanities in 1996. (Commas are used because the clause can be removed from the sentence.) |
| | Here is the book of love poems, **which was given to me by the poet.** |

## ● Practice Your Skills

### *Determining the Function of a Relative Pronoun*

Write each adjectival clause. Then label the use of each relative pronoun, using the following abbreviations. If an adjectival clause begins with an understood *that*, write *(that)* and then write how *that* is used.

subject = *subj.*          object of a preposition = *o.p.*
direct object = d.o.      possession = poss.

1. Robert Frost, whose poetry was awarded the Pulitzer Prize, first published his poems at age thirty-eight.
2. The poet who dressed entirely in white is Emily Dickinson.
3. The poem from which I get my inspiration is "The Road Not Taken" by Frost.
4. The poem you memorized has only six lines.

Uses of Subordinate Clauses • Lesson 2     727

5. The lines "The fog comes / on little cat feet," which open the poem, create a vivid image in my mind.

6. Carl Sandburg, who wrote this short poem, lived from 1878 to 1967.

7. The African-American poet about whom I wrote my essay is Rita Dove.

8. The recordings of her poetry that I heard were on the Internet.

9. Wallace Stevens, who wrote "The Emperor of Ice Cream," dropped out of Harvard and then later went to law school.

10. The students whose essays are the most interesting are the students who felt a true connection with the poets they studied.

# Misplaced Modifiers

To avoid confusion, place an adjectival clause as near as possible to the word it describes.

**16 B.4**  A clause placed too far away from the word it modifies can cause confusion and is called a **misplaced modifier.**

| Misplaced | Tim discovered a park near his new house that included a pond. |
| Correct | Near his new house, Tim discovered a park **that included a pond.** |
| Misplaced | Dennis ran to take the meat off the grill, which was burned to a crisp. |
| Correct | Dennis ran to take the meat, **which was burned to a crisp,** off the grill. |

*You can learn more about misplaced and dangling modifiers on pages 703–704.*

● **Practice Your Skills**

*Identifying Misplaced Modifiers*

Write *MM* for misplaced modifier if the underlined modifier is used incorrectly in the sentence. If the modifier is used correctly, write **C.**

1. Monique packed a picnic basket full of tasty food that was made of straw.

2. Monique's best friend loaded the car with blankets, sunscreen, and a volleyball who was also going on the picnic.

3. I showed the lawn chairs to the girls that I had just bought.

4. My neighbor offered to drive us in his car whom I had invited on the picnic.

5. The car belongs to my neighbor, which has the convertible top.

**6.** The trunk of the car could barely contain all of our picnic supplies, <u>which was the size of a suitcase.</u>

**7.** We spread a cloth over the table <u>that had a red-and-white checkered pattern.</u>

**8.** Some ducks, <u>which were cute and fluffy</u>, begged for food.

**9.** Ed and I tossed a large disk across the grassy clearing <u>that was made of black plastic.</u>

**10.** We feasted on food <u>that was tasty</u> and enjoyed each other's company.

● *Connect to Writing:* **Revising**

### Correcting Misplaced Modifiers

Rewrite the eight incorrect sentences from the preceding exercise, correcting each misplaced modifier. Use a comma or commas where needed.

 **Noun Clauses**

`16 B.5`    A **noun clause** is a subordinate clause that is used as a noun.

A **noun clause** is used in the same ways a single noun can be used. The examples below show some of the uses.

| | |
|---|---|
| **Subject** | **What Jenny planned** was a river cruise. |
| **Direct Object** | Julian knows **that the current is swift.** |
| **Indirect Object** | Give **whoever arrives** a life jacket. |
| **Object of a Preposition** | People are often surprised by **what they find on the river bottom.** |
| **Predicate Nominative** | A challenging trip down the rapids is **what I want right now.** |

The following list contains words that often introduce a noun clause. Remember, though, that *who, whom, whose, which,* and *that* can also be used as relative pronouns to introduce adjectival clauses.

| COMMON INTRODUCTORY WORDS FOR NOUN CLAUSES | | | | |
|---|---|---|---|---|
| how | what | where | who | whomever |
| if | whatever | whether | whoever | whose |
| that | when | which | whom | why |

### Identifying Noun Clauses

Write the noun clause in each sentence.

**1.** How people live in other countries interests many people.
**2.** A trip to the ancient monuments of Egypt is what the historians requested.
**3.** That the tour included the Nile River and Alexandria was pleasing news.
**4.** The tour guide gave the best seats to whoever arrived first.
**5.** Did you know that the Nile is the longest river in the world?

● **Practice Your Skills**

### Determining the Uses of Noun Clauses

Write each noun clause. Then label the use of each one, using the following abbreviations.

subject = *subj.*        object of a preposition = *o.p.*

direct object = *d.o.*       predicate nominative = *p.n.*

indirect object = *i.o.*

**1.** Did you know that heart disease kills people every day?
**2.** How people can learn about heart health interests me.
**3.** That a cardiologist can implant donor or artificial hearts is impressive.
**4.** Nutritionists tell whoever will listen facts about the heart.
**5.** People are often surprised by what they learn from these experts.

✔ *Check Point:* **Mixed Practice**

Write the subordinate clauses in the following sentences. Then label the use of each one, using the following abbreviations.

adverb = *adv.*      adjective = *adj.*     noun = *n.*

**1.** When the earth, moon, and sun are in line, an eclipse occurs.
**2.** What most people associate with Saturn are the rings around the planet.
**3.** Our science teacher, Mrs. Jeffries, told us that Mercury is the planet closest to the sun.
**4.** The planet that is farthest from the sun is Neptune.
**5.** As I built my model of the solar system, I consulted many reference books.
**6.** A thick dictionary with diagrams and charts is what helped me the most.
**7.** Although the sun shone brightly, the weather forecasters maintained that the weekend would be rainy.

**16 C**    A sentence can be **simple, compound, complex, or compound-complex**, depending on the number and the kind of clauses in it.

**16 C.1**    A **simple sentence** consists of one independent clause.

> World War II <u>airplanes</u> <u><u>fascinate</u></u> me.

A simple sentence can have a compound subject, a compound verb, or both. In the examples below, the subject is underlined once and the verb is underlined twice.

> <u>Balloons</u> and <u>blimps</u> <u><u>can carry</u></u> passengers.
> The <u>airplane</u> and the <u>tank</u> <u><u>crashed</u></u> and <u><u>burned</u></u>.

**16 C.2**    A **compound sentence** consists of two or more independent clauses.

A compound sentence should be composed of only closely related independent clauses, usually joined by a coordinating conjunction such as *and, but, for,* or *yet.*

> ┌──────independent clause──────┐    ┌independent clause┐
> <u>I</u> <u><u>ran</u></u> to the airport terminal, but <u>I</u> <u><u>missed</u></u> my plane.
> ┌independent clause┐ ┌──────────independent clause──────────┐
> The <u>pilot</u> <u><u>has arrived</u></u>, the <u>flight attendants</u> <u><u>are checking</u></u> tickets,
>      ┌──────independent clause──────┐
> and the <u>passengers</u> <u><u>may</u></u> now <u><u>board</u></u>.

*You can learn about punctuating a compound sentence on pages 944–945 and 974–976.*

**16 C.3**    A **complex sentence** consists of one independent clause and one or more subordinate clauses.

In a complex sentence, one independent clause and one or more subordinate clauses are connected by a subordinating conjunction, a relative pronoun, or a relative adverb.

> ┌──────independent clause──────┐ ┌─ subordinate clause ─┐
> <u>We</u> <u><u>bought</u></u> a vacation package <u>that</u> <u><u>included</u></u> airfare.
> ┌independent clause┐ ┌──────subordinate clause──────┐ ┌subordinate clause┐
> <u>We</u> <u><u>flew</u></u> to Florida because <u>we</u> <u><u>had</u></u> tickets to a theme park <u>that</u> <u><u>was opening</u></u>.

*You can find a list of subordinating conjunctions on page 721. You can learn about punctuating complex sentences on pages 65, 169, and 736.*

**16 C.4**  A **compound-complex sentence** consists of two or more independent clauses and one or more subordinate clauses.

Conjunctions and punctuation in compound-complex sentences are used in the same way as they are used in compound sentences and in complex sentences.

```
                ┌────────independent clause────────┐      ┌──────independent clause──────┐ ┌──────
                I have dreamed of becoming a pilot, but I have not taken flying lessons because
                ┌────────subordinate clause────────┐
                I am saving the necessary money.
```

## When You Write

A paragraph with nothing but simple sentences becomes dull and monotonous to read. On the other hand, a paragraph with only complex or compound-complex sentences can be confusing. A paragraph that includes a combination of different kinds of sentences is by far the most interesting. Notice the combination of the different kinds of sentences in the following paragraph.

> The plane began its descent to the airport. Passengers looked out the windows, but all they could see was whiteness. The plane bumped through the turbulent air. When the plane was almost over the runway, it finally broke free of the clouds. After landing the plane safely, the pilot turned off the seat-belt sign.

Review a recent composition, making sure that you have varied the types of sentences within your paragraphs.

## ● Practice Your Skills

### *Classifying Sentences*

Label each sentence *simple, compound, complex,* or *compound-complex.*

**1.** In 1984, Byron Lichtenberg, who is a biomedical engineer, became a member of a spacecraft crew.

**2.** Lichtenberg discovered that dealing with zero gravity was difficult.

**3.** The other two astronauts were able to control their movements, but at first Lichtenberg kept bouncing off the walls.

**4.** Lichtenberg found that eating was not easy either.

**5.** He ate with only a spoon because he had to hold onto his food with his other hand.

**6.** Once he tried to make a sandwich, but this task was much harder than he had expected.

**7.** The beef and cheese floated around, but then he clamped them together with the bread.

**8.** Peanuts were the most fun to eat.

**9.** When Lichtenberg tried to pour them down his throat, they escaped and floated around the cabin.

**10.** Eventually he chased them down like a cat and mouse.

## ● *Connect to Writing:* Revising

### *Combining Sentences*

Combine the first three pairs of sentences into compound sentences. Then combine the next three pairs into complex sentences. Combine the last pair of sentences into a compound-complex sentence.

**1.** Mythology associates the winged horse Pegasus with lightning. The modern era associates Pegasus with poetic inspiration.

**2.** An airplane has wings like a bird. They do not flap like a bird's wings.

**3.** Wings can symbolize physical flight above the earth. They can represent rising high above earthly cares and concerns.

**4.** Fairies are seen as dainty creatures. They are drawn with wings of butterflies.

**5.** Wings work in pairs. One is not enough for successful flight.

**6.** The Wright brothers made their first flight in 1903. Flying developed relatively early.

**7.** The afternoon was clear and sunny. I felt like flying a kite. I had homework to do instead.

# Clause Fragments  Lesson 4

**16 D**    Even though a subordinate clause has both a subject and a verb, it does not express a complete thought. A subordinate clause punctuated as a sentence is a **clause fragment.**

To correct a clause fragment, add or change words to express a complete thought or attach the clause to a related sentence.

| | |
|---|---|
| **Adverbial Clause Fragment** | **Whenever I have the opportunity.** I enjoy learning about animals. |
| **Corrected** | Whenever I have the opportunity, I enjoy learning about animals. |
| **Noun Clause Fragment** | **That a cow has four stomachs called the rumen, reticulum, omasum, and abomasum.** I know. |
| **Corrected** | I know that a cow has four stomachs called the rumen, reticulum, omasum, and abomasum. |
| **Adjectival Clause Fragment** | At the workshop she visited booths. **That featured veterinary information.** |
| **Corrected** | At the workshop she visited booths that featured veterinary information. |

*You can learn about other kinds of sentence fragments on pages 661–663 and 705–706.*

## When You Speak and Write

When someone asks you a question that begins with the word *why,* you probably begin your answer with the word *because.*

> Why did you visit the career fair?
>
> **Because** I wanted to learn more about job opportunities.

The example above that begins with *because* is a fragment. While acceptable in conversation, such sentences should be avoided in writing.

● **Practice Your Skills**

### Identifying Clause Fragments

Write *S* if the word group is a sentence. Write *F* if the word group is a clause fragment.

1. Ruminants are animals that chew their cud.
2. As soon as I heard about them.
3. Because I had never seen a moose up close.
4. That the oryx has long, pointed horns that point upward.
5. Whoever drew the picture of the kudu's long spiral horns.
6. I liked the chamois, whose soft skin is sometimes used as a "chamois cloth."
7. That I would never use a real leather chamois cloth again.
8. Until you know the difference between a bison and a musk ox.
9. So that I could also see the stripe-backed duikers.
10. When I saw the gazelles.

oryx

● *Connect to Writing:* **Revising**

### Correcting Clause Fragments

Use each clause fragment in the preceding exercise in a complete sentence. Use a variety of correctly punctuated sentence structures.

**16 E** A **run-on sentence** is two or more sentences that are written as one sentence. A run-on sentence is sometimes seen written as one long sentence with no punctuation. At other times run-ons incorporate punctuation incorrectly.

Run-on sentences result either from writing too fast or from the mistaken idea that very long sentences sound more scholarly. A run-on sentence is often written in one of two ways: with a comma (also known as a **comma splice**) or with no punctuation.

| | |
|---|---|
| **Comma Splice** | Horticulturists grow beautiful plants, they often organize garden shows for interested audiences. |
| **With No Punctuation** | In the winter some trees lose their leaves others do not. |

## ➤ Ways to Correct Run-on Sentences

A run-on sentence can be corrected in several ways. (1) It can be written as two separate sentences. (2) It can be written as a compound sentence with a comma and a conjunction or with a semicolon. (3) It can be written as a complex sentence by changing one part of the run-on sentence into a subordinate clause.

| | |
|---|---|
| **Run-on Sentence** | This botanical garden covers over four acres, it is the second largest in the state. |
| | This botanical garden covers over four acres it is the second largest in the state. |
| **Separate Sentences** | This botanical garden covers over four acres. It is the second largest in the state. |
| **Compound Sentence** | This botanical garden covers over four acres, **and** it is the second largest in the state. (with a comma and a conjunction) |
| | This botanical garden covers over four acres; it is the second largest in the state. (with a semicolon) |
| **Complex Sentence** | This botanical garden, **which covers over four acres,** is the second largest in the state. (adjectival clause) |
| | **Since this botanical garden covers over four acres,** it is the second largest in the state. (adverbial clause) |

### Identifying Run-on Sentences

Label each group of words as *RO* for run-on or *S* for sentence.

1. Many plants have poisonous leaves or fruits, these cause skin irritation or sickness.
2. The belladonna has a beautiful name and poisonous berries, it is also called deadly nightshade.
3. Holly, commonly used for holiday decoration, has poisonous leaves and berries.
4. Another seasonal flower, the lily of the valley, has berries too these should not be eaten by anyone either.
5. Many people love rhubarb pie, they do not know that rhubarb leaves should not be eaten.
6. Like most people, I cannot touch poison ivy, it gives me a rash.
7. Digitalis is a plant used in some medicines the leaves are poisonous when eaten.
8. As a child I learned not to touch the nettle, I learned the hard way.
9. Children and pets don't know the dangers of poisonous plants, some will innocently eat them and become sick or die.
10. English ivy foliage is not poisonous, but the berries are.

poison ivy

● *Connect to Writing:* **Editing**

### Correcting Run-on Sentences

Rewrite the run-on sentences you identified in the preceding exercise as separate sentences, compound sentences, or complex sentences. Use conjunctions and punctuation as needed.

● *Connect to Writing:* **Letter**

### Using Clauses and Sentences

Imagine that you have just discovered an herb whose properties include curing acne, flat feet, migraine, and halitosis. Write a letter to a fellow scientist describing this herb, the experiments you have conducted, and the results of these experiments. Describe the herb in detail, perhaps including a drawing with labels. Check for run-on sentences and fragments. Identify all of the simple sentences, compound sentences, complex sentences, and compound-complex sentences and the types of clauses you have used. Exchange letters with a partner and check each other's work.

# ➤ Diagraming Sentences

Each clause—whether independent or subordinate—is diagramed on a separate baseline like a simple sentence.

**Compound Sentences**  Each independent clause is diagramed like a simple sentence. The clauses are joined at the verbs with a broken line on which the conjunction is written.

> The cafeteria food is good, but I still take my lunch.

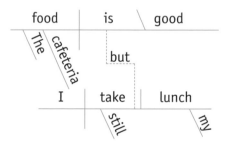

**Complex Sentences**  An adverbial or an adjectival clause in a complex sentence is diagramed beneath the independent clause containing the word or words it modifies. The following diagram contains an adverbial clause. The subordinating conjunction goes on a broken line that connects the verb in the adverbial clause to the modified verb, adverb, or adjective in the independent clause.

> Before I begin my article, I must do more research.

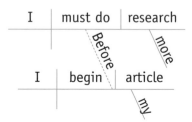

The relative pronoun in an adjectival clause is connected by a broken line to the noun or the pronoun the clause modifies.

We recently bought a clock that chimes on the hour.

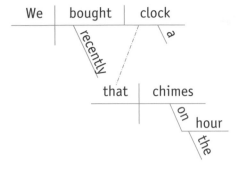

A noun clause is diagramed on a pedestal in the same position as a single noun with the same function, such as a direct object.

Tell us what you want for your birthday.

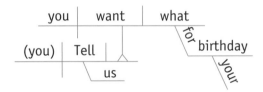

**Compound-Complex Sentences**  To diagram these sentences, apply rules for diagraming compound and complex sentences.

● **Practice Your Skills**

*Diagraming Sentences*

Diagram the following sentences or copy them. If you copy them, draw one line under each subject and two lines under each verb. Then put parentheses around each subordinate clause and label each one adverbial, adjectival, or noun.

**1.** An earthquake begins when underground rocks move.

**2.** This movement creates waves of energy that travel up to the surface.

**3.** Because earthquakes often cause severe damage, architects now can build earthquake-proof buildings.

**4.** Thousands of earthquakes occur during a year, but only a few are large ones.

**5.** What scientists still cannot do is predict earthquakes.

## Assess Your Learning

### Identifying Clauses

Write each subordinate clause. Then label each one adverbial, adjectival, or noun.

1. Although many tornadoes occur throughout the United States, they are quite rare west of the Rockies.
2. Several champion ice-hockey teams have come from Canada, where ice-skating is a very popular sport.
3. I heard that trucks can no longer travel on Grove Street.
4. Wrap that meat in foil before you put it into the freezer.
5. Since I will have a test in Spanish, I went to the language lab.
6. The microphone that he used had a cord attached to it.
7. If you take a trip to Mount Vernon, you will be taken back two centuries into the past.
8. Parachutists often fall a considerable distance before they pull the cord that opens the parachute.
9. Someone once said that an egotist is a person who is "me-deep" in conversation.
10. My mother, who seemed happy and relieved, reported that she had found a new apartment for us.

### Classifying Sentences

Label each sentence simple, compound, complex, or compound-complex.

1. John Paul Jones moved to America to avoid a trial that involved his handling of a mutiny.
2. Although he was born in Scotland, he became a hero of the American Revolution.
3. He battled British ships off the coast of North America.
4. His most famous victory occurred in 1779 aboard the *Bonhomme Richard*.

**5.** His ship was badly damaged, but Jones refused to give up.

**6.** He was urged to surrender, but he called out, "Sir, I have not yet begun to fight," words that have gone down in history.

**7.** Jones was only in his early 30s when he captured the British warships *Drake* and *Serapis*.

**8.** After the war, American shipping became vulnerable to attacks by pirates.

**9.** Thomas Jefferson suggested that John Paul Jones could destroy the pirates.

**10.** He mentioned this in a letter to James Monroe, but nothing came of it.

### ■ Using Sentence Structures

Write five sentences that follow the directions below. (The sentences may come in any order.) Write about an unrecognized hero or a topic of your choice.

**1.** Write a simple sentence.

**2.** Write a complex sentence with an introductory adverbial clause.

**3.** Write a complex sentence with an adjectival clause.

**4.** Write a compound sentence.

**5.** Write a complex sentence with a noun clause.

Label each sentence and check its punctuation.

# Clauses: Posttest

## Directions

Write the letter of the term that correctly identifies each sentence or underlined part of a sentence.

### Stream of Consciousness

**(1)** James Joyce was a great master of stream of consciousness. **(2)** Joyce, however, owed much to a French novelist who had used the technique much earlier. **(3)** Edouard Dujardin experimented with the technique in 1887 when he published *The Laurels Are Cut Down.* **(4)** His novel is rarely read today, but it influenced many writers. **(5)** Dujardin defined his interior monologue as "an unspoken discourse without a hearer present. . . ." **(6)** <u>Some critics distinguish interior monologue from stream of consciousness</u>; they feel that there is a clear difference. **(7)** <u>Although both include a character's thoughts and feelings</u>, interior monologue indicates nothing in the way of a narrator. **(8)** Joyce used both in *Ulysses,* <u>which is one of his finest works.</u> **(9)** <u>If you read Virginia Woolf's work,</u> you will see many examples of stream-of-consciousness writing. **(10)** *To the Lighthouse* alternates between the thoughts of Mr. Ramsay, <u>whose mind works rationally and dispassionately</u>, and those of his wife, a creative, intuitive person.

**1. A** simple sentence
   **B** compound sentence
   **C** complex sentence
   **D** compound-complex sentence

**2. A** simple sentence
   **B** compound sentence
   **C** complex sentence
   **D** compound-complex sentence

**3. A** simple sentence
   **B** compound sentence
   **C** complex sentence
   **D** compound-complex sentence

**4. A** simple sentence
   **B** compound sentence
   **C** complex sentence
   **D** compound-complex sentence

**5. A** simple sentence
   **B** compound sentence
   **C** complex sentence
   **D** compound-complex sentence

**6. A** independent clause
   **B** adverbial clause
   **C** adjectival clause
   **D** noun clause

**7. A** independent clause
   **B** adverbial clause
   **C** adjectival clause
   **D** noun clause

**8. A** independent clause
   **B** adverbial clause
   **C** adjectival clause
   **D** noun clause

**9. A** independent clause
   **B** adverbial clause
   **C** adjectival clause
   **D** noun clause

**10. A** independent clause
   **B** adverbial clause
   **C** adjectival clause
   **D** noun clause

# Writer's Corner

## Snapshot

**16 A**    A **clause** is a group of words that has a subject and predicate. An **independent clause** expresses a complete thought. A **subordinate clause** does not express a complete thought and cannot stand alone as a sentence. (pages 718–719.)

**16 B**    An **adverbial clause** is a subordinate clause functioning as an adverb; an **adjectival clause** is a subordinate clause functioning as an adjective; a **noun clause** is a subordinate clause functioning as a noun. (pages 720–730.)

**16 C**    A **sentence** can be **simple, compound, complex,** or **compound-complex,** depending on the number and the kind of clauses in it. (pages 731–733.)

**16 D**    A **clause fragment** is a subordinate clause that is punctuated like a sentence. (pages 734–735.)

**16 E**    A **run-on sentence** is two or more sentences that are written as one sentence. (pages 736–738.)

## Power Rules

 Fix **sentence fragments** by adding or changing words to express a complete thought or by attaching the fragment to a related sentence. (See pages 734–735.)

| **Before Editing** | **After Editing** |
| --- | --- |
| *Although Sam left early.* He ran into traffic and arrived late. | *Although Sam left early,* he ran into traffic and arrived late. |
| Sam took the train to work yesterday. *Because his car was in the shop.* | Sam took the train to work yesterday *because his car was in the shop.* |

 Revise **run-on sentences** by adding a conjunction and/or punctuation, or by subordinating a clause to an independent clause. (See pages 736–738.)

| **Before Editing** | **After Editing** |
| --- | --- |
| We took the trip in May, *we went to Boston.* | *When we took the trip in May,* we went to Boston. |

# Editing Checklist

Use this checklist when editing your writing.

✓ Did I include a subject and verb in each clause? (See pages 718–719.)

✓ Did I use subordinating conjunctions to show relationships between ideas? (See pages 720–722.)

✓ Did I use noun clauses to make my sentences clear and specific? (See pages 729–730.)

✓ Did I use adverbial and adjectival clauses to add variety and detail to my sentences? (See pages 720–729.)

✓ Did I place adjectival clauses correctly to avoid misplaced modifiers? (See pages 728–729.)

✓ Did I use commas correctly with my clauses? (See pages 721, 727, and 736.)

✓ Did I use a combination of simple, compound, complex, and compound-complex sentences to add variety and interest to my writing? (See pages 731–733.)

✓ Did I correct any clause fragments or run-on sentences? (See pages 734–738.)

## Use the Power

**Think of clauses** as colors. Using various combinations of clauses and types of sentences makes your writing more vivid, just like adding colors to a painting makes it come alive.

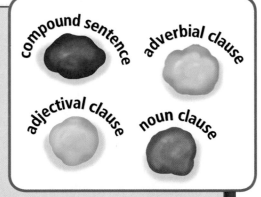

Marco had not traveled much, but he was ready for his adventure to the Atacama Desert. Marco's best friend, who was an expert tour guide, was going to accompany him to the desert because the two had always dreamed about traveling together. When asked, Marco answered that being with his friend for two weeks would not be a problem.

**Revise** a recent composition by adding at least one adverbial clause, one adjectival clause, and one compound sentence.

# Unit 5

# Usage

The architects and builders of the vibrant "city" we call the English language are its speakers and writers—those who create and use its words. The ways to use the language are indeed as varied as the speakers themselves. But the conventional usage presented in this book is important to learn because it will help you communicate powerfully in places such as colleges and workplaces. Now that you have strengthened your understanding of the role verbs, pronouns, adjectives, and adverbs play in sentences, you will build on your understanding and review how to use those words in ways that will help you communicate in the important arenas of your future.

*Language is a city to the building of which every human being brought a stone.*

—*Ralph Waldo Emerson*

# Using Verbs

**How can using verbs in just the right way spark your descriptions and make your writing shine?**

## Using Verbs: Pretest 1

The following draft paragraph about attending an art exhibit is hard to read because it contains errors involving verb usage. The first error has been corrected as an example.

Yesterday I ~~go~~ *went* to an art exhibit, and I have enjoyed it very much. Hearing of the Art Guys, I wanted to see some of their work. I never saw so many unusual sculptures and displays setting in one place before, and I will want to tell you about one of them. One room was designed to be entertaining people. When I had walked into the room, I hear jets flying overhead. As I looked up, I seen the most amazing sight. Televisions were hanging down from the ceiling. Each television was playing a video of jets that had been flying in the sky. I am glad to go to the exhibit. I will intend to return soon. If I was free tomorrow, I would definitely go again.

## Using Verbs: Pretest 2

### Directions

Read the passage and choose the word or group of words that belongs in each underlined space. Write the letter of the correct answer.

In prehistoric times, dancing __(1)__ an early form of artistic expression. Along the shores of the Mediterranean Sea, decorative carvings found in Egyptian tombs __(2)__ that dances __(3)__ during funerals and parades as well as in religious rituals. Dancing always __(4)__ an important part in Greek celebrations. The Romans, too, __(5)__ ceremonial dancing to Italy from Greece, used it in theatrical performances.

During the Middle Ages dance continued __(6)__ an important role in both courtly and village life. The peasants especially __(7)__ performing sword dances, Maypole dances, chain dances, and circle dances. Change, however, __(8)__ in the air. Professional performances __(9)__ as *balletti* originated in the Renaissance and within a few years __(10)__ over all of Europe.

1. **A** have been
   **B** were
   **C** was
   **D** will be

2. **A** reveal
   **B** will be revealing
   **C** are revealing
   **D** do reveal

3. **A** will have been performed
   **B** have been performing
   **C** perform
   **D** were performed

4. **A** has played
   **B** have played
   **C** is played
   **D** were played

5. **A** have brought
   **B** having brought
   **C** brought
   **D** had brought

6. **A** played
   **B** to play
   **C** did play
   **D** having been played

7. **A** have enjoyed
   **B** will enjoy
   **C** enjoy
   **D** enjoyed

8. **A** were
   **B** is
   **C** was
   **D** has been

9. **A** known
   **B** knowing
   **C** knew
   **D** having been known

10. **A** sweep
    **B** have swept
    **C** had swept
    **D** sweeping

# The Principal Parts of Verbs

If you know which word in a sentence is a verb, you can choose to substitute a specific, colorful verb for a dull, general one. Then, however, you must know which form of that verb to use. In this chapter you will learn how to use the correct verb forms.

The four basic forms of a verb are called its **principal parts.** The six tenses of a verb are formed from these principal parts.

> **17 A**    The **principal parts** of a verb are the present, the present participle, the past, and the past participle.

Notice that helping verbs are needed with the present participle and the past participle when they are used as the main verb of the sentence.

| | |
|---|---|
| **Present** | I usually **eat** lunch after drama class. |
| **Present Participle** | I *am* **eating** lunch earlier this week. |
| **Past** | I **ate** lunch an hour ago. |
| **Past Participle** | I *have* already **eaten** lunch. |

## ➤ Regular and Irregular Verbs

Verbs are sometimes classified in two categories: **regular verbs** and **irregular verbs.** The manner in which a verb forms its past and past participle will determine its classification.

> **17 A.1**    A **regular verb** forms its past and past participle by adding *-ed* or *-d* to the present form. An **irregular verb** does not form its past and past participle by adding *-ed* or *-d* to the present form.

## Regular Verbs

Most verbs are classified as regular verbs because they form their past and past participle in the same way—by adding *-ed* or *-d* to the present. The table on the next page lists the four principal parts of the regular verbs *talk, use, equip,* and *commit.* Notice that the present participle is formed by adding *-ing* to the present form, and as the rule says, the past participle is formed by adding *-ed* or *-d* to the present form.

## REGULAR VERBS

| Present | Present Participle | Past | Past Participle |
|---------|-------------------|------|-----------------|
| talk | (is) talking | talked | (have) talked |
| use | (is) using | used | (have) used |
| equip | (is) equipping | equipped | (have) equipped |
| commit | (is) committing | committed | (have) committed |

When endings such as *-ing* and *-ed* are added to some verbs, such as *use, equip,* and *commit,* the spelling changes. If you are unsure of the spelling of a verb form, look it up in the dictionary.

## When You Speak and Write

Get in the habit of pronouncing the *-ed* or *-d* in verb forms such as *asked, helped, looked, seemed, supposed, talked, used,* and *walked* when you are speaking. That way you will be less likely to misspell the word in your writing.

| | |
|---|---|
| **Incorrect** | This was **suppose** to be an ancient pottery exhibit. |
| **Correct** | This was **supposed** to be an ancient pottery exhibit. |

## ● Practice Your Skills

### Determining the Principal Parts of Regular Verbs

Write each verb form. Beside it, label its principal part: *present, present participle, past,* or *past participle.* (Do not include any helping verbs.)

**1.** I sketched too many portraits.

**2.** Thelma is running for Art Club president.

**3.** I have committed to summer art classes.

**4.** I like watercolors.

**5.** Trish is mixing tempera paints.

**6.** She has searched for the perfect still life.

**7.** Tonya and Kyle are arranging fruit in a glass bowl.

**8.** The fruit looks beautiful.

**9.** Everyone else painted fruit yesterday.

**10.** Louis C. Tiffany greatly impacted the Art Nouveau movement with his designs in glass.

# ➤ Irregular Verbs

Some common verbs are classified as irregular because they form their past and past participle in different ways instead of adding *-ed* or *-d* to the present. The irregular verbs have been divided into groups according to the way they form their past and past participle.

Remember that *is* is not part of the present participle and *have* is not part of the past participle. They have been added to the following lists of irregular verbs, however, to remind you that all present and past participles must have a form of one of these helping verbs when they are used as a verb in a sentence.

**Group 1** These irregular verbs have the same form for the present, the past, and the past participle.

| GROUP 1 | | | |
|---|---|---|---|
| **Present** | **Present Part.** | **Past** | **Past Part.** |
| burst | (is) bursting | burst | (have) burst |
| cost | (is) costing | cost | (have) cost |
| hit | (is) hitting | hit | (have) hit |
| hurt | (is) hurting | hurt | (have) hurt |
| let | (is) letting | let | (have) let |
| put | (is) putting | put | (have) put |

**Group 2** These irregular verbs have the same form for the past and the past participle.

| GROUP 2 | | | |
|---|---|---|---|
| **Present** | **Present Part.** | **Past** | **Past Part.** |
| bring | (is) bringing | brought | (have) brought |
| buy | (is) buying | bought | (have) bought |
| catch | (is) catching | caught | (have) caught |
| feel | (is) feeling | felt | (have) felt |
| find | (is) finding | found | (have) found |
| get | (is) getting | got | (have) got or gotten |
| hold | (is) holding | held | (have) held |
| keep | (is) keeping | kept | (have) kept |
| lead | (is) leading | led | (have) led |

| leave | (is) leaving | left | (have) left |
| lose | (is) losing | lost | (have) lost |
| make | (is) making | made | (have) made |
| say | (is) saying | said | (have) said |
| sell | (is) selling | sold | (have) sold |
| send | (is) sending | sent | (have) sent |
| teach | (is) teaching | taught | (have) taught |
| tell | (is) telling | told | (have) told |
| win | (is) winning | won | (have) won |

## ● Practice Your Skills

### Using the Correct Verb Form

Write the *past* or the *past participle* of each underlined verb.

**1.** In 1836, the Mexican General Santa Anna <u>lead</u> his army to the Alamo.

**2.** He had <u>bring</u> with him an army of thousands.

**3.** He <u>find</u> fewer than 200 Texas soldiers at the mission.

**4.** These volunteer freedom fighters had <u>put</u> their lives at risk for their beliefs.

**5.** After 13 days of battle, every soldier in the Alamo had <u>lose</u> his life.

**6.** Despite the bloodshed, they had <u>make</u> history.

**7.** Santa Anna had <u>win</u> the battle, but at great cost.

**8.** One of Santa Anna's colonels <u>say</u> they couldn't afford many more "victories" like the Alamo.

## ● Practice Your Skills

### Determining the Principal Parts of Irregular Verbs

Make four columns on your paper. Label them *Present, Present Participle, Past,* and *Past Participle.* Then write the four principal parts of the following verbs.

**1.** buy      **6.** tell

**2.** keep      **7.** sell

**3.** let      **8.** get

**4.** put      **9.** teach

**5.** hurt      **10.** leave

● *Connect to Writing:* **Editing**

*Correcting Verb Forms*

Rewrite the following paragraph, correcting the incorrect verb forms. (You will correct 8 forms in all.)

**(1)** Francis Scott Key, author of "The Star-Spangled Banner," hold a degree from St. John's College. **(2)** He make his living as a lawyer. **(3)** In 1814, he finded himself aboard a British ship within sight of the British attack on Fort McHenry in Baltimore. **(4)** He had leaved Fort McHenry but could clearly see the bombs. **(5)** Many bursted in the air above, and others hitted the fort. **(6)** Key felt such strong emotions about the battle that he composed "The Star-Spangled Banner." **(7)** After the war he get a job as United States District Attorney. **(8)** In 1843, he contracted pleurisy, which costed him his life.

**Group 3** These irregular verbs form the past participle by adding *-n* to the past.

| GROUP 3 | | | |
|---|---|---|---|
| **Present** | **Present Part.** | **Past** | **Past Part.** |
| break | (is) breaking | broke | (have) broken |
| choose | (is) choosing | chose | (have) chosen |
| freeze | (is) freezing | froze | (have) frozen |
| speak | (is) speaking | spoke | (have) spoken |
| steal | (is) stealing | stole | (have) stolen |

**Group 4** These irregular verbs form the past participle by adding *-n* to the present.

| GROUP 4 | | | |
|---|---|---|---|
| **Present** | **Present Part.** | **Past** | **Past Part.** |
| blow | (is) blowing | blew | (have) blown |
| draw | (is) drawing | drew | (have) drawn |
| drive | (is) driving | drove | (have) driven |
| give | (is) giving | gave | (have) given |
| grow | (is) growing | grew | (have) grown |
| know | (is) knowing | knew | (have) known |
| see | (is) seeing | saw | (have) seen |

| | | | |
|---|---|---|---|
| take | (is) taking | took | (have) taken |
| throw | (is) throwing | threw | (have) thrown |

## ● Practice Your Skills

### *Using the Correct Verb Form*

Write the past or the past participle of each underlined verb.

**1.** Willis has <u>throw</u> three balls through the hoop.

**2.** Brian <u>steal</u> two bases during the sixth inning.

**3.** Every day at camp, we <u>take</u> polo lessons.

**4.** Last night we <u>see</u> the team's most exciting game ever.

**5.** Mom <u>drive</u> us home after the game.

**6.** Chris asked if we had <u>choose</u> a captain yet.

**7.** Last fall I <u>break</u> my arm playing softball.

**8.** My arm has <u>grow</u> stronger with the help of exercise.

## ● Practice Your Skills

### *Determining the Correct Verb Form*

Write the correct form of each underlined verb. Remember that all the action took place the previous summer.

**1.** I <u>buy</u> a bonsai tree at Bao's Bonsai Garden last summer.

**2.** I had <u>see</u> this quaint little nursery before.

**3.** I had <u>take</u> the opportunity and had <u>speak</u> to Bao.

**4.** I <u>find</u> myself thinking about owning a beautiful bonsai.

**5.** Monday, I <u>get</u> up early and <u>make</u> my way to Bao's store.

**6.** I <u>choose</u> a tiny, perfect tree.

**7.** Bao <u>give</u> me a tree-care guide.

**8.** She <u>say</u> most people have never <u>grow</u> a bonsai before.

CHAPTER 17

● *Connect to Writing:* **Editing**

### Using Verb Forms

Rewrite the following paragraph, using past and participle forms. Be sure to change all the present-tense verbs to the past tense. (You will change 21 verb forms in all.)

**(1)** June bursts into the room and makes an announcement. **(2)** She says she had saw a kit for a window-sill herb garden. **(3)** She had drove to the farmer's market and had sold some fresh vegetables she had grew in her large garden. **(4)** Afterwards, she grows interested in the other booths. **(5)** She takes a stroll down the aisles. **(6)** She finds the herb kit and knows she wants it. **(7)** It costs only a few dollars, and so she gives the seller her money. **(8)** She puts her new purchase in the trunk and then finds her car keys in her large bag. **(9)** She feels happy about the herb-garden project. **(10)** She takes the shortcut across the pasture and drives quickly home.

**(11)** June takes the kit into her garage. **(12)** She breaks its seal. **(13)** She finds a calendar schedule for the garden in the directions.

**Group 5** These irregular verbs form the past and the past participle by changing a vowel.

| GROUP 5 | | | |
|---|---|---|---|
| **Present** | **Present Part.** | **Past** | **Past Part.** |
| begin | (is) beginning | began | (have) begun |
| drink | (is) drinking | drank | (have) drunk |
| ring | (is) ringing | rang | (have) rung |
| shrink | (is) shrinking | shrank | (have) shrunk |
| sing | (is) singing | sang | (have) sung |
| sink | (is) sinking | sank | (have) sunk |
| swim | (is) swimming | swam | (have) swum |

**Group 6** These irregular verbs form the past and the past participle in other ways.

| GROUP 6 | | | |
|---|---|---|---|
| **Present** | **Present Part.** | **Past** | **Past Part.** |
| come | (is) coming | came | (have) come |
| do | (is) doing | did | (have) done |
| eat | (is) eating | ate | (have) eaten |
| fall | (is) falling | fell | (have) fallen |
| go | (is) going | went | (have) gone |

| ride | (is) riding | rode | (have) ridden |
|------|-------------|------|---------------|
| run | (is) running | ran | (have) run |
| tear | (is) tearing | tore | (have) torn |
| wear | (is) wearing | wore | (have) worn |
| write | (is) writing | wrote | (have) written |

## *When You Speak*

If you've been around young children much, you know they have difficulty using irregular verbs. They are apt to say proudly, "I **putted** my toys away," or to complain loudly, "She **drinked** my juice." You can help children learn the correct form by rephrasing their statements: "Good! You **put** your toys away" or "She **drank** your juice?"

## ● Practice Your Skills

### *Using the Correct Verb Form*

Write the past or the past participle of each underlined verb.

**1.** Thousands of people go to the rodeo.

**2.** Many come from far away.

**3.** They wear their best boots and a new hat.

**4.** Cowboys had begin practicing for the bull rides long ago.

**5.** These daring men and women had fall many times.

**6.** Some had even tear ligaments or muscles.

**7.** Nevertheless, they had come to the rodeo ready to ride.

**8.** In another show, talented vocalists sing country songs.

## ● Practice Your Skills

### *Supplying the Correct Verb Form*

Complete each pair of sentences by supplying the past or the past participle of the verb in parentheses at the beginning of the sentence.

**1.** (begin) The school play ___ 15 minutes ago. It should have ___ a half hour ago.

**2.** (do) Have you ___ your homework? I ___ mine at school.

**3.** (run) Matthew ___ for Student Council president last year. He should have ___ again this year.

**4.** (drink) We ___ some ice water after cheerleading practice. We should never have ___ it fast.

**5.** (go) Have you ___ to a pep rally yet? Yes, I ___ to one Friday.

The Principal Parts of Verbs • Lesson 1    **757**

### Correcting Verb Forms

Rewrite the following paragraphs, using past and past participle verb forms. (You will change 23 verb forms in all.)

**(1)** Brandy comes to my school last month. **(2)** Before, she had went to another school. **(3)** I speak to her before homeroom because I know what it's like to be new. **(4)** I find Brandy knows sign language. **(5)** She teaches me some before class. **(6)** I see her again at lunch and get up from my seat. **(7)** She sees me and comes over. **(8)** She had already ate her lunch, but she drinks a soda while I eat. **(9)** We write down ideas for a sign language club. **(10)** By the end of lunch period, we had make much progress.

**(11)** Later we send a copy of our plans to the class president. **(12)** He chooses to support our idea. **(13)** He speaks to the student council, and they draw up a plan for the club. **(14)** Brandy and I go to several planning sessions. **(15)** We also begin telling other students about the sign language club. **(16)** The club has became my favorite school activity.

## Power Your Writing: Getting Into the Action

⚡In addition to their function as verbs, participles can also serve as modifiers, often as part of a participial phrase (see pages 693–696). In that form, they add action and colorful detail to writing. When Coretta Scott King relates the story of Rosa Parks (see pages 225–229), she uses a present participial phrase. The participle is highlighted below.

So she sat there, refusing to give up.

Compare that picture to the following version without a participial phrase.

So she sat there. She refused to give up.

Here's another example from that reading about the preparations before the Montgomery bus boycott. Notice the energy added by the participial phrases.

They hustled around town talking with other leaders, arranging with the Negro-owned taxi companies for special bulk fares.

Use participial phrases to power your own writing.

# Six Problem Verbs

Some verbs present problems, not because they are regular or irregular, but because their meanings are easily confused. Always make sure, therefore, that you have chosen the verb that correctly expresses what you want to say or write.

## *lie* and *lay*

*Lie* means "to rest or recline." *Lie* is never followed by a direct object. *Lay* means "to put or set (something) down." *Lay* is usually followed by a direct object.

*You can learn more about direct objects on pages 664–666.*

| Present | Present Part. | Past | Past Part. |
|---------|---------------|------|------------|
| lie | (is) lying | lay | (have) lain |
| lay | (is) laying | laid | (have) laid |

| | |
|---|---|
| **Lie** | Her party dresses **lie** on the floor of the guest bedroom. |
| | They are **lying** in a heap now. |
| | They **lay** there last weekend too. |
| | They **have lain** in the guest bedroom for weeks. |
| **Lay** | **Lay** the servers' aprons on the table. |
| | (You lay what? *Aprons* is the direct object.) |
| | Harry **is laying** the aprons on the table. |
| | Shoshana **laid** the aprons on the table last night. |
| | Usually I **have laid** the aprons on the table. |

## When You Write

When *lie* means "to tell a falsehood," the principal parts are *lie, is lying, lied,* and *(have) lied.* Be sure to include enough information to make the meaning clear because some of the principal parts are the same as those for *to lie* meaning "to rest or recline."

| **Confusing** | Jesse never **lies** about. |
|---------------|------------------------------|
| **Correct** | Jesse never **lies** about his chores. |

## *rise* and *raise*

*Rise* means "to move upward" or "to get up." *Rise* is never followed by a direct object. *Raise* means "to lift (something) up," "to increase," or "to grow something." *Raise* is usually followed by a direct object.

| Present | Present Part. | Past | Past Part. |
|---------|---------------|------|------------|
| rise | (is) rising | rose | (have) risen |
| raise | (is) raising | raised | (have) raised |

**Rise**    **Rise** early for the breakfast shift.

Marianne **is rising** early for her new job.

Marianne **rose** at sunrise yesterday.

She **has risen** early for several weeks.

**Raise**    **Raise** the cattle for the restaurant supplier.

(You raise what? *Cattle* is the direct object.)

He **is raising** the cattle for beef.

He **raised** cattle for the beef suppliers.

He **has raised** cattle for two decades.

## *sit* and *set*

*Sit* means "to rest in an upright position." *Sit* is never followed by a direct object. *Set* means "to put or place (something)." *Set* is usually followed by a direct object.

| Present | Present Part. | Past | Past Part. |
|---------|---------------|------|------------|
| sit | (is) sitting | sat | (have) sat |
| set | (is) setting | set | (have) set |

**Sit**    **Sit** near me at the awards banquet.

She **is sitting** at the head table.

She **sat** there near Tim.

She **has** never **sat** near Tim before tonight.

| **Set** | **Set** the awards on the podium. |
|---|---|
| | (You set what? *Awards* is the direct object.) |
| | He **is setting** the awards on the podium. |
| | He **set** the awards on the podium this morning. |
| | He **has set** the awards on the podium every year. |

*You can learn more about other confusing verbs on pages 752–757.*

## ● Practice Your Skills

### Using the Correct Verb Form

Write the correct verb form from the choices provided.

**1.** I will (lie/lay) on the sofa to rest before the party.

**2.** Why are you (sitting/setting) on the sofa?

**3.** Charlie has (sat/set) the record for hosting the most parties in a summer.

**4.** Tell Jane she must (rise/raise) funds to buy the cake.

**5.** You have (lain/laid) on that sofa for too long.

**6.** Perry, will you (sit/set) the fine china on the table?

**7.** Shelly is (lying/laying) a napkin across her lap.

**8.** I am (rising/raising) to the challenge of entertaining.

**9.** That shy girl has (sat/set) in the corner all evening.

**10.** If you want to play charades, (rise/raise) your hand.

## ✔ *Check Point:* Mixed Practice

Write the past or the past participle of each verb in parentheses.

**1.** For over seven decades, the Harlem Globetrotters have (bring) an unusual dimension to basketball.

**2.** In 1926, the Globetrotters (begin) as a serious team.

**3.** They (play) some of their first games in the Savoy Ballroom in Chicago.

**4.** When the dance hall (fall) on hard times, the team (go) on the road.

**5.** Since that time, the Globetrotters have never (leave) the touring circuit.

**17 B**   The time expressed by a verb is called the **tense** of a verb.

The six tenses are: **present, past, future, present perfect, past perfect,** and **future perfect.**

You can easily form these six tenses by knowing the four principal parts of a verb. In the following examples, the six tenses of *drive* are used to express action at different times.

| | |
|---|---|
| **Present** | Bart **drives** Tad to school. |
| **Past** | Bart **drove** Tad to school yesterday. |
| **Future** | Bart **will drive** Tad to school tomorrow. |
| **Present Perfect** | Bart **has driven** Tad to school all month. |
| **Past Perfect** | Bart **had** never **driven** Tad to school before February. |
| **Future Perfect** | By May, Bart **will have driven** Tad to school for four months. |

## Uses of the Tenses

The six basic tenses—three simple tenses and three perfect tenses—and their various forms have particular uses. As you review the uses, remember that all of the tenses are formed from the four principal parts of a verb and the helping verbs *have, has, had, will,* and *shall.*

**17 B.1**   **Present tense,** the first of the three simple tenses, is used mainly to express (1) an action that is going on now, (2) an action that happens regularly, or (3) an action that is usually constant or the same.

To form the present tense, use the present form (the first principal part of the verb) or add *-s* or *-es* to the present form.

| | |
|---|---|
| **Present Tense** | **Look** at this scuba suit. (current action) |
| | I **dig** for treasure each weekend. (regular action) |
| | Geology class **interests** me. (constant action) |

Occasionally you will also use the present tense when writing history or when writing about literature.

**17 B.2**   **Historical present tense** is used to relate a past action as if it were happening in the present. **Literary present tense** is used when writing about literature.

**History**        Christopher Columbus **encourages** his sailors daily.

**Literature**     In *Beowulf* the poet **tells** of Grendel's underwater lair.

**17 B.3**   **Past tense** is used to express an action that already took place or was completed in the past.

To form the past tense of a regular verb, add *-ed* or *-d* to the present form. To form the past tense of an irregular verb, check a dictionary for the past form or look for it on pages 752–761.

**Past Tense**     I **organized** the artifacts last week.

I **wrote** about my findings.

**17 B.4**   **Future tense** is used to express an action that will take place in the future.

To form the future tense, use the helping verb *shall* or *will* with the present form. In formal English, *shall* is used with *I* and *we,* and *will* is used with *you, he, she, it,* or *they.* In informal speech, however, *shall* and *will* are used interchangeably with *I* and *we*—except *shall* is still often used with *I* and *we* for questions.

**Future Tense**   I **shall organize** the artifacts tomorrow.

Leonore **will write** about the shipwreck.

*You can learn more about* shall *and* will *on page 896.*

*You can learn more about* shall *and* will *on page 896.*

Another way to express a future action is to use a present-tense verb with an adverb or group of words that indicate a future time.

**Future Action**  Leonore **presents** her report to the committee tomorrow.

**17 B.5** **Present perfect tense,** the first of three perfect tenses, has two uses: (1) to express an action that was completed at some indefinite time in the past and (2) to express an action that started in the past and is still going on.

To form the present perfect tense, add *has* or *have* to the past participle.

> **Present Perfect Tense**
>
> I **have organized** several boxes of artifacts.
> (action completed over an indefinite time)
>
> She **has written** the reports for more than five years.
> (action that is still going on)

**17 B.6** **Past perfect tense** expresses an action that took place before some other action.

To form the past perfect tense, add *had* to the past participle.

> **Past Perfect Tense**
>
> I **had organized** the artifacts before I read the instructions.
>
> Leonore **had written** the report by the time I arrived.

**17 B.7** **Future perfect tense** expresses an action that will take place before another future action or time.

To form the future perfect tense, add *shall have* or *will have* to the past participle.

> **Future Perfect Tense**
>
> I **shall have organized** fifty artifacts by tonight.
>
> By next semester, Leonore **will have written** six reports.

## ➤ Verb Conjugation

**17 B.8** A **conjugation** lists all the singular and plural forms of a verb in its various tenses.

A conjugation of the irregular verb *eat* follows.

| CONJUGATION OF *EAT* | |
| --- | --- |
| **Four Principal Parts:** eat, eating, ate, eaten | |
| SIMPLE TENSES | |
| Present | |
| **Singular** | **Plural** |
| I eat | we eat |
| you eat | you eat |
| he, she, it eats | they eat |

## Past

**Singular**

I ate

you ate

he, she, it ate

**Plural**

we ate

you ate

they ate

## Future

**Singular**

I shall/will eat

you will eat

he, she, it will eat

**Plural**

we shall/will eat

you will eat

they will eat

## PERFECT TENSES

### Present Perfect

**Singular**

I have eaten

you have eaten

he, she, it has eaten

**Plural**

we have eaten

you have eaten

they have eaten

### Past Perfect

**Singular**

I had eaten

you had eaten

he, she, it had eaten

**Plural**

we had eaten

you had eaten

they had eaten

### Future Perfect

**Singular**

I shall/will have eaten

you will have eaten

he, she, it will have eaten

**Plural**

we shall/will have eaten

you will have eaten

they will have eaten

*The present participle is used to conjugate only the progressive forms of a verb. You can learn more about the progressive forms of verbs on pages 773–774.*

The principal parts of the verb *be* are highly irregular, as shown in the table below.

| CONJUGATION OF *BE* | |
|---|---|
| **Four Principal Parts:** be, being, was, been | |
| **SIMPLE TENSES** | |
| **Present** | |
| **Singular** | **Plural** |
| I am | we are |
| you are | you are |
| he, she, it is | they are |
| **Past** | |
| **Singular** | **Plural** |
| I was | we were |
| you were | you were |
| he, she, it was | they were |
| **Future** | |
| **Singular** | **Plural** |
| I shall/will be | we shall/will be |
| you will be | you will be |
| he, she, it will be | they will be |
| **PERFECT TENSES** | |
| **Present Perfect** | |
| **Singular** | **Plural** |
| I have been | we have been |
| you have been | you have been |
| he, she, it has been | they have been |
| **Past Perfect** | |
| **Singular** | **Plural** |
| I had been | we had been |
| you had been | you had been |
| he, she, it had been | they had been |

● **Practice Your Skills**

*Identifying Verb Tenses*

Write the tense of each underlined verb.

1. An underwater archaeologist <u>studies</u> shipwrecks and artifacts from watery graves.
2. Archaeologists <u>have found</u> underwater treasures such as jewels, precious metals, and even medical instruments.
3. Radioactive material in the Garigliano River <u>made</u> underwater searches there dangerous.
4. Many students of archaeology <u>will have completed</u> an archaeological dig by graduation.
5. Students <u>will learn</u> about certain underwater worms.
6. These worms <u>eat</u> the wooden parts of a shipwreck.
7. Bodies of water with less salt <u>have provided</u> wooden artifacts in the best condition.
8. Riverbeds and lake bottoms in Europe <u>hold</u> much of the world's riches.
9. After World War II, divers <u>found</u> ammunition beneath old battle sites.
10. The United States government <u>had passed</u> a law about archaeological findings before the ammunition was discovered.

## ● Practice Your Skills

### *Choosing the Correct Tense*

Write the correct form of the verb in parentheses. Beside it, identify its tense using the following abbreviations:

present = *pres.*     present perfect = *pres. p.*
past = *past*         past perfect = *past p.*
future = *fut.*        future perfect = *fut. p.*

1. In a few years, I (shall train/have trained) as a forensic pathologist.
2. By then I (will have achieved/achieved) the same career goals as my role model, Aunt Maya.
3. In college Maya (studies/studied) forensic anthropology.
4. This science (applied/applies) physical anthropology to the legal process.
5. She (has become/became) an expert in her field over the past five years.
6. A forensic pathologist (helped/helps) solve murders.
7. Now Maya (took/has taken) a job as a forensic pathologist.
8. I often (ask/had asked) her questions about her job.
9. She once (determines/determined) the age and gender of a victim by studying the bones.

## ✔ *Check Point:* Mixed Practice

Write each verb and label its tense using the following abbreviations:

present = *pres.*     present perfect = *pres. p.*
past = *past*         past perfect = *past p.*
future = *fut.*        future perfect = *fut. p.*

1. After this week I will have learned about several cultural holidays.
2. I look forward to next May.
3. I had heard about *Cinco de Mayo* before this week.
4. Some friends excitedly described this Mexican holiday.
5. Now I have learned more information about the *Cinco de Mayo* celebration.
6. Spanish speakers will translate the name as Fifth of May.
7. On this date in 1862, a Mexican army defeated a French army at the Battle of Puebla.
8. The French eventually occupied Mexico after all.
9. Nevertheless, this battle has become a symbol of Mexican unity and pride.

# Common Problems Using Tenses

Knowing the tenses of verbs and their uses will eliminate most of the verb errors you may have been making. There are, however, a few special problems you should keep in mind when you edit your writing.

**17 B.9**   The tense of the verbs you use depends on the meaning you want to express.

## Past Tenses

If you want to express two past events that happened at the same time, use the past tense for both. Sometimes, however, you will want to tell about an action that happened before another action in the past. In such a situation, use the past perfect to express the action that happened first.

| | |
|---|---|
| **Past/Past** | When the author **arrived**, we **cheered.** |
| | (Both events happened at the same time.) |
| **Past/Past Perfect** | I **wrote** the play after I **had gone** to Broadway. |
| | (I went to Broadway before I wrote the play.) |

*When You Speak*

A common error in speaking is to use the words *would have* in a clause starting with *if* when that clause expresses the earlier of two past actions. You should instead use the past perfect tense to express the earlier action.

| | |
|---|---|
| **Incorrect** | If John **would have studied,** he might have passed the literature test. |
| **Correct** | If John **had studied,** he might have passed the literature test. (The past perfect shows that studying would have come before passing the test.) |

# Present and Past Tenses

**17 B.10** Occasionally, you will have to use a combination of present and past tense verbs to express an exact meaning.

**Present/Past**

┌present┐    ┌─past─┐
Kelly **knows** that I **borrowed** her book yesterday.
(*Knows* is in the present tense because it describes action that is happening now, but *borrowed* is in the past tense because it happened at a definite time in the past.)

**Past/Present Perfect**

┌─past─┐                              present perfect
Ever since I **discovered** *Wuthering Heights,* I **have read** that book every year.
(*Discovered* is in the past tense because it occurred at a definite time in the past, but *have read* is in the present perfect because it started in the past and is still going on.)

## ● Practice Your Skills

### *Identifying Combinations of Tenses*

Write the tense of each underlined verb.

Be prepared to explain why the tense is correct.

present = *pres.*     present perfect = *pres. p.*
past = *past*         past perfect = *past p.*
future = *fut.*       future perfect = *fut. p.*

1. I <u>went</u> to class and I <u>received</u> a copy of *The Canterbury Tales.*
2. I <u>smiled</u> because I <u>had heard</u> of the tales before.
3. I <u>hope</u> we <u>read</u> "The Pardoner's Tale."
4. My classmates <u>discovered</u> that Geoffrey Chaucer <u>had written</u> the tales in verse form.
5. Chaucer <u>began</u> *The Canterbury Tales* after he <u>had penned</u> *Troilus and Criseyde.*

# Present and Past Participles

Like verbs, participles used as adjectives have present and past tenses to express specific time.

| PARTICIPLES OF *EAT* | |
|---|---|
| **Present Participle** | eating |
| **Past Participle** | eaten |

**17 B.11**   Use *having* with a past participle in a participial phrase to show that one action was completed before another one.

**Incorrect**   **Applying** for the job, she waited for the manager's phone call. (The use of *applying,* the present participle, implies illogically that she was still applying while she waited for the phone call.)

**Correct**   **Having applied** for the job, she waited for the manager's phone call. (The use of *having* with the past participle *applied* shows that she applied for the job before she waited for the phone call.)

*You can learn more about participial phrases on pages 241 and 694–696.*

# Present and Perfect Infinitives

Like participles, infinitives also have different forms.

| INFINITIVES OF *EAT* | |
|---|---|
| **Present Infinitive** | to eat |
| **Perfect Infinitive** | to have eaten |

**17 B.12**   To express an action that takes place *after* another action, use the **present infinitive;** to express an action that takes place *before* another action, use the **perfect infinitive.**

**Present Infinitive**   For a year I waited **to apply** for a job on the school newspaper. (The applying came *after* the waiting.)

**Perfect Infinitive**   I feel very happy **to have applied** for a job in journalism. (The applying came *before* the feeling of happiness.)

*You can learn more about infinitives on pages 699–702.*

## ● Practice Your Skills

### *Identifying Correct Tenses of Participles and Infinitives*

If the tense of the underlined participle or infinitive is incorrect, write *I*. If the sentence is correct, write *C*.

**1.** I am happy <u>to view</u> Leonardo da Vinci's *Mona Lisa*.

**2.** Da Vinci was one of the most interesting artists <u>having lived</u> during the Italian Renaissance.

**3.** The Duke of Milan was confident enough in Da Vinci <u>to suggest</u> that Da Vinci create a great sculpture of a horse in honor of the duke's father.

**4.** <u>Creating</u> the design, Da Vinci named it *Il Cavallo,* meaning "The Horse" in Italian.

**5.** <u>Approving</u> Da Vinci's drawing, the duke set about collecting the seventy tons of bronze it would take to cast the horse.

**6.** Using the drawing as a guide, Da Vinci began <u>to sculpt</u> a massive model out of clay.

**7.** When war erupted between France and Milan, the duke was forced <u>to have used</u> the bronze to make cannons.

**8.** Da Vinci was forced <u>to have left</u> *Il Cavallo* unfinished when he fled Milan in 1499.

## ● *Connect to Writing:* Editing

### *Correcting the Tenses of Participles and Infinitives*

Rewrite the incorrect sentences in the preceding exercise, correcting the tenses of the participles and infinitives.

**Progressive and Emphatic Verb Forms**

In addition to the six basic tenses, every verb has six progressive forms and an emphatic form for the present and past tenses.

## Progressive Forms

**17 B.13**    The **progressive forms** are used to express continuing or ongoing action. To write the progressive forms, add a present or perfect tense of the verb *be* to the present participle.

Notice in the following examples that all of the progressive forms end in *-ing*.

| | |
|---|---|
| **Present Progressive** | I am eating. |
| **Past Progressive** | I was eating. |
| **Future Progressive** | I will (shall) be eating. |
| **Present Perfect Progressive** | I have been eating. |
| **Past Perfect Progressive** | I had been eating. |
| **Future Perfect Progressive** | I will (shall) have been eating. |

The **present progressive** form shows an ongoing action that is taking place now.

I **am playing** volleyball now.

Occasionally the present progressive can also show action in the future when the sentence contains an adverb or a phrase that indicates the future—such as *tomorrow* or *next month*.

I **am playing** volleyball after school tomorrow.

The **past progressive** form shows an ongoing action that took place in the past.

I **was playing** volleyball when the rain began.

The **future progressive** form shows an ongoing action that will take place in the future.

I **will be playing** volleyball when you have your party.

The **present perfect progressive** form shows an ongoing action that is continuing in the present.

> I **have been playing** volleyball for the past two and a half years.

The **past perfect progressive** form shows an ongoing action in the past that was interrupted by another past action.

> I **had been playing** volleyball when Coach Williams asked me to play basketball instead.

The **future perfect progressive** form shows a future ongoing action that will have taken place by a stated future time.

> By next summer **I will have been playing** volleyball for over three years.

## Emphatic Forms

**17 B.14**   The **emphatic forms** of the present and past tenses of verbs are mainly used to show emphasis or force. To write the present emphatic, add *do* or *does* to the present tense of a verb. To write the past emphatic, add *did* to the present tense.

> **Present**               I **eat** lunch every day at twelve o'clock.
>
> **Present Emphatic**      I **do eat** lunch every day at twelve o'clock.
>
> **Past**                  I **ate** lunch yesterday.
>
> **Past Emphatic**         I **did eat** lunch yesterday.

The emphatic forms are also used in some questions and negative statements.

> **Questions**             **Do** you **eat** lunch every day?
>
> **Negative Statement**    I **did** not **eat** lunch Monday.

Do you remember *Green Eggs and Ham* by Dr. Seuss? One of the things that makes the story fun to listen to is the emphatic verb forms.

> **Do** you **like** green eggs and ham?
> I **do** not **like** them, Sam-I-am. I **do** not **like** green eggs and ham.
> I **do** not **like** them in a house. I **do** not **like** them with a mouse. I **do** not **like** them here or there. I **do** not **like** them anywhere.
>
> —Dr. Seuss, *Green Eggs and Ham*

## ● Practice Your Skills

### *Identifying Progressive and Emphatic Forms*

Write the progressive or emphatic form in each sentence. Beside it write *P* for progressive or *E* for emphatic.

**1.** Did you go to the swim meet?

**2.** I will be buying season tickets tomorrow.

**3.** I have been saving my money all month.

**4.** Coach Chang didn't know about the new uniforms.

**5.** He will have been looking for the old uniforms for two hours.

**6.** He does look frantic.

**7.** I am going to the football game.

**8.** I shall be sitting at the fifty yard line.

**9.** I had been running track until I sprained my ankle.

**10.** I didn't have a sports bandage for my ankle.

**11.** Stephanie is jogging tomorrow afternoon.

**12.** She does love that activity.

**13.** She will have been jogging for one hour by dark.

**14.** Jon has been timing her laps.

**15.** Marcos will be lifting weights two days a week.

● *Connect to Writing:* **Drafting**

### Using Emphatic Verbs

Brainstorm five ideas that you emphatically agree or disagree with. Write an emphatic statement expressing each of these ideas. Underline the emphatic form of the verb in each statement.

✓ *Check Point:* **Mixed Practice**

Write the tense of each underlined verb.

**1.** In health class we <u>are learning</u> about vegetarian diets.

**2.** I <u>have</u> always <u>wanted</u> to learn about this topic.

**3.** In college Ms. Summers <u>had taken</u> a nutrition class.

**4.** Afterward she <u>designed</u> a lesson plan on vegetarian diets.

**5.** The class <u>was taking</u> careful notes.

**6.** We <u>will be planning</u> a vegetarian banquet for our class on Friday.

**7.** *Vegans,* or strict vegetarians, <u>do</u> not <u>consume</u> meat or animal products of any kind.

**8.** By the end of the school year, Ms. Summers <u>will have been following</u> a vegan diet for ten years.

**9.** I <u>am</u> not <u>feeling</u> comfortable with the vegan diet.

**10.** Lacto vegetarians always <u>have eaten</u> milk, cheese, and other dairy products.

**11.** Lacto vegetarians <u>don't eat</u> meats, poultry, or eggs.

**12.** My friend Kandie <u>resolved</u> to be a lacto vegetarian.

**13.** By the end of class, she <u>had changed</u> her mind.

**14.** An ovo lacto vegetarian <u>will eat</u> eggs and dairy products.

CHAPTER 17

# Active and Passive Voice

Some action verbs can be in the **active voice** or the **passive voice.**

**17 C** **The active voice indicates that the subject is performing the action. The passive voice indicates that the action of the verb is being performed upon the subject.**

In the following examples, the verb in the active voice has a direct object, making it a **transitive verb.** However, the verb in the passive voice does not have a direct object.

| | |
|---|---|
| **Active Voice** | Horace **found** a silver dollar. |
| **Passive Voice** | A silver dollar **was found** by Horace. (no direct object) |
| **Active Voice** | Marie **sent** the money by courier. |
| **Passive Voice** | The money **was sent** by courier. (no direct object) |

*You can learn about transitive verbs on pages 625–626.*

When you change a verb from active to passive voice, the direct object usually becomes the subject. In the example above, *money* was the direct object when the verb was active, but it became the subject when the verb became passive. Notice that verbs in the passive voice consist of a form of the verb *to be* plus a past participle, such as *was found* and *was sent.*

Some transitive verbs can also have an indirect object. When such a verb and its objects are changed to the passive voice, either of the two objects can become the subject of the sentence. If the other object remains an object of the verb, it is called a **retained object.**

| | |
|---|---|
| **Active Voice** | The judges gave each **winner** fifty **dollars.** |
| **Passive Voice** | Each winner was given fifty **dollars** by the judges. |
| **Passive Voice** | Fifty dollars was given to each **winner** by the judges. |

### Identifying Active and Passive Voice

Write the verb in each sentence. Then label each one *A* for *active* or *P* for *passive.*

1. The early American colonists used currencies from several different countries.
2. America once issued a five-cent bill.
3. The first Continental coin was designed by Benjamin Franklin.
4. The dies for that coin were engraved by Abel Buell.
5. Tobacco was used as money in Virginia and Maryland.
6. Martha Washington may have donated several of her silver forks and spoons for the minting of a series of half dimes.
7. The buffalo nickel was designed by James Earle Fraser, a famous sculptor.
8. Fraser's model for the nickel had been borrowed from the Bronx Zoo.
9. Nickels contain mostly copper.
10. The average United States dollar bill has a life span of less than one year.

## ➤ Use of Voice in Writing

Because verbs in the active voice are more forceful and have greater impact than verbs in the passive voice, you should use the active voice as much as possible.

**17 C.1**   Use **active voice** to increase the force and impact of your writing.

The passive voice does have some uses.

**17 C.2**   Use the **passive voice** in the following situations: (1) when the doer of the action is unknown or unimportant and (2) when you want to emphasize the receiver of the action or the results.

The extra tickets **were sold** at a profit. (doer unknown or unimportant)

The crumbling currency **was made** during the Civil War. (emphasis on the results)

# ● Practice Your Skills

### Using Active and Passive Voices

Write the verb in each sentence. Then label each one *A* for *active* or *P* for *passive*.

1. An interesting novel was given to my class by our literature teacher.
2. *Robinson Crusoe* was written by Daniel Defoe.
3. In the story, Robinson Crusoe is shipwrecked on an island.
4. Later, the character Friday befriends Crusoe.
5. This novel was published in 1719.
6. It is judged by scholars to be one of the first English novels ever written.
7. Before this time period, stories were written in verse form by authors.
8. Defoe was born in London in 1660.
9. His father named him Daniel Foe.
10. Around 1695, the name was changed to Defoe by Daniel.

## ● *Connect to Writing:* Revising

### Using Active and Passive Voice

Rewrite the passive-voice sentences in the preceding exercise, changing the passive voice to the active voice if appropriate. If a sentence is better In the passive voice, write C.

## ● *Connect to Speaking and Writing:* Vocabulary Review

### Using the Vocabulary of Grammar

With a partner, talk about the difference between active voice and passive voice. Then write short definitions of the two terms. Finally, write a sentence in active voice. Exchange sentences with your partner and change your partner's sentence from active to passive voice.

**17 D** The **mood** of a verb is the way in which the verb expresses an idea.

In English there are three moods: **indicative, imperative,** and **subjunctive.**

**17 D.1** The **indicative mood** is used to state a fact or to ask a question.

**17 D.2** The **imperative mood** is used to give a command or to make a request.

Since the indicative mood is used to state facts or ask questions, it is the mood that is used most often in both writing and speaking.

| | |
|---|---|
| **Indicative** | A national park **makes** a good vacation spot. |
| | What **makes** camping so much fun? |
| **Imperative** | **Look** at this brochure on Yellowstone National Park. |
| | **Consider** a trip to Mesa Verde. |

**17 D.3** The **subjunctive mood** is used to express wishes, ideas contrary to fact, doubts, possibilities, proposals, and demands or requests after the word *that*.

| | |
|---|---|
| **Contrary To Fact** | If I **were** you, I'd pack a water bottle. |
| | (I am not you.) |
| | If Karla **were** here, she could go with us. |
| | (She is not here.) |
| **A Wish** | I wish I **were** a better skier. |
| | I wish that **were** our flight. |
| **Command/Request Beginning With *That*** | I demand *that* we **be** given a better camp site. |
| | (If not in the subjunctive mood, the subject and verb would be *we are given*.) |
| | She ordered *that* nobody **hike** without proper boots. |
| | (If not in the subjunctive mood, the subject and verb would be *nobody hikes*.) |

In English, the subjunctive verb forms differ from the indicative forms in only two situations.

The **present subjunctive** uses the base form of the verb for all persons and numbers, including the third-person singular, but indicative verbs use the -s form.

**Indicative**    She **puts** out the campfire.

**Subjunctive**    The park ranger suggested that she **put** out the campfire.

In the present subjunctive, the verb *to be* is always *be*.

He recommended that all canoe trips **be** in the afternoon.

The **past subjunctive** form of the verb *to be* is *were* for all persons and numbers.

If my grandfather **were** here, he would enjoy the horseback riding.

Although the subjunctive mood is not used much today, it still shows up in a number of idiomatic expressions such as the following.

**Subjunctive Expressions**    **Be** that as it may, . . .

Far **be** it from me to . . .

## When You Speak and Write

The subjunctive voice is a persuasive tool. It can be used to soften a suggestion or strengthen a command.

I wish I were going to the park.

I demand that she take me to the park.

Practice using the subjunctive with a partner by exchanging wishes and statements contrary to fact. Use these sentence starters:

If I were a _____, I would _____.

I wish I were _____.

● **Practice Your Skills**

*Using the Subjunctive Mood*

Write the correct form of the verb in parentheses.

**1.** I wish I (was, were) brave enough to ski the steep slopes.

**2.** Tom talks as if he (was, were) the hike leader.

**3.** I wish Earl (was, were) here.

**4.** If I (was, were) you, I'd wear a life jacket.

**5.** I suggest that you (be, are) at the dock in an hour.

**6.** Lisa wished she (was, were) at the beach right now.

**7.** Marnie requested that he (be, is) in the boat.

**8.** After ten minutes in the sun, my skin felt as though it (was, were) already burned.

**9.** Cheryl asked that we (be, are) ready at noon.

**10.** If Todd (was, were) here, he would want to surf.

● *Connect to Writing:* **Revising**

*Using Subjunctive and Indicative Mood in Sentences*

Write each sentence using either the subjunctive or the indicative mood of the verb form. Then write *S* for *subjunctive* or *I* for *indicative*.

**1.** Yosemite National Park (be) a national treasure.

**2.** If I (be) you, I'd hike up Bridal Veil Falls.

**3.** I wish I (be) a mountain climber.

**4.** I demand that we (allow) to climb El Capitan.

**5.** If I (be) you, I would not climb El Capitan.

## Assess Your Learning

### ▪ Using the Correct Verb Form

Write the past or past participle of each verb in parentheses.

**1.** We (speak) to her before she (drive) to New York.

**2.** I should have (know) his name because we both (grow) up in Park Ridge.

**3.** She (write) to the manufacturer after the boat had (sink) for the second time.

**4.** Grandmother (make) two blueberry pies and (take) them to the fair.

**5.** I (begin) thinking about entering the race because I have (ride) bicycles for ten years.

### ▪ Correcting Verb Tenses

Write the correct form of any incorrect verb in each sentence.

**1.** Ever since 1787, the bald eagle was America's national bird.

**2.** If that dog was mine, I would take better care of him.

**3.** Mike just realized that he left his books in Leroy's car.

**4.** Since the senator has been reelected, Pam is happy to work on her campaign.

**5.** Because Karen sleep late, she missed the bus again.

**6.** Since I was young, I was afraid of bees.

**7.** As the buzzers sounded, the quarterback has thrown a pass into the end zone.

**8.** I wish I was already graduated from high school.

**9.** Raymond noticed that he saw the same red car pass by our house twice.

**10.** Dad knows I have worked hard yesterday.

## Determining Active and Passive Voice

Write the verb in each sentence and label it *active* or *passive*. Then rewrite any sentence in the passive voice that should be in the active voice.

**1.** Because of the severe ice storm, the school was closed for the day.

**2.** An interesting experiment was performed by us in chemistry.

**3.** In 1863, Lincoln made Thanksgiving a national holiday.

**4.** Great interest in space exploration has been shown by the United States.

**5.** The SATs were taken by many seniors on Saturday.

## Writing Sentences

Write five sentences that follow the directions below.

**1.** Write a sentence with a perfect participle and a verb in the future tense.

**2.** Write a sentence in the subjunctive mood.

**3.** Write an imperative sentence. Use one verb in the present tense along with an infinitive.

**4.** Write a sentence with one verb in the passive voice and another in the active voice.

**5.** Write a sentence using both the verb *rise* and the verb *sit* in the past tense.

# Using Verbs: Posttest

## Directions

Read the passage and choose the word or group of words that belongs in each underlined space. Write the letter of the correct answer.

Did you know that modern universities __(1)__ from schools that originated in Europe during the Middle Ages? Such schools __(2)__ their name from the Latin word *universitas*, meaning "a group of people assembled for a common purpose." In early English schools, colleges __(3)__ within universities to provide living quarters and dining rooms for various groups of students. Such students __(4)__ members of a college and a university at the same time. Today, however, both colleges and universities __(5)__ teaching institutions.

My friend Paul __(6)__ to attend a small liberal arts college. I __(7)__ a university with several colleges, or branches, each offering course work in a different discipline. Freshmen and sophomores must take certain basic courses before __(8)__ on a major. If it __(9)__ not for this regulation, students might make poor choices. __(10)__ for two years to select a major, for example, my sister Tawnee knew she really wanted to major in chemistry even though she had also been interested in physics and engineering.

1. **A** develop
   **B** will have developed
   **C** developed
   **D** develops

2. **A** took
   **B** has taken
   **C** taking
   **D** were taking

3. **A** form
   **B** have been formed
   **C** will be formed
   **D** were formed

4. **A** were becoming
   **B** have become
   **C** become
   **D** became

5. **A** were
   **B** are
   **C** will be
   **D** was

6. **A** choose
   **B** chosen
   **C** were chosen
   **D** chose

7. **A** have selected
   **B** will have selected
   **C** selecting
   **D** to select

8. **A** decide
   **B** decided
   **C** deciding
   **D** having been decided

9. **A** was
   **B** were
   **C** have been
   **D** is

10. **A** Waiting
    **B** To wait
    **C** Having waited
    **D** Waited

# Writer's Corner

## Snapshot

**17 A**  The **principal parts of a verb** are the present, the present participle, the past, and the past participle. (pages 750–761)

**17 B**  The time expressed by a verb is called the **tense** of a verb. (pages 762–776)

**17 C**  The **active voice** indicates that the subject is performing the action. The **passive voice** indicates that the action of the verb is being performed upon the subject. (pages 777–779)

**17 D**  The **mood** of a verb—**indicative, imperative,** or **subjunctive**—is the way in which a verb expresses an idea. (pages 780–782)

## Power Rules

Memorize irregular verbs forms to avoid mistakes. (pages 752–761)

| **Before Editing** | **After Editing** |
|---|---|
| They *was* late to school. | They *were* late to school. |
| The balloon *bursted* when he sat on it. | The balloon *burst* when he sat on it. |

Keep a **consistent verb tense** unless a change in tense is necessary. (pages 762–776)

| **Before Editing** | **After Editing** |
|---|---|
| I *opened* the door, and the dog *runs* out. | I *opened* the door, and the dog *ran* out. |

Use the word *have* or its contraction *'ve* instead of the word *of* after a helping verb such as *could, might,* or *should*. (page 889)

| **Before Editing** | **After Editing** |
|---|---|
| If I had finished my homework, I *could of* gone to the movies. | If I had finished my homework, I *could have* gone to the movies. |

## Editing Checklist

Use this checklist when editing your writing.

✓ Did I use use specific verbs rather than general ones? (See page 750.)
✓ Did I use the correct verb forms? (See pages 750–761.)
✓ Did I use the six basic verb tenses correctly? (See pages 762–772.)
✓ Did I avoid unnecessary shifts in tense? (See pages 762–776.)
✓ Did I use the progressive verb forms correctly? (See pages 773–774.)
✓ Did I use the emphatic past and present verb forms correctly? (See pages 774–776.)
✓ Did I use active voice to make my sentences more powerful? (See pages 777–779.)
✓ Did I use the indicative, imperative, and subjunctive moods effectively and correctly? (See pages 780–782.)

## Use the Power

Use this chart to help you form verb tenses correctly.

| | Past | Present | Future |
|---|---|---|---|
| **Simple** | past tense form<br>*He drove.* | base form<br>*He drives.* | *will* + base form<br>*He will drive.* |
| **Progressive** | *was* or *were* + present participle<br>*He was driving.* | *am, is,* or *are* + present participle<br>*He is driving.* | *will be* + present participle<br>*He will be driving.* |
| **Perfect** | *had* + past participle<br>*He had driven.* | *has* or *have* + past participle<br>*He has driven.* | *will have* + past participle<br>*He will have driven.* |
| **Perfect Progressive** | *had been* + present participle<br>*He had been driving.* | *has* or *have been* + present participle<br>*He has been driving.* | *will have been* + present participle<br>*He will have been driving.* |
| **Emphatic** | *did* + present tense<br>*He did drive.* | *do* + present tense<br>*He does drive.* | *No future emphatic form.* |

# Using Pronouns

**How can you use pronouns to make your writing coherent and accurate?**

## Using Pronouns: Pretest 1

The following draft paragraph is hard to read because it contains several errors involving pronouns. Revise the paragraph so that it reads more smoothly. The first error has been corrected as an example.

My mother and ~~me~~ *I* bought a large supply of oil paints before beginning my art course, knowing I would enjoy them. It said that beginners were welcome. That was me. The teacher told we students to let our imaginations flow. Although the instructor said to experiment with color, when I saw the colors in your paintings, I decided I didn't like them. I don't like it when you feel completely lost when they're doing a new project. Next I tried to create an impressionist painting of flowers in vases, but they looked like cartoon creatures to myself. When I showed my paintings to Minnie and Leo, they were sitting by the windows. The two of they admired my sketches, and that encouraged myself to create more. Both were pleased to give his opinion.

# CHAPTER 18

## Using Pronouns: Pretest 2

### Directions

Read the passage and choose the pronoun that belongs in each underlined space. Write the letter of the correct answer.

___(1)___ are Wilbur and Orville Wright? As everyone knows, these men from Dayton, Ohio, became famous when ___(2)___ invented ___(3)___ most famous invention, the airplane. Before 1900, most people could not even imagine ___(4)___ flying through the air like a bird! Of course, it took two extraordinary individuals to create such an inconceivable machine. Each of the brothers brought ___(5)___ own unique talents and qualities to the collaboration. Wilbur, ___(6)___ few knew well because of his quietness, was the visionary of the two. ___(7)___ was the one ___(8)___ first dreamed of flying. Orville, on the other hand, was more mechanically minded than ___(9)___. It was also Orville's enthusiasm that carried ___(10)___ throughout the long years preceding their first flight at Kitty Hawk, North Carolina.

1. **A** Who
   **B** Whom
   **C** Whose
   **D** Whomever

2. **A** them
   **B** they
   **C** theirs
   **D** their

3. **A** them
   **B** they
   **C** theirs
   **D** their

4. **A** them
   **B** they
   **C** theirs
   **D** themselves

5. **A** his
   **B** his or her
   **C** their
   **D** theirs

6. **A** whoever
   **B** whomever
   **C** who
   **D** whom

7. **A** He
   **B** Him
   **C** His
   **D** Their

8. **A** who
   **B** whom
   **C** whose
   **D** whoever

9. **A** he
   **B** him
   **C** their
   **D** them

10. **A** they
    **B** them
    **C** their
    **D** he

Many pronouns have a different form and a different function for each case. When you use a particular form of a pronoun, therefore, you are signaling to a reader or a listener how that pronoun is being used in a sentence. (Nouns change form only in the possessive case. For example, *girl* becomes *girl's* in the possessive case.)

**18 A**   **Case is the form of a noun or a pronoun that indicates its use in a sentence.**

English has three cases: **the nominative case, the objective case,** and **the possessive case.** Many pronouns change form for each of the cases. Notice, though, that *you* and *it* are the same in both the nominative and the objective cases.

### NOMINATIVE CASE

(Used for subjects and predicate nominatives)

| | |
|---|---|
| **Singular** | I, you, he, she, it |
| **Plural** | we, you, they |

### OBJECTIVE CASE

(Used for direct objects, indirect objects, objects of prepositions, and objects of verbals)

| | |
|---|---|
| **Singular** | me, you, him, her, it |
| **Plural** | us, you, them |

### POSSESSIVE CASE

(Used to show ownership or possession)

| | |
|---|---|
| **Singular** | my, mine, your, yours, his, her, hers, its |
| **Plural** | our, ours, your, yours, their, theirs |

## ➤ The Nominative Case

**Nominative Case Personal Pronouns**   I, you, he, she, it, we, they

**18 A.1**   The **nominative case** is used for subjects and predicate nominatives.

# Pronouns as Subjects

A pronoun can be used as a subject of a simple sentence or a clause.

> **Simple Sentence** **We** applied for jobs in the campus bookstore.
>
> **Clause** Mrs. Mendez hired Paul as soon as **he** had filled out the application.

The case of a pronoun that is part of a compound subject is sometimes not as obvious as a single-subject pronoun. Double-check any pronoun in a compound subject to make sure that it is in the nominative case. To do this, say the nominative and the objective pronouns separately—to find out which one is correct.

> Jason and (he, him) cashed the paychecks.
>
> **He** cashed the paychecks.
>
> **Him** cashed the paychecks.

The nominative case *he* is the correct form to use.

> Jason and **he** cashed the paychecks.

This method of checking for the correct case also works if both subjects are pronouns.

> He and (she, her) worked at the campus bookstore.
>
> **She** worked at the campus bookstore.
>
> **Her** worked at the campus bookstore.

The nominative case *she* is the correct form to use.

> He and **she** worked at the campus bookstore.

# Pronouns as Predicate Nominatives

A **predicate nominative** follows a linking verb and identifies, renames, or explains the subject.

> That was **I** who won the scholarship.

The preceding example probably sounds extremely formal—or even incorrect—to you. However, while *That was me* or *It's me* is common usage in conversation, it should be avoided in written work.

It was **she.**     That is **he.**     The winners are **they.**

To decide whether the pronoun in a compound predicate nominative is in the correct case, turn the sentence around to make the predicate nominative the subject. Then say the nominative and the objective pronouns separately to find out which one is correct.

The finalists for the essay award are Ben and (she, her).

Ben and (she, her) are the finalists for the essay award.

**She** is a finalist.

**Her** is a finalist.

The finalists for the essay award are Ben and **she.**

Sometimes the wording of a sentence becomes awkward when pronouns or compound pronouns are used as predicate nominatives. You can avoid this awkwardness by turning the sentence around.

**Awkward**          The financial aid officer is **she.**

**Turned Around**    **She** is the financial aid officer.

**Awkward**          The financial aid recipients are Di and **he.**

**Turned Around**    Di and **he** are the financial aid recipients.

*You can learn more about predicate nominatives on pages 667–668. Also, you can find lists of common linking verbs on page 628–629.*

# Nominative Case Pronouns Followed by Appositives

An **appositive** is a noun or a pronoun that renames or identifies the noun or pronoun next to it in a sentence. Occasionally when *we* is used as a subject or a predicate nominative, a noun or a pronoun functions as the appositive of *we*. The noun appositive that follows *we* never affects the case of *we*.

The best way to check whether you have used the correct pronoun is to drop the appositive mentally from the sentence.

**We** language specialists thoroughly enjoy our jobs.

(We thoroughly enjoy our jobs.)

The newest college students on campus are **we** freshmen.

(The newest college students on campus are we.)

## *When You Speak and Write*

An appositive is an excellent tool for clarifying information for the reader or listener.

| | |
|---|---|
| **Vague** | We completed our applications. |
| **More Specific** | We students completed our applications. |

In a current or recent composition, look for places to add appositives to clarify.

## Nominative Case Pronouns as Appositives

An appositive is in the same case as the noun or pronoun to which it refers.

**18 A.2**  When a pronoun is part of an appositive to a subject or a predicate nominative, the pronoun should be in the nominative case.

The exchange students, Yuri and **he,** work in the language lab.

*Yuri* and *he* are appositives to the subject *students*. Since the subject is in the nominative case, an appositive to the subject is also in the nominative case.

*Using Pronouns in the Nominative Case*

Write the correct form of the pronoun in parentheses.

1. The students concerned about the cost of college are (we, us) seniors.
2. Several financial aid advisors, Victor and (they, them), spoke to us.
3. Todd and (him, he) described the best ideas.
4. Neither Ava nor (me, I) is worried about college fees.
5. Of all our classmates, (her, she) and (I, me) are the ones who immediately took the advisors' suggestions.
6. It was (me, I) who learned about college work-study.
7. It was (she, her) who got the application forms.
8. The recipients of grant money are Ava and (I, me).
9. Maddy and (he, him) will apply for athletic scholarships.
10. The champions of our track meet are (them, they).
11. It wasn't (me, I) who applied for an academic scholarship at the university.
12. Suzanne believes that both (she, her) and Jake will be awarded scholarships.
13. The valedictorian and salutatorian of our class are (them, they).
14. (We, Us) students from lower-income families applied for need-based financial aid.
15. Trisha said that (her, she) and Tyrone would apply for guaranteed student loans.

● *Connect to Writing:* **Editing**

*Using the Nominative Case*

If an underlined pronoun is in the wrong case, write it correctly. If it is in the correct case, write **C**.

1. Mom said that Monica and <u>him</u> would get summer jobs.
2. The new burger chefs are Ben and <u>her</u>.
3. <u>We</u> workers are saving our money for college.
4. Last summer, Juan and <u>him</u> saved enough for tuition.
5. Gloria and <u>me</u> will live in the dorms to save money.
6. The people awarded the internships are Holly and <u>she</u>.
7. Their parents and <u>them</u> are visiting the campus soon.
8. The students who most appreciate their education are <u>us</u> workers.
9. Two friends, Amy and <u>him</u>, pay their own expenses.
10. The new lab assistants are <u>her</u> and <u>me</u>.

## ✅ Check Point: Mixed Practice

If an underlined pronoun is in the wrong case, write it correctly. If it is in the correct case, write **C.**

**1.** Me and him went to the zoo last weekend.
**2.** The tour guides are them.
**3.** Us animal lovers never tire of observing the zoo's inhabitants.
**4.** The ticket-takers, Arnold and she, are in our high-school biology class.
**5.** Them and us sometimes help feed the lambs in the petting zoo.
**6.** It was me who noticed the new reptile exhibit.
**7.** The reptile caretakers, Lynn and her, told us about the heat lamps.
**8.** Lynn said, "The luckiest employees here are we snake handlers!"
**9.** Petra and him watched the poison arrow frogs.
**10.** This frog sweats poison when he senses danger.
**11.** They, the frogs, live in South America.
**12.** One of this frog's enemies is us humans.
**13.** My friend Jeremy and him enjoy visiting the lions.
**14.** Monique and her, two of my good friends, found us by the orangutans.
**15.** We students watched the orangutans eat fruit.

# ➤ The Objective Case

| Objective Case Personal Pronouns | me, you, him, her, it, us, them |
|---|---|

**18 A.3** The **objective case** is used for direct objects, indirect objects, objects of prepositions, and objects of verbals.

## Pronouns as Direct and Indirect Objects

**18 A.4** A pronoun that is used as a direct object will follow an action verb and answer the question *Whom?* A pronoun that is used as a direct object is in the objective case.

**18 A.5** A pronoun that is used as an indirect object will answer the question *To whom?* or *For whom?* after the direct object. A pronoun that is used as an indirect object is in the objective case.

|  |  |
|---|---|
| **Direct Objects** | Dad will drive **us** to work. |
|  | The optician will assist **her** now. |
| **Indirect Objects** | i.o.     d.o.<br>The cashier gave **me** a receipt. |
|  | i.o.                    d.o.<br>Give **him** those eyeglass frames. |

To check for the correct case of a compound direct object, say the nominative and the objective case pronouns in separate sentences.

Jason saw the Dyers and (they, them) at the optical store.

Jason saw **they** at the optical store.

Jason saw **them** at the optical store.

The objective case *them* is the correct form to use.

Jason saw the Dyers and **them** at the optical store.

Compound indirect objects can be checked in the same way.

i.o.        i.o.            d.o.<br>Fred gave Beth and (I, me) new sunglasses.

Fred gave **I** new sunglasses.

Fred gave **me** new sunglasses.

The objective case *me* is the correct form to use.

i.o.        i.o.          d.o.<br>Fred gave Beth and **me** new sunglasses.

*You can learn more about direct objects and indirect objects on pages 664–666.*

# Pronouns as Objects of Prepositions

A prepositional phrase begins with a preposition and ends with a noun or a pronoun called the object of a preposition.

**18 A.6**    A pronoun that is used as an object of a preposition is in the objective case.

> You can ride to work with **us.**
> (*With us* is the prepositional phrase.)
> Is this lab coat for **me?**
> (*For me* is the prepositional phrase.)
> The patient gave his insurance card to **you.**
> (*To you* is the prepositional phrase.)

You can check to see that a pronoun in a compound object of a preposition is in the objective case by saying the nominative and objective case pronouns separately.

> The ophthalmologist wrote prescriptions for David and (she, her).
> The ophthalmologist wrote prescriptions for **she.**
> The ophthalmologist wrote prescriptions for **her.**

The objective case *her* is the correct form to use.

> The ophthalmologist wrote prescriptions for David and **her.**

You might have noticed that sometimes people will use nominative case pronouns after the preposition *between* in an effort to sound formal or correct. However, all pronouns used as objects of a preposition should be in the objective case.

> **Incorrect**    The sales agreement was between **he** and **I.**
> **Correct**    The sales agreement was between **him** and **me.**

*You can learn more about objects of prepositions on pages 640 and 684. Also, you can find a list of common prepositions on pages 639–640.*

### Using Pronouns as Objects

Write the correct form of the pronoun in parentheses. Then write how the pronoun is used, using the following abbreviations.

direct object = *d.o.*          indirect object = *i.o.*
object of a preposition = *o.p.*

**1.** Like you and (I, me), Yvonne is looking for a job.
**2.** The manager hired Tim and (I, me) as opticians.
**3.** Dad called Megan and (he, him) to tell them about our jobs as interns.
**4.** We should talk to Rebecca and (she, her), our coworkers.
**5.** For four hours I waited on Mr. Stuart and (they, them), my best customers.
**6.** Give the customer and (we, us) copies of the receipt.
**7.** Between you and (I, me), I plan to become the assistant manager.
**8.** Mrs. Samuelson will pay (they, them) or (we, us) fifteen dollars to repair her antique spectacles.
**9.** Would you like to go to the training seminar with Tom and (we, us)?
**10.** Why did you disagree with the experienced lens cutter and (he, him)?

## Pronouns as Objects of Verbals

Because participles, gerunds, and infinitives are verb forms, they can take objects.

**18 A.7**    A pronoun that is the direct object of a verbal is in the objective case.

| | |
|---|---|
| **Participial Phrase** | *Seeing **her** in the restaurant,* Jeff asks the tennis star for her autograph. (The phrase is *seeing her in the restaurant.* *Her* is the object of the participle *seeing.*) |
| **Gerund Phrase** | I don't recall *seeing **him** at practice.* (The phrase is *seeing him at practice.* *Him* is the object of the gerund *seeing.*) |
| **Infinitive Phrase** | I want *to watch **them** soon,* but I am very busy. (The phrase is *to watch them soon.* *Them* is the object of the infinitive *to watch.*) |

A pronoun in a compound object of a verbal can be checked by saying the nominative and objective case pronouns in separate sentences.

I hope to see Bill and (she, her) at the game.

I hope to see **she** at the game.

I hope to see **her** at the game.

I hope to see Bill and **her** at the game.

*You can learn more about verbals on pages 693–702.*

## Objective Case Pronouns Followed by Appositives

An appositive of the pronoun *us* does not affect the case of *us*. To check whether you have used the correct pronoun, mentally drop the appositive from the sentence.

Give **us** fans those season tickets.

(Give us those season tickets. *Us* is used as an indirect object, and *fans* is the appositive.)

## Objective Case Pronouns as Appositives

**18 A.8**    When a pronoun is part of an appositive to a direct object, an indirect object, or an object of a preposition, the pronoun should be in the objective case.

d.o.

We found two volunteers, Gladys and **him,** to work at the refreshment stand.

(*Gladys* and *him* are the appositives to the direct object *volunteers.* Since a direct object is in the objective case, an appositive to the direct object is also in the objective case.)

● **Practice Your Skills**

*Using Objective Case Pronouns*

Write the correct form of the pronoun in parentheses.

**1.** Making (he, him) the shortstop was a wise decision.

**2.** The principal asked (we, us) athletes for our opinion on the new gymnasium.

**3.** Finding (he, him) in the weight room, the coach helped the bodybuilder.

**4.** Be sure to tell Carrie and (she, her) about the basketball game after school.

5. At the awards ceremony, the coach gave special recognition to two athletes, Pedro and (he, him).

6. It was a great disappointment to (we, us) fans when Mason struck out.

7. Alex tried in vain to find Sarah and (he, him) in the crowded stadium.

8. I don't recall seeing Nat and (they, them) at the soccer game last week.

9. They interviewed two of my favorite baseball players, Mark and (he, him), for the evening newscast.

10. Watching Liz and (they, them) on the field, Mom was very proud.

11. We asked several baseball players, Andy and (they, them), to help out with Little League.

12. I remember helping Terrence and (she, her) learn to spike a volleyball.

13. I don't want to coach Sammy and (they, them) in the drizzling rain.

14. Meeting the pro wrestler and (him, he) in person was a memorable event.

15. Giving the boys and (she, her) our tickets, we went back home.

## Connect to Writing: Editing

### Using Objective Case Pronouns

If an underlined pronoun is in the wrong case, write it correctly. If it is in the correct case, write **C.**

1. Please save seats for <u>he</u> and Sharon.
2. Will you show Marcia and <u>I</u> your canoe over the holiday weekend?
3. Dad had warned you and <u>she</u> about that thin ice!
4. The assistant coach explained the plays to <u>we</u> quarterbacks.
5. Will Roger be able to drive <u>us</u> home after the game?
6. We saw the performances of the two finalists, Pat and <u>he</u>.
7. He should never have taken <u>her</u> and the dog rafting.
8. We saw Dad watching our cousin and <u>they</u> on the balance beams.
9. Mom sent Harold and <u>I</u> to summer basketball camp.
10. Be sure to call <u>we</u> parents when you get to the ball park.

## Check Point: Mixed Practice

Write each underlined pronoun that is incorrectly used; beside it, write the correct objective case pronoun.

1. Taking <u>they</u> to the counter, I paid for the guitar picks with my allowance.
2. Dad bought new CDs by our favorite rock group for Leslie and <u>I</u>.

**3.** Photographing <u>she</u> and <u>he</u> during their concert is my job.

**4.** The ticket agents sold <u>we</u> country-western fans discount tickets.

**5.** I wanted to invite the new band members, Steve and <u>they</u>, to the party.

**6.** Mr. Vernon trained Valerie and <u>he</u> on the cello.

**7.** I forgot to wish the drummers, <u>she</u> and Emily, good luck on their audition.

**8.** After telling my brother and <u>they</u> about my new baby grand piano, I invited them over to see it.

**9.** I laughed when Peter said, "Take <u>we</u> groupies backstage!"

**10.** We asked two people, <u>he</u> and Kathy, to take turns driving the tour bus.

## ➤ The Possessive Case

| | |
|---|---|
| **Possessive Case Personal Pronouns** | my, mine, your, yours, his, her, hers, its, our, ours, their, theirs |

**18 A.9**  The **possessive case** is used to show ownership or possession.

Possessive case pronouns are most often used before a noun or by themselves.

**Before A Noun**  This is **my** poem.

**By Themselves**  These are **mine,** but which are **his?**

Be careful not to confuse certain possessive pronouns with contractions. A personal pronoun in the possessive case never includes an apostrophe. *Its, your, their,* and *theirs* are possessive pronouns. *It's, you're, they're,* and *there's* are contractions.

## Possessive Pronouns with Gerunds

As you may recall, a gerund is a verb form ending in *-ing* that is used in all the ways a noun is used.

**18 A.10**  If a pronoun comes directly in front of a gerund, it should be in the possessive case—in just the same way a possessive pronoun would come in front of a regular noun.

gerund

We were pleased at ***his** writing the story.*

(The whole gerund phrase is *his writing the story.* It is used as an object of the preposition *at.* Since *writing* is a gerund, it is preceded by a possessive pronoun: *his writing.*)

A big surprise was *their publishing his story.*
(The whole gerund phrase is *their publishing his story.* It is used as a predicate nominative. Since *publishing* is a gerund, it is preceded by a possessive pronoun: *their publishing.*)

A common error is to put a nominative or an objective case pronoun before a gerund instead of a possessive case pronoun.

| **Incorrect** | We were pleased at **him** writing the story. |
| **Incorrect** | A big surprise was **they** publishing his story. |

Another possible error is confusing a gerund with a present participle because both are verb forms that end in *-ing*. However, since a participle is used as an adjective, it would never be preceded by a possessive pronoun.

| **Gerund** | The children enjoyed ***our** reading to them.* |
| | (The gerund phrase is the direct object. The children enjoyed what? *Our reading to them.* Since *reading* is a gerund, it is preceded by a possessive pronoun.) |
| **Participle** | We baby-sat the children and watched ***them** reading to one another.* |
| | (*Them* is a direct object in this sentence. We watched whom? *Them.* Since *them* is a direct object, it is in the objective case. The participial phrase is used as an adjective to describe *them.*) |

*You can learn more about gerunds on pages 697–699. You can find out more about participles on pages 693–696.*

● **Practice Your Skills**

***Using Pronouns in the Possessive Case***

Write the correct pronoun in parentheses.

**1.** (Theirs, There's) is the remodeled bookstore on Pier 21.
**2.** We were surprised at (them, their) buying the building.
**3.** (Him, His) renovating it was a smart business move.
**4.** This shelf and (its, it's) hardware are covered in rust.

**5.** Is there any chance of (you, your) getting a job at the Recycled Books and More store?

**6.** That shipment of used books must be (ours, our's).

**7.** Dan was surprised at (me, my) knowing so much about bookbinding.

**8.** I hadn't heard about (him, his) getting hired as assistant manager.

**9.** We all appreciated (you, your) explaining the employee insurance benefits to us.

**10.** My parents are pleased at (me, my) learning the bookstore business.

**11.** The idea of buying used textbooks for the store was (hers, her's).

**12.** (Him, His) stocking the shelves with the recycled textbooks was my suggestion.

**13.** The job of buying used CDs for the music section is (their's, theirs).

**14.** (Her, She) finding the true crime section of the store took five minutes.

**15.** These paperbacks are (your's, yours), but the hardbacks are mine.

## *Connect to Writing:* Revising

### Using Possessive Pronouns

Write each sentence, replacing the possessive nouns with possessive pronouns.

**1.** The National Book Foundation awards the National Book Award each year for The National Book Foundation's choice of best fiction in the United States.

**2.** In 1951, William Faulkner won the National Book Award for William Faulkner's *Collected Stories*.

**3.** Alice Walker won the National Book Award in 1983 for Alice Walker's novel *The Color Purple*.

**4.** Authors in the British Commonwealth of Nations are eligible to win the British Commonwealth of Nations' Booker Prize for the authors' full-length novels.

**5.** In 1992, Michael Ondaatje and Barry Unsworth were each awarded the Booker Prize for Michael Ondaatje's and Barry Unsworth's novels *The English Patient* and *Sacred Hunger*.

**6.** Ondaatje later agreed to let Ondaatje's novel be made into a film that received much critical acclaim and several Academy Award nominations.

**7.** Since Nobel prizes are awarded internationally, writers in any country may be given the award for the writers' literary work.

**8.** Joseph Pulitzer established the Pulitzer Prize through Joseph Pulitzer's endowment to Columbia University.

### ✔ *Check Point:* Mixed Practice

Write each pronoun that is in the wrong case. Then write it correctly. If a sentence is correct, write **C**.

1. Mr. Ayers, the librarian, showed Alicia and I some books about holidays.
2. Them will be enjoyable to read.
3. I listened to Mr. Ayers and she discussing Kwanzaa.
4. Tell we listeners about the seven principles of Kwanzaa.
5. Him and me are planning a Kwanzaa celebration.
6. Notifying them of the plans will take time.
7. The sets for the Christmas play were painted by two people, Carmen and I.
8. In the car, dressed in red and green, were Ben and her.
9. Everyone was glad to hear of me joining the choir.
10. We latke lovers will serve crispy latkes to our guests during Hanukkah.
11. Kyle and them enjoy the eight days of Hanukkah.
12. Is there any chance of you lending me your extra silver menorah?

CHAPTER 18

## Pronoun Problems  Lesson 2

Has anyone at the other end of the telephone ever said to you, "Whom may I say is calling"? The next time you hear that expression, you will know that the speaker has just made a pronoun error.

**18 B** Common pronoun problems include the misuse of *who* and *whom*, incomplete comparisons, and the misuse of reflexive and intensive pronouns.

### ➡ *Who* or *Whom*?

**18 B.1** The correct case of *who* is determined by how the pronoun is used in a question or a clause.

Like personal pronouns, the pronouns *who* and *whoever* change their forms—depending upon how they are used within a sentence.

| WHO AND WHOEVER | |
|---|---|
| **Nominative Case** | who, whoever |
| **Objective Case** | whom, whomever |
| **Possessive Case** | whose |

**18 B.2** *Who* and *whoever* and their related pronouns are used in questions and in subordinate clauses.

In questions *who* and *whoever* and their related pronouns are frequently used. The case you should use depends upon how the pronoun is used.

| | |
|---|---|
| **Nominative Case** | **Who** volunteered for Meals on Wheels? (subject) |
| **Objective Case** | **Whom** did you assist at the shelter? (direct object) |
| | To **whom** did you donate the shoes? (object of the preposition *to*) |

When deciding which case to use, turn a question around to its natural order.

| | |
|---|---|
| **Question** | **Whom** did you assist? |
| **Natural Order** | You did assist **whom.** |

CHAPTER 18

In casual conversation you might hear people say, "**Who** did you invite?" instead of "**Whom** did you invite?" This informal usage is accepted in most casual settings; however, in your formal written work, you should use **whom**.

Go back to a recent formal composition. Check to be sure you have used *who* and *whom* correctly.

**18 B.3**   In an adjectival or a noun clause, the way *who* (and its related pronouns) is used determines its case.

The following examples show how forms of *who* are used in adjectival clauses.

| | |
|---|---|
| **Nominative Case** | Eva is a girl **who enjoys helping others.** |
| | (*Who* is the subject of *enjoys.*) |
| **Objective Case** | Mr. Jenkins is the man **whom the community theater group consulted.** |
| | (*Whom* is the direct object of *consulted.* The theater group consulted whom.) |
| | Peg is the health aide **from whom I learned about candystripers.** |
| | (*Whom* is the object of the preposition *from. From* is part of the clause.) |

The following examples show how forms of *who* and *whoever* are used in noun clauses.

| | |
|---|---|
| **Nominative Case** | **Whoever collects clothing for the charity drive** will receive a free lunch. |
| | (*Whoever* is the subject of *collects.*) |
| | Jerry didn't know **who the new volunteer was.** |
| | (*Who* is a predicate nominative. The volunteer was who.) |
| **Objective Case** | Invite **whomever you want.** |
| | (*Whomever* is the direct object of *want.* You want whomever.) |
| | At the soup kitchen, Ray gives help to **whomever he sees.** |
| | (The entire clause is the object of the preposition *to. Whomever* is the direct object of *sees.*) |

Sometimes an interrupting expression such as *I believe, we know, do you suppose,* or *I hope* appears in a question or a clause. Mentally drop this expression to avoid any confusion.

> **Who** *do you suppose* will win the fundraiser raffle?
>
> (Who will win the fundraiser raffle? *Who* is the subject of *will win.*)
>
> Otis, **who** *I think* is a volunteer at the YMCA, is a senior.
>
> (Otis, who is a volunteer at the YMCA, is a senior. *Who* is the subject of *is.*)

*You can learn more about adjectival and noun clauses on pages 724–730.*

### ● Practice Your Skills

**Using Who and Its Related Pronouns**

Write each form of *who* or *whoever* that is used incorrectly. If a sentence is correct, write **C.**

1. Whom may I say is volunteering for the campus cleanup on Saturday?
2. I met Roth, who is a community service director.
3. Tell whoever you see about the neighborhood playground project.
4. Did they say whom the sponsors of Paint the Playground Day are?
5. With who did you work at the park?
6. Who did you nominate as volunteer of the year?
7. Do you know who the event director is?
8. The school board will give 50 dollars to whomever organizes a school-improvement event.
9. With whom did you travel recently to the Volunteer America conference?
10. Mr. Davis is the social worker who we know from the homeless shelter.
11. Aaron usually likes whoever he works for.
12. From who should we request a new supply of the drug education materials?

### ● *Connect to Writing:* Editing

**Using Forms of Who and Whoever**

Rewrite the incorrect sentences in the preceding exercise, using the correct form of *who* or *whoever.* Then, using the following abbreviations, write how each pronoun is used.

subject = *subj.*          predicate nominative = *p.n.*

direct object = *d.o.*          object of the preposition = *o.p.*

# ⮕ Pronouns in Comparisons

Pronouns are often used in comparisons. A problem sometimes arises when a comparison is made but not said or written out completely. The result is an **elliptical clause.**

**18 B.4**    An **elliptical clause** is a subordinate clause that begins with the word *than* or *as* and that leaves out the verb or part of the verb as understood.

Although words are omitted from an elliptical clause, they are still understood to be in the clause.

> Mr. Lee coached Eric more **than I.**
>
> Mr. Lee coached Eric more **than me.**

Depending upon what meaning is intended, both of the preceding examples are correct.

> Mr. Lee coached Eric more **than I coached Eric.**
>
> (*I* is correct because it is the subject of *coached.*)
>
> Mr. Lee coached Eric more **than he coached me.**
>
> (*Me* is correct because it is the direct object of *coached.*)

**18 B.5**    In an elliptical clause, use the form of the pronoun you would use if the clause were completed.

To decide which pronoun to use in an elliptical clause, mentally complete the clause. Then choose the form of the pronoun that expresses the meaning you want.

An elliptical clause, however, can sometimes correctly express only one meaning.

> Do you think David Greene shoots hoops as well as (I, me)?
>
> Do you think David Greene shoots hoops as well **as I shoot hoops?**

*You can learn more about elliptical clauses on pages 723–724.*

## ● Practice Your Skills

### *Using Pronouns in Elliptical Clauses*

Write each pronoun that is used incorrectly in an elliptical clause. If a sentence is correct, write **C.**

**1.** Amy ran more laps than me.

**2.** In the tryouts I think Susannah did better than her.

**3.** When coaching Little League, Barry has more patience than him.

**4.** Andrea is as experienced a gymnast as me.

**5.** Martha likes the softball uniforms more than us.

**6.** At the track meet, Anna earned more ribbons than me.

**7.** Coach Ferguson trained that player better than he.

**8.** Ben is not as tall as her, but he runs much faster.

**9.** My sister was always better in sports than me.

**10.** Mary cheered for Doug more than him.

● *Connect to Writing:* **Editing**

*Using Pronouns in Comparisons*

For each of the preceding sentences, complete the elliptical clause with the correct pronoun. If a clause can be completed two ways, write them both.

## ➤ Reflexive and Intensive Pronouns

Because reflexive and intensive pronouns end in *-self* or *-selves,* they are easy to recognize. These pronouns are often used for emphasis.

| REFLEXIVE AND INTENSIVE PRONOUNS | |
|---|---|
| **Singular** | myself, yourself, himself, herself, itself |
| **Plural** | ourselves, yourselves, themselves |

**18 B.6** **Reflexive pronouns** always refer back to a previous noun or pronoun in the sentence.

**Reflexive Pronouns**   Tiffany voted for **herself.**

They saw **themselves** as rivals.

**18 B.7**   **Intensive pronouns** are used to emphasize a noun or another pronoun in the sentence.

**Intensive Pronouns**

Ben **himself** was elected homecoming king.

They **themselves** decorated the gym.

Never use reflexive or intensive pronouns by themselves. They always have to have an antecedent in the same sentence.

**Incorrect**   Laura and **myself** are the only candidates. (*Myself* has no antecedent in the sentence.)

**Correct**   Laura and **I** are the only delegates.

## When You Speak

In daily conversation, you may hear *theirself* used as a reflexive or an intensive pronoun. For example, a friend may say, "When they laughed in class, they couldn't help theirself." *Theirself,* however, is not a word; you should always use the pronoun *themselves* instead. Similarly, you would never say, "He cut *hisself.*" Instead, you would say "He cut *himself.*"

● **Practice Your Skills**

*Using Reflexive and Intensive Pronouns*

Write the reflexive and intensive pronouns in the following sentences. Then write *I* if the pronoun is incorrect and **C** if the pronoun is correct.

**1.** The nominees for homecoming queen are Amber Stockton and myself.

**2.** I can see myself in the crown already.

**3.** I noticed themselves in the top row of the bleachers.

**4.** The football team and ourselves marched onto the field.

**5.** The quarterback bought hisself a new tux.

**6.** The former homecoming queen will perform the crowning herself.

**7.** When last year's homecoming king arrived, the announcer said, "Himself is here."

**8.** I myself did not see himself.

**9.** The band of my corsage had tangled itself on my ring.

**10.** The girls in the court admired theirself in the mirrors.

## ✔ Check Point: Mixed Practice

Write each pronoun that is used incorrectly. Then write it correctly. If a sentence is correct, write **C**.

1. I answered the telephone by saying, "Whom may I say is calling?"
2. A salesperson asked to speak to whomever was "the lady of the house."
3. If they could hear theirself talk, salespeople wouldn't say things like that.
4. This is the kind of telemarketer whom I believe should be banned.
5. Maria and I have spoken to more salespeople than her.
6. Do you think she is more sympathetic to pushy salespeople than I?
7. Whom do you think buys useless junk?
8. Wayne, who everyone knows is too trusting, buys whatever a salesperson shows him.
9. No one has more encyclopedias than him.
10. Maria and myself use the encyclopedias at school.

## Power Your Writing: Who or What?

An appositive phrase adds details—the who or the what— about the word that immediately precedes it. This extra information helps readers stay involved and interested in your ideas. In the sentence below from Russell Baker's "Little Red Riding Hood Revisited," the appositive phrase in bold type adds important (and humorous) information about the grandmother. The appositive phrase is set off by a comma.

> Once upon a point in time, a small person named Little Red Riding Hood initiated plans for the preparation, delivery, and transportation of foodstuffs to her grandmother, **a senior citizen residing at a place of residence in a forest of indeterminate dimension.**

Use appositive phrases in your own writing to add necessary information. Try your hand at writing a humorous description using an appositive phrase.

A pronoun's **antecedent** is the word that the pronoun refers to or replaces.

**18 C**  A pronoun and its antecedent must agree in **number** and **gender** since they both are referring to the same person, place, or thing.

**Number** is the term used to indicate whether a noun or a pronoun is singular (one) or plural (more than one). **Gender** is the term used to indicate whether a noun or a pronoun is masculine, feminine, or neuter.

| GENDER | | | |
|---|---|---|---|
| **Masculine** | he | him | his |
| **Feminine** | she | her | hers |
| **Neuter** | it | its | |

To make a pronoun agree with its antecedent, first find the antecedent. Then determine its number and gender. Making a pronoun agree with a single-word antecedent usually is not a problem.

**Nancy** must plant **her** vegetable garden soon.
(*Nancy* is singular and feminine; therefore, *her* is correct because it also is singular and feminine.)

**Members** of the landscape team presented **their** ideas at a special meeting.
(*Members* is plural; therefore, *their* is plural.)

If the antecedent of a pronoun is more than one word, you need to remember two rules.

**18 C.1**  If two or more singular antecedents are joined by *or, nor, either/or,* or *neither/nor,* use a singular pronoun to refer to them.

All the conjunctions listed in this rule indicate a choice—one *or* the other. In the following example, Harold *or* Cliff gave me his shovel—not both of them. As a result the pronoun must be singular.

Either Harold or Cliff gave me **his** shovel.

**18 C.2**   When one antecedent is singular and the other is plural, the pronoun agrees with the closer antecedent.

Neither Sue nor the other two gardeners planted **their** begonias in the proper soil.

Neither my brothers nor my father brought **his** rake.

**18 C.3**   If two or more singular antecedents are joined by **and** or **both/and,** use a plural pronoun to refer to them.

The conjunctions *and* and *both/and* indicate more than one. In the following example, both Greta *and* Mavis—two people—planted their spring flowers too early. Because the antecedent is plural, the plural pronoun must be used.

Both Greta and Mavis planted **their** spring flowers too early.

The gender of most antecedents is obvious. *Harold* and *Cliff* are masculine; *Greta* and *Mavis* are feminine. The gender of some antecedents, however, is not as obvious. Standard English solves the agreement problem in such cases by using the phrase *his or her* to refer to antecedents of unknown gender.

Each horticulturist should photograph **his or her** prize roses.

Overusing *his or her* in a short passage can make writing sound awkward. You can often avoid this problem by rewriting such sentences, using plural forms.

All horticulturists should photograph **their** prize roses.

*You can learn more about pronouns and antecedents on page 621.*

## Practice Your Skills

### *Making Pronouns Agree with Their Antecedents*

Write the pronoun that correctly completes each sentence.

1. Every American should know what ____ state flower is.
2. Texans see ____ state flower, the bluebonnet, bloom in March and April.
3. Both Florida and Delaware have fruit blossoms as ____ state flowers.
4. Florida claims the orange blossom as ____ state flower, and Delaware claims the peach blossom.
5. Each member of the Women's Garden Club in Rhode Island makes sure that ____ grows the state flower, the violet, in ____ garden.

## *Connect to Writing:* Editing

### *Making Pronouns and Antecedents Agree*

Rewrite the paragraphs, correcting errors in pronoun and antecedent agreement.

(1) A gardener should test their soil to see if they should add fertilizer or compost. (2) A local garden center should have testing kits on their shelves. (3) If the gardener's soil is too alkaline or acidic, they can buy additives to mix into them. (4) Smart gardeners develop soil that crumbles easily in its hands. (5) Sometimes they have to add sand, clay, or compost to create rich soil. (6) Both my neighbor, Mrs. Kent, and I turn their soil with a shovel and mix in other soil types.

(7) I learned that soil that sticks together when you press it probably has too much clay in them. (8) Clumpy, sticky clay packs too tightly around a plant's roots, and they cannot drain properly. (9) Conversely, a loose and sandy soil loses his nutrients, and the plants can't get what it will need to thrive. (10) Loam is the best kind of soil because she is not too sticky or sandy. (11) Either leaves or manure will provide their nutrients to any soil you mix them into. (12) A gardening center stocks bags of compost and fertilizer on their shelves.

#  Indefinite Pronouns as Antecedents

Based on their number, the common indefinite pronouns have been divided into the following three groups.

| COMMON INDEFINITE PRONOUNS | |
| --- | --- |
| **Singular** | anybody, another, anyone, anything, each, either, everybody, everyone, everything, neither, nobody, no one, nothing, one, somebody, someone, something |
| **Plural** | both, few, many, several |
| **Singular/Plural** | all, any, enough, more, most, none, some |

**18 C.4**  A personal pronoun must be singular if its antecedent is one of the singular indefinite pronouns.

**Each** of the girls is bathing **her** puppy.

**18 C.5**  A personal pronoun must be plural if its antecedent is one of the plural indefinite pronouns.

**Both** of the brothers donated **their** time to the humane society.

**18 C.6**  If the antecedent of a personal pronoun is one of the singular/plural indefinite pronouns, the personal pronoun agrees in number and gender with the noun to which the indefinite pronoun refers (shown in italics in the examples below).

**Some** of the dog *food* has ants in **it.** (singular)

**Some** of the cat *owners* have declawed **their** pets. (plural)

Sometimes the gender of a singular indefinite pronoun is not indicated by other words in the sentence. Standard English solves this problem by using *his or her* to refer to antecedents of unknown gender. You can also rewrite the sentence, using the plural form.

**Each** of the riders must register **his or her** horse by Monday.

**All** of the riders must register **their** horses by Monday.

CHAPTER 18

● **Practice Your Skills**

*Making Pronouns Agree*

Write the pronoun that correctly completes each sentence.

1. Neither of the squirrels has had ___ dinner of sunflower seeds and strawberries.
2. All of the parakeets had green feathers on ___ wings.
3. Both of my parrots recently learned to say ___ names.
4. Most of the lizards sat cozily beneath ___ heat lamps.
5. Each of the Siamese fighting fish must have ___ own bowl in which to swim.
6. If any of these shells will work, put ___ in the hermit crab's cage.
7. Several of my cats have torn apart ___ cat toys.
8. One of the boys said that ___ would groom my poodle.
9. Most of the floor of the rabbits's cage had alfalfa on ___.
10. Either of the women should place broccoli in ___ turtle's food dish.

✔ *Check Point:* **Mixed Practice**

Write a pronoun that correctly completes each sentence.

1. Participants in the auto show should bring ___ vehicles to the lot by Saturday.
2. All of my sisters received cars on ___ sixteenth birthdays.
3. Both Ray and Otis forgot ___ keys today.
4. Most of these abandoned vehicles will never be claimed by ___ owners.
5. Somebody who owns the red convertible has left ___ car unlocked.
6. Some of the girls are riding to the game with ___ friends.
7. Many of the boys in the shop class have already rebuilt ___ carburetors.
8. Susan and Julie asked ___ father for a ride to the library.
9. Neither of my brothers could find ___ spare tire.
10. Several of my friends drive ___ cars to school every day.

● *Connect to Writing:* **Letter**

### Correcting Antecedent Problems

One of your friends is in the hospital, and you want to cheer him or her up. Write an amusing letter describing your recent school experiences. (Feel free to embellish them.) Use the pronouns you studied in this section: the *who/whom* pronouns, pronouns in comparisons, reflexive and intensive pronouns, and indefinite pronouns. Edit your letter for mistakes in pronoun usage, and then write the final copy.

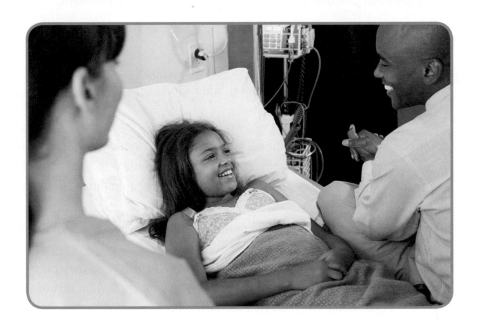

● *Connect to Writing:* **Persuasive Essay**

### Using Pronouns and Antecedents

Write a persuasive essay about testing products on animals. Convince your classmates to see the issue as you do. For example, do you believe testing on animals is never okay? Is it acceptable when developing life-saving medicine, but unacceptable when developing a new kind of mascara? Use specific examples to illustrate your opinions. Check for pronoun and antecedent agreement before you write your final copy.

Not only does a pronoun have to agree in number and gender with its antecedent, but that antecedent must also be very clear. If an antecedent is hard to determine or if it is missing entirely, then your writing will become confusing or even misleading. As part of your editing, you should look for unclear, missing, or confusing antecedents.

**18 D**   **Every personal pronoun should clearly refer to a specific antecedent.**

## ➤ Unclear Antecedents

**18 D.1**   Although words such as *it, they, this,* and *that* might vaguely refer to antecedents within a piece of writing, you need to use more specific words to avoid any confusion.

| | |
|---|---|
| **Unclear** | Chuck is a tour guide, but none of his friends chose **it** as a career. (The antecedent of *it* is not clear. The context of the sentence only suggests that the pronoun *it* refers to guiding tours as a profession.) |
| **Clear** | Chuck is a tour guide, but none of his friends chose **guiding tours** as a career. |
| **Unclear** | The recreation director pulled the bell cords, and **they** rang out loudly. (The antecedent of *they* is not clear. The context of the sentence suggests that the antecedent is *bells*.) |
| **Clear** | The recreation director pulled the bell cords, and the **bells** rang out loudly. |
| **Unclear** | I spent the summer at a horse ranch. **This** convinced me I wanted to become a veterinarian. (*This* has no clear antecedent, but it suggests the experience of being at the horse ranch.) |
| **Clear** | I spent the summer at a horse ranch. **This experience** convinced me I wanted to become a veterinarian. |

Some writers mistakenly use the pronoun *you* to refer to themselves. As a result, the pronoun *you* does not have a clear antecedent. Recast such sentences using the pronoun *I*.

| | |
|---|---|
| **Unclear** | I work at the YMCA camp because **you** can be outdoors all summer. |
| **Clear** | I work at the YMCA camp because **I** can be outdoors all summer. |

#  Missing Antecedents

**18 D.2**   When pronouns are written without any antecedents at all, you often have to rewrite the sentence and replace the pronoun with a noun.

**Missing**    In the book **it** shows how to restring a guitar.
(The antecedent of *it* is missing.)

**Clear**    The **book** shows how to restring a guitar.

**Missing**    In the spring **they** are offering public recitals at the music academy. (The antecedent of *they* is missing.)

**Clear**    In the spring **the music academy** is offering public recitals.

# Confusing Antecedents

**18 D.3**   When a pronoun has more than one possible antecedent, rewrite the sentence and replace the pronoun with a specific noun to clarify the sentence's meaning.

**Confusing**    As Paulo was showing Mike the boat, **he** fell into the water.
(Who fell in, Paulo or Mike?)

**Clear**    As Paulo was showing Mike the boat, **Mike** fell into the water.

**Confusing**    Rita had oars in both hands, but now **they** have disappeared.
(What disappeared, the oars or her hands?)

**Clear**    Rita had oars in both hands, but now **the oars** have disappeared.

---

● *Connect to Speaking and Writing:* **Vocabulary Review**

*Using the Vocabulary of Grammar*

With a partner, review the grammar terms introduced in this chapter. (Hint: Important terms are in purple type.) Then quiz each other on the terms until you have them memorized.

## Practice Your Skills

### Identifying Unclear, Missing, and Confusing Antecedents

Write *I* if the sentence contains a pronoun-antecedent error and **C** if the sentence is correct.

**1.** When Jane told Shawna about the new jet skis, she was very excited.

**2.** After my father and grandfather stowed the gear, he said, "All aboard!"

**3.** The Virgin Islands are our destination, and you can snorkel there.

**4.** I could hardly see the jellyfish and stingray underwater because it was cloudy.

**5.** Later I told Michelle and Marla about our trip, and they said it sounded enjoyable.

**6.** Wearing flippers on both feet, Geoffrey jumped into the water and then they fell off.

**7.** I packed a sun hat and tanning lotion, and it spilled inside my bag.

**8.** I asked Erica or Joanne to lend me a towel, and she offered me one.

**9.** After I took the fish off the hooks, I threw them into the water.

**10.** When the boat hit the rock, it was a disaster.

## *Connect to Writing:* Revising

### Correcting Antecedent Problems

Rewrite the sentences from the preceding exercise, correcting unclear, missing, or confusing antecedents.

## *Check Point:* Mixed Practice

Rewrite each sentence, correcting unclear, missing, or confusing antecedents.

**1.** On the map of South Padre Island, it shows where the best swimming areas are.

**2.** Clark and Billy bought hamburgers for the swimmers and then ate them.

**3.** When my friends and I tossed cheese puffs to the seagulls, they flew through the air.

**4.** It says "No Diving" on the sign at the end of the dock.

**5.** Shari and Shane do not want sunburns, so they used plenty of sunblock.

## Assess Your Learning

### ■ Using Pronouns in the Correct Case

Write the correct form of the pronoun in parentheses.

**1.** Mrs. Winters asked my friend Raymond to mow the lawn (himself, herself).

**2.** (Who, Whom) do you think will win the award for best singer?

**3.** Roy knows more about both folk music and country music than (she, her).

**4.** Was it Ken or (she, her) who saved that man's life at the beach yesterday?

**5.** Daniel, (who, whom) the coach promoted from junior varsity, has become one of Reading's best players.

**6.** The mayor promised three seniors, Carla, Al, and (he, him), summer jobs at City Hall.

**7.** Is Spencer older than (she, her)?

**8.** Show your pass to (whoever, whomever) is at the entrance to the estate.

**9.** Three of (we, us) boys volunteered to help load the moving van for Mr. Rodriguez.

**10.** Both Mom and Dad were surprised at (me, my) offering to clean the garage.

**11.** (Who, Whom) did you visit in Albany?

**12.** Neither the blue jay nor the sparrow abandoned (its, their) nest during the storm.

**13.** The only ones in the store were Kim and (he, him).

**14.** Both Lynn and Donna brought (her, their) umbrellas to the baseball game.

## ■ Editing for Pronoun Problems

Find at least one error in each sentence below. Write the sentences correctly.

**1.** With who are you going to the senior prom?
**2.** Daniel talks to Beth more than she talks to he.
**3.** Whom do you suppose will replace Mrs. Bennett?
**4.** E-mailing Antoine probably would be much easier than phoning himself.
**5.** Our friend Barbara asked whom the man in the blue seersucker suit was.

## ■ Making Pronouns Agree with Antecedents

Write the pronoun that correctly completes each sentence.

**1.** All the girls on the softball team packed ___ gear into the minivan.
**2.** Every duck in the pond had a piece of bread in ___ beak.
**3.** Neither Jeremiah nor Vincenzo submitted ___ history report on time.
**4.** One of the girls must have sold ___ bicycle.
**5.** Dogs perspire through ___ paw pads.

## ■ Writing Sentences

Write five sentences that follow the directions below.

**1.** Write a sentence using a form of the word *you* preceding a gerund.
**2.** Write a sentence with two pronouns in an appositive that agrees with the subject.
**3.** Write a sentence that correctly uses the word *whomever*.
**4.** Write a sentence that includes a personal pronoun used as a subject or object in an elliptical clause.
**5.** Write a sentence using a form of *we* followed by an appositive.

## Directions

Read the passage and choose the pronoun that belongs in each underlined space. Write the letter of the correct answer.

Most young people today have seen __(1)__ fair share of full-length animated movies, such as *The Lion King* or *A Bug's Life*. In fact, you probably remember __(2)__ seeing movies such as *Cinderella* and *Toy Story* when you were younger. However, before 1937, a full-length cartoon feature had never been made. It was Walt Disney, of course, __(3)__ produced the first one, *Snow White and the Seven Dwarfs*.

Back then, no one thought __(4)__ idea would succeed. For example, Walt's brother and business partner Roy O. Disney, who was more conservative than __(5)__, feared financial ruin. Nevertheless, Walt was confident that __(6)__ watched his cartoon would love it, and Walt wanted to show Roy that __(7)__ and everyone else were wrong.

For three years the animators in Disney's employ worked hard on __(8)__ drawings of Snow White. Walt gave __(9)__ high standards to follow, but all of the difficult work eventually paid off. When the movie ended its first showing, the members of the audience rose from __(10)__ seats and cheered wildly.

**1. A** they
   **B** them
   **C** their
   **D** theirs

**2. A** you
   **B** your
   **C** yours
   **D** their

**3. A** who
   **B** whom
   **C** whoever
   **D** whoever

**4. A** he
   **B** him
   **C** his
   **D** himself

**5. A** he
   **B** him
   **C** his
   **D** their

**6. A** who
   **B** whoever
   **C** whom
   **D** whomever

**7. A** he
   **B** his
   **C** him
   **D** their

**8. A** their
   **B** theirs
   **C** his
   **D** him

**9. A** him
   **B** his
   **C** they
   **D** them

**10. A** they
    **B** them
    **C** their
    **D** theirs

## Snapshot

**18 A**  **Case**—nominative, objective, or possessive—is the form of a noun or pronoun that indicates its use in the sentence. (pages 790–804)

**18 B**  Common problems with pronouns include the misuse of forms of *who* and *whom,* incomplete comparisons, and misuse of reflexive and intensive pronouns. The correct case of **who** or a related pronoun is determined by how the pronoun is used in a question or clause. (pages 805–811)

**18 C**  A pronoun's **antecedent** is the word that the pronoun refers to or replaces. A pronoun and its antecedent must agree in number and gender. (pages 812–817)

**18 D**  Every personal pronoun should clearly refer to a specific antecedent to avoid unclear, missing, or confusing references. (pages 818–820)

## Power Rules

 Use **subject forms of pronouns** in the subject position. Use the **object form** when the pronoun is a direct object, an indirect object, or an object of a preposition. (pages 790–801)

| **Before Editing** | **After Editing** |
| --- | --- |
| Melinda and *her* were group leaders. | Melinda and *she* were group leaders. |
| They want you and *I* to join. | They want you and *me* to join. |

 Several pronouns **sound like** other words. When you write, be sure you use the word with the correct meaning. Saying contractions as two words can help you decide which word is correct. (pages 801-802)

| **Before Editing** | **After Editing** |
| --- | --- |
| Are those *you're* books? (*you're* is a contraction of *you are*) | Are those *your* books? (*your* is the possessive form of *you*) |
| *Their* studying at the library. (*their* is the possessive form of *they*) | *They're* studying at the library. (*they're* is the contraction of *they are*) |
| *Its* time for a study break. (*its* is the possessive form of *it*) | *It's* time for a study break. (*it's* is the contraction of *it is*) |

## Editing Checklist

Use this checklist when editing your writing.

✓ Did I use use nominative pronouns as subjects? (See pages 790–795.)

✓ Did I use objective pronouns as objects of prepositions, direct objects, indirect objects, and objects of verbals? (See pages 795–801.)

✓ Did I use possessive pronouns to show ownership? (See pages 801–804.)

✓ Did I use forms of *who* and *whom* correctly? (See pages 805–807.)

✓ Did I use pronouns correctly when making comparisons? (See pages 808–809.)

✓ Did I use reflexive pronouns correctly? (See pages 809–811.)

✓ Did I use intensive pronouns to emphasize a noun or pronoun in a sentence? (See pages 809–811.)

✓ Did I make each pronoun agree with its antecedent both in number and gender? (See pages 812–817.)

✓ Did I make sure all pronouns have clear antecedents? (See pages 818–820.)

## Use the Power

**Problems with pronouns** often occur in compound constructions. Using your knowledge of academic language, find the compound elements and separate them into their parts. For example, many people think that the following usage is correct (the compound element is highlighted):

Her and Nadine went to the movies.

Those same people, however, would never say, "Her went to the movies." Similarly, in the case of a compound object, people might say:

They threw a party for Miguel and I when we graduated.

They would never say, "They threw a party for I when I graduated."

**Divide** compound subjects or objects into their separate parts and test each with the rest of the sentence. You'll likely be able to hear the right one.

# Subject and Verb Agreement

**How can accurate subject-verb agreement help your writing achieve clarity and focus?**

## Subject and Verb Agreement: Pretest 1

The following draft of a letter to a magazine editor contains several errors in subject and verb agreement. The first error has been corrected. How would you revise the remaining errors?

Dear Ms. Anderson:

    I have written a detective story about Liza Wingsmith and her partner, Cal Hobbes. Both Liza and Cal is eager to track down a neighborhood bicycle thief. I sincerely hopes I can interest you in publishing it. The stories in your magazine, *The Magic of Mystery,* often features clever and quirky detectives like Liza and Cal. Sometimes Liza and her partner, a computer ace, uses disguises while spying on suspects. Both the Internet and the local library serves as resources for their detective work. Liza's motto, "No criminal is too clever to catch," hang in her office in Austin, Texas. As she investigates, Liza's skill and determination proves successful. She and Cal both displays good humor and a positive attitude. Will you or an associate responds to me if you are interested in my story? Enclosed is an outline. Two weeks are what I'd need to fully polish my story. I enjoy your magazine and believe it provide a good home for my story.

Sincerely,
Deanna Deene

# Subject and Verb Agreement: Pretest 2

## Directions

Write the letter of the best way to write the underlined verb(s) in each sentence. If the underlined part contains no error, write D.

**1.** Storm trackers track hurricanes and <u>map</u> their locations.

**2.** The data compiled by storm trackers <u>are</u> both extensive and important.

**3.** Hurricanes in the eastern U.S. <u>has caused</u> great damage.

**4.** Each of the hurricanes <u>seem</u> worse than the one before.

**5.** One hundred miles inland <u>are</u> a common distance for a storm to travel.

**6.** An area struck by either of these storms often <u>suffer</u> great damage.

**7.** Neither storms nor other bad weather <u>are avoided</u> by a move to another state.

**8.** The media <u>inform</u> us that storms occur everywhere.

**1. A** maps
   **B** is mapping
   **C** has mapped
   **D** No error

**2. A** is
   **B** has proven
   **C** was proven
   **D** No error

**3. A** was caused
   **B** is causing
   **C** have caused
   **D** No error

**4. A** seems
   **B** have seem
   **C** do seem
   **D** No error

**5. A** is
   **B** seem
   **C** were
   **D** No error

**6. A** suffers
   **B** has suffered
   **C** suffering
   **D** No error

**7. A** were avoided
   **B** be avoided
   **C** is avoided
   **D** No error

**8. A** has informed
   **B** was informing
   **C** informing
   **D** No error

# Agreement of Subjects and Verbs

How many times have you seen the "perfect" pair of jeans, tried them on, and then discovered to your great disappointment that they were either too loose or too short? "Perfect" as they are, you cannot wear them because they do not fit. In a way, subjects and verbs are like people and jeans. Some fit together; others do not. When words do fit together, they are said to be in **agreement.** This chapter will review the different types of subjects and verbs. Then it will show you which agree and which do not.

**19 A**   A verb must agree with its subject in **number.**

**Number** determines whether a word is singular (one) or plural (more than one). A subject and a verb agree when they have the same number.

To understand agreement, you must know the singular and plural forms of nouns, pronouns, and verbs. The plurals of most nouns are formed by adding –s or –es to the singular form. Some nouns, however, form their plurals irregularly. For example, *children* is the plural of *child*. Certain pronouns also form their plurals by changing form.

| NOUNS | | PRONOUNS | |
|---|---|---|---|
| **Singular** | **Plural** | **Singular** | **Plural** |
| lion | lions | I | we |
| fox | foxes | you | you |
| goose | geese | he, she, it | they |

Verbs also have singular and plural forms, but only present tense verbs change endings. The third-person singular of present tense verbs ends in –s or –es. However, most plural forms of present tense verbs do not end in –s or –es. Notice that *I* and *you* take the plural form of the verb.

**Third Person Singular**   (He, She, It) sits.

**Others**   (I, You, We, They) sit.

The box on the next page shows the singular and the plural forms of the irregular verbs *be, have,* and *do* in the present tense. Notice that *be* also has irregular forms for both the singular and the plural in the past tense.

| PRESENT TENSE | PAST TENSE |
|---|---|
| **Singular** | **Singular** |
| I **am, have, do** | I **was, had, did** |
| you **are, have, do** | you **were, had, did** |
| he, she, it **is, has, does** | he, she, it **was, had, did** |
| **Plural** | **Plural** |
| we **are, have, do** | we **were, had, did** |
| you **are, have, do** | you **were, had, did** |
| they **are, have, do** | they **were, had, did** |

Since a subject and a verb both have number, they must agree in a sentence.

**19 A.1**   A singular subject takes a singular verb. A plural subject takes a plural verb.

> The <u>lion</u> <u>pounces</u>.   The <u>lions</u> <u>pounce</u>.
> The <u>fox</u> <u>hides</u>.   The <u>foxes</u> <u>hide</u>.
> The <u>goose</u> <u>flies</u>.   The <u>geese</u> <u>fly</u>.
> <u>It</u> <u>is</u> a hawk.   <u>They</u> <u>are</u> hawks.

*Be, have*, and *do* are often used as helping verbs. When they are, they must agree in number with the subject.

**19 A.2**   The first helping verb must agree in number with its subject.

> <u>Pamela</u> **is** <u>studying</u> primates in science class.
> The baby <u>gorillas</u> **were** <u>found</u> in the jungle.
> The <u>birds</u> **have** <u>flown</u> away.
> <u>Mark</u> **does** <u>have</u> a pet cockatoo.

*You can learn more about regular and irregular verbs on pages 750–761.*

Mark Twain is known for breaking rules of grammar in the dialogue of his characters. For example, Huckleberry Finn tells the reader that when "Mr. Mark Twain" wrote *Tom Sawyer,*

"There was things which he stretched, but mainly he told the truth."

You know that the correct grammar would be "There *were* things that he stretched." Twain's misuse of subject and verb agreement is one aspect of **local color writing.** With this type of writing, authors write sentences exactly as the people in a particular region would speak them.

Write a paragraph in which characters speak the way people do in your region.

## ● Practice Your Skills

### *Making Subjects and Verbs Agree*

Write the correct form of the verb in parentheses.

**1.** Alex (is, are) a 22-year-old gray parrot.

**2.** Trainers (talks, talk) to Alex every day.

**3.** Irene Pepperberg (train, trains) Alex to speak and reason.

**4.** The teacher (hold, holds) a tray of wood, plastic, and wool items.

**5.** She (asks, ask) Alex, "How many wood?"

**6.** Alex (respond, responds) with the correct number of wooden objects.

**7.** As a reward, Irene (gives, give) a wooden object to Alex to play with.

**8.** Sometimes Alex (want, wants) a treat instead of a toy.

**9.** On these occasions, the parrot (say, says), "Wanna nut."

**10.** Some scientists believe that gray parrots (rival, rivals) apes in intelligence.

## ● *Connect to Writing:* Editing

### *Using Subject and Verb Agreement*

Edit the sentences in the following paragraphs for subject-verb agreement. If a subject and verb do not agree in number, write the sentence correctly.

**(1)** Koko were born in 1971. **(2)** She are a black gorilla, and she weigh about 280 pounds. **(3)** Her handlers has taught her to understand over 2,000 words of American Sign Language. **(4)** The teachers shows Koko how to form the words, or they molds Koko's hands into the proper shape. **(5)** The techniques is very similar to teaching sign language to a human. **(6)** Koko speak to people using over 1,000 signs. **(7)** Koko's gorilla friend Michael also have learned some sign language—over 500 signs. **(8)** Sometimes, the two gorillas communicates with each other in this way.

**(9)** Koko were able to name her own pet kitten, whom she called All Ball. **(10)** Her favorite color are red, and her favorite toys is rubber alligators. **(11)** She love to watch *Wild Kingdom* on television, and she also like films about children and animals, such as *Free Willy*. **(12)** Koko's caregivers at the Gorilla Foundation has noticed that the gorilla's favorite book are *The Three Little Kittens*.

## ➤ Interrupting Words

Often a subject and a verb are side by side in a sentence. When they are, agreement between them is usually easy to recognize. Many times, however, a phrase or a clause modifying the subject separates it from the verb. In these sentences, there may be a temptation to make the verb agree with the word closest to it rather than with its subject. To avoid making this mistake in agreement, find the subject and make the verb agree with it.

**19 A.3**    The agreement of a verb with its subject is not changed by any interrupting words.

Notice in each of the following examples that the subject and the verb agree in number—regardless of any interrupting words.

| | |
|---|---|
| **Prepositional Phrase** | The <u>games</u> on the computer **<u>were</u>** installed. <br> (The plural helping verb *were* agrees with the plural subject *games,* even though the singular noun *computer* is closer to the verb.) |
| **Participial Phrase** | The <u>monitor</u>, covered with notes, **<u>is</u>** mine. <br> (*Is* agrees with *monitor,* not *notes.*) |
| **Negative Statements** | The program <u>architects</u>, not their manager, **<u>design</u>** the project. <br> (*Design* agrees with *architects,* not *manager.*) |
| **Adjectival Clauses** | Computer <u>programs</u> that compose music **<u>are</u>** a form of artificial intelligence. <br> (*Are* agrees with *programs,* not *music.*) |

A compound preposition—such as *in addition to, as well as, along with,* and *together with*—will often interrupt a subject and a verb. Make sure the verb always agrees with the subject, not the object of the compound preposition.

Gail, together with her sisters, **is** starting a computer software company.

(*Is* agrees with *Gail,* not *sisters.*)

The boys, as well as my uncle, **are** installing the satellite dish.

(*Are* agrees with *boys,* not *uncle.*)

● **Practice Your Skills**

*Making Interrupted Subjects and Verbs Agree*

Write the subject in each sentence. Next to each subject, write the form of the verb in parentheses that agrees with it.

1. Many students at the science fair (was, were) honored for their technological creations.
2. The inventions, arranged on a table, (includes, include) telephones, speakers, and other electronics.
3. The cost of each project (averages, average) one hundred dollars.
4. Tyrone Purdy, unlike other students, (has, have) a parent who is a scientist.
5. Dr. Purdy, so helpful to us students, (hands, hand) out the awards while a photographer takes pictures.
6. The telephone that "speaks" the names of callers (is, are) my favorite invention.
7. The pager-on-a-necklace, including ports for phone jacks and printers, (wins, win) an award as well.
8. The underwater fisher's camera, not the musical earrings, (was, were) the first-place winner.
9. The lucky students who won first, second, and third place (was, were) given scholarships for college.
10. The second-place winner, as well as several other participants, (plan, plans) to attend M.I.T.

● *Connect to Writing:* **Editing**

*Using Subject and Verb Agreement*

Write each verb that does not agree with its subject. Beside the verb, write its correct form.

(1) Scientists who work at universities and laboratories regularly invents amazing items. (2) Their expensive inventions, often funded by grants, introduces creative applications for technology. (3) Scientists at the Massachusetts Institute of Technology Media Lab was able to create "intelligent clothes." (4) For example,

a television reporter, together with other journalists, are now able to stay ahead of the competition by wearing gloves! **(5)** The reporter wear a glove equipped with a video camera in the palm. **(6)** A pair of special glasses show the image being recorded.

**(7)** These scientists at M.I.T. has created other wearable technology. **(8)** People who travel to a foreign country has the option of wearing a translation vest. **(9)** These vests, not a foreign language dictionary, is what will translate the tourists' speech. **(10)** A speaker wearing the vest talk normally. **(11)** Microphones built into the vest records the spoken words, and speakers at shoulder level relays the translation.

## *Connect to Writing:* Description

### *Making Subjects and Verbs Agree*

Write a description of your own idea for a piece of "intelligent" clothing. Describe its purpose, how it works, and where a person might wear the clothing. Edit your writing for agreement between subjects and verbs. Write a neat final copy, and share it with your class.

## ✔ *Check Point:* Mixed Practice

Write the subject in each sentence. Then write the form of the underlined verb that agrees with the subject. If the verb is correct, write **C**.

**1.** This lawn, covered with weeds, <u>need</u> Rodney's attention and expertise.

**2.** Rodney, one of my neighbors, <u>own</u> a lawn care and landscaping business.

**3.** His customers <u>is impressed</u> by his knowledge and skill.

**4.** Rodney <u>have told</u> me how he learned the business.

**5.** Informative books, not luck, <u>explains</u> his success.

**6.** The books in the library <u>were</u> the key to his business endeavors.

**7.** Now, his accounts in the bank <u>reflects</u> that financial success.

**19 B**  Compound subjects, indefinite pronouns as subjects, and subjects in inverted order can pose agreement problems.

## Compound Subjects

When you make two or more subjects agree with a verb, you should remember two rules.

**19 B.1**  When subjects are joined by *or, nor, either/or,* or *neither/nor,* the verb agrees with the closer subject.

> Either <u>you</u> or <u>Lola</u> <u>buys</u> vegetables at the Vine Street Farmers' Market.
> (*Buys* agrees with the closer subject *Lola.*)
> A <u>ladybug</u> or an <u>earthworm</u> <u>is</u> a helpful creature for a vegetable garden.
> (*Is* agrees with the closer subject *earthworm.*)

The same rule applies when one subject is singular and the other subject is plural.

> Neither the <u>trowel</u> nor our <u>shovels</u> <u>were</u> in sight.
> (*Were* agrees with the closer subject *shovels*—even though *trowel* is singular.)

When compound subjects are joined by other conjunctions, however, a different rule applies.

**19 B.2**  When subjects are joined by *and* or *both/and,* the verb is plural.

These conjunctions always indicate more than one. Since more than one is plural, the verb must be plural also.

> The <u>mulch</u> and the <u>fertilizer</u> <u>are</u> in the barn.
> (*Two* items—the *mulch* and the *fertilizer*—are in the barn.
> The verb must be plural to agree with both of them.)
> Both the <u>rakes</u> and that <u>wheelbarrow</u> **were** <u>left</u> in the rain.
> (Even though *wheelbarrow* is singular, the verb is still plural because the
> wheelbarrow and the rakes—together—were left in the rain.)

The second rule has certain exceptions. Two subjects joined by *and* occasionally refer to only one person or one thing. In such a case, the verb must be singular.

Fruit and cheese is my mom's favorite dessert.
(*Fruit and cheese* is considered one item.)
Strawberries and cream is also very good.
(*Strawberries and cream* is considered one item.)

Another exception involves the words *every* and *each*. If one of these words comes before a compound subject that is joined by *and,* each subject is considered separately. As a result, the verb must be singular to agree with a singular subject.

Every barn and fence receives a fresh coat of paint.
Each pond and creek brims with rainwater.

## ● Practice Your Skills

### Making Verbs Agree with Compound Subjects

Write the correct form of the verb in parentheses.

1. Wheat and corn (grows, grow) well in Washington.
2. For some reason, neither snails nor slugs (crawl, crawls) over crushed eggshells.
3. Each flower garden and vegetable plot (was, were) sprinkled with eggshells.
4. Either chicken wire or a wooden fence (form, forms) a good garden enclosure.
5. On a busy farm, every man, woman, and child (is, are) given duties.
6. Bacon and eggs (are, is) many farmers' favorite breakfast food.
7. Neither chemical fertilizers nor chemical pesticides (is, are) used in organic gardens.
8. Every horticulturist and gardener (know, knows) that lavender repels insects in the garden and moths in the closet.
9. Peanuts or potatoes (grow, grows) on many of Oklahoma's farms.
10. Both cantaloupe and spinach (flourishes, flourish) in southwest Texas along the border of Mexico.

# ➤ Indefinite Pronouns as Subjects

**19 B.3**   A verb must agree in number with an indefinite pronoun used as a subject.

The indefinite pronouns in the following chart have been grouped according to number.

| COMMON INDEFINITE PRONOUNS | |
|---|---|
| **Singular** | another, anybody, anyone, anything, each, either, everybody, everyone, everything, much, neither, nobody, no one, one, somebody, someone, something |
| **Plural** | both, few, many, others, several |
| **Singular/Plural** | all, any, most, none, some |

A singular verb agrees with a singular indefinite pronoun, and a plural verb agrees with a plural indefinite pronoun.

**Singular**   One of my golf balls **is** muddy.

**Plural**   Many of my golf balls are muddy.

The number of an indefinite pronoun in the singular/plural group is determined by the object of the prepositional phrase that follows it.

**Singular**   Some of the equipment is on sale.

**or Plural**   Most of the barbells are on sale.

## ● Practice Your Skills

### *Making Verbs Agree with Indefinite Pronoun Subjects*

Write the subject in each sentence. Next to it, write the form of the verb in parentheses that agrees with the subject.

**1.** All of the players (has, have) received their letters.

**2.** Everybody at the pep rally (are, is) wearing the school colors, green and gold.

**3.** Both of the teams (wear, wears) green jerseys.

**4.** Most of the opposing team (have, has) the flu.

**5.** Neither of those footballs (is, are) mine.

**6.** Some of the basketball fans (has, have) arrived.

**7.** Others (plans, plan) to be here soon.

**8.** Everyone, including the band, (was, were) thirsty during halftime.

**9.** Any parts of the game plan (is, are) open to revision.

**10.** Another of my teammates (has, have) become severely dehydrated.

**11.** Several of the rackets (was, were) damaged.

**12.** Something left in one of these gymnasium lockers (smell, smells) horrible.

**13.** Each of those skates (needs, need) new blades.

## ● *Connect to Writing:* Revising

### *Making Verbs and Indefinite Pronouns Agree*

Rewrite each sentence twice. First, add a prepositional phrase with a plural object. Second, add a prepositional phrase with a singular object. Be sure to check that all subjects and verbs agree.

**1.** Some have finished the marathon.

**2.** Any are welcome.

**3.** None is accused of cheating.

**4.** Most train all day.

**5.** All is in the locker.

## Subjects in Inverted Order

A sentence is said to be in **inverted order** when the verb or part of the verb phrase comes before the subject. Even though a verb may precede a subject, it still must agree with the subject in number.

**19 B.4**   The subject and the verb of an inverted sentence must agree in number.

There are several types of inverted sentences. When you are looking for the subject in an inverted sentence, turn the sentence around to its natural order. To have the sentence make sense, you must occasionally drop *here* or *there* when putting the sentence into its natural order.

| | |
|---|---|
| **Inverted Order** | In the valley is a babbling brook. |
| | (A babbling *brook is* in the valley.) |
| **Question** | Was the mountain visible in the fog? |
| | (The *mountain was* visible in the fog.) |
| **Sentences Beginning with *Here* or *There*** | Here are the hiking trails. |
| | (The *hiking trails* are here.) |
| | There is a waterfall on the edge of the cliff. |
| | (Drop *there*. A *waterfall is* on the edge of the cliff.) |

*You can learn more about sentences written in inverted order on pages 656–658.*

### ● Practice Your Skills

#### Making Subjects and Verbs in Inverted Order Agree

Write the subject in each sentence. Next to it write the form of the verb in parentheses that agrees with the subject.

**1.** Along the Tennessee-North Carolina border (run, runs) a mountain range.

**2.** (Has, Have) you ever heard anyone talk about the Great Smoky Mountains?

**3.** There (is, are) a park called Great Smoky Mountains National Park that includes the highest peak.

**4.** (Do, Does) they know that the Great Basin between the Sierra Nevada and Wasatch Range in the western United States has no outlet to the sea?

**5.** Here (is, are) colorful, current maps of the five Great Lakes: Superior, Michigan, Huron, Erie, and Ontario.

**6.** (Were, Was) souvenir shops selling pieces of the demolished Berlin Wall?

**7.** Across western Australia (stretches, stretch) the Great Sandy Desert.

**8.** (Is, Are) the tour scheduled to visit the Greater Antilles, a group of islands in the West Indies?

9. There (is, are) a seaport called Great Yarmouth on the eastern coast of England in Norfolk.

10. Off the northeast coast of Australia (lies, lie) the Great Barrier Reef, a coral reef 1,250 miles long.

## Connect to Writing: Oral Presentation

### *Writing Sentences in Inverted Order*

Using the preceding exercise as a reference, choose a geographical location that interests you. Write six sentences in inverted order to ask questions you would like answered about this place. One example might be "What is the average temperature in Australia?" Research to find the answers, and write and give an oral presentation detailing what you learned.

## ✔ Check Point: Mixed Practice

Write each sentence, using the correct present tense form of the verb in parentheses.

1. (is) Both Sherlock Holmes and Dr. Watson ___ characters in a popular series of mystery stories.

2. (read) Many of the world's mystery fans ___ these stories by Arthur Conan Doyle.

3. (investigate) Throughout London and the surrounding countryside, Holmes ___ murders and thefts.

4. (is) There ___ cases such as the murderous "speckled band" and the disappearance of a horse called Silver Blaze.

5. (find) Across a windowsill, Hilton Cubitt ___ drawings of mysterious little stick-figure men.

6. (is) All of the drawings ___ interpreted by Holmes.

# Other Agreement Problems  Lesson 3

> **19 C** Other situations that cause agreement problems include contractions, collective nouns, words expressing time, and titles.

## Collective Nouns

You may recall that a **collective noun** names a group of people or things. A collective noun may be either singular or plural—depending on how it is used in a sentence.

| COMMON COLLECTIVE NOUNS | | | |
|---|---|---|---|
| band | congregation | flock | orchestra |
| class | crew | gang | swarm |
| committee | crowd | herd | team |
| colony | family | league | tribe |

> **19 C.1** Use a singular verb with a collective-noun subject that is treated as a unit. Use a plural verb with a collective-noun subject that is treated as individual parts.

The class **is** presently holding elections.
(The class is working together as a whole unit in this sentence. As a result, the verb is singular.)

The class **are** casting their ballots today.
(The members of the class are acting independently—each one casting a ballot. As a result, the verb is plural.)

## Words Expressing Amounts or Times

Subjects that express amounts, measurements, weights, or times usually are considered to be a single unit. However, they often have plural forms.

> **19 C.2** A subject that expresses an amount, a measurement, a weight, or a time is usually considered singular and takes a singular verb.

| Quantity | **Ten** <u>dollars</u> <u>is</u> the amount of my campaign contribution. |
| --- | --- |
| | (one amount of money) |
| | **Five** <u>miles</u> <u>is</u> the distance from my house to City Hall. |
| | (one unit of distance) |
| | **Two** <u>pounds</u> <u>is</u> the weight of this box of campaign buttons. (one |
| | unit of weight) |
| Time | **Six** <u>months</u> **<u>is</u> <u>needed</u>** to prepare the candidates. |
| | (one period of time) |
| | **Thirty** <u>minutes</u> <u>is</u> how long the legislator spoke. |
| | (one period of time) |

If an amount, measurement, weight, or time is treated in its individual parts, then the verb must be plural.

| Quantity | **Two** <u>pounds</u> of pencils **<u>were</u>** lost. |
| --- | --- |
| | **Ten** <u>dollars</u> **<u>were</u>** in the treasurer's hand. |
| Time | **Six** <u>months</u> **<u>have</u> <u>passed</u>** since the election. |

When the subject is a fraction or a percent, the verb agrees with the object of the prepositional phrase that follows the subject.

| Singular | <u>One third</u> of my salary <u>goes</u> to taxes. |
| --- | --- |
| Plural | <u>One fourth</u> of the seniors <u>are</u> old enough to vote. |

# ➤ The Number of, A Number of

Although the expressions *the number of* and *a number of* are very similar, one expression takes a singular verb and one takes a plural verb.

**19 C.3**   Use a singular verb with *the number of* and a plural verb with *a number of.*

**The <u>number</u> of** students touring the White House <u>is</u> surprising. (singular)

**A <u>number</u> of** high school students <u>intend</u> to go into city government. (plural)

Be sure to choose the correct expression for your writing purpose. **A number of tourists visit yearly** focuses on the action of the tourists. **The number of tourists escalates yearly** focuses on the action of the **number.** Look at a piece of writing you are working on and be sure the way you express number reflects your purpose.

## ➤ Singular Nouns That Have Plural Forms

Even though a word ends in *–s,* it may not take a plural verb. Some nouns are plural in form but singular in meaning because they name a single thing—one area of knowledge or one type of disease, for example.

| SINGULAR NOUNS WITH PLURAL FORMS | | | |
|---|---|---|---|
| civics | economics | gymnastics | mathematics |
| measles | molasses | mumps | news |
| physics | social studies | the United States | |

**19 C.4**  Use a singular verb with certain subjects that are plural in form but singular in meaning.

Civics is the study of citizens' rights and responsibilities.

The local news covers the mayor's weekly activities.

A second group of similar nouns are usually plural, as their form indicates. A third group can be either singular or plural, depending on how they are used in a sentence. If you are confused about a particular noun, it sometimes helps to check the dictionary.

| SIMILAR NOUNS | |
|---|---|
| **Usually Plural** | barracks, data, eyeglasses, media, pliers, scissors, shears, slacks, thanks, trousers |
| **Singular/Plural** | acoustics, athletics, headquarters, ethics, politics, tactics |

Your <u>eyeglasses</u> **were** <u>found</u> in the courtroom. (plural)

The <u>headquarters</u> for the United Nations **is** <u>located</u> in New York City. (singular—an administrative center)

The <u>headquarters</u> **are** <u>located</u> on the outskirts of the town. (plural—a group of buildings)

Notice that if the word *pair* precedes a word that is usually plural, the verb is nevertheless singular because the verb then agrees with the singular noun *pair*.

**Singular**    That <u>pair</u> of scissors <u>is</u> dull.

**Plural**    Those <u>scissors</u> <u>are</u> dull.

## *When You Speak and Write*

Although *data* and *media* are both plural nouns, many people use them as singular nouns in informal speech. However, in your formal speaking and writing, it is best to use *data* and *media* as plural nouns; their singular forms are *datum* and *medium*.

| | |
|---|---|
| **Singular** | My favorite <u>medium</u> of communication <u>is</u> the newspaper. |
| **Plural** | Various <u>media</u> <u>are</u> radio, television, and print. |
| **Singular** | This <u>datum</u> <u>is</u> not the result I expected. |
| **Plural** | The <u>data</u> I collected <u>are</u> accurate. |

## ● Practice Your Skills

### *Making Subjects and Verbs Agree*

Write the correct form of the verb in parentheses.

**1.** A large number of the candidates (is, are) female.

**2.** Campaigning for school government (takes, take) up most of my sister's spare time.

**3.** Two-thirds of the people in town (does, do) not vote.

**4.** Ten minutes (was, were) not a long wait to vote.

**5.** Sixty percent of the student body (has, have) voted in student government elections.

6. Three miles (is, are) the distance from here to the governor's mansion.

7. The jury (was, were) in complete disagreement throughout the deliberations.

8. The headquarters for Steve's campaign for class president (is, are) the corner pizza parlor.

9. The city government news (is, are) broadcast at five o'clock.

10. Almost three-fourths of the apples in the basket (was, were) used in pies at the mayor's reception dinner.

## ● *Connect to Writing:* Editing

### Correcting Subject and Verb Agreement Problems

Write the subject and the correct verb form. If a sentence is correct, write C.

1. A swarm of reporters want to question the politician.

2. "Mumps are preventable with a vaccine," said the new county health commissioner.

3. Approximately four dollars was paid for each nominee's campaign poster.

4. The number of candidates for Student Council is surprisingly large.

5. The committee was arguing about the details of the voting procedure.

6. A group of students from the twelfth grade are ready to vote.

7. That pair of red suspenders look good on the senator.

8. Economics are Kevin's major at the University of Florida in Gainesville.

9. The media are distorting the candidate's remarks.

10. A number of students is planning for political careers.

# ➤ Doesn't or Don't?

*Doesn't* and *don't* are contractions. When checking for agreement with a subject, say the two words of a contraction separately. Also keep in mind which contractions are singular and which are plural.

| CONTRACTIONS | |
|---|---|
| **Singular** | doesn't, hasn't, isn't, wasn't |
| **Plural** | don't, haven't, aren't, weren't |

**19 C.5**    The verb part of a contraction must agree in number with the subject.

> This cold <u>weather</u> **does**n't <u>bother</u> me at all.
>
> These <u>rainstorms</u> **do**n't <u>alter</u> my plans.

## ➤ Subjects with Linking Verbs

A predicate nominative follows a linking verb and identifies, renames, or explains the subject. Occasionally, however, a subject and its predicate nominative will not have the same number. The verb, nevertheless, agrees with the subject.

**19 C.6**    A verb agrees with the subject of a sentence, not with the predicate nominative.

> <u>Hail</u> <u>is</u> small pieces of ice in a thunderstorm.
>
> (The singular verb *is* agrees with the singular subject *hail*—even though the predicate nominative *pieces* is plural.)
>
> Small <u>pieces</u> of ice in a thunderstorm <u>are</u> hail.
>
> (*Are* agrees with the plural subject *pieces*—not with the singular predicate nominative *hail*.)

*When You Write*

When writing, avoid creating sentences in which the subject and the predicate nominative do not agree in number.

| | |
|---|---|
| **Incorrect** | <u>Hailstones</u> <u>are</u> a small **piece** of ice. |
| **Correct** | <u>Hailstones</u> <u>are</u> small **pieces** of ice. |

Look back at a recent composition to be sure predicate nominatives and their subjects agree in number.

*You can find lists of linking verbs on pages 628–629.*

## ➤ Titles

Some titles may seem plural because they are composed of several words. A title, nevertheless, is the name of only one book, poem, play, work of art, country, or the like. As a result, a title is singular and takes a singular verb. Most multiword names of businesses and organizations are also considered singular.

A title is singular and takes a singular verb.

| | |
|---|---|
| **Book** | *Great Expectations* is a novel by Charles Dickens. |
| **Poem** | "The Planters" is a poem by Margaret Atwood. |
| **Play** | *Death of a Salesman* is my favorite play. |
| **Work of Art** | *Midsummer* is an oil painting by Albert Joseph Moore. |
| **Country** | The Netherlands is an interesting vacation destination. |
| **Company** | Barrett's Book Barn is having a sale on mystery novels. |

● **Practice Your Skills**

*Making Subjects and Verbs Agree*

Write the correct form of the verb in parentheses.

**1.** Snowy ski slopes (is, are) a great attraction in Colorado.

**2.** He (doesn't, don't) know the way through the fog.

**3.** *The Iceman Cometh,* a play in four acts, (is, are) Eugene O'Neill's most celebrated work.

**4.** These rain boots (is, are) the perfect gift.

**5.** Ick! The snow (feel, feels) slushy and grainy.

**6.** (Doesn't, Don't) the weather bureau issue tornado warnings?

**7.** A tornado spinning across fields (look, looks) violent.

**8.** *Human Figure with Two Birds* (was, were) created from scrap wood, black paper, emery paper, and oil paints by Max Ernst.

**9.** Car Haven (is, are) the store for snow tires.

**10.** (Doesn't, Don't) daylight saving time start tonight?

# ➤ *Who, Which,* and *That*

*Who, which,* and *that* are often used as relative pronouns to begin an adjectival clause. When one of these words is the subject of the clause, the number of its verb will depend upon the number of the pronoun's antecedent.

In an adjectival clause in which the relative pronoun *who, which,* or *that* is used as the subject, the verb agrees with the antecedent of the relative pronoun.

Bobby read a nonfiction **book** that was a thousand pages long.

(The antecedent of *that* is *book*. Since *book* is singular, *was* is also singular.)

Find the titles of three **books** that deal with space exploration.

(The antecedent of *that* is *books*. Since *books* is plural, *deal* is also plural.)

If an adjectival clause is preceded by the expression *one of,* the verb in the clause is usually plural.

Alfred, Lord Tennyson is *one of* the **poets** who **were** appointed poet laureate of England. (The antecedent of *who* is *poets,* not *one.*)

*You can learn more about adjectival clauses on pages 724–729.*

## ● Practice Your Skills

### *Making Verbs Agree with Relative Pronouns*

Write the correct form of the verb in parentheses.

**1.** I liked the film that (was, were) adapted from Charlotte Brontë's *Jane Eyre.*

**2.** Jane Eyre and Mr. Rochester, who (is, are) the primary characters, grow to love each other.

**3.** A mysterious, ghostlike woman, who (is, are) locked in the attic, sets Jane's room afire.

**4.** *Wide Sargasso Sea,* which (were, was) written by Jean Rhys, creates a story around this mysterious woman.

**5.** *Shirley* is another of the novels that (was, were) written by Charlotte Brontë.

**6.** This author had two sisters who (was, were) also writers.

**7.** *Wuthering Heights* is the novel that (was, were) published under Emily Brontë's pen name, Ellis Bell.

**8.** This is a story that (contain, contains) love and hate, riches and poverty,

**9.** Anne Brontë's novel *The Tenant of Wildfell Hall,* which (is, are) one of her two novels, was published in 1848.

## ● *Connect to Writing:* Character Essay

### *Subject and Verb Agreement*

You are writing a story for a mystery magazine. Write a letter to the publisher of the magazine outlining your ideas for the two main characters in this story. Offer details about the plot, setting, time period, and the conflicts the characters face. Include the opening paragraph of your story to send along to the publisher.

### Using Subject and Verb Agreement

Write the correct form of the verb in parentheses.

1. (is) Miss Marple and Hercule Poirot, who ____ Agatha Christie's most famous creations, both solve crimes.
2. (is) These fictional characters, which ____ beloved by many, are featured in separate mystery series.
3. (discover) Jane Marple is an elderly woman who ____ murders and other crimes in unexpected places.
4. (is) *Murder at the Vicarage,* which ____ her first adventure, chronicles a murder investigation.
5. (occur) The victim of a murder that ____ at the vicarage is Colonel Protheroe.

## ✔ *Check Point:* **Mixed Practice**

Write the verbs that do not agree with their subjects. Then write those verbs correctly.

(1) What does you know about trees? (2) Do you know that the leaves on a tree has several functions? (3) One of these functions are to make food for the tree. (4) Carbon dioxide from the air is taken in by the leaves. (5) Water and minerals from the soil is taken in by the roots. (6) The chlorophyll in leaves absorbs energy from the sun and then change the carbon dioxide and water into glucose, or food.

(7) Leaves also give off enormous quantities of water. (8) Some of the water that flow from the roots to the leaves are used to make food. (9) Most of the rest of the water in leaves evaporate through tiny holes on the surface of the leaves.

## ● *Connect to Writing:* **Basic Vocabulary**

### Using Subjects and Verbs That Agree

When writing in English, you must be sure verbs agree with their subjects. Go over the meanings of the terms *compound subject, indefinite pronoun, inverted order, contraction,* and *collective noun* to understand how they impact subject verb agreement. Next, write two sentences, each of which contains one of the following.

• a compound subject

• an indefinite pronoun as a subject

• a collective noun

## Assess Your Learning

### ▪ Correcting Errors with Modifiers

Write the correct form of each verb in parentheses.

1. Rome—with its ornate architecture, marvelous food, and fascinating history—(attracts, attract) many tourists from around the world.
2. One of my presents (was, were) a gift certificate from the huge video store on Madison Avenue.
3. (Was, Were) many world records broken in the 1984 Olympics in Los Angeles?
4. Both the hockey team and the baseball team (has, have) won state championships this year.
5. Mathematics (is, are) a special kind of language.
6. (Is, Are) ten dollars too much for this paperback book?
7. My uncle, not my cousins, (was, were) visiting at the end of August.
8. A grouping of millions of stars (is, are) called a galaxy.
9. Ham and eggs (makes, make) a hearty breakfast for our family.
10. In the basket (was, were) two apples, a pear, and a bunch of grapes.
11. (Doesn't, Don't) Richard play on the varsity basketball team anymore?
12. There (is, are) more than 19 species of buzzards.
13. Neither the center nor the guard (knows, know) that play well.

### ▪ Correcting Errors with Subject-Verb Agreement

Write the following sentences, correcting each mistake. If a sentence is correct, write **C** after the number.

1. Either a bookcase or some shelves is needed.
2. Two-thirds of the students has voted.
3. Has all the applicants been interviewed?
4. This week there have been several warm days.
5. Don't the movie start at 5:30?
6. Neither of these reports has any footnotes.

### ■ Writing Sentences

Write five sentences that follow the directions below.

**1.** Write a sentence in which the subject is a number of miles.

**2.** Write a sentence with a collective noun as a subject. Write the sentence so that the members of the group act independently.

**3.** Write a question that begins with *doesn't* or *don't*.

**4.** Write a sentence in which the subject and the verb are separated by a participial phrase.

**5.** Write a sentence that contains a subordinate clause beginning with *that*. Make the subject in the independent clause singular.

# Subject and Verb Agreement: Posttest

### Directions

Write the letter of the best way to write the underlined verb in each sentence. If the underlined part contains no error, write D.

**1.** Some traffic signs <u>is understood</u> in all countries.

**2.** At least a fourth of Dad's salary <u>go</u> into the savings account every month.

**3.** The number of honor students <u>are growing</u> year by year at our school.

**4.** Neither my brother nor his friends <u>wants</u> to dance.

**5.** Amy, not her friends, <u>supports</u> my position on this issue.

**6.** Long grain white rice, along with cheese and pine nuts, <u>are</u> my favorite side dish.

**7.** <u>Has</u> the audience <u>been seated</u>?

**8.** A number of students in this class <u>has</u> consistently <u>appeared</u> on the honor roll.

**1. A** was understood
   **B** has been understood
   **C** are understood
   **D** No error

**2. A** have gone
   **B** goes
   **C** were going
   **D** No error

**3. A** were growing
   **B** is growing
   **C** have been growing
   **D** No error

**4. A** want
   **B** has wanted
   **C** does want
   **D** No error

**5. A** support
   **B** have supported
   **C** were supporting
   **D** No error

**6. A** were
   **B** have
   **C** is
   **D** No error

**7. A** Have been seated
   **B** Were seated
   **C** Were being seated
   **D** No error

**8. A** is appearing
   **B** have appeared
   **C** was appearing
   **D** No error

# Writer's Corner

## Snapshot

**19 A**  A verb must agree with its subject in number. (pages 828–833)

**19 B**  Compound subjects, indefinite pronouns as subjects, and subjects in inverted order can pose agreement problems. (pages 834–839)

**19 C**  Other situations that cause agreement problems include contractions, collective nouns, words expressing time, and titles. (pages 840–848)

## Power Rules

Be sure that every sentence has a subject and predicate. **The subject and verb must agree.** (pages 826–853)

| **Before Editing** | **After Editing** |
|---|---|
| Each of the employees *plan* to take a vacation. | Each of the employees *plans* to take a vacation. |
| The group *want* to go to somewhere warm and sunny. | The group *wants* to go somewhere warm and sunny. |
| The owner or the managers *makes* the schedules. | The owner or the managers *make* the schedules. |

Use **subject forms of pronouns** in the subject position. Use the **object form** when the pronoun is a direct object, indirect object, or object of a preposition. (pages 790–801)

| **Before Editing** | **After Editing** |
|---|---|
| *Him* and Jackson play football. | *He* and Jackson play football. |
| Lila and *her* always go to the games. | Lila and *she* always go to the games. |
| They want to sit by you and *I*. | They want to sit by you and *me*. |

## Editing Checklist

Use this checklist when editing your writing.

✓ Did I write sentences in which the verb always agrees with the subject in number? (pages 828–831)

✓ Did I make singular subjects take singular verbs and plural subjects take plural verbs? (pages 828–831)

✓ Did I make verbs agree with compound subjects? (pages 834–836)

✓ Did I use singular verbs with singular indefinite pronouns and plural verbs with plural indefinite pronouns? (pages 836–837)

✓ Did I make subjects and verbs in inverted order agree? (pages 838–839)

✓ Did I use verbs that agreed with collective nouns? (page 840)

✓ Did I make verbs agree with singular nouns that have plural forms? (pages 842–844)

## Use the Power

**Some subjects and verbs** fit together, and others do not. Use these puzzle diagrams to help you understand rules for subject and verb agreement.

**Rule:** When subjects are joined by *or, nor, either/or,* or *neither/nor,* the verb agrees with the closer subject.

**Rule:** A verb must agree in number with an indefinite pronoun used as a subject.

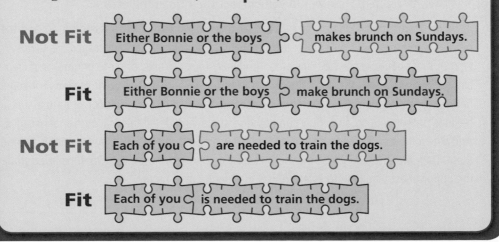

**Not Fit** — Either Bonnie or the boys makes brunch on Sundays.

**Fit** — Either Bonnie or the boys make brunch on Sundays.

**Not Fit** — Each of you are needed to train the dogs.

**Fit** — Each of you is needed to train the dogs.

# Using Adjectives and Adverbs

How can you write with clarity using adjectives, adverbs, and comparisons?

## Using Adjectives and Adverbs: Pretest 1

The first draft below has several errors in the use of adjectives and adverbs. The first error has been corrected. How would you correct the remaining errors?

Vincent van Gogh is one of the popularist artists in the world. His passion for art and the natural world was more great than any painter. When he looked at landscapes, he saw a kind of raw beauty, which he translated into heavy brush strokes of more brighter and clear colors. Each of us sees the natural world from our own most unique point of view. For some, nature's beauty creates the most powerfulest feelings of joy. For these people, nature stirs feelings of wonder and awe. They can describe in glowing detail their favoritest landscapes. And yet, some people haven't never thought much about the beauty they encounter around them. Their emotions might be most aroused by a song or a novel. Van Gogh believed that the importanest language to listen to was the language of nature.

# Using Adjectives and Adverbs: Pretest 2

## Directions

Read the passage and choose the word or group of words that belongs in each numbered, underlined space. Write the letter of the correct answer.

In 1803, Luke Howard, an English scientist, devised the basic system of cloud classification. This system of ten kinds of clouds still works ___(1)___ even today. In fact, for over 200 years, his cloud classification system remains better than ___(2)___ system. The ___(3)___ clouds are nimbostratus clouds, which are called rain clouds. They are often ___(4)___ than other clouds, and they ___(5)___ exceed an altitude of one mile. Because these clouds often produce rain or snow, they look ___(6)___ to people with outdoor plans. ___(7)___ threatening are stratus clouds. The rain in these clouds is always less than ___(8)___ clouds. Stratus clouds are ___(9)___ because they only produce drizzle or mist. The ___(10)___ clouds of all, of course, are the cumulus clouds, which are called fair-weather clouds.

1. **A** well
   **B** good
   **C** better
   **D** best

2. **A** any
   **B** a
   **C** any other
   **D** this

3. **A** closer and most familiar
   **B** closest and more familiar
   **C** closer and more familiar
   **D** closest and most familiar

4. **A** darker
   **B** most darker
   **C** more darker
   **D** more darkerer

5. **A** don't never
   **B** don't ever
   **C** don't hardly
   **D** don't barely

6. **A** bad
   **B** badly
   **C** more bad
   **D** more badly

7. **A** Little
   **B** Less
   **C** Lesser
   **D** Least

8. **A** other
   **B** in other
   **C** the rain in other
   **D** the rain in

9. **A** nice
   **B** nicer
   **C** more nicer
   **D** most nicest

10. **A** most best
    **B** best
    **C** bestest
    **D** most better

# Comparison of Adjectives and Adverbs

Everyone has preferences. You may feel, for example, that meat loaf tastes *good,* spaghetti tastes *better,* and grilled salmon tastes the *best* of all. Adjectives and adverbs have more than one form to express such preferences. This chapter will review the different forms of comparison, as well as some problems you might have with making comparisons.

The three forms that most adjectives and adverbs take to show the degrees of comparison are **the positive, the comparative,** and **the superlative.**

**20 A**   Adjectives and adverbs are **modifiers.** Most modifiers show degrees of comparison by changing their form.

The basic form of an adjective or an adverb is the **positive degree.** It is used when no comparison is being made—when you simply are making a statement about a person or a thing.

> **Adjective**   This route to the track meet is **quick.**
>
> **Adverb**   Brad can run **fast.**

When two people, things, or actions are being compared, the **comparative degree** is used. Notice that *-er* has been added to *quick* and *fast.*

> **Adjective**   Of the two routes to the track meet, this one is **quicker.**
>
> **Adverb**   Of the two runners, Brad can run **faster.**

When more than two people, things, or actions are being compared, the **superlative degree** is used. Notice that *-est* has been added to *quick* and *fast.*

> **Adjective**   Of the three routes to the track meet, this one is **quickest.**
>
> **Adverb**   Of all the runners in the race, Brad can run **fastest.**

*You can learn more about adjectives and adverbs on pages 631–638.*

#  Regular Comparison

Most adjectives and adverbs form their comparative and superlative degrees the same way. The comparative and superlative forms of most modifiers are determined by the number of syllables an adjective or adverb has.

## One-Syllable Modifiers

**20 A.1**  Add *-er* to form the comparative degree and *-est* to form the superlative degree of one-syllable modifiers.

| ONE-SYLLABLE MODIFIERS | | |
|---|---|---|
| **Positive** | **Comparative** | **Superlative** |
| young | younger | youngest |
| hot | hotter | hottest |
| soon | sooner | soonest |
| green | greener | greenest |

A spelling change sometimes occurs when an ending is added to a modifier. If you are not sure how to form the comparative or superlative degree of a modifier, check the dictionary.

Most two-syllable words form their comparative degree by adding *-er* and their superlative degree by adding *-est*. Some of these words, however, use *more* and *most* because the words would sound awkward—or be impossible to pronounce—if *-er* or *-est* were added. *More* and *most* are also used with all adverbs that end in *-ly*.

## Two-Syllable Modifiers

**20 A.2**  Use *-er* or *more* to form the comparative degree and *-est* or *most* to form the superlative degree of two-syllable modifiers.

| TWO-SYLLABLE MODIFIERS | | |
|---|---|---|
| **Positive** | **Comparative** | **Superlative** |
| graceful | more graceful | most graceful |
| early | earlier | earliest |
| slowly | more slowly | most slowly |

# Three-Syllable Modifiers

**20 A.3**   Use *more* to form the comparative degree and *most* to form the superlative degree of modifiers with three or more syllables.

| MODIFIERS WITH THREE OR MORE SYLLABLES | | |
|---|---|---|
| **Positive** | **Comparative** | **Superlative** |
| dangerous | more dangerous | most dangerous |
| rapidly | more rapidly | most rapidly |
| furious | more furious | most furious |

*Less* and *least* are used to form negative comparisons.

| NEGATIVE COMPARISONS | | |
|---|---|---|
| **Positive** | **Comparative** | **Superlative** |
| tasty | less tasty | least tasty |
| steadily | less steadily | least steadily |

## Irregular Comparison

**20 A.4**   Never add *-er* and *-est* to the comparative and superlative degrees of irregular modifiers.

**Incorrect**     I liked that movie the mostest.

**Correct**     I liked that movie the most.

The following adjectives and adverbs change form completely for the comparative and superlative degrees.

| IRREGULAR MODIFIERS | | |
|---|---|---|
| **Positive** | **Comparative** | **Superlative** |
| bad/badly/ill | worse | worst |
| good/well | better | best |
| little | less | least |
| many/much | more | most |

## Practice Your Skills

### Forming the Comparison of Modifiers

Write each modifier. Beside it, write its comparative and superlative forms.

| | | |
|---|---|---|
| **1.** weak | **6.** light | **11.** little |
| **2.** hurriedly | **7.** different | **12.** quickly |
| **3.** good | **8.** bad | **13.** clever |
| **4.** horrible | **9.** great | **14.** many |
| **5.** busy | **10.** unsafe | **15.** swift |

## Practice Your Skills

### Using the Correct Form of Comparison

Write the correct form of the modifier in parentheses.

**1.** Of the three boys, Colin devised the (better, best) game plan.

**2.** Rita's, not Amy's, kite flew (higher, highest).

**3.** Jan swam across the pool (more, most) rapidly than Ty.

**4.** Which sport do you like (better, best): football, basketball, or tennis?

**5.** Which has the (more, most) photogenic mascot, our high school or theirs?

**6.** Of your two friends who play soccer, which one is (more, most) athletic?

**7.** Which city has the (larger, largest) sports arena: Dallas or San Francisco?

**8.** Since there are two acceptable candidates for team captain, the coach has to choose the (better, best) one.

**9.** I don't know which I like (less, least), running laps or doing push-ups.

**10.** Alex is the (louder, loudest) of all the fans.

● *Connect to Writing:* **Editing**

### Using Comparisons

Write each of the seven incorrect modifiers. Beside each, write the correct form.

(1) On October 17, 1989, baseball fans attended what would become their more memorable game ever. (2) On this fateful day, over 62,000 fans packed Candlestick Park for the third game of the World Series. (3) As the game wore on, the fans became most excited, stomping their feet and doing the wave. (4) At 5:04 p.m., a Richter-magnitude 7.1 earthquake struck. (5) At first, fans did not suspect anything dangerouser than the bleachers' shaking from stomping feet. (6) Then they realized that an event most life-threatening than rumbling bleachers had occurred: an earthquake had shaken the entire San Francisco Bay area. (7) This 20-second earthquake was the baddest quake in years. (8) Its shocks reached San Francisco from the epicenter, 60 miles to the south. (9) Six years earlier, in 1983, Candlestick Park had been examined and then reinforced to a more high level of structural integrity. (10) The 1989 Loma Prieta Earthquake, therefore, did not cause extensiver damage to the ballpark than could be repaired in a short time.

✔ *Check Point:* **Mixed Practice**

Write the correct form of the modifier in parentheses.

1. Which is (longer, longest), a yard or a meter?
2. Which one—George, Thomas, or Ken—ran (faster, fastest)?
3. Since there were two liters of juice, I drank the (older, oldest) one first.
4. Your talk on the metric system was (more, most) informative than mine.
5. Who do you think is the (heavier, heaviest) boy, Lewis or James?
6. Which is (shorter, shortest): the centimeter, the millimeter, or the inch?
7. I think the inch is the (more, most) useful unit of measure.
8. Which costs (less, least), the ruler or the yardstick?
9. Of the centipede and the millipede, which has (more, most) legs?
10. The races include the one-kilometer, the two-kilometer, and the five-kilometer; the two-kilometer race would be (better, best) for you.

● *Connect to Writing:* **Content-Based Vocabulary**

### Using Adjectives and Adverbs in Comparisons

Write an explanatory paragraph describing what you have learned about the three degrees of comparison: positive, comparative, and superlative. Then write three sentences: one with an adverb in the positive, one with an adjective in the comparative, and one using an adjective and an adverb in the superlative.

20 B     When using adjectives and adverbs for comparison, avoid making double comparisons, illogical comparisons, and comparisons of members of a group to themselves.

## ➤ Double Comparisons

Use only one method of forming the comparative and superlative degrees at a time. Using both methods simultaneously results in a **double comparison.**

20 B.1     Do not use both *-er* and *more* to form the comparative degree, or both *-est* and *most* to form the superlative degree of modifiers.

| | |
|---|---|
| **Double Comparison** | That snake is **more longer** than this one. |
| **Correct** | That snake is **longer** than this one. |
| **Double Comparison** | This is the **most loudest** parrot. |
| **Correct** | This is the **loudest** parrot. |

## ➤ Illogical Comparisons

When you write a comparison, be sure you compare two or more similar things. When you compare different things, the comparison becomes illogical.

20 B.2     Compare only items of a similar kind.

| | |
|---|---|
| **Illogical Comparison** | A dachshund's **legs** are shorter than most other **dogs.** (*Legs* are being compared with *dogs.*) |
| **Logical Comparison** | A dachshund's **legs** are shorter than most other dogs' **legs.** (*Legs* are now being compared with *legs.*) |
| **Logical Comparison** | A dachshund's **legs** are shorter than most other **dogs'.** (With the possessive *dogs',* *legs* is understood; therefore, *legs* are being compared with *legs.*) |
| **Logical Comparison** | A dachshund's **legs** are shorter than **those** of other dogs. (The demonstrative pronoun *those* takes the place of *legs;* therefore, *legs* are being compared with *legs.*) |

*You can learn about using an apostrophe with possessives on pages 964–971.*

## *Other* and *Else* in Comparisons

Very often, one or more people or things will be compared with other people or things in the same group. When you make such a comparison, be sure you do not appear to compare a person or a thing with itself.

**20 B.3**  Add *other* or *else* when comparing a member of a group with the rest of the group.

| | |
|---|---|
| **Incorrect** | In today's show Greased Lightning has won more awards than any horse. (Since Greased Lightning is a horse in the show, it is being compared with itself.) |
| **Correct** | In today's show Greased Lightning has won more awards than any **other** horse. (Greased Lightning is now being compared only with the *other* horses.) |
| **Incorrect** | The pet store manager, Mandy, knows more about fish than anyone in the store. (Since Mandy is in the store, she is being compared with herself.) |
| **Correct** | The pet store manager, Mandy, knows more about fish than anyone **else** in the store. (Mandy is now being compared only with the *other* people in the store.) |

● *Connect to Writing:* **Writing to Compare and Contrast**

*Using Adjectives and Adverbs*

Choose two images in this book that you would like to write about. Note the colors, shapes, composition, and perspective used in each of the images. In what ways are these images alike? In what ways are they different? Think about what you find interesting in each image, and why. Write a paragraph comparing and contrasting the two images point by point.

*When You Read*

Some advertisers give you the first half of a comparison but not the second half.

Our pizza is the best because it has more toppings. (It has more toppings than what?)

When you see such ads, finish the comparison and then decide for yourself if the product is a superior one!

## ● Practice Your Skills

### *Identifying Mistakes with Comparisons*

Using the following abbreviations, write the type of each mistake. If a sentence is correct, write *C*.

double comparison = *d.c.*          illogical comparison = *i.c.*

needs *other* or *else* in comparison = *o.e.*

1. Fifi jumps higher and farther than any dog in the show.
2. A properly fed animal will perform more better than one indulged with unhealthy snacks.
3. Nathan has more pets than anyone on the obedience school staff.
4. Though not the prettiest canines, pit bulls are perhaps more popular watchdogs than any dog.
5. I think a rabbit's fur is more softer than even a cat's fur.
6. The beauty of this stray mutt is greater than the purebred Great Dane.
7. Andrew is fairer than any other judge on the regional cat show panel.
8. The African elephant probably has larger eyes than any animal in the world.
9. This dog-walkers' club is the most wonderful idea of the summer!
10. Chu is kinder to animals than anyone in his family.

## ● *Connect to Writing:* Editing

### *Correcting Mistakes with Comparisons*

Write the incorrect sentences in the preceding exercise, correcting the mistakes in the use of comparisons.

## ✔ *Check Point:* Mixed Practice

Write each sentence, correcting the mistakes in comparisons. If a sentence is correct, write *C*.

1. Primary colors like blue and red are more purer than secondary colors like purple and orange.
2. Yellow and green can be seen more readily by the human eye than any colors.
3. Isn't hot pink much more brighter than pastel pink?
4. These greens and yellows are more cheerful than black and silver.
5. Yellow, red, and orange hues are the most brightest colors of all.

# Problems with Modifiers

**20 C**  Be aware of problems when using adjectives and adverbs, such as when to use them, and when to use *good* or *well* and *bad* or *badly*. Avoid double negatives.

## ➤ Adjective or Adverb?

Although adjectives and adverbs are both modifiers, they are very different in many other ways. You learned in the grammar section of this book that an adjective describes a noun or pronoun. You also learned that an adjective usually comes before the noun or pronoun it describes, or it follows a linking verb. Adjectives are usually easy for you to recognize because they answer the following questions.

| | |
|---|---|
| **Which One?** | **That** recipe is easy. |
| **What Kind?** | This lemonade tastes **sweet.** |
| **How Many?** | I have **three** cookies. |
| **How Much?** | I need **more** butter for this frosting. |

Some verbs—such as *feel, smell,* and *taste*—can be either linking verbs or action verbs. When they are used as linking verbs, they are often followed by an adjective.

| | |
|---|---|
| **Linking Verb** | The milk **smelled** sour. |
| | (*Smelled* links *milk* and *sour*—sour milk.) |
| **Action Verb** | I **smelled** the milk. |
| | (*Smelled* is used as an action verb.) |

If you are not sure whether a verb is being used as a linking verb or as an action verb, substitute the verb *is*. If the sentence makes sense, the verb is a linking verb. If it does not make sense, the verb is an action verb.

*You can find a list of common linking verbs and a list of additional linking verbs on pages 628–629.*

Adverbs describe verbs, adjectives, and other adverbs. Because adverbs can be placed almost anywhere in a sentence, ask the questions on the next page to find them.

| Where? | Place the carved roast **here.** |
|---|---|
| When? | **Yesterday** I made butterscotch pudding. |
| How? | **Briskly** whisk the eggs. |
| To What Extent? | Please don't stir the muffin batter **too long.** |
| | I'll have another of those **wonderfully** tasty crab puffs! |

Because so many adverbs end in *-ly,* they are usually easy to recognize. Remember, however, that a few adjectives—such as *early* and *lively*—also end in *-ly.*

| Adverb | He cooks breakfast **daily.** |
|---|---|
| | (*Daily* tells when he cooks breakfast.) |
| Adjective | His **daily** ritual includes a healthful breakfast. |
| | (*Daily* tells what kind of ritual it is.) |

A few words—such as *first, hard, high, late,* and *long*—do not change form whether they are used as an adjective or an adverb.

| Adverb | Eat **first** and then wash the pans. |
|---|---|
| | (*First* tells when you should eat.) |
| Adjective | His **first** omelet was a success. |
| | (*First* tells which omelet was successful.) |

## ➤ *Good* or *Well?*

*Good* is always an adjective. *Well* is usually used as an adverb. *Well* is used as an adjective, however, when it means "in good health" or "satisfactory."

**20 C.1** Use *good* as an adjective; use *well* as an adverb unless it means "in good health" or "satisfactory."

| Adjective | Sally is a **good** cook. |
|---|---|
| Adverb | Sally cooks **well.** |
| Adjective | Sally doesn't feel **well** today. (in good health) |

 ## Bad or Badly?

*Bad* is an adjective and often follows a linking verb. *Badly* is used as an adverb.

**Adjective**   This egg smells **bad.**

**Adverb**   Oh! I've **badly** jammed the garbage disposal.

> **20 C.2**   Use *bad* as an adjective; use *badly* as an adverb.

### When You Speak and Write

In casual conversation, it is acceptable to use *bad* or *badly* after the verb *feel*. In formal writing, however, always use *bad* as an adjective and *badly* as an adverb.

**In Writing**   I feel **bad** about taking the last cookie.

**In Conversation**   I feel **badly** about taking the last cookie.

## Double Negatives

Some words are considered negatives. In most sentences two negatives, called a **double negative,** should not be used together.

> **20 C.3**   Avoid using double negatives.

| COMMON NEGATIVES | |
|---|---|
| but (meaning "only") | none |
| barely | no one |
| hardly | not (and its contraction *n't*) |
| neither | nothing |
| never | only |
| no | scarcely |

| | |
|---|---|
| **Double Negative** | Sue does**n't** have **no** choice in this meal. |
| **Correct** | Sue does**n't** have any choice in this meal. |
| **Double Negative** | There is**n't hardly** any reason to eat now. |
| **Correct** | There is**n't any** reason to eat now. |
| **Correct** | There is **hardly** any reason to eat now. |

● **Practice Your Skills**

### Identifying Mistakes in the Use of Modifiers

Using the following abbreviations, write the type of each mistake. If a sentence is correct, write *C.*

adjective or adverb = *a. a.*          *good* or *well* = *g. w.*

*bad* or *badly* = *b. b.*          double negative = *d. n.*

1. Everyone did good on the home economics final exam.
2. Jeff looked hungry at the enchiladas the class prepared.
3. Liza did quite well in baking crab puffs.
4. No one knew nothing about making chocolate mousse.
5. Those who arrived to class early got the best utensils.
6. "The early bird gets the worm!" shouted Shelly, grabbing the best of the three mixers.
7. Don't feel bad if your first piecrust is a little tough.
8. That marmalade tastes bitterly.
9. There ain't no reason why you can't help wash dishes.
10. That fish casserole smells rather strongly.
11. I don't have hardly any sugar left.
12. Gareth felt bad about burning the cinnamon rolls.
13. Because of Don's confusing directions, we could not hardly make a successful soufflé.
14. Don't you think this frosted cake looks well?

● *Connect to Writing:* **Editing**

### Correcting Mistakes in Comparisons

Write the incorrect sentences in the preceding exercise, correcting the mistakes in the use of comparisons.

Inexperienced writers often use comparisons that have become clichés through overuse. Similes such as "black as night," "flat as a pancake," and "thin as a rail" have been used so often that they no longer create any special image in a reader's mind. Look back at a recent composition and be sure your comparisons are fresh, surprising, and vivid. The extra thought is worth the results!

## ✔ *Check Point:* **Mixed Practice**

Write the following paragraphs, correcting each error in the use of comparisons.

**(1)** Venus has been called Earth's twin. **(2)** Second in distance from the sun, Venus comes more nearer to Earth than any planet. **(3)** Venus's diameter, density, mass, and gravity are all close to Earth. **(4)** Venus's year is about three-fifths as long as Earth's. **(5)** Venus's rotation, however, is from east to west, while Earth and most planets rotate from west to east.

**(6)** Venus is masked by dense clouds. **(7)** Astronomers knew hardly nothing about Venus's atmosphere and surface until radar and unpiloted spacecraft penetrated the clouds. **(8)** Despite Venus's clouds, its surface gets much more hotter than Earth. **(9)** The temperature on Venus can reach 460°C.

**(10)** Because Venus is more closer to the sun than Earth is, you can see it only when you face in the general direction of the sun. **(11)** During most of the daytime, the sun shines too vivid to allow you to see Venus. **(12)** When Venus is east of the sun, however, the sun sets before it. **(13)** Then Venus can be seen clear in the twilight of the western sky.

## ● *Connect to Speaking and Listening:* **Classroom Materials**

### *Using Adjectives and Adverbs*

Discuss with a partner the difference between adjectives and adverbs. What questions does an adjective answer? What questions does an adverb answer? Take turns creating sentences that use the words *intense, luxurious, extremely, scarcely, annually,* and *badly.* Ask your partner to identify whether each of these words is used as an adverb or an adjective. Decide together if each answer is correct, and why or why not.

## Assess Your Learning

### Correcting Errors with Modifiers

Write the following sentences, correcting each error. If a sentence is correct, write *C* after the number.

**1.** We couldn't go swimming this morning because there wasn't no lifeguard on duty.

**2.** Which tastes worse, that bitter cough medicine or warm milk?

**3.** Today I feel the bestest I have felt in over a week.

**4.** Why haven't you never learned to swim?

**5.** After her argument with her brother Michael, Marsha felt badly.

**6.** Rich can paint both figures and landscapes better than anyone I know.

### Editing for Correct Use of Modifiers

Read the following paragraphs. Then find and write the nine errors in the use of adjectives or adverbs. Beside each error write the correct form.

(1) Mercury is the planet most nearest the sun. (2) Its diameter is about one-third that of Earth. (3) Because of its smaller size, Mercury's gravity is also much weaker than Earth. (4) One hundred kilograms on Earth, for example, would weigh only about 37 kilograms on Mercury.

(5) Scientists knew hardly nothing about the surface of Mercury until *Mariner 10*, an unmanned spacecraft, made flyby observations in 1974 and 1975. (6) The photographs it took of Mercury turned out good. (7) They showed that Mercury's surface was similar to the moon. (8) Mercury's rocky landscape is marked by broad plains, a few large-ringed basins, and highlands studded with more smaller craters. (9) The plains were formed by lava. (10) The basins and most of the craters were formed when rock masses from space collided forceful with Mercury. (11) The most largest basin has a diameter of 1,300 kilometers and is ringed by mountains 2 kilometers high.

## Writing Sentences

Write five sentences that follow the directions below.

**1.** Write a sentence using the superlative degree of *good* and the comparative degree of *little*.

**2.** Write a sentence using the word *taste* first as an action verb and then as a linking verb.

**3.** Write a sentence using both *bad* and *badly*.

**4.** Write a sentence about a river, lake, or ocean. Use a positive adverb and a comparative adjective.

**5.** Write a sentence using *well* as an adjective.

# Using Adjectives and Adverbs: Posttest

## Directions

Read the passage and choose the word or group of words that belongs in each numbered, underlined space. Write the letter of the correct answer.

Weather forecasters are __(1)__ today than they were even 25 years ago. __(2)__ have a hard time understanding why. Because of satellites and other technological advances, forecasters have __(3)__ information available to them than their predecessors did. They are now able to predict violent storms such as tornadoes much __(4)__. Tornadoes, by far, are more destructive than __(5)__ storm on Earth! They are __(6)__ on the plain states than __(7)__ in the U.S. In 1925, one of the __(8)__ tornadoes of all times killed 700 people in only three and a half hours! Tornadoes cause so much destruction because their winds are stronger __(9)__ storms! Listen __(10)__ to this advice: If a tornado is approaching, go to a cellar or a closet far away from the outside walls of your house!

1. A more smarter
   B smarter
   C smartest
   D most smarter

2. A No one scarcely would
   B No one hardly would
   C No one wouldn't
   D No one would

3. A more
   B most
   C morer
   D much

4. A more better
   B more well
   C better
   D more good

5. A any
   B a
   C any other
   D this

6. A more common
   B more commoner
   C most common
   D most commoner

7. A anywhere
   B anywhere else
   C everywhere
   D nowhere

8. A bad
   B badly
   C worse
   D worst

9. A than other
   B than those of other
   C than all other
   D than most

10. A good
    B better
    C well
    D most well

## Snapshot

**20 A**   Adjectives and adverbs are modifiers. They show degrees of comparison by changing their form, which can be **positive, comparative, or superlative.** (pages 856–860)

**20 B**   **Double comparisons, illogical comparisons,** and *other/else* comparisons are problems that can occur when adjectives and adverbs are used in comparisons. (pages 861–863)

**20 C**   Be aware of problems when using adjectives and adverbs: when to use them, and when to use *good* or *well* and *bad* or *badly.* Avoid **double negatives.** (pages 864–868)

## Power Rules

**Avoid using double negatives.** Use only one negative form for a single negative idea. (pages 866–867)

| **Before Editing** | **After Editing** |
|---|---|
| Travis won*'t* say *nothing.* | Travis won't say *anything.* |
| They did*n't* plan *nothing* to do over spring break. | They didn't plan *anything* to do over spring break. |
| It *won't hardly* matter if we're late. | It *won't* matter if we're late. |
| They *couldn't scarcely* see because it was so dark. | They *could scarcely* see because it was so dark. |

## Editing Checklist

Use this checklist when editing your writing.

✓ Did I use the correct forms of adjectives and adverbs to show degrees of comparison? (See pages 856–860.)

✓ Did I avoid double comparisons? (See page 861.)

✓ Did I compare similar things in my writing? (See page 861.)

✓ Did I use *other* or *else* when comparing a member of a group with the rest of the group? (See page 862.)

✓ Did I use adverbs and adjectives correctly in my writing? (See pages 864–865.)

✓ Did I generally use *good* as an adjective and *well* as an adverb? Did I use *bad* as an adjective and *badly* as an adverb? (See pages 865–866.)

✓ Did I avoid using double negatives? (See pages 866–867.)

## Use the Power

Use the sentences below to help you remember the regular and irregular comparative and superlative forms.

**Regular Comparative:** LeTroy is faster than Sam and always beats him in the 50-yard dash.

**Irregular Comparative:** Sam has many track medals, but LeTroy has more medals than Sam.

**Regular Superlative:** Grace is steadier than Jill on the balance beam.

**Irregular Superlative:** Grace has the best coach in town.

Part of the growing process is learning that some behavior is appropriate and some is not. Everyone quickly learns as a child, for example, that throwing food on the floor is definitely not acceptable or appropriate behavior.

As children grow older, most learning becomes more complicated. No longer is everything either good or bad, right or wrong. Some behavior is appropriate in some situations but inappropriate in others. Using your fingers, for example, to eat fried chicken may be appropriate behavior at home, but it may become inappropriate at a fancy restaurant.

Different expressions of the English language are somewhat like certain types of behavior; they may be appropriate with one audience but not with another. Using contractions in your conversations, for example, is standard and acceptable, but using contractions in a research paper is not appropriate.

Professor Higgins in *My Fair Lady* prided himself on his ability to name the towns where people were born by analyzing their dialects. **Dialect** is a regional variety of language that includes grammar, vocabulary, and pronunciation. Like the English, Americans have different dialects. The accents and expressions of people from parts of Texas, for example, are quite different from the accents and expressions of people from parts of Massachusetts. In spite of these variations in dialect, though, people from Texas and people from Massachusetts can easily understand and communicate with each other.

The place of your birth, however, is not the only influence on the way you speak. Your ethnic and educational backgrounds, as well as other factors, also contribute to the particular way you speak. All of these combined factors add a richness and a vibrant diversity to the English language. These factors have also created the need for different levels of expression. Traditionally these levels are recognized as standard and nonstandard.

**Standard English** is used in public by almost all professional people—such as writers, television and radio personalities, government officials, and other notable figures. Standard English uses all the rules and conventions of usage that are accepted most widely by English-speaking people throughout the world. (They are the same rules and conventions that are taught in this text.) The use of Standard English varies, nevertheless, in formal and informal situations.

**Formal English,** which follows the conventional rules of grammar, usage, and mechanics, is the standard for all written work. It is used mainly in such written work as formal reports, essays, scholarly writings, research papers, and business letters. Formal English may include some words that are not normally used in everyday conversation and frequently may employ long sentences with complex structures. To maintain a formal tone of writing, most writers avoid contractions, colloquialisms, and certain other common verbal expressions. The following example of formal English is an excerpt from one of Carson McCullers's essays.

> Whether in the pastoral joys of country life or in the labyrinthine city, we Americans are always seeking. We wander, question. But the answer waits in each separate heart—the answer of our own identity and the way by which we can master loneliness and feel that at last we belong.
> —Carson McCullers, *The Mortgaged Heart*

**Informal English** does not mean "inferior English." Just like formal English, informal English follows the rules and the conventions of Standard English; however, it follows them less rigidly. It includes some words and expressions, such as contractions, that would sound out of place in formal writing. English-speaking people around the world generally use informal English in their everyday conversation. It is also used in magazines, newspapers, advertising, and much of the fiction that is written today. The following example of informal English is a diary entry that was written by Admiral Byrd during one of his expeditions to Antarctica.

> Something—I don't know what—is getting me down. I've been strangely irritable all day, and since supper I have been depressed. . . . This would not seem important if I could only put my finger on the trouble, but I can't find any single thing to account for the mood. Yet it has been there; and tonight, for the first time, I must admit that the problem of keeping my mind on an even keel is a serious one.
> —Richard Byrd, *Alone*

**Nonstandard English,** which is suitable in certain instances, incorporates the many variations produced by regional dialects, slang, and colloquial expressions. However, it should be used in limited situations and only if the use of Standard English, as set forth in the preceding section, is not required. Since nonstandard English lacks uniformity from one section of the country to the next and from year to year, you should always use Standard English when you write in academic and other formal situations. Some fiction authors use nonstandard English, however, to recreate the conversation of people from a particular locale or time period. This, for example, was Eudora Welty's purpose when she wrote the following passage.

> "This is what come to me to do," she said. "I going to the store and buy my child a little windmill they sells, made out of paper. He going to find it hard to believe there such a thing in the world. I'll march myself back where he waiting, holding it straight up in this hand."
>
> —Eudora Welty, "The Worn Path"

Some of the entries in the following glossary of usage make reference to Standard and nonstandard English, the terms discussed in the previous section. Since the glossary has been arranged alphabetically, you can use it easily.

**a, an** Use *a* before a word beginning with a consonant sound. Use *an* before a word beginning with a vowel sound. Always keep in mind that this rule applies to sounds, not letters. For example, *an hour ago* is correct because the *h* is silent.

> He finished painting **a** home on our block.
>
> Then he asked for **an** honest evaluation of his work.

**accept, except** *Accept* is a verb that means "to receive with consent." *Except* is usually a preposition that means "but" or "other than." *Acceptance* and *exception* are the noun forms.

> The players will **accept** all the new rules **except** one.

**adapt, adopt** Both of these words are verbs. *Adapt* means "to adjust." *Adopt* means "to take as your own." *Adaption, adaptation,* and *adoption* are the noun forms.

> We can **adapt** to our new environment if we **adopt** some new habits.

**advice, advise** *Advice* is a noun that means "a recommendation." *Advise* is a verb that means "to recommend."

> What **advice** would you give to a freshman?
>
> I would **advise** any freshman to get involved in school activities.

**affect, effect** *Affect* is usually a verb that means "to influence" or "to act upon." *Effect* is usually a noun that means "a result" or "an influence." As a verb, *effect* means "to accomplish" or "to produce."

> Eastern Kansas was seriously **affected** by the storm.
>
> The **effects** of the storm cost the state millions of dollars.
>
> The fear of mud slides **effected** detours.

**all ready, already** *All ready* means "completely ready." *Already* means "previously."

> Are the children **all ready** to go?
>
> Yes, they have **already** changed their clothes.

**all together, altogether** *All together* means "in a group." *Altogether* means "wholly" or "thoroughly."

> The members of our group were **all together** at the concert.
>
> The concert was **altogether** enjoyable.

**allusion, illusion** Both of these words are nouns. An *allusion* is "an implied or indirect reference; a hint." An *illusion* is "something that deceives or misleads."

> I noticed many biblical and mythological **allusions** in the film.
>
> I learned that movement in motion pictures is created by an optical **illusion.**

## When You Use Technology

The spell check feature on your word processing or e-mail software can be very helpful. It can help you check your spelling as you compose or edit your writing. Be careful, however, because a spelling check will not edit your work. For example, spell check will not flag your writing when you incorrectly use *affect* when you really mean to use *effect*. You can usually find the spelling feature in the Edit or the Tools menu of your software. You can also set most current programs to mark misspelled words as you type. Look in the Preferences menu to activate this feature.

● *Connect to Writing*

### Allusions

An **allusion** is a reference to another text or to a body of common knowledge. Professional writers use allusions for several reasons—perhaps to add depth to a work, to create a link to the past, or to add humor. The fantasy writer Terry Pratchett is a master of the humorous allusion. In a conversation among wandering "heroes," one of the company alludes to the epic *Beowulf* while complaining about how "heroing" isn't what it used to be.

... Monsters are getting more uppity, too. I heard where this guy, he killed this monster in this lake, no problem, stick its arm up over the door.

... [Y]ou know what? Its mum come and complained. Its actual mum come right down to the hall next day and *complained*. Actually *complained*. That's the respect you get.

—Terry Pratchett, *Guards! Guards!*

When attempting an allusion in your own writing, be sure to refer to a work or body of knowledge that your audience will know. Otherwise the allusion will be lost.

**a lot** These two words are often written as one word. There is no such word as "alot." *A lot* should be avoided in formal writing. (Do not confuse *a lot* with *allot*, which is a verb that means "to distribute by shares.")

| | |
|---|---|
| **Informal** | Do you miss them **a lot?** |
| **Formal** | Do you miss them **very much?** |
| | I hope they will **allot** the chores equally. |

**among, between** Both of these words are prepositions. *Among* is used when referring to three or more people or things. *Between* is usually used when referring to two people or things.

The senator moved **among** the people in the crowd.

He divided his time **between** shaking hands and speaking.

**amount, number** *Amount* refers to a quantity. *Number* refers to things that can be counted.

A small **number** of students raised a large **amount** of money for the arts.

## Practice Your Skills

### Finding the Correct Word

Write the word in parentheses that correctly (formally) completes each sentence.

1. The (affect, effect) of the recent Globe Theatre restoration has been to heighten interest (a lot, considerably) in this (all ready, already) well-known Elizabethan theater.

2. The Globe, which opened in 1599, was also known as "The Wooden O," (a, an) (allusion, illusion) to its shape.

3. Built to accommodate a large (amount, number) of people, the Globe could hold approximately three thousand people (all together, altogether).

4. William Shakespeare was (among, between) the five actors who (all together, altogether) owned half interest in the theater.

5. Although the exact (amount, number) of performances (ain't, isn't) known, Shakespeare's plays were often enacted at the Globe.

6. In 1613, the (affect, effect) of a malfunctioning cannon during a performance was the burning down of the theater.

## Connect to the Writing Process: Revising

### Recognizing Correct Usage

Rewrite the following paragraphs, changing the words that are used incorrectly. There are 11 usage errors.

Adoption to the theatrical conventions of the Elizabethan era had a affect on the design of the Globe. For example, the adoption of an trapdoor in the center of the stage provided for the entrance and exit into "Hell." Two pillars, located among the two sides of the stage, held up "Heaven." At the rear of the stage was a gallery that was already for musicians or for a balcony scene. The stage itself extended out about thirty feet all together into the courtyard. Since the yard was an open area, the weather sometimes effected performances.

In this area there were a lot of spectators who were called groundlings. To be admitted, groundlings paid the amount of one penny. They stood through an entire performance and could move around accept when it was too crowded. Although often disruptive, the conduct of the groundlings was altogether accepted by the actors for economic reasons. The people who sat among the seven galleries upstairs had to pay the number of two pence for their seats.

**any more, anymore** Do not use *any more* for *anymore*. *Any more* refers to quantity. The adverb *anymore* means "from now on" or "at present."

Is there **any more** lettuce in the garden?

No, I don't raise lettuce **anymore.**

**anywhere, everywhere, nowhere, somewhere** Do not add *s* to any of these words.

| **Nonstandard** | Melanie wants to travel **everywheres.** |
| **Standard** | Melanie wants to travel **everywhere.** |

**as far as** This expression is sometimes confused with "all the farther," which is nonstandard English.

| **Nonstandard** | Is a mile **all the farther** you can walk? |
| **Standard** | Is a mile **as far as** you can walk? |

**at** Do not use *at* after *where*.

| **Nonstandard** | Let me know **where** the keys are **at.** |
| **Standard** | Let me know **where** the keys are. |

**a while, awhile** *A while* is an expression made up of an article and a noun. It must be used after the prepositions *for* and *in*. *Awhile* is an adverb and is not used after a preposition.

You won't get your test results for **a while.**

I think you should wait **awhile** before calling again.

**bad, badly** *Bad* is an adjective and often follows a linking verb. *Badly* is used as an adverb and often follows an action verb. In the first two examples, *felt* is a linking verb.

| **Nonstandard** | My sister felt **badly** about missing us. |
| **Standard** | My sister felt **bad** about missing us. |
| **Standard** | She was so upset that she burned the dinner **badly.** |

*You can learn more about using adjectives and adverbs on pages 631–638 and pages 854–873.*

**because** Do not use *because* after *the reason*. Use one or the other.

| Nonstandard | **The reason** he joined the exercise class was **because** he wanted to feel more energetic. |
| Standard | He joined the exercise class **because** he wanted to feel more energetic. |
| Standard | **The reason** he joined the exercise class was **that** he wanted to feel more energetic. |

**being as, being that** These expressions should be replaced with *because* or *since*.

| Nonstandard | **Being as** it rained on Saturday, I didn't run. |
| Standard | **Since** it rained on Saturday, I didn't run. |

**beside, besides** *Beside* is a preposition that means "by the side of." As a preposition, *besides* means "in addition to." As an adverb, *besides* means "also" or "moreover."

Sit **beside** me at the PTA meeting. (by the side of)

**Besides** meeting the teachers, we also will tour the new facilities. (in addition to)

The school has a swimming pool, tennis courts, and an indoor track **besides.** (also)

**both** Never use *the* before *both*.

| Nonstandard | We saw **the both** of you at the mall. |
| Standard | We saw **both** of you at the mall. |

**both, each** *Both* refers to two persons or objects together, but *each* refers to an individual person or object.

**Both** office buildings were designed by the same architect; however, **each** building is quite different.

**bring, take** *Bring* indicates motion toward the speaker. *Take* indicates motion away from the speaker.

**Bring** me a stamp and then **take** this letter to the mailbox.

● **Practice Your Skills**

*Finding the Correct Word*

Write the word in parentheses that correctly completes each sentence.

**1.** (Beside, Besides) the preliminary audition, those trying out for a high school musical usually have to attend a callback audition.

**2.** (Both, Each) of them are essential to the casting process; (both, each) has a different procedure.

**3.** (Both, The both) require student performance, but with certain important differences.

**4.** For example, when going to the preliminary audition, students usually may (bring, take) their own music or may use a selection from the musical.

**5.** At the callback audition, students do not have a choice (any more, anymore), (being as, since) the musical theater team decides which selections it wishes to hear each student perform.

**6.** Similarly, for (a while, awhile), students have the option to read for any part they choose; however, at the callback, no matter how (bad, badly) they may want a particular role, the choice may not be theirs.

**7.** Even if permitted to read their favorite part, students may be asked to read dialogue from several other parts (beside, besides).

**8.** In the preliminary, to prevent students from feeling (bad, badly), they usually perform only in front of the drama director, choreographer, and musical director.

**9.** At callback, other students who are waiting to audition again are (everywhere, everywheres) while an individual is auditioning.

**10.** After (a while, awhile), students get used to having others (beside, besides) them while they're performing, thus helping to prevent the actors from having (any more, anymore) stage fright.

### Recognizing Correct Usage

Rewrite the following paragraphs, changing the words that are used incorrectly. There are nine usage errors.

A musical theater team would assure you that nowheres is teamwork required any more than in a musical production. Collaboration begins with the drama director, choreographer, and musical director being that they must model cooperative behavior for their students. Even though they bring individual expertise to the production, together they take responsibility for evaluating, casting, encouraging, and critiquing the performers. After a while, students begin to understand how bad teamwork is needed to coordinate the details.

In many high schools, the students go all the farther promoting ticket sales, distributing posters, and coordinating costumes. Many productions even have two student stage managers, the both of whom share responsibilities. In other words, although both are involved with the smooth operation of every scene, each stage manager has particular duties. For example, one might instruct a performer where to stand at, while the other might place props besides a piece of scenery. Beside being stage managers, students often operate both the lighting and sound equipment. Ultimately, the reason a production is successful is because each person contributes to the whole.

## ● Practice Your Skills

### Explanatory Writing: Correct Usage

The concept of collaboration, working together to create a desired result, may be applied in many subject areas. You have probably worked together at one time or another in your classes to produce a collaborative assignment. Some students prefer working together, while others prefer doing independent work. Compose an original paragraph explaining your personal preference concerning collaborative assignments. In your explanation, include at least five of the following words.

- *advice/advise*
- *affect/effect*
- *all together/altogether*
- *among/between*
- *both/each*

**can, may** *Can* expresses ability. *May* expresses possibility or permission.

**Can** you see the third line of the eye chart?

**May** I try one more time?

**can't help but** In this expression use a gerund instead of *but*.

> **Nonstandard**    I **can't help but** notice your new haircut.
>
> **Standard**    I **can't help** noticing your new haircut.

**capital, capitol** A *capital* is the chief city of a state. Also, names are written with *capital* letters, people invest *capital,* and a person can receive *capital* punishment. A *capitol* is the building in which the legislature meets.

> The name of the **capital** of Florida is written in **capital** letters on the **capitol** building in Tallahassee.

**coarse, course** *Coarse* is an adjective that means "loose or rough in texture" or "crude and unrefined." *Course* is a noun that means "a way of acting or proceeding" or "a path, road, or route." Also, people play golf on a *course;* an appetizer is one *course* of a meal; and students take *courses* in school. *Course* is also the word used in the parenthetical expression *of course.*

> Many people heard his **coarse** remarks after the tennis match.
>
> What **course** of action would you take to stop his behavior?

**continual, continuous** Both of these words are adjectives. *Continual* means "frequently repeated." *Continuous* means "uninterrupted."

> The **continual** bolts of lightning frightened me.
>
> The rain was **continuous** for over ten hours.

**different from** Use this form instead of *different than. Different than,* however, can be used informally when it is followed by a clause.

> **Informal**    My sweater is **different than** the one Gram knitted for Maureen.
>
> **Formal**    My sweater is **different from** the one Gram knitted for Maureen.
>
> **Standard**    Her jacket is **different from** mine also.

**discover, invent** Both of these words are verbs. *Discover* means "to find or get knowledge of for the first time." *Invent* means "to create or produce for the first time." Something that is discovered has always existed but it was unknown. Something that is invented has never existed before. The noun forms of these words are *discovery* and *invention.*

> I learned that Isaac Newton **discovered** the law of gravity and that Benjamin Franklin **invented** bifocal glasses.

**doesn't, don't** *Doesn't* is singular and should be used only with singular nouns and the personal pronouns *he, she,* and *it. Don't* is plural and should be used with plural nouns and the personal pronouns *I, you, we,* and *they.*

| | |
|---|---|
| **Nonstandard** | He **don't** need any help. |
| **Standard** | He **doesn't** need any help. |
| **Nonstandard** | An apple a day **don't** keep the doctor away. |
| **Standard** | An apple a day **doesn't** keep the doctor away. |

**done** *Done* is the past participle of the verb *do.* So, when *done* is used as a verb, it must be used with one or more helping verbs.

| | |
|---|---|
| **Nonstandard** | Eli **done** exactly what the doctor told him. |
| **Standard** | Eli **has done** exactly what the doctor told him. |

**double negative** Words such as *hardly, never, no, not,* and *nobody* are considered negatives. Do not use two negatives to express one negative meaning.

| | |
|---|---|
| **Nonstandard** | He doesn**'t hardly** have any spare time. |
| **Standard** | He doesn**'t** have any spare time. |
| **Standard** | He **never** has any spare time. |

*You can learn more about the use of negatives on pages 866–867.*

**emigrate, immigrate** Both of these words are verbs. *Emigrate* means "to leave a country to settle elsewhere." *Immigrate* means "to enter a foreign country to live there." A person emigrates *from* a country and immigrates *to* another country. *Emigrant* and *immigrant* are the noun forms.

> Kin Fujii **emigrated** from Japan ten years ago.
>
> Did he **immigrate** to this country for economic reasons?

**etc.** *Etc.* is an abbreviation for a Latin phrase, *et cetera,* that means "and other things." Never use the word *and* with *etc.* If you do, what you are really saying is "and and other things." It is best, however, not to use this abbreviation at all in formal writing.

> **Informal**      For the salad we need grapes, oranges, **etc.**
>
> **Formal**          For the salad we need grapes, oranges, **and other fruits.**

**farther, further** *Farther* refers to distance. *Further* means "additional" or "to a greater degree or extent."

> How much **farther** will we travel tonight?
>
> The tour guide will give us **further** instructions shortly.

**fewer, less** *Fewer* is plural and refers to things that can be counted. *Less* is singular and refers to quantities and qualities that cannot be counted.

> I scored **fewer** points in basketball this year than last year.
>
> You should place **less** importance on the mistakes you make.

**former, latter** *Former* is the first of two people or things. *Latter* is the second of two people or things. (Use *first* and *last* when referring to three or more.)

> For the main course, we had a choice of roast beef or pork chops. We learned that the portions for the **former** would be larger than the portions for the **latter.**

*Finding the Correct Word*

Write the word in parentheses that correctly completes each sentence.

1. One of the most dramatic occurrences of the Great Depression (can, may) be the Dust Bowl.

2. The (former, latter) affected the entire nation; the (former, latter) affected only the Great Plains states.

3. During the 1930s, no (fewer, less) than a million people were uprooted from their land and charted their (coarse, course) to California.

4. The combination of fear and hope they experienced (doesn't, don't) seem a great deal (different from, different than) that felt by the (emigrants, immigrants) to America in the 19th and early 20th centuries.

5. Of (coarse, course), the exodus to California was a result of a (continual, continuous) drought that plagued the Great Plains.

6. Unknowingly, many farmers (done, had done) irreversible damage to the land by uprooting the natural sod that provided drought protection for the soil.

7. The drought gave rise to (farther, further) problems, as enormous quantities of dust swirled across the plains, forcing the farmers (farther, further) away from home.

8. The name "Okie" was (discovered, invented) to describe the migrating people, even though many came from other states besides Oklahoma.

9. Today we (can hardly, can't hardly) imagine the endless lines of homeless people traveling away from the plains in search of a new life.

10. Many (discovered, invented) that the stories of abundant jobs had been (discovered, invented) by wealthy landowners looking for cheap labor.

USAGE GLOSSARY

*Recognizing Correct Usage*

Rewrite the following paragraphs, changing the words that are used incorrectly.

Born in Salinas, California, John Steinbeck had an opportunity to discover the continuous plight of migrant workers. By living among them, he gained farther knowledge of them and their working conditions. He had done his research thoroughly; from those experiences, he discovered the characters for several of his works. Some critics considered his characters to be course and common. Others, however, felt Steinbeck had special empathy for the lonely, the mistreated, the poor, and others who suffered. Readers can't help but recognize this continuous theme in works such as *Tortilla Flat, Of Mice and Men*, and *The Grapes of Wrath*.

No other account of the Dust Bowl migration has had more impact than John Steinbeck's *The Grapes of Wrath*. Although some consider this work a social protest, it can more accurately be described as a work of art. In 1940, the film version of the novel was well received even though the ending was different than the novel's. Steinbeck received no less than the Pulitzer Prize for this novel in the same year. Its artistic value hasn't never decreased; in fact, it has increased over the years. His literary acclaim spread farther when he received the Nobel Prize for his life's work in 1962.

**good, well** *Good* is an adjective and often follows a linking verb. *Well* is an adverb and often follows an action verb. However, when *well* means "in good health" or "satisfactory," it is used as an adjective.

Do you feel **good** this morning? (adjective)

Yes, I work **well** in the morning. (adverb)

Pat doesn't feel **well.** ("in good health")

*You can learn more about using adjectives and adverbs on pages 631–638 and 854–873.*

**had of** Do not use *of* after *had.*

| | |
|---|---|
| **Nonstandard** | I would have taken my umbrella if **I had of** listened to the weather forecast. |
| **Standard** | I would have taken my umbrella if **I had** listened to the weather forecast. |

**have, of** Never substitute *of* for the verb *have*. When speaking, many people make a contraction of *have*. For example, someone might say, "We should've left sooner." Because *'ve* sounds like *of*, *of* is often incorrectly substituted for *have*.

> **Nonstandard**    You should **of** roasted the potatoes.
>
> **Standard**    You should **have** roasted the potatoes.

**hear, here** *Hear* is a verb that means "to perceive by listening." *Here* is an adverb that means "in this place."

> If you stand over **here,** can you **hear** the phone ring?

**hole, whole** *Hole* is an opening in something. *Whole* means "complete or entire."

> The **whole** time I watched the **hole,** no animal went in.

**imply, infer** Both of these words are verbs. *Imply* means "to suggest" or "to hint." *Infer* means "to draw a conclusion by reasoning or from evidence." A speaker implies; a listener infers. *Implication* and *inference* are the noun forms.

> Grandmother **implied** that she might be visiting soon.
>
> We **inferred** from what she said that she was excited.

**in, into** Use *into* when you want to express motion from one place to another.

> The mixture **in** the bowl should be put **into** the blender.

**irregardless** Do not substitute this word for *regardless*.

> **Nonstandard**    **Irregardless** of anything you say, I still think he was telling the truth.
>
> **Standard**    **Regardless** of anything you say, I still think he was telling the truth.

**its, it's** *Its* is a possessive pronoun. *It's* is a contraction for *it is*.

> The committee will announce **its** findings on Friday.
>
> **It's** going to be a controversial report.

**kind, sort, type** These words are singular and should be preceded by *this* or *that*. *Kinds, sorts,* and *types* are plural and should be preceded by *these* or *those*.

> Joan likes **that type** of book bag.
>
> Joan likes **those types** of book bags.

**kind of, sort of** Never substitute these expressions for *rather* or *somewhat* in formal writing.

> **Nonstandard**    Calculus was **sort of** difficult for me.
>
> **Standard**    Calculus was **rather** difficult for me.

**knew, new** *Knew,* the past tense of the verb *know,* means "was acquainted with." *New* is an adjective that means "recently made" or "just found."

> We **knew** all along that a **new** gym would be built.

**learn, teach** Both of these words are verbs. *Learn* means "to acquire knowledge." *Teach* means "to instruct."

> **Nonstandard**    Who **learned** you how to water ski?
>
> **Standard**    Who **taught** you how to water ski?
>
> **Standard**    I **learned** how to water ski from my sister.

**leave, let** Both of these words are verbs. *Leave* means "to depart." *Let* means "to allow" or "to permit."

> **Nonstandard**    **Leave** me fix dinner before the game.
>
> **Standard**    **Let** me fix dinner before the game.
>
> **Standard**    I want to **leave** early to get a good seat.

## Practice Your Skills

### Finding the Correct Word

Write the word in parentheses that correctly completes each sentence.

1. Environmental issues, ranging from ocean pollution to a (hole, whole) in the ozone layer, plague the (hole, whole) world.
2. As our population grows, these (type, types) of issues will increase.
3. We (hear, here) horror stories every day about companies that pollute, (irregardless, regardless) of environmental regulations.
4. (Its, It's) not unusual to have specials on TV that warn us about the damaging (implications, inferences) of air and water pollution.
5. (Its, It's) importance is (kind of, rather) difficult to (learn, teach) the public.
6. From the indifference displayed by many, we can only (imply, infer) that some people don't care about (learning, teaching).
7. Community projects, such as going (in, into) the streams to remove trash, (let, leave) us have an opportunity to help.
8. Promoting recognition of environmentally safe products (in, into) the community works (good, well).
9. More (knew, new) and innovative approaches are needed to make people feel (good, well) about their involvement.
10. We could (have, of) made more rapid progress if we had known how to increase public support.

## Connect to the Writing Process: Revising

### Recognizing Correct Usage

Rewrite the following paragraph, changing the words that are used incorrectly.

One woman who new well how to raise public awareness was writer and scientist Rachel Carson. She is a well example of how it's possible to combine our interests with our learning to produce results. Drawn to nature as a child, she later wrote about it's wonders and also managed to learn a hole generation about environmental dangers. Also, she put a hole in the accepted theory in the 1920s that science was a profession kind of ill-suited for women. Irregardless of her gender, she earned a master's degree in zoology from Johns Hopkins University and went in the field of aquatic biology. With *The Sea Around Us,* she opened up a new world to the reading public. However, from the inferences in *The Silent Spring* about the harmful effects of pesticides, the public implied the threat to our environment.

### Describing a Scene

Rachel Carson's love of nature led her to write *The Sea Around Us*. The California coastline epitomizes the power and beauty of the sea. Imagine that you are seated on a shoreline along the West Coast of the United States. You want to preserve the memory of the moment. Using at least six of the following words, describe in detail what you see and how it makes you feel.

- *can/may*
- *continual/continuous*
- *farther/further*
- *hole/whole*
- *kind/sort/type*
- *learn/teach*

**lie, lay** *Lie* means "to rest or recline." *Lie* is never followed by a direct object. Its principal parts are *lie, lying, lay,* and *lain. Lay* means "to put or set (something) down." *Lay* is usually followed by a direct object. Its principal parts are *lay, laying, laid,* and *laid.*

Don't **lie** down now.

The workers will **lay** the new carpet in your room.

*You can learn more about using the verbs* lie *and* lay *on page 759.*

**like, as** *Like* can be used as a preposition to introduce a prepositional phrase. *As* is usually a subordinating conjunction that introduces an adverbial clause. Although *like* is sometimes used informally as a conjunction, it should be avoided in formal situations.

| | |
|---|---|
| **Informal** | The room is perfect just **like** it is. (clause) |
| **Formal** | The room is perfect just **as** it is. |
| **Formal** | The wallpaper is gray-striped **like** mine. (prepositional phrase) |

**loose, lose** *Loose* is usually an adjective that means "not tight." *Lose* is a verb that means "to misplace" or "not to have any longer."

Your tooth is very **loose.**

I hope you don't **lose** it before class pictures are taken.

**may be, maybe** *May be* is a form of the verb *be*. *Maybe* is an adverb that means "perhaps."

> The chance of a lifetime **may be** in this envelope.
>
> **Maybe** we have won the expense-paid vacation to Greece.

**most, almost** *Most* is a noun, a pronoun, or an adjective that modifies a noun or a pronoun. *Almost*, which means "nearly," is an adverb. Do not substitute *most* for *almost*.

> **Nonstandard**    Did you type **most** all of your term paper?
>
> **Standard**    Did you type **almost** all of your term paper?
>
> **Standard**    I spent **most** of the weekend on the computer.

**nor, or** Use *neither* with *nor* and *either* with *or*.

> **Neither** Fred **nor** Jane is coming to the party.
>
> They are going to **either** the movies **or** the concert.

**of** Prepositions such as *inside, outside,* and *off* should not be followed by *of*.

> **Nonstandard**    The ball rolled **off of** the chair.
>
> **Standard**    The ball rolled **off** the chair.

**ought** Never use *have* or *had* with *ought*.

> **Nonstandard**    Ben **hadn't ought** to drive so fast.
>
> **Standard**    Ben **ought not** to drive so fast.

**passed, past** *Passed* is the past tense of the verb *pass*. As a noun, *past* means "a time gone by." As an adjective, *past* means "just gone" or "elapsed." As a preposition, *past* means "beyond."

> In the **past,** she always **passed** her courses with *A*'s. (*past* as a noun)
>
> For the **past** several mornings, I have walked **past** the park on my way to school.
>
> (past as an adjective and then as a preposition)

**precede, proceed** Both of these words are verbs. *Precede* means "to be, go, or come ahead of something else." *Proceed* means "to move along a course," "to advance," or "to continue after a pause or an interruption."

> One guide will **precede** our group down the mountain.
>
> **Proceed** down the steep mountain with great caution.

**principal, principle** As an adjective *principal* means "main" or "chief." As a noun *principal* means "the head of a school" or "a leader." *Principle* is a noun that is synonymous with *law, truth, doctrine,* or *code of conduct.*

> The **principal** reason he stayed in school was because of the advice given by the **principal** at Atlantic High.
>
> Roberto decided to stick by the **principles** his parents had instilled in him.

**respectfully, respectively** *Respectfully* is related to the noun *respect,* which means "high regard or esteem." *Respectively* means "in the order given."

> **Respectfully,** the guide inquired about my destination.
>
> I replied that it would be London and Paris, **respectively.**

**rise, raise** *Rise* means "to move upward" or "to get up." *Rise* is never followed by a direct object. Its principal parts are *rise, rising, rose,* and *risen. Raise* means "to lift up," "to increase," or "to grow something." *Raise* is usually followed by a direct object. Its principal parts are *raise, raising, raised,* and *raised.*

> The spectators always **rise** when the judge enters the courtroom.
>
> They wondered if the attorney would **raise** the same issue that he brought up yesterday.

*You can learn more about using the verbs* rise *and* raise *on page 760.*

*Finding the Correct Word*

Write the word in parentheses that correctly completes each sentence.

1. (Almost, Most) all people agree that poetry (may be, maybe) described in a variety of ways.

2. Neither poets (nor, or) readers of poetry agree on how it (had ought, ought) to be defined.

3. Words, of (coarse, course), are the (principal, principle) components of poetry.

4. This fact (raises, rises) the question as to why one poem isn't basically (as, like) another.

5. However, in the usage and pattern of those words (lays, lies) the uniqueness of each poem.

6. In the (passed, past), some argued that a poem (ain't, isn't) true poetry unless it (passed, past) certain criteria—namely, the use of elevated language.

7. In the late 1800s, Walt Whitman (preceded, proceeded) to use the language of the common people.

8. The (loose, lose) style of Whitman's poetry, known as free verse, did not cause it to (loose, lose) a rhythmical quality.

● *Connect to the Writing Process:* **Revising**

*Recognizing Correct Usage*

Rewrite the following paragraphs, changing the words that are used incorrectly.

Sonnets, revered in the passed, continue to be a principal part of poetry. The names of two major forms, Petrarchan and Shakespearean, proceed from their extensive use by Petrarch and Shakespeare. These are known also as either the Italian sonnet or the English sonnet, respectfully. Although each contains fourteen lines, they loose their similarity in most other elements.

Ballads, another fixed form, are based in principal on songs that tell a story; they may be one of the oldest forms of poetry. Proceeding the others, the first stanza typically ought to present the characters and the problem; the rest of the stanzas proceed to solve the dilemma presented by the first.

In contrast, the intent of the five-line limerick, whose name comes from a city in Ireland, is to amuse. May be the varied forms of poems ensure that poetry doesn't ever loose its universal appeal.

**says, said** Do not use *says,* the present tense of the verb *say,* when you should use the past tense, *said.*

> **Nonstandard**  Then she **says,** "I want to go with you."
>
> **Standard**  Then she **said,** "I want to go with you."

**–self, –selves** A reflexive or an intensive pronoun that ends in *-self* or *-selves* should not be used as a subject. (Never use "hisself" or "theirselves.")

> **Nonstandard**  Ken and **myself** were chosen.
>
> **Standard**  Ken and **I** were chosen.

**shall, will** Formal English uses *shall* with first-person pronouns and *will* with second- and third-person pronouns. Today, however, *shall* and *will* are used interchangeably with *I* and *we,* except that *shall* is usually still used with first-person pronouns for questions.

> **Shall** I meet you at the mall?
>
> **Will** you meet me at the mall?

**sit, set** *Sit* means "to rest in an upright position." *Sit* is never followed by a direct object. Its principal parts are *sit, sitting, sat,* and *sat. Set* means "to put or place (something)." *Set* is usually followed by a direct object. Its principal parts are *set, setting, set,* and *set.*

> **Sit** down and rest for a while.
>
> I'll **set** the dishes on the shelf.

*You can learn more about using the verbs* sit *and* set *on pages 760–761.*

**some, somewhat** *Some* is either a pronoun or an adjective that modifies a noun or a pronoun. *Somewhat* is an adverb.

> **Nonstandard**  School enrollment has declined **some.**
>
> **Standard**  School enrollment has declined **somewhat.**

**suppose to, supposed to** Be sure to add the *d* to *suppose* when it is followed by *to.*

> **Nonstandard**  I was **suppose to** finish my project today.
>
> **Standard**  I was **supposed to** finish my project today.

**than, then** *Than* is usually a subordinating conjunction and is used for comparisons. *Then* is an adverb that means "at that time" or "next."

> I didn't think I would finish sooner **than** you.
>
> Finish your homework and **then** call me.

**that, which, who** These words are often used as relative pronouns to introduce adjective clauses. *That* refers to animals and things and usually begins an essential clause. *Which* refers to animals and things. *Who* refers to people.

> The ad **that** was posted on the board sounds interesting.
>
> That ad, **which** also runs on radio, will attract many people.
>
> Anyone **who** responds to the ad may fill out an application.

**their, there, they're** *Their* is a possessive pronoun. *There* is usually an adverb, and sometimes it will begin an inverted sentence. *They're* is a contraction for *they are.*

> **Their** car is parked over **there,** ready for the trip.
>
> **They're** leaving for Mobile tomorrow.

**theirs, there's** *Theirs* is a possessive pronoun. *There's* is a contraction for *there is.*

> **There's** an easy solution to my problem, but what about **theirs?**

**them, those** Never use *them* as a subject or an adjective.

> **Nonstandard**  **Them** are from whose garden? (subject)
>
> **Standard**  **Those** are from whose garden?
>
> **Nonstandard**  Rachel grew **them** tomatoes. (adjective)
>
> **Standard**  Rachel grew **those** tomatoes.

**this here, that there** Avoid using *here* and *there* in addition to *this* and *that.*

> **Nonstandard**  **That there** sunset looks beautiful.
>
> **Standard**  **That** sunset looks beautiful.
>
> **Nonstandard**  **This here** saddle is mine.
>
> **Standard**  **This** saddle is mine.

A Writer's Glossary of Usage     **897**

**this, that, these, those** *This* and *that* are singular and should modify singular nouns. *These* and *those* are plural and should modify plural nouns.

> **Nonstandard** Does the Sport Shop sell **those** kind of bats?
>
> **Standard** Does the Sport Shop sell **that** kind of bat?

**threw, through** *Threw* is the past tense of the verb *throw*. *Through* is a preposition that means "in one side and out the other."

> I hope no one **threw** Sunday's newspaper away.
>
> Look **through** the stack of papers on the table.

## ● Practice Your Skills

### *Finding the Correct Word*

Write the word in parentheses that correctly completes each sentence.

1. It would be classified as an understatement if someone (said, says) that interest in soccer had increased (some, somewhat) in the United States.
2. In fact, most (shall, will) agree the sport has gone (threw, through) an amazing transformation.
3. Actually, soccer has increased in popularity more (than, then) any other sport.
4. (This, This here) transformation began taking place in the 1950s; before (than, then), it was simply known as the favorite sport of Europe and South America.
5. The 1994 World Cup, held in the United States, (set, sit) in motion a nationwide interest.
6. At the matches, fans (threw, through) (their selves, themselves) energetically into the excitement.
7. (These sort of, This sort of) excitement spilled over to playgrounds, recreation centers, and schools.
8. Many spectators (setting, sitting) in the stands had to learn the rules of soccer.
9. (These, These sort of) rules are actually much simpler (than, then) rules for American football.
10. (Shall, Will) we some day find that soccer has become the national sport of the United States?

**to, too, two**  *To* is a preposition. *To* also begins an infinitive. *Too* is an adverb that modifies an adjective or another adverb. *Two* is a number.

**Two** more people are **too** many **to** take in our car.

We hurried **to** the picnic area before it got **too** crowded.

**try to**  Use *try to* instead of *try and,* which is nonstandard.

| | |
|---|---|
| **Nonstandard** | Please **try and** be there on time. |
| **Standard** | Please **try to** be there on time. |

**use to, used to**  Be sure to add the *-d* to *use.*

| | |
|---|---|
| **Nonstandard** | I **use to** paint with watercolors. |
| **Standard** | I **used to** paint with watercolors. |

**way, ways**  Do not substitute *ways* for *way* when referring to a distance.

| | |
|---|---|
| **Nonstandard** | Aren't you a long **ways** from home? |
| **Standard** | Aren't you a long **way** from home? |

**weak, week**  *Weak* is an adjective that means "not strong" or "likely to break." *Week* is a noun that means "a time period of seven days."

For the first **week** after your surgery, you'll feel quite **weak.**

**what**  Do not substitute *what* for *that*.

> **Nonstandard**  The car **what** you bought was too expensive.
>
> **Standard**  The car **that** you bought was too expensive.

**when, where**  Do not use *when* or *where* directly after a linking verb in a definition.

> **Nonstandard**  In the North, October is **when** you should plant tulip bulbs.
>
> **Standard**  In the North, October is the **month when** you should plant tulip bulbs.
>
> **Nonstandard**  The Hall of Mirrors is **where** the Treaty of Versailles was signed.
>
> **Standard**  The Hall of Mirrors is the **room where** the Treaty of Versailles was signed.
>
> **Nonstandard**  A harvest is **when** the farmers bring in their crops.
>
> **Standard**  A harvest is **the time when** the farmers bring in their crops.

**where**  Do not substitute *where* for *that*.

> **Nonstandard**  I read **where** bowling is the number one participant sport in the United States.
>
> **Standard**  I read **that** bowling is the number one participant sport in the United States.

**who, whom**  *Who,* a pronoun in the nominative case, is used either as a subject or as a predicate nominative. *Whom,* a pronoun in the objective case, is used mainly as a direct object, an indirect object, or an object of a preposition.

> **Who** is waving at you? (subject)
>
> It is Howard, **whom** I have known all my life. (direct object of the verb *have known* in the adjective clause)
>
> To **whom** will you give permission to drive? (object of the preposition *to*)

Except when using nonstandard English for special effect, professional writers use standard English even in the titles of their works. Notice the correct usage of *who* in the nominative case and *whom* in the objective case in these titles.

*For* **Whom** *the Bell Tolls* by Ernest Hemingway

*The Man* **Who** *Came to Dinner* by Moss Hart

**whose, who's** *Whose* is a possessive pronoun. *Who's* is a contraction for *who is*.

**Whose** suitcase is that?

It belongs to the man **who's** walking this way.

**your, you're** *Your* is a possessive pronoun. *You're* is a contraction for *you are*.

**You're** sure you put **your** baseball glove in the car?

● **Practice Your Skills**

*Finding the Correct Word*

Write the word in parentheses that correctly completes each sentence.

1. (Your, You're) senior year is one of the most important years, and one of the most memorable years (to, too, two).
2. Many (who, whom) previously thought they had a long (way, ways) to go before graduation realize that the time is rapidly approaching.
3. It is essential that you (try and, try to) keep a focus on the goals (that, what) you have set.
4. (Your, You're) certain (to, too, two) discover that all decisions about (your, you're) future need careful consideration.
5. (Whose, Who's) qualified to help with college or career decisions should determine (whose, who) help you seek.
6. If you should find yourself (weak, week) in a certain subject, find out (who, whom) can provide tutoring.
7. When in doubt, remember that (to, too, two) excellent sources from (who, whom) you can seek advice are your parents and guidance counselors.
8. If you are (use to, used to) letting decisions slide, (try and, try to) practice self-discipline.

### Recognizing Correct Usage

Rewrite the following paragraph, changing the words that are used incorrectly.

Be sure to participate in senior activities leading up too you're graduation; they're two special to miss. The memories what you accumulate will last a lifetime. One event, the junior-senior prom, is where the junior class honors graduating seniors. The king and queen are the couple who juniors and seniors recognize symbolically at the dance. The academic awards program is designed to try to give recognition to those who are deserving. The yearbook signing is when seniors write final messages to one another. You're sure to have teachers, too, who wish to add congratulatory notes. This informal party, usually held the last weak of school, is a special memory before the formal activities of graduation actually begin.

## ● Practice Your Skills

### Personal Response: Correct Usage

The following words of George Will, a *Washington Post* columnist, are an excerpt from his column and the advice he offered his daughter's graduating class. Examine this excerpt and then read the instructions that follow.

Well, we live and learn. Indeed, the happiest people live to learn. They live for the delightful astonishments that never stop coming to those who never stop learning.

So, go through life with, figuratively speaking, a crick in your neck from looking back at the path by which humanity got to today. It is a path littered with true stories that astonish. Understand that happiness is a talent, one that immunizes you against being bored. Boredom is sinful because, as a character says in a Saul Bellow novel, "Boredom is the shriek of unused capacities."

—George Will, "Will's Way"

Using any ten of the glossary words from *lie/lay* through *your/you're,* write a personal response to George Will's commencement advice. Underline the words you chose, checking that you used the correct form.

## ✔ *Check Point:* **Mixed Practice**

Write the word in parentheses that correctly completes each sentence.

1. While the rituals of (passed, past) high school graduations may have changed (some, somewhat), the excitement and solemnity of the occasion have not.

2. The importance of graduation is reflected in the (amount, number) of preparations made during the (preceding, proceeding) (weak, week).

3. The salutatorian and valedictorian usually make (farther, further) revisions to (their, they're) speeches.

4. A proper fit of the mortarboard is essential; if (it's, its) (to, too, two) (loose, lose), you might (loose, lose) it.

5. (To, Too, Two) achieve the full (affect, effect) and ensure that it fits (good, well), try on the robe also.

6. Graduation practices are held to (learn, teach) graduates how to walk (all together, altogether) in the processional march.

7. At practice the coordinator (can, may) even (raise, rise) the issue of when and how to (raise, rise) at the proper time.

8. The coordinator also (learns, teaches) you how to properly adjust the tassel after receiving (you're, your) diploma.

9. Special instructions that (lay, lie) out important details are available (beside, besides) the stage.

10. As these preparations (infer, imply), the (hole, whole) ceremony is carefully planned.

# Unit 6

# Mechanics

Imagine speech without pauses. Pauses in spoken and written communicaton are "precious" because they separate thoughts into manageable units. Just like the occasional stops to enjoy the scenery during a long hike, pauses in written communication help readers absorb meaning and prepare for the ideas and information to come. In this unit you will gain, among other skills, the skill to choose the right punctuation marks for each situation—the ones that will herd your words together, separate them from others, and form the "precious" pauses necessary for clear communication.

*The most precious things in speech are pauses.*

—*Ralph Richardson*

# Capital Letters

scene from: *The Color Purple*

**How can you use capital letters to clarify your writing?**

## Capital Letters: Pretest 1

The letter below contains several errors in capitalization. The three lines under the first error indicate a capital *D*. Revise the rest of the letter so that all capitalization is correct.

dear Ms. Walker,

Our school, Webster Academy, will be hosting a literary event on may 12. As Director, i'm extremely pleased to invite you to serve as our Featured author of the Day. We would like You to read a selection from *the Color Purple*. The theme this year will be "our Cultural Histories." You can contact me, Paul Rodell, Reader's theater Director, Webster academy, 209 Phineas road, Princeton, Rhode Island, 02906. To get to our school from Green Airport, you should take Cumberland avenue North and exit on Route 23 East. Stay on that for two miles. That will take you right into Princeton. Turn Left onto Webster, and you'll see our School. We hope you will be able to come. please let me know as soon as possible.

sincerely,

Paul Rodell
Director

## Capital Letters: Pretest 2

### Directions

Read the passage and decide which word or words should be capitalized in each underlined part. Write the letter of the correct answer. If the underlined part contains no error, write D.

On the **(1)** <u>continent of Antarctica, the sun shines for half a year</u>. I don't know if **(2)** <u>i could endure the other six months of darkness, although</u> the experience would be interesting. **(3)** <u>human populations do not live in Antarctica</u>, but penguins and seals do. Can you picture yourself writing letters that begin, **(4)** <u>"dear mom, Here I am</u> on a **(5)** <u>giant glacier far from civilization</u>"?

**1. A** Sun
   **B** Continent
   **C** Year
   **D** No error

**2. A** I
   **B** Although
   **C** Darkness
   **D** No error

**3. A** Populations
   **B** Human
   **C** Human, Populations
   **D** No error

**4. A** Dear
   **B** Mom
   **C** Dear Mom,
   **D** No error

**5. A** Giant
   **B** Glacier
   **C** Civilization
   **D** No error

Until the advent of printing in the fifteenth century, words were written in all capital letters, and no punctuation was used. When scribes wrote, they ran words TOGETHERLIKETHIS.

With the printing press came specific uses for capitalization as well as the introduction of punctuation. Not only could people read faster, but they could also understand more easily what they read. The correct use of capitalization and punctuation will add clarity to your writing also, forestalling any misunderstanding of your meaning.

Today a capital letter marks the beginning of certain constructions and emphasizes the importance of certain words.

**21 A**  **Capitalize the beginning of a sentence or a line of poetry, parts of a letter or an outline, and the pronoun *I*.**

## ➤ Sentences and Poetry

Capital letters draw a reader's attention to the beginning of a sentence or of a new line of poetry.

**21 A.1**  **Capitalize the first word of a sentence and of a line of poetry.**

| | |
|---|---|
| **Sentence** | Teenagers in our community have become increasingly involved in poetry readings. |
| **Poetry** | The panther is like a leopard,<br>Except it hasn't been peppered.<br>Should you behold a panther crouch,<br>Prepare to say Ouch.<br>Better yet, if called by a panther,<br>Don't anther.<br>　　　　　　　　*—Ogden Nash* |

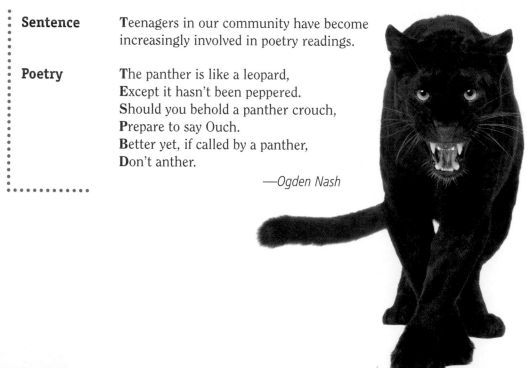

When only two or three lines of poetry are quoted, they can be written with a slash ( / ) between each line. Each new line after a slash begins with a capital letter.

"God in His wisdom made the fly / **A**nd then forgot to tell us why."
—*Ogden Nash*

**21 A.2**    Capitalize the first word when a direct quotation is used.

Marvin asked, "**D**o you understand this essay by Orwell?"

*You can learn more about capitalization in direct quotations on pages 990–991.*

Some poets deliberately misuse or eliminate capital letters. For example, in her poem "The Sky is low—the Clouds are mean," Emily Dickinson capitalizes common nouns, perhaps to personify them or to give them prominence.

The **S**ky is low—the **C**louds are mean.
A **T**ravelling **F**lake of **S**now
Across a **B**arn or through a **R**ut
Debates if it will go—

—Emily Dickinson, "The Sky is low—the Clouds are mean"

William Carlos Williams, on the other hand, wrote entire poems without using a single capital letter.

so much depends
upon
a red wheel
barrow
glazed with rain
water
beside the white
chickens
—William Carlos Williams, "The Red Wheelbarrow"

These unusual capitalizations contribute to the beauty and meaning of the poems. When you quote poetry in your writing, duplicate the author's capitalization and punctuation, even if it "breaks the rules."

## ➤ Parts of a Letter

**21 A.3** Capitalize the first word of a greeting of a letter, and the first word in the closing of a letter.

| PARTS OF A LETTER | | |
|---|---|---|
| **Greetings** | Dear Sir or Madam: | Attention Subscriber: |
| | Dear Mr. Rogers: | My dearest Jimmy, |
| **Closings** | Sincerely yours, | Best regards, |
| | Your friend, | Cordially, |

## ➤ Outlines

Capital letters draw the reader's attention to the beginning of each heading in an outline.

**21 A.4** Capitalize the first word of each item in an outline and the letters that begin major subsections of the outline.

    I. Argument for a student bookstore-café
        A. Encourages reading for relaxation
        B. Provides space for poetry readings
        C. Provides school supplies and snacks

## ➤ Formal Resolutions

A formal resolution is an opinion or intention, often in writing, agreed upon by a committee or other formal group. Some formal resolutions are constructed as clauses instead of sentences; nevertheless, the first word of the resolution is usually capitalized.

**21 A.5** Capitalize the first word in a formal resolution that follows the word *Resolved.*

Resolved: That this school should build a bookstore-café for the use of all students.

**Some Formal Statements**

Formal statements are sometimes introduced with phrases ending in colons, such as *The decision is this:* and *The question was this:* In these situations, the formal statement usually begins with a capital letter.

**21 A.6**   Capitalize the first word of a formal statement that follows a colon.

> The question was this: **C**ould we afford to pay a speaker as prestigious as Maya Angelou?
>
> The committee issued the following statement: **D**onations to the guest speaker's fund are needed.

*You can learn more about using colons on pages 979–982.*

 **The Pronoun *I***

The pronoun *I* is always capitalized, no matter its position in a sentence or a line of poetry.

**21 A.7**   Capitalize the pronoun *I*, both alone and in contractions.

> **I**'m sure **I** saw her in English class.
>
> **I** don't know if **I**'ll want to read my poem aloud.

*The first word of a direct quotation is also capitalized. You can learn more about capitalization with quotations on pages 990–991.*

## *When You Write*

When writing a narrative in first-person, such as an autobiography, use the pronoun *I* sparingly unless you are striving for self-emphasis.

| | |
|---|---|
| **Self-Emphasis** | **I** write poetry, **I** critique books, and **I** teach literature classes. |
| **Subject Emphasis** | **I** write poetry, critique books, and teach literature classes. |

Check over a recent personal essay to be sure you do not use the pronoun *I* too often.

## ● Practice Your Skills

### Using Capitalization with First Words and I

Choose the item in each pair that is capitalized correctly. Then write the letter of each correct item.

**1. a.** I sign all my letters "yours sincerely."

　　**b.** I sign all my letters "Yours sincerely."

**2. a.** Resolved: That the first day of spring be Poetry Day at our school.

　　**b.** Resolved: that the first day of spring be Poetry Day at our school.

**3. a.** We have been assigned to write to an author whose work we enjoy. perhaps I will write to Terry Pratchett.

　　**b.** We have been assigned to write to an author whose work we enjoy. Perhaps I will write to Terry Pratchett.

**4. a.** I. Ideas for Poetry Day　　　　**b.** I. Ideas for Poetry Day
　　　　A. Guest poet　　　　　　　　　　　A. guest poet
　　　　B. Public reading　　　　　　　　　B. public reading
　　　　C. Contest　　　　　　　　　　　　C. contest

## ● *Connect to Writing:* Editing

### Using Capitalization

Write each item using correct capitalization.

**1.** T. S. Eliot's character J. Alfred Prufrock says, "I should have been a pair of ragged claws / scuttling across the floors of silent seas."

**2.** in "Shooting an Elephant" Orwell writes, "in Moulmein, in Lower Burma, I was hated by large numbers of people—the only time in my life that I have been important enough for this to happen to me."

**3.** the narrator in O'Brien's "Sister Imelda" makes the following statement: "in our deepest moments, we say the most inadequate things."

**4.** Resolved: that "Mutability" by Shelley be the official poem of the senior class.

## ● *Connect to Speaking and Writing:* Peer Consultation

### Using Capitals in an Outline

With a partner, write an outline for a short skit you would like to perform for your classmates and teacher. Talk about what you will include in the skit, and then work on the outline together. Use capital letters correctly when creating your outline.

Beginning a noun with a capital letter can tell a reader that it is a **proper noun**—that it names a particular person, place, or thing.

**21 B**    **Capitalize proper nouns and their abbreviations.**

Proper nouns include names of particular persons, geographical names, and names of time periods. The rule for each type of proper noun follows.

## Names of Particular Persons and Animals

**21 B.1**    Names of particular persons and animals should be capitalized. Also capitalize the initials that stand for people's names.

| NAMES | |
|---|---|
| **Persons** | James, Jocelyn Weiss, Allison **R. F**errara |
| **Animals** | Rex, Felix, Spot, **D**ancer, Thunderbolt |

Surnames that begin with *De, Mc, Mac, 0',* or *St.* usually contain two capital letters. These names can vary, so ask the individuals how their names are spelled and capitalized.

| NAMES WITH TWO CAPITAL LETTERS | | | | |
|---|---|---|---|---|
| DeJong | McGuire | MacInnis | O'Hara | St. James |

Capitalize descriptive names or nicknames used as proper nouns or parts of proper nouns.

| DESCRIPTIVE NAMES | | |
|---|---|---|
| Calamity Jane | Honest Abe | the Cornhusker State |

Capitalize abbreviations that follow a person's name.

> Stephanie Wong, **M.D.,** will be tonight's guest speaker.

Capitalize common nouns that are clearly personified, such as in "one who loves Nature."

**Geographical Names**

**21 B.2**   Geographical names, including the names of particular places, bodies of water, and celestial bodies, should be capitalized.

| GEOGRAPHICAL NAMES | |
|---|---|
| **Streets, Highways** | Tremont Street (**St.**), Meridian Turnpike (**Tpk.**), Route (**Rt.**) 77, Montgomery Freeway (**Frwy.**), Interstate Highway 35 (**I-35**), Charleton Boulevard (**Blvd.**), Sunshine Highway (**Hwy.**), Michigan Avenue (**Ave.**), Thirty-second Street (The second part of a hyphenated numbered street is not capitalized.) |
| **Cities, States** | Rapid City, South Dakota (**SD**); Washington, **D.C.** |
| **Townships, Counties, Parishes** | Pottsville Township, Broward County, New Hope Parish |
| **Countries** | Saudi Arabia, Thailand, Ireland, Canada |
| **Sections of a Country** | the Northwest, New England, the South, the Sun Belt (Compass directions do not begin with a capital letter: *Go east on Route 23.*) |
| **Continents** | South America, Africa, Australia |
| **World Regions** | Northern Hemisphere, South Pole, the Far East |
| **Islands** | Long Island, the Philippine Islands |
| **Mountains** | Mount (**Mt.**) Hood, the Allegheny Mountains (**Mts.**) |
| **Parks** | Bryce Canyon National Park |
| **Bodies of Water** | Pacific Ocean, South China Sea, Persian Gulf, Ohio River, Cedar Lake |
| **Stars** | Sirius, Nova Hercules, North Star |
| **Constellations** | Big Dipper, Ursa Minor, Orion |
| **Planets** | Venus, Neptune, Saturn, Earth (Do not capitalize *sun* or *moon*. Also do not capitalize *earth* preceded by *the.*) |

Words such as *street, mountain, river, island,* and *county* are capitalized only when they are part of a proper noun.

*You can learn more about proper nouns on page 619.*

Which lake is larger, Lake Superior or Lake Michigan?

Which county is central, Travis County or Randall County?

## ● Practice Your Skills

### *Using Capital Letters*

Write the following items, using capital letters where needed.

**1.** the columbia river

**2.** mountains in the east

**3.** the milky way

**4.** fifty-third st.

**5.** the earth and mars

**6.** madrid, spain

**7.** north on hayes highway

**8.** his horse dusty

**9.** alfred moses, jr.

**10.** lake Victoria

## ● Practice Your Skills

### *Using Capital Letters*

Correctly write each word that should be capitalized.

**1.** Woodrow Wilson, born in staunton, va, had a pet ram named old ike.

**2.** Barack Obama and his family invited a dog named bo into the White House.

**3.** The rocky mountains were once called the stony mountains.

**4.** The first woman to swim the english channel in both directions was Florence Chadwick of california.

**5.** Old north church, or Christ Church, is boston's oldest standing church.

**6.** It is where the signal lantern for the midnight ride of paul revere was hung.

**7.** Henry wadsworth longfellow wrote a poem about the famous ride.

**8.** The capital of texas was changed 15 times before austin was finally chosen.

## ● *Connect to Writing:* Grade-Level Vocabulary

### *Using Capitals in Geographical Names*

With a partner, look over all the types of geographical names listed in the chart on the left page. Go down the list together and write two additional names for each entry on the chart. For example, at "Countries" you might add Egypt and Macedonia and at "Islands" you might add St. Thomas and Hawaii. Once you have completed your chart, write a short account of which entry was the hardest to find additional examples for, and why.

## ➤ Names of Groups

**21 B.3**   Names of groups, including the names of organizations, businesses, institutions, government bodies, political parties, and teams, should be capitalized.

## NAMES OF GROUPS

| | |
|---|---|
| **Organizations** | the **A**merican **R**ed **C**ross, the **B**oy **S**couts of **A**merica, the **A**ir **N**ational **G**uard |
| **Businesses** | **F**ly **N**ow **A**irlines, **T**he **G**old and **S**ilver **C**ompany, **H**awthorne's **G**reenery, **T**aft **S&L** |
| **Institutions** | **H**awthorne **H**igh **S**chool, **L**akeview **H**ospital, the **U**niversity (**U**niv.) of **T**exas, **N**ew **Y**ork **U**niversity **(NYU)** (Words such as *school, hospital,* and *university* are not capitalized unless they are part of a proper noun.) |
| **Government Bodies or Agencies** | the **U**nited **S**tates **S**upreme **C**ourt, **C**ongress, the **S**enate, the **V**eterans **A**dministration, **P**arliament, **NASA** |
| **Political Parties** | the **D**emocratic party, a **R**epublican |
| **Teams** | the **S**eattle **S**eahawks, the **H**ouston **R**ockets, the **A**mes **L**ittle **L**eague |

## ➤ Specific Time Periods, Events, and Documents

**21 B.4**  Specific time periods, including the days and months of the year, holidays, special events, and historical events, periods, and documents, are capitalized.

## TIME PERIODS, EVENTS, AND DOCUMENTS

| | |
|---|---|
| **Days, Months** | **T**uesday (**T**ues.), **W**ednesday (**W**ed.), **F**ebruary (**F**eb.), **D**ecember (**D**ec.) (Do not capitalize the seasons of the year— such as summer and winter—unless they are part of a proper noun: Brooks Summer Fair.) |
| **Holidays** | **M**emorial **D**ay, **T**hanksgiving, **P**resident's **D**ay |
| **Special Events** | the **O**range **B**owl **P**arade, the **O**lympics, the **B**oston **M**arathon |
| **Historical Events** | the **T**rojan **W**ar, the **B**oston **T**ea **P**arty, the **L**ouisiana **P**urchase, **D**-**D**ay |
| **Time Periods** | the **M**iddle **A**ges, the **A**ge of **R**eason, the **G**reat **D**epression, **R**econstruction |
| **Time Abbreviations** | **B.C./B.C.E./A.D., AM/PM, CST** (**C**entral **S**tandard **T**ime) |
| **Documents** | the **T**ruman **D**octrine, the **T**reaty of **P**aris, the **F**irst **A**mendment, the **C**ivil **R**ights **A**ct |

Prepositions that are part of a proper noun are not usually capitalized.

# Names of Nationalities, Races, Languages, and Religions

**21 B.5** Names of nationalities, races, languages, and religions, including religious holidays and references, are capitalized.

| NATIONALITIES, RACES, LANGUAGES, AND RELIGIONS | |
| --- | --- |
| **Nationalities and Races** | Chinese, Mexican, Norwegian, Canadian, Irish, Dutch, Portuguese, Caucasian, Asian, African, Cherokee |
| **Languages and Computer Languages** | Spanish, Greek, Russian, Latin, Arabic, C++, Hyper Text Markup Language **(HTML)**, Cobol, Java |
| **Religions** | Roman Catholicism, Judaism, Lutheranism, Islam |
| **Religious Holidays and References** | Purim, Kwanzaa, Christmas, Ramadan, the Bible, the New Testament, the Torah, the Koran, Buddha, God<br>(Do not capitalize *god* when it refers to a polytheistic god.) |

## When You Write

You may have noticed that some writers capitalize the pronouns *he* and *him* when referring to God. Other writers do not capitalize these pronouns.

God told Pharaoh to let **H**is people go.

God told Pharaoh to let **h**is people go.

Also, religious writers sometimes capitalize *thy, thine,* and *thou* (archaic words for *your, yours*, and *you*) when they use pronouns in direct address to God. Whatever decision you make regarding capitalization of such pronouns, you should be consistent.

Check for consistent use of capitalization of pronouns in one of your recent compositions.

 **Other Proper Nouns**

**21 B.6** Other proper nouns should also begin with capital letters.

| OTHER PROPER NOUNS | |
|---|---|
| **Awards** | the **N**obel **P**rize, the **D**avis **C**up |
| **Brand Names** | a **T**rifect computer, **P**eaches soap (The product itself is not capitalized.) |
| **Structures, Memorials, Monuments** | **G**olden **G**ate **B**ridge, **E**iffel **T**ower, **V**ietnam **M**emorial, **W**ashington **M**onument, **M**ount **R**ushmore |
| **Ships, Trains, Aircraft, Spacecraft** | *SS Minnow, Orient Express, Spirit of St. Louis, Apollo 13, Challenger* |
| **Technological Terms** | **I**nternet, **W**eb, **W**orld **W**ide **W**eb, **W**eb site, **W**eb page, |
| **Names of Courses** | **C**hemistry II, **D**rafting I, **D**rawing 101 |

Unnumbered courses such as *history, science,* and *art* are not capitalized. Language courses such as *Spanish* and *English,* however, are always capitalized because the name of a language is always capitalized. Also, do not capitalize class names such as *freshman* or *senior* unless they are part of a proper noun: *Senior Class Picnic.*

● **Practice Your Skills**

*Capitalizing Proper Nouns*

Write the following items, using capital letters only where needed.

1. math and Spanish
2. the eiffel tower in paris
3. turkey on thanksgiving
4. dec.
5. the stone age
6. computer sciences corp.
7. the god zeus

8. computer book on java
9. harvard college
10. spring and summer
11. the supreme court
12. a jewish rabbi
13. web site on the internet
14. friday

● *Connect to Writing:* **Autobiography**

*Proper Nouns*

One's cultural heritage is important to most people. Writing about your own heritage can help you get more deeply in touch with it. Describe an aspect of your culture that has contributed to who you are. Use correct capitalization when writing names of particular people and places, time periods, and so on.

## ● Practice Your Skills

### Using Capital Letters

Correctly write each word that should begin with a capital letter.

**1.** Edith Wharton won a pulitzer prize for her fiction.

**2.** John Adams was a member of the federalist party.

**3.** Dolley Madison was voted a seat in the house of representatives on january 9, 1844.

**4.** When my sister graduated from purdue university, she got a job with a computer company.

**5.** Did you visit mount vernon, george washington's home?

**6.** Ty Cobb of the detroit tigers made 4,191 base hits during his career.

**7.** Last year, when I was a junior, I enjoyed french, creative writing, and art II.

**8.** J. R. Andrews was captain of the *derwent,* which sailed between sydney and london in the 1880s and 1890s.

**9.** Stephanie Louise Kwolek, a scientist, was inducted into the national inventors hall of fame on july 22, 1995.

**10.** Do you think any inventor will ever be as well known as Thomas alva Edison?

## ● *Connect to Writing:* Editing

### Capitalizing Proper Nouns

Rewrite the following sentences, capitalizing the proper nouns and using lowercase letters for words that are incorrectly capitalized.

**1.** A famous tourist attraction in italy is the Leaning Tower of pisa.

**2.** This Tower continues to lean each year.

**3.** The Cathedral of notre dame is a very famous Cathedral in Paris, france.

**4.** It is located on the île de la Cité, a small Island off the Seine river.

**5.** The phrase *Notre dame* means "our lady" in french.

### ✔ *Check Point:* **Mixed Practice**

Correctly write each word that should begin with a capital letter.

1. In an average year, santa fe, new mexico, receives 17 more inches of snow than fairbanks, alaska.

2. The first college for women, which opened in 1834, was wheaton college in norton, massachusetts.

3. andrew jackson fought in the revolutionary war when he was only thirteen years old.

4. the largest natural history museum in the world is the american museum of natural history.

5. The closest planet to the sun, mercury, is about one-third the size of earth.

6. John glenn's space capsule, *friendship 7*, was picked up by the recovery ship *noah*.

7. The people of philadelphia first celebrated the fourth of july a year after the declaration of independence had been adopted by the continental congress.

8. In 1888 in new york, george eastman invented a box camera that held rolled film.

9. The philadelphia eagles started playing in the national football league in 1933.

10. The last state to join the union before alaska and hawaii was arizona, which was admitted on valentine's day in 1912.

11. Charles Lindbergh flew the *spirit of st. louis* solo from the U.S. to Paris in May 1927.

12. Gold was discovered by accident at sutter's mill in California on January 24, 1848.

13. The statue of liberty was a gift from the french to celebrate the first centennial of independence in the U.S.

14. The *titanic* sank on April 14, 1912.

15. Toni Morrison won the 1993 nobel prize in literature for her six visionary and poetic novels.

# Proper Adjectives — Lesson 3

Because proper adjectives are formed from proper nouns, they should be capitalized in the same way that proper nouns are capitalized.

**21 C    Capitalize most proper adjectives.**

| PROPER NOUNS AND ADJECTIVES | |
| --- | --- |
| **Proper Nouns** | Spain, Idaho |
| **Proper Adjectives** | Spanish rice, Idaho potatoes |

When adjectives are formed from the words that refer to the compass directions, such as *east,* no capital letters are used.

> The wind was blowing from an **e**asterly direction.

Some proper adjectives derived from proper nouns are so familiar that they are no longer capitalized.

| COMMONPLACE PROPER ADJECTIVES | | |
| --- | --- | --- |
| china plates | pasteurized milk | quixotic vision |

When a proper adjective is part of a hyphenated adjective, capitalize only the part that is a proper adjective. Sometimes, however, both parts of a hyphenated adjective are proper adjectives.

| HYPHENATED PROPER ADJECTIVES | |
| --- | --- |
| all-American team | trans-Siberian journey |
| Indo-European languages | African-American literature |
| Nobel-Prize-winning scientist | |

### Capitalizing Proper Adjectives

Correctly write each word that should begin with a capital letter. If a sentence is correct, write C.

**1.** The olympic athletes first competed in Greece.

**2.** Also popular were the Isthmian Games, which were held near the Isthmus of Corinth.

**3.** Baseball is often called the all-american game.

**4.** Nemesio Guillot is said to have introduced cuban baseball in 1864.

**5.** Guillot taught his fellow Cubans to play the game after learning it from Americans in the U.S.

**6.** American soccer is equivalent to the latin-american game of football.

**7.** In 1959, Rong Guotuan won a gold medal in table tennis, becoming the first athlete in chinese history to be a world champion.

**8.** Some activities we enjoy today—swimming, equestrian sports, rowing— were also popular ancient egyptian sports.

**9.** Cricket, tennis, and kabaddi (a combination of wrestling and rugby) are popular indian athletic activities.

**10.** A relatively cold climate encourages canadian youngsters to play ice hockey.

● *Connect to Writing:* **Editing**

### Capitalizing Proper Nouns and Adjectives

Write each sentence, capitalizing the nouns and adjectives correctly. If a sentence is correct, write C.

**1.** A republican senator spoke at assembly today.

**2.** The friday afternoon traffic near my school is heavy.

**3.** "An Anglophile loves all things english," said my english teacher, Miss Gilbert.

**4.** Should I use roman numerals or arabic numerals?

**5.** I received a french dictionary for graduation.

**6.** Our class is going to hike in the appalachian mountains.

## Titles Lesson 4

Capital letters signal the importance of titles of persons and works of art.

**21 D**   Capitalize the titles of persons and works of art.

## ➤ Titles Used with Names of Persons

**21 D.1**   Capitalize a title showing office, rank, or profession when it comes before a person's name.

| | |
|---|---|
| **Before a Name** | Is **J**udge Abraham Goodell in his chambers this morning? |
| **Used Alone** | Who was the **j**udge at the recent grand larceny trial? |
| **Before a Name** | I worked on **S**enator Sheridan Ames's re-election campaign. |
| **Used Alone** | The **s**enator from our district is running for re-election. |

Do not capitalize the prefix *ex-* or the suffix *-elect* when either is connected to a title.

The patriotic parade honored **ex**-Senator Hillmann and Governor-**e**lect Baray.

## ➤ Titles Used Alone

**21 D.2**   Capitalize a title that is used alone when it is substituted for a person's name in direct address or when it is used as a name.

The titles for the current United States President and Vice President, for the Chief Justice, and for the Queen of England are almost always capitalized when they are being substituted for the person's name.

| | |
|---|---|
| **Used as a Name** | How is the patient in room 114 this evening, **D**octor? |
| **Not Used as a Name** | The **d**octor will speak to you before she leaves. |
| **High Government Official** | The **P**resident and the **V**ice **P**resident will attend the summit meeting next month. |
| | The **Q**ueen will be giving a speech this week. |

Remember that *president* and *vice president* are capitalized when they stand alone only if they refer to the *current* president and vice president.

Was John F. Kennedy the youngest **p**resident ever to hold office?

## ⇒ Titles Showing Family Relationships

**21 D.3**   Capitalize a title showing a family relationship when it comes before a person's name, when it is used as a name, or when it is substituted for a person's name.

| | |
|---|---|
| **Before a Name** | When did **U**ncle Ron and **A**unt Mary leave? |
| **Used as a Name** | Please tell **M**om that she has a visitor. |
| **Direct Address** | I'll help you paint the porch, **D**ad. |

Titles showing family relationships should not be capitalized when they are preceded by a possessive noun or pronoun—unless they are considered part of a person's name.

| | |
|---|---|
| **No Capital** | My **a**unt lives in California. Aaron is taking Phil's **s**ister to the prom. |
| **Capital** | When does your **U**ncle Ralph get home from work? (*Uncle* is considered part of Ralph's name.) |

## ⇒ Titles of Written Works and Other Works of Art

**21 D.4**   Capitalize the first word, the last word, and all important words that are used in the following titles: books, stories, poems, newspapers and newspaper articles, magazines and magazine articles, movies, plays, television series, musical songs and compositions, and works of art.

Short prepositions, coordinating conjunctions, and articles should not be capitalized unless they are the first or last words in a title.

## TITLES OF WORKS

| | |
|---|---|
| **Books and Parts of Books** | *Pride and Prejudice, Dictionary of Desktop Publishing,* Chapter 11, Vol. V, No. 4, Part IV |
| **Short Stories** | "The Train from Rhodesia" by Nadine Gordimer |
| **Poems** | "The Road Not Taken" by Robert Frost |
| **Newspapers and Newspaper Articles** | the *Chicago Tribune* (The word *the* before the title of a newspaper is usually not capitalized.), "New City Park Opens," "A Day in the Life of Our Mayor" |
| **Magazines and Magazine Articles** | *Discover Magazine, Newsweek,* "The Two Things Every High School Senior Should Know" |
| **Movies** | *Men in Black, Gone with the Wind* |
| **Plays** | *Hamlet, The Importance of Being Earnest* |
| **Television Series** | *Heroes, Dateline, Tom and Jerry* |
| **Musical Songs and Compositions** | "Amazing Grace," "The Star-Spangled Banner," "Violin Concerto in E Minor" |
| **Works of Art** | *Water Lilies* (painting by Claude Monet), *Sleeping Muse* (sculpture by Constantin Brancusi), *McPherson's Woods* (photograph by Matthew Brady) |

*You can learn about punctuating titles on pages 983–988.*

● **Practice Your Skills**

*Capitalizing Titles*

Correctly write each word that should begin with a capital letter. If an item is correct, write C.

**1.** justice ruth bader ginsburg

**2.** *I never saw another butterfly,* a play by Celeste Raspunti

**3.** my science professor

**4.** *uncle tom's cabin,* a novel by Harriet Beecher Stowe

**5.** my best friend's uncle sam

**6.** *the office,* a series on television

**7.** *the thinker,* a sculpture by Auguste Rodin

**8.** the albuquerque journal

**9.** "the forgotten city," a poem by William Carlos Williams

**10.** ex-speaker of the house of representatives

**11.** *tv guide*

**12.** "what a wonderful world," a song made popular by Louis Armstrong

## ✔ *Check Point:* Mixed Practice

Correctly write each word that should begin with a capital letter. Then answer each question, if you can!

**1.** was alan b. shepard, jr., or john glenn the first american to orbit the earth?

**2.** was it the pilgrims or the puritans who landed at plymouth rock in 1620?

**3.** which is the most westerly state in the u.s., Alaska or hawaii?

**4.** who is the author of *great expectations,* a novel written during queen victoria's reign in england?

**5.** in what country were the first olympic games held?

**6.** was william mckinley or theodore roosevelt the first president elected in the twentieth century?

**7.** what was the name of dorothy's dog in *the wizard of oz?*

**8.** is the geyser old faithful in wyoming or nevada?

**9.** "i want to hold your hand" was the first american number-one single of what british group?

**10.** did world war II end in 1942 or 1945?

**11.** is the cy young award given in baseball or football?

**12.** is sacramento or los angeles the capital of california?

**13.** general lee surrendered to general grant at the appomattox court house in what American state?

**14.** did clark kent work for the *metropolis journal* or the *daily planet?*

**15.** what was the russian equivalent of the u.s. central intelligence agency?

## ● *Connect to Writing:* Invitation

### *Using Correct Capitalization*

Write an invitation to your family explaining that your drama group is giving a performance of an original play. Give information about the play, including the title, the names of the authors, actors, and director, and a short plot synopsis. Ask the recipient of the invitation to let you know if they will be coming (seating is limited). Also, provide directions to your school. Include major highways, roads, and landmarks. When you finish, edit your invitation for mistakes in capitalization, and then write the final copy.

## Assess Your Learning

### Using Capital Letters Correctly

Correctly write each word that should begin with a capital letter.

**1.** dalia's address is 43 thirty-third street, kokomo, indiana.

**2.** school usually starts on the wednesday after labor day.

**3.** the mediterranean sea is one of the most polluted seas on earth.

**4.** mount desert island, off the coast of maine, was discovered in 1604 by champlain, a french explorer.

**5.** have you any tickets for the chicago white sox game on saturday?

**6.** when i was a junior, my favorite course was biology, but this year i like english best.

**7.** the oscar weighs 7 pounds and is 10 inches high.

**8.** minnesota is called the land of 10,000 lakes, but it actually contains more than 11,000 lakes.

**9.** there really was a molly pitcher, but her real name was mary hayes mccauley.

**10.** during the battle of monmouth, she carried water in a pitcher to thirsty american soldiers.

**11.** when my parents went to canada last summer, they visited the small nova scotian town where mother was born.

**12.** have you ever read elizabeth jennings' poem "in memory of anyone unknown to me"?

**13.** last month the vice president represented the president on a tour of the far east.

**14.** the *andrea doria* collided with a swedish ship off the coast of nantucket in 1956.

### ◼ Editing for the Correct Use of Capital Letters

Correctly write each word that should begin with a capital letter. Do not include words that are already capitalized.

How did the state of idaho get its name? Some believe it is a shoshoni indian word meaning "gem of the mountains." The idaho state historical society, though, insists that the state's name does not have any meaning. It was first coined by a mining lobbyist in 1860 as a good name for a new territory in the pikes peak mining country. However, just before congress voted in washington, d.c., the hoax was discovered. That territory was then named colorado. The word idaho, nevertheless, kept popping up in the pacific northwest. For example, a steamboat that carried prospectors up and down the columbia river was named the *idaho*. As a result, three years later the name was again suggested to congress, but this time it was accepted.

### ◼ Writing Sentences

At the library find a fact that pertains to each of the following topics. Each fact should include a proper noun, a proper adjective, or a title.

Write a sentence that includes . . .
1. a fact about a famous bridge.
2. a fact about a holiday.
3. a fact about a state capital.
4. a fact about an English poet.
5. a fact about basketball.

## Directions

Read the passage and decide which word or words should be capitalized in each underlined part. Write the letter of the correct answer. If the underlined part contains no error, write D.

The term **(1)** "morse code" refers to the method of communication using dots, dashes, and spaces to represent letters and numbers. **(2)** in electrical telegraphy, this code consists of short and long pulses; the code can be translated to short and long flashes of light, too. The **(3)** telegraph, invented in the u.s. in the 1830s by morse, uses electrical telegraphy. Similarly, **(4)** ships can use bright lights to flash messages across long distances when radio communications are down. Many people know the **(5)** code for the distress call, sos.

**1. A** Morse Code
   **B** Morse
   **C** Method, Communication
   **D** No error

**2. A** Electrical Telegraphy
   **B** In, Code
   **C** In
   **D** No error

**3. A** U.S., Morse
   **B** Telegraph, U.S.
   **C** Electrical Telegraphy
   **D** No error

**4. A** Ships
   **B** Long Distances
   **C** Bright Lights
   **D** No error

**5. A** SOS
   **B** Distress Call, SOS
   **C** Distress Call
   **D** No error

# Writer's Corner

## Snapshot

**21 A** Use capital letters at the beginning of a sentence or a line of poetry, in parts of a letter or an outline, and in the pronoun *I*. (pages 908–912)

**21 B** Capitalize proper nouns and their abbreviations. (pages 913–920)

**21 C** Capitalize most proper adjectives. (pages 921–922)

**21 D** Capitalize the titles of persons and works of art. (pages 923–926)

## Power Rules

 Be sure that every statement in your writing that **begins with a capital letter** is a complete sentence, not a sentence fragment.

| Before Editing | After Editing |
| --- | --- |
| *When I'm done with this project.* I'll go for a bike ride. | *When I'm done with this project,* I'll go for a bike ride. |
| *The photographer. My friend's aunt.* Offered to photograph our science project. | *The photographer, my friend's aunt,* offered to photograph our science project. |
| I built my own bookshelves. *Because I didn't have any money to spare.* | I built my own bookshelves *because I didn't have any money to spare.* |

 Check for **run-on sentences** and separate them by capitalizing the first word of the second sentence or making other appropriate changes, such as adding a conjunction and/or punctuation. (pages 736–738)

| Before Editing | After Editing |
| --- | --- |
| Mike picked out a place for lunch, Aramis found a trail to hike. | Mike picked out a place for lunch, *and* Aramis found a trail to hike. |
| We went to the concert, we got seats in the front row. | *When we went to the concert,* we got seats in the front row. |

## Editing Checklist

Use this checklist when editing your writing.

✓ Did I capitalize first words in each sentence and the pronoun *I?* (pages 908–912)
✓ Did I correctly capitalize proper nouns and their abbreviations? (pages 913–920)
✓ Did I capitalize proper adjectives? (pages 921–922)
✓ Did I correctly capitalize the titles of persons and works of art? (pages 923–926)
✓ Did I edit my work for mistakes in capitalization? (pages 906–931)
✓ Did I use capitalization to make my writing more precise? (pages 906–931)

## Use the Power

Capital letters draw attention to certain words and the beginnings of sentences. Use the graphics and rules below to help you understand how to use correct capitalization in your writing.

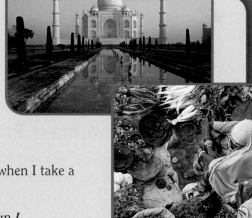

**Rule:** Capitalize the **first word** in every sentence.
Adventure is my main goal when I take a vacation.

**Rule:** Always capitalize the pronoun *I.*
When I have time and money, I'll travel overseas.

**Rule:** Capitalize **proper nouns.**
Someday, I'd like to see the Taj Majal in India.

**Rule:** Capitalize **proper adjectives.**
Maybe I could prepare for a trip by sampling some Indian food.

**Rule:** Capitalize most **titles.**
I just finished reading a fascinating travel book called *The Rough Guide to India.*

# CHAPTER 22

# End Marks and Commas

**How can you create meaning through the careful use of end marks and commas?**

## End Marks and Commas: Pretest 1

The following e-mail is about a new Web site. It is a first draft that contains several errors in the use of end marks and commas. The first two errors have been corrected. How would you revise the e-mail to correct the remaining errors?

Alex ^!^

Wow~You won't believe what I just found? You know how I'm supposed to be writing that report in science class: I found the perfect place to get all my information. It is this great dinosaur Web site that has dozens of links to dinosaur information. Reliable information. A few of the links are broken but most of them are up to date! You can look at photos of fossils bones and nests and then print them out? The Webmaster a "virtual geologist" will answer any questions you send in.

By the way aren't you and your family going camping somewhere this summer. You will want to follow the link to Dinosaur National Monument. This is a park on the border of Colorado and Utah where you can inspect dinosaur bones up close. Do you think your family would want to take me along. That of course would be great.

See you later,

Matt

# End Marks and Commas: Pretest

## Directions

Read the passage and choose the mark of punctuation that belongs in each underlined space. Write the letter of the correct answer.

Wow __(1)__ Look over there by the tree at that huge beetle. It must be a Hercules beetle __(2)__ Did you know that a Hercules beetle has a horn that grows up to four inches long __(3)__ My science teacher, Dr __(4)__ Carpenter, told us these facts. Only the male beetle, not the female __(5)__ has this horn. Look at this picture of the beetle on the Internet __(6)__ Scarab beetles, which include the Hercules beetle, are found worldwide __(7)__ Other members of the scarab family are June bugs, Japanese beetles, rhinoceros beetles __(8)__ and dung beetles. Don't these beetles usually have a brilliantly colored body __(9)__ The female Hercules beetle has a layer of red hairs __(10)__ and the Japanese beetle is a shiny green and brown.

**1. A** period
   **B** question mark
   **C** exclamation point
   **D** comma

**2. A** period
   **B** question mark
   **C** exclamation point
   **D** comma

**3. A** period
   **B** question mark
   **C** exclamation point
   **D** comma

**4. A** period
   **B** question mark
   **C** exclamation point
   **D** comma

**5. A** period
   **B** question mark
   **C** exclamation point
   **D** comma

**6. A** period
   **B** question mark
   **C** exclamation point
   **D** comma

**7. A** period
   **B** question mark
   **C** exclamation point
   **D** comma

**8. A** period
   **B** question mark
   **C** exclamation point
   **D** comma

**9. A** period
   **B** question mark
   **C** exclamation point
   **D** comma

**10. A** period
   **B** question mark
   **C** exclamation point
   **D** comma

A sentence has one of four different functions. It can make a statement, give a command, ask a question, or express strong feeling.

**22 A** Depending on its function, a sentence may be **declarative, imperative, interrogative,** or **exclamatory.**

The end mark you use with a particular sentence is determined by the function of that sentence. Most sentences make a statement or express an opinion.

**22 A.1** A **declarative sentence** makes a statement or expresses an opinion and ends with a period ( **.** ).

The following examples are both declarative sentences, even though the second example contains an indirect question.

Dinosaurs have fascinated people for many years.

I am not sure when dinosaurs lived.

(The direct question would be *When did dinosaurs live?*)

The second function of a sentence is to give directions, make requests, or give commands. Generally *you* is the understood subject of these sentences.

**22 A.2** An **imperative sentence** gives a direction, makes a request, or gives a command. It ends with a period or an exclamation point ( **.** or **!** ).

If a command is given in a normal tone of voice, it is followed by a period when written. If it expresses strong feeling, it is followed by an exclamation point.

Use this map to get to Dinosaur, Colorado.
(normal tone of voice)

Don't touch my video camera again!
(emotional tone of voice)

Occasionally an imperative sentence is stated as a question, but no reply is expected. Since the purpose of the sentence remains the same—to make a request—the sentence is followed by a period or by an exclamation point.

> Will you please hand me that book on dinosaur extinction.

The third function of a sentence is to ask a question—whether it is completely or incompletely expressed.

**22 A.3**    An interrogative sentence asks a question and ends with a question mark ( **?** ).

> Have you seen the dinosaur display**?**
>
> Where**?** Did I pass it**?**

## When You Read

Watch for interrogative sentences in advertising—both in print and on television. A company will draw you in by asking you a question. Most people feel obligated to answer a question, and so they pay attention to the ad. For example, a magazine page is covered with photos of individual potato chips, and at the top you read, "Can you tell which chip is the fat-free chip?" For a moment, you're tempted to try to answer the question—and the chip company wins your attention!

Look at a recent persuasive essay you have written. Try using an interrogative sentence to draw the reader in. Do you think this technique would help accomplish your goal?

The fourth function of a sentence is to express strong feeling, such as excitement or anger. Avoid overusing this type of sentence, for it can very quickly lose its impact.

**22 A.4**    An **exclamatory sentence** expresses strong feeling or emotion and ends with an exclamation point ( **!** ).

> I think I've found a fossil**!**

An interjection that expresses strong feeling or emotion, such as *Wow* or *Oh,* is followed by an exclamation point.

> Ouch**!** This cat has teeth like a tiger's.

*You can learn more about punctuation with interjections on page 643.*

Fiction writers are especially attentive to their use of end marks when they write dialogue. End marks help give the conversation dynamics—a sense of action—by conveying the speaker's emotions and attitudes quickly through punctuation. Consider the emotions related by the following lines:

**"Stop,"** he said.

**"Stop!"** he said.

Simply by looking at end marks, you can tell that the first speaker feels thoughtful and is in no particular hurry, while the second speaker feels a sense of urgent danger or excitement. Check your own writing to be sure you've used similar end marks effectively.

● **Practice Your Skills**

*Classifying Sentences*

Using the following abbreviations, label each sentence. (Since none of the sentences end with punctuation marks, you will need to label each sentence according to its meaning.)

declarative = *d.*      imperative = *imp.*

interrogative = *int.*      exclamatory = *ex.*

1. Paleontologists study life from the geological past
2. Do you know that fossilized footprints tell us about how dinosaurs moved
3. Will you look at this cast of a footprint
4. Wow, look at the size of it
5. Read the next chapter in your geology textbook
6. What caused the dinosaur extinction at the Cretaceous/Tertiary boundary
7. Everything from asteroids to volcanoes has been blamed
8. I wonder what it was like to watch dinosaurs roam
9. What an exciting time it must have been
10. Dinosaur bones have been discovered in Colorado

● *Connect to Writing:* **Editing**

*Punctuating Sentences*

Rewrite the sentences in the preceding exercise, adding the correct end punctuation.

 **Other Uses of Periods**

Periods have several uses in addition to ending a sentence.

## With Abbreviations

Using abbreviations is a good way to write faster when you are taking notes, but they should usually be avoided in formal writing, such as in essays and research papers.

**22 A.5**  Use a period after most abbreviations.

The following list contains some abbreviations that are acceptable in formal writing. Use the dictionary to check the spelling and punctuation of other abbreviations.

| ABBREVIATIONS | | | | | |
|---|---|---|---|---|---|
| **Titles with Names** | Mr. | Ms. | Mrs. | Rev. | Dr. |
| | Lt. | Col. | Prof. | Gov. | Sr. |
| **Initials for Names** | A. E. Housman | | | J. R. R. Tolkien | |
| | Samuel T. Coleridge | | | | |
| **Times with Numbers** | a.m. | p.m. | B.C. | B.C.E. | A.D. |
| **Addresses** | Ave. | St. | Blvd. | Rt. | Dept. |
| | Rd. | Dr. | Ct. | P.O. Box | |
| **Organizations and Companies** | Co. | Inc. | Corp. | Assoc. | |

Some organizations and companies are known by abbreviations that stand for their full names. The majority of these abbreviations do not use periods. A few other common abbreviations also do not include periods.

| ABBREVIATIONS WITHOUT PERIODS | |
|---|---|
| FBI = Federal Bureau of Investigation | km = kilometer |
| USAF = United States Air Force | mph = miles per hour |
| ISP = Internet Service Provider | |

● *Connect to Writing:* **Letter to the Editor**

*Using End Marks and Abbreviations*

Write a letter to the editor of your local paper detailing your opinion about an ongoing civic issue. Give reasons for your opinion, and back it up with facts. Be sure to address the editor formally and use appropriate end marks in your letter.

If a statement ends with an abbreviation, only one period is needed at the end of the sentence. If an interrogative or an exclamatory sentence ends with an abbreviation, both a period and a question mark, or a period and an exclamation point, are needed.

> The graduation ceremony begins at 7:00 p.m.
>
> Does the graduation ceremony begin at 7:00 p.m.?

Today, almost everyone uses the post office's two-letter state abbreviations that do not include periods. You can find a list of these state abbreviations at the front of most telephone books. The following list includes a few examples.

| STATE ABBREVIATIONS | | |
| --- | --- | --- |
| AK = Alaska | MD = Maryland | OR = Oregon |
| CA = California | MO = Missouri | TX = Texas |
| CO = Colorado | NJ = New Jersey | UT = Utah |
| HI = Hawaii | OK = Oklahoma | VT = Vermont |

## With Outlines

Periods are used in outlines to help mark each major and minor division.

**22 A.6**   Use a period after each number or letter that shows a division in an outline.

> I. Popular entertainment awards on television
>   A. MTV Music Awards
>     1. New Group
>     2. Female Solo Artist
>   B. Vision Fashion Awards
>     1. Fall Collection
>     2. Designer
> II. Film Industry Awards
>   A. Drama
>     1. Original Screenplay
>     2. Adapted Screenplay
>   B. Comedy

## Practice Your Skills

### Using Periods

Write each item, using abbreviations and periods. If you are unsure of the spelling or the punctuation of an abbreviation, look it up in the dictionary.

**1.** George Bush, Senior

**2.** New Jersey

**3.** Carlson Lumber Company

**4.** September

**5.** Captain Ahab

**6.** III Conclusion

**7.** Park Avenue

**8.** et cetera

**9.** a liter of milk

**10.** cash on delivery

## *Connect to Writing:* Editing

### Using Abbreviations and End Marks

Write each sentence, abbreviating the underlined items and using end marks correctly.

**1.** For the ribbon-cutting ceremony, we bought a 100-<u>foot</u> red ribbon

**2.** My friends and I were honored by <u>Governor</u> Richmond for cleaning up the old playground at 1300 Elm <u>Avenue</u>

**3.** At exactly 2:00 *post meridiem*, I will announce the contest winners

**4.** Kay will receive her <u>Bachelor of Arts</u> degree from the university in June

**5.** Have you applied for a summer intern position with the <u>Department</u> of Parks and Recreation in Boston, <u>Massachusetts</u>

## *Connect to Writing:* Outline of a Five-Year Plan

### Using End Marks

What do you want your life to be like five years from now? Write a statement that tells what you want to be doing at that time. Then make an outline of your five-year plan that shows how you intend to get there. In your outline, name the school or schools you hope to attend, the degrees you will pursue, the company you hope to work for, the job title you aspire to, and so on. Indicate how these will help you achieve your goal. Use abbreviations and proper end marks, and double-check your work for accuracy.

**22 B**    Commas have two basic purposes: to separate and to enclose items.

## Commas That Separate

If commas did not separate certain items from each other, all writing would be subject to constant misunderstanding. There is a difference, for example, between *pineapple juice and cheese* and *pineapple, juice, and cheese.* The following specific situations are places in which commas should be used to separate items.

## Items in a Series

A **series** is three or more similar items listed in consecutive order. Words, phrases, clauses, or short sentences that are written as a series are separated by commas.

**22 B.1**    Use commas to separate items in a series.

| | |
|---|---|
| **Words** | Dinner, movies, and parties are popular date ideas. (nouns) |
| | We joked, laughed, and talked all evening. (verbs) |
| **Phrases** | I searched for his phone number in my notebook, on my desk, in my book bag, and throughout my house. |
| **Subordinate Clauses** | We aren't sure who should drive, where we should go, or how late we should stay out. |
| **Short Sentences** | The curtain fell, a brief silence followed, and then we applauded loudly. |

When a conjunction connects the last two items in a series, a comma is optional. It is always best, however, to include the comma before the conjunction in order to eliminate any possible confusion or misunderstanding.

| | |
|---|---|
| **Confusing** | My boyfriend makes delicious pea, chicken, tomato and onion soups. (Does he make tomato soup or tomato and onion soup?) |
| **Clear** | My boyfriend makes delicious pea, chicken, tomato, and onion soups. (The last comma makes the meaning clear.) |

If conjunctions connect all the items in a series, no commas are needed unless they make the sentence clearer.

> This dance is fast **and** difficult **and** fun!

Some expressions, such as *needle and thread,* are thought of as a single item. If one of these pairs of words appears in a series, it should be considered one item.

> For our picnic we packed yogurt, fruit and cheese, and oatmeal cookies.
>
> Did you remember the chicken, bread, and ice cream and cake?

## Ordinal Numbers

**22 B.2**  Use commas after the words *first, second,* and similar words when they introduce items in a series.

> Josh's surprise party should include three key things: **first,** a live band; **second,** his favorite food; and **third,** all his close friends.

Notice that when the items in a series have internal commas, the items are separated by semicolons to avoid any confusion.

*You can learn more about semicolons on pages 974–979.*

## When You Write

You have probably noticed that newspaper headlines are usually very short—not even a sentence. When headline writers need to write longer headlines, they use commas to join ideas. This usage of commas is similar to using commas to join items in a series. With a headline, however, the "series" may be only two items long. This headline has a two-item "series" of short sentences:

Mayor Wins Budget, More Lies Ahead

This headline has a two item "series" of subjects:

Mayor, City Council Tussle Over Budget

Try writing several headlines about events happening at school. Use commas to join ideas.

# Adjectives Before a Noun

A conjunction sometimes connects two adjectives before a noun. When the conjunction is omitted, a comma is often used instead.

> A busy, enjoyable evening awaits us.

**22 B.3**  Use a comma sometimes to separate two adjectives that directly precede a noun and that are not joined by a conjunction.

There is a test you can use to decide whether a comma should be placed between two adjectives before a noun. Read the sentence inserting *and* between the adjectives. If the sentence sounds natural, a comma is needed.

| | |
|---|---|
| **Comma Needed** | I'll wear my old, comfortable boots to the dance. (*Old and comfortable* sounds natural. When a comma is needed, you can also reverse the adjectives: *comfortable and old*.) |
| **Comma Not Needed** | I'll wear my new black boots to the dance. (*New and black* does not sound natural, nor could you reverse the adjectives to read *black and new*.) |

Usually no comma is needed after a number or after an adjective that refers to size, shape, or age. For example, no commas are needed in the following expressions.

| ADJECTIVE EXPRESSIONS | |
|---|---|
| four square boxes | a large Mexican hat |

## *Connect to Writing:* Recipes

### *Commas That Separate*

Your class is selling a cookbook as a fund-raiser. Write the recipe for a dish you enjoy making—pizza with the works, maybe, or nine-layer dip. Follow the format of the recipe on the next page. Write a list of ingredients with any necessary adjectives. Follow the ingredients' list with the instructions. Edit your recipe for commas and end marks.

### Using Commas to Separate

Write each series or each pair of adjectives, adding a comma or commas where needed. If commas in a sentence are used correctly, write C.

**1.** Owen and Daisy ate a dinner of rice beef and cheese enchiladas and salad.

**2.** I wore a red white and blue shirt to Stan's Fourth of July picnic.

**3.** Before picking up Marcia, Danny washed and waxed the car and vacuumed the floor mats.

**4.** For our first date, we didn't know whether to see a movie go to the park or eat dinner.

**5.** The local dinner theater production of *An Ideal Husband* was a brilliant date idea.

**6.** Stacey's prom dress was made of red satin and tulle and lace.

**7.** Stacey and Eric shared a sleek white limousine with Clark and Tabitha.

**8.** "I have no idea where they went what they are doing or when they'll be back," said Stacey's younger sister Janelle.

**9.** Shawn and Kelly rode the horses down the hill around the lake and through the trees.

**10.** The food is planned, the date is set, and the invitations are in the mail.

● *Connect to Writing:* **Editing**

### Using Commas That Separate

Write the following recipe. Insert commas where needed.

**Crunchy Nutty Granola Cereal**

| | | |
|---|---|---|
| 14 oz. oats not instant | ½ cup raisins | 1 tsp. vanilla |
| ½ cup dark brown sugar | ¼ cup wheat germ | ½ cup honey |
| ½ cup cracked wheat | ⅓ cup peanuts chopped fine | 1 cup 7-grain cereal |
| ¼ cup bran oats or wheat | 1 stick (¼ lb.) butter | |

Combine oats brown sugar cracked wheat bran raisins wheat germ and peanuts. Set aside. Melt butter. Stir together the butter vanilla and honey. Pour over cereal mixture stir until well moistened and add the 7-grain cereal. Mix well. Then spread mixture on two cookie sheets. Bake at 325°, stirring frequently, until lightly browned, about 10–15 minutes.

# Compound Sentences

The independent clauses in a compound sentence can be combined in several ways. One way is to join them with a comma and one of the coordinating conjunctions—*and, but, or, nor, for, so,* or *yet.*

**22 B.4**   Use a comma to separate the independent clauses of a compound sentence if the clauses are joined by a coordinating conjunction.

My sister has caught two fish**,** **but** I haven't caught any.

Friday is Sandy's birthday**,** **and** I will give her a hermit crab.

She wants a horse**,** **yet** she's scared to ride one.

No comma is needed in a very short compound sentence—unless the conjunction *yet* or *for* separates the independent clauses.

**No Comma**   The car backfired **and** Buster barked.

**Comma**   Tiger hissed**,** **for** I'd startled her.

Do not confuse a sentence that has one subject and a compound verb with a compound sentence that has two sets of subjects and verbs. A comma is not placed between the parts of a compound verb when there is only one subject.

**Compound Sentence**   I feed the cows each evening**,** and John milks them each morning. (comma needed)

**Compound Verb**   I worked last night and couldn't feed the cows. (no comma needed)

*A semicolon, or a semicolon and a transitional word, can also be used between independent clauses that are not separated by a conjunction. You can learn more about punctuation with clauses on pages 721, 727.*

## ● Practice Your Skills

### *Using Commas with Compound Sentences*

Write *I* if commas are used incorrectly in a sentence. Write *C* if commas are used correctly.

1. Wild pigs will eat almost anything but they won't overeat.

2. Give the dog some water or he'll dehydrate.

3. The gestation period for an elephant is 21 months and the newborn weighs 90 kilograms.

4. A hippo spends most of its time in water yet grazes for grass on land at night.

5. The cheetah can reach a speed of up to 60 miles per hour, and maintain it for nearly half a mile.

6. The silkworm isn't a worm, but is actually a caterpillar.

7. Frogs breathe through their lungs as well as through their skins.

8. At first glance the desert may seem to lack life but it actually is alive with many plants and animals.

9. Cod can lay up to five million eggs at one time, but very few of the eggs hatch and mature.

10. The giant panda is a relative of the raccoon, but can weigh up to 300 pounds.

11. The horseshoe crab is a prehistoric creature, and it has blue blood.

12. Monarch caterpillars have a bitter taste from eating milkweed so birds spit them out.

13. Adult manatees can eat up to 108 pounds of vegetation daily for they are herbivores.

## ● *Connect to Writing:* Editing

### *Using Commas with Compounds*

Rewrite the Incorrect sentences from the preceding exercise, adding or deleting commas as needed.

# Introductory Structures

A comma is needed to separate certain introductory words, phrases, and clauses from the rest of the sentence.

**22 B.5**   Use a comma after certain introductory structures.

| | |
|---|---|
| **Words** | **Yes,** that is my calculator. (*No, now, oh, well,* and *why* are other introductory words that are set off by commas—unless they contribute to the meaning of a sentence: Yes *was her answer*.) |
| **Prepositional Phrase** | **Throughout the entire math class,** Jessie coughed and sneezed. (A comma comes after an introductory prepositional phrase of four or more words.) |
| **Participial Phrase** | **Hunting for my protractor,** I found a long-lost pair of gloves. |
| **Infinitive Phrase Used as an Adverb** | **To help Ellen,** I showed her how to find a cube root. (A comma does not follow an infinitive phrase that is used as the subject of a sentence: *To pass the math test was* my only concern.) |
| **Adverbial Clause** | **Before they left,** they figured out the amount for a 20 percent tip. |

Notice in the following examples that the punctuation of shorter phrases varies. Also, never place a comma after a phrase or phrases followed by a verb.

| | |
|---|---|
| **Other** | **In June 2010,** 320 students applied for math scholarships. (A comma follows a phrase that ends with a date or number.) |
| | **Up above,** the compass lay forgotten on the shelf. (A comma is used to avoid confusion.) |
| | **Across the board** was the longest equation I've ever seen. (No comma is used because the verb follows the introductory phrase.) |

## Practice Your Skills

### Using Commas with Introductory Structures

Write the introductory structures that should be followed by a comma.
If a sentence is correct, write C after the number.

**1.** Living in France in the early 1600s René Descartes applied algebraic concepts to geometry.

**2.** Nowadays we call Descartes' mathematical ideas Cartesian geometry.

**3.** From Euclid of Alexandria we get Euclidean geometry.

**4.** Called the leading mathematician of antiquity Euclid explained geometry concepts in *The Elements*.

**5.** To explain the parallel axiom Euclid said only one line can be drawn through a point parallel to a given line.

**6.** After leaving Samos around 532 B.C., the Greek Pythagoras lived in Italy.

**7.** A thousand years earlier the Babylonians had known about the theorem we call Pythagoras's theorem.

**8.** To prove the theorem was a challenge reserved for Pythagoras.

**9.** In 1750 Maria Gaëtana Agnesi held the chair of mathematics at the University of Bologna.

**10.** Noted for her work in differential calculus Agnesi was the first woman to occupy a chair of mathematics.

## *Connect to Writing:* Editing

### Using Commas with Introductory Structures

Write the following paragraph, inserting commas after introductory structures where needed.

**(1)** Consisting of a frame with beads on vertical wires the abacus is an ancient arithmetic calculator. **(2)** Used in China even today the abacus can be found in shops and classrooms. **(3)** To tally bills quickly a merchant can use an abacus. **(4)** To teach arithmetic to children a teacher can use an abacus to show, rather than tell, how addition and subtraction work. **(5)** Oh this handy instrument needs neither batteries nor solar power. **(6)** For more information you can search for tutorials on the Internet.

 **Commonly Used Commas**

Commas are used to separate the items in a date or an address, and they are also used in letters.

## With Dates and Addresses

**22 B.6**  Use commas to separate the elements in dates and addresses.

Notice in the following examples that a comma is also used to separate the last item in a date or the last item in an address from the rest of the sentence.

> On Monday, October 12, 1999, we founded the Community Music Network.
>
> Send your résumé to Ms. Faye Buscone, Meals on Wheels, 520 Johnson Street, Madison, Wisconsin 53703, before June 30.
>
> (No comma is placed between the state and the ZIP Code.)

If items in an address are joined by a preposition, no comma is needed to separate them.

> A homeless shelter has opened at 45 Jackson Boulevard in Tacoma, Washington.

No comma is needed when just the month and the year are given.

> Project Youth Horizons will reach its ten-year anniversary in July 2018.

## In Letters

Commas are used in the salutation of many letters and in the closing of all letters.

**22 B.7**  Use a comma after the salutation of a friendly letter and after the closing of all letters.

| SALUTATIONS AND CLOSINGS | | |
|---|---|---|
| **Salutations** | Dear David, | Dear Grandmother, |
| **Closings** | Sincerely yours, | Love, |

## When You Write

E-mail messages should follow the same rules of punctuation as other messages do. Since some people exchange e-mail messages with friends or coworkers much of the day, they tend to use very informal salutations and closings. A message might begin "David," or "Hi," instead of "Dear David," but it still uses the comma. Likewise, the closing may be "Later," instead of "Sincerely yours," but the comma is still used to mark the signing off.

Write an e-mail to a friend, following the standard rules of punctuation you would use in a letter.

Often the use of too many commas is as confusing as not using enough commas. Use commas only where a rule indicates they are needed. In other words, use commas only where they make the meaning of your writing clear.

## ● Practice Your Skills

### *Identifying Commonly Used Commas*

Write *a* or *b* to indicate the sentence that uses commas correctly.

**1. a.** You can write to me at the Columbia Children's Refuge, Box 1254, Columbia, Missouri, 65201, after September 1.

  **b.** You can write to me at the Columbia Children's Refuge, Box 1254, Columbia, Missouri 65201, after September 1.

**2. a.** Dear Professor Tucker, You are invited to attend the ninth annual International Food Fair on February 9 2011.

  **b.** Dear Professor Tucker, You are invited to attend the ninth annual International Food Fair on February 9, 2011.

**3. a.** In 1844 George Williams founded the first YMCA.

  **b.** In 1844, George Williams founded the first YMCA.

**4. a.** On March 30, 1937, Franklin Roosevelt established the Okefenokee Swamp as a national wildlife refuge.

  **b.** On March 30 1937, Franklin Roosevelt established the Okefenokee Swamp as a national wildlife refuge.

**5. a.** Write to Student Study Support (SSS), 843 Woodcove Avenue, Pittsburgh, Pennsylvania 15216 for free study guides.

  **b.** Write to Student Study Support (SSS), 843 Woodcove Avenue, Pittsburgh, Pennsylvania 15216, for free study guides.

## ● *Connect to Writing:* Editing

### Using Commas

Rewrite the following friendly letter, inserting commas where needed.

Dear Friends

   Thank you for your hard work on Saturday June 9. The cleanup for Oak Park 247 Oak Avenue was a success. I want to invite all of you to the first Park Play Day this Saturday June 16. A picnic will be held in Oak Park from noon to 5:00 p.m. Please RSVP. Write me at 203 W. 15th St. Durant OK 74701 by Wednesday.

   Best regards

   Tiffany

## ✔ *Check Point:* Mixed Practice

Write each sentence, adding a comma or commas where needed. If a sentence is correct, write *C*.

1. Among the inventions of Thomas Edison are the light switch an electric pen and the microphone.
2. The parking meter was invented in Oklahoma City by Carlton Magee.
3. To pay off a debt Walter Hunt invented the safety pin.
4. Margaret E. Knight patented an improved paper machine and invented a machine for cutting out shoes.
5. James Watt was not the inventor of the first steam engine but he did improve the steam engine in 1769.
6. After Humphrey O'Sullivan had walked all day on the hot hard pavements of Boston he invented the rubber heel.
7. Joseph Friedman invented the first flexible plastic straw.
8. Amanda Theodosia Jones invented the vacuum process of preserving food and tried to establish a factory that would use her process.
9. To improve methods of farming Englishman Thomas Coke invented a new method of crop rotation during the 1700s.

## ● *Connect to Reading, Speaking, and Listening:* Vocabulary

### Using Inflection to Understand Sentences

You use inflection to create meaning when you speak. In writing, you use commas and end marks. Read a few lines from a written text using no inflection. Have a partner reword these lines as a question, a statement, and an exclamation. You must indicate where commas are needed and what end mark should be used.

#  Commas That Enclose

Some sentences contain expressions that interrupt the flow. These expressions usually supply information that is not necessary for understanding the main idea of a sentence.

When an interrupting expression comes in the middle of a sentence, use two commas to set it off. If an interrupting expression comes at the beginning or at the end of a sentence, use only one comma.

## Direct Address

Any name, title, or other word that is used to address someone directly is set off by commas. These interrupting expressions are called nouns of **direct address.**

**22 B.8**    Use commas to set off nouns of direct address.

> **Kenneth,** what did you do with my new book?
>
> Hurry, **Mandy,** or we'll miss Anne Rice's autograph session.
>
> What is your favorite poem, **Maria?**

## Parenthetical Expressions

**22 B.9**    Use commas to set off parenthetical expressions.

> **By the way,** did you read Tony's new story?
>
> Your essay, **of course,** was beautifully written.
>
> We will proceed as planned, **nevertheless.**

Following is a list of common parenthetical expressions.

| COMMON PARENTHETICAL EXPRESSIONS | | | |
|---|---|---|---|
| after all | for instance | I know | moreover |
| at any rate | however | in fact | nevertheless |
| by the way | I believe | in my opinion | of course |
| consequently | I guess | on the contrary | therefore |
| for example | I hope | on the other hand | |

Commas are used to set off an expression *only* if it interrupts the flow of the sentence. If the words are an essential part of the sentence, do not use commas.

| | |
|---|---|
| **Comma** | **On the other hand,** we did enjoy the author's book exhibit. |
| **No Comma** | Wear that glove **on the other hand.** (*On the other hand* is necessary to the meaning of the sentence.) |
| **Commas** | I noticed, **however,** that the boy never paid for the book. |
| **No Commas** | Our book club will wait in line for **however** long it takes! (*However* is part of a phrase that is necessary to the meaning of the sentence.) |

Expressions other than those listed in the box on the previous page can also be parenthetical if they interrupt the flow of the sentence.

> Novels, **like movies,** can change your view of life.

Contrasting expressions, which often begin with *not, but, but not,* or *though not,* are also considered parenthetical expressions.

> Peggy, **not Angela,** will recite a poem at graduation.
>
> The actor, **though not well known,** will star in the play.

Occasionally an adverbial clause will also interrupt a sentence.

> His novel sales, **if they hit nine million today,** will set a national record.

Parenthetical expressions can also be used to join two independent clauses. When they do so, they are preceded by a semicolon and followed by a comma.

> I searched the library for hours; **nevertheless,** I could not find the information.
>
> I invited Professor Dinny to my reading; **after all,** she inspired me to write.

*To learn more about joining two independent clauses, see pages 944–945, 974 and 980. Parentheses and dashes are also used to set off parenthetical expressions. To learn more, see pages 1007–1008.*

# Appositives

An **appositive,** including its modifiers, identifies or explains a noun or a pronoun in a sentence.

**22 B.10**   Use commas to set off most appositives and their modifiers.

> Mr. James, **my English teacher,** attended Ohio State.
>
> I read Harper Lee's only novel, *To Kill a Mockingbird.*

An appositive is occasionally preceded by the word *or, particularly, notably,* or *especially.* Some appositives that are introduced by *such as* are also set off by commas.

> Many students, **especially freshmen,** have entered the story contest.
>
> Use visual aids, **such as photos of the author.**

An appositive is not set off by commas if it identifies a person or a thing by telling which one or ones. Often these appositives are names and have no modifiers.

> The verb *write* is an irregular verb. (Which verb?)
>
> My cousin **Lucy** is writing a screenplay. (Which cousin?)

When adjectives are in the appositive position, they are set off by commas.

> The limerick, **short and funny,** is Wanda's.

Titles and degrees following a name are usually set off by commas.

> Alicia Ray, **Ph.D.,** an author, is married to Frank Moore, **Sr.,** an editor.

The trend is not to set off titles such as *Jr., Sr.,* and *III* with commas. The individual's preference, if known, should be respected.

### ● *Connect to Writing:* Opinion Essay

#### *Using Commas that Enclose*

What animal do you think is the most beautiful in the world? Prepare an opinion essay for your classmates. Describe the animal and then explain your opinion. Be sure to use appositives correctly.

### Using Commas with Interrupters

Write the word or words in each sentence that should be enclosed in commas. If a sentence does not need any additional commas, write C.

1. William Carlos Williams M.D. was a noted poet.
2. Uriah Heep the villain in Charles Dickens's *David Copperfield* was the focus of my English composition.
3. The great playwright Lillian Hellman was born in 1905.
4. Lydia have you met Toni Morrison author of *Beloved?*
5. The poet Shel Silverstein died I believe in May 1999.
6. He wrote my favorite book *The Giving Tree* about nature.
7. *Apocalypse Now* Francis Ford Coppola's controversial film on the Vietnam War was based on Conrad's novel *Heart of Darkness*.
8. Epic poetry long and complex usually contains references to mythological gods, battles, and heroes.
9. I recommend poems by authors such as Edna St. Vincent Millay and Robert Frost.
10. Our book club selection for this month by the way is *Remains of the Day* by Kazuo Ishiguro.

## ● *Connect to Writing:* Editing

### Using Commas with Interrupters

Rewrite each sentence, using the interrupter in parentheses. Use commas where needed.

1. Edmund Spenser wrote *The Faerie Queene*. (not William Shakespeare)
2. Coleridge considered his friend the greatest poet since Milton. (Wordsworth)
3. John Locke is well-known for his essays. (like Jonathan Swift)
4. "A Modest Proposal" is Swift's best-known essay. (I believe)
5. Many readers didn't realize Swift was being satirical. (not literal)

# Nonessential Elements

Like other interrupters, some participial phrases and some clauses are not needed to make the meaning of a sentence clear or complete. Such phrases and clauses are **nonessential** or **nonrestrictive.**

**22 B.11**  Use commas to set off a **nonessential** or **nonrestrictive** participial phrase or clause.

To decide whether a phrase or a clause is or is not essential, read the sentence without it. If the phrase or the clause could be removed without changing the basic meaning of the sentence, it is nonessential. A phrase or a clause that modifies a proper noun is almost always nonessential.

| | |
|---|---|
| **Nonessential Participial Phrase** | Birds' nests, **made from grass and twigs,** were visible in the trees. (*Birds' nests were visible in the trees.*) |
| **Nonessential Adjectival Clause** | A dog, **which is my favorite kind of pet,** is more loyal than a cat. (*A dog is more loyal than a cat.*) |

A clause or phrase is **essential** or **restrictive** if it identifies a person or thing by answering the question *Which one?* If the phrase or the clause were removed, the meaning of the sentence would be unclear or incomplete. An adjectival clause that begins with *that* is usually essential.

**22 B.12**  No commas are used if a participial phrase or a clause is **nonrestrictive (essential)** to the meaning of a sentence.

| | |
|---|---|
| **Essential Participial Phrase** | The horse **named Prince** should be removed from the show. (*The horse should be removed from the show.* The phrase is needed to identify which of many horses should be removed.) |
| **Essential Adjectival Clause** | The parakeets **that you wanted** were already sold. (*The parakeets were already sold.* The clause is needed to identify which parakeets were already sold.) |

● **Practice Your Skills**

*Using Commas with Nonessential Elements*

Find each interrupter and state whether it is *essential (E)* or *nonessential (N)*. (Note that the commas that should enclose nonessential elements are not present.)

**1.** The lizard called the gecko can grow a new tail.

**2.** The carrier pigeon which was a common message carrier is now extinct.

**3.** Ralph Winters fishing in Beaver Brook caught a trout.

**4.** Scientists who classify insects are called entomologists.

**5.** We watched the geese flying south.

**6.** A tarantula's bite which is not usually fatal still causes a great deal of pain.

**7.** The ostrich which is the largest of all birds can outrun a horse.

## ● *Connect to Writing:* Editing

### *Using Commas with Nonessential Elements*

Write each sentence in the preceding exercise that has a nonessential element, adding a comma or commas where needed.

## ● *Connect to Writing:* Revising

### *Adding Phrases to Sentences*

Rewrite each sentence twice. First, add a nonessential phrase or clause to the sentence. Second, add an essential phrase or clause. Use commas where needed.

**1.** The dog is next door.

**2.** The mouse is trapped.

**3.** The giraffes are majestic.

**4.** My pet snake got loose.

## ✔ *Check Point:* Mixed Practice

Write the following paragraphs, adding commas where needed. (You will add 21 commas in all.)

Elizabeth Blackwell was the first woman to earn a medical degree but she had to travel a long hard road to get that degree. Even though 29 medical schools had refused to admit her she persisted. After three years of private study Blackwell was finally accepted to the Medical Institute of Geneva New York. The director doubtful and concerned passed her application on to the students for their approval. Thinking it was a joke everyone agreed to admit her. When Blackwell arrived however she was greeted with shock and anger. She was ridiculed ignored refused lodging and barred from some classroom activities.

Graduating at the head of her class on January 23 1849 Blackwell continued her studies in London and Paris. She finally returned to New York City and there she opened a hospital in 1853. Called the New York Infirmary for Women and Children it was staffed by women. With the help of Emily her younger sister Blackwell added a medical college for women to the site in 1868.

As a pioneer in medicine Blackwell opened the door for women in the medical field. She required that female students work harder than male students to establish themselves in the medical community. Because of her courage many women comfortably practice medicine today.

## Assess Your Learning

### Using Commas Correctly

Write each sentence, adding a comma or commas where needed. If a sentence needs no commas, write **C**.

**1.** Among the heroes of the American Revolution was a gallant young Frenchman who risked his life and fortune.

**2.** Lafayette was born in Chavaniac France on September 6 1757.

**3.** Although at the age of nineteen he was both a French army captain and a popular nobleman he was not satisfied with life.

**4.** When the American colonies declared their independence from England France's ancient foe Lafayette sailed for America.

**5.** He offered his enthusiastic heartfelt services to Congress which rewarded him with the rank of major general.

**6.** Lafayette served under Washington who became his friend.

**7.** Lafayette who proved to be a good officer was slightly wounded in 1777 in his first battle the Battle of Brandywine.

**8.** His great achievement for the colonies was a treaty of alliance that he persuaded the French government to sign in 1778.

**9.** When he returned to France after the surrender of Cornwallis at Yorktown he joined the French Revolution.

**10.** He served as commander-in-chief of the National Guard which was organized to safeguard the revolution.

### Kinds of Sentences and End Marks

Write each sentence and its appropriate end mark. Then label each one *D* for declarative, *IM* for imperative, *IN* for interrogative, or *E* for exclamatory.

**1.** Scientists estimate that about 100 acres of the remaining tropical rain forests are being cleared every minute

**2.** How big is an acre

**3.** In your mind, picture a football field minus the end zones

**4.** Now picture 100 of these football fields

**5.** That's how much of the remaining rain forests is being destroyed every single minute

6. Tropical rain forests are found in only seven percent of the world, but they play a vital part in sustaining many life forms

7. Why are rain forests so important

8. The trees provide huge amounts of the earth's oxygen, and the forests are great sources for many needed medicines

9. Of course, the rain forests are also the homes of many endangered species of animals and insects

10. Find out what you can do to stop the destruction of these vital rain forests

## Writing Sentences

Write five sentences that follow the directions below. Write about one of the following topics or a topic of your choice: an interesting person from history or an environmental issue such as the rain forests.

Write a sentence that …

1. includes a series of nouns.
2. includes two adjectives before a noun.
3. includes an introductory participial phrase.
4. includes an introductory adverbial phrase.
5. includes an appositive.

# End Marks and Commas: Posttest

## Directions

Read the passage and write the letter of the answer that correctly punctuates each underlined part. If the underlined part contains no error, write D.

Many **(1)** <u>people including teenagers are</u> unaware of the amount of sugar they consume. Foods like candy, soda, and maple syrup may contain more sugar than you think. **(2)** <u>For example suppose</u> you drink a twelve-ounce can of **(3)** <u>soda</u> You have drunk the equivalent of ten teaspoons of sugar. Are you **(4)** <u>surprised</u> If you are not surprised by that **(5)** <u>fact perhaps</u> this one will surprise you. Foods such as **(6)** <u>muffins, salad dressings,</u> **(7)** <u>yogurt and cheese spread</u> may have added sugar. **(8)** <u>Wow</u> Who would have guessed **(9)** <u>this</u> Nutritionists suggest a simple response to sugar. If you are in good health, eat it in **(10)** <u>moderation</u> If you are overweight, eat sugar sparingly.

**1. A** people, including teenagers, are
    **B** people including teenagers, are
    **C** people, including teenagers are
    **D** No error

**2. A** For example suppose,
    **B** For example! suppose
    **C** For example, suppose
    **D** No error

**3. A** soda,
    **B** soda.
    **C** soda?
    **D** No error

**4. A** surprised!
    **B** surprised?
    **C** surprised.
    **D** No error

**5. A** fact, perhaps
    **B** fact, perhaps,
    **C** fact. perhaps
    **D** No error

**6. A** muffins, salad dressings
    **B** muffins salad, dressings
    **C** muffins salad dressings
    **D** No error

**7. A** yogurt and cheese, spread
    **B** yogurt, and cheese spread
    **C** yogurt and cheese spread,
    **D** No error

**8. A** Wow,
    **B** Wow!
    **C** Wow.
    **D** No error

**9. A** this?
    **B** this,
    **C** this.
    **D** No error

**10. A** moderation!
    **B** moderation?
    **C** moderation.
    **D** No error

# Writer's Corner

## Snapshot

**22 A** Depending on its function, a sentence may be **declarative, imperative, interrogative,** or **exclamatory.** The function determines the punctuation mark. (pages 934–939)

**22 B** **Commas** have two basic purposes: to **separate** and to **enclose** items. (pages 940–956)

## Power Rules

 Be sure that every statement in your writing is a **complete sentence, not a fragment.** You can fix a fragment by adding a conjunction and/or a comma to join it to an independent clause. (pages 661–663)

### Before Editing

*If I can earn extra money.* I'll buy new running shoes.

Our neighbor. *A marathon runner.* Offered to help me train for the race.

### After Editing

*If I can earn extra money,* I'll buy new running shoes.

Our neighbor, *a marathon runner,* offered to help me train for the race.

 Check for **run-on sentences** and fix them by adding a conjunction and/or a comma or by separating the sentences into two complete sentences with the proper end marks. (pages 736–738)

### Before Editing

Tony handed out fliers, Sandra invited people to sign the petition.

They worked hard to get Leslie elected class president, she was really grateful.

### After Editing

Tony handed out fliers, *and* Sandra invited people to sign the petition.

They worked hard to get Leslie elected class president. *She was very grateful.*

# Editing Checklist

Use this checklist when editing your writing.

✓ Did I use a period to end sentences that made a statement or expressed an opinion? (See page 934.)

✓ Did I use a period or exclamation point to end sentences that gave a direction or command or made a request? (See pages 934–935.)

✓ Did I use a question mark to end sentences that asked a question? (See page 935.)

✓ Did I use an exclamation point to end sentences that expressed strong feelings? (See page 935.)

✓ Did I use commas to separate items in my writing? (See pages 940–947.)

✓ Did I use commas where they were needed to make my writing clear? (See pages 940–956.)

✓ Did I use commas to enclose expressions that interrupted the flow of the sentence? (See pages 951–956.)

# Use the Power

Use the sentences below to help you remember which end marks to use. The function of each sentence tells you what type of end mark to use.

**Declarative:** This is a good beach for surfing.

**Interrogative:** Will you help me learn how to stand up on the board?

**Exclamatory:** That was a huge wave!

**Imperative:** Once you stand up, don't look back.

# Other Punctuation

**How can you use apostrophes, semicolons, colons, hyphens, and other punctuation to communicate precisely and to enhance your writing style?**

## Other Punctuation: Pretest 1

The following first draft contains several punctuation errors. The first error has been corrected. How would you revise the draft to correct the remaining errors?

Being abandoned by a friend is no fun. For this article, I recently asked junior James Webb if a friend had ever deserted him. "Yes and it really hurt," said James. "We'd been friends' for a long time—and I never expected something like this to happen". I asked James for a few details. He explained that his buddy really changed after he made final cuts on the varsity football team. His friend started hanging out with a different crowd; mostly athletes. "He canceled a backpacking trip we'd been planning for months, said James. Just said he was busy." James story is not unusual... About one third of the people I asked had stories about a friends disloyalty. Maybe thats' why theres a book about it; "How to Survive the Loss of a Friend." I thought it was ten dollar's worth of good information.

## Other Punctuation: Pretest

### Directions

Each underlined part in the passage lacks one type of punctuation. Write the letter of the answer with the punctuation that correctly completes the underlined part.

(1) Variety and <u>creativity these</u> are the elements that make a vegetarian diet appealing. Many (2) <u>people and I include myself</u> think a dinner of only vegetables would be boring. Go to a Japanese or Thai restaurant and notice this (3) <u>restaurants use</u> of flavorings in vegetable dishes. You might taste the (4) <u>following spices garlic, cayenne pepper, and ginger.</u> (5) <u>Youll get plenty of ideas</u> for your own vegetarian cuisine.

1. **A** Dash
   **B** Apostrophe
   **C** Hyphen
   **D** Brackets

2. **A** Apostrophe
   **B** Parentheses
   **C** Italics
   **D** Semicolon

3. **A** Colon
   **B** Semicolon
   **C** Dash
   **D** Apostrophe

4. **A** Colon
   **B** Italics
   **C** Parentheses
   **D** Quotation marks

5. **A** Brackets
   **B** Italics
   **C** Apostrophe
   **D** Hyphen

Although end marks and commas are the punctuation marks most commonly used, all marks of punctuation are important. Failure to use apostrophes to show possession or to form contractions, for example, will confuse readers.

**23 A** The **apostrophe ( ' )** is used to show possession and in contractions.

## ➤ Apostrophes to Show Possession

By using apostrophes, you can indicate that nouns and some pronouns show possession.

### Possessive Forms of Nouns

The possessive of a singular noun is usually formed differently than the possessive of a plural noun.

**23 A.1** Add **'s** to form the possessive of a singular noun.

To form the possessive of a singular noun, write the noun without adding or omitting any letters. Then add *'s* at the end.

> friend + **'s** = friend**'s**        This is my friend**'s** cabin.
>
> business + **'s** = business**'s**    The business**'s** walls need paint.

Singular compound nouns and the names of most businesses and organizations form their possessives in the way other singular nouns do.

> Her mother-in-law**'s** lakeside barbecue is tomorrow.
>
> The Uptown Meat Market**'s** ribs are the best!

To form the possessive of a plural noun, look at the ending of the plural noun. The ending determines the way you form the possessive. If the noun ends in *s*, add an apostrophe.

**23 A.2** Add only an apostrophe to form the possessive of a plural noun that ends in *s*.

> girls + **'** = girls**'**        The girls**'** rowing team has won!
>
> Nelsons + **'** = Nelsons**'**    The Nelsons**'** raft seats two.

**23 A.3**   Add **'s** to form the possessive of a plural noun that does not end in *s*.

If a plural noun does not end in *s*, add *'s* to form the possessive—just as you would to a singular noun.

> men + **'s** = men**'s**        Where are the men**'s** hiking boots?
>
> cacti + **'s** = cacti**'s**        The cacti**'s** blossoms are pink.

Do not confuse a plural possessive with the simple plural form of a noun.

> **Possessive**    Marty is the **twins'** rowing coach.
>
> **Plural**    Marty coaches the **twins.**

## ● Practice Your Skills

### *Forming Possessive Nouns*

Write the possessive form of each noun.

| | | |
|---|---|---|
| **1.** mother | **6.** oxen | **11.** beaches |
| **2.** sister-in-law | **7.** women | **12.** officers |
| **3.** Karen | **8.** city | **13.** birch |
| **4.** Palmers | **9.** geese | **14.** children |
| **5.** editor-in-chief | **10.** world | **15.** babies |

## ● Practice Your Skills

### Using Possessive Nouns

Write the correct possessive noun in parentheses.

**1.** The two (boys', boy's) canoe was bright orange.

**2.** (Terrys', Terry's) backpack is waterproof.

**3.** The primitive campsite is at (Papa Bear's Campground, Papa Bear Campground's).

**4.** Do you want my life jacket or (Suzys', Suzy's)?

**5.** This life (jackets', jacket's) strap is broken.

**6.** All the life (jackets', jacket's) straps are broken.

**7.** Why don't we rent new life jackets from those (women's, womens') supply booth?

**8.** Look! I see the (McKlintocks', McKlintock's) camper!

**9.** Later I want to visit the (horse's, horses') stables.

**10.** Your (brother's-in-law, brother-in-law's) trail map is too old to be useful.

## ● *Connect to Writing:* Editing

### Using Apostrophes

Correctly write each word that needs an apostrophe or an apostrophe and an *s*.

**1.** A hunter jacket is usually made of camouflage fabric.

**2.** Who has November hunting itinerary?

**3.** The tent metal poles are in good condition.

**4.** The poles construction is of aluminum.

**5.** How long will your father-in-law hunting trip last?

**6.** We appreciated the other men offer of firewood.

**7.** Charlies Market on Highway 52 will buy our venison.

**8.** Is that bag of corn Paul?

**9.** He brought it for the deer feeding trough.

**10.** Mr. Wong four-wheel-drive vehicle saved us from being stuck in that mud hole.

# Possessive Forms of Pronouns

Personal pronouns and the pronoun *who* show possession by changing form, not by adding an apostrophe.

> **23 A.4** The possessive forms of personal pronouns and the pronoun *who* do not use apostrophes.

This is **his** yearbook, but **whose** is that?

None of the following possessive personal pronouns include apostrophes.

| POSSESSIVE PERSONAL PRONOUNS | | | |
|---|---|---|---|
| my, mine | his | its | their, theirs |
| your, yours | her, hers | our, ours | |

Do not confuse a contraction with a possessive personal pronoun. A possessive personal pronoun does not include an apostrophe, but a contraction does. *Its, your, their,* and *theirs* are possessive personal pronouns. *It's, you're, they're,* and *there's* are contractions.

*You can learn more about possessive pronouns on pages 801–804.*

An indefinite pronoun forms its possessive in the same way a singular noun does—by adding *'s*.

No one**'s** yearbook is signed yet.

Did you ask for anyone**'s** signature?

*You can find a list of common indefinite pronouns on page 623.*

## When You Write

Writers often use mnemonic phrases to help them remember the spelling of difficult words. The following sentence, for example, might help someone remember the spelling of the possessive pronoun *theirs:* "The *heirs* in *theirs* did not inherit an apostrophe."

Think up your own mnemonic device to help you remember a word or words that you have difficulty spelling. Share your idea with your classmates.

## ● Practice Your Skills

### *Using Possessive Pronouns*

Write the correct form of each possessive pronoun in parentheses.

**1.** (You're, Your) research papers are due on Friday.

**2.** (Everyone's, Every ones') speech should be given by Tuesday.

**3.** I think this ruler is missing (it's, its) markings.

**4.** (Who's, Whose) is this sketch?

**5.** (There's, Theirs) is the classroom with the purple walls.

**6.** This new globe is (hers, her's).

**7.** (Your's, Yours) arrived first thing this morning.

**8.** (Someone's, Someones') jacket was left in the bleachers.

**9.** (Their, They're) report cards should be put over there.

**10.** (Her, Her's) photograph won a prize.

## ● *Connect to Writing:* Editing

### *Using Possessive Pronouns*

Rewrite any incorrectly written possessive pronouns. If all of the pronouns in a sentence are written correctly, write *C*.

**1.** The responsibility for sales of the yearbook is our's.

**2.** Soliciting advertising, however, is you're responsibility.

**3.** Theirs is a difficult job.

**4.** They must judge hundreds of amateur photos on each ones' merits.

**5.** That colorful photo of Mark spiking a volleyball is mine.

**6.** Who will design the cover is anybodies' guess.

**7.** The cover design I like best is your's.

**8.** All of the yearbook members can design there own page of highlights.

**9.** Some bodys' page design will win a prize of $100.

**10.** We want this year's book to have its own unique look.

# Apostrophes to Show Joint or Separate Ownership

In written work apostrophes can signal either joint or separate ownership. One apostrophe is used to show joint ownership. Two or more apostrophes are used to show separate ownership.

**23 A.5**    Add **'s** to only the last word to show joint ownership. Add **'s** to each word to show separate ownership.

In the following example, the audiobook belongs to Paul and Craig. Since both people own the audiobook, an apostrophe is added to the second name only.

> Paul and Craig**'s** audiobook has been returned.

If one of the words in a phrase showing joint ownership is a possessive pronoun, the noun must also show possession.

> Paul**'s** and **his** audiobook has been returned.

In the following example, Paul and Craig own separate audiobooks; therefore, an apostrophe is added to each name.

> Paul**'s** and Craig**'s** audiobooks have been returned.

# Apostrophes with Nouns Expressing Times or Amounts

When you use a noun that expresses time or amount as an adjective, write it in the possessive form.

**23 A.6**    Use an apostrophe with the possessive form of a noun that expresses time or amount.

> She lost a week**'s** time by reading the wrong book.
> I spent nine dollar**s'** worth of quarters on the new book.

Other words that express time include *minute, hour, day, month,* and *year.*

# Practice Your Skills

## Using Apostrophes Correctly

Write the correct possessive form of the noun or pronoun in parentheses.

**1.** My grandparents always read ___ fairy tales to me. (the Grimm brothers and Andersen)

**2.** *Middlemarch* by George Eliot might be several ___ worth of reading. (month)

**3.** There is an interesting article about *Treasure Island* in ___ paper. (Sunday)

**4.** *Jude the Obscure* is one of ___ favorite novels. (LuAnn and her)

**5.** One of that ___ bestsellers is *A Night Without Armor* by Jewel. (year)

# *Connect to Writing:* Editing

## Using Possessive Nouns and Pronouns

Rewrite any incorrectly written possessive noun or pronoun. If all possessive forms in a sentence are written correctly, write C.

**1.** This weeks assignment is to write a poem.

**2.** Brandy and Kristen's poems will both serve as examples.

**3.** Kristen's and her works have been published frequently.

**4.** The first-place winner and the second-place winner's poems will be considered for publication.

**5.** The newspaper editor and English teacher's decisions are final.

**6.** She will have several hour's worth of reading to do.

**7.** Stan's and mine poems are both candidates for prizes.

**8.** Give me a days time to prepare my acceptance speech.

**9.** Becca or Nancy's poem will probably win third place.

**10.** Becca's and Nancy's poems are too somber for my taste.

# *Connect to Writing:* Legal Document

## Apostrophes

One of your best friends has asked you to share an apartment after high school graduation. You agree with your friend to write a statement of ownership regarding furniture, dishes, sound equipment, and so on. What will belong to you jointly, and what will you possess individually? What will be your rights in using one another's personal possessions and food? Write a fair statement of ownership, using apostrophes to show possession. Edit for mistakes in punctuation and then write the final copy.

Correctly write each word that should be in possessive form.

**1.** Alfred applied for the cashier position at the corner gas station.

**2.** The manager and assistant manager impressions of him were favorable.

**3.** He begins his shift by breaking open two dollars worth of nickels, fifty cents worth of pennies, and other rolled coins.

**4.** His job also includes keeping the women and men restrooms stocked with paper towels and soap.

**5.** The employees uniform is a lime-green smock.

**6.** Everyone distaste for the color is apparent.

**7.** Alfred and Paul decision to ask for new uniforms was applauded by the staff.

# ➤ Other Uses of Apostrophes

In addition to showing possession, apostrophes have several other uses.

## Apostrophes with Contractions

**23 A.7**    Use an apostrophe in a contraction to show where one or more letters have been omitted.

| CONTRACTIONS | | |
|---|---|---|
| are not = aren't | that is = that's | I will = I'll |
| we have = we've | let us = let's | of the clock = o'clock |

The only contraction in which any letters are changed or added is the contraction for *will not,* which is *won't.*

● **Practice Your Skills**

*Writing Contractions*

Write the contraction for each pair of words.

**1.** do not        **6.** who is        **11.** were not

**2.** I have        **7.** they are        **12.** it is

**3.** did not        **8.** will not        **13.** you are

**4.** let us        **9.** I am        **14.** has not

**5.** we will        **10.** is not        **15.** I would

● *Connect to Writing:* **Editing**

### Using Contractions

Write the words in each sentence that may be replaced with a contraction. Then write the contraction. Some sentences contain more than one possible contraction.

**1.** I cannot see the racetrack from here.

**2.** They are about to start the race.

**3.** We will move to better seats.

**4.** The race will begin at three of the clock sharp.

**5.** There will be a chance to meet the winners afterward.

**6.** They will accept their trophies and then mingle with the crowd.

**7.** I will be sure to get my picture taken next to the champion horse.

**8.** I have always wanted a horse of my own, but I am not sure I would know how to ride in a race.

**9.** Let us talk later about how we will buy a horse together and who is going to build the stable in his backyard!

**10.** I have not had this much fun in weeks, and I will not miss a minute of this race!

## Apostrophes with Certain Plurals

To prevent confusion, certain items form their plurals by adding *'s.*

**23 A.8**    Add **'s** to form the plural of lowercase letters, some capital letters, and some words used as words.

Are these letters *s***'s** or *e***'s?**

Should *O***'s** be round or oval?

Your *A***'s** look very sloppy.

The plurals of most other letters, symbols, numerals, and words used as words can be formed by adding an *s.*

The Beatles led the British invasion in the 1960**s.**

Entrepreneurs see $**s** when they recognize a popular fad.

Your paper contains too many *if***s.**

# Apostrophes with Certain Dates

An apostrophe is also used when numbers are dropped from a date.

**23 A.9**  Use an apostrophe to show that numbers are omitted in a date.

> We bought this personal computer in '09. (2009)
>
> Our old PC was manufactured in '02. (2002)

## ● Practice Your Skills

### *Using Apostrophes*

Write each underlined item in its plural form, and shorten all dates to a two-digit form (such as '05).

**1.** The binary numbering system used by computers consists of _0_ and _1_.

**2.** When I write quick e-mails, I use _&_ for _and_.

**3.** How many _@_ are in an e-mail address?

**4.** I've had my e-mail account since the late _1990_.

**5.** In 2008, I changed my ISP.

## ✔ *Check Point:* Mixed Practice

Rewrite each incorrectly written letter or word. If a sentence is correct, write C.

**1.** A student's life is very busy.

**2.** Diego's composition was well written, was'nt it?

**3.** The freshmen and seniors lockers were just painted.

**4.** The Queen of Englands coronation picture is hanging in my homeroom.

**5.** Teenager's interests in most areas have changed over the past fifty years.

**6.** There's their neighbor, waiting at the bus stop.

## ● *Connect to Writing:* E-mail

### *Apostrophes*

You purchased a "refurbished" laptop computer, and many of the keyboard keys are faulty. Some type the wrong letter, and others do not work at all. Write an e-mail to the technical support division of Global PCs. Describe the keys that are not working correctly, and give the date you purchased the computer. Use plurals of all letters, symbols, and words used as words.

By using the **semicolon** and the **colon,** you can create sentence variety and clarity in your writing.

## Semicolons

**23 B**   A **semicolon (;)** is used between the clauses of a compound sentence when they are not joined by a conjunction. A **colon (:)** is used to introduce lists and long quotations and to separate certain independent clauses.

Two independent clauses not properly joined result in a **run-on sentence.** A run-on sentence can be corrected in several ways. One way to correct a run-on sentence is to join the clauses with a coordinating conjunction and a comma.

> **Run-On**     The goldfish is my pet the cat is my mom's.
>
> **Corrected**     The goldfish is my pet, **and** the cat is my mom's.

The clauses in a compound sentence can be joined by a semicolon when there is no conjunction.

> A goldfish is a great pet; it demands only food and water from its caretaker.
>
> A cat requires a little time; it needs to be pampered by whoever owns it.
>
> The earthworm has no lungs; it breathes through its skin.

Only closely related clauses should be joined by a semicolon. Ideas not closely related belong in separate sentences.

> **Not Closely Related**     Ferrets make wonderful pets. Everyone should have a pet.
>
> **Closely Related**     Ferrets make wonderful pets; they are friendly and use a litter box just as cats do.

*You can learn more about correcting run-on sentences on pages 736–738.*

# Semicolons with Conjunctive Adverbs and Transitional Words

The clauses in a compound sentence can also be joined by a semicolon and certain conjunctive adverbs or transitional words.

**23 B.1**  Use a **semicolon** between the clauses in a compound sentence when they are joined by certain conjunctive adverbs or transitional words.

In the examples below, the conjunctive adverb *however* and the transitional words *for example* are preceded by a semicolon and followed by a comma.

He told me the dog was friendly**;** **however,** it barked ferociously at me.

The kitten's markings could inspire a name**;** **for example,** you could call her Stripes.

Following are lists of common conjunctive adverbs and transitional words.

| COMMON CONJUNCTIVE ADVERBS | | |
| --- | --- | --- |
| accordingly | furthermore | otherwise |
| also | hence | similarly |
| besides | however | still |
| consequently | instead | therefore |
| finally | nevertheless | thus |
| **COMMON TRANSITIONAL WORDS** | | |
| as a result | in addition | in other words |
| for example | in fact | on the other hand |

Some of the conjunctive adverbs and transitional words above can also be used as parenthetical expressions within a single clause.

**Joining Clauses**  A katydid looks much like a harmless green grasshopper**;** **consequently,** people are surprised when it bites them.
(A semicolon comes before the transitional word, and a comma follows it.)

**Within Clauses**  The grasshopper**,** **however,** doesn't bite.
(A comma comes before and after the conjunctive adverb.)

*You can learn more about parenthetical expressions on pages 951–952.*

*Using Semicolons and Commas*

Write *I* if the sentence does not use semicolons and commas correctly. Write *C* if the sentence is correct.

1. Plankton floats at the ocean's surface other sea animals rely on it for food.
2. The bivalve mollusk has two shells hinged together, similarly oysters and mussels have hinged shells.
3. Oysters are prized for the pearls they produce; as a result oyster beds are cultivated as "pearl farms."
4. The sponge is a plantlike animal, and it grows only in an underwater habitat.
5. Jellyfish are stunningly beautiful on the other hand; their sting is stunningly painful.
6. Coral looks like porous rock; however, it is a skeleton secreted by living marine polyps.
7. Polyps such as the sea anemone live individually, others live in colonies and form coral reefs.
8. The octopus has a smooth body with a mouth on the underside furthermore it has eight arms covered with suckers.
9. The ten-armed squid is often used as fish bait; consequently; *squidding* means "to fish for squid" or "to fish with squid as bait."
10. A sea horse's head and neck resemble those of a horse, it swims with its head held upright like a horse's, and its tail curled beneath.

# Semicolons to Avoid Confusion

To make your meaning clear, you may have to substitute a semicolon for a comma.

**23 B.2**   Use a semicolon instead of a comma to avoid possible confusion in certain situations.

A semicolon is used instead of a comma between the clauses of a compound sentence if there are commas within a clause.

Military uniforms are often blue, gray, or black; but those are not the only colors used. (Normally, a comma comes before a conjunction separating the clauses in a compound sentence.)

Semicolons are also used instead of commas between items in a series if the items themselves contain commas.

> The President's schedule includes stops in London, England; Paris, France; Florence, Italy; Geneva, Switzerland; and New Delhi, India.
> (Normally, commas separate the items in a series.)

*You can learn more about using commas on pages 940–956.*

## ● Practice Your Skills

### *Using Semicolons*

Write each word that should be followed by a semicolon and then add the semicolon. You may need to replace a comma or commas with semicolons.

1. Armistice Day is November 11, 1918 it is the anniversary of the cease-fire of World War I, which occurred during the eleventh day of the eleventh month at eleven o'clock.

2. The site of the 1898 Klondike gold rush wasn't Alaska in fact, it was the Yukon Territory of Canada.

3. Pocahontas's real name was said to be Matoak *Pocahontas* was a family name.

4. I want to write my research paper on General Douglas MacArthur, General George S. Patton, or General Robert E. Lee however, I can't decide which general interests me the most.

5. Robert E. Lee's personal home was made into Arlington National Cemetery during the Civil War therefore, he never went home again.

6. The French and Indian War was 1754–1763 the American Revolutionary War was 1775–1783.

7. Reenactments of battles of the Civil War (1861–1865) will be performed on Saturday, June 8 Sunday, June 9 and Monday, June 10.

8. Alaska was bought from Russia in 1867 for 2.5 cents per acre however, it was not admitted into the Union as a state until 1959.

9. Hawaii also was admitted as a state in 1959 it consists of several islands, has its capital in Honolulu, and is 6,424 square miles.

10. The Great Wall of China is more than just stone and mortar in fact, it has over 10,000 watchtowers, hundreds of passes, a rich historical value, and strong cultural influence.

● **Practice Your Skills**

*Using Semicolons and Commas*

Write each word that should be followed by a semicolon or comma and then add the semicolon or comma.

1. The Sahara covers an area of about 3,500,000 square miles Europe covers about 4,100,000 square miles.

2. Florida is not the southernmost state in the United States Hawaii is farther south.

3. I have lived in Detroit Michigan Lincoln Nebraska and Ames Iowa.

4. Some people call Texas the biggest state in the Union on the contrary Alaska is the biggest state.

5. Death Valley contains the lowest point in the Western Hemisphere this point is 282 feet below sea level.

6. Death Valley is not confined to one state it stretches across parts of eastern California and southern Nevada.

7. Popular European vacation destinations include Paris, France Rome, Italy and London, England however some tourists visit other destinations such as Brussels, Belgium.

8. Unmapped areas of the world include jungles in New Guinea submerged caves in Wakulla Springs, Florida and areas of the Nahanni National Park in Canada.

9. The map of the world in other words is not complete.

10. The United States contains many parks and natural wonders furthermore you don't need a passport to see them.

11. Carlsbad Caverns National Park in New Mexico for example, has one of the world's largest underground chambers and the nation's deepest limestone cave.

### Using Semicolons and Commas

Write the following paragraphs, adding semicolons and commas where needed.

> The Bermuda Triangle is a mysterious, triangle-shaped area of the North Atlantic Ocean it is located off the coast of Florida. Many ships, planes, and people have disappeared without a trace in this triangle in fact some say there is a powerful vortex beneath the water. Despite numerous accounts of disappearances within the Bermuda Triangle, the U.S. Board of Geographic Names does not record "Bermuda Triangle" as an official name moreover it does not maintain an official file on the area.
>
> The Department of the Navy however acknowledges that there is an area of water where unexplained disappearances occur. The Navy maintains a Web site at *http://www.history.navy.mil* called the Bermuda Triangle Fact Sheet. Follow the link for the "Frequently Asked Questions" page and then the "Bermuda Triangle" page. The FAQ sheet specifies the triangle's three corners as Miami, Florida San Juan, Puerto Rico and the island of Bermuda furthermore the sheet mentions Coast Guard searches for missing people and ships in that area. A group of five U.S. Navy Avenger Torpedo Bombers for example left Ft. Lauderdale, Florida, on a training mission and never returned. The flight lieutenant's compass failed while over the triangle he is reported to have sent a message before the planes disappeared forever. One of the rescue planes searching for the five planes also disappeared.

#  Colons

Colons are used with lists, independent clauses, long quotations, and in certain conventional situations.

## Colons with Lists

A **colon** is used most often to introduce a list of items that will follow in a sentence.

**23 B.3**  Use a **colon (:)** before most lists of items, especially when a list comes after an expression such as *the following*.

When I think of California, I think of the following**:** beaches, sunshine, and surfing.

My favorite beaches are these**:** Huntington Beach, Malibu Beach, and Redondo Beach.

A colon, however, does not follow a verb or a preposition.

| **No Colon** | Ocean water **includes** salt, seaweed, and jellyfish. |
| **Colon** | Ocean water includes the following: salt, seaweed, and jellyfish. |
| **No Colon** | Salt is used **for** making glass, building roads, and tanning leather. |
| **Colon** | Salt is used in the following processes: making glass, building roads, and tanning leather. |

*Remember that commas usually separate items in a series. You can learn more about items in a series on pages 940–941.*

## Colons with Certain Independent Clauses

**23 B.4**  Use a colon between independent clauses when the second clause explains or restates the first.

We learned why sodas sell so well: the United States consumes more soft drinks than any country but Mexico.

We now know why she named her new soft drink Key West Cola: she lives in Key West, Florida.

## Colons with Long, Formal Quotations and Formal Statements or Propositions

**23 B.5**  Use a colon to introduce a long, formal quotation or a formal statement or proposition.

Maimonides, the wise Jewish philosopher who lived from 1135 to 1204, wrote this advice: "Do not consider it proof just because it is written in books, for a liar who will deceive with his tongue will not hesitate to do the same with his pen."

The issue before the committee was this: It is necessary that more students be recruited to participate in next month's Trivia Scavenger Trek.
(The formal statement begins with a capital letter.)

*You can learn more about long quotations on page 998.*

# Colons with Conventional Situations

**23 B.6**    Use a colon in certain conventional situations.

| COLONS IN CONVENTIONAL SITUATIONS | |
|---|---|
| **Between Hours and Minutes** | 7**:**30 a.m. |
| **Between Biblical Chapters and Verses** | Psalms 46**:**10 |
| **Between Periodical Volumes and Pages** | *Futura* 16**:**3–8 |
| **After Salutations in Business Letters** | Dear Sir or Madam**:** |
| **Between Titles and Subtitles** | *Star Wars***:** *The Phantom Menace* (movie) <br> *The Chieftains***:** *Tears of Stone* (recording) |

*When You Write*

More and more employers are giving job applicants the option of submitting cover letters and résumés through e-mail. Most people attach their résumé as a file attachment and write out the cover letter as an e-mail message. These e-mail letters should follow the same rules for punctuating salutations and closings as typed letters; that is, use a colon after the salutation and a comma after the closing. Look at an e-mail cover letter you are working on. Be sure you follow the standards used in writing any business letter.

## Practice Your Skills

### Using Colons

Write each word or number that should be followed by a colon and add the colon.

**1.** Answer this question How much U.S. trivia do you know?

**2.** The last showing of *Star Wars IV A New Hope* is at 9 14 p.m.

**3.** The following words are all twentieth-century creations *beautician, highbrow,* and *superhighway.*

**4.** Theodore Roosevelt stated "The only man who never makes a mistake is the man who never does anything."

**5.** I had a revelation on my eighteenth birthday I was now old enough to vote.

### Using Colons

Write each sentence, adding colons where appropriate. If a sentence is correct, write C.

**1.** The assignment is this Write a paper about U.S. trivia or culture.

**2.** I'll expect your finished papers on Friday by 2 00 sharp.

**3.** You can get help with your research from the librarian, a tutor, or me.

**4.** Other research paper ideas are these life on an American farm, five American poets, or Native American culture.

**5.** The principal is making the following announcement Students who submit their research papers for publication in the school newsletter must do so by 2 45 on Wednesday.

### ✔ *Check Point:* **Mixed Practice**

Write the following sentences, adding semicolons, colons, and commas where needed.

**1.** The average adult male needs about 2,000 to 2,400 calories a day the average teenage male needs about 2,400 to 2,800 calories.

**2.** The Surgeon General has issued the following warning Smoking by pregnant women may result in fetal injury, premature birth, and low birth weight.

**3.** Bones are vital to the circulatory system they produce blood cells within their marrow.

**4.** The brain has these three parts the cerebrum, the cerebellum, and the cerebral cortex.

**5.** I knew that the heart, liver, and kidneys are organs I did not realize that skin is an organ.

**6.** The skin is in fact the body's largest organ.

**7.** The blood bank's plea is this Donate blood today.

**8.** Babies don't develop the cells necessary to see in color until they are six to eight months old therefore everyone is colorblind at birth.

**9.** A meal eaten at 6 00 PM is in some part of the digestive system until 6 00–9 00 AM the following day.

# Italics (Underlining)

**Italics** are printed letters that slant to the right. If you are writing by hand, you should underline anything that needs to be italicized.

**23 C** **Italics (underlining) are used to indicate certain titles and names, foreign words, and a word used as a word.**

| | |
|---|---|
| **Italics** | Have you read *Dubliners* by James Joyce? |
| **Underlining** | Have you read <u>Dubliners</u> by James Joyce? |

**23 C.1** Italicize (underline) letters, numbers, and words used as words. Also underline foreign words that are not generally used in English.

| | |
|---|---|
| **Letters, Numbers** | When you write your compositions, your capital *Q*'s look like *2*s. (Only the *Q* and the *2* are italicized— not the 's or s.) |
| **Words, Phrases** | In Shakespeare's time the word *gentle* meant "noble." |
| | In the same era the word <u>forsooth</u> meant "in truth" or "indeed." |
| **Foreign Words** | In Hebrew *shalom* means "peace." |

**23 C.2** Italicize (underline) the titles of long written works or musical compositions that are published as a single unit. Also italicize (underline) the titles of paintings and sculptures and the names of vehicles.

Long works include books, periodicals, newspapers, full-length plays, and very long poems. Long musical compositions include operas, symphonies, ballets, and albums. Vehicles include airplanes, ships, trains, and spacecraft. Titles of movies and radio and TV series should also be italicized (underlined).

| | |
|---|---|
| **Books** | George Eliot wrote *Silas Marner.* |
| | May I use your <u>Dictionary of Symbolism</u>? |
| **Magazines** | I subscribe to *Poets & Writers.* |
| | I also subscribe to <u>Poetry Horizons</u>. |
| **Newspapers** | I enjoy the movie reviews in the *Philadelphia Bulletin*. |
| | Ari reads the comics in the <u>Chicago Tribune</u>. |
| | (*The* is generally not considered part of the title of a newspaper or a magazine.) |

CHAPTER 23

| | |
|---|---|
| **Plays and Movies** | Henrik Ibsen's plays *Hedda Gabler* and *A Doll's House* were written in the late 1800s. |
| | The movie <u>Where the Wild Things Are</u> is based on a book by Maurice Sendak. |
| **Television Series** | The series *Biography* on A&E featured Vincent van Gogh. |
| | <u>Star Trek: The Next Generation</u> included quotations of Shakespeare and references to his plays. |
| **Long Musical Compositions** | Wolfgang Amadeus Mozart composed the opera *Don Giovanni* in Italian. |
| | Mozart composed <u>The Magic Flute</u> in German. |
| **Works of Art** | *Story Cloth,* embroidered by Yang Fang Nhu, is fiber art. |
| | <u>Listening</u> is an oil on cardboard by Gabriele Münter. |
| **Names of Vehicles** | The *Gudgeon* was the first submarine to circle the earth. |
| | Charles Lindbergh flew the <u>Spirit of St. Louis</u>. |

## When You Write

Word-processing programs allow you to use italics and other special text. These italics *replace* underlining—use one or the other. Be sure to use one method–underlining or italics—consistently throughout your paper; that is, do not write <u>Romeo and Juliet</u> in one paragraph and *Romeo and Juliet* in another paragraph.

## ● Practice Your Skills

### Using Italics (Underlining)

Write and underline each letter, word, or group of words that should be italicized.

1. Often, The Learning Channel will air a series called Great Books.
2. Kaddara, an opera produced in 1921, is about Eskimos.
3. Charles Schulz, who created the character Charlie Brown, was once a cartoonist for a well-known magazine, the Saturday Evening Post.
4. The character Snoopy in You're a Good Man, Charlie Brown would be a fun part to act.
5. Leonardo da Vinci's painting The Last Supper is considered one of the great art treasures of the world.

6. Why does my English teacher always say I must mind my p's and q's?

7. Biblioteca is Spanish for "library."

8. The name White House was given to the presidential residence by Theodore Roosevelt.

9. The Wall Street Journal offers reports on businesses and the stock market.

10. I read a travelogue on the Queen Elizabeth 2 in Outside magazine.

11. Children on the Beach is a painting by American Impressionist Mary Cassatt.

12. Do you subscribe to Popular Photography?

13. Of all Dickens's books that I have read, I enjoyed Oliver Twist the most.

14. The Sunday editions of major newspapers (like the Chicago Tribune) have a section on "Life and Arts."

## *Connect to Writing:* Editing

### Using Italics (Underlining)

Write the following paragraph, adding italics (underlining) as needed.

My goal is to manage a large bookstore that carries books, music, and periodicals. I would devote funds to a magnificent young adult section with plenty of bestsellers like The Giver by Lois Lowry and The Outsiders by S. E. Hinton. I would feature weekly displays of magazines such as Discover and Writer's Digest and carry major newspapers, including USA Today, the Chicago Tribune, and the Miami Herald. The overhead speaker system would play music from the store's music section. Handel's Messiah would be a good choice during the holidays. Posters of colorful, classical art such as A Sunday Afternoon on the Island of La Grande Jatte by Georges Seurat would adorn the walls of the classical music section. The science and technology section would feature books about Liberty Bell 7 (the second manned spacecraft) and other overlooked spacecraft. A bookstore with this much variety would require me to dot every i and cross every t, but I could do it.

## *Connect to Writing:* Description

### Italics (Underlining)

An online ad agency has asked you to write a description of your interests in books, magazines, newspapers, plays, movies, television, music, and art. Mention a favorite in each category, using italics (underlining) correctly.

Knowing how to use quotation marks correctly when you write fiction is important because conversations cannot be written without them. Authors often use conversation, or **dialogue,** to reveal important information about the characters and to add realism to fiction.

Quotation marks are also essential in research papers. If you omit or incorrectly use quotation marks, you may, unwittingly, be plagiarizing someone else's words. Quotation marks show that the words you are writing belong to someone else.

**23 D**    **Quotation marks (" ") come in pairs. They are placed at the beginning and at the end of uninterrupted quotations and certain titles. Ellipses (. . .) indicate that words have been removed.**

## ➤ Quotation Marks with Titles

**23 D.1**    Use quotation marks to enclose the titles of chapters, articles, stories, one-act plays, short poems, and songs.

The titles of long works of art and publications are italicized (underlined). These long works, however, are usually composed of smaller parts. A newspaper has articles, for example, and a book can include chapters, short stories, short plays, or poems. When the titles of these smaller parts are written, they should be enclosed in quotation marks.

Quotation marks are also placed around the titles of essays, compositions, episodes from TV series, and movements from long musical compositions.

| | |
|---|---|
| **Chapters in a Book** | "I Observe" is my favorite chapter in *David Copperfield* by Charles Dickens. |
| **Poems** | Yesterday we read Robert Browning's poem "My Star" in our anthology *English Literature.* |
| **Articles in Magazines or Newspapers** | "Facing the Future" was an informative article in *Time.*<br><br>For homework please read "The Life of a Small-Town Writer" in the local newspaper. |
| **Television Episodes** | Tonight's episode of *The Simpsons* is "Lisa the Iconoclast." |
| **Songs** | I often listen to "Candle in the Wind" on Elton John's album *Goodbye Yellow Brick Road.* |

CHAPTER 23

## Practice Your Skills

### Using Quotation Marks with Titles

Find and write each title, adding quotation marks or italics (underlining) where needed.

1. I'm using Automation on the Line, an illustrated article in the Detroit News, in my research paper.
2. The drama class presented the one-act play The Happy Journey to Trenton and Camden by Thornton Wilder.
3. The band played Yankee Doodle as we marched by.
4. You can find the short story The Bear in the book The Works of William Faulkner.
5. The Elizabethan Stage was the title of my essay.
6. Are we supposed to read Keats's poem To Autumn or Shelley's poem To a Skylark for class tomorrow?
7. In film class I learned that As Time Goes By is the famous song in the movie Casablanca.
8. In music class we're learning Cloudburst, the last movement from Grofé's Grand Canyon Suite.
9. Have you read the chapter The Turning Point in our textbook The History of the World?
10. As soon as I passed my driver's test, I read the article Buying a Used Car.

## Connect to Writing: Prewriting

### Brainstorming Using Quotation Marks

List the titles of all the printed and recorded materials you have read or listened to in the past week. If you read a poem in an anthology, for example, you would list the anthology's title and the poem's title. Use quotation marks and italics (underlining) correctly.

## Check Point: Mixed Practice

Write each title, adding quotation marks or italics (underlining) where needed.

1. I enjoyed the story The Necklace by Guy de Maupassant.
2. It is in Fiction: A Longman Pocket Anthology, just after The Cask of Amontillado by Poe.
3. Have you read Alfred Noyes's tragic poem The Highwayman?

4. Loreena McKennitt set The Highwayman to music on her album The Book of Secrets.
5. The last episode of this TV show was called Graduation.
6. There is an article called Fairy Tale or Marketing Ploy? in Hollywood Weekly; it's about celebrity weddings.
7. I've read up to the chapter A Wedding Night in The Hunchback of Notre Dame.
8. Wasn't Roy Orbison's performance of Oh, Pretty Woman used in the movie Pretty Woman?
9. I read the chapter entitled Elements of the Novel.
10. I found a great article called How to Write a Poem.
11. The poem When the Frost Is on the Punkin by James Whitcomb Riley paints a picture of fall in the Midwest.
12. I'll analyze the chapter News from Lake Wobegon Days by Garrison Keillor.
13. Some songs from the very long poem The Princess by Alfred Lord Tennyson are included in the collection Victorian Poetry and Poetics.

# ➤ Quotation Marks with Direct Quotations

**23 D.2**     Use quotation marks to enclose a person's exact words.

Quotation marks are placed around a **direct quotation**—the exact words of a person. They are not placed around an **indirect quotation**—a paraphrase of someone's words.

| | |
|---|---|
| **Direct Quotation** | Bill said, "I'm almost ready." |
| **Indirect Quotation** | Bill said that he was almost ready. |
| | (The word *that* often signals an indirect quotation.) |

A one-sentence direct quotation can be placed before or after a **speaker tag,** a phrase such as *said Marcus* or *Skye asked,* that indicates who is speaking. It can also be interrupted by a speaker tag. In all three cases, quotation marks enclose only the person's exact words. In the third sentence below, two sets of quotation marks are needed because quotation marks enclose only a person's exact words, not the speaker tag.

| | |
|---|---|
| **Before** | "The game was very suspenseful," Marcus said. |
| **After** | Marcus said, "The game was very suspenseful." |
| **Interrupted** | "The game," Marcus said, "was very suspenseful." |

Only one set of quotation marks is needed to enclose any number of quoted sentences—unless they are interrupted by a speaker tag.

Marcus said, **"**The game was very suspenseful. We were tied in the last inning. Then Will hit a home run.**"**

## ● Practice Your Skills

### *Using Quotation Marks with Direct Quotations*

Write *I* if quotation marks are used incorrectly. Write *C* if quotation marks are used correctly.

**1.** "The volleyballs are low on air, Coach Mabry said."

**2.** "I'm not sure," I said, "where the air pump is."

**3.** Someone said "that the pump is in the supply closet."

**4.** The crowd chanted, "Two, four, six, eight! "Whom do we appreciate? The Rockets!

**5.** Did you say that you're going to resign as team captain?

**6.** I certainly did not say that, "Mark protested."

**7.** I replied, "Go ask Tyler. He heard it too."

**8.** "The new gym, our principal promised, will be everything we've hoped for."

**9.** "The builders said that the gym is nearly finished."

**10.** "Do fifty push-ups and no cheating, the coach commanded." "Then run ten laps around the track."

**11.** I can hardly breathe, puffed Taylor.

**12.** Chris added, "I prefer running laps over doing push-ups."

**13.** Raquel asked, "What's next?"

**14.** "I'd like," Suzanne suggested, "to practice my relay.

**15.** "Finish warming up! Coach shouted. You haven't even begun to work!"

## ● *Connect to Writing:* Editing

### *Using Quotation Marks with Direct Quotations*

Rewrite the incorrect sentences from the preceding exercise, using quotation marks correctly. In this exercise place a comma or an end mark that follows a quotation inside the closing quotation marks.

# Capital Letters with Direct Quotations

A capital letter begins a quoted sentence—just as it begins a regular sentence.

**23 D.3**   Begin each sentence of a direct quotation with a capital letter.

> **"H**appiness is a long Saturday with nothing to do,**"** Priscilla said.
>
> Priscilla said, **"H**appiness is a long Saturday with nothing to do.**"**
> (*Two* capital letters are needed: one for the first word of the sentence and one for the first word of the quotation.)
>
> **"H**appiness,**"** Priscilla said, **"i**s a long Saturday with nothing to do.**"**
> (*Is* does not begin with a capital letter because it is in the middle of the quotation.)
>
> **"H**appiness is a long Saturday with nothing to do,**"** Priscilla said. **"T**hat is the best antidote to stress I can give you.**"**
> (*That* is capitalized because it starts a new sentence.)

● **Practice Your Skills**

*Using Capital Letters with Direct Quotations*

Write *I* if the sentence does not use capital letters and quotation marks correctly. Write *C* if it is correct.

**1.** "the happy do not believe in miracles," Goethe stated.

**2.** "Happiness is not a state to arrive at, but a manner of traveling," Commented Margaret Run beck.

**3.** "Those who won our independence . . . believed liberty to be the secret of happiness and courage to be the secret of liberty," declared Justice Louis D. Brandeis.

**4.** "When one is happy, there is no time to be fatigued. being happy engrosses the whole attention, E. F. Benson said."

**5.** Don Marquis mused, "Happiness is the interval between periods of unhappiness."

**6.** "When a happy moment, complete and rounded as a pearl, falls into the tossing ocean of life," Agnes Repplier once said, "it is never wholly lost."

**7.** Happiness is not being pained in body or troubled in mind, commented Thomas Jefferson.

**8.** C. P. Snow said, "the pursuit of happiness is a most ridiculous phrase. If you pursue it, you'll never find it."

9. William Lyon Phelps mused, "If happiness truly consisted in physical ease and freedom from care, then the happiest individual, I think, Would be an American cow."

10. "happiness is not a matter of events. it depends upon the tides of the mind," Alice Meynell once said.

# Commas with Direct Quotations

A comma is used to separate a direct quotation from a speaker tag.

**23 D.4**   Use a comma to separate a direct quotation from a speaker tag. Place the comma inside the closing quotation marks.

Notice in the following examples that when the speaker tag follows the quotation, the comma goes *inside* the closing quotation marks.

"You should enter the story contest**,**" she said.
(The comma goes *inside* the closing quotation marks.)

She said**,** "You should enter the story contest."
(The comma follows the speaker tag.)

"You should**,**" she said**,** "enter the story contest."
(*Two* commas are needed to separate the speaker tag from the interrupted quotation. The first comma goes *inside* the closing quotation marks.)

● **Practice Your Skills**

*Using Commas with Direct Quotations*

Write *I* if the sentence uses commas, capital letters, or quotation marks incorrectly. Write *C* if the sentence is correct.

1. Agatha Christie said, "The best time for planning a book is while you're doing the dishes."

2. "I see but one rule: to be clear", wrote Stendhal. "If I am not clear, all my world crumbles to nothing."

3. Aristotle once said "The greatest thing in style is to have a command of metaphor."

4. "A book ought to be an ice pick" wrote Kafka, "to break up the frozen sea within us."

5. "Regarding writing," Guy de Maupassant advises "get black on white."

6. Isaac Bashevis Singer commented, "A story to me means a plot where there is some surprise . . . because that is how life is–full of surprises."

7. "One writes to make a home for oneself," Says Alfred Kazin, on paper, in time and in others' minds."

8. Fitzgerald wrote, "You don't write because you want to say something; you write because you've got something to say."

9. "When you're writing, you're trying to find out something which you don't know", James Baldwin commented.

10. Baldwin went on to explain "The whole language of writing for me is finding out what you don't want to know, what you don't want to find out. But something forces you to anyway."

## Connect to Writing: Editing

### Punctuating Direct Quotations

Rewrite the incorrect sentences from the preceding exercise, using commas, capital letters, and quotation marks correctly.

## End Marks with Direct Quotations

A period marks the end of a statement or an opinion, and it also marks the end of a quoted statement or opinion. The period is *always* placed inside the quotation marks.

**23 D.5**    Place a period inside the closing quotation marks when the end of the quotation comes at the end of the sentence.

He said, **"**I think I'll order lasagna**."**
(The period goes *inside* the closing quotation marks.)

**"**I think I'll order lasagna,**"** he said**.**
(The period follows the speaker tag, and a comma separates the quotation from the speaker tag.)

**"**I think,**"** he said, **"**I'll order lasagna**."**
(The period goes *inside* the closing quotation marks.)

If a quotation asks a question or shows strong feeling, the question mark or the exclamation point goes inside the closing quotation marks. Notice that the question mark goes *inside* the closing quotation marks in the three examples that follow.

> She asked, **"**Where did you pick the apples**?"**
>
> **"**Where did you pick the apples**?"** she asked.
>
> **"**Where,**"** she asked, **"**did you pick the apples**?"**

The exclamation point also goes *inside* the closing quotation marks in the following three examples.

> He exclaimed, **"**It is time for dessert**!"**
>
> **"**It is time for dessert**!"** he exclaimed.
>
> **"**It is,**"** he exclaimed, **"**time for dessert**!"**

A quotation of two or more sentences can include various end marks.

> **"**Did you see the cooking exhibit**?"** Laura asked. **"**I accidentally knocked over the wok**!"**

Occasionally a question or an exclamatory statement will include a direct quotation. In such cases the end mark goes *outside* the closing quotation marks.

> Did Nancy say, **"**The Chinese food has arrived**"?**
>
> (The whole sentence—not the quotation—is the question.)
>
> I couldn't believe it when Ben said, **"**They forgot our egg rolls**"!**
>
> (The whole sentence—not the quotation—is exclamatory.)

**23 D.6** Place the question mark or the exclamation point *outside* the closing quotation marks when the sentence itself is a question or an exclamation.

## ● *Connect to Speaking and Listening:* **Classroom Interaction**

### *Using Quotation Marks*

Find a novel with dialogue that uses quotation marks. With a partner, take turns reading the conversation between characters. As you read, indicate where the quotation marks are placed by saying "Begin quote" and "End quote." Tell your partner beforehand that you will be indicating a few quotation marks where they do not belong, and that it is his or her job to correct you when this happens.

Semicolons and colons go *outside* closing quotation marks.

My dad specifically said, **"**No parties while I'm gone**"**; therefore, I'll plan the pizza party for this weekend.

The following are today's **"**savory selections**"**: baked beans, creamed corn, and mini-sausages.

## Practice Your Skills

### Using End Marks and Commas with Direct Quotations

Write *I* if end marks and commas are used incorrectly. Write *C* if the sentence is correct.

1. "Where is the saltshaker," Cindy asked.
2. I shouted "Don't touch that—it's hot"
3. "Those fresh tomatoes were delicious," Megan said. "Did you grow them yourself?"
4. Who said "Taste this unusual fruit."
5. "Wow" exclaimed Andie "Are these luscious brownies made from scratch"
6. "First you blend the dry ingredients," explained my mom. "Then you add the milk."
7. I asked "Should we use buttermilk or whole milk"
8. Did I actually hear you say, "I promise to wash all the dishes after dinner"?
9. "Yeast" she said "is what makes the dough rise".
10. He walked through the kitchen shouting "Brownies! Brownies! Who wants a brownie"
11. Do you think we use chocolate chips? asked Megan, I think we use cocoa.
12. I'm sure Mom said, "Use baking powder for your rising agent," so we don't need the yeast.
13. Max called out, "Make some ham and cheese sandwiches too!"
14. Did Bart say, The Pattersons have arrived?"
15. "Is the food ready? Emily asked, I'm starving?"

## *Connect to Writing:* Editing

### Using End Marks and Commas with Direct Quotations

Rewrite the incorrect sentences from the preceding exercise, using end marks and commas as needed.

## ✓ Check Point: Mixed Practice

Rewrite each sentence, adding capital letters, quotation marks, and other punctuation marks where needed.

**1.** the applause of a single human being is of great consequence Samuel Johnson said

**2.** the most beautiful adventures explained Robert Louis Stevenson are not those we go to seek

**3.** we need to restore the full meaning of the old word duty Pearl Buck remarked it is the other side of rights

**4.** Joseph Conrad stated an ideal is often but a flaming vision of reality

**5.** make up your mind to act decisively and take the consequences no good is ever done in this world by hesitation Thomas Huxley warned

**6.** Janet Erskine Stuart said to aim at the best and to remain essentially ourselves are one and the same thing

**7.** welcome everything that comes to you André Gide advised but do not long for anything else

**8.** can anything be sadder than work left unfinished Christina Rossetti asked yes, work never begun

**9.** did the poet W. B. Yeats say good conversation unrolls itself like the dawn

**10.** when people talk, listen completely stated Ernest Hemingway most people never listen

## ● *Connect to Writing:* Interview

### Direct Quotations

You are writing an article for the school newspaper, and you need several direct quotations to make the article come alive. Interview a classmate about a topic of your choice. (Possible topics include favorite bands, career choices, or how to keep a friend.) Write down your interviewee's statements exactly, using quotation marks and end marks correctly. Then write a short article that incorporates some of the direct quotations from your interview. Edit for correct use of all punctuation and compose the final copy.

# Other Uses of Quotation Marks

In addition to titles and direct quotations, quotation marks have many special applications.

## Unusual Uses of Words

Quotation marks can draw attention to a word that is used in an unusual way.

**23 D.7**　Use quotation marks to enclose slang words, technical terms, and other unusual uses of words.

| | |
|---|---|
| **Slang** | "Surfing channels" and "surfing the Net" are slang expressions for watching TV and browsing the Internet. |
| **Technical Terms** | A computer "crash" is a system failure. You will probably need to "reboot" your computer. |
| **Invented Words** | He plays so many computer games that I call him a "game-oholic." |
| **Irony and Sarcasm** | Please don't "help" me anymore. You crashed my system! |

## Dictionary Definitions

When you write a dictionary definition within a piece of writing, you must include both italics (underlining) and quotation marks.

**23 D.8**　When writing a word and its definition in a sentence, italicize (underline) the word but use quotation marks to enclose the definition.

| | |
|---|---|
| **Definitions of Words** | The word *mouse* can mean either "a computer input device" or "a small, furry rodent." |

## Dialogue

**Dialogue** is the vocal interaction between two or more people. Good dialogue conveys mood, information, and insight into the people involved.

**23 D.9**　When writing **dialogue,** begin a new paragraph each time the speaker changes.

In the example below, the actions or descriptions of the speakers are sometimes included within the same paragraph in which each one speaks.

> "Class," said Ms. Spoffard, turning from the board with a smile, "who would like to help design the official Web site for our school?"
>
> "I'll help," said Stephen, who had already designed his own site.
>
> "Excellent!" said Ms. Spoffard. "Who else?"
>
> "I volunteer David," said Alma, smiling brightly. She added, "He already works part time as a Webmaster."

If the speaker's sentences form more than one paragraph, begin each paragraph with a quotation mark, but place a closing quotation mark at the end of the last paragraph only.

> Ms. Spoffard said, "Let me begin by telling you what the major sections of the Web site will be.
>
> "First, we need an attractive home page, where people can find basic information and links to other pages.
>
> "Next, we need pages on each major aspect of our school, including sports, clubs, social activities, and even the week's cafeteria menu.
>
> "Finally, we need a map of the school."
>
> The students sat silently, eagerly taking notes.
>
> "May I design the map?" Jordan asked. "I have a few ideas I'd like to share."
>
> "We need a floor plan of the actual structure," continued Ms. Spoffard, "that the viewer could surf through.
>
> "In addition, we need realistic details, which will require an observant team."

## Long Passages

Whenever you are quoting a passage of five or more lines, use a block quote. In a **block quote,** the quoted material is set off from the body of the text by indenting either the left margin or both the left and right margins. Notice in the example below that no quotation marks are used around a block quote.

> In his book *Editing Your Newsletter,* Mark Beach explains that with illustrations, you can have too much of a good thing:
>
> > Clip art was developed for display ads, not editorial matter. When using clip art in a newsletter, keep your objectives clear. Novice editors tend to use too many illustrations and to place them poorly. Even some experienced designers think readers like lots of drawings scattered at random.
>
> Beach urges newsletter editors to use clip art sparingly.

As you have learned, there is more than one way to format a long quoted passage. When you write a research paper, therefore, be sure to consult your teacher's guidelines or the style handbook that your class uses to learn what format you should use. Then follow that format consistently.

*You can learn more about using colons with formal quotations and with formal statements and propositions on page 980. You can learn about citing sources on pages 443–449.*

## Quotations Within Quotations

If a title or a quotation is included within another quotation, a distinction must be made between the two sets of quotation marks.

**23 D.10**   To avoid any confusion, use single quotation marks to enclose a quotation or certain titles within a quotation.

> "Is the chapter 'Graphics and the Newsletter' a long one?" Li asked.
>
> Lou said, "I heard him say, 'The answers are on page 101.'"
>
> Lou asked, "Did he say, 'The answers are on page 101'?"

Notice in the second example above that the closing single quotation mark and the closing double quotation marks come together. The period is inside both of them.

### Using Quotation Marks

Write *I* if quotation marks are used incorrectly. Write *C* if the sentence is correct.

**1.** A "mouse potato' is someone who sits at the computer all day.

**2.** "Faith asked, Did someone say, Reboot all the computers now?"

**3.** From my point of view, your work looks like personal e-mails.

**4.** A "computer virus" or "computer bug" causes a program to malfunction.

**5.** You probably remember hearing the news hype about the 'millennium bug.'

**6.** The word *click* "means to press a button on the mouse."

**7.** Does *netiquette* mean etiquette for the Internet?

**8.** The computer lab monitor said, "Print the warning that begins, 'Software piracy will be prosecuted.'"

**9.** A 'chat room' is a location on the Internet where you exchange written dialogue with other computer users.

**10.** When your computer is connected to the Internet, you are "online."

**11.** "I heard Garrett say, 'The Internet is a technical highway of computerized information."

**12.** The word *e-mail* means 'electronic mail.'

**13.** Jason likes to "surf the net."

## *Connect to Writing:* Editing

### Using Quotation Marks

Rewrite each incorrect sentence from the preceding exercise, using quotation marks correctly.

## *Connect to Writing:* Drafting

### Writing Quotations Using Quotation Marks

Write ten quotations of statements people have made to you in the past two days. Include at least two quotations within quotations. Use quotation marks where needed.

Correctly rewrite the following dialogue between Ebenezer Scrooge and Bob Cratchit. Add punctuation and indentation as needed.

Hallo growled Scrooge in his accustomed voice as near as he could feign it. What do you mean by coming here at this time of day? I am very sorry, sir said Bob. I am behind my time. . . . Yes. I think you are. Step this way, sir, if you please It's only once a year, sir pleaded Bob, appearing from the tank. It shall not be repeated. I was making rather merry yesterday, sir. Now, I'll tell you what, my friend said Scrooge. I am not going to tolerate this sort of thing any longer. Therefore . . . I am about to raise your salary!

—Charles Dickens, *A Christmas Carol*

# Ellipses

Most often **ellipses** are used with quotations to show that part of a complete quotation has been dropped.

**23 D.11**   Use **ellipses** ( **. . .** ) to indicate any omission in a quoted passage or a pause in a written passage.

| | |
|---|---|
| **Quoted Passage** | "With malice toward none **. . .** let us strive on to finish the work we are in**. . . .**" Abraham Lincoln |
| | (Notice that part of the quotation is omitted at the end of the statement; the three ellipses are followed by a period.) |
| **Written Passage** | "Well **. . .** I don't know who won the election," said the ballot-counter. |

● *Connect to Writing:* **Dialogue**

*Quotation Marks and Ellipses*

Make up a dialogue between two friends who are having troubles in their friendship. (Topics could be a third person taking up the time of one of the friends, or one of the friends feeling hurt by something the other one said.) Write the dialogue using proper quotation marks and paragraph breaks. Also use ellipses to indicate places where pauses and breaks in the conversation take place.

## Practice Your Skills

### Using Ellipses

Write the following paragraphs, omitting the underlined portions and inserting ellipses as needed.

Four score and seven years ago our fathers brought forth <u>on this continent</u> a new nation, <u>conceived in Liberty, and</u> dedicated to the proposition that all men are created equal.

Now we are engaged in a great civil war, testing whether that nation<u>, or any nation so conceived and so dedicated,</u> can long endure. We are met on a great battlefield <u>of that war. We have come</u> to dedicate a portion of that field, as a final resting place for those who here gave their lives <u>that that nation might live</u>. It is altogether fitting <u>and proper</u> that we should do this.

—Abraham Lincoln, "The Gettysburg Address"

## *Connect to Writing:* Revising

### Using Ellipses

Write a shortened version of this paragraph, using ellipses to indicate where you omit words.

The other day, one of the gentlemen from Georgia, an eloquent man, and a man of learning, so far as I can judge, not being learned myself, came down upon us astonishingly. He spoke in what the Baltimore American calls the "scathing and withering style." At the end of his second severe flash I was struck blind, and found myself feeling with my fingers for an assurance of my continued physical existence. A little of the bone was left, and I gradually revived. He eulogized Mr. Clay in high and beautiful terms, and then declared that we had deserted all our principles, and had turned Henry Clay out, like an old horse, to root. This is terribly severe. It cannot be answered by argument; at least, I cannot so answer it. I merely wish to ask the gentleman if the Whigs are the only party he can think of, who sometimes turn old horses out to root. Is not a certain Martin Van Buren an old horse, which your own party have turned out to root? and is he not rooting a little to your discomfort about now?

—Abraham Lincoln (from a speech in the House of Representatives)

# Other Marks of Punctuation  Lesson 5

**23 E**  A **hyphen** divides a word at the end of a line and separates parts of a compound word. **Dashes, parentheses,** and **brackets** separate words from the rest of the sentence.

## ➤ Hyphens

A **hyphen** (-) has several uses besides its most common use, dividing a word at the end of a line.

## Hyphens with Divided Words

**23 E.1**  Use a hyphen to divide a word at the end of a line.

To understand how to divide a word, use the following guidelines.

| GUIDELINES FOR DIVIDING WORDS |
|---|
| **1. Divide words only between syllables.**<br>hu·mor·ous = hu-morous or humor-ous |
| **2. Never divide a one-syllable word.**<br>laugh　　　　brought　　　　save　　　　lead |
| **3. Never separate a one-letter syllable from the rest of the word.**<br>Do Not Break　　a·dore　　　　e·mit　　　　I·ris |
| **4. Hyphenate after two letters at the end of a line, but do not carry a two-letter word ending to the next line.**<br>Break　　　　be-lieve　　re-call　　in-vite<br>Do Not Break　　tight·en　　shov·el　　over·ly |
| **5. Usually divide words containing double consonants between the double consonants.**<br>shim-mer　　oc-cur　　ship-ping　　stag-ger |
| **6. Divide hyphenated words only after the hyphens.**<br>spur-of-the-moment　　father-in-law　　self-confident |
| **7. Do not divide a proper noun or a proper adjective.**<br>Olivero　　Yonkers　　Himalayan　　Polish |

If you do not know how to hyphenate certain words, check a dictionary.

**Practice Your Skills**

*Using Hyphens to Divide Words*

Write each word, using a hyphen or hyphens to show where the word can be divided at the end of a line. If a word should not be divided, write *no*.

| | | |
|---|---|---|
| **1.** educate | **6.** governor | **11.** puzzle |
| **2.** squeeze | **7.** octave | **12.** immune |
| **3.** follow | **8.** permit | **13.** dress |
| **4.** event | **9.** planet | **14.** Nigerian |
| **5.** holiday | **10.** traitor | **15.** tuition |

● *Connect to Writing:* **Editing**

*Editing for Hyphens That Divide Words*

Some of the following words have been divided incorrectly. Rewrite each word, using a hyphen or hyphens to show where the word can be divided. If a word is correct, write *C*.

| | | |
|---|---|---|
| **1.** pepp-er | **6.** John-son | **11.** envelo-pe |
| **2.** yes-terday | **7.** thre-ad | **12.** tab-let |
| **3.** tele-vision | **8.** a-void | **13.** sweat-er |
| **4.** tab-le | **9.** ampli-fier | **14.** mer-ry-go-round |
| **5.** Lin-coln | **10.** bask-etball | **15.** ba-tter |

CHAPTER 23

# Hyphens with Certain Numbers

Hyphens are needed when you write out certain numbers.

**23 E.2**   Use a hyphen when writing out the numbers *twenty-one* through *ninety-nine.*

**Seventy-four** new math textbooks were shipped to us today.

Since we ordered **eighty-nine,** we are missing fifteen.

# Hyphens with Some Compound Nouns and Adjectives

Some compound nouns and adjectives need one or more hyphens.

**23 E.3**   Use one or more hyphens to separate the parts of some compound nouns and adjectives. Also use one or more hyphens between words that make up a compound adjective located before a noun.

| HYPHENATED COMPOUND WORDS | |
|---|---|
| **Compound Nouns** | sister-in-law, flare-up, secretary-general |
| **Compound Adjectives** | skin-deep, long-term, run-of-the-mill |

A hyphen is usually used only when a compound adjective comes before a noun—not when it follows a linking verb and comes after the noun it describes.

**Adjective Before a Noun**   This is a **fact-filled** paper on Pythagoras.

**Adjective After a Noun**   This paper on Pythagoras is **fact filled.**

A hyphen is used only when a fraction is used as an adjective—*not* when it is used as a noun.

**Fraction Used as an Adjective**   A **one-fourth** minority of the students knows Pythagoras's theorem.

**Fraction Used as a Noun**   **Three fourths** of the students had never heard of Pythagoras.

Never use a hyphen between an adjective and an adverb ending in *–ly*.

That **fairly difficult** geometry test yielded no low scores. (no hyphen)

# Hyphens with Certain Prefixes

Several prefixes and one suffix are always separated from their root words by a hyphen.

**23 E.4** Use a hyphen after the prefixes *ex-*, *self-*, and *all-* and before the suffix *-elect*.

A hyphen is used with all prefixes before most proper nouns or proper adjectives.

| HYPHENS WITH PREFIXES AND SUFFIXES | | | |
|---|---|---|---|
| ex-champion | self-control | all-around | mayor-elect |
| mid-Atlantic | pre-Columbian | pro-American | |

## ● Practice Your Skills

### *Using Hyphens*

Correctly write each word that should be hyphenated. If no word in the sentence needs a hyphen, write C.

**1.** Is Maya Nenno the write in candidate for class president?

**2.** The ex mayor of Morrisville teaches trigonometry at the University of Nebraska.

**3.** I still must work twenty five more equations.

**4.** Fifty six bushels of corn were picked today.

**5.** Have you heard of this mathematician from the mid Victorian era?

**6.** The metal used in the sculpture is one fourth copper.

## ● *Connect to Writing:* Editing

### *Using Hyphens*

Some of the hyphens in these sentences are used incorrectly; others are missing. Correctly write each word that should be hyphenated. If a sentence is correct, write C.

**1.** Thirty nine seniors are enrolled in honors math.

**2.** A three-fourths majority voted to host a free math clinic for the nearby junior high.

**3.** We expect only one-half of those who signed up actually to attend the clinic.

**4.** The student assistants at the math clinic must be self motivated-workers.

**5.** The day's program is all encompassing, including beginning and advanced skills.

**6.** This all encompassing format should meet the needs of every student.

# Hyphens to Avoid Confusion

Without a hyphen, some words would be difficult to read.

**23 E.5**    Use a hyphen to prevent confusion or awkwardness.

re-edit, anti-irritant, semi-invalid

(prevents awkwardness of two consecutive identical vowels)

co-operator of equipment (prevents confusion with the word *cooperator*)

re-sign the contract (prevents confusion with the word *resign*)

## ● Practice Your Skills

### *Using Hyphens*

Correctly write each word that should be hyphenated. If a sentence is correct, write C.

**1.** I would like to reexamine those photographs.

**2.** At least one half of these photographs are of historical buildings in town.

**3.** Many of the buildings are of pre World War II construction.

**4.** We should repetition the town hall to hang these photos in the lobby.

**5.** A three fourths portion of the wall space is now covered in tattered travel posters.

**6.** These quality photographs would create a much improved look.

**7.** If the photo display is long term, perhaps it will attract customers to your gallery.

**8.** After all, the run of the mill citizen goes inside the town hall only occasionally.

#  Dashes, Parentheses, and Brackets

Although **dashes, parentheses,** and **brackets** are used to separate words and phrases, do not overuse these punctuation marks and do not substitute them for other marks of punctuation, such as commas or colons.

## Dashes

Like a comma, a **dash** (—) is used to separate words or expressions. A dash, however, indicates a greater separation than a comma does. Dashes should be used in the following situations.

**23 E.6**   Use dashes to set off an abrupt change in thought.

> Several students—there were five—applied for the job.
>
> I've misplaced the book—oh, I see you have it.

**23 E.7**   Use dashes to set off an appositive that is introduced by words such as *that is, for example,* or *for instance.*

> If an item is lost—for example, a book or a tape—pay the fee.
>
> Sam's job—that is, assistant librarian—is interesting.

**23 E.8**   Use dashes to set off a parenthetical expression or an appositive that includes commas. Also use dashes to call special attention to a phrase.

> Let's find a novel—mystery or historical—for you.
>
> You can return the novel to me Monday or Wednesday—or Friday, for that matter—right after school.

**23 E.9**   Use dashes to set off a phrase or a clause that summarizes or emphasizes what has preceded it.

> June 6, 7, and 8—these are the dates of the book auction.
>
> A book and a T-shirt—I received these gifts for my birthday.

## Power Your Writing: Dash It All

⚡ The dash should be used sparingly, but can be used effectively to separate words and phrases from the rest of the sentence, as in these examples from "Quality" by John Galsworthy (pages 317–322):

> For to make boots—such boots as he made—seemed to me then, and still seems to me, mysterious and wonderful.

> When at last I went I was surprised that . . . another name was painted, also that of a bootmaker—making, of course, for the Royal Family.

Experiment with dashes in your own writing.

## Parentheses

**Parentheses** (**( )**) separate information that is not necessary to the meaning of the sentence. Definitions and dates, for example, are sometimes enclosed by parentheses. When using parentheses, remember to use pairs.

**23 E.10**   Use parentheses to enclose information that is not related closely to the meaning in a sentence.

To decide whether you should use parentheses, read the sentence without the parenthetical material. If the meaning and structure of the sentence are not changed, then add parentheses. Parenthetical expressions slow readers down. You should limit the use of parenthetical material in any one piece of writing.

> Dylan Thomas **(**1914–1953**)** read his own poetry brilliantly.
>
> Samuel Clemens did not invent the name Mark Twain **(**which means "a depth of 2 fathoms, or 12 feet"**)**.

**23 E.11**   Use parentheses to identify a source of information such as a reference to an author or a page number.

> "Arthur Conan Doyle realized he could make more money writing mystery stories than practicing ophthalmology" **(**Garrett 22**)**.

When the closing parenthesis comes at the end of a sentence, the end mark usually goes outside of the parentheses. However, occasionally the end mark goes inside the parentheses if the end mark actually belongs with the parenthetical material.

> Many people enjoy Doyle's mystery stories. **(**I'm not one of them, though.**)**

# Brackets

Brackets (**[ ]**) come in pairs, just like quotation marks and parentheses. They are used to enclose certain specific information. When you write a research paper that includes quoted passages, you may need to use brackets.

**23 E.12**   Use brackets to enclose an explanation within quoted material that is not part of the quotation.

> Richard Ellman wrote, "He **[**W. B. Yeats**]** displayed and interpreted the direction in which poetry was to go."

The following summary may help you decide when to use certain kinds of punctuation.

---

## PUNCTUATING PARENTHETICAL INFORMATION

Parenthetical (nonessential) information is always set off from the rest of the sentence by special punctuation. Depending on how important the parenthetical material is, use one of the following marks of punctuation.

- Use commas ( **,** ) to enclose information that is loosely related to the rest of the sentence yet is nonessential. This method is the most common.
- Use parentheses **( )** to enclose information that is not essential to the meaning of the sentence but that adds an interesting point.
- Use dashes (**—**) to signal a break in the train of thought.
- Use brackets **[ ]** to enclose your own words inserted into a quotation.

---

## ● Practice Your Skills

### Using Dashes, Parentheses, and Brackets

Write *I* if the sentence is punctuated incorrectly. Write *C* if it is punctuated correctly.

1. The Victorian poet, Alfred Lord Tennyson 1809–1892, wrote *In Memoriam* over a period of seventeen years.
2. "Mariana," "Ulysses," and "Maud" all these are poems by Tennyson.
3. A number of Victorian authors—for example, Charles Dickens, Wilkie Collins, and Arthur Conan Doyle—wrote mystery stories.
4. At Dickens's death he died in 1870 his novel *The Mystery of Edwin Drood* was unfinished.
5. One of the most interesting characters was what was her name? Her Royal Highness the Princess Puffer.

● *Connect to Writing:* **Editing**

### *Using Dashes, Parentheses, and Brackets*

Rewrite the incorrect sentences from the preceding exercise, using commas, dashes, parentheses, and brackets correctly.

## ✔ *Check Point:* **Mixed Practice**

Write the following sentences, inserting hyphens, parentheses, dashes, and brackets as needed.

1. Running, swimming, and riding these are good forms of exercise.
2. We need to add forty eight chairs that's four dozen.
3. I think you are shall we say too short to be good at basketball.
4. The dates for some of this year's competitions football, tennis, and track have already been set.
5. Who was it that said, "He Tom Landry was the greatest football coach of all time"?

## ✔ *Check Point:* **Mixed Practice**

Write the following paragraphs, adding any punctuation marks and capital letters that are needed.

There arent any hard and fast statistics nevertheless the expression OK is probably the most widely used American expression in the world. For example, during World War II, there was a special international soccer match. One team was composed of members from the following four countries Poland, Czechoslovakia, Denmark, and Norway. The team had serious difficulties because of the language differences. Finally one of Polands players shouted, OK! Feeling confident that everyone finally understood the same thing, the team members went on to win the game.

Despite its international acceptance, the expression OK is really an all American expression. It first appeared in print in 1839 in a Boston newspaper, the Morning Post. A year later President Martin Van Buren he was born in Kinderhook, New York ran for a second term of office. He was called Old Kinderhook by his backers. The initials of his nickname were then used during the campaign. Later OK came into wide use as a catchword meaning all is right.

## Assess Your Learning

### ▣ Using Correct Punctuation

Write each sentence, adding punctuation where needed.

1. The conservation department puts rainbow trout into the streams the lakes are stocked with salmon, herring, pickerel, and perch.
2. The prop committee still hasnt found the following items a straw hat, a wicker chair, and a large desk.
3. Everyones enthusiasm at the pep rally encouraged the players on Newtons all star team.
4. In the code the 2s stood for es.
5. The Eighteenth Amendment the prohibition amendment was not ratified by Connecticut and Rhode Island.
6. Most insects have no eyelids thus, their eyes are always open.
7. Six, forty, and ten these are the three correct answers.
8. Its time to apply for the dogs new license.
9. We have our choice of pink, aqua, or lavender unfortunately, we dont know which color would be best for the room.
10. A tree snake appears to fly through the air however it merely glides on air currents.
11. We couldnt possibly be at your house by 7 30.
12. Shiny metals for example, tin and copper turn into black powders when finely ground aluminum is an exception.
13. Gregor Mendel 1822–1884 was the Austrian botanist who developed the basic laws of heredity.
14. Bobs and Teds scores in their last bowling game were the best they ve ever had.
15. Only two copies of the works of the Greek sculptor Myron have survived one of those is the sculpture Discus Thrower.

## ◼ Punctuating Direct Quotations

Write each sentence correctly, adding end marks, commas, and quotations marks where needed.

**1.** Ogden Nash mused, I marvel that such small ribs as these can cage such vast desire to please

**2.** A dog's ideal is a life of active uselessness stated William Phelps

**3.** If dogs could talk Karel Capek said perhaps we would find it as hard to get along with them as we do with people.

**4.** A dog is a lion on his own street states a Hindu proverb

**5.** When did a dog ever turn up his nose at a smell asked C. E. Montague

## ◼ Writing Sentences

Write five sentences that follow the directions below.

Write a sentence that . . .

**1.** includes the possessive form of the nouns *cousins* and *six months*.

**2.** includes the joint ownership of something.

**3.** includes a series of dates, including month, day, and year.

**4.** includes a colon at the beginning of a list.

**5.** includes a dash or pair of dashes.

# Other Punctuation: Posttest

## Directions

Each underlined part in the passage may lack one type of punctuation. Write the letter of the answer with the punctuation that correctly completes the underlined part. If the underlined part contains no error, write **D**.

(1) René Magritte 1898–1967 was a Belgian artist who established a reputation as a talented artist in the Surrealist style. Horror, comedy, and (2) mystery these are some of the moods he created in his paintings. If you study a number of his paintings, you'll notice certain symbols are repeated (3) throughout many of them the female torso, the bowler hat, the castle, and others. (4) Although Magrittes work is famous today, he had to work earnestly for his success. His humble beginnings included (5) nonglamorous jobs such as designing wallpaper and sketching advertisements.

**1. A** Parentheses
  **B** Quotation marks
  **C** Italics
  **D** No error

**2. A** Italics
  **B** Parentheses
  **C** Dash
  **D** No error

**3. A** Hyphen
  **B** Semicolon
  **C** Colon
  **D** No error

**4. A** Semicolon
  **B** Dash
  **C** Apostrophe
  **D** No error

**5. A** Semicolon
  **B** Colon
  **C** Dash
  **D** No error

# Writer's Corner

## Snapshot

**23 A**  An **apostrophe** is used to show possession and in contractions. (pages 964–973)

**23 B**  A **semicolon** is used between the clauses of a compound sentence when they are not joined by a conjunction. A **colon** is used to introduce lists and long quotations and to separate certain independent clauses. (pages 974–982)

**23 C**  **Italics** are used to indicate certain titles and names, foreign words, and a word used as a word. If you are writing by hand, **underline** whatever should be italicized. (pages 983–985)

**23 D**  **Quotation marks** come in pairs. Use them at the beginning and at the end of certain titles and to indicate quotations and dialogue. (pages 986–1001)

**23 E**  A **hyphen** divides a word at the end of a line. **Dashes, parentheses,** and **brackets** separate certain words or groups of words from the rest of the sentence. (pages 1002–1010)

## Power Rules

 Use standard ways to make nouns possessive. When you use a **noun to show ownership,** add an *'s* to singular nouns and plural nouns that don't end in an *s*. Add only an apostrophe to plural nouns ending in an *s*. (pages 964–966)

| **Before Editing** | **After Editing** |
| --- | --- |
| My *sister* friends are coming with us. | My *sister's* friends are coming with us. |
| We are borrowing my *parents* car. | We are borrowing my *parents'* car. |

 Check for **run-on sentences** and fix them by adding a conjunction, a conjunctive adverb, a transitional word, and/or punctuation. (pages 736–738)

| **Before Editing** | **After Editing** |
| --- | --- |
| Josh's favorite kind of dog is a boxer *mine is a Dalmatian.* | Josh's favorite kind of dog is a boxer; *mine is a Dalmatian.* |
| Dalmatians are very active *they make wonderful pets.* | Dalmatians are very active; *nevertheless, they make wonderful pets.* |

## Editing Checklist

Use this checklist when editing your writing.

✓ Did I use apostrophes correctly with possessive nouns and with contractions? (See pages 964–972.)

✓ Did I use semicolons and colons correctly with lists, independent clauses, and long quotations? (See pages 974–982.)

✓ Did I use italics or underlining for certain words and titles? (See pages 983–985.)

✓ Did I use quotation marks with titles and direct quotations? (See pages 986–995.)

✓ Did I use hyphens to divide words and in compound nouns and numbers? (See pages 1002–1004.)

✓ Did I use dashes, parentheses, and brackets correctly? (See pages 1007–1010.)

## Use the Power

**These graphics** can help you remember how to use punctuation in everyday life.

| | |
|---|---|
| "Quotation Marks" | "The Wasteland" is my favorite poem. |
| Apostrophe ' | Are you going to Tina's party? |
| Dash — | My brother went skydiving—and lived to tell about it! |
| Semicolon ; | We visited Paris, France; Venice, Italy; and Madrid, Spain. |
| Colon : | Dear Madam: |
| Italics *abc* | Have you ever read *On the Road?* |
| Hyphen – | I can't wait until I turn twenty–one. |
| Ellipsis . . . | I could live on pizza . . . if it were more nutritious. |
| [ Brackets ] | "He [ the director ] told us exactly what to do." |
| ( Parentheses ) | Read about the stock market in the last chapter ( pages 22–28 ). |

# Spelling Correctly

**How can you communicate your message effectively by using accurate spelling?**

## Spelling Correctly: Pretest 1

The following first draft contains several spelling errors. The first error has been corrected. Revise the rest of the draft to correct the remaining spelling errors.

Of all the ~~stringged~~ *stringed* instruments, the violin is truely the most versatile. It is unussual to see violas and celloes in a country music group, and you will rarly see iether banjoes or guitars in the symphony orcestra. Violins, however, have dual lifes. Going by the name of "fiddles," they do themselfes proud, playing with folk or bluegrass comboes. As violins, they are the principle voices in symphonys, sonatas, and concertoes. Alone, they can play soloes. With a cello and a viola, they can play trios. They are almost as versatile and popular as pianoes, and they are much more potable!

# Spelling Correctly: Pretest 2

## Directions

Read the passage. Write the letter of the answer that correctly respells each underlined word. If the word is correct, write D.

 We **(1)** recentally read a poem by John Keats called "Ode to a Nightingale." This **(2)** melencholy poem expresses the poet's **(3)** emoteons as he listens to the bird's song. He remarks that the bird is **(4)** imortal and that the same song he hears was heard by ancient **(5)** emporers. The poet speaks of the **(6)** numbness he feels at the **(7)** tyrany of time. His heartache contrasts with the **(8)** happyness of the bird's melody. He speaks of flying to the bird on the **(9)** invisable wings of poetry. In **(10)** dispair, he wonders whether he is awake or dreaming.

1. **A** recently
   **B** recenttly
   **C** reccently
   **D** No error

2. **A** melancoly
   **B** melancholy
   **C** melancholly
   **D** No error

3. **A** emoteions
   **B** emotions
   **C** emottions
   **D** No error

4. **A** imortle
   **B** inmortal
   **C** immortal
   **D** No error

5. **A** emperors
   **B** empirers
   **C** emporrers
   **D** No error

6. **A** numness
   **B** nummness
   **C** numbeness
   **D** No error

7. **A** tirrany
   **B** tiranny
   **C** tyranny
   **D** No error

8. **A** happiness
   **B** hapiness
   **C** happynes
   **D** No error

9. **A** invizable
   **B** invissable
   **C** invisible
   **D** No error

10. **A** despair
    **B** dispare
    **C** despare
    **D** No error

# Strategies for Learning to Spell

Learning to spell involves a variety of senses. You use your senses of hearing, sight, and touch to spell a word correctly. Here is a five-step strategy that many people have used successfully as they learned to spell unfamiliar words.

## 1  Auditory

**Say the word aloud. Answer these questions.**

- Where have I heard or read this word before?
- What was the context in which I heard or read the word?

## 2  Visual

**Look at the word. Answer these questions.**

- Does this word divide into parts? Is it a compound word? Does it have a prefix or a suffix?
- Does this word look like any other word I know? Could it be part of a word family I would recognize?

## 3  Auditory

**Spell the word to yourself. Say the word the way it is spelled. Answer these questions.**

- How is each sound spelled?
- Are there any surprises? Does the word follow spelling rules I know, or does it break the rules?

## 4  Visual/Kinesthetic

**Write the word as you look at it. Answer these questions.**

- Have I written the word clearly?
- Are my letters formed correctly?

## 5  Visual/Kinesthetic

**Cover up the word. Visualize it. Write it. Answer this question.**

- Did I write the word correctly?

**If the answer is no, return to step 1.**

# Spelling Strategies

Being a good speller is an ongoing process. As you read and build your vocabulary, you also increase the number of words whose spellings you will want to master. The strategies in this chapter will help you spell new words as well as familiar words.

**Use a dictionary.** If you're not sure how to spell a word, or if a word you've written doesn't "look right," check the word in a dictionary. If you don't want to stop and check a word while you are writing, that is okay. Instead, circle the word and look it up when you finish.

**Proofread your writing carefully.** Read your paper one word at a time, looking only for spelling errors. Also, watch for words you're not sure you spelled correctly. If you are working on a computer, you can use the spell checker.

**Be sure you are pronouncing words correctly.** "Swallowing" syllables or adding extra syllables can cause you to misspell a word.

**Make up mnemonic devices.** A sentence like "**Ants** have many descend**ants**" can help you remember that *descendant* ends with *ant*. "There are a pair of *ll's* in **parallel**" can help you remember where the double *l's* belong in *parallel*.

**Keep a spelling journal.** Use it to record the words that you've had trouble spelling. Here are some steps for organizing your spelling journal.

- Write the word correctly.
- Write the word again, underlining or circling the part of the word that gave you trouble.
- Write a tip that will help you remember how to spell the word in the future.

| colossal | colossal | Colossal has two o's, two l's, and two s's, but only the s's are side by side |
| --- | --- | --- |

## ● Practice Your Skills

### *Recognizing Misspelled Words*

Identify the misspelled word in each set. Then write the word correctly.

|     |                  |               |                 |
| --- | ---------------- | ------------- | --------------- |
| **1.** | (a) occurrence | (b) neice     | (c) stretch     |
| **2.** | (a) fiery       | (b) drought   | (c) arial       |
| **3.** | (a) condemn     | (b) weight    | (c) interupt    |
| **4.** | (a) courtesy    | (b) milage    | (c) regrettable |
| **5.** | (a) assistence  | (b) biscuit   | (c) carriage    |
| **6.** | (a) immigrant   | (b) fasinate  | (c) pitiful     |
| **7.** | (a) business    | (b) bargain   | (c) campain     |
| **8.** | (a) ilustrate   | (b) seize     | (c) reference   |
| **9.** | (a) chord       | (b) luxury    | (c) napsack     |
| **10.** | (a) analyze    | (b) ordinery  | (c) cooperate   |

## ● Practice Your Skills

### *Pronouncing Words*

Practice saying each syllable in the following words to help you spell the words correctly.

| | |
| --- | --- |
| **1.** am•big•u•ous | **6.** li•ai•son |
| **2.** si•mul•ta•ne•ous | **7.** a•non•y•mous |
| **3.** phe•nom•e•non | **8.** fo•li•age |
| **4.** ca•tas•tro•phe | **9.** pop•u•lar•i•ty |
| **5.** bank•rupt•cy | **10.** sim•i•le |

Spelling generalizations are rules that apply to many different words. Knowing these generalizations can help you spell many words correctly. The information that follows will help you decide when to use certain letter patterns, how to form plurals, and how to add prefixes and suffixes.

**24 A**  **Spelling patterns**—such as *i* before *e* except after *c*—apply to many words and can help you spell many different words correctly.

## Words with *ie* and *ei*

**24 A.1**  When the vowel sound is long *e*, write *ei* after *c* and *ie* after other consonant letters.

| *IE* AND *EI* | | | | | |
|---|---|---|---|---|---|
| **Examples** | ceiling | receive | deceive | field | believe |
| | conceit | achieve | deceit | chief | grieve |
| **Exceptions** | seize | either | neither | leisure | protein | weird |

**24 A.2**  When the sound is long *a* or any vowel sound other than long *e*, write *ei*.

| VOWEL SOUNDS OTHER THAN LONG *E* | | | |
|---|---|---|---|
| **Examples** | weigh | neighbor | freight | reign |
| | height | heir | forfeit | heifer |
| **Exceptions** | view | friend | mischief | ancient |
| | sieve | fierce | tie | pier |

The generalizations do not apply if the *i* and *e* are in different syllables.

| *IE* AND *EI* IN DIFFERENT SYLLABLES | | | |
|---|---|---|---|
| be•ing | de•ice | re•imburse | re•iterate |
| pi•ety | fi•esta | di•et | sci•ence |

# Words with -sede, -ceed, and -cede

**24 A.3** The syllable that sounds like "seed" is usually spelled -cede, but it can be spelled -ceed or -sede.

| *-SEDE, -CEED,* AND *-CEDE* | | |
|---|---|---|
| *-sede* (only one example) | super**sede** | |
| *-ceed* (only three examples) | ex**ceed** | pro**ceed** | suc**ceed** |
| *-cede* (all other words) | ac**cede** | con**cede** | pre**cede** |

There is no *-seed* ending except in words derived from the noun *seed*, such as *reseed*, which means "to sow again."

## ● Practice Your Skills

### *Using Spelling Patterns*

Write each word, adding *ie* or *ei*. If you are unsure about a spelling, check the dictionary.

**1.** br ▨ f
**2.** for ▨ gn
**3.** th ▨ r
**4.** n ▨ ce
**5.** rec ▨ pt
**6.** p ▨ ce
**7.** l ▨ sure

**8.** perc ▨ ve
**9.** w ▨ gh
**10.** y ▨ ld
**11.** s ▨ ge
**12.** hyg ▨ ne
**13.** s ▨ zure
**14.** rec ▨ ve

**15.** conc ▨ t
**16.** dec ▨ ve
**17.** ▨ ther
**18.** med ▨ val
**19.** rel ▨ ve
**20.** counterf ▨ t

## ● Practice Your Skills

### *Using Spelling Patterns*

Write each word, adding *-sede, -ceed,* or *-cede*.

**1.** re ▨
**2.** con ▨
**3.** ex ▨
**4.** inter ▨
**5.** super ▨

**6.** pro ▨
**7.** se ▨
**8.** ac ▨
**9.** suc ▨
**10.** pre ▨

## ● *Connect to Writing:* **Editing**

### *Using Spelling Patterns*

Read this article, paying particular attention to the underlined words. Decide whether they are spelled correctly. Then rewrite those that are misspelled.

Today much is known about the culture of <u>ancient</u> Egypt. Two centuries of study have <u>yeilded</u> a wealth of information about the religious <u>beliefs</u> and practices of Egypt of long ago. At the beginning of the nineteenth century, Egyptian civilization was <u>veiled</u> in mystery. Jean-François Champollion was the first scholar to work in this <u>field</u>. He is <u>veiwed</u> as the founder of Egyptology.

Champollion worked with the Rosetta Stone to <u>piece</u> together the principles of <u>heiroglyphics</u>. The Rosetta Stone, which was discovered by Napoleon's troops near Alexandria, had been inscribed by <u>preists</u> of Ptolemy V. Using the stone, Champollion <u>proceded</u> to compare the Egyptian text to the Greek text on the stone and <u>succeded</u> in figuring out the key to the <u>heiroglyphic</u> symbols. For the study of ancient Egypt, this was an <u>excedingly</u> important <u>acheivement</u>.

There are a number of useful generalizations that will help you spell the plural of most nouns.

**24 B** **To form the plural of most nouns, add *s* or *es*. Some nouns form their plurals in other ways.**

## Regular Nouns

**24 B.1** To form the plural of most nouns, add *s*.

| | | MOST NOUNS | | | |
|---|---|---|---|---|---|
| **Singular** | geologist | frog | bicycle | rose | puzzle |
| **Plural** | geologists | frogs | bicycles | roses | puzzles |

**24 B.2** To form the plural of most nouns ending in *s, ch, sh, x,* or *z*, add *es*.

| | | S, CH, SH, X, AND Z | | | |
|---|---|---|---|---|---|
| **Singular** | moss | beach | wish | tax | waltz |
| **Plural** | mosses | beaches | wishes | taxes | waltzes |

Add just *s* to words that end in a *ch* pronounced like a *k: monarchs, epochs*.

## WORD ALERT

The following related plurals are alike, except one ends in *s* and the other in *es*. Form the plurals carefully because their meanings differ.

**cloths**—[plural noun] pieces of fabric with specific uses; often part of a compound word: *tablecloths, dishcloths, washcloths*

There are cleaning **cloths** in the broom closet.

**clothes**—[plural noun] garments or apparel, usually made of cloth

Everyone wore formal **clothes** to the prom.

# Nouns Ending with *y*

**24 B.3**   Add *s* to form the plural of a noun ending with a vowel and *y*.

| VOWELS AND *Y* | | | | |
|---|---|---|---|---|
| **Singular** | ess**ay** | journ**ey** | all**oy** | monk**ey** |
| **Plural** | essay**s** | journey**s** | alloy**s** | monkey**s** |

**24 B.4**   Change the *y* to *i* and add *es* to a noun ending in a consonant and *y*.

| CONSONANTS AND *Y* | | | | |
|---|---|---|---|---|
| **Singular** | ene**my** | falla**cy** | catego**ry** | supp**ly** |
| **Plural** | ene**mies** | falla**cies** | catego**ries** | supp**lies** |
| **Exceptions** | For proper nouns ending with *y,* just add *s.* | | | |
| | Jeremy | Avery | Kennedy | |
| | Jeremy**s** | Avery**s** | Kennedy**s** | |

## ● Practice Your Skills

### *Forming Plurals*

Write the plural form of each noun. Use a dictionary to check your work.

| | | | |
|---|---|---|---|
| **1.** fantasy | **6.** fox | **11.** casualty | **16.** bench |
| **2.** editor | **7.** alley | **12.** holiday | **17.** six |
| **3.** latch | **8.** phrase | **13.** ally | **18.** sketch |
| **4.** thistle | **9.** hoax | **14.** railway | **19.** melee |
| **5.** tragedy | **10.** reply | **15.** class | **20.** blueberry |

## ● *Connect to Writing:* Editing

### *Spelling Plural Nouns*

Edit this paragraph, changing the underlined nouns from singular to plural.

The names people give their baby go in and out of fashion. This is true of names given to both sex, but switch in popularity are particularly common for very old names given to boy. Consider Henry. The name Henry has been around for century. It means "one who rules the home and estate (amassed property)." History is full of famous Henry. There were eight monarch of England named Henry and six Holy Roman emperor. Other recent historical personality include Henry Ford and Henry Kissinger. But for a while, during the middle decade of the twentieth century, the name Henry was not very popular. There were many Gary and Barry, but not very many Henry. Today family are once again naming their baby Henry. How many Henry do you know?

# Nouns Ending with *o*

**24 B.5**    Add *s* to form the plural of a noun ending with a vowel and *o*.

| VOWELS AND O | | | |
|---|---|---|---|
| **Singular** | stud**io** | rat**io** | ster**eo** | kangar**oo** |
| **Plural** | stud**ios** | rat**ios** | ster**eos** | kangar**oos** |

**24 B.6**    Add *es* to form the plural of many nouns that end with a consonant and *o*.

| CONSONANTS AND O | | | |
|---|---|---|---|
| **Singular** | toma**to** | torpe**do** | he**ro** | ec**ho** |
| **Plural** | toma**toes** | torpe**does** | he**roes** | ec**hoes** |

**24 B.7**    Add *s* to form the plural of musical terms, proper nouns, and some other nouns that end in a consonant and *o*.

| MUSICAL TERMS, FOODS, ETC. | | | |
|---|---|---|---|
| **Singular** | picco**lo** | tange**lo** | ta**co** | Poco**no** |
| **Plural** | picco**los** | tange**los** | ta**cos** | Poco**nos** |

When dictionaries give two forms for the plurals of some nouns ending in a consonant and *o,* the first form is the preferred one.

| PREFERRED FORMS | | |
|---|---|---|
| **Singular** | tornad**o** | zer**o** | mosquit**o** |
| **Plural** | tornad**oes** or tornados | zeros or zeroes | mosquit**oes** or mosquitos |

# Nouns Ending in *f* or *fe*

**24 B.9** To form the plural of some nouns ending in *f* or *fe,* just add *s.*

| *F* OR *FE* | | | | |
|---|---|---|---|---|
| **Singular** | che**f** | staf**f** | roo**f** | wai**f** | giraf**fe** |
| **Plural** | che**fs** | staf**fs** | roo**fs** | wai**fs** | giraf**fes** |

**24 B.10** For some nouns ending in *f* or *fe,* change the *f* or *fe* to *v* and add *es.*

| *F* OR *FE* TO *V* | | | | |
|---|---|---|---|---|
| **Singular** | shel**f** | lea**f** | hoo**f** | wi**fe** | kni**fe** |
| **Plural** | shel**ves** | lea**ves** | hoo**ves** | wi**ves** | kni**ves** |

When unsure which rule applies, consult a dictionary to find out the correct plural form of a word that ends with *f* or *fe.*

## ● Practice Your Skills

*Forming Plurals*

Write the plural form of each of these nouns. Check a dictionary to be sure you've formed the plural correctly.

| | | | |
|---|---|---|---|
| **1.** half | **6.** placebo | **11.** belief | **16.** gulf |
| **2.** cello | **7.** scenario | **12.** banjo | **17.** proof |
| **3.** tomato | **8.** soprano | **13.** silo | **18.** self |
| **4.** burrito | **9.** pimento | **14.** wharf | **19.** folio |
| **5.** sheriff | **10.** ratio | **15.** stereo | **20.** radio |

# Numerals, Letters, Symbols, and Words Used as Words

**24 B.11** To form the plurals of most numerals, letters, symbols, and words used as words, add an *s*. With some lowercase letters, some capital letters, and some words used as words, use an apostrophe and *s*.

**Examples** The *7***s** in this column should be *4***s**. Interest rates were high in the 1980**s**. Ampersands (*&***s**) replace *and***s** in some company names. There will be no *but***s** about it.

**Exceptions** If *e'***s** are closed at the top, they look like *i'***s**. (Without the apostrophe, *i'*s become *is*.)

*A'***s** are easy letters to write. (*A'*s become *As*.)

Some writers prefer to add *'s* to form the plural of all numerals, letters, symbols, and words used as words.

# Other Plural Forms

**24 B.12** Irregular plurals are not formed by adding *s* or *es*.

| IRREGULAR PLURALS | | | | |
|---|---|---|---|---|
| **Singular** | child | woman | tooth | mouse |
| **Plural** | child**ren** | wom**en** | t**eeth** | m**ice** |

**24 B.13** For some nouns, the singular and the plural forms are the same.

| SAME SINGULAR AND PLURAL | | | | |
|---|---|---|---|---|
| sheep | moose | corps | scissors | Chinese |
| salmon | trout | species | series | Swiss |

# Compound Nouns

**24 B.14** The plurals of most compound nouns are formed in the same way other plural nouns are formed.

| MOST COMPOUND NOUNS | | |
|---|---|---|
| **Singular** | stepchild | eyetooth | bookshelf |
| **Plural** | step**children** | eye**teeth** | book**shelves** |

**24 B.15**  In compound words in which one part of the compound word modifies the other, make the word that is modified the plural.

| SELF-MODIFYING COMPOUNDS | | | |
|---|---|---|---|
| **Singular** | musk-ox | son-in-law | runner-up |
| **Plural** | musk-**oxen** | **sons**-in-law | **runners**-up |

# Foreign Plurals

**24 B.16**  The plurals of some foreign words are formed as they are in their original language. For some foreign words, there are two ways to form the plural.

| FOREIGN WORDS | | | | |
|---|---|---|---|---|
| **Singular** | alga | alumnus | bacterium | ellipsis |
| **Plural** | algae | alumni | bacteria | ellipses |
| **Singular** | formula | index | hippopotamus | |
| **Plural** | formulas or formulae | indexes or indices | hippopotamuses or hippopotami | |

Check a dictionary when writing the plural of foreign words. When two forms are given, the first one is preferred.

## WORD ALERT

Listen and watch for foreign words that are becoming more commonly used. If you use them in your writing, be sure to form the plurals correctly. Check a dictionary to be sure you have written a plural form correctly.

**chapeau**—[noun, plural *chapeaux,* French] a hat
Brett and Olivia put their **chapeaux** on the shelf.

**cravat**—[noun, plural *cravats,* French] a scarf or a tie
He bought two **cravats** in the shirt department.

*Forming Plurals*

Write the plural form for each item. If you are not sure about the correct form, check a dictionary.

| | | |
|---|---|---|
| **1.** memorandum | **6.** but | **11.** die |
| **2.** genus | **7.** 8 | **12.** ? |
| **3.** stylus | **8.** 1890 | **13.** goose |
| **4.** thesis | **9.** dormouse | **14.** goldfinch |
| **5.** nucleus | **10.** grandchild | **15.** tempo |

● *Connect to Writing:* **Editing**

*Forming Plurals*

Decide if the underlined plurals in these paragraphs are formed correctly. Check a dictionary if you're not certain. If any of the underlined plurals are incorrectly formed, write the correct forms.

Everyone knows something about dude ranches, where tenderfoots go to pretend they are cowpokes. Probably fewer people have heard of tourist farms because there hasn't been much publicity in the medium. Tourist farms are one of the vacation phenomenons of the late 1990s. These farms offer city-dwellers who spend their workdays in offices the opportunity to experience life as their forefathers (and foremothers) might have in the 1890's. Parents and their childs spend their vacations on working farms, not as bystanders or looker-ons, but as farmhands. They plow fields and plant crops. They feed the poultries and collect the eggs. They milk the dairy cattles. They pick fruit from orchards. They learn the importance of windmills and other farm apparatusses to traditional farms. If the windmills do not turn, the guests will help figure out how to pump water for the sheeps and other farm animals. Familys might spend mornings picking buckets of blackberrys, which later become pies, jellys, and jams. Farms may not be ideal vacation spots for couch potatoes or fuddy-duddys, but for people looking for relief from stress, farms can be ideal.

● *Connect to Reading and Writing:* **Classroom Vocabulary**

*Spelling with New Vocabulary*

This chapter has introduced you to new terms you will use often in your study of English grammar. To keep track of these new words and phrases, such as *compound nouns, words used as words, foreign plurals, prefixes,* and *suffixes,* make a booklet that lists and tells about them.

# Spelling Numbers  Lesson 3

**24 C**    **Some numbers are written as numerals while other numbers are written as words.**

The following generalizations can help you decide how to write numbers in your compositions.

## Numerals or Number Words

**24 C.1**    Spell out numbers that can be written in one or two words. Use numerals for other numbers. Always spell out a number that begins a sentence.

> Our journey lasted **fifteen** days.
>
> We traveled **3,220** miles, from Portland, Maine, to Portland, Oregon.
>
> **Three hundred eighty-seven** miles was the farthest we traveled in one day.

Be consistent. When you have many numbers in a passage, use numerals for them all.

> We traveled an average of **230** miles a day, but one day we went **387** miles and another day we traveled only **95** miles.

## Ordinal Numbers

**24 C.2**    Always spell out numbers used to tell the order.

> On the **first** day, we got a very late start.
>
> By the **tenth** day, we were getting tired of traveling.

### WORD ALERT

> Use ordinal words to represent the names of streets numbered first through tenth. For street names greater than *tenth,* use ordinal figures: numbers ending in *st, nd, rd,* and *th.*
>
> Fifth Avenue      44th Street      83rd Street      First Street

# Other Uses of Numerals

**24 C.3** Use numerals in dates, addresses, times of day, and measurements and for numbers that identify.

| USES OF NUMERALS | | | |
|---|---|---|---|
| **Dates** | September **9, 2001** | A.D. **1066** | **500** B.C. |
| **Addresses** | **220** West End Avenue Hudson, OH **43210-2104** | | |
| **Time** | **9:45** A.M. | **7:15** P.M. | |
| | (If you use *o'clock,* then write the hour: **six** o'clock) | | |
| **Measurements** | **90** degrees<br>**51** percent | **16** ounces<br>**47** points | |
| **Numbers That Identify** | Route **66**<br>Box **549** | Channel **11**<br>pages **11–17** | Room **213** |

● **Practice Your Skills**

*Spelling Numbers*

If the underlined number is written correctly, write **C.** If it is written incorrectly, rewrite it correctly.

**1.** Grandma received <u>80</u> birthday cards on her <u>eightieth</u> birthday.

**2.** On the <u>17th</u> of July, the hottest day of the summer, the temperature soared to a humid <u>ninety-nine</u> degrees.

**3.** Our <u>1st</u> dog weighed <u>47</u> pounds, but the new puppy will weigh about <u>80</u> pounds when it is grown.

**4.** It's almost <u>5</u> o'clock, and in <u>60</u> minutes, <u>12</u> people will walk through that door, expecting dinner.

**5.** The drawing on page <u>thirty-nine</u> shows the Great Pyramid of Khufu, which may have been built in <u>twenty-six eighty</u> B.C. and is one of the <u>Seven</u> Wonders of the Ancient World.

**6.** A sonnet is <u>14</u> lines of iambic pentameter; each line has <u>10</u> beats and every <u>2nd</u> beat is emphasized.

**7.** The final score was <u>ninety-five</u> to <u>ninety-three</u>, and Channel <u>Three</u> is showing game highlights at <u>11</u> o'clock.

**8.** Phillis Wheatley, the <u>1st</u> published African-American poet, was kidnapped from Africa when she was <u>7</u>; she published her first book of poems when she was <u>17</u>.

**9.** In 1803, the United States purchased <u>eight hundred twenty-eight thousand</u> square miles of land from France at a cost of about <u>four</u> cents an acre.

**10.** For <u>36</u> seasons, the Major League record for home runs was <u>61</u>, but Negro League player Josh Gibson, who died in <u>1947</u>, had a season record of <u>89</u> homers.

## *Connect to Writing:* Editing

### *Writing Numbers*

Rewrite this paragraph, correcting any mistakes in writing numbers.

Of the 48 contiguous United States, Minnesota is the state located farthest north. Minnesota covers a total of eighty-four thousand four hundred two square miles, and an estimated 5,266,774 people lived there in 2010, making Minnesota the 12th largest in size and 21st in population.

53 percent of all Minnesotans are estimated to live in the Minneapolis/St. Paul area. With a population of two hundred seventy-seven thousand two hundred fifty-one, St. Paul is the 2nd most populous city in Minnesota. It ranks among the 50 largest U.S. cities. Both Minneapolis and St. Paul rank high when it comes to quality of life. Well over 6,000 acres of the city are devoted to parks, and over 6 square miles are covered by water. There are 12 lakes within the city limits of Minneapolis.

Lake Calhoun

**24 D**  A **prefix** is one or more syllables placed in front of a base word to form a new word. A **suffix** is one or more syllables placed after a base word to form a new word.

**24 D.1**  When you add a **prefix,** the spelling of the base word does not change.

| PREFIXES | |
|---|---|
| **anti** + toxin = **anti**toxin | **re** + enact = **re**enact |
| **re** + introduce = **re**introduce | **over** + rule = **over**rule |
| **pre** + suppose = **pre**suppose | **in** + animate = **in**animate |

When the prefix *re-* is followed by a word that begins with *e,* some writers prefer to hyphenate the word: re + enact = re-enact.

## WORD ALERT

The prefix *anti-* and the prefix *ante-* sound alike, but their meanings are different.

**anti**—[prefix] adds the meaning "against" or "opposite"

Many college students were part of the **antiwar** movement of the 1960s.

Vitamin K is a common **antitoxin.**

**ante**—[prefix] adds the meaning "before" or "prior"

In architecture, *antebellum* means before the Civil War and *prewar* means before World War II. Many buildings in Boston **antedate** the Revolutionary War.

**24 D.2**  Most of the time when adding a **suffix,** simply affix it to the end of the word.

## Suffixes -*ness* and -*ly*

**24 D.3**  The suffixes -*ness* and -*ly* are added to most base words without any spelling changes.

| SUFFIXES -NESS AND -LY | |
|---|---|
| keen + **ness** = keen**ness** | light + **ly** = light**ly** |
| kind + **ness** = kind**ness** | soft + **ly** + soft**ly** |
| fond + **ness** = fond**ness** | |

# Words Ending in *e*

**24 D.4** Drop the final e in the base word when adding a suffix that begins with a vowel.

### SUFFIXES WITH VOWELS

imagine + **ary** = imagin**ary**          note + **able** = not**able**

refuse + **al** = refus**al**          destine + **y** = destin**y**

**24 D.5** Keep the final e when the suffix begins with a consonant.

### SUFFIXES WITH CONSONANTS

| | |
|---|---|
| **Examples** | excite + **ment** = excite**ment** |
| | grace + **ful** = grace**ful** |
| **Exceptions** | judge + **ment** = judg**ment**          awe + **ful** = aw**ful** |
| | true + **ly** = tru**ly** |

**24 D.6** When the base word ends with *ce* or *ge,* the final e must stay to retain the soft sound of the consonant. In some base words ending with *ce,* the e is changed to *i* before adding a suffix that begins with a vowel.

### *CE* OR *GE*

change + **able** = chang**eable**          courage + **ous** = courag**eous**

notice + **able** = notic**eable**          grace + **ous** = grac**ious**

## WORD ALERT

Pronounce the difference between *ref´ use* and *re fuse´* by stressing the correct syllable. If you add a suffix to *ref´use* and mispronounce it, the word will not make sense.

**refuse´**—[verb] to express unwillingness to believe or to participate

I **refuse´** to watch the news coverage.

**ref´use**—[noun] trash or garbage

The disaster left **ref´use** throughout the city.

**refuse´ + al = refus´al**

I accept your **refus´al** to watch.

### Adding Prefixes and Suffixes

Combine these base words and prefixes or suffixes. Remember to make any necessary spelling changes.

| | | |
|---|---|---|
| **1.** dis + appear | **8.** under + rate | **15.** final + ly |
| **2.** re + elect | **9.** space + ous | **16.** true + ly |
| **3.** nerve + ous | **10.** store + age | **17.** co + operate |
| **4.** imitate + ion | **11.** argue + ment | **18.** race + al |
| **5.** ir + regular | **12.** manage + able | **19.** style + ish |
| **6.** use + able | **13.** outrage + ous | **20.** arrange + ment |
| **7.** im + mobile + ity | **14.** grieve + ous | |

● *Connect to Writing:* **Editing**

### Spelling Words with Prefixes and Suffixes

Locate the words in this paragraph that have prefixes or suffixes, and rewrite correctly those that are misspelled.

The nineteenth century saw the establishment of many utopian communities. Often founded in lovly locations, these communities were based on a combineation of socialism and religious commitment. "From each according to his gifts, to each according to his needs" is a statment of the harmony and fairness these communities truely struggled to attain. Each member worked for the benefit and betterment of all members. Unfortuneately, self-interest is more natureal to humankind than concern for communal good. Too often selfishness and self-involvment stood in opposetion to the achievment of true community. As a result, many utopian communities ultimatly failed.

# Words Ending with *y*

**24 D.7**  Keep the *y* when adding a suffix to words that end in a vowel and *y*. Change *y* to *i* when adding a suffix to words that end in a consonant and *y*.

| SUFFIXES WITH *Y* | | | |
|---|---|---|---|
| **Examples** | employ + **able** = employ**able** | ally + **ance** = all**iance** | |
| | pay + **ment** = pay**ment** | merry + **ly** = merr**ily** | |
| **Exceptions** | twenty + **ish** = twenty**ish** | day + **ly** = da**ily** | |
| | hobby + **ist** = hobby**ist** | shy + **ness** = shy**ness** | |

# Doubling the Final Consonant

**24 D.8** Double the final consonant when adding a suffix that begins with a vowel if the base word satisfies both these conditions: (1) It has only one syllable or is stressed on the final syllable and (2) It ends in one consonant preceded by one vowel.

| DOUBLE CONSONANTS | |
|---|---|
| **One-Syllable Words** | hop + er = ho**pp**er<br>wet + est = we**tt**est<br>fog + y = fo**gg**y |
| **Final Syllable Stressed** | upset + ing = upse**tt**ing<br>admit + ance = admi**tt**ance<br>rebel + ion = rebe**ll**ion |

# Words Ending with *c*

**24 D.9** When adding a suffix that begins with *e, i,* or *y* to a word that ends with a vowel and *c*, do not double the final *c*. Instead add the letter *k* after the *c* to retain the hard *c* sound.

| FINAL C | |
|---|---|
| picnic + **er** = picni**ck**er | colic + **y** = coli**ck**y |

## ● Practice Your Skills

### Adding Suffixes

Combine these base words and suffixes. Remember to make any necessary spelling changes.

**1.** lobby + ist

**2.** deny + al

**3.** vary + ance

**4.** steady + ly

**5.** gold + en

**6.** transmit + al

**7.** compel + ing

**8.** regret + able

**9.** colic + y

**10.** worry + some

**11.** deter + ent

**12.** occur + ence

**13.** rely + able

**14.** real + ist

**15.** thirty + ish

**16.** person + al

**17.** panic + y

**18.** apply + ance

**19.** mimic + er

**20.** profit + able

● *Connect to Writing:* **Editing**

### Using Suffixes and Other Endings

Read these paragraphs, looking for words that are spelled incorrectly. Write each word correctly.

Many people experience recuring dreams. These dreams sometimes reveal things about the dreamer's personallity. Some people's recurring dreams are undenyably their very own. They are unique and unlike any other. Other people have dreams that are shared, with some personnal varyation, by many people.

A common recurring dream is the one in which the dreamer must take the final exam in a course she either didn't know or forgot she was registerred for. This can be a very upseting dream, and the dreamer is often panicing when he or she wakes up. Experts say that this dream is typically experienced by people who are worried—sometimes excessively—about doing well.

Another dream that is reported frequentely to experts includes the action of jumping or flying. The dreamer often is comforted by the upward movement. Experts say that this dream usualy reveals a subconscious acknowledgment of the ability to overcome obstacles or to move beyond challenging situations. Those who have recuring dreams of this kind are sincerly appreciatetive of the positive explanation.

✔ *Check Point:* **Mixed Practice**

Add the prefix or suffix to each of these base words, and write the new word.

**1.** admit + ance

**2.** lazy + ness

**3.** day + ly

**4.** argue + ment

**5.** un + notice + able

**6.** repel + ant

**7.** hobby + ist

**8.** acknowledge + ment

**9.** buoy + ancy

**10.** re + place + able

**11.** courage + ous

**12.** lonely + ness

**13.** face + al

**14.** panic + y

**15.** picnic + er

**16.** mis + spell

**17.** infer + ence

**18.** il + logical

**19.** even + ness

**20.** study + ous

# Words to Master

Make it your goal to learn to spell these fifty words this year. Use them in your writing, and practice writing them until spelling them correctly comes automatically.

| | | |
|---|---|---|
| accommodate | espionage | perceive |
| adolescence | fission | physician |
| allegiance | fulfill | plagiarism |
| anonymous | guarantee | psychology |
| atmosphere | harassment | reminiscent |
| bibliography | hypocrisy | rendezvous |
| bizarre | initiative | specimen |
| boulevard | interference | strategic |
| camouflage | larynx | symbolic |
| caricature | maintenance | symmetrical |
| complexion | maneuver | theoretical |
| conscientious | melancholy | thesaurus |
| curriculum | mischievous | tyranny |
| despair | naive | unscrupulous |
| dilemma | obsolete | vehicle |
| dilettante | orchestra | villain |
| environment | parallelism | |

## Assess Your Learning

### Spelling Words Correctly

Write the letter preceding the misspelled word in each group. Then write the word, spelling it correctly.

1. (a) proceed (b) sharing (c) stereos
   (d) acurracy (e) rendezvous

2. (a) deceive (b) occurred (c) managable
   (d) eyeglasses (e) forgettable

3. (a) piece (b) excede (c) feign
   d) fifes (e) echoes

4. (a) thesaurus (b) usualy (c) descendant
   (d) gauge (e) notaries public

5. (a) rarity (b) chefs (c) alloys
   (d) rein (e) rehersal

6. (a) apparant (b) concede (c) referral
   (d) patios (e) outrageous

7. (a) releive (b) seize (c) veil
   (d) wives (e) thesis

8. (a) leisure (b) overrule (c) alumnuses
   (d) obedient (e) bizarre

9. (a) changeable (b) disimilar (c) loneliness
   (d) mosquito (e) bushes

10. (a) recurence (b) license (c) overture
    (d) sieve (e) neither

## Directions

Read the passage. Write the letter of the answer that correctly respells each underlined word. If the word is correct, write D.

*The Catcher in the Rye* is an **(1)** extreamly popular book about **(2)** adolesence and coming of age. The hero, Holden Caulfield, runs away from his prep school as Christmas **(3)** vacation begins. On the **(4)** bulavards of New York, he finds himself involved in a **(5)** serie of adventures.

Holden is a **(6)** fascinateing character, at once both worldly and **(7)** niave. His **(8)** disatisfaction with the adult world around him is evident as he rails against **(9)** hypocracy and dishonesty. Holden's feelings are **(10)** remaniscent of the teenage rebellions that took place in the 1960s.

**1. A** extremally
   **B** extremely
   **C** exstreamly
   **D** No error

**2. A** adolescence
   **B** adolecense
   **C** adolesense
   **D** No error

**3. A** vacasion
   **B** vaccasion
   **C** vacateon
   **D** No error

**4. A** boulevards
   **B** bullavards
   **C** boulavards
   **D** No error

**5. A** series
   **B** serieses
   **C** seria
   **D** No error

**6. A** fastenating
   **B** fascinating
   **C** fascanating
   **D** No error

**7. A** nyive
   **B** naiv
   **C** naive
   **D** No error

**8. A** disatissfaction
   **B** dissatisfaction
   **C** dissatisfashion
   **D** No error

**9. A** hippocracy
   **B** hypocrasy
   **C** hypocrisy
   **D** No error

**10. A** reminiscent
    **B** remeniscent
    **C** reminicent
    **D** No error

# Writer's Corner

## Snapshot

**24 A**   **Spelling patterns**—such as *i* before *e* except after *c*—apply to many words and can help you spell many different words correctly. (pages 1021–1023)

**24 B**   **To form the plural** of most nouns, **add *s* or *es*.** Some nouns form their plurals in other ways. (pages 1024–1030)

**24 C**   Some numbers are written as numerals while other numbers are written as words. (pages 1031–1033)

**24 D**   A **prefix** is one or more syllables placed in front of a base word to form a new word. A **suffix** is one or more syllables placed after a base word to form a new word. (pages 1034–1038)

## Power Rules

**Homophones** are **words that sound alike** but have different meanings. When you write, be sure you use the word with your intended meaning. It often helps to say contractions as two words. (pages 874–903)

| Before Editing | After Editing |
| --- | --- |
| We went *too* the library yesterday. (*Too* means *also* or *in addition.*) | We went *to* the library yesterday. (*To* shows direction.) |
| Can I borrow *you're* book? (*You're* is a contraction of *you are.*) | Can I borrow *your* book? (*Your* is the possessive form of *you.*) |
| *Its* almost time to go home. (*Its* is the possessive form of *it.*) | *It's* almost time to go home. (*It's* is a contraction of *it is.*) |

When you write, avoid misusing or misspelling these **commonly confused words.** (pages 874–903)

| Before Editing | After Editing |
| --- | --- |
| Everyone went camping *accept* Tara. (*Accept* means *to agree to something.*) | Everyone went camping *except* Tara. (*Except* means *not including.*) |
| Tim ran *further* than Ryan. (*Further* refers *to something additional.*) | Tim ran *farther* than Ryan. (*Farther* refers to *distance.*) |
| *Less* than twenty people came. (*Less* refers to an *amount, degree, or value.*) | *Fewer* than twenty people came. (*Fewer* refers to *things that can be counted.*) |

## Editing Checklist

Use this checklist when editing your writing.

✓ Did I pay attention to spelling patterns in my writing? (See pages 1021–1023.)
✓ Did I correctly form regular and irregular plurals of nouns? (See pages 1024–1030.)
✓ Did I use spelling generalizations to form plurals of compound and foreign words and other plurals? (See pages 1028–1030.)
✓ Did I use a dictionary to check spellings I was unsure of? (See page 1019.)
✓ Did I change the spelling of base words if needed when adding suffixes? (See pages 1034–1038.)
✓ Did I carefully edit my writing for misspelled words? (See pages 1016–1043.)

## Use the Power

Some words or word parts sound the same but are spelled differently. Use a mnemonic device to help you remember how to spell difficult words.

| WORD | MNEMONIC DEVICE |
|---|---|
| chief, ceiling, receipt, leisure, protein, neither | *i* before *e* except after *c* (unless **nEIther** applies) |
| their, there | **Their** feet take them **here** and t**here**. (*Here* and *there* are places.) |
| succeed, proceed, exceed (*-ceed* vs. *-cede*) | Full sp**EED** ahead. |
| desert, dessert | Two sugars please—for two **ss's** in de**SS**ert. |
| personal, personnel | A person**AL** matter was handled in the personn**EL** office. (*a* before *e*) |
| stationary, stationery | Station**A**ry is p**A**rked c**A**rs; station**E**ry is **E**nvelopes and p**E**ns. |

# Language QuickGuide

Researchers have found that certain patterns of language used offend educated people more than others and therefore affect how people perceive you. Since these patterns of language use have such an impact on future success, you should learn how to edit for the more widely accepted forms. The list below identifies ten of the most important conventions to master the Power Rules. Always check for them when you edit.

**1. Use only one negative form for a single negative idea.** (See pages 866–867.)

**Before Editing**

Max looked through his binoculars but didn't *see nothing*.
There *wasn't* scarcely any time to call.

**After Editing**

Max looked through his binoculars but didn't see *anything*.
There *was* scarcely any time to call.

**2. Use mainstream past tense forms of regular and irregular verbs.** (See pages 750–776.) You might try to recite and memorize the parts of the most common irregular verbs.

**Before Editing**

Amelia *eat* at my house last night.
Alicia *walk* Wags around the block.
We *have did* nothing all day.
I *thinked* about it all night.

**After Editing**

Amelia *ate* at my house last night.
Alicia *walked* Wags around the block.
We *have done* nothing all day.
I *thought* about it all night.

**3. Use verbs that agree with the subject.** (See pages 826–853.)

**Before Editing**

I *shovels* the driveway after each snow.
My cats and my dog *eats* from the same bowl.
Either the guitars or the tuba *are* out of tune.
Neither Marsha nor the Bryan brothers *is singing* in tune.

**After Editing**

I *shovel* the driveway after each snow.
My cats and my dog *eat* from the same bowl.
Either the guitars or the tuba *is* out of tune.
Neither Marsha nor the Bryan brothers *are singing* in tune.

**4.** Use subject forms of pronouns in subject position. Use object forms of pronouns in object position. (See pages 790–801.)

**Before Editing**

*Her* and Chase have been deputized.
*Him* and his posse look ridiculous.
*Her* and *me* are soul sisters.

**After Editing**

*She* and Chase have been deputized.
*He* and his posse look ridiculous.
*She* and *I* are soul sisters.

**5.** Use standard ways to make nouns possessive. (See pages 964–966.)

**Before Editing**

The *cups* handle is broken.
All the *cup's* handles are broken.
The *earths* texture is quite loamy.
I just love that *bottles* color.
*Conans* favorite dessert is lima bean pie.

**After Editing**

The *cup's* handle is broken.
All the *cups'* handles are broken.
The *earth's* texture is quite loamy.
I just love that *bottle's* color.
*Conan's* favorite dessert is lima bean pie.

**6.** Use a consistent verb tense except when a change is clearly necessary. (See pages 762–776.)

**Before Editing**

I *dive* off the board when I *went swimming* last night.
Dinah was walking home when she *hears* the siren.

**After Editing**

I *dove* off the board when I *went swimming* last night.
Dinah was walking home when she *heard* the siren.

**7.** Use sentence fragments only the way professional writers do, after the sentence they refer to and usually to emphasize a point. Fix all sentence fragments that occur before the sentence they refer to and ones that occur in the middle of a sentence. (See pages 661-663.)

**Before Editing**

*Today.* Zippy is hiding in his cage.
Studying for a test. *When I'm at a football game is distracting.* So I better study at home.
We cancelled our subscription. *The reason being that we didn't like the magazine.*

**After Editing**

*Today,* Zippy is hiding in his cage.
Studying for a test *when I'm at a football game is distracting, so* I better study at home.
We cancelled our subscription *because we didn't like the magazine.*

**8.** Use the best conjunction and/or punctuation for the meaning when connecting two sentences. Revise run-on sentences. (See pages 736–738.)

**Before Editing**

Grant rubbed the lantern, a genie came out.

The rain started pouring, I put on my poncho.

I called, Heidi answered.

**After Editing**

*When* Grant rubbed the lantern, a genie came out.

*After* the rain started pouring, I put on my poncho.

I called, *and* Heidi answered.

**9.** Use the contraction *'ve* (not *of*) when the correct word is *have,* or use the full word *have.* Use *supposed* instead of *suppose* and *used* instead of *use* when appropriate. (See pages 889, 896 and 899.)

**Before Editing**

Hammond should *of* ordered rice and beans.

We might *of* studied too hard for this test.

Haywood would *of* come over if we'd invited him.

I am *suppose* to be home by nine o'clock.

I *use* to like my pancakes with syrup, but now I prefer them with chocolate chips.

**After Editing**

Hammond *should've* ordered rice and beans.

We might *have* studied too hard for this test.

Haywood would *have* come over if we'd invited him.

I am *supposed* to be home by nine o'clock.

I *used* to like my pancakes with syrup, but now I prefer them with chocolate chips.

**10.** For sound-alikes and certain words that sound almost alike, choose the word with your intended meaning. (See pages 874–903.)

**Before Editing**

Rhoda wanted *too* drive my new car. (*too* means "also" or "in addition")

*You're* new phone looks fancy. (*you're* is a contraction of *you are*)

*They're* phones were not charged. (*they're* is a contraction of *they are*)

*Their* goes my weekend. (*their* is the possessive form of *they*)

*Its* possible that Stella will win the prize. (*its* is the possessive form of *it*)

**After Editing**

Rhoda wanted *to* drive my new car. (*to* is part of the infinitive *to drive*)

*Your* new phone looks fancy. (*your* is the possessive form of *you*)

*Their* phones were not charged. (*their* is the possessive form of *they*)

*There* goes my weekend. (*there* means "in that place")

*It's* possible that Stella will win the prize. (*it's* is a contraction of *it is*)

# Nine Tools for Powerful Writing ●●●●●●●●

In addition to using Power Rules to help you avoid errors, try using these nine powerful tools to help you turn good writing into excellent writing.

**1.** **Set the scene** with adverbial clauses. (See page 169.)

Grab your readers' attention with scene-setting information in the form of adverbial clauses, which start with such words as *if, because, until, while, since,* and *although.*

> **While Edgar Allan Poe's work shares key features of all Gothic works,** it is also credited with elevating this popular genre into the realm of literature.

**2.** Less is more: **avoid wordiness.** (See page 367.)

With editorial scissors in hand, cut out all unnecessary words as you revise.

> The fact that Poe's stories and poems have endured through the ages is due to the efficiency of their ability to probe the dark recesses of the human psyche.

> **Poe's stories and poems have endured because they efficiently probe the dark recesses of the human psyche.**

**3.** Use the **power of 3s** to add style and emphasis with **parallelism.** (See pages 120, 301.)

One way to add power is to use a writing device called *parallelism.* Parallelism is the use of the same kind of word or group of words in a series of three or more.

> As his characters **relive hideous crimes, mourn lost loves, and await death** . . .

**4.** Create emphasis by **dashing it all.** (See page 340.)

Dashes can create abrupt breaks that emphasize a word or group of words.

> . . . they grapple not only with a dark physical world, but the equally dark— **perhaps even darker**—psychological world within themselves.

**5.** Zoom in with **absolutes**. (See page 142.)

Absolutes are phrases that zoom in on details. Construct them with a noun or nouns, an action word that ends in *-ing,* and a modifier.

> Poe's works also endure because they are tightly constructed, **each element moving readers toward the chilling conclusion.**

**6.** Add detail to your sentences with **adjectives and adjectival phrases come lately.** (See page 193.)

Adjectives work well when placed before the nouns they modify. When adjectives or adjectival phrases "come lately," though, sentences can become more graceful.

> First-person narrators, **unreliable and often deranged,** pull readers into the psychological drama.

**7.** Elaborate by **explaining who or what with appositives.** (See page 61.)

An appositive is a noun or pronoun phrase that identifies or adds identifying information to the preceding noun. Use them to streamline your prose.

> Who can forget the distraught narrator descending into madness in the poem "The Raven," **one of Poe's best known works**?

**8.** **Get into the action** with participial phrases. (See page 241.)

You can pack a lot of action into your sentences if you include an *-ing* verb, or *"-ing* modifier." Formally called a *present participial phrase,* these *-ing* modifiers describe a person, thing, or action in a sentence.

> **Using mood, voice, and other elements,** Poe conducts an unsettling tour of the Gothic world within the human mind.

**9.** Write with variety and coherence and **let it flow.** (See page 430.)

Vary the length, structure, and beginnings of your sentences and use connecting words to help your writing flow smoothly.

> While Edgar Allan Poe's work shares the key features of all Gothic works, it is also credited with elevating this popular genre into the realm of literature. Poe's stories and poems have endured because they efficiently probe the dark recesses of the human psyche. As his characters relive crimes, mourn lost loves, and await death, they grapple not only with a dark physical world, but the equally dark—perhaps even darker—psychological world within themselves. Poe's works also endure because they are tightly constructed, each element moving readers toward the chilling conclusion. Sentence structure and sound techniques darken mood. First-person narrators, unreliable and often deranged, pull readers into the psychological drama. Who can forget the distraught narrator descending into madness in the poem "The Raven," one of Poe's best known works? Using mood, voice, and other elements, Poe conducts an unsettling tour of the Gothic world within the human mind.

Nine Tools for Powerful Writing    **1049**

# Grammar QuickGuide

This section presents an easy-to-use reference for the definitions of grammatical terms. The number on the colored tab tells you the chapter covering that topic. The page number to the right of each definition refers to the place in the chapter where you can find additional instruction, examples, and applications to writing.

## 13 The Parts of Speech

**How can you combine the parts of speech to create vivid and exact sentences?**

### Nouns and Pronouns

| | | |
|---|---|---|
| **13 A** | A **noun** is the name of a person, place, thing, or idea. | 618 |
| **13 A.1** | A **concrete noun** names a person or an object that can actually be seen, touched, tasted, heard, or smelled. An **abstract noun** names qualities, conditions, and ideas that cannot be perceived through the senses. | 618 |
| **13 A.2** | A **common noun** names any person, place, or thing. A **proper noun** always begins with a capital letter and names a particular person, place, or thing. | 619 |
| **13 A.3** | A **compound noun** is made up of more than one word. | 619 |
| **13 A.4** | A **collective noun** names a group of people or things. | 619 |
| **13 A.5** | A **pronoun** is a word that takes the place of one or more nouns. | 621 |
| **13 A.6** | A **reflexive pronoun** refers to the noun or pronoun that is the subject of the sentence. It is an essential part of the sentence. An **intensive pronoun** is included in a sentence to add emphasis—or intensity—to a noun or another pronoun. | 622 |
| **13 A.7** | **Indefinite pronouns** often refer to unnamed persons or things and usually do not have specific antecedents. | 623 |
| **13 A.8** | A **demonstrative pronoun** is used to point out a specific person, place, or object in the same sentence or in another sentence. | 623 |
| **13 A.9** | An **interrogative pronoun** is used to ask a question. | 624 |

QUICKGUIDE

# Verbs

# Adjectives and Adverbs

# Other Parts of Speech

# 14 The Sentence Base

How can you use sentences to paint powerful images and tell interesting stories?

## Subjects and Predicates

## Sentence Fragments

## Complements

QUICKGUIDE

# 15 Phrases

How can you use phrases to add variety, clarity, and vitality to your writing?

## Prepositional Phrases

## Appositives and Appositive Phrases

## Verbals and Verbal Phrases

QUICKGUIDE

## Misplaced and Dangling Modifiers

## Phrase Fragments

# 16 Clauses

How can you use clauses to express subtle and precise meaning?

## Independent and Subordinate Clauses

## Uses of Subordinate Clauses

# Kinds of Sentence Structure

**16 C**    A sentence can be **simple, compound, complex, or compound-complex,** depending on the number and the kind of clauses in it.    731

     **16 C.1**    A **simple sentence** consists of one independent clause.    731

     **16 C.2**    A **compound sentence** consists of two or more independent clauses.    731

     **16 C.3**    A **complex sentence** consists of one independent clause and one or more subordinate clauses.    731

     **16 C.4**    A **compound-complex sentence** consists of two or more independent clauses and one or more subordinate clauses.    732

# Clause Fragments

**16 D**    Even though a subordinate clause has both a subject and a verb, it does not express a complete thought. A subordinate clause punctuated as a sentence is a **clause fragment.**    734

# Run-on Sentences

**16 E**    A **run-on sentence** is two or more sentences that are written as one sentence. A run-on sentence is sometimes seen written as one long sentence with no punctuation. At other times run-ons incorporate punctuation incorrectly.    736

This section presents an easy-to-use reference for the explanations of how various grammatical elements are and should be used. The number on the colored tab tells you the chapter covering that topic. The page number to the right of each definition refers to the place in the chapter where you can find additional instruction, examples, and applications to writing. You can also refer to the Writer's Glossary of Usage (pages 874-903) for help with commonly confused usage items.

## 17 Using Verbs

**How can using verbs in just the right way spark your descriptions and make your writing shine?**

### The Principal Parts of Verbs

**17 A**    The **principal parts** of a verb are the present, the present participle, the past, and the past participle.    750

     **17 A.1**    A **regular verb** forms its past and past participle by adding *-ed* or *-d* to the present form. An **irregular verb** does not form its past and past participle by adding *-ed* or *-d* to the present form.    750

### Verb Tense

**17 B**    The time expressed by a verb is called the **tense** of a verb.    762

     **17 B.1**    **Present tense,** the first of the three simple tenses, is used mainly to express (1) an action that is going on now, (2) an action that happens regularly, or (3) an action that is usually constant or the same.    762

     **17 B.2**    **Historical present tense** is used to relate a past action as if it were happening in the present. **Literary present tense** is used when writing about literature.    763

     **17 B.3**    **Past tense** is used to express an action that already took place or was completed in the past.    763

     **17 B.4**    **Future tense** is used to express an action that will take place in the future.    763

     **17 B.5**    **Present perfect tense,** the first of three perfect tenses, has two uses: (1) to express an action that was completed at some indefinite time in the past and (2) to express an action that started in the past and is still going on.    764

QUICKGUIDE

## Active and Passive Voice

## Mood

# 18 Using Pronouns

How can you use pronouns to make your writing coherent and accurate?

## The Cases of Personal Pronouns

QUICKGUIDE

# Pronoun Problems

**18 B**    Common pronoun problems include the misuse of *who* and *whom*,     **805**
incomplete comparisons, and the misuse of reflexive and intensive
pronouns.

> **18 B.1**    The correct case of *who* is determined by how the pronoun is     **805**
> used in a question or a clause.

> **18 B.2**    *Who* and *whoever* and their related pronouns are used in     **805**
> questions and in subordinate clauses.

> **18 B.3**    In an adjectival or a noun clause, the way *who* (and its related     **806**
> pronouns) is used determines its case.

> **18 B.4**    An **elliptical clause** is a subordinate clause that begins with     **808**
> the word *than* or *as* and that leaves out the verb or part of the
> verb as understood.

> **18 B.5**    In an elliptical clause, use the form of the pronoun you would     **808**
> use if the clause were completed.

> **18 B.6**    **Reflexive pronouns** always refer back to a previous noun     **809**
> or pronoun in the sentence.

> **18 B.7**    **Intensive pronouns** are used to emphasize a noun or     **810**
> another pronoun in the sentence.

# Pronouns and Their Antecedents

**18 C**    A pronoun and its antecedent must agree in **number** and **gender** since     **812**
they both refer to the same person, place, or thing.

> **18 C.1**    If two or more singular antecedents are joined by *or, nor, either/*     **812**
> *or,* or *neither/nor,* use a singular pronoun to refer to them.

> **18 C.2**    When one antecedent is singular and the other is plural, the     **813**
> pronoun agrees with the closer antecedent.

> **18 C.3**    If two or more singular antecedents are joined by *and* or *both/*     **813**
> *and,* use a plural pronoun to refer to them.

> **18 C.4**    A personal pronoun must be singular if its antecedent is one of     **815**
> the singular indefinite pronouns.

> **18 C.5**    A personal pronoun must be plural if its antecedent is one of     **815**
> the plural indefinite pronouns.

## Unclear, Missing, or Confusing Antecedents

# 19 Subject and Verb Agreement

How can accurate subject-verb agreement help your writing achieve clarity and focus?

## Agreement of Subjects and Verbs

## Common Agreement Problems

# 20 Using Adjectives and Adverbs

How can you write with clarity using adjectives, adverbs, and comparisons?

## Comparison of Adjectives and Adverbs

**20 A.4**  Never add *-er* and *-est* to the comparative and superlative      858
degrees of irregular modifiers.

## Problems with Comparisons

**20 B**  When using adjectives and adverbs for comparison, avoid making double      861
comparisons, illogical comparisons, and comparisons of members of a
group to themselves.

**20 B.1**  Do not use both *-er* and *more* to form the comparative degree, or      861
both *-est* and *most* to form the superlative degree of modifiers.

**20 B.2**  Compare only items of a similar kind.      861

**20 B.3**  Add *other* or *else* when comparing a member of a group with the      862
rest of the group.

## Problems with Modifiers

**20 C**  Be aware of problems when using adjectives and adverbs, such as when to      864
use them, and when to use *good* or *well* and *bad* or *badly*. Avoid double
negatives.

**20 C.1**  Use *good* as an adjective; use *well* as an adverb unless it means      865
"in good health" or "satisfactory."

**20 C.2**  Use *bad* as an adjective; use *badly* as an adverb.      866

**20 C.3**  Avoid using double negatives.      866

# Mechanics QuickGuide ● ● ● ● ● ● ● ● ● ● ● ● ● ● ● ● ● ● ● ●

This section presents an easy-to-use reference for the mechanics of writing: capitalization, punctuation, and spelling. The number on the colored tab tells you the chapter covering that topic. The page number to the right of each definition refers to the place in the chapter where you can find additional instruction, examples, and applications to writing.

## 21 Capital Letters

**How can you use capital letters to clarify your writing?**

### First Words and the Pronoun *I*

**21 A** Capitalize the beginning of a sentence or a line of poetry, parts of a letter or an outline, and the pronoun *I*. — 908

> **21 A.1** Capitalize the first word of a sentence and of a line of poetry. — 908

> **21 A.2** Capitalize the first word when a direct quotation is used. — 909

> **21 A.3** Capitalize the first word in a greeting of a letter and the first word in the closing of a letter. — 910

> **21 A.4** Capitalize the first word of each item in an outline and the letters that begin major subsections of the outline. — 910

> **21 A.5** Capitalize the first word in a formal resolution that follows the word *Resolved.* — 910

> **21 A.6** Capitalize the first word of a formal statement that follows a colon. — 911

> **21 A.7** Capitalize the pronoun *I*, both alone and in contractions. — 911

### Proper Nouns

**21 B** Capitalize proper nouns and their abbreviations. — 913

> **21 B.1** Names of particular persons and animals should be capitalized. Also capitalize the initials that stand for people's names. — 913

> **21 B.2** Geographical names, including the names of particular places, bodies of water, and celestial bodies, should be capitalized. — 914

> **21 B.3** Names of groups, including the names of organizations, businesses, institutions, government bodies, political parties, and teams, should be capitalized. — 915

# 22 End Marks and Commas

How can you create meaning through the careful use of end marks and commas?

## Kinds of Sentences and End Marks

# Commas

QUICKGUIDE

# 23 Other Punctuation

How can you use apostrophes, semicolons, colons, hyphens, and other punctuation to communicate precisely and to enhance your writing style?

## Apostrophes

**23 A**   The **apostrophe ( ' )** is used to show possession and in contractions.   964

  **23 A.1**   Add **'s** to form the possessive of a singular noun.   964

  **23 A.2**   Add only an apostrophe to form the possessive of a plural noun that ends in *s*.   964

  **23 A.3**   Add **'s** to form the possessive of a plural noun that does not end in *s*.   965

  **23 A.4**   The possessive forms of personal pronouns and the pronoun *who* do not use apostrophes.   967

  **23 A.5**   Add **'s** to only the last word to show joint ownership. Add **'s** to each word to show separate ownership.   969

  **23 A.6**   Use an apostrophe with the possessive form of a noun that expresses time or amount.   969

  **23 A.7**   Use an apostrophe in a contraction to show where one or more letters have been omitted.   971

  **23 A.8**   Add **'s** to form the plural of lowercase letters, some capital letters, and some words used as words.   972

  **23 A.9**   Use an apostrophe to show that numbers are omitted in a date.   973

## Semicolons and Colons

**23 B**   A **semicolon (;)** is used between the clauses of a compound sentence when they are not joined by a conjunction. A **colon (:)** is used to introduce lists and long quotations and to separate independent clauses.   974

  **23 B.1**   Use a semicolon between the clauses in a compound sentence when they are joined by certain conjunctive adverbs or transitional words.   975

  **23 B.2**   Use a semicolon instead of a comma to avoid possible confusion in certain situations.   976

  **23 B.3**   Use a colon before most lists of items, especially when a list comes after an expression such as *the following*.   979

## Italics (Underlining)

## Quotation Marks and Ellipses

QUICKGUIDE

| **23 D.9** | When writing **dialogue,** begin a new paragraph each time the speaker changes. | 996 |
|---|---|---|
| **23 D.10** | To avoid any confusion, use single quotation marks to enclose a quotation or certain titles within a quotation. | 998 |
| **23 D.11** | Use an **ellipsis** ( **. . .** ) to indicate any omission in a quoted passage or a pause in a written passage. | 1000 |

## Other Marks of Punctuation

| **23 E** | A **hyphen** divides a word at the end of a line and separates parts of a compound word. **Dashes, parentheses,** and **brackets** separate words from the rest of the sentence. | 1002 |
|---|---|---|
| **23 E.1** | Use a hyphen to divide a word at the end of a line. | 1002 |
| **23 E.2** | Use a hyphen when writing out the compound numbers between *twenty-one* and *ninety-nine.* | 1003 |
| **23 E.3** | Use one or more hyphens to separate the parts of some compound nouns and adjectives. Also use one or more hyphens between words that make up a compound adjective located before a noun. | 1004 |
| **23 E.4** | Use a hyphen after the prefixes *ex-, self-,* and *all-* and before the suffix *-elect.* | 1005 |
| **23 E.5** | Use a hyphen to prevent confusion. | 1006 |
| **23 E.6** | Use dashes to set off an abrupt change in thought. | 1007 |
| **23 E.7** | Use dashes to set off an appositive that is introduced by words such as *that is, for example,* or *for instance.* | 1007 |
| **23 E.8** | Use dashes to set off a parenthetical expression or an appositive that includes commas or to call special attention to a phrase. | 1007 |
| **23 E.9** | Use dashes to set off a phrase or a clause that summarizes or emphasizes what has preceded it. | 1007 |
| **23 E.10** | Use parentheses to enclose information that is not related closely to the meaning in a sentence. | 1008 |
| **23 E.11** | Use parentheses to identify a source of information such as a reference to an author or a page number. | 1008 |
| **23 E.12** | Use brackets to enclose an explanation within quoted material that is not part of the quotation. | 1009 |

# 24 Spelling Correctly

How can you communicate your message effectively by using accurate spelling?

## Spelling Patterns

**24 A**     **Spelling patterns**—such as *i* before *e* except after *c*—apply to many words and can help you spell many different words correctly.    1021

     **24 A.1**    When the vowel sound is long *e*, write *ei* after *c* and *ie* after other consonant letters.    1021

     **24 A.2**    When the sound is long *a* or any vowel sound other than long *e*, write *ei*.    1021

     **24 A.3**    The syllable that sounds like "seed" is usually spelled *-ceed*, but it can be spelled *-sede or -cede*.    1022

## Plurals

**24 B**     To form the plural of most nouns, add *s* or *es*. Some nouns form their plurals in other ways.    1024

     **24 B.1**    To form the plural of most nouns, add *s*.    1024

     **24 B.2**    To form the plural of nouns ending in *s, ch, sh, x*, or *z*, add *es*.    1024

     **24 B.3**    Add *s* to form the plural of a noun ending with a vowel and *y*.    1025

     **24 B.4**    Change the *y* to *i* and add *es* to a noun ending in a consonant and *y*.    1025

     **24 B.5**    Add *s* to form the plural of a noun ending with a vowel and *o*.    1026

     **24 B.6**    Add *es* to form the plural of many nouns that end with a consonant and *o*.    1026

     **24 B.7**    Add *s* to form the plural of musical terms, proper nouns, and some other nouns that end in *o*.    1026

     **24 B.8**    When dictionaries give two forms for the plurals of some nouns ending in a consonant and *o*, the first form is the preferred one.    1027

     **24 B.9**    To form the plural of some nouns ending in *f* or *fe*, just add *s*.    1027

     **24 B.10**    For some nouns ending in *f* or *fe*, change the *f* to *v* and add *es* or *s*.    1027

     **24 B.11**    To form the plurals of most numerals, letters, symbols, and words used as words, add an *s*. With some lowercase letters, some capital letters, and some words used as words, use an apostrophe and *s*.    1028

QUICKGUIDE

**24 D.7**  Keep the *y* when adding a suffix to words that end in a vowel    1036
and *y*. Change *y* to *i* when adding a suffix to words that end in a
consonant and *y*.

**24 D.8**  Double the final consonant when adding a suffix that begins    1037
with a vowel if the base word satisfies both these conditions: (1)
It has only one syllable or is stressed on the final syllable and (2)
It ends in one consonant preceded by one vowel.

**24 D.9**  When adding a suffix that begins with *e, i,* or *y* to a word that    1037
ends with a vowel and *c,* do not double the final *c.* Instead add
the letter *k* after the *c* to retain the hard *c* sound.

# Glossary

## A

**abbreviation** shortened form of a word that generally begins with a capital letter and ends with a period

**abstract** summary of points of writing, presented in skeletal form

**abstract noun** noun that cannot be seen or touched, such as an idea, quality, or characteristic

**acronym** an abbreviation formed by using the initial letters of a phrase or name (CIA—Central Intelligence Agency)

**action verb** verb that tells what action a subject is performing

**active voice** voice the verb is in when it expresses that the subject is performing the action

**adequate development** quality of good writing in which sufficient supporting details develop the main idea

**adjectival clause** subordinate clause used to modify a noun or pronoun

**adjectival phrase** prepositional phrase that modifies a noun or a pronoun

**adjective** word that modifies a noun or a pronoun

**abreviatura** forma reducida de una palabra que generalmente comienza con mayúscula y termina en punto

**síntesis** resumen de los puntos principales de un texto, presentados en forma de esquema

**austantivo abstracto** sustantivo que no puede verse ni tocarse, como una idea, una cualidad o una característica

**acrónimo** abreviatura que se forma al usar las letras iniciales de una frase o de un nombre (CIA—Central Intelligence Agency [Agencia Central de Inteligencia])

**verbo de acción** verbo que indica qué acción realiza el sujeto

**voz activa** voz en que está el verbo cuando expresa que el sujeto está realizando la acción

**desarrollo adecuado** cualidad de un texto bien escrito, en cual suficientes detalles de apoyo desarrollan la idea principal

**cláusula adjetiva** cláusula subordinada utilizada para modificar a un sustantivo o a un pronombre

**frase adjetiva** frase preposicional que modifica a un sustantivo o a un pronombre

**adjetivo** palabra que modifica a un sustantivo o a un pronombre

| English | Español |
|---------|---------|
| **adverb** word that modifies a verb, an adjective, or another adverb | **adverbio** palabra que modifica a un verbo, a un adjetivo o a otro adverbio |
| **adverbial clause** subordinate clause that is used mainly to modify a verb | **cláusula adverbial** cláusula subordinada que se utiliza principalmente para modificar a un verbo |
| **adverbial phrase** prepositional phrase that is used mainly to modify a verb | **frase adverbial** frase preposicional que se utiliza principalmente para modificar a un verbo |
| **aesthetics** study of beauty and artistic quality | **estética** estudio de la belleza y de las características del arte |
| **alliteration** repetition of a consonant sound at the beginning of a series of words | **aliteración** repetición de un sonido consonántico al comienzo de una serie de palabras |
| **allusion** reference to persons or events in the past or in literature | **alusión** referencia a personas o sucesos del pasado o de la literatura |
| **analogy** logical relationship between a pair of words | **analogía** relación lógica entre una pareja de palabras |
| **analysis** the process of breaking a whole into parts to see how the parts fit and work together | **análisis** proceso de separación de las partes de un todo para examinar cómo encajan y cómo funcionan juntas |
| **antecedent** word or group of words to which a pronoun refers | **antecedente** palabra o grupo de palabras a que hace referencia un pronombre |
| **antithesis** in literature, using contrasting words, phrases, sentences, or ideas for emphasis: *She was tough as nails and soft as spun sugar.* | **antítesis** en literatura, el uso de palabras, frases, oraciones o ideas contrastantes para producir énfasis: *Era dura como una piedra y con un corazón de oro.* |
| **antonym** word that means the opposite of another word | **antónimo** palabra que significa lo opuesto de otra palabra |

| English | Español |
|---|---|
| **appositive** noun or pronoun that identifies or explains another noun or pronoun in a sentence | **aposición** sustantivo o pronombre que especifica o explica a otro sustantivo o pronombre en una oración |
| **article** the special adjectives *a, an, the* | **artículo** adjetivos especiales *a (un/una), an (un/una) y the (el/la/los/las)* |
| **assonance** repetition of a vowel sound within words | **asonancia** repetición de un sonido vocálico en las palabras |
| **audience** person or persons who will read your work or hear your speech | **público** persona o personas que leerán tu trabajo o escucharán tu discurso |
| **autobiography** account of a person's life, written by that person | **autobiografía** relato de la vida de una persona, escrito por esa misma persona |

## B

| English | Español |
|---|---|
| **ballad** a narrative song or poem. A *folk ballad* may be passed down by word of mouth for generations before being written down. A *literary ballad* is written in a style to imitate a folk ballad but has a known author. | **balada** canción o poema narrativo. Una *balada folclórica* puede transmitirse oralmente de generación en generación antes de que se ponga por escrito. Una *balada literaria* está escrita en un estilo que imita a la balada folclórica, pero se sabe quién es su autor. |
| **bandwagon statement** appeal that leads the reader to believe that everyone is using a certain product | **enunciado de arrastre** enunciado apelativo que lleva al lector a creer que todos usan cierto producto |
| **bibliographic information** information about a source, such as author, title, publisher, date of publication, and Internet address | **información bibliográfica** datos sobre una fuente: autor, título, editorial, fecha de publicación, dirección de Internet, etc |
| **body** one or more paragraphs composed of details, facts, and examples that support the main idea | **cuerpo** uno o más párrafos compuestos de detalles, hechos y ejemplos que apoyan la idea principal |

| English | Español |
|---|---|
| **brackets** punctuation marks [ ] used to enclose information added to text or to indicate new text replacing the original quoted text; always used in pairs | **corchetes** signos de puntuación [ ] utilizados para encerrar la información añadida al texto o para indicar el texto nuevo que reemplaza al texto original citado; siempre se usan en parejas |
| **brainstorming** prewriting technique of writing down ideas that come to mind about a given subject | **intercambio de ideas** técnica de preparación para la escritura que consiste en anotar las ideas que surgen sobre un tema |
| **business letter** formal letter that asks for action on the part of the receiver and includes an inside address, heading, salutation, body, closing, and signature | **carta de negocios** carta formal que solicita al destinatario que realice una acción e incluye dirección del destinatario, membrete, saludo, cuerpo, despedida y firma |

**C**

| | |
|---|---|
| **case** form of a noun or a pronoun that indicates its use in a sentence. In English there are three cases: the nominative case, the objective case, and the possessive case. | **caso** forma de un sustantivo o de un pronombre que indica su uso en una oración. En inglés hay tres casos: nominativo, objetivo y posesivo. |
| **cause and effect** method of development in which details are grouped according to what happens and why it happens | **causa y efecto** método de desarrollo en cual los detalles están agrupados según lo que sucede y por qué sucede |
| **central idea** the main or controlling idea of an essay | **idea central** idea principal o fundamental de un ensayo |
| **characterization** variety of techniques used by writers to show the personality of a character | **caracterización** varias técnicas utilizadas por los escritores para mostrar la personalidad de un personaje |
| **chronological order** the order in which events occur | **orden cronológico** orden en el que ocurren los sucesos |
| **citation** note that gives credit to the source of another person's paraphrased or quoted ideas | **cita** nota que menciona la fuente de donde se extrajeron las ideas, parafraseadas o textuales, de otra persona |

**claim** in a persuasive speech or essay, a main position or statement supported with one or more examples and warrants

**afirmación** en un discurso o ensayo persuasivo, punto de vista o enunciado principal fundamentado con uno o más ejemplos y justificaciones

**clarity** the quality of being clear

**claridad** cualidad de un texto de ser claro

**classics** literary works that withstand the test of time and appeal to readers from generation to generation and from century to century

**clásicos** obras literarias que superan la prueba del tiempo y atraen a los lectores de generación en generación y de un siglo a otro

**classification** method of development in which details are grouped into categories

**clasificación** método de desarrollo en el que los detalles están agrupados en categorías

**clause fragment** subordinate clause standing alone

**fragmento de cláusula** cláusula subordinada que aparece de forma independiente

**clause** group of words that has a subject and verb and is used as part of a sentence

**cláusula** grupo de palabras que tiene sujeto y verbo y se utiliza como parte de una oración

**cliché** overused expression that is no longer fresh or interesting to the reader

**cliché** expresión demasiado usada que ya no resulta original ni interesante para el lector

**close reading** reading carefully to locate specific information, follow an argument's logic, or comprehend the meaning of information

**lectura atenta** lectura minuciosa para identificar información específica, seguir un argumento lógico o comprender el significado de la información

**clustering** visual strategy a writer uses to organize ideas and details connected to the subject

**agrupación** estrategia visual que emplea un escritor para organizar las ideas y los detalles relacionados con el tema

**coherence** logical and smooth flow of ideas connected with clear transitions

**coherencia** flujo lógico de ideas que discurren conectadas con transiciones claras

| English | Español |
|---|---|
| **collaboration** in writing, the working together of several individuals on one piece of writing, usually done during prewriting, including brainstorming and revising | **colaboración** en el ámbito de la escritura, el trabajo en común de varios individuos en un texto, usualmente durante la etapa de preparación para la escritura, incluida la técnica de intercambio de ideas y la tarea de revisión |
| **collective noun** noun that names a group of people or things | **sustantivo colectivo** sustantivo que designa un grupo de personas o cosas |
| **colloquialism** informal phrase or colorful expression not meant to be taken literally but understood to have particular non-literal meaning | **coloquialismo** frase informal o expresión pintoresca que no debe tomarse literalmente, pues tiene un significado figurado específico |
| **common noun** names any person, place, or thing | **sustantivo común** designa cualquier persona, lugar o cosa |
| **comparative degree** modification of an adjective or adverb used when two people, things, or actions are compared | **grado comparativo** forma de un adjetivo o adverbio que se usa cuando se comparan dos personas, cosas o acciones |
| **compare and contrast** method of development in which the writer examines similarities and differences between two subjects | **compara y contraste** método de desarrollo en cual el escritor examina las semejanzas y las diferencias entre dos temas |
| **complement** word or group of words used to complete a predicate | **complemento** palabra o grupo de palabras utilizadas para completar un predicado |
| **complete predicate** all the words that tell what the subject is doing or that tell something about the subject | **predicado completo** todas las palabras que expresan qué hace el sujeto o dicen algo acerca del sujeto |
| **complete subject** all the words used to identify the person, place, thing, or idea that the sentence is about | **sujeto completo** todas las palabras utilizadas para identificar la persona, el lugar, la cosa o la idea de la que trata la oración |

| English | Español |
|---|---|
| **complex sentence** sentence that consists of a dependent and an independent clause | **oración compleja** oración que consiste de una cláusula dependiente y una independiente |
| **composition** writing form that presents and develops one main idea | **composición** tipo de texto que presenta y desarrolla una idea principal |
| **compound adjective** adjective made up of more than one word | **adjetivo compuesto** adjetivo formado por más de una palabra |
| **compound noun** a single noun comprised of several words | **sustantivo compuesto** sustantivo individual formado por varias palabras |
| **compound sentence** consists of two simple sentences, usually joined by a comma and the coordinating conjunction *and, but, or,* or *yet* | **oración compuesta** consiste de dos oraciones simples, unidas generalmente por una coma y la conjunción coordinante and (y), but (pero), or (o) y yet (sin embargo) |
| **compound subject** two or more subjects in a sentence that have the same verb and are joined by a conjunction | **sujeto compuesto** dos o más sujetos en una oración que tienen el mismo verbo y están unidos por una conjunción |
| **compound verb** two or more verbs in one sentence that have the same subject and are joined by a conjunction | **verbo compuesto** dos o más verbos en una oración que tienen el mismo sujeto y están unidos por una conjunción |
| **compound-complex sentence** two or more independent clauses and one or more subordinate clauses | **oración compuesta-compleja** dos o más cláusulas independientes y una o más cláusulas subordinadas |
| **concluding sentence** a strong ending added to a paragraph that summarizes the major points, refers to the main idea, or adds an insight | **oración conclusiva** un final que se añade a un párrafo y que resume los puntos principales, se refiere a la idea principal o añade una reflexión. |
| **conclusion** a strong ending added to a paragraph or composition that summarizes the major points, refers to the main idea, and adds an insight | **conclusión** un final fuerte que se añade a un párrafo o a una composición y que resume los puntos principales, se refiere a la idea principal y añade una reflexión |

| English | Español |
|---|---|
| **concrete noun** person, place, or thing that can be seen or touched | **sustantivo concreto** una persona, un lugar o una cosa que puede verse o tocarse |
| **conflict** struggle between opposing forces around which the action of a work of literature revolves | **conflicto** lucha entre fuerzas opuestas alrededor de cual gira la acción de una obra literaria |
| **conjunction** word that joins together sentences, clauses, phrases, or other words | **conjunción** palabra que une dos oraciones, cláusulas, frases u otras palabras |
| **conjunctive adverb** an adverb used to connect two clauses | **adverbio conjuntivo** adverbio utilizado para conectar dos cláusulas |
| **connotation** meaning that comes from attitudes attached to a word | **connotación** significado que proviene de los valores vinculados a una palabra |
| **consonance** repetition of a consonant sound, usually in the middle or at the end of words | **consonancia** repetición de un sonido consonántico, usualmente en el medio o al final de las palabras |
| **context clue** clues to a word's meaning provided by the sentence, the surrounding words, or the situation in which the word occurs | **clave del contexto** pistas sobre el significado de una palabra proporcionadas por la oración, las palabras que la rodean o la situación en la que aparece la palabra |
| **contraction** word that combines two words into one and uses an apostrophe to replace one or more missing letters | **contracción** palabra que combina dos palabras en una y utiliza un apóstrofo en lugar de la(s) letra(s) faltante(s) |
| **contradiction** in a persuasive speech or essay, a logical incompatibility between two propositions made by the author | **contradicción** en un discurso o ensayo persuasivo, incompatibilidad lógica entre dos proposiciones hechas por el autor |
| **controlling idea** the main idea or thesis of an essay | **idea dominante** idea principal o tesis de un ensayo |
| **cooperative learning** strategy in which a group works together to achieve a common goal or accomplish a single task | **aprendizaje cooperativo** estrategia mediante cual los miembros de un grupo trabajan juntos para alcanzar una meta en común o llevar a cabo una tarea |

**coordinating conjunction** single connecting word used to join words or groups of words

**conjunción coordinante** palabra de conexión usada para unir palabras o grupos de palabras

**correlative conjunction** pairs of conjunctions used to connect compound subjects, compound verbs, and compound sentences

**conjunción correlativa** pares de conjunciones usadas para conectar los sujetos compuestos, los verbos compuestos y las oraciones compuestas

**count noun** a noun that names an object that can be counted (*grains of rice, storms, songs*)

**sustantivo contable** sustantivo que designa un objeto que se puede contar (granos de arroz, tormentas, canciones)

**counter-argument** argument offered to address opposing views in a persuasive composition

**contraargumento** argumento que se ofrece para tratar las opiniones contrarias en una composición persuasiva

**creative writing** writing style in which the writer creates characters, events, and images within stories, plays, or poems to express feelings, perceptions, and points of view

**escritura creativa** estilo de escritura en cual el escritor crea los personajes, los sucesos y las imágenes de cuentos, obras de teatro o poemas para expresar sentimientos, percepciones y puntos de vista

**critique** a detailed analysis and assessment of a work such as a piece of writing

**crítica** análisis detallado y evaluación de una obra, como un texto escrito

### D

**dangling modifier** phrase that has nothing to describe in a sentence

**modificador mal ubicado** frase que no describe nada en una oración

**dash** punctuation mark that indicates a greater separation of words than a comma

**raya** signo de puntuación que indica una separación mayor entre las palabras que una coma

**declarative sentence** a statement or expression of an opinion. It ends with a period.

**oración enunciativa** enunciado o expresión de una opinión. Termina en punto.

GLOSSARY

**definition** method of development in which the nature and characteristics of a word, object, concept, or phenomenon are explained

**demonstrative pronoun** word that substitutes for a noun and points out a person or thing

**denotation** literal meaning of a word

**descriptive writing** writing that creates a vivid picture of a person, an object, or a scene by stimulating the reader's senses

**developmental order** information that is organized so that one idea grows out of the preceding idea

**Dewey decimal system** system by which nonfiction books are arranged on shelves in numerical order according to ten general subject categories

**dialect** regional variation of a language distinguished by distinctive pronunciation and some differences in word meanings

**dialogue** conversation between two or more people in a story or play

**direct object** noun or a pronoun that answers the question *What?* or *Whom?* after an action verb

**direct quotation** passage, sentence, or words stated exactly as the person wrote or said them

**definición** método de desarrollo en cual se explican la naturaleza y las características de una palabra, objeto, concepto o fenómeno

**pronombre demostrativo** palabra que está en lugar de un sustantivo y señala una persona o cosa

**denotación** significado literal de una palabra

**texto descriptivo** texto que crea una imagen vívida de una persona, un objeto o una escena estimulando los sentidos del lector

**orden de desarrollo** información que está organizada de tal manera que una idea surge de la precedente

**Sistema decimal de Dewey** sistema por cual los libros de no ficción se ubican en los estantes en orden numérico según diez categorías temáticas generales

**dialecto** variación regional de un idioma caracterizada por una pronunciación distintiva y algunas diferencias en el significado de las palabras

**diálogo** conversación entre dos o más personas en un cuento o en una obra de teatro

**objeto directo** sustantivo o pronombre que responde la pregunta ¿Qué? (*What?*) o ¿Quién? (*Whom?*) después de un verbo de acción

**cita directa** pasaje, oración o palabras enunciadas exactamente como la persona las escribió o las dijo

## English

**documentary** a work composed of pieces of primary source materials or first-hand accounts such as interviews, diaries, photographs, film clips, etc.

**documentary** images, interviews, and narration put together to create a powerful report

**double negative** use of two negative words to express an idea when only one is needed

**drafting** stage of the writing process in which the writer expresses ideas in sentences, forming a beginning, a middle, and an ending of a composition

### E

**e-mail** electronic mail that can be sent all over the world from one computer to another

**editing** stage of the writing process in which the writer polishes his or her work by correcting errors in grammar, usage, mechanics, and spelling

**elaboration** addition of explanatory or descriptive information to a piece of writing, such as supporting details, examples, facts, and descriptions

## Español

**documental** obra compuesta por fragmentos de fuentes primarias o relatos de primera mano, como entrevistas, diarios, fotografías, fragmentos de películas, etc.

**documental** imágenes, entrevistas y narración que se combinan para crear un informe poderoso

**negación doble** uso de dos palabras negativas para expresar una idea cuando sólo una es necesaria

**borrador** etapa del proceso de escritura en la cual el escritor expresa sus ideas en oraciones que forman el principio, el medio y el final de una composición

**correo electrónico** mensaje electrónico que puede enviarse a cualquier lugar del mundo desde una computadora a otra

**edición** etapa del proceso de escritura en la cual el escritor mejora su trabajo y corrige los errores de gramática, uso del lenguaje, aspectos prácticos y ortografía

**explicación** agregar información explicativa o descriptiva a un texto, como detalles de apoyo, ejemplos, hechos y descripciones

| English | Español |
|---|---|
| **electronic publishing** various ways to present information through the use of technology. It includes desktop publishing (creating printed documents on a computer), audio and video recordings, and online publishing (creating a Web site). | **publicación electrónica o Ciberedición** varias maneras de presentar la información por el uso de la tecnología. Incluye la autoedición (crear documentos impresos en una computadora), las grabaciones de audio y video y la publicación en línea (crear un sitio web). |
| **ellipses** punctuation marks ( . . . ) used to indicate where text has been removed from quoted material or to indicate a pause or interruption in speech | **puntos suspensivos** signos de puntuación (. . .) utilizados para indicar dónde se ha quitado parte del texto de una cita o para indicar una pausa o una interrupción en el discurso |
| **elliptical clause** subordinate clause in which words are omitted but understood to be there | **cláusula elíptica** cláusula subordinada en cual se omiten palabras, pero se comprende que están implícitas |
| **emoticons** symbols used by e-mail users to convey emotions | **emoticonos** símbolos utilizados por los usuarios del correo electrónico para transmitir emociones |
| **encyclopedia** print or online reference that contains general information about a variety of subjects | **enciclopedia** obra de referencia, impresa o en línea, que contiene información general sobre varios temas |
| **endnote** complete citation of the source of borrowed material at the end of a research report | **nota final** cita completa de la fuente de la que se tomó información, colocada al final de un informe de investigación |
| **essay** composition of three or more paragraphs that presents and develops one main idea | **ensayo** composición de tres o más párrafos que presenta y desarrolla una idea principal |
| **essential phrase or clause** group of words essential to the meaning of a sentence; therefore, not set off with commas | **frase o cláusula esencial** grupo de palabras esencial para el significado de una oración; por lo tanto, no está encerrado entre comas |
| **etymology** history of a word, from its earliest recorded use to its present use | **etimología** historia de una palabra, desde su uso registrado más antiguo hasta su uso actual |

| English | Español |
|---|---|
| **evidence** facts and examples used to support a statement or proposition | **evidencia** hechos y ejemplos utilizados para fundamentar un enunciado o proposición |
| **exclamatory sentence** expression of strong feeling that ends with an exclamation point | **oración exclamativa** expresión de sentimiento intenso que termina con signo de exclamación |
| **expository writing** prose that explains or informs with facts and examples or gives directions | **texto expositivo** texto en prosa que explica o informa con hechos y ejemplos o da instrucciones |
| **external coherence** organization of the major components of a written piece (introduction, body, conclusion) in a logical sequence and flow, progressing from one idea to another while holding true to the central idea of the composition | **coherencia externa** organización de las partes principales de un trabajo escrito (introducción, cuerpo, conclusión) en una secuencia lógica que presenta fluidez y avanza de una idea a otra, pero sustentando la idea central de la composición |

**F**

| | |
|---|---|
| **fable** story in which animal characters act like people to teach a lesson or moral | **fábula** relato en cual los personajes son animales que actúan como personas para enseñar una lección o una moraleja |
| **fact** statement that can be proven | **hecho** enunciado que puede probarse |
| **feedback** written or verbal reaction to an idea, a work, a performance, and so on, often used as a basis for improvement | **realimentación** reacción escrita u oral respecto de una idea, obra, representación, etc., que suele utilizarse como base para mejorarla |
| **fiction** prose works of literature, such as short stories and novels, which are partly or totally imaginary | **ficción** obras literarias en prosa, como cuentos y novelas, que son parcial o totalmente imaginarias |
| **figurative language** language that uses such devices as imagery, metaphor, simile, hyperbole, personification, or analogy to convey a sense beyond the literal meaning of the words | **lenguaje figurado** lenguaje que emplea recursos tales como imágenes, metáforas, símiles, hipérboles, personificación o analogía para transmitir un sentido que va más allá del sentido literal de las palabras |

**flashback** an interruption of the normal chronological order of the plot to narrate events that occurred earlier

**folktale** story that was told aloud long before it was written

**footnote** complete citation of the source of borrowed material at the bottom of a page in a research report

**foreshadowing** the use of hints or clues about what will happen later in the plot

**formal English** conventional rules of grammar, usage, and mechanics

**format (page)** the way in which page elements, such as margins, heads, subheads, and sidebars, are arranged

**fragment** group of words that does not express a complete thought

**free verse** poetry without meter or a regular, patterned beat

**freewriting** prewriting technique of writing freely without concern for mistakes made

**friendly letter** writing form that may use informal language and includes a heading, greeting (salutation), body, closing, and signature

**flash-back** interrupción del orden cronológico normal del argumento para narrar sucesos que ocurrieron anteriormente

**cuento folclórico** relato que se contaba en voz alta mucho antes de que fuera puesto por escrito

**nota al pie** cita completa de la fuente de la que se tomó información, colocada en la parte inferior de una página de un informe de investigación

**presagio** uso de pistas o claves sobre lo que sucederá posteriormente en el argumento

**inglés formal** reglas convencionales de gramática, uso del lenguaje y aspectos prácticos de la escritura

**formato (página)** forma en que están organizados los elementos de la página, como los márgenes, encabezados, subtítulos y recuadros

**fragmento** grupo de palabras que no expresa un pensamiento completo

**verso libre** poesía sin metro fijo o patrón rítmico regular

**escritura libre** técnica de preparación para la escritura que consiste en escribir libremente sin preocuparse por los errores cometidos

**carta amistosa** tipo de texto que puede usar un lenguaje informal e incluye membrete, saludo, cuerpo, despedida y firma

GLOSSARY

| English | Español |
|---|---|
| **G** | |
| **generalization** a conclusion based on facts, examples, or instances | **generalización** conclusión basada en hechos, ejemplos o casos |
| **generalizing** forming an overall idea that explains something specific | **generalizando** formar una idea general que explica algo específico |
| **genre** a distinctive type or category of literature such as the epic, mystery, or science fiction | **género** tipo distintivo o categoría literaria, como la épica, las novelas de misterio, o la ciencia ficción |
| **genre** a distinctive type or category of text, such as personal narrative, expository essay, or short story | **género** tipo distintivo o categoría de texto, como la narración personal, el ensayo expositivo o el cuento |
| **gerund phrase** a gerund with its modifiers and complements working together as a noun | **frase de gerundio** un gerundio con sus modificadores y complementos, que funcionan juntos como un sustantivo |
| **gerund** verb form ending in –*ing* that is used as a noun | **gerundio** forma verbal que termina en –*ing* y puede usarse como sustantivo |
| **glittering generality** word or phrase that most people associate with virtue and goodness that is used to trick people into feeling positively about a subject | **generalidad entusiasta** palabra o frase que la mayoría de la gente asocia con la virtud y la bondad, y que se utiliza con el fin de engañar a las personas para que tengan una reacción positiva respecto de cierto tema |
| **graphic elements (in poetry)** in poetry, use of word position, line length, and overall text layout to express or reflect meaning | **elementos gráficos (en la poesía)** en poesía, el uso de la ubicación de las palabras, la extensión de los versos y la disposición general del texto para expresar o mostrar el significado |
| **H** | |
| **helping verb** auxiliary verb that combines with the main verb to make up a verb phrase | **verbo auxiliar** verbo que se emplea junto con el verbo principal para formar una frase verbal |

| English | Español |
|---------|---------|
| **homographs** words that are spelled alike but have different meanings and pronunciations | **homógrafos** palabras que se escriben de igual manera, pero tienen significados y pronunciaciones diferentes |
| **homophones** words that sound alike but have different meanings and spellings | **homófonos** palabras que suenan de igual manera, pero tienen significados diferentes y se escriben de manera distinta |
| **hyperbole** use of exaggeration or overstatement | **hipérbole** uso de la exageración o amplificación |
| **hyphen** punctuation mark used to divide words at the end of a line | **guión** signo ortográfico usado para separar las palabras al final de un renglón |

**I**

| | |
|---------|---------|
| **idiom** phrase or expression that has a meaning different from what the words suggest in their usual meanings | **modismo** frase o expresión que tiene un significado diferente de lo que sugieren habitualmente las palabras que la forman |
| **imagery** use of concrete details to create a picture or appeal to senses other than sight | **imaginería** uso de detalles concretos para crear una imagen o apelar a los otros sentidos además de la vista |
| **imperative mood** verb form used to give a command or to make a request | **modo imperativo** forma verbal usada para dar una orden u hacer un pedido |
| **imperative sentence** a request or command that ends with either a period or an exclamation point | **oración imperativa** pedido u orden que termina en punto con signo de exclamación |
| **indefinite pronoun** word that substitutes for a noun and refers to unnamed persons or things | **pronombre indefinido** palabra que sustituye a un sustantivo y alude a personas o cosas que no han sido identificadas |
| **independent clause** group of words that can stand alone as a sentence because it expresses a complete thought | **cláusula independiente** grupo de palabras que pueden formar por sí solas una oración porque expresan un pensamiento completo |

| English | Español |
|---|---|
| **indicative mood** verb form used to state a fact or to ask a question | **modo indicativo** forma verbal usada para enunciar un hecho o hacer una pregunta |
| **indirect object** noun or a pronoun that answers the question *To or from whom?* or *To or for what?* after an action word | **objeto indirecto** nombre o pronombre que responde la pregunta ¿A quién o para quién? (*To or from whom?*) o ¿A qué o para qué? (*To or for what?*) después de una palabra de acción |
| **inference** a reasonable conclusion drawn by the reader based on clues in a literary work | **inferencia** conclusión razonable que saca el lector basándose en las pistas de una obra literaria |
| **infinitive** verb form that usually begins with *to* and can be used as a noun, adjective, or adverb | **infinitivo** forma verbal que generalmente empieza con *to* y se puede usar como sustantivo, adjetivo o adverbio |
| **informative writing** writing that explains with facts and examples, gives directions, or lists steps in a process | **texto informativo** texto que explica algo con hechos y ejemplos, da instrucciones o enumera los pasos de un proceso |
| **inquiring** a prewriting technique in which the writer asks questions such as *Who? What? Where? Why?* and *When?* | **indagar** técnica de preparación para la escritura en cual el escritor hace preguntas como ¿Quién? (*Who?*), ¿Qué? (*What?*), ¿Dónde? (*Where?*), ¿Por qué? (*Why?*) y ¿Cuándo? (*When?*) |
| **intensive pronoun** word that adds emphasis to a noun or another pronoun in the sentence | **pronombre enfático** en una oración, palabra que añade énfasis a un sustantivo o a otro pronombre |
| **interjection** word that expresses strong feeling | **interjección** palabra que expresa un sentimiento intenso |
| **internal coherence** in a written piece, organization of ideas and/or sentences in a logical sequence and with a fluid progression | **coherencia interna** en un texto escrito, la organización de las ideas y/o de las oraciones en una secuencia lógica y con un desarrollo fluido |

GLOSSARY

## English

**Internet** global network of computers that are connected to one another with high speed data lines and telephone lines

**interrogative pronoun** pronoun used to ask a question

**interrogative sentence** a question. It ends with a question mark.

**intransitive verb** action verb that does not pass the action from a doer to a receiver

**introduction** one or more paragraphs in an essay that introduce a subject, state or imply a purpose, and present a main idea

**introduction** first paragraph of a composition that catches the reader's attention and states the main idea

**inverted order** condition when the subject follows the verb or part of the verb phrase

**irony** a recognition and heightening of the difference between appearance and reality. *Situational irony* occurs when events turn out differently from what is expected; *dramatic irony* occurs when the audience has important information that a main character lacks.

**irregular verb** verb that does not form its past and past participle by adding *–ed* or *–d* to the present tense

## Español

**internet** red mundial de computadoras que están conectadas entre sí con líneas de datos y líneas telefónicas de alta velocidad

**pronombre interrogativo** pronombre utilizado para hacer una pregunta

**oración interrogativa** pregunta. Empieza y termina con signos de interrogación en español y termina con signo de interrogación en inglés.

**verbo intransitivo** verbo de acción que no transfiere la acción del agente a un receptor

**introducción** en un ensayo, uno o más párrafos que presentan un tema, enuncian o sugieren un propósito y presentan una idea principal

**introducción** primer párrafo de una composición que capta la atención del lector y enuncia la idea principal

**orden invertido** circunstancia en la que el sujeto sigue al verbo o a una parte de la frase verbal

**ironía** reconocimiento e intensificación de la diferencia entre la apariencia y la realidad. La *ironía situacional* ocurre cuando los sucesos resultan de manera diferente de lo esperado; la *ironía dramática* ocurre cuando el público tiene información importante de la que carece el personaje principal.

**verbo irregular** verbo que no forma el pasado o el participio pasado al agregar *–ed* o *–d* al tiempo presente

| English | Español |
|---|---|
| **English** | **Español** |

##  J

**jargon** specialized vocabulary used by a particular group of people

**journal** daily notebook in which a writer records thoughts and feelings

**juxtaposition** two or more things placed side by side, generally in an unexpected combination

**jerga** vocabulario especializado usado por un grupo específico de personas

**diario** cuaderno en el que un escritor anota cada día sus pensamientos y sentimientos

**yuxtaposición** dos o más cosas ubicadas una junto a la otra, generalmente en una combinación inesperada

## L

**linking verb** verb that links the subject with another word that renames or describes the subject

**listening** the process of comprehending, evaluating, organizing, and remembering information presented orally

**literary analysis** interpretation of a work of literature supported with appropriate details and quotations from the work

**loaded words** words carefully chosen to appeal to one's hopes or fears rather than to reason or logic

**verbo copulativo** verbo que conecta al sujeto con otra palabra que vuelve a nombrar o describe al sujeto

**escuchar** proceso de comprender, evaluar, organizar y recordar la información presentada oralmente

**análisis literario** interpretación de una obra literaria fundamentada con detalles apropiados y citas de la obra

**palabras tendenciosas** palabras escogidas cuidadosamente para apelar a las esperanzas o los temores del destinatario, en lugar de la razón o la lógica

## M

**memo** short for *memorandum*, a concise form of communication used to disseminate decisions, plans, policies and the like; used frequently in business settings

**memo** abreviatura de *memorándum*, forma concisa de comunicación usada para difundir decisiones, planes, políticas y cuestiones similares; utilizada frecuentemente en el ambiente de los negocios

GLOSSARY

| English | Español |
|---|---|
| **metaphor** figure of speech that compares by implying that one thing is another | **metáfora** figura retórica que hace una comparación implícita entre dos cosas |
| **meter** rhythm of a specific beat of stressed and unstressed syllables found in many poems | **metro** ritmo con una cadencia específica de sílabas tónicas (acentuadas) y átonas (inacentuadas) que se halla en muchos poemas |
| **misplaced modifier** phrase or a clause that is placed too far away from the word it modifies, thus creating an unclear sentence | **modificador mal colocado** frase o cláusula ubicada demasiado lejos de la palabra que modifica, por lo que crea una oración poco clara |
| **modifier** word that makes the meaning of another word more precise | **modificador** palabra que hace más preciso el significado de otra palabra |
| **mood** overall atmosphere or feeling created by a work of literature | **atmósfera** clima o sentimiento general creado por una obra literaria |
| **multimedia** the use of more than one medium of expression or communication such as a presentation composed of visual images and audio soundtrack | **multimedia** uso de más de un medio de expresión o comunicación, como una presentación compuesta por imágenes visuales y una banda sonora de audio |

## N

| English | Español |
|---|---|
| **narrative writing** writing that tells a real or an imaginary story with a clear beginning, middle, and ending | **texto narrativo** texto que relata una historia real o imaginaria con un principio, un medio y un final |
| **narrator** the person whose voice is telling the story | **narrador** persona cuya voz cuenta la historia |
| **network** a system of interconnected computers | **red** sistema de computadoras interconectadas |
| **noncount noun** a noun that names something that cannot be counted (*health, weather, music*) | **sustantivo no contable** sustantivo que designa algo que no se puede contar (*la salud, el clima, la música*) |

**nonessential phrase or clause** group of words that is not essential to the meaning of a sentence and is therefore set off with commas (also called *nonrestrictive phrase or clause*)

**nonfiction** prose writing that contains facts about real people and real events

**nonstandard English** less formal language used by people of varying regions and dialects; not appropriate for use in writing

**noun** a word that names a person, place, thing, or idea. A common noun gives a general name. A proper noun names a specific person, place, or thing and always begins with a capital letter. Concrete nouns can be seen or touched; abstract nouns can not.

**noun clause** a subordinate clause used like a noun

**novel** a long work of narrative fiction

**nuance** a small or subtle distinction in meaning

**O**

**object pronoun** type of pronoun used for direct objects, indirect objects, and objects of prepositions

**frase o cláusula incidental** grupo de palabras que no es esencial para el significado de una oración y, por lo tanto, está encerrada entre comas (también llamada *frase o cláusula no restrictiva*)

**no ficción** texto en prosa que contiene hechos sobre gente real y sucesos reales

**inglés no estándar** lenguaje menos formal utilizado por personas de diversas regiones y dialectos; inapropiado para usarlo en la escritura

**sustantivo** palabra que designa una persona, un lugar, una cosa o una idea. Un sustantivo común expresa un nombre general. Un sustantivo propio nombra una persona, un lugar o una cosa específica y siempre comienza con mayúscula. Los sustantivos concretos designan cosas que pueden verse o tocarse, mientras que los sustantivos abstractos no lo hacen.

**cláusula nominal** cláusula subordinada usada como sustantivo

**novela** obra extensa de ficción narrativa

**matiz** diferencia de significado pequeña o sutil

**pronombre objeto** tipo de pronombre utilizado para los objetos directos, objetos indirectos y objetos de preposiciones

**object** word that answers the question *What?* or *Whom?*

**objective** not based on an individual's opinions or judgments

**objective complement** a noun or an adjective that renames or describes the direct object

**observing** prewriting technique that helps a writer use the powers of observation to gather details

**occasion** motivation for composing; the factor that prompts communication

**online** connected to the Internet via a line modem connection

**onomatopoeia** the use of words whose sounds suggest their meaning

**opinion** a judgment or belief that cannot be absolutely proven

**oral interpretation** performance or expressive reading of a literary work

**order of importance or size** way of organizing information by arranging details in the order of least to most (or most to least) pertinent

**outline** information about a subject organized into main topics and subtopics

**objeto** palabra que responde la pregunta ¿Qué? *(What?)* o ¿Quién? *(Whom?)*

**objetivo** no basado en las opiniones o juicios de un individuo

**complemento objetivo** sustantivo o adjetivo que vuelve a nombrar o describe al objeto directo

**observación** técnica de preparación para la escritura que ayuda a un escritor a usar su capacidad de observación para reunir detalles

**ocasión** motivación para componer; factor que da lugar a la comunicación

**en línea** conectado a la Internet a través de una conexión de módem

**onomatopeya** uso de palabras cuyos sonidos sugieren su significado

**opinión** juicio o creencia que no se puede probar completamente

**interpretación oral** representación o lectura expresiva de una obra literaria

**orden de importancia o tamaño** manera de organizar la información poniendo los detalles en orden de menor a mayor (o de mayor a menor) pertinencia

**esquema** información sobre un tema organizada en temas principales y subtemas

| English | Español |
|---|---|
|  **P** | |
| **paragraph** group of related sentences that present and develop one main idea | **párrafo** grupo de oraciones relacionadas que presentan y desarrollan una idea principal |
| **parallelism** repetition of two or more similar words, phrases, or clauses creating emphasis in a piece of writing and easing readability | **paralelismo** repetición de dos o más palabras, frases o cláusulas similares que crea énfasis en un texto escrito y facilita su lectura |
| **paraphrase** restatement of an original work in one's own words | **paráfrasis** reescritura de una obra original con las propias palabras |
| **parentheses** punctuation marks ( ) used to enclose supplementary information not essential to the meaning of the sentence; always used in pairs | **paréntesis** signos de puntuación ( ) utilizados para encerrar información adicional que no es esencial para el significado de la oración; se usan siempre en parejas |
| **parenthetical citation** source title and page number given in parentheses within a sentence to credit the source of the information | **cita parentética** título de la fuente y número de página escritos entre paréntesis dentro de una oración para dar a conocer la fuente de la información |
| **parody** humorous imitation of a serious work | **parodia** imitación humorística de una obra seria |
| **participial phrase** participle that works together with its modifier and complement as an adjective | **frase participial** participio que funciona junto con su modificador y su complemento como adjetivo |
| **participle** verb form that is used as an adjective | **participio** forma verbal que se utiliza como adjetivo |
| **parts of speech** eight categories into which all words can be placed: noun, pronoun, verb, adjective, adverb, preposition, conjunction, and interjection | **categorías gramaticales** ocho categorías en las que pueden clasificarse todas las palabras: sustantivo, pronombre, verbo, adjetivo, adverbio, preposición, conjunción e interjección |
| **passive voice** the voice a verb is in when it expresses that the action of the verb is being performed upon the subject | **voz pasiva** voz en que está el verbo cuando expresa que la acción del verbo se realiza sobre el sujeto |

**play** a piece of writing to be performed on a stage by actors

**obra de teatro** texto escrito para que los actores lo representen en un escenario

**plot** sequence of events leading to the outcome or point of the story; contains a climax or high point, a resolution, and an outcome or ending

**argumento** secuencia de sucesos que lleva a la resolución del relato o propósito del mismo; contiene un clímax o momento culminante y una resolución o final

**plural** form of a noun used to indicate two or more

**plural** forma del sustantivo utilizada para indicar dos o más personas o cosas

**poem** highly structured composition that expresses powerful feeling with condensed, vivid language, figures of speech, and often the use of meter and rhyme

**poema** composición muy estructurada que expresa un sentimiento intenso mediante un lenguaje condensado y vívido, figuras retóricas y, frecuentemente, el uso de metro y rima

**poetry** form of writing that uses rhythm, rhyme, and vivid imagery to express feelings and ideas

**poesía** tipo de texto que utiliza ritmo, rima e imágenes vívidas para expresar sentimientos e ideas

**point of view** vantage point from which a writer tells a story or describes a subject

**punto de vista** posición de ventaja desde cual un escritor narra una historia o describe un tema

**portfolio** collection of work representing various types of writing and the progress made on them

**carpeta de trabajos** colección de obras que representan varios tipos de textos y el progreso realizado en ellos

**positive degree** adjective or adverb used when no comparison is being made

**grado positivo** adjetivo o adverbio usado cuando no se realiza una comparación

**possessive pronoun** a pronoun used to show ownership or possession

**pronombre posesivo** pronombre utilizado para indicar propiedad o posesión

**predicate adjective** adjective that follows a linking verb and modifies, or describes, the subject

**adjetivo predicativo** adjetivo que sigue a un verbo copulativo y modifica, o describe, al sujeto

GLOSSARY

**predicate nominative** noun or a pronoun that follows a linking verb and identifies, renames, or explains the subject

**predicate** part of a sentence that tells what a subject is or does

**prefix** one or more syllables placed in front of a base word to form a new word

**preposition** word that shows the relationship between a noun or a pronoun and another word in the sentence

**prepositional phrase** a group of words made up of a preposition, its object, and any words that describe the object (modifiers)

**prewriting** invention stage of the writing process in which the writer plans for drafting based on the subject, occasion, audience, and purpose for writing

**principal parts of a verb** the present, the past, and the past participle. The principal parts help form the tenses of verbs.

**progressive verb form** verbs used to express continuing or ongoing action. Each of the six verb tenses has a progressive form.

**pronoun** word that takes the place of one or more nouns. Three types of pronouns are *personal, reflexive,* and *intensive.*

**predicado nominal** sustantivo o pronombre que sigue a un verbo copulativo e identifica, vuelve a nombrar o explica al sujeto

**predicado** parte de la oración que indica qué es o qué hace el sujeto

**prefijo** una o más sílabas colocadas adelante de la raíz de una palabra para formar una palabra nueva

**preposición** palabra que muestra la relación entre un sustantivo o un pronombre y otra palabra de la oración

**frase preposicional** grupo de palabras formado por una preposición, su objeto y todas las palabras que describan al objeto (modificadores)

**preescritura** etapa de invención del proceso de escritura en la cual el escritor planea un borrador basándose en el tema, la ocasión, el público y el propósito para escribir

**partes principales de un verbo** presente, pasado y participio pasado. Las partes principales ayudan a formar los tiempos verbales.

**forma verbal progresiva** verbos usados para expresar una acción que continúa o está en curso. Cada uno de los seis tiempos verbales tiene una forma progresiva.

**pronombre** palabra que está en lugar de uno o más sustantivos. Entre los tipos de pronombres están los pronombres personales, reflexivos y enfáticos.

**proofreading** carefully rereading and making corrections in grammar, usage, spelling, and mechanics in a piece of writing

**corregir** relectura atenta de un texto y corrección de la gramática, del uso del lenguaje, de la ortografía y de los aspectos prácticos de la escritura

**proofreading symbols** a kind of shorthand that writers use to correct their mistakes while editing

**símbolos de corrección de textos** tipo de taquigrafía que usan los escritores para corregir sus errores cuando revisan un texto

**propaganda** effort to persuade by distorting and misrepresenting information or by disguising opinions as facts

**propaganda** intento de persuadir distorsionando y tergiversando la información o disfrazando de hechos las opiniones

**proper adjective** adjective formed from a proper noun

**adjetivo propio** adjetivo formado a partir de un sustantivo propio

**protagonist** the principal character in a story

**protagonista** personaje principal de un relato

**publishing** stage of the writing process in which the writer may choose to share the work with an audience

**publicar** etapa del proceso de escritura en la cual el escritor puede escoger dar a conocer su trabajo a un público

**purpose** reason for writing or speaking on a given subject

**propósito** razón para escribir o hablar sobre un tema dado

## Q

**quatrain** four-line stanza in a poem

**cuarteta** en un poema, estrofa de cuatro versos

## R

**reader-friendly formatting** page elements such as fonts, bullet points, line length, and heads adding to the ease of reading

**formato de fácil lectura** elementos que se agregan a la página escrita, como tipo de letra, viñetas, extensión de los renglones y encabezados para facilitar la lectura

**Readers' Guide to Periodical Literature** a print or online index of magazine and journal articles

**Guía para el lector de publicaciones periódicas** índice impreso o en línea de artículos de diarios y revistas

GLOSSARY

| English | Español |
|---|---|
| **reflecting** act of thinking quietly and calmly about an experience | **reflexionar** acción de pensar en silencio y con calma sobre una experiencia |
| **reflexive pronoun** pronoun formed by adding *–self* or *–selves* to a personal pronoun; it is used to refer to or emphasize a noun or pronoun | **pronombre reflexivo** pronombre que se forma al agregar *–self* o *–selves* al pronombre personal; se usa para aludir a un sustantivo o a un pronombre o enfatizarlos |
| **regular verb** verb that forms its past and past participle by adding *–ed* or *–d* to the present | **verbo regular** verbo que forma el pasado o participio pasado al agregar *–ed* o *–d* al tiempo presente |
| **relative pronoun** pronoun that begins most adjectival clauses and relates the adjectival clause to the noun or pronoun it describes | **pronombre relativo** pronombre con el que comienza la mayoría de las cláusulas adjetivas y que relaciona la cláusula adjetiva con el sustantivo o pronombre que describe |
| **repetition** repeat of a word or phrase for poetic effect | **repetición** repetir una palabra o frase para lograr un efecto poético |
| **report** a composition of three or more paragraphs that uses specific information from books, magazines, and other sources | **informe** composición de tres o más párrafos que emplea información específica extraída de libros, revistas y otras fuentes |
| **research paper** a composition of three or more paragraphs that uses information drawn from books, periodicals, media sources, and interviews with experts | **artículo de investigación** composición de tres o más párrafos que utiliza información obtenida en libros, publicaciones periódicas, medios de comunicación y entrevistas con expertos en el tema |
| **resolution** the point at which the chief conflict or complication of a story is worked out | **resolución** momento en el que se resuelve el conflicto principal o complicación de un cuento |
| **restrictive phrase or clause** group of words essential to the meaning of a sentence; therefore, not set off with commas (also called *essential phrase or clause*) | **frase o cláusula restrictiva** grupo de palabras esencial para el significado de una oración; por lo tanto, no está encerrado entre comas (también llamada *frase o cláusula esencial*) |

**S**

| English | Español |
|---|---|
| **script** the written form of a dramatic performance, written by a playwright | **guión** forma escrita de un espectáculo dramático, realizada por un dramaturgo |
| **sensory details** descriptive details that appeal to one of the five senses: seeing, hearing, touching, tasting, and smelling | **detalles sensoriales** detalles descriptivos que apelan a uno de los cinco sentidos: vista, oído, tacto, gusto y olfato |
| **sentence** group of words that expresses a complete thought | **oración** grupo de palabras que expresa un pensamiento completo |
| **sentence base** a subject, a verb, and a complement | **base de la oración** un sujeto, un verbo y un complemento |
| **sentence combining** method of combining short sentences into longer, more fluent sentences by using phrases and clauses | **combinación de oraciones** método de combinar oraciones breves para formar oraciones más largas y fluidas mediante el uso de frases y cláusulas |
| **sentence fragment** group of words that does not express a complete thought | **fragmento de oración** grupo de palabras que no expresa un pensamiento completo |
| **sentence** group of words that expresses a complete thought | **oración** grupo de palabras que expresa un pensamiento completo |
| **sequential order** the order in which details are arranged according to when they take place or when they are done | **orden secuencial** orden en que están organizados los detalles de acuerdo con el momento en que tienen lugar o cuándo se realizan |
| **setting** the place and time of a story | **ambiente** lugar y tiempo de un relato |
| **short story** well-developed story about characters facing a conflict or problem | **relato corto** relato bien desarrollado sobre personajes que se enfrentan a un conflicto o problema |
| **simile** figure of speech comparing two objects using the words *like* or *as* | **símil** figura retórica que compara dos objetos usando la palabra como (*like* or *as*) |
| **simple predicate** the main word or phrase in the complete predicate | **predicado simple** la palabra o la frase principal en el predicado completo |

GLOSSARY

**style** visual or verbal expression that is distinctive to an artist or writer

**subject (composition)** topic of a composition or essay

**subject (grammar)** word or group of words that names the person, place, thing, or idea that the sentence is about

**subject complement** renames or describes the subject and follows a linking verb. The two kinds are predicate nominatives and predicate adjectives.

**subjunctive mood** words such as *if, as if,* or *as though* that are used to express a condition contrary to fact or to express a wish

**subordinate clause** group of words that cannot stand alone as a sentence because it does not express a complete thought

**subordinating conjunction** single connecting word used in a sentence to introduce a dependent clause which is an idea of less importance than the main idea

**subplot** a secondary plot line that reinforces the main plot line

**subtle meaning** refined, intricate, or deep meaning, sometimes not noticed during the first encounter with a work of art

**estilo** expresión visual o verbal que es propia de un artista o escritor

**tema** idea principal de una composición o ensayo

**sujeto** palabra o grupo de palabras que nombran la persona, el lugar, la cosa o la idea de la que trata la oración

**complemento predicativo subjetivo** vuelve a nombrar o describe al sujeto y está a continuación de un verbo copulativo. Los dos tipos son los predicados nominales y los adjetivos predicativos.

**modo subjuntivo** palabras como *if* (si), *as if* (como si) o *as though* (como si) que se usan para expresar la subjetividad o un deseo

**cláusula subordinada** grupo de palabras que no puede funcionar por sí solo como una oración porque no expresa un pensamiento completo

**conjunción subordinante** palabra de conexión usada en una oración para introducir una cláusula dependiente que expresa una idea de menor importancia que la idea principal

**subargumento** argumento secundario que refuerza la línea argumental principal

**significado sutil** significado delicado, intrincado o profundo que a veces no se nota durante el primer encuentro con una obra de arte

| English | Español |
|---|---|
| **suffix** one or more syllables placed after a base word to change its part of speech and possibly its meaning. | **sufijo** una o más sílabas colocadas después de la raíz de una palabra para modificar su categoría gramatical y, posiblemente, su significado |
| **summary** information written in a condensed, concise form, touching only on the main ideas | **resumen** información escrita en forma condensada y concisa, que incluye sólo las ideas principales |
| **superlative degree** modification of an adjective or adverb used when more than two people, things, or actions are compared | **grado superlativo** forma de un adjetivo o adverbio que se usa cuando se comparan más de dos personas, cosas o acciones |
| **supporting sentence** sentence that explains or proves the topic sentence with specific details, facts, examples, or reasons | **oración de apoyo** oración que explica o prueba la oración principal con detalles específicos, hechos, ejemplos o razones |
| **suspense** in drama, fiction, and nonfiction, a build-up of uncertainty, anxiety, and tension about the outcome of the story or scene | **suspenso** en las obras de teatro, de ficción y de no ficción, acumulación de incertidumbre, ansiedad y tensión acerca de la resolución de la historia o escena |
| **symbol** an object, an event, or a character that stands for a universal idea or quality | **símbolo** objeto, suceso o personaje que representa una idea o cualidad universal |
| **synonym** word that has nearly the same meaning as another word | **sinónimo** palabra que significa casi lo mismo que otra palabra |
| **synthesizing** process by which information from various sources is merged into one whole | **sintetizar** proceso por cual se integra en un todo la información proveniente de varias fuentes |

**T**

| | |
|---|---|
| **tense** the form a verb takes to show time. The six tenses are the *present, past, future, present perfect, past perfect,* and *future perfect* | **tiempo verbal** forma que toma un verbo para expresar el tiempo en que ocurre la acción. Los seis tiempos verbales son: presente, pasado, futuro, presente perfecto, pretérito perfecto y futuro perfecto |

| English | Español |
|---|---|
| **testimonial** persuasive strategy in which a famous person encourages the purchase of a certain product | **testimonial** estrategia persuasiva en cual una persona famosa alienta a comprar un cierto producto |
| **theme** underlying idea, message, or meaning of a work of literature | **tema** idea, mensaje o significado subyacente de una obra literaria |
| **thesaurus** online or print reference that gives synonyms for words | **tesauro** (Diccionario de sinónimos) material de referencia en línea o impreso que ofrece alternativas para las palabras |
| **thesis statement** statement of the main idea that makes the writing purpose clear | **enunciado de tesis** enunciado de la idea principal que pone en claro el propósito para escribir |
| **tired word** a word that has been so overused that it has been drained of meaning | **palabra gastada** palabra que se ha usado tanto que se ha vaciado de significado |
| **tone** writer's attitude toward the subject and audience of a composition (may also be referred to as the writer's *voice*) | **tono** actitud del escritor hacia el tema y destinatario de una composición (también puede denominarse voz del escritor) |
| **topic sentence** a sentence that states the main idea of the paragraph | **oración principal** oración que enuncia la idea principal del párrafo |
| **transitions** words and phrases that show how ideas are related | **elementos de transición** palabras y frases que muestran las ideas cómo están relacionadas |
| **transitive verb** an action verb that passes the action from a doer to a receiver | **verbo transitivo** verbo de acción que transfiere la acción de un agente a un destinatario |
| **trope** in literature, a common or overused theme, motif, figure of speech, plot device, etc. | **tropo** en literatura, un tema, motivo, figura retórica, recurso argumental, etc. muy común o muy usado |

**U**

| | |
|---|---|
| **understatement** an expression that contains less emotion than would be expected | **minimización** expresión que contiene menos emoción que la esperada |
| **understood subject** a subject of a sentence that is not stated | **sujeto tácito** sujeto de una oración que no está explícito |

| English | Español |
|---|---|
| **unity** combination or ordering of parts in a composition so that all the sentences or paragraphs work together as a whole to support one main idea | **unidad** combinación u ordenamiento de las partes de una composición de tal manera que todas las oraciones o párrafos funcionen juntos como un todo para fundamentar una idea principal |

## V

| English | Español |
|---|---|
| **verb phrase** main verb plus one or more helping verbs | **frase verbal** verbo principal más uno o más verbos auxiliares |
| **verb** word used to express an action or state of being | **verbo** palabra usada para expresar una acción o un estado del ser |
| **verbal** verb form that acts like another part of speech, such as an adjective or noun | **verbal** forma del verbo que funciona como otra categoría gramatical, tal como un adjetivo o un sustantivo |
| **voice** the particular sound and rhythm of the language the writer uses (closely related to *tone*) | **voz** sonido y ritmo particular del lenguaje que usa un escritor (estrechamente vinculado al tono) |

## W

| English | Español |
|---|---|
| **warrant** in a persuasive speech or essay, connection made between a claim and the examples used to support the claim | **justificación** en un discurso o ensayo persuasivo, conexión que se hace entre una afirmación y los ejemplos usados para fundamentarla |
| **wordiness** use of words and expressions that add nothing to the meaning of a sentence | **palabrería** uso de palabras y expresiones que no añaden nada al significado de una oración |
| **working thesis** statement that expresses the possible main idea of a composition or research report | **hipótesis de trabajo** enunciado que expresa la posible idea principal de una composición o de un informe de investigación |
| **works-cited page** alphabetical listing of sources cited in a research paper | **página de obras citadas** lista alfabética de las fuentes citadas en un artículo de investigación |

GLOSSARY

## English

**World Wide Web** network of computers within the Internet capable of delivering multimedia content and text over communication lines into personal computers all over the globe

**writing process** recursive stages that a writer proceeds through in his or her own way when developing ideas and discovering the best way to express them

## Español

**red mundial de comunicación** red de computadoras dentro de la Internet capaz de transmitir contenido multimedia y textos, a través de líneas de comunicación, a las computadoras personales de todas partes del mundo

**proceso de escritura** etapas recurrentes que un escritor sigue a su manera cuando desarrolla ideas y descubre la mejor manera de expresarlas

# Index

*Note: Italic locators (page numbers) indicate skill sets*

INDEX

*Note: Italic locators (page numbers) indicate skill sets*

*Note: Italic locators (page numbers) indicate skill sets*

*Note: Italic locators (page numbers) indicate skill sets*

search engine, 421-422, 607
thesaurus, online, 420
video editing program, 601
Web site software program, 603
word-processing program, 589
Concept outline, for audiovisual
production, 596
Concluding sentence
composition, 87, 106
descriptive paragraph, 100
expository paragraph, 102
model, 87, 98, 100, 102, 104
narrative paragraph, 98
persuasive paragraph, 104
Conclusion
clincher, 249
composition, 122
defined, 122
descriptive writing, 158
drafting, 146, 249
expository writing, 249
invalid, 289
literary analysis, 324, 341
model, 122, 146, 249
personal narrative, 146
persuasive writing, 279
speech, 576
and thesis statement, 122, 324, 341
Concrete noun, 618, 1050
Condensing, 368-370
Conducting an interview, for research
report, 393-394
Conferencing
defined, 27
guidelines, 27
revising, 28
Conflict
central, 184
in play, 207
in short story, 183-185, 191
Conjugation, 764-768, 1057
Conjunctions, 62-64, 73-76, 641-642,
713-714, 1029
and adjectives before a noun, 942,
1065
with adverbial clauses, 720
with compound subjects, 658, 834,
1052
with compound verbs, 658, 1052
coordinating, 62, 73-74, 641
correlative, 641
defined, 641, 1051
diagramed, 673-676, 739
exercises, *642, 646, 722*
with independent clauses, 731, 944,
974, 1065-1066
with items in a series, 940-941
subordinating, 63-64, 75-76, 123,
437, 720-722
Conjunctive adverb, 975, 1066

Connotation, 50
Consonance, 215
Context clues/context of a word, 510-
513
*Continual, continuous*, 884
Contractions, 252, 627, 801, 844-845,
889, 911, 964, 967, 971-972, 1061,
1063, 1066
Contrasting expression, 952
Controlling idea, 20, 111
Cookies, on Internet, 606
Cooperative learning, 586
Coordinating conjunction, 62, 73-74,
77, 641, 731, 924, 944, 974, 1065
Coordination, faulty, 73-74
Copyright page, as research tool, 412
Correlative conjunction, 77, 641
*Cost*, principal parts, 752
Counter-argument, 298, 436
Cover letter, 538
Creative writing, 178-223. *See also* Play;
Poetry; Short story.
analyzing, 183
building suspense, 195
camera directions, 211
characters, 187, 191, 195, 199, 209
chronological order, 191
climax, 191
conflict
central, 184
defined, 183
types of, 184, 191
dialogue, 194, 210
drafting, 194-197
editing, 202
exercises, *178-179, 181-183,
185-187, 190-193, 197-201, 203,
208-212, 214, 216, 218, 220-223*
figurative language, 217-218
flashback, 196
foreshadowing, 196
free verse, 216, 220
half rhyme, 219
iambic pentameter, 216
idea chart, 213
implying, 192
interactive poem, 221
juxtaposition, 196
meter, 216
model, 179, 205
mood, 188, 200, 210
narrator, 189-190
page design, 203
play, 205-212
plot, 191, 196, 198
poetry, 213-221
point of view, 189-190
prewriting, 184-193
publishing, 203
resolution, 183, 191

revising, 198-201
rhyme scheme, 219
scene, 207
schemes, 215
screenplay, 205
setting, 188, 191, 209
short story, 183-204
story outline, 191
story within a story, 196
sound devices, 215
stage directions, 211
stanza, 219
style, 200
subplot, 196
theme, 186, 208
title, 191
tone, 200, 210
tropes, 216
Critical analysis. *See* Literary analysis.
Critical thinking. *See* Think Critically.
Cutaway shot, in video production, 600
Cyberbullying, 613
Cyberspace, 604-606

**D**

Dangling modifier, 703-704, 1054
Dashes, 340, 1007-1008, 1068
Database, online, 393, 413-423
Dates, 948, 973, 1008, 1032, 1065,
1070
Declarative sentence, 934, 1064
Definition. *See also* Meaning of a word.
from context, 510-513
in dictionary, 508
and italics, 996, 1067
and quotation marks, 996, 1067
and parentheses, 1008, 1067
Definition text, 266-267
Degrees of comparison, 508, 517,
856-860, 1061
exercises, *859-860*
Demonstrative pronoun, 623, 634, 1050
Denotation, 50
Dependent clause. *See* Subordinate
clause.
Derivational suffix, 517
Derived words, in dictionary, 509
Descriptive details, 140-141, 145,
158-159, 162, 194, 199, 269
Descriptive writing, 100-101, 154-177,
486-487
exercises, *101, 156-157, 159-161,
163-177*
Desktop publishing, 589-595
Details
background, 141
brainstorming, 18
in characterization, 187, 195, 199
classifying, 20-21

*Note: Italic locators (page numbers) indicate skill sets*

first draft, 22-23, 148, 197, 212, 214, 341-344, 368, 431, 442
introduction, 108-112, 143-144, 243-244
journal entry, 13
literary analysis, 341-348
model, 22-23
from outline, 170, 242, 245, 247-248, 302, 431, 438, 442
personal narrative writing, 143-147
persuasive writing, 302-303
poem, 214
research report, 431-449
second draft, 345-348
short story, 194-197
strategies, 22
summary, 368-372
supporting sentences, 87, 90, 98, 100, 102, 104
thesis statement, 110-112, 242, 302-303, 431-432
title, 23, 249
topic sentence, 87-89, 98, 100, 102, 104
transitions, 94-95, 145, 170, 198, 247-248, 302, 341, 442
works cited, 441-442, 447-449
Drag and drop, on Web site, 603
Drama. *See* Creative writing; Play.
Draw conclusions, 461
*Draw*, principal parts, 754
*Drink*, principal parts, 756
*Drive*, principal parts, 754

**E**

*Eat*, principal parts, 756
Editing
checklist, 30, 651, 681, 715, 745, 787, 825, 853, 873, 931, 961, 1015, 1043
composition, 124
descriptive writing, 171-172
essay tests, 492
expository writing, 252
literary analysis, 351
for mainstream conventions, 8-10
personal narrative, 149
personalized editing checklist, 31
persuasive writing, 310, 312
research report, 451
short story, 202
summary, 374-375
using a manual of style, 31
video production, 601
for wordiness, 30
writing process, 30-32
Editorial, 279-283
*Ei, ie*, spelling rule for, 1021, 1069

Either-or fallacy, 304
Elaborating, 24
Electronic publishing, 589-603. *See also* Publishing.
Ellipsis, 342, 723, 1000-1001, 1068
*Else, other*, in comparisons, 862, 1062
E-mail
attachments, 610
business, 534
guidelines, 534
versus paper letter, 530
versus paper memo, 566
defined, 606
descriptive, 177
following up on, 610
guidelines, 610
informative, 255
instructions, 609
mailing lists, 611-612
netiquette, 607, 612-613
options, 610-611
persuasive, 315
style, 609-610
using, 609-611
*Emigrate, immigrate*, 886
Emotional appeals
loaded language, 55
persuasive essay, 104, 293, 297, 302-303
Empathic listening, 580
Emphasis, 119, 250
Emphatic forms of verbs, 774-776, 1057
Employment letters, 534-535
Empty expressions, 68
Encyclopedias, 415-416
citing, 446-447
online, 416
as research tool, 393, 575
specialized, 416-417
End marks, 932-939, 992-994, 1064-1065
with direct quotations, 992-994
exercises, *932-933, 936-937, 939, 957-959, 993-994*
with parentheses, 445, 1008
Ending. *See* Conclusion.
Endnotes, 445-446
English language
American English, 45-46, 502-505
antonym, 524, 527
cliché, 55
colloquialisms, 45
computer language, 917
connotation, 50
denotation, 50
derived words, 509
dialects of, 44-45
dictionaries, 506-510
English in the 21st century, 505

etymology, 509
euphemism, 55
figures of speech, 51-54, 160-161, 216-218, 327
formal compared with informal, 45, 875
history, 497-505
idioms, 45
inflected forms, 508
jargon, 45
literal language, 51
loaded language, 56
Middle English (1150-1500), 498-500
Modern English (1500-Present), 500-501
nonstandard English, 57, 875
Old English (450-1150), 498
slang, 45, 996
standard English, 45, 57, 874
synonym, 419, 524, 527
and television, 58
thesaurus, 419-420, 524
tired words, 55
Entry, in dictionary, 506-509
Entry word, 506
Envelopes, for business letter, 533
*Equip*, principal parts, 751
Error recognition, 480
Essay tests, 485-493
Essential clause or phrase, 61, 691, 695, 727, 952, 955, 1065
Establishing believability, 303
Establishing shot, in video production, 599-600
*Etc.*, 886
Ethical beliefs, appealing to, 293
Ethos, 303
Etymology, 509
Euphemism, 55
Evaluating. *See also* Revising.
composition writing, 121
creative writing, 201, 212
descriptive writing, 173
details, 372
documentary, 455
dramatic scene, 212
and drawing conclusions, 461
evidence, 299
expository writing, 251, 253
literature, 329-330
main ideas, 372
oral presentation, 578-580
peers, 144
personal narrative writing, 148, 150
persuasive writing, 309, 313
photo essay, 175
research report, 450, 452
reviewing drafts, 121
sentence fluency, 66

*Note: Italic locators (page numbers) indicate skill sets*

*Note: Italic locators (page numbers) indicate skill sets*

*Note: Italic locators (page numbers) indicate skill sets*

*Note: Italic locators (page numbers) indicate skill sets*

*Note: Italic locators (page numbers) indicate skill sets*

*Note: Italic locators (page numbers) indicate skill sets*

*Note: Italic locators (page numbers) indicate skill sets*

*Note: Italic locators (page numbers) indicate skill sets*

INDEX

*Note: Italic locators (page numbers) indicate skill sets*

*Note: Italic locators (page numbers) indicate skill sets*

Research report (*continued*)
quoting and paraphrasing, 370-371,
400-403, 433-435
research questions, 392
revising, 450
sources
evaluating, 396-398
finding, 393-394, 406-423
primary, 393, 397, 449
secondary, 393, 397, 449
using, 433-435
subject, choosing and limiting,
389-391
summarizing, 362-375, 400-403
summary, 358-376
synthesizing, 425
taking notes, 400-403
thesis, 426, 431-432
works cited, 441-449
Resolution, as literary element, 183, 191
*Respectfully, respectively*, 894
Restrictive clause or phrase. *See*
Essential clause or phrase.
Résumé, 538-539
Revising, 24-29
adding, 24, 250
for adequate development, 90-91,
115-116
characters, 199
checklist, 26, 148, 171, 201, 251,
309, 349-350, 373, 450, 492
for clarity, 24
for coherence, 94-96, 119, 250
composition, 124
through conferencing, 27
deleting, 24, 250
descriptive writing, 171-172
elaborating, 24
for emphasis, 119, 250
essay tests, 486-487, 492
expository writing, 250-251
literary analysis, 349-350
model, 26
paragraph, 350
peer response, 28, 93, 173, 350
personal narrative, 148-149
persuasive writing, 304-309
play, 212
poetry, 218, 220
for propaganda, 307-308
rearranging, 24, 250
research report, 450
sentence structures, 67
sentences, 60-79, 350
short stories, 198-201
speeches, 577
strategies, 24, 148, 250, 450
style, 200
substituting, 24, 250
summary, 373

thesis, 242, 244, 341, 431-432
for unity, 93, 119, 250
using feedback, 28-29, 66, 77, 79,
124, 149, 172-173, 203, 251,
309, 373, 450
words, 350
Revision-in-context question, 483-484
Rhyme, 215, 219-220, 326, 328
Rhyme scheme, 219, 326, 328
Rhythm, 59, 216-218, 328
*Ride*, principal parts, 757
*Ring*, principal parts, 756
*Rise*, principal parts, 760, 894
*Rise, raise*, 760, 894
Root words, 513-514, 520-522
from Greek, 514, 521
from Latin, 513, 520
Rubrics, 25
compositions, 124
descriptive writing, 173
expository writing, 253
fluency, 66
idea, 92
literary analysis, 352
organization, 97
personal narratives, 150
persuasive writing, 313
research reports, 452
screenplay, 212
six-trait, 25, 124, 150, 173, 204,
253, 313, 352, 452
stories, 204
word choice, 57
*Run*, principal parts, 757
Run-on sentence, 10, 123, 736-738,
744, 930, 960, 974, 1014, 1055

## S

Salutation, in a letter, 532-534, 910,
948, 981, 1065
*Say*, principal parts, 753
*Says, said*, 896
Scene, 205, 207
Scheme, in writing, 215
Screenplay, 205
Script, 205
Search engine, defined, 607
*-Sede, -ceed, and -cede*, word ending,
1002
*See*, principal parts, 754
*-Self, -selves*, 622, 809, 896
*Sell*, principal parts, 753
Semicolon
combining sentences, 736, 1066
compound sentences, 974, 1014,
1066
conjunctive adverbs, 975
exercises, *976-979*
independent clause, 301, 974, 1066

instead of a comma, 976-977, 1066
items in a series, 941, 1066
transitional words, 975
usage, 974-979
*Send*, principal parts, 753
Sensory details
description, 158, 168
in short story, 188, 195
types, 159
in writing process, 90, 100-101, 140,
158, 170, 487
Sentence. *See also* Run-on sentence;
Sentence fragment; Sentence parts.
beginnings, varying, 59-66
capitalization, 906-931
clincher, 249
combining
by coordinating, 62, 75
with phrases, 60
by subordinating, 63
complement, 664-670, 674-676
complete, 654-655, 661-662
completion tests, 472-474
complex, 65, 731, 744, 1055
compound, 65, 744, 1055
compound-complex, 65, 732, 744,
1055
concise, 67-72
concluding, 87, 90, 98, 100, 102,
104, 106
correcting, 73-79, 482-483, 735,
738, 820, 863
declarative, 934, 960, 1064
defined, 654, 1052
diagramed, 673-676, 707-710,
739-740
end marks, 445, 932-939, 992-993,
1064-1065
exclamatory, 934-935, 960,
1064-1065
fluency, 6, 430, 663
fragment, 9, 351, 654, 661-663, 680,
705-706, 734-735, 1046, 1052,
1054
imperative, 934, 960, 1064
interrogative, 934-935, 960,
1064-1065
inverted order, 656-657, 834,
838-839, 1060
kinds of sentences, 65, 731-733,
744, 934-939, 1055, 1064-1065
natural order, 656-657, 838
numbers, 937, 941, 973, 983, 1003,
1066-1068
patterns, 671-672
punctuating, 610, 661, 680, 688,
691, 695, 721, 727, 732, 734,
736, 932-1015
rambling, 67
recognizing, 480

*Note: Italic locators (page numbers) indicate skill sets*

INDEX

*Note: Italic locators (page numbers) indicate skill sets*

*Note: Italic locators (page numbers) indicate skill sets*

Usage labels, in dictionary, 507
Usage QuickGuide, 1056-1062
*Use*, principal parts, 751
*Use to, used to*, 899

# V

Valid inference, 118, 246-247
Variant spelling, 506
Variety in sentences
    varying sentence beginnings, 65
    varying sentence length, 59, 65
    varying sentence structure, 59, 65
Venn diagram, 260
Verb
    action, 625-626, 629, 655, 664-665,
        777, 864, 1051-1052
    active voice, 6, 78-79, 777-778,
        786, 1057
    agreement with subject, 310,
        826-853, 1060-1061
    auxiliary, 626
    common helping, 626
    common linking, 628-629
    complete predicate, 654-655, 1052
    compound, 62, 658, 661, 731, 944,
        1052
    conjugation, 764-768, 1057
    defined, 625, 650, 1051
    diagramed, 673-676, 739-740
    exercises, *79, 626, 656, 658-660,*
        *751, 753-758, 761, 767-768,*
        *770, 772, 775-776, 778-779,*
        *782, 830-833, 835-839,*
        *843-844, 848*
    helping, 626, 750, 752, 762-763,
        829, 885, 1051, 1060
    intransitive, 625-626, 1051
    irregular, 8, 451, 752-761, 764-765,
        786, 828-829, 1045, 1056
    linking, 628-630, 655, 664, 667,
        669, 791, 845, 864, 866, 880,
        888, 900, 1004, 1051-1052
    mood, 780-782, 786, 1057-1058
    number, 828-829, 831, 836, 838,
        841-842, 845-846, 852,
        1060-1061
    passive voice, 78-79, 777-778, 786,
        1057
    position in sentence, 655-656, 673
    principal parts, 750-761, 1056
        irregular verb, 750-761, 1056
        regular verb, 750-751, 1056
    problem verbs, 759-761
    progressive form, 773-774, 1057
    regular, 750-751, 1056
    simple predicate, 654-655, 1052
    specific, 49-50

tense, 9-10, 152, 259, 352, 461,
    753-766, 776, 816-817,
    1023-1024, 1035
transitive, 625-626, 777, 1051
used as adjective, 693-694, 699-700,
    714, 1053
verb phrase, 626-628, 1051
vivid, 5, 47
Verb phrase
    defined, 626, 1051
    identifying, 627-628, 721
    order, 838
    parallelism, 77, 120, 301, 1048
    in questions, 635
Verb tense
    conjugation, 764-768, 1057
    consistent, 9, 149, 451, 786, 1046
    emphatic form, 774-775, 1057
    future, 762-763, 765-766, 1056
    future perfect, 762, 764-765, 767,
        1057
    future perfect progressive, 774
    future progressive, 773
    historical present tense, 763, 1056
    literary present tense, 763, 1056
    past, 762-763, 765-766, 1056
    past perfect, 762, 764-766, 1057
    past perfect progressive, 774
    past progressive, 773
    perfect infinitive, 771-772, 1057
    present, 762, 764-766, 1056
    present infinitive, 771-772, 1057
    present perfect, 762, 764-766, 1056
    present perfect progressive, 774
    present progressive, 773
    principal parts, 750-761, 1056
    progressive form, 773-774, 1057
    shifts in, 769-772
    uses of, 762-764
Verbal phrase, 693-702, 1053
    and comma, 695-696
    gerund phrase, 697-699, 714, 1053
    identifying, 711-712
    infinitive phrase, 699-702, 714, 1053
    participial phrase, 693-696, 714,
        1053
Verbals, 693-702, 1053
    defined, 693, 714
    gerunds, 697, 1053
    infinitives, 699, 1053
    participle, 693-694, 1053
Verb-subject agreement. *See* Agreement,
    subject-verb.
Vertical file, 413, 420
Video files, on Web site, 610
Video production
    assemble editing, 601
    audio tasks, 597
    background music, 601
    brief, 596

camera moves, 598-599
camera shots, 597-599
camera techniques, 599
computer editing, 601
concept outline, 596
cutaway shot, 600
cuts, 599
dissolve, 601
establishing shot, 599-600
fade, 601
final cut, 601
forms, 588
in-camera editing, 601
insert editing, 601
panning, 599
post-production, 601
pre-production, 596-598
pre-production checklist, 597
pre-production tasks, 597
reaction shot, 600
script, 597
special effects, 598
storyboard, 597
titles, 597
tracking, 599
treatment, 596
video editing programs, 601
video production schedule, 598
video tasks, 597
voiceover narration, 601
zooming, 599
Videoconference, 570
Visual composition, 125
Visual representations
    analyze, audience response,
        578-580
    charts, 554-557, 594-595
    creating a project, 574-578
    presenting a project, 578
    reflecting critically on work
        produced, 58
    using a variety of forms, 576
    using a variety of technologies, 495,
        573, 576
Vivid words, 47-56
Vocabulary, 497-528. *See also* Word
    parts.
    acronyms, 16
    American dialects, 44
    analogies, 90, 160, 234, 305, 350,
        469-471, 527-528
    antonyms, 419, 506, 524, 527
    base words, 1034-1038, 1042,
        1070-1071
    borrowed words, 433, 443
    clichés, 51, 55-56
    colloquialisms, 45-46, 875
    compound words, 1004, 1024, 1029,
        1068, 1070
    computer language, 917

INDEX

*Note: Italic locators (page numbers) indicate skill sets*

Note: Italic locators (page numbers) indicate skill sets

INDEX

# Image Credits

Art Resource: p. 854 Wheatfield with Crows, 1890. Vincent Van Gogh. Van Gogh Museum, Amersterdam, The Netherlands, Art Resource, NY

Corbis: pp. 696 © Reuters / CORBIS

Dreamstime: pp. 3, 7, 31, 32, 48, 49, 55, 59, 74, 79, 80, 94, 100, 112, 117, 119, 134, 151, 152, 157, 166, 167, 180, 185, 196, 217, 234, 264, 266, 268, 282, 291, 292, 294, 298, 300, 314, 319, 335, 347, 349, 357, 362, 375, 378, 424, 432, 455, 456, 475, 615, 616, 640, 646, 651, 668, 681, 686, 704, 716, 719, 735, 738, 747, 755, 778, 788, 811, 817, 826, 833, 848, 859, 917, 932, 978, 1023, 1025, 1033, 1043, 1043

Getty Images: pp. 453 Amos Morgan / Photodisc / Getty Images, 229 SuperStock / Getty Images

iStockphoto: pp. 4, 16, 27, 28, 35, 36, 41, 43, 54, 58, 75, 116, 129, 170, 175, 176, 182, 201, 211, 222, 232, 254, 312, 346, 354, 360, 362, 376, 378, 388, 391, 395, 399, 403, 435, 436, 456, 473, 479, 483, 484, 572, 652, 659, 678, 682, 687, 690, 700, 748, 776, 779, 782, 784, 804, 839, 850, 905, 908, 958, 961, 962, 965, 997, 1006, 1049

Jupiter Images: pp. 52, 137, 190, 197, 214, 218, 222, 258, 262, 270, 272, 321, 330, 331, 372, 387, 459, 467, 491, 495, 496, 511, 531, 549, 577, 648, 712, 715, 732, 737, 742, 809, 822, 824, 837, 928, 931, 931, 944, 1012, 1016

Library of Congress: pp. 50, 630

NASA: p. 868

Picture Desk: p. 906 WARNER BROS / THE KOBAL COLLECTION

SuperStock: p. 968 © Brand X/SuperStock

Wikimedia Commons: pp. 63, 125